THROUGH WOMEN'S EYES

An American History

WITH DOCUMENTS

D0348480

THROUGH WOMEN'S EYES

An American History
WITH DOCUMENTS

Ellen Carol DuBois

UNIVERSITY OF CALIFORNIA,
LOS ANGELES

Lynn Dumenil

OCCIDENTAL COLLEGE

BEDFORD/ST. MARTIN'S
Boston ◆ New York

For Bedford/St. Martin's

Executive Editor for History: Mary Dougherty
Director of Development for History: Jane Knetzger
Executive Developmental Editor: Elizabeth M. Welch
Production Editor: Arthur Johnson
Production Supervisor: Yexenia Markland
Senior Marketing Manager: Jenna Bookin Barry
Editorial Assistant: Elizabeth Wallace
Production Assistants: Kristen Merrill and Amy Derjue
Copyeditor: Lisa Wehrle
Text Design: Anna Palchik
Indexer: Julie Grady
Cover Design: Billy Boardman and Donna Lee Dennison
Cover Art: (Top row, from left) Latina office manager: © Shades of L.A. Archives/Los Angeles Public Library. Sarah Winnemucca: © Nevada Historical Society. Sojourner Truth: © Bettmann/CORBIS. Dolores Huerta: © AP/Wide World Photos. Eleanor Roosevelt: © Bettmann/CORBIS. (Bottom row, from left) Amy Tan: © Reuters/CORBIS; G. Reed Schumann, photographer. Ida B. Wells: Special Collections Research Center, University of Chicago Library. Mercy Otis Warren: John Singleton Copley, *Mrs. James Warren (Mercy Otis),* about 1763, oil on canvas; Museum of Fine Arts, Boston, bequest of Winslow Warren, 31.212; photograph © 2004 Museum of Fine Arts. Elizabeth Cady Stanton: © Bettmann/CORBIS. Sharecropper: © Library of Congress, LC-USF-3301-006218. (On spine) "Migrant Mother": © Library of Congress, LC-USF34-009058-C.
Composition: Pine Tree Composition, Inc.
Cartography: Mapping Specialists Ltd.
Printing and Binding: R.R. Donnelley & Sons Company

President: Joan E. Feinberg
Editorial Director: Denise B. Wydra
Director of Marketing: Karen Melton Soeltz
Director of Editing, Design, and Production: Marcia Cohen
Managing Editor: Elizabeth M. Schaaf

Library of Congress Control Number: 2004107879

0   9   8   7   6   5
f   e   d   c   b   a

For information, write: Bedford/St. Martin's, 75 Arlington Street, Boston, MA 02116 (617-399-4000)

ISBN: 0–312–24731–1
EAN: 978–0–312–24731–7

For Our Mothers and Our Sisters

PREFACE
FOR INSTRUCTORS

WHEN MARY BEARD ASSEMBLED *America Through Women's Eyes* in 1933, she had to present her bold vision of a women-centered American history from the colonial era to the Great Depression by creating an anthology of excerpts from original sources and selections from a few other historians' writings. She expressed the hope that the result would "illustrate, if in a fragmentary way, the share of women in the development of American Society—their activity, their thought about their labor, and their thought about the history they have helped to make or have observed in the making."[1] In this textbook, we have self-consciously followed Beard's lead in constructing a narrative of U.S. history from the point of view of American women with resources she could barely imagine, a rich body of scholarly literature developed over the past forty years to investigate numerous aspects of American women's history.

APPROACH AND FORMAT

Through Women's Eyes: An American History, with Documents is intended to challenge the separation of "women's history" from what students, in our experience, think of as "real history." We treat all central developments of American history, always through women's eyes, so that students may experience the broad sweep of the nation's past from a new and illuminating perspective. *Through Women's Eyes* combines in-depth treatment of well-known aspects of the history of women, such as the experiences of Lowell mill girls and slave women, the cult of true womanhood, and the rise of feminism, with developments of U.S. history not usually considered from the perspective of women, including the American Revolution, Civil War battlefields, post–World War II anti-communism, and the civil rights movement. Our goal of a full integration of women's history and U.S. history is pragmatic as well as principled. We recognize that the students who read *Through Women's Eyes* may have little background in U.S. history, that they will be learning the nation's history as they follow women through it.

At the same time that we broaden the conception of women's and U.S. history, we offer an inclusive view of the lives of American women. We have decentered the narrative from an emphasis on white privileged women to bring ethnic and racial minorities and wage earning women from the margins to the center of our story.

---

[1]Mary Ritter Beard, ed., *America Through Women's Eyes* (New York: Macmillan Co., 1933), 9.

In providing an integrated analysis of the rich variety of women that includes ethnic and racial diversity and class, immigrant status, geographical, and sexual orientation differences, we have also explored the dynamics of relationships between women. Examples of sisterhood emerge from our pages, but so too do the hierarchical relations of class and race and other sources of tensions that erected barriers between women.

Our plans for the treatment of written and visual primary sources—so basic to the book—are equally ambitious. Just as many of our students hold preconceived notions of women's history as an intriguing adjunct to "real history," they often equate the historian's finished product with historical "truth." We were determined to reveal the relationship between secondary and original sources, to show history as a dynamic process of investigation and interpretation rather than a set body of facts and figures. To this end, we divide each of our chapters into narrative text and primary-source essays. Of the essays, 18 center on written documents, providing more than 70 readings ranging from diaries, letters, and memoirs to poems, newspaper accounts, and public testimony. Our 16 visual essays collect over 120 images extending from artifacts, engravings, and portraits to photographs, cartoons, and television screen shots. Together, the sources reveal to students the wide variety of primary evidence from which history is crafted. Our documentary and visual essays not only allow for focused treatment of many topics—for example, the experience of Native American women before and after European conquest, women on the Civil War battlefields, the Great Migration of African Americans in the World War I era, women's use of public spaces in the early twentieth century, popular culture in the 1950s, and the "third wave" feminist revival of the 1990s— but they also provide ample guidance for students to analyze historical documents thoughtfully. Each essay offers advice about evaluating the sources presented and poses questions for analysis intended to foster students' ability to think independently and critically. Substantive headnotes to the sources and plentiful cross-references between the narrative and the essays further encourage students to appreciate the relationship between historical sources and historical writing.

The process of selecting these documents and images has been particularly rewarding. We have been delighted to uncover fresh sources with which to augment the classic works that have become women's history staples. Consider the subject of antebellum westward expansion, which we take up in Chapter 4. The tendency in women's history has been to focus on the role and experience of U.S. women from the East, during the 1840s and 1850s, crossing the Oregon Trail through the Indian lands of the Great Plains to reach the Pacific Coast. The primary sources here are abundant, as Yankee settlers, women as well as men, left innumerable trail diaries and memoirs of their pioneering experience, which subsequent generations treasured, archived, and published. But using only these materials does not give a sufficiently rich portrait of the Pacific Coast experience from the beginning of the Mexican War through the Gold Rush and California statehood. We had to find a way to suggest more of the multicultural confrontations of this period and not rely solely on the perspectives of American pioneers. We did so by constructing a set of primary sources that juxtapose three accounts from roughly the same place and time (California, 1847–1850), taken from a native Piute woman, a Mexican Californiana woman, and an Anglo settler. Although these three women did not literally encounter one another, the combination encourages students to imagine their diverse experiences within a shared field of historical experience and to think about the relations of unequal power among them.

FEATURES AND PEDAGOGY

We are proud as well of the pedagogical features we provide to help students enter into and absorb the text. Each chapter opens with a *thematic introduction* that starts with a particular person or moment in time chosen to pique students' interest and segues into a clear statement of the central issues and ideas of the chapter. An *illustrated chapter timeline* alerts students to the main events covered in the narrative and relates women's experience to U.S. history by visually linking key developments. At the close of each narrative section, an *analytic conclusion* revisits central themes and provides a bridge to the next chapter.

Beyond the visual sources presented in the essays, *over 70 historical images* and *12 maps and graphs* extend and enliven the narrative, accompanied by substantive captions that relate the illustration to the text and help students unlock the image. Also animating the narrative while complementing the documentary essays are *29 primary-source excerpts drawn from classic texts* by women such as Mary Jemison, Elizabeth Cady Stanton, Sojourner Truth, and Betty Friedan. At the end of each chapter, we provide *plentiful footnotes* and an *annotated bibliography* that combines print works and Web sites to give students a myriad of opportunities for reading and research beyond the boundaries of the textbook.

In addition, we open the book with an *Introduction for Students* that discusses the evolution of women's history as a field and the approach we took in capturing its exciting state today. An *extensive Appendix* includes not only tables and charts focused on U.S. women's experience over time but, in keeping with our mission to integrate women's history and American history, fundamental documents relating to U.S. history: the Declaration of Independence, the U.S. Constitution and its amendments, the Seneca Falls Declaration of Sentiments, a compendium of presidential administrations, and annotated extracts of Supreme Court cases of major relevance to U.S. history "through women's eyes."

Although we view *Through Women's Eyes* as an exciting new departure, we also recognize that it would not have been possible without the dynamic developments and extraordinary output in the field of U.S. women's history since Mary Beard wrote her book. In 1933 Beard acknowledged that the "collection, editing, sifting and cataloguing of sources dealing with women's work and thought in the making of civilization" was ground as yet uncultivated.[2] We have been fortunate to reap a rich harvest from the scholarly literature of the last thirty years, a literature that has

---

[2]Ibid.

allowed us to express the diversity of women's lives and to conceive of U.S. history from a gendered perspective.

ADDITIONAL RESOURCES

Bedford/St. Martin's has published both online and print resources relevant to the women's history course that complement our textbook.

Book Companion Site at bedfordstmartins.com/duboisdumenil   The book companion site for *Through Women's Eyes* extends the goals of the text by integrating maps, selected images, primary documents, links to relevant Web sites, and online research resources at a single Web address. Resources can be selected and stored for later use or published to a unique Web address.

Bedford Series in History and Culture   Over 70 American titles in this highly praised series, including a number focused on women's history, combine first-rate scholarship, historical narrative, and important primary documents for undergraduate courses. Each book is brief, inexpensive, and focused on a specific topic or period. Package discounts are available.

Historians at Work   In this series, unabridged selections by distinguished historians, each with a different perspective, provide a unique structure within which to examine an important historical issue, such as *Who Were the Progressives?*, edited by Glenda Gilmore, and *What Did the Internment of Japanese Americans Mean?*, edited by Alice Yang Murray. With headnotes and questions to guide their reading and complete, original footnotes, students are able to engage in discussion that captures the intellectual excitement of historical research and interpretation. Package discounts are available.

ACKNOWLEDGMENTS

Textbooks are for learning, and writing this one has taught us a great deal. We have learned from each other and have enjoyed the richness of the collaborative process. But we have also benefited immensely from the opportunity to read and assess the works of literally hundreds of scholars whose research and insights have made this book possible.

We are grateful to friends and colleagues who have critiqued portions of the manuscript. Barbara Loomis read Chapters 1 and 2 in the early stages of the project. Her perceptions and encouragement meant a great deal. For Chapter 9, Daniel Horowitz shared his expertise on Betty Friedan and the postwar era. We are thankful not only for his encouragement but also for his role in introducing the two of us sixteen years ago. Allison Sneider and Alice Echols contributed significantly to Chapter 10. Norman Cohen, who brought his historical insights and editing skills to many of these chapters, also fed us wonderful meals after our many meetings on the project. As always, Lynn thanks him for his patience, humor, and love.

Numerous colleagues, former students, researchers, and archivists graciously answered frenzied phone and e-mail queries, helping us to find facts, quotations, images, and references. In listing the names, we apologize in advance in case our collective memory fails us. Thanks to Steve Aron, Jacalyn Blume, Paul Boyer, Walter Brem, Ellen Broidy, Kathleen Brown, Victoria Bissell Brown, Colin Calloway, Marisela Chavez, Jerry Clark, Lawrence Culver, Tom Dublin, Jo Duffy, Rebecca Edwards, Cynthia Enloe, Lillian Faderman, Claudia Goldin, Deena J. González, Ann Gordon, James Grossman, Lisbeth Haas, P. Jane Halen, Darlene Clark Hine, Akasha Hull, Karla Jay, Jane Kamensky, Elizabeth Kennedy, Linda Kerber, Carol Lasser, Marco Leone, Linda Lumsden, Valerie Matsumoto, Elaine Tyler May, Rebecca Mead, Ann Mellor, Melissa Meyer, Beth Meyers, Elisabeth Muhlenfeld, Theda Perdue, Laura Pierce, Ted Porter, George Rable, Janice Reiff, Yolanda Retter, Seth Rockman, Vicki Ruiz, Martha Severns, Tom Sitton, Kathryn Sklar, Clyde Spillenger, Brenda Stevenson, Sally Wagner, Michele Wallace, Devra Weber, Deborah Welch, Lesley Wischmann, the women of the June L. Mazer Lesbian Archives, Rumi Yasutake, Xiao-huang Yin, Nanci Young, Henry Yu, and Judy Yung.

Bedford/St. Martin's commissioned numerous reviews of chapters, and we were uniformly impressed with the great care these scholars brought to their evaluation of the manuscript. Although space constraints meant that we could not adopt all of their excellent suggestions, the book is much stronger for their insights. Our gratitude to: Robert Dinkin, *California State University, Fresno;* Jacqueline Dirks, *Reed College;* Nancy Gabin, *Purdue University;* Gayle Gullett, *Arizona State University;* Johanna Hume, *Alvin Community College;* Colette Hyman, *Winona State University;* Elizabeth Leonard, *Colby College;* Lucy Murphy, *Ohio State University;* Sherri Patton, *Sacramento City College;* Sarah M. S. Pearsall, *St. Andrews University;* Heather Prescott, *Central Connecticut State University;* Marguerite Renner, *Glendale Community College;* Myra Rich, *University of Colorado at Denver;* Johanna Schoen, *University of Iowa;* David Silverman, *George Washington University;* Sharon Strom, *University of Rhode Island;* and Laura Woodworth-Ney, *Idaho State University.* We would also like to thank Eliza Reilly, *Franklin and Marshall College,* who took on a special task by giving us invaluable advice on how to encourage students to evaluate images as historical sources and helping us to draft the visual source essays for Chapter 6. We are grateful as well to the following scholars for taking the time to read page proof and to preview the project: Victoria Bissell Brown, *Grinnell College;* Patricia Cline Cohen, *University of California, Santa Barbara;* Susan Glenn, *University of Washington;* Vivian Gornick; Jacquelyn Dowd Hall, *University of North Carolina at Chapel Hill;* Susan Hartmann, *Ohio State University;* Nancy Hewitt, *Rutgers University;* Daniel Horowitz, *Smith College;* Alice Kessler-Harris, *Columbia University;* Joanne Meyerowitz, *Yale University;* Vicki Ruiz, *University of California, Irvine;* Brenda Stevenson, *University of California, Los Angeles.*

A number of students served as research assistants, and they were particularly helpful in finding primary sources. We thank Erin Blakemore, Anastasia

Christman, Kimberly Earhart, G. Mehara Gerardo, Maria Hernandez, Natalie Joy, Anne Lescoulie, Chelsea Neel, Deirdre Cooper Owens, and Melanie Riccobene. Nancy Grubb, of Occidental College, helped immensely with timely secretarial assistance. Michael Kerwin and Jennifer Johnson, also of Occidental College, Ann Gordon of the Stanton/Anthony Papers, Holly Reed of the National Archives, Marva Felchin of the Autry Library, Jack Herlihy of Lowell National Historical Park, Martha Mayo of the Center for Lowell History, John Calhoon of the Seaver Center for Western History Research, and Robert Cooney provided valuable assistance in obtaining and identifying images.

We have a great deal of admiration for the people at Bedford/St. Martin's who have worked so hard to bring this book to fruition. Former president Charles H. Christensen and current president Joan E. Feinberg have been warmly enthusiastic, as have editorial director Denise Wydra, sponsoring editor Mary Dougherty, director of development Jane Knetzger, and senior marketing manager Jenna Bookin Barry. We are grateful to Katherine E. Kurzman, who first asked us to write a women's history textbook, and to Patricia A. Rossi, who helped conceptualize its format. Jessica Angell and Ann Grogg edited a number of chapters with great care. Elizabeth Wallace kept track of all the complex pieces of the book, keeping everyone involved organized. Robin Raffer researched photo images; Sandy Schechter arranged for text permissions; Lisa Wehrle copyedited the manuscript; Anna Palchik designed the interior of the book; Billy Boardman and Donna Dennison designed the cover; and Arthur Johnson oversaw the production process. Finally, we are deeply indebted to Elizabeth M. Welch, the senior developmental editor in charge of the book, who served as critic, cheerleader, and friend. She devoted enormous amounts of energy to improving the book at every stage of the way, with good humor, great tact, and keen intelligence.

We have dedicated *Through Women's Eyes* to "our mothers and our sisters." We wanted to honor Mildred DuBois and the memory of Margaret Brosius Dumenil, both impressive women and working mothers, whose stories are part of the history we tell here. We also wanted to acknowledge the support of our sisters, both literally (Gwen DuBois; Karen Kotloff, Helen Dumenil Chaney, Irene Dumenil, and Frances Pasmanick) and also figuratively, as we thank our individual networks of women friends who have enriched our professional and personal lives.

Ellen Carol DuBois • Lynn Dumenil
Los Angeles, August 2004

BRIEF CONTENTS

C O N T E N T S

CHAPTER 1
"New World" Women, to 1750
2

CHAPTER 2
Mothers and Daughters
of the Revolution, 1750–1800
70

CHAPTER 5
Reconstructing Women's Lives North and South, 1865–1900
270

CHAPTER 6
Women in an Expanding Nation: Consolidation of the West, Mass Immigration, and the Crisis of the 1890s
340

SPECIAL FEATURES

INTRODUCTION
FOR STUDENTS

IN READING THIS TEXTBOOK, you will encounter a rich array of source materials and a narrative informed by a wealth of scholarship, so you may be surprised to learn that women's history is a comparatively new field. When Mary Ritter Beard, the founding mother of women's history in the United States, assembled *America Through Women's Eyes* in 1933, she argued that an accurate understanding of the nation's past required as much consideration of women's experience as of men's. But so limited were the sources available to her that she had no choice but to present the first women-centered American history as a spotty anthology of primary and secondary writings by a handful of women writers. Not until the 1970s, with the resurgence of feminism that you will read about in Chapter 10, did researchers start to give extensive attention to women's history. In that decade, history, along with other academic disciplines such as literature and sociology, underwent significant change as feminist scholars' desire to analyze as well as to protest women's unequal status fueled an extraordinary surge of investigation into women's experiences. Feminist theorists revived an obscure grammatical term, "gender," to distinguish the meaning that a particular society attaches to differences between men and women from "sex," or the unchanging biological differences between men and women. Because gender meaning varies over time and among societies, gender differences are both socially constructed and subject to change.

The concept of gender and the tools of history go together. If we are to move past the notion that what it means to be a woman never changes, we must look to the varying settings in which people assume female and male roles, with all their attendant expectations. Definitions of femininity and masculinity, family structures, what work is considered properly female or male, understandings of motherhood and of marriage, and women's involvement in public affairs all vary tremendously across time, are subject to large forces like economic development and warfare, and can themselves shape the direction of history. As historian Joan Scott forcefully argues, gender can be used as a tool of historical analysis, to explore not only how societies interpret differences between women and men but also how these distinctions can work to legitimize other hierarchical relations of power.[1]

This textbook draws on the rich theoretical and historical work of the past forty years to present a synthesis of American women's experiences. We begin with an ancient Pueblo American origins story and end with a set of images that place women in the context of the globalized world of the twenty-first century. In

---

[1]Joan Wallach Scott, "Gender: A Useful Category of Historical Analysis," *American Historical Review* 91, no. 5 (December 1986): 1067.

between we highlight both the broad patterns of change concerning women's political, economic, and family lives and the diversity of American women's experiences.

As its title suggests, however, *Through Women's Eyes: An American History, with Documents* aims for more than an account of U.S. women's history. Beyond weaving together the wealth of scholarship available to U.S. women's historians, we seek to fulfill Mary Beard's vision of a text that covers the total range of the nation's history, placing women — their experiences, contributions, and observations — at the center. We examine major economic developments, such as the emergence of slavery as a labor system, the rise of factories in the early nineteenth century, the growth of an immigrant labor force, and the shift to corporate capitalism. We explore major political themes, from reform movements to political party realignments to the nation's many wars. We look at transformations in family and personal life, the rise of consumer and mass culture, the racial and ethnic heterogeneity of the nation's peoples, and shifting attitudes about sexuality. But as we do so, we analyze how women experienced these national developments and how they contributed to and shaped them.

THE HISTORY OF WOMEN'S HISTORY: FROM SEPARATE SPHERES TO MULTICULTURALISM

When the field of U.S. women's history began to take off as a scholarly endeavor in the 1970s, one particular form of gender analysis was especially influential. The "separate spheres" paradigm, as historians termed it, focused on the nineteenth-century ideology that divided social life into two mutually exclusive arenas: the private world of home and family, identified with women, and the public world of business and politics, identified with men. In a second phase, as scholarship on women of color increased, the primacy of the separate spheres interpretation gave way to a more nuanced interpretation of the diversity of women's experiences.

Separate Spheres and the Nineteenth-Century Gender System

Women's historians of the 1970s found in the nineteenth-century system of separate spheres the roots of the gender distinctions of their own time. They observed that although ideas about separate spheres had been of enormous importance in the nineteenth century, these ideas had received little to no attention in historical accounts. The approach that women's historians took was to re-vision this nineteenth-century gender system through women's eyes. They found that, although women's lives were tightly constricted by assumptions about their proper place within the family, expectations of female moral influence and a common sense of womanhood allowed women collectively to achieve a surprising degree of social authority.

The separate spheres paradigm proved a valuable approach, but it hid as much as it yielded about women's lives. Early on, historian Gerda Lerner observed that it was no coincidence that the notion of women's exclusive domesticity flourished just as factories were opening up and young women were going to work in them.[2] Because adherence to the ideology of separate spheres helped to distinguish the social standing of middle-class women from their factory-working contemporaries, Lerner urged that class relations and the growth of the female labor force be taken into account in understanding the influence that such ideas held. Subsequent historians have observed that the idealization of women within the domestic sphere coincided exactly with the decline of the economic importance of family production relative to factory production; and that just as class inequality began to challenge the nation's democratic self-understanding, American society came to define itself in terms of the separate spheres of men and women.

Additional problems emerged in the reliance on the separate spheres paradigm as the dominant basis for nineteenth-century U.S. women's history. Historian Nancy Hewitt contends that whatever sense of female community developed among nineteenth-century women rarely crossed class or race lines. On the contrary, hierarchical relationships—slave to mistress, immigrant factory worker to moneyed consumer, nanny to professional woman—have been central to the intricate tapestry of the historical female experience in America.[3] Even among the middle-class wives and mothers who did not work outside the home and whose family-based lives made them the central focus of separate spheres ideology, Linda Kerber urges historians not to confuse rhetoric with reality, ideological values with individual actions.[4] The lasting contribution of the historical exploration of separate spheres ideology is the recognition of the vital impact of gender differentiation on American history; the challenge posed by its critics is to develop a more complex set of portraits of women who lived in, around, and against these notions. As it matures, the field of women's history is able to move from appreciating the centrality of gender systems to accommodating and exploring conflicts and inequalities among women.

Toward a More Inclusive Women's History: Race and Ethnicity

The field of U.S. women's history has struggled to come to terms with the structures of racial inequality so central to the American national experience. As Peggy Pascoe observes, modern scholars have learned to think about race and gender in similar ways, no longer treating either as unchanging biological essences around which history forms but as social constructions that change meaning and content over time and place.[5] Building on a century-long scholarly tradition in African

---

[2]Gerda Lerner, "The Lady and the Mill Girl," *Midcontinent American Studies Journal* 10 (1969): 5–15.
[3]Nancy Hewitt, "Beyond the Search for Sisterhood: American Women's History in the 1990s," in Vicki Ruiz and Ellen Carol DuBois, eds., *Unequal Sisters: A Multicultural Reader in U.S. Women's History,* 3rd ed. (New York: Routledge, 2000), 1–19.
[4]Linda K. Kerber, "Separate Spheres, Female Worlds, Woman's Place: The Rhetoric of Women's History," *Journal of American History* 75, no. 1 (June 1988): 9–39.
[5]Peggy Pascoe, "Gender," in Richard Wightman Fox and James Kloppenberg, eds., *A Companion to American Thought* (Cambridge, MA: Blackwell, 1995), 273.

American history, black women scholars started in the 1980s to chart new territory as they explored the interactions between systems of racial and gender inequality. Analyzing the implications of the denial to late nineteenth-century black women of the privileges granted white women, Evelyn Brooks Higginbotham observes that "gender identity is inextricably linked to and even determined by racial identity."[6]

Other scholars of color, especially Chicana feminists, advanced this thinking about racial hierarchy and its intersections with the structures of gender. They made it clear that the history of Chicanas could not be understood within the prevailing black-white model of racial interaction. The outlines of a multivocal narrative of U.S. women's history that acknowledge women's diversity in terms of race, class, ethnicity, and sexual orientation are advanced by *Unequal Sisters: A Multicultural Reader in U.S. Women's History,* coedited by Vicki Ruiz and one of the authors of this text, Ellen Carol DuBois. This anthology of pathbreaking research pays particular attention to the historical experiences of Western women, noting that "the confluence of many cultures and races in this region—Native American, Mexican, Asian, Black, and Anglo"—required "grappling with race" from a multicultural perspective.[7] By using her own southwestern experience, Gloria Anzaldúa added the influential metaphor of "borderlands" to this approach to suggest that the division between different communities and personal identities is somewhat arbitrary and sometimes shifting.[8] This new approach took the logic of the historical construction of gender, so important to the beginning of women's history, and pushed it further by emphasizing an even greater fluidity of social positioning.

APPROACHING HISTORY *THROUGH WOMEN'S EYES*

How then to bring together a historical narrative told from such diverse and at times conflicting viewpoints? All written histories rely on unifying themes to organize what is otherwise a chaotic assembly of facts, observations, incidents, and people. Traditionally, American history employed a framework of steady national progress, from the colonial revolt against England to modern times. Starting in the 1960s, the writing of American history emphasized an alternative story line of the struggles of workers, slaves, Indians, and (to some degree) women, to overcome enduring inequalities. Initially, women's history emphasized the rise and fall of the system of separate gender spheres, the limits of which we suggest above. In organizing *Through Women's Eyes,* we employ another framework, one that emphasizes

---

[6]Evelyn Brooks Higginbotham, "African American Women's History and the Metalanguage of Race," *Signs* 17, no. 2 (Winter 1992): 254.

[7]DuBois and Ruiz, *Unequal Sisters,* xii. This reader has two later editions (1994, 2000) that include substantially different articles.

[8]Gloria Anzaldúa, *La Frontera/Borderlands: The New Mestiza* (1987; San Francisco: Aunt Lute Books, 1999).

three major themes that shaped the diversity of women's lives in American history—work, politics, and family and personal life.

Work and the Sexual Division of Labor

The theme of women's work reveals both stubborn continuities and dramatic changes. Women have always labored, always contributed to the productive capacity of their communities. Throughout American history, women's work has taken three basic forms—unpaid labor within the home, chattel slavery, and paid labor. The steady growth of paid labor, from the beginning of American industrialization in the 1830s to the present day (women now constitute essentially half of America's workforce), is one of the fundamental developments in this history. As the female labor force grew, its composition changed, by age, race, ethnicity, and class. By the mid-twentieth century, the working mother had taken over where once the working girl had predominated. We have also followed the repeated efforts of wage earning women to organize collectively in order to counter the power of their employers, doing so sometimes in conjunction with male workers and sometimes on their own. Always a small percentage of union members compared to men, women exhibited unanticipated militancy and radicalism in their fight with employers over union recognition and fair wages and hours.

Most societies divide women's work from men's, and America's history has been no exception. Feminist scholars designate this gender distinction as the "sexual division of labor." Yet the content of the sexual division of labor varies from culture to culture, a point made beginning with the discussion of Native American communities in the precolonial and colonial eras. When women first began to take on paid labor in large numbers, they did so primarily as servants and seamstresses; the nature of their work thus generally followed the household sexual division of labor. The persistence of sex segregation in the workforce has had many sources of support: employers' desire to have a cheap, flexible supply of labor; male workers' control over better jobs and higher wages; and women's own assumptions about their proper place.

The division between male and female work continued, and with it the low wages and limited opportunities on the women's side of the line. This was true even as what counted as women's jobs began to expand, and teaching and secretarial labor, once securely on the male side of the line, crossed over to become "feminized" job categories. American feminism in the late twentieth century has been committed to eroding this long-standing principle that work should be divided into male and female categories. As historian Alice Kessler Harris puts it, feminists "introduced the language of sex discrimination onto the national stage, casting a new light on seemingly natural patterns of accommodating sex difference."[9] The degree to which the sexual division of labor has been substantially breached—

---

[9]Alice Kessler Harris, *In Pursuit of Equity: Women, Men, and the Quest for Economic Citizenship in 20th-Century America* (New York: Oxford University Press, 2001), 245–46.

whether it is half achieved or half undone — we leave to our readers, who are part of this process, to determine.

Gender and the Meaning of Politics

The theme of politics in women's historical experience presents a different sort of challenge, for it is the *exclusion* of women from formal politics that is the obvious development in U.S. women's history, at least until 1920 when the Nineteenth Amendment granting woman suffrage was ratified. While the story of women's campaign for the vote plays an important role in our historical account, we have not portrayed the suffrage movement as a monolithic effort. Rather, we have attended to the inequalities of class and race and the strategic and ideological conflicts that ran throughout the movement. We have also stressed the varying political contexts, ranging from Reconstruction in the 1860s to the Populist upsurge in the 1890s to Progressivism in the 1910s, within which women fought for their voting rights. Finally, we have traced the significance of voting in U.S. women's history after the right to it was formally secured, following women's efforts to find their place—as voters and as office holders—in the American political system.

U.S. women's historians have gone beyond the drama surrounding the vote, its denial and its uses, to a more expansive sense of the political dimension of women's historical experience. Feminist scholars have forged a definition of politics that looks beyond the formal electoral arena to other sorts of collective efforts to change society, alter the distribution of power between groups, create and govern important institutions, and shape public policy. Women's historians have given concrete substance to this broad approach to female political involvement by investigating the tremendous social activism and civic engagement that thrived among women, especially through the long period during which they lacked formal political rights. "In order to bring together the history of women and politics," writes Paula Baker, "we need a more inclusive definition of politics . . . to include any action, formal or informal, taken to affect the course or behavior of government or the community."[10]

From this perspective, the importance of women in the realm of politics reaches back to the Iroquois women who elected chiefs and participated in decisions to go to war and the European women colonists who provided the crucial support necessary to sustain pre-Revolutionary boycotts against British goods in the struggle for national independence. Just a small sampling of this rich tradition of women's civic activity through the nineteenth century includes the thousands of New England women who before the Civil War signed petitions against slavery and Indian removal; the campaign begun by Ida B. Wells against the lynching of southern blacks; the ambitious late nineteenth-century national reform agenda of Frances Willard's Woman's Christian Temperance Union; and Jane Addams's lead-

---

[10]Paula Baker, "The Domestication of Politics: Women and American Political Society, 1780–1920," *American Historical Review* 89 (June 1984): 622.

ership in addressing problems of the urban immigrant poor and on behalf of international peace. "Women's organizations pioneered in, accepted and polished modern methods of pressure-group politics," observes historian Nancy Cott.[11]

Indeed, this sort of extra-electoral political activism extended into the twentieth century, incorporating women's challenges to the arms race of the post–World War II era and the civil rights leadership of women such as Ella Baker of the Southern Conference Leadership Committee in the 1950s and Dolores Huerta of the United Farm Workers union in the 1960s. This inclusive sense of what constitutes "politics" has not only enriched our understanding of women's history, but it has generated a more complex understanding of the nature of political power and process within U.S. history in general.

Given the theme of politics as one of the major frames for this book, what is the place of the politics of feminism in the tale we tell? There are many definitions of feminism, but perhaps the clearest is the tradition of organized social change by which women challenge gender inequality. The term "feminism" itself arose just as the woman suffrage movement was nearing victory, but the tradition to which it refers reaches back to the women's rights movements of the nineteenth century. Historical research has unearthed a great deal of breadth and diversity in the many campaigns and protests through which women from different groups, in different times and places, dealing with different challenges, expressed their discontent with the social roles allotted to them and pursued their ambitions for wider options, more individual freedom, and greater social authority.

Feminism and women's history are mutually informing. Feminism is one of the important subjects of women's history, and history is one of feminism's best tools. Knowing what the past has been for women, doing the scholarship that Anne Firor Scott calls "making the invisible woman visible," is a necessary resource in pressing for further change.[12] But feminism is also a method by which historians examine the past in terms of women's efforts to challenge, struggle, make change, and sometimes achieve progress. Like so many of the scholars on whom the authors of this text rely, we have worked from such a perspective, and the passion we have brought to this work has its roots in a feminist commitment to highlighting—and encouraging—women's active social role and contribution to history. For us, however, a women's history informed by feminism is not a simple exercise of celebration, but a continuing and critical examination of what we choose to examine in the past and the methods we use to do so.

The Role of Family and Personal Life

The third integrating category of *Through Women's Eyes* is the theme of family and personal life. In contrast to the categories of labor and politics, which have been recognized in all narratives of the nation's past, women's historians took the

[11]Nancy Cott, *The Grounding of American Feminism* (New Haven: Yale University Press, 1987), 95.
[12]Anne Firor Scott, "Making the Invisible Woman Visible: An Essay Review," *Journal of Southern History* 38, no. 4 (November 1972): 629–38.

lead in bringing family and personal life into the mainstream of American history. Indeed, one of the fundamental contributions of feminist scholarship has been to demonstrate that kinship and sexuality have not been static elements of human nature but have their own complex histories. We try to make this clear by discussing the variety of family patterns evident among Native Americans, immigrants, African Americans, white middle-class Americans, and other ethnic groups.

Over the span of American history, family life has gone from the very center of political power and economic production in the seventeenth and eighteenth centuries to a privileged arena of emotional life in the early twenty-first century. As we write this introduction, family life—who can marry whom, what forms of sexuality should be tolerated, who should care for children and how—have become topics of intense public contest and political positioning. Thus concepts and experiences of family and sexual life, once viewed as the essence of women's separate sphere, are increasingly understood as a major connection between private concerns and public issues.

The histories of both motherhood and female sexuality reveal this connection. Motherhood not only has been central to women's individual family lives but also has served larger functions as well. Within slave communities, mothers taught their children how to survive within and fight against their servitude. Among middle-class women in the nineteenth and early twentieth centuries, motherhood became an effective way to claim female public authority. In the 1950s, at the start of the Cold War between the United States and the former Soviet Union, radical women subverted intense anti-Communist interrogations under the cloak of motherhood, thus trumping one of the decade's most dramatic themes with another. The social significance of motherhood has been used for conservative political purposes as well, with claims about the centrality of women's maternal role to social order providing the fuel of the anti-feminist backlash of the 1970s and through it the emergence of a new political right.

When it comes to the subject of sexuality, historians have proved particularly innovative in learning to read through the euphemisms and silences that obscure women's sexual lives even more than men's. They have delved into documents left by guardians of sexual propriety about prostitutes and by lascivious masters about slave women, in order to imagine how the objects of these judgments themselves experienced these encounters. When historians set aside modern attitudes toward sexuality and reexamined the lives of seemingly prudish nineteenth-century middle-class women, they found, as Linda Gordon demonstrates, the origins of the American birth control movement and all the radical changes in women's lives that flowed from it.[13] No longer content to portray the history of female sexuality as a simple move from repression to freedom, historians have examined the changing understandings of female sexuality and its shifting purposes in the twentieth century, as it played a major role in advancing new standards of consumerism, and in

---

[13]Linda Gordon, *The Moral Property of Women: A History of Birth Control Politics in America* (1976; Urbana: University of Illinois Press, 2004).

modernizing—though not necessarily making more egalitarian—relations between men and women.

Perhaps historians of women have been most creative in learning to look beyond the heterosexual relations that traditionally have defined sexuality to explore the intimate, romantic, and ambiguously sexual relations among women themselves. Carroll Smith Rosenberg pioneered in demonstrating how common romantic friendships among women were in the nineteenth century, describing them as "an intriguing and almost alien form of human relation, [which] flourished in a different social structure and amidst different sexual norms."[14] Historical work into what has come to be called "homosociality" has deepened understandings of sexuality overall. Thus, as with the concepts of gender and race, women's history has led us to view sexuality itself as socially constructed, not as biologically prescribed.

Sexuality has been an especially important site for historians to locate the intersections of race and gender. Middle-class white women's historical prominence rested in considerable part on the contrast between their reputed sexual innocence and propriety and the supposedly disreputable (and titillating) sexuality of women of color on the margins, such as black slaves, so-called Indian squaws, and Asian prostitutes. This intersection between sexuality and race has also been investigated from the position of women who found themselves on the other side of the vice-virtue divide. As historian Paula Giddings argues, the rising up of recently freed African American women against their reputations as sexually available and that of African American men as sexually predatory helped to generate the creation of a black middle class and "a distinctive mix which underlined Black women's activism for generations to come."[15]

These and other discoveries in the field of U.S. women's history have made this textbook possible. The rich body of scholarly literature developed over the past decades has also enabled us to achieve our goal of integrating women's history into U.S. history, of showing how material once separated as "women's history" contributes to a broader understanding of the nation's history. In *America Through Women's Eyes,* Mary Beard insisted that women not be rendered as the passive objects of men's actions but as makers of history themselves; and that they not be removed from the historical flow into a separate narrative, but that their history be understood as part and parcel of the full range of national experience. This has been our guiding principle in writing this textbook—and the reason we have titled it an American history "through women's eyes."

---

[14]Carroll Smith Rosenberg, "The Female World of Love and Ritual," *Signs* 1 (1979): 1–29.
[15]Paula Giddings, *When and Where I Enter: The Impact of Black Women on Race and Sex in America* (New York: William Morrow, 1984), 50.

THROUGH WOMEN'S EYES

An American History

WITH DOCUMENTS

1

"New World" Women

TO 1750

ACCORDING TO THE ACOMA PUEBLO INDIANS' ORIGIN story, the first women in the world were two sisters, born underneath the ground and sent above by Tsichtinako (Thought Woman). She first taught them to plant corn, tend and harvest it, grind it for food, and use fire to cook it. They next learned how to turn the animal figurines their father had given them into living creatures. Eventually, one of the sisters, Iatiku, the Mother of the Corn Clan, married her nephew Tiamuni. They gave their daughters clan names: Sky, Water, Fire, and Corn, symbolizing the four elements that formed the basis of the Acomas' religious cosmology.

Among the widely diverse indigenous peoples of North America, there were innumerable stories detailing the origin of humans and their environment, each reflecting a distinctive culture. With this strong sense of themselves and their past, Native Americans could hardly be said to inhabit what the Europeans who began arriving around 1500 termed "the New World." Yet for indigenous peoples, the Europeans brought such dramatic change that their world seemed new. As Europeans seized land, settled in the Americas, and began importing Africans as slaves, women from three continents interacted and faced new challenges. One commonality they shared was the significant disruption to their accustomed ways of life.

Contact and ultimately conquest by the Europeans transformed Native Americans' economies and profoundly altered their communities. African women not only endured captivity, a traumatic voyage, and the adjustments to a new environment, but many also witnessed firsthand the piecemeal institutionalization of a system that made most of them and their children perpetual slaves. For European women, the degree of hardship they faced varied with individual circumstance, but all confronted high mortality rates, harsh living conditions, and periodic Indian raids. Although we may find other points of similarities among women, such as activities connected to childbirth and childrearing or the limited access to political power, the differences are equally striking. Race, ethnicity, class, location, religion, and age powerfully shaped the lives of "New World" women. This chapter explores the distinct patterns that characterized their experiences.

NATIVE AMERICAN WOMEN

With an estimated two hundred language groups existing in North America on the eve of European conquest, the world of Native Americans defies simple generalization. Historians usually analyze Native Americans in the context of region and economic activities. Thus, in the Southwest were the agricultural peoples, the Pueblos. In California were the hunter-gatherers, the Chumash; in the Northwest, the fishing Nootkas, and in the Great Plains, hunters such as the Crows. In the Great Lakes region, groups such as the Ojibwas emphasized fur trapping. In the eastern woodlands, dominated by agriculture, the Iroquois lived in the Northeast and the Algonquins on the Atlantic coast (see Map 1.1). The heterogeneity of native peoples is also evident in their gender system—the construction of roles assigned to men and to women—which varied from group to group. No matter what specific tasks were included, roles related to economic activities were a powerful determinant of native women's lives. The system of kinship, whether lineage was traced through the female line (matrilineal) or through the male (patrilineal), was another. Once the process of European conquest and colonization began, native women's lives were also powerfully shaped by the impact of the invaders on their traditional societies.

3

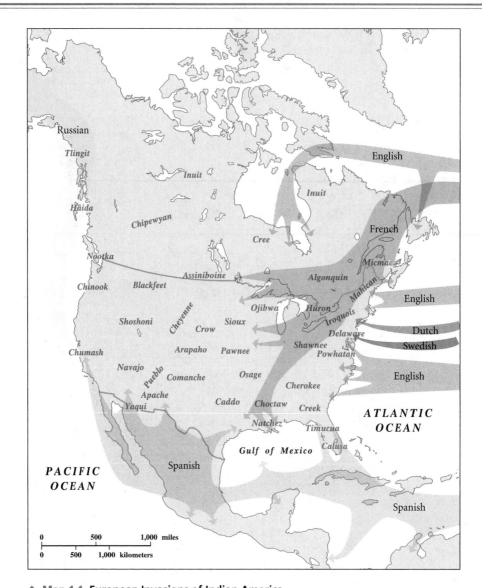

◆ **Map 1.1 European Invasions of Indian America**

At different times in the course of the sixteenth, seventeenth, and eighteenth centuries, various major European nations penetrated North America. Their intrusion set off ripple effects throughout Indian country, often affecting the lives of Indian people who had never laid eyes on a European. Shown here are only some examples of the estimated two hundred language groups living in North America when the Europeans arrived.

Worlds Collide: Indigenous Peoples and European Invaders

Archaeological evidence indicates that at least 14,000 years ago Native Americans migrated across a land bridge between Siberia and Alaska that once united Asia and North America. Historians believe that in the fifteenth century as many as 18 million indigenous people lived in the region of North America that eventually became the United States. Although popular images of Native Americans depict them primarily as hunter-gatherers or nomadic hunters, a significant number engaged in farming, with some combination of fishing or hunting. In these agricultural communities, women fulfilled crucial roles in planting, harvesting, and processing food. Before the arrival of Europeans, some indigenous groups hunted bison on the Great Plains by using fires to stampede the animals over cliffs. It was not until native groups like the Comanches, Arapahos, Cheyennes, and Sioux, living on the borders of the Plains, had access to the horses the Spaniards imported that significant numbers of native peoples migrated to the Great Plains and became nomadic bison hunters. In all groups that emphasized hunting, men hunted, while women skinned the animals and processed the meat for food.

Wherever they lived, these indigenous Americans were not a static people, frozen in time waiting for Europeans to "discover" them. Historians have mapped out an amazing array of Indian trails that crisscrossed the continent. Trading in shells, furs, agricultural products, pottery, salt, copper, and slaves, Native Americans had contact with and knowledge of many other groups with whom they shared the continent. Although trade was peaceful, Native Americans sometimes warred with one another over land and resources. This violence had special meaning for women since they and children were often taken captive and sometimes adopted by their captors. Both warfare and ecological pressures such as drought prompted significant migration, the merging of communities to create new native groups, and the rise and fall of powerful Indian nations.

Although accustomed to flux and even to absorbing new peoples into their communities, changes to the worlds of Native American women and their families were of an entirely different order following the European conquest that began with Christopher Columbus's landing on the Caribbean island of San Salvador in 1492. This conquest formed part of a larger search for wealth and commerce that had first led rival European nations to seek trading opportunities in Asia and Africa. In the New World, the Spanish, French, Portuguese, Swedish, Dutch, and English hoped to find gold, slaves, furs, timber, and other valuable products. By the early seventeenth century, they had established a number of permanent colonial settlements, most notably the Spanish founding of St. Augustine (1565) in Florida and Santa Fe (1610) in New Mexico, the French establishment of Quebec (1608), and the English colonies of Jamestown (1607), Plymouth (1620), and Massachusetts Bay (1630). While Europeans sought to control native peoples through force, coerced labor, and at times enslavement, perhaps the most devastating impact of the conquest was the unintentional spread of diseases such as smallpox, for which Native Americans had no immunity. Historians estimate that between 1492 and 1800, over 70 percent of the native population was wiped out.

Significant differences marked the colonial systems of the three major nations engaged in conquering the continent. The Catholic countries of France and Spain had a powerful missionary presence designed to convert and domesticate the Indians. Unlike England's more commercially driven efforts, the French and Spanish came as military units with few women accompanying them. Their colonial systems produced what historians term a "frontier of inclusion" in which they incorporated indigenous peoples into their colonies, though in distinctly subordinate positions. In particular, European men cohabited with and married native women, producing mixed-race, or what the French called *métis* and the Spanish *meztizo,* children. In contrast, the English created "frontiers of exclusion," bringing in white women and generally pushing Native Americans out to make room for their own settlements.

All Europeans assumed the superiority of European culture and characterized indigenous peoples as savages with inferior civilizations. This vision shaped their understanding, or misunderstanding, of Native American societies and especially of Native American women. Witnessing some native women's sexual freedom, Europeans interpreted it as sexual depravity. And when Europeans saw the hard physical labor of native women and what they incorrectly took to be the idleness of men, who hunted rather than farmed, they assumed that lazy husbands had made drudges of their wives. In the early seventeenth century, Englishman William Wood described New England Native American women as "their husbands Caterers, trudging to the Clamm bankes for their belly timber, and their Porters to lugge home their Venison which their lazinesse exposed to the Woolves till they impole it upon their wives shoulders. They likewise sew their husbands shooes, and weaves coates of Turkie fathers, besides all their ordinary household drudgeries which daily lies upon them."[1]

Native American women's lives, however, were more complex than European observers comprehended. Although we have virtually no documents written by the women themselves, a cautious reading of European eyewitness accounts of the communities they encountered has provided historians with insights into early American native lives in the sixteenth and seventeenth centuries. (See Visual Sources: Images of Native American Women, pp. 38–49.) In many Indian nations, women had more power and more sexual equality than most European women of their time. An examination of two well-documented groups provides insight into the diverse lives of Native American women and their cultures.

The Pueblo Peoples

Perched on cliffs in present-day Colorado are the remains of prehistoric dwellings of the native people called Anasazi, who settled in the area as early as 300 B.C. From their distinctive multistoried, mud-plastered buildings came the generic name *Pueblos,* which the Spanish gave to Anasazi descendants such as the Zuni, Hopi, Acoma, and similar peoples who were living in the American Southwest (New Mexico, Arizona, Colorado, and Utah) by A.D. 1250. When the Spanish arrived in the region in the mid-sixteenth century, there were close to 250,000

Pueblo people living in more than one hundred towns and villages. Pueblos encompassed seven language groups, and undoubtedly customs and rituals varied from tribe to tribe, despite many points of similarity. Like many other Indian peoples, the Pueblos apparently experienced much social disruption in the years preceding the conquest. The hostile incursions of more nomadic Apaches from the Great Plains into their region may have been one of the causes for significant Pueblo migration and change in the region during the thirteenth and fourteenth centuries.

By the 1500s, the Pueblos already practiced intensive agriculture, growing corn, squash, and beans. As with other societies, a sexual division of labor characterized their social organization. Men's responsibilities included trade and defense. They also tended the corn crop. Men collected and placed the timbers for the construction of their homes, but women plastered the walls. Women's work centered on what went on within those walls, the "inside" of the community. They created pottery, made moccasins and blankets, and, most crucially, prepared the food. Grinding the dried corn was women's work, a task that daughters and mothers shared. Women viewed their production of food as something vital to their people, as something spiritual, a point reinforced by the Acoma Pueblo origin story that begins this chapter.

In addition to its association with corn and the earth's fertility, women's spirituality—and men's—was tied to their sexuality. Intercourse often held ritualistic

◆ **Anasazi Ladle**
This ceramic Anasazi ladle dates from 900–1300 and was discovered in a cave in Canyon de Chelly, Arizona. The striking black and white design is typical of the pottery of these early cliff-dwellers who were the ancestors of the Pueblo peoples. *Brooklyn Museum of Art, Museum Expedition 1903. Purchased with funds given by A. Augustus Healy and George Foster Peabody. 03.325.10847.*

and religious meanings. It was not only the source of life but also a means of taming bad spirits in nature and of integrating outsiders into the tribe. It helped to maintain the cosmic balance. Pueblo ideology, then, recognized women's sexual power, a factor, like women's role in food production, that contributed to a relatively egalitarian relationship between the sexes.

Women's position in their community was consolidated by the matrilineal lineage system that traced ancestry and access to land through the female line. Like most native peoples, the Pueblos believed that land was occupied communally by families and, in their case, passed through the female line. Control of the land was tied to use, not to some abstract concept of ownership. In addition to being matrilineal, Pueblos were matrifocal, meaning that men left their mothers' homes to marry and moved in with their wives' family. In Pueblo society, men and women could leave their marriages and choose new partners without stigma, an arrangement in accord with the understanding that an individual's primary identity was defined by his or her mother's identity, not a marriage bond. Older women, then, were particularly influential members of the community. While men dominated the "outside" realm—trade, defense, and war—women dominated the inside world of the pueblo walls they had constructed.

Pueblo men's and women's lives changed dramatically with the arrival of the Spanish. In the first decades of the sixteenth century, Spanish forces brutally conquered the Aztecs in Mexico, seizing their wealth and enslaving them. In 1540, a group of Spaniards from central Mexico led by Vásquez de Coronado ventured north into the Pueblo region. Failing to find the gold they had expected, Coronado's men departed but not before they had looted, raped, and massacred Pueblo peoples. In 1598, with the hope of finding another rich empire of Native Americans, the Spaniards returned to what they now called New Mexico, bringing priests, soldiers, and some settlers to the area. They subdued the Pueblos by force and made New Mexico a Spanish colony. Franciscan friars pressured the Pueblos to participate in Catholic Christian rites and suppressed traditional religion. For native women, this meant an attack on key aspects of their culture: fertility cults and rituals tied to sexuality and spirituality. The Church tried to impose a patriarchal system on these women by attempting to restructure the division of labor to model it after European notions of proper gender roles. They urged men to take over building and farming tasks that formerly had been women's work. The friars also called for monogamous, life-long marriages and for female modesty and reserve.

The Pueblo peoples faced other pressures as well. The Spanish demanded tribute, or *encomienda,* in the form of labor, food, and crafts, a strain on the natives' economy that threatened women's control of land and household production. Their hardships were compounded by raids by hostile Apaches and Navajos, who took women and children captives. At the same time, Pueblo women were raped and sexually exploited by Spanish men. What the Pueblos saw as women's gift of a marital alliance, Spanish men saw as their patriarchal right. When the Spanish kept demanding tributes and women's bodies without offering appropriate exchanges, the Pueblos' anger mounted. Eventually, in 1680, the various tribes came together in one of the most effective Indian resistance movements in American history, the Pueblo Revolt, which kept the Spanish out for twelve years.

When the Spanish reasserted their control in 1692, their rule was more relaxed. Meddling less with religious and cultural values, they primarily required *encomienda,* to which most of the Pueblos acceded. Pueblo women's skills at pottery and weaving became important for trade and exchange. Native women also continued to form willing as well as unwilling sexual alliances with Spanish men. Because Pueblos viewed sexual intercourse as a means for a woman to share in her partner's power, sexual relations with Spaniards likely were seen as benefiting the Pueblos as well. Thus, while rape remained common, women also allied themselves with Spanish men as a way of improving their own and their family's economic position. Most telling about the impact of Spanish rule on women is that those groups with the most contact with the colonizers were the most likely to abandon the matrilineal system and substitute Spanish-style patriarchy that gave men more control over women. Spain ruled the American Southwest until 1821 when Mexico achieved its independence and the region came under that nation's control.

The Iroquois Five Nation Confederacy

Far away from the southwestern Pueblos, the Iroquois Five Nations Confederacy—consisting of the Seneca, Cayuga, Oneida, Onondaga, and Mohawk people—constructed another version of native life. In the forests of what became New York State and Ontario, Canada, an estimated 20,000 to 30,000 people lived in perhaps ten villages at the turn of the seventeenth century. The Iroquois were unique among native peoples for their Great League of Peace and Power, founded in 1451, which linked them in an elaborate system of confederation. Another distinctive characteristic of Iroquois culture was the powerful political position given to women. The Iroquois matrilineal system emphasized women's importance for establishing identity and rights to the use of land in each clan. Several families lived together in longhouses, their bark and log dwellings, which were supervised by clans' elder women, or matrons, of the lineage.

The sexual division of labor reinforced women's dominance in the village. Men prepared fields for planting, but their major duties took them to the forests where they hunted, conducted trade, and warred with hostile tribes. Women's responsibilities centered in the village where they raised crops (corn, beans, and squash); gathered mushrooms, berries, and nuts; prepared food; distributed the results of men's hunting; and made baskets, pottery, and other implements. They worked hard but communally. According to Mary Jemison, an Englishwoman captive who lived among them (see box, "Living among the Seneca"), "In order to expedite their business, and at the same time enjoy each other's company, they all work together in one field, or at whatever job they may have on hand." In the spring, Jemison continued, "they chose an older woman to be their driver and overseer, when at labor, for the ensuing year. She accepts the honor, and they consider themselves bound to obey her."[2]

Mary Jemison
Living among the Seneca

Mary Jemison (1743–1833) was captured by Seneca Indians when she was fifteen years old. They adopted her, following a common Iroquoi pattern of viewing captives as replacements for deceased relatives—in Jemison's case, the brother of two women who claimed her. Dickewamis, her Indian name, had opportunities to return to white society after the American Revolution, but she chose to stay with the Senecas. In her old age, Jemison dictated her story, which was first published in 1824. This passage describes her daily life among the Seneca.

I had then been with the Indians four summers and four winters, and had become so far accustomed to their mode of living, habits and dispositions, that my anxiety to get away, to be set at liberty, and leave them, had almost subsided. With them was my home; my family was there, and there I had many friends to whom I was warmly attached in consideration of the favors, affection and friendship with which they had uniformly treated me, from the time of my adoption. Our labor was not severe; and that of one year was exactly similar, in almost every respect, to that of the others, without that endless variety that is to be observed in the common labor of the white people. Notwithstanding the Indian women have all the fuel and bread to procure, and the cooking to perform, their task is probably not harder than that of white women, who have those articles provided for them; and their cares certainly are not half as numerous, nor as great. In the summer season, we planted, tended and harvested our corn, and generally had all our children with us; but had no master to oversee or drive us, so that we could work as leisurely as we pleased. We had no ploughs on the Ohio; but performed the whole

Elder women of the clans played a powerful public role. They selected which males became village chiefs while retaining the right to depose them. Only men served on the Council of Elders, but eligibility for these positions passed through the female line. Women also had a significant voice in religious activities. For example, Seneca women formed Chanters of the Dead, a group that interpreted dreams and participated in numerous rituals. In other ways Iroquois women influenced what might be termed the political side of life. Because they controlled food supplies—both current crops and the food they had carefully preserved and storehoused—they provisioned warriors and thus had a say in plans for raids and wars. They also determined adoptions into the tribe—a means of integrating cap-

process of planting and hoeing with a small tool that resembled, in some respects, a hoe with a very short handle.

Our cooking consisted in pounding our corn into samp or hommany, boiling the hommany, making now and then a cake and baking it in the ashes, and in boiling or roasting our venison. As our cooking and eating utensils consisted of a hommany block and pestle, a small kettle, a knife or two, and a few vessels of bark or wood, it required but little time to keep them in order for use.

Spinning, weaving, sewing, stocking knitting, and the like, are arts which have never been practised in the Indian tribes generally. After the revolutionary war, I learned to sew, so that I could make my own clothing after a poor fashion; but the other domestic arts I have been wholly ignorant of the application of, since my captivity. In the season of hunting, it was our business, in addition to our cooking, to bring home the game that was taken by the Indians, dress it, and carefully preserve the eatable meat, and prepare or dress the skins. Our clothing was fastened together with strings of deer skin, and tied on with the same. . . .

One thing only marred my happiness, while I lived with them on the Ohio; and that was the recollection that I had once had tender parents, and a home that I loved. Aside from that consideration, or, if I had been taken in infancy, I should have been contented in my situation. Notwithstanding all that has been said against the Indians, in consequence of their cruelties to their enemies — cruelties that I have witnessed, and had abundant proof of — it is a fact that they are naturally kind, tender and peaceable towards their friends, and strictly honest; and that those cruelties have been practised, only upon their enemies, according to their idea of justice.

SOURCE: James E. Seaver, *A Narrative of the Life of Mary Jemison: Deh-He-Wä-Mis,* 4th ed. (1824; repr., New York: Miller, Orton, and Mulligan, 1856), 72–74.

tives and minimizing losses due to disease and warfare — and could call for the avenging of deaths in their own families, thus initiating raids and warfare.

Iroquois women's political power impressed European observers. Father Joseph-François Lafitau, a French Jesuit missionary in Canada, noted in 1724 that "nothing, however, is more real than this superiority of the women. . . . The land, the fields and their harvest all belong to them. They are the souls of the Councils, the arbiters of peace and of war. They have charge of the public treasury. To them are given the slaves. They arrange marriages. The children are their domain, and it is through their blood that the order of succession is transmitted."[3] (See Figure 1.6, p. 42.)

The encroachment of Europeans—the English, French, and Dutch—had a major impact on the Iroquois, although they were able to resist far longer than other peoples in the region. Desire to control the lucrative European fur trade that had begun early in the seventeenth century led the Iroquois to a century-long warfare with neighboring groups such as the Mahicans and the Hurons. Participation in this trade had long-term implications, as concentrating on fur for barter undercut Iroquois' self-sufficiency and introduced European goods into daily life. The warfare around the fur trade created severe disruptions for many Indian nations. Ironically, in the short run, this warfare may have increased women's power by removing men from the villages for longer periods of time. New European-made goods, such as metal utensils, pots, needles, thread, cloth, and finished clothing, also lightened the burden of women's work. In the long run, however, the dominance of the fur trade undermined agricultural production and helped to devalue women's contributions to their communities.

The chaos caused by warfare and disease may have been a factor in encouraging many Iroquois men and women to leave their villages for the mission communities established by French Jesuits in Canada. Like the Franciscans in the Southwest, however, Jesuits made every to effort to suppress the sexual expression of the Iroquois and to encourage them to adopt European-style marriages. Many women seemed to have been especially attracted to Catholicism, in part because of the honored position of the Virgin Mary and female saints (see Figure 1.10, p. 46). But the Catholicism of the Iroquois incorporated many distinctive native elements, such as music and decoration. Here, as in the secular facets of life, the Iroquois learned to accommodate to the European presence, but this accommodation became increasingly difficult in the eighteenth century as pressures on the Native Americans mounted.

Native Women's Worlds

Pueblo and Iroquois women lived far apart. Their economic systems and their environments varied dramatically, as did their social structures. Iroquois women had more formal power than Pueblo women. But the similarities in their lives are instructive and provide a starting point for sketching a few broad generalizations about indigenous women of North America in the era of conquest. What were their economic roles? What can we know of their sexual lives? What political and religious influence did they exert within their communities? What impact did the European invasion have on them?

Women's economic significance was a common denominator most indigenous peoples shared. Among the coastal Algonquins, women not only tended crops but also participated in the fishing vital to their people's survival. They fashioned mats and baskets and other essential artifacts of daily life. Among the groups that emphasized hunting, like the Ojibwas of the Great Lakes region or the Apaches of the Great Plains, men's role as hunters were the more highly valued. But women cured the meat and dressed the skins, gathered feathers from birds, fashioned moccasins, and sometimes bartered in the increasingly important fur trade. In 1632, a French cleric, Paul Le Jeune, observed: "The women know what they are to do, and the men also; and one never meddles with the work of the others." As one man reported to Le Jeune, "To live among us without a wife . . . is to live without help, without home, and to be always wandering."[4]

Many indigenous groups embraced a range of sexual expression that shocked European observers, especially when it came to women. With women's fertility understood as part of the earth's fertility, Indians saw women as sexually potent. Matrilineal native societies, which were less concerned with establishing the paternity of children (always a worry for European males), were more likely to tolerate open female sexuality. According to a French observer of the matrilineal Alqonguins, "A Young Woman, say they, is Master of her own Body, and by her Natural Right of Liberty is free to do what she pleases."[5] In some European communities, married women experienced more restrictions, including stiff penalties for adultery, but since native marriages were usually easily dissolved, many native women simply left unhappy relationships. Europeans were also shocked by some groups' polygyny, whereby a man might have multiple wives who were often sisters. Wives may have encouraged this practice because it offered them companionship and someone with whom to share their work.

Formal political power eluded most Native American women. The Iroquois matrons were one exception; another were the few Algonquian women like Wetamo, a sachem (chief) of the Wampanoag people of New England, or Cockacoeske, queen of the Pamunkey Indians of Virginia, who actually held direct authority and power. Informally, women's influence was often significant, especially in the many native communities that emphasized consensus in decision making and allowed the voices of women, particularly older ones, to be heard. As one historian has noted, speaking of the Indians of the East Coast, "The women's power normally operated more covertly, though often no less effectively than the men's, for they were the acknowledged guardians of tradition and peace in societies whose survival depended in large measure on both."[6] In religious matters, women's access to high-status roles varied from group to group. In some groups, they might be healers, crucial to the well-being of their people, while in others they were religious leaders.

Whatever their roles in their societies, Native American women, like men, faced extraordinary challenges in the wake of the European invasion. Historians often describe the collision of the two worlds of indigenous peoples and Europeans in the context of a "Columbian exchange." Europeans imported to the Americas various foods such as wheat and sugar, animals such as horses, devastating diseases, and manufactured goods, including cloth, guns, and metalwork. Enslaved Africans and European settlers were the human part of the exchange. From the New World, the Europeans took the precious metals gold and silver, furs, and crops such as corn, potatoes, and tobacco. The meanings for indigenous peoples of this complex process of collision and exchange varied. The coastal Algonquins, who stood in the way of English colonists' desire for land, experienced a far more rapid assault on their way of life than, for example, the Iroquois Five Nations, whose geographic position, political strength, and protection through the buffering of other tribes helped maintain their independence. Fur- and skins-trading groups, like the Hurons of the Great Lakes or the Creeks of the Southeast, had special pressures of their own as they became more dependent on European goods that they received in return for furs.

Native American women were drawn into contact with Europeans with un-even results. English colonizers in Massachusetts and Virginia, as well as Spaniards in New Mexico, for example, depended heavily on the foodstuffs, especially corn, that Native American women produced. In fur-trading regions, as the hunt for fur intensified, whole tribes became more nomadic. This change disrupted women's influential sphere in the home village and their agricultural contributions to the community, although their role of dressing the fur pelts was still valued. In some regions, such as the Great Lakes, women helped to diversify their communities' economies by producing maple sugar (see Figure 1.6), selling feathers, and developing commercial lead mining. Women's productivity linked them to the Atlantic trading network, making them participants in a far-flung trading enterprise.

Women also frequently became the sexual partners of the white traders, forming long-term unions known as "country marriages." Among the Creek peoples of Alabama, Georgia, and northern Florida, for example, many women married French and English traders. Coosaponokeesa, or Mary Musgrove Matthews Bosonworth, was herself of mixed blood and possibly the daughter of one of the first English traders in the Creek country. She had three sequential marriages to white Georgians, was fluent in her native language of Muskogee and in English, and with her husbands maintained an important trading post. She was instrumental in persuading her people to give land to the founder of the colony of Georgia. Coosaponokeesa and others like her in the frontier trading regions throughout the continent served as human bridges between the Europeans and their own people. These women gave their husbands, in the words of one historian, "an entrée into the cultures and communities of their own people. In this way, Indian women were the first important mediators of meaning between the cultures of two worlds."[7]

Another commonality seems to have been women's role in helping their communities adapt to change. As warfare and trade disrupted external worlds, women's responsibility for maintaining traditional ways at home took on even greater importance. They incorporated enticing European goods into native life, using metal implements to facilitate traditional basket work or using colorful cloth in constructing native apparel. Even in religion, they wove together native practices with the new, fashioning distinctive versions of Christianity. The sexual division of labor, which entrusted so much of daily life to native women, made women conservators of culture in the context of crisis.

SOUTHERN COLONIES

Both the French and the Spaniards continued to be a force on the North American continent well into the early nineteenth century. The Dutch, too, with their settlements and lucrative control of the fur trade in the Hudson River area, exerted considerable influence in northeastern America. Sweden established a lesser stake in the Delaware region, and in the eighteenth century the Russians became a presence in the Northwest (see Map 1.1). Although colonists came from many European nations, the English dominated the eastern seaboard region, which eventually formed the political foundation of the United States as the thirteen English colonies.

English cultural values were particularly influential in shaping early American assumptions concerning women's proper place. Women's work was expected to be confined to household production, even though these notions concerning the sexual division of labor were not always met—particularly among the poor. Both Protestant religious values and English law, especially as it related to property, reinforced women's subordination to men. These ideas about women's gender roles framed the experiences of the Englishwomen who came as settlers to Britain's colonies as well as the African women who came bound as slaves. But the special circumstances of the New World, particularly demographic factors and the economic realities of frontier life itself, also powerfully shaped migrant women's lives.

The English did not succeed in establishing a permanent beachhead on the continent until 1607, when a group of English merchants, armed with a charter from the British crown and calling themselves the London (later Virginia) Company, founded Jamestown (see Map 1.2). These merchants hoped that trade with the Native Americans, especially for precious metals, would reap a fortune for the investors and settlers alike. It was not until 1613 that the colonists finally found a marketable commodity: tobacco. This crop, as well as other staples such as rice and indigo, served a crucial role in the economies of future southern colonies: Maryland (1634); the Carolinas (1663); and Georgia (1732).

White Women Newcomers

The merchants who sought to exploit the perceived wealth of North America needed a steady supply of laborers to make their venture a success. A population explosion in England and rising levels of poverty facilitated the recruitment of thousands willing to make the hazardous journey. The newcomers were overwhelmingly male. To redress this imbalance, in 1620 and 1621 the company imported approximately 150 "tobacco brides"—"respectable" young women, whose passages were paid for with 120 pounds of tobacco by men eager to acquire wives who could serve not only as sexual partners but also as another pair of hands on the farm. Historians are not able to track these women, but their disappearance from historical records suggests that many died, mostly from disease and starvation in the hardship years of 1622–1623. The brides made hardly a dent in improving the balance between the sexes. Women continued to immigrate in small numbers compared to men (in 1635, only 14 percent of the 2,010 arriving from London were women). Maryland, founded to provide refuge for Catholics, had an even greater disproportion of men to women. In the colony's first decade, men outnumbered women by 6 to 1; after 1650, the ratio was 3 to 1. In Maryland and

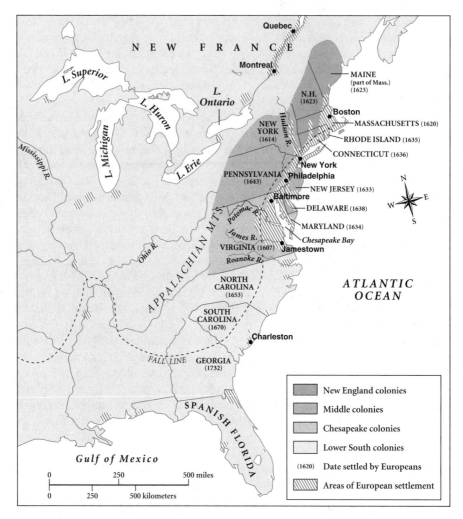

◆ **Map 1.2 American Colonies, 1732**
By 1732, settlers inhabited a narrow band of land that stretched along the eastern seaboard from Maine to Florida. The colonies' claims to tracts of land to the west were contested by Native Americans as well as by the ambitions of France and Spain.

Virginia, it was not until after 1700, when male immigration had slowed and subsequent generations began to reproduce, that the sex ratio came into balance.

Mortality rates remained exceptionally high in the Chesapeake throughout the seventeenth century as a result of harsh conditions, especially the prevalence of diseases such as malaria and dysentery. Men's average life span was 48 years; women's was 39. (The hazards of childbirth caused the disparity; women who survived their childbearing years lived much longer than men.) The death of a spouse often cut marriages short; in Maryland, for example, only one in three couples could expect their marriage to last ten years. With a large pool of prospective mates, widows remarried quickly, creating complicated households of stepsisters and stepbrothers.

The circumstances of the Chesapeake made it difficult to reestablish as strong a patriarchal system as the one that flourished in England. The many children who came to adulthood with just one parent alive had unusual freedom from parental oversight in their marriage choices. In the scattered homesteads of the southern colonies, with little communal oversight given to young couples, premarital sex was probably common. The availability of land and the uncertainty of life induced many Chesapeake fathers to leave land to their daughters as well as to their sons.

Married women, however, generally were just as subordinate to their husbands as in England. Under English common law, which the Chesapeake colonies followed, a married woman became a *feme covert* who subordinated her legal identity to her husband. Without any separate legal identity, married women could not sue or be sued, hold public office, or vote; their husbands had legal control over their property, their children, and even their bodies. When a married woman was brought before the court for an offense, her husband was held responsible, even if the alleged crime was adultery. Those few women who remained single or who were widowed had the status of *feme sole,* which gave them more individual rights in law. A woman lost control of her property when she married, but on her husband's death she did receive a small portion—a dower right, which was no less than one third of the estate—for the duration of her lifetime.

In actuality, Chesapeake widows had better opportunities than widows in England or New England to improve their circumstances by marrying well (or, if they survived more than one husband, by marrying well again). Husbands often left their wives more than the accustomed one-third dower rights—perhaps because they were so uncertain that their children would live to adulthood—and made wives executrices of their estates. Thus, astute women could amass wealth and achieve a degree of economic autonomy. Elizabeth Digges, the widow of the former governor of Virginia, had an estate valued at 1,100 pounds, which was the largest in York County. Other wealthy widows made a name for themselves: they appeared in court to transact legal business connected to their estates and ran ads in colonial newspapers, offering land or slaves for sale.

The most famous Chesapeake woman who acted independently was not a widow, but unmarried. Margaret Brent, a well-connected English Catholic, came to Maryland in 1638. Both she and her sister Mary acquired substantial landholdings that they managed independently. Margaret Brent actively exercised her *feme sole* rights, appearing in court to reclaim debts, making contracts, and conducting her business freely. Her business acumen, her high status as a large landholder and English gentlewoman, and the lack of an appropriate male without political entanglements led the governor of Maryland, Lord Calvert, to name her as his executrix in his will. When he died in 1647, Maryland had recently experienced a local rebellion, and the troops that had put it down had yet to be paid. The responsibility of bringing order to the colony fell to Brent. The Maryland assembly passed a resolution that "the colony was safer in her hands than any man's in the

Province . . . she rather deserves favor and thanks from your honour for her so much concerning for the public safety."[8] Despite this show of trust and respect, the assembly refused in 1647 to honor Brent's novel demand that she be given two votes in the assembly, one based on her role as landowner and another on her role as representative of her male clients. Soon afterwards, Brent relocated to Virginia. Although Brent's story illustrates the fluid Chesapeake circumstances that allowed women to have unusual economic power, and in rare cases even limited political power, it is clearly an exceptional one.

In contrast to Brent, the vast majority of the early white immigrants to the Chesapeake — male and female — came as indentured servants. In Virginia, Maryland, the Carolinas, and Georgia, a system of "bound" labor predominated. Impoverished young people, seeking opportunities unavailable in the Old World, bound themselves in a legal document (an indenture) to masters for fixed periods of time — usually between four and seven years — exchanging their labor for their passage to the colonies and their keep. Recognizing the importance of women in creating a stable colony, the Virginia Company eagerly recruited young women by using propaganda that assured them that they would be treated well, would find it easy to marry at the conclusion of their service, and would not be "put into the ground to worke, but occupie such domestique imployments and housewifery as in England."[9]

As many as three-quarters of the women who migrated to the Chesapeake were indentured. Despite the promises of the colonies' promoters, indentured women servants found life harsh (see box, "The Trappan'd Maiden: or, The Distressed Damsel"). Their responsibilities for food preparation and housekeeping were carried out in primitive ways in small dwellings. In the early years, the zeal to produce a cash crop overrode the English sensibilities about proper gender roles. Instead of concentrating on domestic production, women servants often were sent into the tobacco fields — planting seedlings, hoeing, weeding, and, at harvest, stripping and processing the leaves for market.

In addition to the arduous work expected of these women, the conditions of their servitude increased their hardships. Routinely punished and sometimes severely beaten by masters, women had difficulty securing legal protection because of their bound status. Prohibited from marrying, they were subject to sexual exploitation, although not necessarily by their masters, for whom a pregnant servant or one with an infant was an encumbrance rather than a help. When women became pregnant — and an estimated 20 percent of indentured servants did — they were punished with a public whipping and a fine. Those unable to pay the fine had their time of servitude extended, usually by one to two years. A servant who claimed that the master was the father of her child was not released from service; the Virginia assembly, for instance, worried that if a "woman got with child by her master should be freed from that service it might probably induce such loose persons to lay all their bastards to their masters."[10] Rather, her indenture was transferred to a new master, who paid the county for her services.

Because of the indenture system, most young women who came to the Chesapeake married relatively late, at age 24 or 25. Marriage helped to mark a woman's

◆ **Curing and Drying Tobacco**

This image of tobacco processing depicts a common aspect of women's work in the early Chesapeake, the laborious process of growing and harvesting tobacco. Five slaves in the background, including a child and possibly a woman, hang tobacco leaves to dry. One of the white women in front strips the cured leaves while the other packs them. Tobacco required nearly constant attention, so even though work changed with the season, there was always more than enough. *Culver Pictures.*

freedom from bound labor, but it did not necessarily lighten her load. Some women married "up"—and found themselves the mistress of servants—but others married men less well off than their former masters and found their circumstances reduced. In addition to the added responsibility of childbirth and childcare, wives maintained the household and, in poorer families, often worked in the fields. Many women took on the role of "deputy husband," conducting business and trade during their husbands' absences. Wives' contributions to the household economy were valued, but as elsewhere in the English world, married women lived highly circumscribed lives.

The Trappan'd Maiden: or, The Distressed Damsel

This traditional ballad about the girl who "was cunningly Trappan'd" and "sent to Virginny from England, Where she doth Harship undergo" may or may not have actually been composed by a woman servant, but its lyrics capture the harsh quality of countless indentured women's lives. Note that instead of the customary young woman's lament of betrayal by a lover, this maiden's betrayer is an employer. Folk materials like this ballad form an important resource for historians in the attempt to reconstruct the lives of ordinary people who rarely left written records behind.

Give ear unto a Maid, that lately was betray'd,
And sent into Virginny, O:
In brief I shall declare, what I have suffer'd there,
When that I was weary, weary, weary, weary, O.

[Since] that first I came to this Land of Fame,
Which is called Virginny, O,
The Axe and the Hoe have wrought my overthrow,
When that I was weary, weary, weary, weary, O.

Five years served I, under Master Guy,
In the land of Virginny, O,
Which made me for to know sorrow, grief and woe,
When that I was weary, weary, weary, weary, O.

When my Dame says "Go" then I must do so,
In the land of Virginny, O;
When she sits at Meat, then I have none to eat,
When that I am weary, weary, weary, weary, O. . . .

By 1700, as a native-born generation came to maturity, the imbalanced sex ratio began to right itself. Gender roles lost their flexibility and became more like the restrictive patterns of the English world the colonists had left behind. In established settlements, white women increasingly retreated from arduous work in the fields and shifted their labor to domestic chores. More women engaged in household production, contributing to the family's economy in new ways. A few white women, wealthy enough to have a large retinue of slaves for household tasks, devoted time to such pursuits as studying French, playing music, writing letters, doing needlework, and tending their children. These wealthy women also began to participate in a growing consumer economy, importing gowns, china, silver, and furniture. In Charleston, South Carolina, a flourishing port and the South's largest

If my Dame says "Go!" I dare not say no,
In the Land of Virginny, O;
The Water from the Spring, upon my head I bring,
When that I am weary, weary, weary, weary, O.

When the Mill doth stand, I'm ready at command,
In the Land of Virginny, O;
The Water for to make, which makes my heart to ake,
When that I am weary, weary, weary, weary, O.

When the Child doth cry, I must sing "By-a-by!"
In the Land of Virginny, O;
No rest that I can have, whilst I am here a Slave,
When that I am weary, weary, weary, weary, O.

A thousand woes beside, that I do here abide,
In the Land of Virginny, O;
In misery I spend my time that hath no end,
When that I am weary, weary, weary, weary, O.

Then let Maids beware, all by my ill-fare,
In the Land of Virginny, O;
Be sure to stay at home, for if yon do here come,
You all will be weary, weary, weary, weary, O.

But if it be my chance, Homewards to advance,
From the Land of Virginny, O;
If that I, once more, land on English Shore,
I'll no more be weary, weary, weary, weary, O.

SOURCE: Charles Harding Firth, ed., *An American Garland: Being a Collection of Ballads Relating to America, 1563–1759* (Oxford: Blackwell, 1915), 251–53.

city, elite women hosted elaborate entertainments such as the 1741 "elegant Supper and Ball, at which was a very numerous and gay Appearance of Ladies."[11] Privileged white women's attention to hospitality and fashion, as well as to domesticity and maternal duties, eventually became essential elements in the notion of the genteel lady that reinforced southern patriarchal culture.

Perhaps the biggest change in the lives of white women of all classes was the growth of slavery. By the 1680s, planters turned increasingly to the purchase of African slaves for their labor supply. This momentous transformation came about in part because of a greater availability of slaves at the same time that the supply of European indentured servants began to shrink as employment conditions in England improved. The increased use of African men and women in the fields allowed the planters to reinstitute what they thought were proper gender roles for white women, so that by 1722 Virginian William Beverly could write that "slaves of both sexes are employed together in tilling and manuring the ground" while "a white woman is rarely or never put to work in the ground."[12]

African Women

Whether they were slaveowners or not, white women's lives were inextricably tied up with slavery. Until the mid-seventeenth century, relatively few Africans had been imported into North America, and the historical records on them are spotty. One of the first African women was "Mary," who arrived in Virginia in 1622 and ended up at the same plantation as "Antonio a Negro." Although the details are unknown, eventually the two won their freedom, married, adopted the surname *Johnson*, raised a large family, and became modest landowners. The couple's experience points to an important fact about early African servitude: initially the system was a fluid one that allowed some blacks opportunities for freedom and created a small nucleus of free blacks in the region.

Historians have debated at length over the origins of the American system of chattel slavery, whereby human beings became the permanent legal property of their owners. How crucial was Europeans' sense of Africans' racial inferiority? How vital was the region's labor shortage? At what precise time did Africans move from a servant status shared with indentured whites to a distinctive condition where they and their children were perpetually enslaved? Virginia's laws concerning black women servants are exceptionally revealing of the steps the Chesapeake colonies took toward institutionalizing slavery (see pp. 63–64). The 1643 law that explicitly placed a tax on the labor of African women, for example, placed them in the same category as paid male (European and African) labor. White women were exempted from this tax, under the assumption that they worked in the homes, not in the fields—more the ideal than the reality, as the picture on page 19 suggests. By making a sharp distinction between black and white women's roles, the law thus contributed to the view of Africans as fundamentally distinct from Europeans. As one historian explains, "lawmakers assumed that the English gender division of labor—the one they continued to hope would take hold in the colony—did not and need not apply to Africans."[13]

This first encoding of the distinction between black and white women was followed by others. Particularly important was the 1662 law that made bondage heritable from one generation to the next: "all children borne in this country shall be held bond or free only according to the condition of the mother."[14] A major break with English precedent, which held that children followed their father's condition, this law made the paternity of a slave woman's child legally irrelevant. In essence, enslavement was now not limited to an individual's lifetime but passed to offspring through the female parent. This devaluation of paternity also increased the slave woman's vulnerability to rape, even though the 1662 law imposed stiff penalties on whites who had sexual intercourse with blacks. Not all of the piecemeal legislation that created the institution of perpetual slavery centered on women and their bodies, but these two laws indicate the intertwining roles that gender, sexuality, and reproduction played in drawing the lines between free and enslaved, between white and black.

The harshness of African women's American existence began when they were kidnapped or sold into slavery by African slave traders who supplied them to Europeans in search of laborers for their colonial dominions. They suffered the horrific "midpassage" across the Atlantic where men were packed into the stultifying holds and women often were held on the decks. There they faced less congestion but were more vulnerable to crew members' sexual attacks. African women's adjustment to their new environment was made more difficult by language and cultural barriers. While most came from West Africa, they represented numerous groups and languages and could not easily communicate among themselves.

Once in America, slaves were sold to planters for work in the tobacco fields. In contrast to the large plantations with numerous slaves that developed in the 1700s, most black slaves in the 1600s lived and worked in small isolated groups. Slaves' fertility was low in the seventeenth century: they bore an average of three children. Marriage between slaves was not permitted by law, and stable unions were difficult to form in the face of the threat of sale and the reality of widely dispersed residences. In all likelihood, women raised their children alone, away from their mates. In this, their patterns bore some similarity to West African family practices, where women and their children lived with the mother's family and fathers lived nearby. But unlike the African situation, women in the New World lacked the supporting kinship network. Later in the history of slavery, women relied heavily on a network of real and fictive kin on plantations to share in childrearing, but in the early days, African women were isolated and slave communities rare.

The peoples of West Africa valued women's agricultural expertise, and thus African female slaves were already used to farm labor. In the Chesapeake, they worked alongside men in labor gangs in the tobacco fields. The records of planter Robert Parnafee indicate that the value of his "servant wench's" tobacco crop was 1,140 pounds, comparable to his male slaves' production. In South Carolina—where slave importation was so dramatic after 1700 that Africans formed a majority in the population—African women helped to introduce rice cultivation, which was widespread in West Africa. In South Carolina, women borrowed from African techniques as they planted rice by digging a hole with their heel and then using their foot to cover the seeds with soil. Their hoeing in unison to work songs and the flat coiled baskets they made for threshing the rice drew also on African traditions.

Slavery was far from a static system. In the South, the most significant historical change was the gradual process of institutionalizing perpetual slavery, which was firmly in place by the turn of the eighteenth century. Another important development was the emergence of a "creole" (that is, native-born African American) group. Because of the initially skewed sex ratio and the low fertility of African immigrant women, slaves did not begin to have enough children to offset their deaths and increase their numbers until the 1720s. Better nutrition and the recognition by masters that slave reproduction added to their own wealth contributed to increased fertility of second-generation women, who on average had nine children. As plantations

◆ **West Africa Women Hulling Rice**
This eighteenth-century engraving shows West African women hulling rice using the technology and skills that they brought with them to America. After placing the grain in a large mortar hollowed from the trunk of a pine or cypress tree, the women pound it with long wooden pestles, removing the husks and whitening the grains. Such prodigious labor made possible the highly successful Carolinas rice industry. By the 1770s, slaves were annually processing 75 million tons of rice for export and millions more for their own consumption.
Library of Congress.

became larger and demanded more slaves, more opportunities for slave communities developed. Planters instituted a more distinct sexual division of labor. Men worked in skilled or semiskilled trades or were assigned to plowing; women hoed and performed other less skilled jobs such as spreading manure and building fences. It was still relatively rare in the seventeenth century for slave women to serve exclusively as house servants on large plantations, but their numbers were increasing, and many slave women became important in household textile production as well.

After two centuries of English colonization, tobacco and rice plantations and the slave labor that sustained them had created a distinctive economy and culture in the Chesapeake and Carolinas. This slave society profoundly affected women's lives both black and white. At the same time, other English colonies had developed distinctive economies and cultures in which slavery existed but as only one form of labor. In New England and the middle colonies, however, as in the southern colonies, unique circumstances of frontier life impinged on traditional English notions of women's gender roles.

NEW ENGLAND COLONIES

Despite their common English origins, the colonies of New England differed dramatically from the Chesapeake and Carolina settlements. Although climate and geography accounted for some of the differences—New England did not offer possibilities for staple crop agriculture—at the center of the distinctive quality of New England was its early settlers' religion. Unlike in the southern colonies, economic motives, although present, were not foremost.

The people who founded Plymouth (1620), Massachusetts Bay (1630), Connecticut (1635), and New Hampshire (1638) were "Puritans," separatist dissenters from the established Anglican Church of England. Subject to religious persecution and inspired by the idea of creating a harmonious Christian commonwealth in the New World—what Puritan leader John Winthrop described as "a city on a hill" that would be a model for all peoples—nearly 50,000 Puritans left England between 1620 and 1640. Dedicating themselves to a righteous and disciplined life based on a covenant with God, they established a society in which church and state intertwined, giving the religious and moral values of Puritanism the force of law. If in the Southeast demography was one of the defining factors shaping women's lives, in New England, religion served as a powerful force constructing gender roles and framing women's experiences.

The Puritan Search for Order: The Family and the Law

The Puritans' religious beliefs facilitated the rapid establishment of stable communities. Nearly three-quarters of Puritan settlers migrated in family groups that included wives and daughters, in contrast to the Chesapeake colonists, where the vast majority of migrants were men. Even so, as many as one-third of the adult male settlers came as unmarried men, creating a skewed sex ratio of single men to single women of approximately 4 to 1 that led to an early age of marriage for women. However, New Englanders soon began to reproduce. They had high and rising rates of childbirth (first-generation Plymouth women bore an average of 7.8 children, the majority of whom lived to adulthood) and long marriages, both of which contrasted with the Chesapeake. Within Puritan ideology, the family stood as a lynchpin of social order, a value that was magnified in the frontier conditions of the New World as the colonists encountered physical hardships, disease, and persistent conflicts with Native Americans. Although Puritans encouraged love and respect between husbands and wives, they nonetheless embraced hierarchical notions of family, with each person's role clearly delineated. So crucial to social order was the family unit that the relatively rare adult single man or woman was required to live within a family to ensure his or her righteous behavior.

Religious ideas also shaped the Puritan legal framework. The Massachusetts colonies followed the English principle of *feme covert*, so, as in the Chesapeake and Carolinas, married women had few legal rights. New England widows had more opportunities to control their wealth than those in England, but New England courts often oversaw the process, frequently insisting that widows be of good character before gaining unimpeded access to their dower rights. In some ways, New England laws at least initially were more favorable to women than in the old country or in other colonies. Because Puritans, as part of their dissent from the Church of England, viewed marriage as a civil contract rather than as a religious sacrament, they permitted divorce and allowed partners to remarry. Preventing bigamy

◆ **The Cheney Family**

This elaborate family portrait by an unknown artist dates from the late eighteenth century. The number and age spread of the children suggests the long period of childbearing and childrearing typical for colonial women and may account for the worn look on Mrs. Cheney's face. Her eldest daughter, seated next to her, is married to the man standing at the rear and holds two of her own children, who are not much younger than her siblings. *The Cheney Family, Gift of Edgar William and Bernice Chrysler Garbisch, Image © 2004 Board of Trustees, National Gallery of Art, Washington.*

among men and women unable to secure legal dissolution of unhappy marriages was also a factor in shaping colonial New Englanders' approach to divorce. Women were more likely to obtain divorces if they could claim that men failed to meet expectations for proper male behavior, for instance, through desertion or impotence. Although Puritan divorce practices offered women more legal protection than they had in England, women did not thereby gain power in marriage. As one scholar of early eighteenth-century Connecticut law concludes, "A long-suffering wife could be freed from a husband who utterly neglected his familial responsibilities, but a woman who challenged her spouse's decisions, no matter how abusive his behavior, received no relief from the divorce law."[15]

The Puritan moral code, at least in the early years of settlement, punished both men and women—though not equally—for sexual crimes such as intercourse outside of marriage. Premarital pregnancy, as long as the couple married, was not harshly condemned. In the absence of marriage, however, a woman in childbirth was pressured to name the father so he could be held as accountable as the mother and so that the child's and mother's financial needs could be met. But the Puritans did not avoid a sexual double standard. A married man's liaison with an unmarried woman was a less serious offense than a married women's relationship with an unmarried man. As Puritan William Gouge put it, her crime created "greater infamy before men, worse disturbance of the family, more mistaking of legitimate, or illegitimate children."[16] Similarly, rape of a married woman was regarded, in the words of one historian, as "not the offense against the woman but the offense against her husband."[17]

That women were subordinate to men was evident throughout Puritan society. New England colonies mandated by law that all children be taught to read, and women did have a high literacy rate. Yet rosters indicate that few girls attended school; those who did were not encouraged to learn to write. Not surprisingly, few women wrote diaries or books. (See Documents: By and About Colonial Women, pp. 50–64.) Of the 911 books produced in seventeenth-century New England, only 4 were by women. Of these, the most famous was Anne Bradstreet's *Several Poems Compiled with Great Variety of Wit and Learning* (1678). Bradstreet's brother, the pastor Thomas Parker, wrote to Bradstreet, "Your printing of a Book, beyond the custom of your sex, doth rankly smell."[18] Perhaps in response, Bradstreet wryly noted in one of her poems:

I am obnoxious to each carping tongue
Who says my hand a needle better fits,
A Poets pen all scorn I should thus wrong
for such despite they cast on female wits.[19]

Mary Rowlandson's *A True History of the Captivity and Restoration of Mrs. Mary Rowlandson* (1677) was another of these books. Although part of what made it so successful was a horrified fascination with the details of a white woman's sojourn among people the colonists viewed as savages, another reason is that Rowlandson's survival was seen as a sign of God's blessing on the Puritan community. Rowlandson herself expressed the meaning of her ordeal in the context of faith: "The Lord hath shewn me the vanity of these outward things . . . that they are but a shadow, a blast, a bubble, and things of no continuance. That we must rely upon God himself, and our whole dependence must be upon him."[20] But if Puritan leaders valued Rowlandson for her pious example, they drew clear boundaries to contain women who presumed to offer their own doctrinal interpretations. Even though Puritan women shared with men the right to be members of the church once they satisfactorily testified to their salvation, the clergy and other male community leaders periodically punished or banished heretical women who challenged male authority.

Disorderly Women

In the 1630s, Massachusetts leaders faced a major controversy that challenged both religious orthodoxy and gender assumptions: the case of Anne Hutchinson. Hutchinson believed that people were "saved" by a direct and sudden infusion of God's spirit, not by mere adherence to the Puritan moral code. Thus she challenged not only religious doctrine but also the clergy who interpreted it and the magistrates who enforced Massachusetts colony laws. Her provocation went even deeper; she also contested the subordinate status of women in the Puritan religious world. Hutchinson arrived in the colony with her merchant husband in 1634 and began her religious proselytizing in conjunction with her role as midwife in the all-female groups that customarily attended women in childbirth. From this venue, hidden from male eyes, Hutchinson moved on to have informal religious meetings in her home, where she expounded on her theological interpretations to large mixed-sex groups. As her popularity mounted, clergymen and other male leaders worried that her radical religious views were becoming a threat to the colony. Using their power—both religious and civil—they tried to make her see her theological errors and cease her disruptive activities.

Hutchinson's refusal led to her dramatic trial for heresy in 1637. The prominent minister John Cotton preached to Boston women that Hutchinson "is but a Woman and many unsound and dayngerous principles are held by her." The formal accusation brought against her charged that "you have rather been a Husband than a Wife and a preacher than a Hearer; and a Magistrate than a Subject."[21] Trial records indicate that Hutchinson ably defended both her religious ideas and a woman's right to expound upon them, to no avail. Excommunicated and banished, she moved to Rhode Island, established in 1636 as a haven for the growing number of refugees from Massachusetts orthodoxy.

Although Hutchinson was unusually charismatic and her case especially dramatic, she represented not just a religious controversy that attracted men and women but also an undercurrent of female rebelliousness that community leaders felt compelled to repress. In the aftermath of her trial, churches began to drop the requirement that women make their conversion statements publicly. Instead they could relay their experience privately to their ministers who, in turn, would convey their words to the congregation. Moreover, one historian has found that during this crisis the percentage of female defendants brought before the courts rose significantly. Either women were more assertive or the magistrates were more determined to discipline women, especially those influenced by religious heresy.

The most dramatic crime associated with women was witchcraft. Of the 344 people accused of being witches in the colonial period, 80 percent were female; of the men accused, half were relatives of accused female witches. Two major outbreaks of witch-hunting occurred in New England: one during the period 1647–1663 in which 79 people were accused and 15 hanged, and another in 1692, centered in Salem, Massachusetts, in which over 200 were accused and 19 were hanged.

Witchcraft was a complex crime. Sometimes women charged with being Satan's servants were associated with heresy. Many of Anne Hutchinson's critics, for example, never formally accused her but hinted that she was a witch. For others, it was less their religious positions than their *maleficium,* or malicious actions against their neighbors, that brought them to trial. Did milk sour, an animal die, a child take sick? Did a midwife assist—or perhaps cause—a deformed birth? Did young girls have fits and see an unpopular village woman in spirit form? Did men believe themselves sexually ravaged by a neighbor woman with supernatural powers?

The finger often pointed at an older, often poor and powerless, woman. She might have a reputation for being argumentative, discontented, or prideful. She might also be suspected of causing abortion and infanticide, or if she were a midwife, of using her healing power for ill, instead of good. Another major category of witches—more evident in the Salem cases—were those with some measure of authority or prestige. For example, a widow engaged in a dispute with her husband's heirs over property rights was a likely candidate for suspicion. Indeed, as the frenzy escalated in Salem, the accused included many elite men and women. Their accusers were often young women who claimed the witches had "possessed" them. The young women's accusations gave them an unprecedented opportunity to influence community affairs and to exercise a degree of power, thus complicating the gender dimensions of the incidents. Indeed, the situation quickly spun out of the control of the clergy and magistrates, who ceased to support the prosecutions. Eventually, the governor of Massachusetts interceded and brought the trials to a halt in 1692.

What accounts for these tumultuous outbursts of witch-hunting? Most historians believe that societal tensions laid the groundwork. Concern about religious dissent created anxiety about the social order and made colonial leaders eager to suppress possible minions of Satan in their midst. In the Salem cases, religious dissent had already been squelched, but other issues operated. Many Salem residents were refugees from violent Indian wars on the southern Maine frontier. Their prominence in the Salem cases suggests a link between the community's susceptibility to believing in the malevolent power of witches among them (and those witches' ability, for example, to aid the "heathen" Indians in massacring the Christian settlers) and the insecurities of living near the frontier at a time of heightened Indian resistance to colonial encroachment. In addition, by the 1690s the stability of New England's Puritan order was being eroded by the growth of trade, an influx of immigrants, and the inroads of secularism and materialism. These tensions were compounded by a growth in population that put pressure on available land, which in turn created intergenerational tensions as young people chafed at the older generation's control of family property. While these sources of anxieties help to explain the dynamics of the Salem furor, they do not fully acknowledge that the witch hunts had a strong gendered component. Much of their frenzy was directed toward older women who were viewed as either deviant or powerful; in either case, accused witches seemingly violated their female gender roles.

Women's Work and Consumption Patterns

Only a small minority of women were involved in the dramatic events connected to mid- to late seventeenth-century witch-hunts or religious dissents. Most New England women led ordinary, work-filled lives. Wealthier women's labor was less physically demanding than rural women's, but all women's work was valued for its contribution to the family economy. The division of labor followed English patterns: men's duties concentrated outside the home in farming, fishing, or trade; women's duties centered within the home around food preparation, childbearing, and childrearing. "Goodwives," as hard-working married women were called, tended domestic animals and vegetable gardens, and fashioned meals with the few cooking utensils available. They produced candles and soap and worked at spinning and clothes making.

Women created networks of female friends and relatives to help with their tasks. Since few women were mistresses of all necessary household trades, they usually bartered among themselves for household necessities, especially in more remote areas where women's lives were harder and their time more constrained. Women trained their own daughters in wifely responsibilities and often took in daughters of neighbors to apprentice them in exchange for their household labor. And in another form of distinctly female labor, childbirth, women came together in close communion, often spending days at a prospective mother's home, giving practical assistance and emotional comfort during a time when between almost one in ten New England women died of childbirth or related complications.

Midwives were central figures in the New England world of women and demonstrate that women could and did engage in work beyond their own homes. They generally were highly respected and often served as doctors for a variety of ailments, tending the sick with herbal remedies. Payment for their assistance was received as goods-in-kind—chickens, eggs, cloth, sugar, and so on—or as coin from more prosperous citizens. Other women too moved outside the sexual division of labor. If her husband was away hunting, serving in the militia, or trading, the wife conducted family business and represented the husband in legal matters. Widows, who as *femes sole* could act on their own, often ran taverns, inns, or printing establishments. Many took pride in their abilities to manage their estates. Bostonian Ann Pollard reported that by her "own proper gettings by my Labour and Industry" the estate of her husband "is Considerably Advanced and bettered."[22]

As the colonies' commerce increased, colonial mercantile cities such as New York, Philadelphia, Boston, and Charleston grew in size and importance. At the same time, King William's War (1689–1697) and Queen Anne's War (1702–1713), European conflicts that also played out in the American colonial empires, created a dramatic rise in widows, who with their children often moved to urban centers like Boston, where widows represented 16 percent of the population by 1725. Poorer town women, encouraged to work by community leaders eager to keep them off the charity rolls, found employment as seamstresses and in other trades that drew on their wifely skills. Shopkeeping was another avenue for women, and historians estimate that between 1740 and 1775, over ninety Boston women operated commercial enterprises.

A small proportion of working women in the New England colonies were African slaves. In the eighteenth century, slaves probably constituted between 2 and 3 percent of New England's population. (Slavery was abolished in most of New England in the late eighteenth century.) Although some slave women in the North labored in the fields, more commonly they worked as domestic servants, especially in the growing cities. In contrast to southern slaves, they were also more likely to be trained in skilled housewifery. One advertisement offering a woman for sale described her as skilled in all "household arts and especially talented in needlework."[23] Even more obviously than in the early South, the labor of black women slaves in New England contributed to the leisure of their white mistresses, usually the wives of merchants, professionals, and craftsmen.

For these prosperous women and their daughters, increased free time contributed to changes in their daily life. Some took up activities like fancy needlework that demonstrated their genteel feminine skills. Well-to-do women increasingly bought what they needed instead of making it themselves, and imported goods were especially popular. Boston milliner and merchant Elizabeth Murray offered satin gloves, ebony fans, and ermine muffs. Although this kind of opulence was still unusual, it pointed to the emergence of a consumer culture in urban areas.

◆ **The Potter Family**
This mid-eighteenth-century painting reveals the prosperity of the Potter family of Matunuck, Rhode Island. The young boy serving them tea is either a slave or a servant and demonstrates how northern women and their families benefited from the labor of African Americans. *The Newport Historical Society (53.3).*

◆ Sarah Bradstreet's "Adam and Eve" Sampler

The first American examples of needlework samplers were simple ones that contained rows of letters and numbers and were made by young girls as part of their training in housewifery. By the end of the seventeenth century in New England, however, a distinctive female art form—needlepoint "fancy" work—became widespread among more prosperous women and was often taught in schools for girls that emphasized such skills as drawing and embroidery. In eighteenth-century Boston a school of needlepoint emerged that featured a popular religious topic, Adam and Eve in the Garden of Eden. This example created by Sarah Bradstreet in 1754 indicates the way in which young women began to move beyond plain needlework to needlepoint by including artwork in their designs and using fine embroidery yarn. *Courtesy of Historic Deerfield, Inc. Photograph by Amanda Merullo.*

This consumer culture was part of a broad pattern of economic change evident in New England life, especially after 1700. Population increases and immigration from numerous nations had swelled the population of what were now four colonies (Massachusetts, Connecticut, Rhode Island, and New Hampshire) to almost 100,000. As urban areas and commerce grew and class distinctions increased, the region became less distinctly Puritan and more diverse in its religious character. Ministers complained about the decline in faith and morality. Men, increasingly focused on economic success, moved away from religion, leaving women to predominate in most churches and beginning a distinctive association with moral and spiritual matters that deepened over time (see Chapter 3). Puritans' political control slipped as well, as the British crown revoked the Massachusetts charter in 1684 and soon established the short-lived Dominion of New England, which constricted the colonists' self-government. In a new charter of 1692, the influence of the Puritan church was greatly reduced when property holding, not church membership, became the basis for freeman — and voting — status.

Some scholars argue that the breakdown of the Puritan commonwealth also eroded the power of the patriarchal family, giving women a greater degree of freedom. Certainly new prosperity and urban growth stimulated female education and opened increased economic opportunities for some women. Changes in church membership patterns gave women more voice in the religious sphere of life, but at a time when church influence was declining. Perhaps the most significant change toward the end of the colonial period in New England was the increased diversification in women's lives — the continued hard labor on the farms, the variety of work in the cities, the increased presence of female slaves as servants, and new goods for consumption for prosperous urban women. These patterns pointed to the segmentation of women's communities that would persist throughout the course of American history, in New England and beyond.

MIDDLE COLONIES

From initial settlements in Virginia and Massachusetts in the early seventeenth century, the English in America expanded all along the eastern seaboard by 1750. Maryland, Virginia, the Carolinas, and Georgia were organized around staple crop agriculture and slave labor. The economy of New England was centered in commerce. In between, the Dutch colony of New Netherland was conquered by the English in 1664 and renamed New York. From New York, New Jersey emerged as an independent colony in the 1680s. In 1681 the Quaker William Penn received a charter from the British king giving him authority to establish Pennsylvania. These new "middle colonies" infused variety into English colonies. New York's complex mix included the Dutch, Germans, French Huguenots, Africans, and Jews. Pennsylvania also attracted a diverse group of nationalities, and, because of Penn's desire to preserve religious freedom for Quakers, had a policy of religious toleration that encouraged diversity.

Women in New Netherland and New York

The middle colonies' heterogeneity produced some distinctive patterns for women. Among the most dramatic was married women's legal status under the Dutch. In contrast to the British concept of *feme covert,* Dutch women could choose their form of marriage, either *mantus* or *usus.* In the former, they accepted their husband's authority over them; in the latter, women were considered equal partners in marriage and maintained their legal identity and their maiden name. They viewed their possessions as community property, or in the words of one couple, Lawrence Zachaarison Sluijs and Annetie Oenen, they felt that they had "gained together their estate." Both husband and wife usually constructed a mutual will, in which each left the estate to the other, postponing the children's inheritance until both died. Married women could and did own property and manage their own businesses. Margaret Hardenbroeck perfectly exemplified the New Netherland businesswomen. She immigrated to America in 1659 and established herself as a successful trader who represented other merchants as well. When she married Pieter Rudolhus DeVries, she maintained her business and at his death became a very wealthy widow. In her second marriage, to Frederick Philipsen, the couple drew up a *usus* contract that delineated her private property rights and ensured that she would be able to continue her commercial activities. The couple were highly successful traders and partners in their own shipping line who often acted as each other's agent in business matters and in court.

When the English conquered New Netherland, they decreed that Dutch inheritance laws could be sustained and Dutch contracts honored. But women's positions changed significantly in just a few decades. As more English men and women settled in New York, they implemented English common law practices that circumscribed married women's property rights. Even Dutch women gradually became less visible in the public sphere. In Albany, for example, forty-six women were listed as traders before the British conquest, but by the turn of the century, there were none. Women's names also became less prevalent in the rosters of skilled artisans and proprietors—brewers, bakers, and the like—and women were less likely to appear in court representing themselves or others. Margaret Hardenbroeck continued her business ventures, but when she bought land in New Jersey, her husband had to make the purchase for her.

As Dutch men began to transfer more of their wealth to their adult children rather than to their wives, they also began to distinguish between male and female heirs, leaving sons real property and daughters cash and moveable goods; such inheritances were equal in value but different in kind. The biggest losers, however, were wives. As an increasingly competitive economy placed more pressures on the colonial family, the distinctive rights of Dutch married women gave way to the dominant culture. In 1710, the New York assembly passed a law that lumped married women together with minors and with those judged of unsound mind, all of whom presumably were not capable of acting on their own.

Women in Pennsylvania

The women of Pennsylvania represent yet another pattern. In this colony, Quakers were numerous and influential. Unlike the Dutch, Quaker women had no distinctive economic privileges, yet religious values made their society unusually egalitarian. George Fox, the seventeenth-century English founder of the Quakers, argued that before the "fall" that ousted Adam and Eve from Eden, men and women were "both meett helpes, and they was both to have Dominion over all that God made."[24] Fox's radical emphasis on equality between husband and wife was in keeping with Quaker ideas that criticized hierarchical relations in general and in religion specifically. The Quakers believed that "the Inner Light of Christ" was available to all equally as an intimate, revelatory experience of God. In the words of one historian, this inner light experience "could include revelations beyond scripture, making the personal, individual relationship to God superior to any other experience of worship, such as liturgy and sermonizing."[25] Among American Quakers, a number of women, such as Elizabeth Norris of Philadelphia, were noted for eloquently articulating that women should not be subordinated to men in religion or the family. Most Quakers did not fully embrace the radical implications for men's and women's status that their theology embodied, but the religion did offer women unusual opportunities to challenge conventional expectations about their roles.

Thus women in Quaker communities could achieve public religious authority, both in England and in the colonies. In contrast to the Puritan effort to suppress women's religious speech, among Quakers women were often respected religious teachers, in part because religious ministry was not ordained or institutionalized among them. It was not unusual for women such as Sarah Morris or Jane Fenn to travel back and forth across the Atlantic and throughout the colonies on their religious missions. Quaker institutions reflected women's high status. In Pennsylvania, women's local monthly groups sent representatives to quarterly meetings, which in turn sent representatives to a yearly convocation in Philadelphia. Created "for the better management of the discipline and other affairs of the church more proper to be inspected by their sex," the meetings monitored family life in the community.[26] In particular, they forwarded petitions for marriage that determined whether the couple embraced appropriate Quaker values. By formalizing the responsibility of some Quaker matrons to monitor the behavior of other women, Quaker practice offered an additional degree of religious power to women.

Not all Pennsylvania women were Quakers. The region's success in wheat and rye production attracted English, Welsh, Swedish, Ulster Scots, and German settlers to its fertile land. Rural farm women were likely to put in at least some time in the fields, as did the white women of the Chesapeake. And here, too, there seems to have been a large servant population that included many women. Wives of tenant farmers often assisted in the harvest or did domestic work in other people's homes, and white women were also indentured or free servants in rural areas. In addition, Pennsylvania and other middle colonies relied on male and female slaves for agricultural work; slave women not only worked in the fields but also served as

◆ **Dutch Farm Family**
Martin Van Bergen of Leeds, New York, celebrated his prosperity by commissioning this painting of his farm in the Hudson River valley. The family's wealth is evident in the fine clothing the farmer and his wife (center) are wearing, the size of their home, and the presence of black slaves among their workers. Many Dutch farmers in the Hudson River valley prospered at the expense of slaves, whom they owned in much greater numbers than did their English neighbors. *Fenimore Art Museum, Cooperstown, New York.*

domestics and as dairy maids. Before 1750 about 20 to 30 percent of Pennsylvania's labor force were slaves.

As was the case in New England, slave women were particularly evident in the burgeoning cities of the middle colonies. In 1664, when the English conquered New Netherlands, over 20 percent of New York's population were slaves. Philadelphia, Boston, and Newport also had significant slave populations in the late seventeenth and early eighteenth centuries, as well as small free black populations. Free and enslaved black women served primarily as domestic labor, but they may also have assisted in small shops under the supervision of white women merchants. By the mid-eighteenth century, about 12 percent of Philadelphia households were headed by a woman, often a widow who had independent means or was engaged in retail trade or in running lodging houses. The growing number of white female servants reflected the increase in class stratification evident throughout the British colonies on the eve of the Revolution.

CONCLUSION: The Diversity of American Women

As diverse as the women who inhabited North America from 1600 to 1750 were, their lives did share some commonalities. All women operated within a fairly rigid sexual division of labor, although the actual tasks assigned to them varied from culture to culture. Most women's roles included childbearing, childrearing, and food preparing. Within their communities, women tended to form strong bonds with other women in similar circumstances—the corn grinders of the Pueblos, the planters of the Iroquois, the female bartering networks of New Englanders, and the supportive communities of slave women are among the most obvious examples. With some exceptions, women shared an exclusion from direct political participation. They also shared the burdens—although they varied widely—of adjusting to the New World environment that European conquest and settlement of North American created.

Despite these basic commonalities, the differences among women of this period were striking. Not only were there significant variations among Native, African, and European women, but there were differences within each group. Native American women encompassed perhaps the richest cultural variety. But Africans, as well, represented various languages and cultural groups. Among European women, too, distinctions emerged. Between first- and second-generation settlers, there were major differences in quality of life, especially in the southern colonies. Beyond that, ethnic, religious, and regional differences proved powerful determinants of women's legal and economic circumstances. And by the mid-eighteenth century, class—both in growing cities and in the plantation regions of the South—had become as important as any other factor that shaped women's experiences.

Historians in the past were tempted to see the colonial period as a monolithic one in which women's lives were static. Reading back from nineteenth-century middle-class gender roles, which relegated women firmly to the private world of the home, historians viewed the white colonial woman's participation in a pre-industrial household economy as empowering. A similar tendency to romanticize the hard life of Native American women contrasted their freedom and influence with the patriarchal structure within which European women lived. Although comparisons are perhaps inevitable, they can obscure the complexities of women's lives—both the diversity that characterized them and the points of common ground they shared. Such comparisons also deflect attention from the historical changes that shaped these women's lives: the conquest of Native Americans, the importation and enslavement of Africans, the massive migration of Europeans, and the economic and political maturing of the British colonies. The period covered by the next chapter, the revolutionary era of 1750–1800, was also thick with changes that powerfully affected the lives of women.

VISUAL SOURCES

Images of Native American Women

A MAJOR OBSTACLE facing historians of women is a lack of *primary* or original sources. Because they were less literate and usually less engaged than men in public life, women were not as likely to create written records. When they did write, their words were infrequently published or saved. The material we do have is overwhelmingly by elite or middle-class women. The voices of the poor and of the nonliterate, including Native Americans and Africans, are particularly obscured, especially in the early colonial period. But historians of the "bottom up," of men and women outside the realm of leadership and power, are very resourceful. These historians mine demographic data, scour court records and wills, borrow from ethnographers and folklorists, and examine material culture, or artifacts, to reconstruct the lives of people who have left relatively few traditional historical documents behind.

In exploring the lives of early native American women, historians use two major sources: one is the archaeological record of artifacts created by indigenous groups before the European invasion; the second are the images and narratives produced by Europeans eager to describe the peoples they encountered in what they viewed as the New World. As this essay on images of native women suggests, both sources have their limitations in conveying women's lives accurately and clearly.

Figure 1.1, a stone effigy pipe of a woman grinding corn, dates from about 1200 and came from the Spiro Mound people of what is now Oklahoma. Figure 1.2, a similar pipe showing the

◆ Figure 1.1 **Effigy Pipe from Spiro Mound, Oklahoma (c. 1200)**
Werner Forman/Art Resource, New York. National Museum of the American Indian, Smithsonian Institution.

◆ Figure 1.2 **Effigy Pipe from Cahokia Mound, Illinois (c. 1200–1400)**
Collection of Dr. Kent Westbrook. Photo by John T. Pafford.

same corn motif, came from the Cahokia Mound area in today's Madison County, Illinois. Based on what you have already read about corn cultivation and Native American women, what is the significance of this type of depiction? Fortunately, historians are not totally dependent on guesswork in interpreting such images, as they can build upon a wide range of archaeological evidence. The people of Spiro and Cahokia were part of a large group of people whom historians call Mississippian. They lived in the Mississippi and Ohio River valleys in North America's eastern woodlands from roughly 1000 to 1730, with the height of the culture spanning the years 1100–1400. Distinguished by the large earthen mounds they built for ceremonial, political, and residential purposes, they apparently had a highly stratified social structure and complex culture. Artifacts recovered from the mounds, especially ones designed to be buried with the deceased, reveal a wide variety of artisanal crafts including pottery and stonework. Some of these goods may have been produced by women. In addition, the mounds contained "foreign" material such as marine-shell beads and copperware that indicate a trading network extending to the Great Lakes in the north, Florida in the east, and the Rocky Mountains in the west.

Although archaeological evidence such as food remains, human bones, and pollen provides little specific detail about women's lives in Mississippian culture, it does indicate the centrality of maize—what Europeans called Indian corn.[27] Maize constituted 50 percent of these people's diets, and their pottery was used to cook it and to store it in pits. For reasons that historians debate, such as climatic change or warfare, the mound-builders had largely disappeared by the time of European contact. But the native peoples Europeans encountered in these regions continued to rely heavily on the corn produced by women. This corn became a vital staple for Europeans as well. What do these effigy pipe artifacts indicate about women's role in Mississippian mound-builders' society?

Figure 1.3, a meticulously carved ceramic bottle in the shape of a nursing mother, dates from the same period and was also found in Illinois.

◆ Figure 1.3 **Effigy Bottle, Cahokia Mound, Illinois (c. 1200–1400)**
From the Henry Whelpley Memorial Collection at the St. Louis Science Center.

◆ **Figure 1.4 Theodor Galle, *America* (c. 1580)**
The Burndy Library, Dibner Institute for the History of Science and Technology, Cambridge, Massachusetts.

Presumably it was not made to hold liquid for everyday use but for ritualistic or symbolic purposes—perhaps it was placed in a grave for use in the afterlife. What insight into Mississippian women's lives and culture does the image offer?

Representations of Native American women by Europeans tell us less about these women themselves than about European perceptions of their conquest of the Americas. Allegorical depictions, such as Figure 1.4, were not intended to portray a real woman. Rather, this image uses a device common in western European art—employing the female form to symbolize a country or abstract qualities such as virtue or liberty. Images of America that depicted a symbolic Native American woman were so popular that they appeared in decorations for sixteenth-century European palaces and in other unlikely places such as the 1594 Geneva Triumphal Arch. The illustration here, entitled *America,* is an engraving created around 1580 by Theodor Galle, based on a drawing from circa 1574 by Jan van der Straet. The striking image represents Amerigo Vespucci, the Italian explorer whose name was eventually given to the land mass he first explored in 1499,° as he awakens America. The animal at bottom right is a sloth, and in the background naked people are roasting a human leg on a spit. The engraving projects America as a bountiful land, but with savage peoples. The phrase in Latin may be translated in two ways,

°Historians dispute the exact year of Vespucci's arrival in the Americas.

depending on the reader's interpretation of the word *retexit:* "Amerigo rediscovers America; he called her once and thenceforth she was always awake" or "Amerigo laid bare America; once he called her thenceforth she was always aroused." How do these different translations affect the viewer's interpretation of the engraving? What is the significance of Vespucci being clothed and standing while the woman representing America is largely naked and reclining? Why would Europeans choose to depict America as a woman? What does the engraving reveal about European society and values?

More helpful to us in understanding the reality of indigenous women's lives than allegorical depictions are the illustrations and descriptions made by Europeans who encountered them in the sixteenth and seventeenth centuries. Often these accounts aimed at promoting enthusiasm and funding for exploration, colonization, or missionary activity, so they presented Native American peoples in ways that would appeal to their readers. Publications such as Theodor de Bry's multivolumed *Great Voyages* (1590) provided texts with illustrations detailing geography, information about flora and fauna, and accounts of native peoples. A native of Flanders, de Bry was a Protestant refugee in Germany with a fervent interest in promoting the colonization schemes of Protestant nations on a continent where the Catholic French and Spanish had already established a foothold. His depiction in Figure 1.5 must be analyzed with his point of view and purpose in mind. The image is based on the work of artist Jacques Le Moyne de Morgues, who had spent

◆ Figure 1.5 **Indians Planting Corn, from Theodor de Bry, *Great Voyages* (1590)**
Library of Congress, LC-DIG-ppmsca-02937.

◆ Figure 1.6 **Canadian Iroquois Women Making Maple Sugar, from Joseph-François Lafitau, *Moeurs des Sauvages Amériquains* (1724)**
General Research Division, the New York Public Library, Astor, Lenox, and Tilden Foundations.

time in Florida when the French had an outpost there. The drawing purports to describe the Timucua, part of the Muskogean language group. Timucuas were a matrilineal, agricultural people who raised corn, beans, and squash. Scholars believe that some details in this image may be accurate, such as the dress, the baskets, and the use of sticks to punch holes in the ground for planting, but the straight rows are apparently modeled after the plowed fields of Europe, and the hoes depicted are Flemish tools. What does this image suggest about the Timucuas' sexual division of labor?

A much later depiction of women's work (Figure 1.6) appeared in *Moeurs des Sauvages Amériquains* (1724) by Joseph-François Lafitau, a Jesuit missionary in

◆ **Figure 1.7 John White, _Theire sitting at meate_ (c. 1585–1586)**
Library of Congress, LC-USZ62-570.

the region of Montreal, Canada. Accompanying his illustration of Canadian Iroquois women making maple sugar, Lafitau wrote, "The women are busy going to get the vessels which are already full of the sap which drips from the trees, taking this sap and pouring it into the kettles which are on the fire. One woman is watching over the kettles while another one, seated, is kneading with her hands this sap which is thickening and in condition to be put in the shape of sugar loaves. Beyond the camp and the woods appear the fields as they look at the end of winter. We can see the women busy putting the fields into shape for the first time and sowing their corn."[28] What does this drawing and description suggest about the work patterns of these Iroquois women?

Perhaps the most comprehensive set of North American drawings are those of John White, who became governor of Roanoke, the short-lived, first English attempt to create a colony in North America. But White was also an artist whom Sir Walter Raleigh commissioned to illustrate plant and animal life and the native peoples encountered in the Roanoke voyages of 1584–1590. Not all of White's watercolors have survived, but those that have, such as the piece shown in Figure 1.7, appear to have been accurately drawn from his careful observations of the coastal

◆ Figure 1.8 **Theodor de Bry, *Their sitting at meate* (1590), Based on a Drawing by John White**
Courtesy of the John Carter Brown Library at Brown University.

Algonquins, who lived near the island of Roanoke on the Outer Banks of today's North Carolina. Theodor de Bry modified White's drawings when he published them in 1590 (see, for example, Figure 1.8). What are the most significant differences between the two versions of the image *Theire sitting at meate*? Why might de Bry have changed White's original drawing?

De Bry's version of White's image also depicts specific items, including fish, corn, and a gourd, thus indicating some of the foods and implements available to these Algonquins. The couple is seated on a mat; whom do you suppose made it? Both White's original version and de Bry's reproduction echo a common convention of depicting a couple, perhaps revealing the Europeans' emphasis on the marital bond as opposed to the natives' emphasis on family lineage.

White's detailed depiction of clothing and ornamentation is particularly valuable. Why might the English have been so interested in such careful attention? Figure 1.9, *A Chief Lady of Pomeiooc and Her Daughter*, features the wife of the chief in an Algonquin town in what is now North Carolina. Although not clear from the drawing, the accompanying text written by Thomas Harriott indicates

◆ Figure 1.9 *A Chief Lady of Pomeiooc and Her Daughter*
Library of Congress, LC-USZ62-570.

◆ **Figure 1.10 Claude Chauchetière, *Blessed Kateri Tekakwitha* (1682–1693)**
Photo by Anne M. Scheuerman, Pittsford, New York.

that the marks on the woman's arms and face are "pownced" or tattooed. Her skirt is made of skins, trimmed in beads. She is wearing two three-stand necklaces of beads, one closely fitting around her neck, the other hanging to her waist. Her daughter also wears a beaded necklace and carries a doll—a European one, dressed in Elizabethan clothing. A caption for a similar illustration that appeared in de Bry's volume concludes with a comment concerning the doll: "They are greatley Diligted [delighted] with puppetts, and babes which wear [were] brought oute of England."[29] What is the significance of the inclusion of this European item?

Trade goods represented one important European influence on Native Americans' lives. Another was religion. Figure 1.10 depicts Kateri Tekakwitha, who exemplifies the attraction Catholicism held for many Iroquois women. Kateri's mother, an Algonquin Christian convert, had been captured by the Iroquois and then married a Mohawk chief. When Kateri arrived in the Jesuit mission of Caughnawaga near Montreal in 1677, she was already a convert. There she developed a cult following of native women who physically tortured themselves to demonstrate their faith. After her death in 1680, she became associated with miracles and healing, heightening the veneration she is still accorded today (she was beatified by Pope John Paul II in 1980). Although Kateri's commitment to her new religion was intense, like many other converts, aspects of native religion shaped her Catholicism. As one historian explains, "The practices of Kateri and her followers resembled native 'vision quests,' in which young Iroquois sought spiritual knowledge through self-denial and deprivation."[30] Everything historians know about Kateri is filtered through the accounts of the Jesuit missionaries who held her up as an example of their successful efforts to convert Native Americans. The portrait in Figure 1.10 was painted shortly after her death by Father Claude Chauchetière, a Jesuit who knew her well. He claimed that she appeared to him six days after her death and asked him to "publicize her life and to spread her image among the people of the colony."[31] There is little in this portrait to suggest Kateri's native past or the "real" Kateri. In what ways does the painting reflect Chauchetière's goals in creating it?

Pocahontas of the Algonquin Powhatan people in Virginia is perhaps the most famous native American woman and is often depicted. Figure 1.11 represents the famous story of how she convinced her father, the powerful chief Powhatan, to spare the life of Captain John Smith. As Smith recounted it, "At last they brought him [Smith] to Meronocomo, where was Powhatan their Emperor. Here more than two hundred of those grim Courtiers stood wondering at him, as he had beene a monster; till Powhatan and his trayne had put themselves in their greatest braveries . . . having feasted him after their best barbarous manner they could, a long consultation was held, but the conclusion was, two great stones were brought before Powhatan; then as many as could laid hands on him, dragged him to them, and thereon laid his head, and being ready with their clubs, to beate out his braines, Pocahontas the Kings dearest daughter, when no intreaty could prevaile, got his head in her armes, and laid her owne upon his to save hime from death. . . ."[32] What similarities can you find between this illustration of Pocahontas and those of the Algonquin women drawn by John White?

King Powhatan *comands* C. Smith *to be flayne his*
daughter Pokahontas *beggs his life his thankfullnefs*
and how he Subiected 39 *of their kings reade y hiſtor*

◆ Figure 1.11 **Pocahontas Convinces Her Father, Chief Powhatan, to Spare the Life of Captain John Smith, from John Smith,** *Generall Historie of Virginia* **(1624)**
© *Bettmann/CORBIS.*

Although Smith reported the story of Pocahontas and included the illustration in his *Generall Historie of Virginia* (1624), it may not be true: Smith did not mention her when he first described his adventures among the Powhatans. But Smith and other propagandists of the Virginia colony drew on the story of Pocahontas on a number of occasions, especially when, during a period of British captivity in 1613, she converted to Christianity and subsequently married a Virginia tobacco planter, John Rolfe. Rolfe and Pocahontas, now Rebecca, had a child together and made a visit to England. There, the former Indian princess was much displayed. Figure 1.12, a 1616 portrait painted of her during her London stay and shortly before her death of pneumonia, represents her as John Smith later described her: "a gracious lady" with a "very formall and civill . . . English manner."[33] The Virginia Company, which sponsored her trip and presumably commissioned the portrait, spent lavishly on her costume, with its rich lace and braid on her tapestry fabric dress and an expensive white felt hat. Why might Smith and others of the Virginia Company have sponsored this type of representation of Pocahontas?

The real woman behind the myth remains obscure, but in the active role Pocahontas took in interacting with the Virginian colonists, serving as translator and mediator, she was similar to many other native women who acted as bridges between cultures. Her marriage to Rolfe made perfect sense from a native point of view. Many native groups used marriage to build alliances with potentially threatening enemies. Pocahontas may well have viewed her liaison with Rolfe as a means of helping her people.

◆ **Figure 1.12** *Pocahontas* **(1616)**
National Portrait Gallery, Smithsonian Institution/Art Resource, New York.

QUESTIONS FOR ANALYSIS

1. How do we recapture the lives of people who left no written records? This visual essay features images of early native American women and cautions that we must "read" these images carefully in using them to understand indigenous women's lives. What limitations do these images have as historical sources?

2. What commonalities do you find among the different representations of native American women? What differences?

3. One important characteristic of native societies was the sexual division of labor. In what ways do these images depict women's economic participation in their communities?

DOCUMENTS

By and About Colonial Women

LITTLE MATERIAL WRITTEN BY AMERICAN WOMEN in the seventeenth century is available to historians. Even in New England, where literacy was prized and most women were taught to read, relatively few women could write, as historians who have examined the signatures on deeds and other legal documents have discovered. In seventeenth-century New England, women produced only 4 books and only 2 of the 57 surviving diaries from that period. More records exist from the mid-eighteenth century, when education opportunities for women expanded slightly. But for most of the period from 1600 to 1750, men wrote much of the material we rely on to learn about women's experiences. Even our knowledge of a famous and educated woman such as Anne Hutchinson comes from accounts written by men, such as ministers like John Cotton and John Winthrop.

MANUALS OF ADVICE

ONE CATEGORY OF MATERIAL written by men that gives us some insight into colonial women's lives is *prescriptive* literature—that is, works in which the authors prescribe, as opposed to describe, women's proper roles and actions. While these prescriptive writings do not tell us about how real women acted, they do reveal the expectations that society held for women and often suggest that male leaders were worried about women staying in their proper place. Puritan ministers paid special attention to the subject: between 1668 and 1735, clerics such as Cotton Mather produced approximately seventy-five printed sermons and tracts about women. Another major source of prescriptive notions were the numerous published guides to housewifery.

In the seventeenth century, most of the reading material available to the colonists came from England and serves as a reminder that these first settlers were English in culture and values. One particularly popular guide was Gervase Markham's *Countrey Contentments* (1615), which was divided into two books, the first for men on such topics as hunting and the second, titled "The English Huswife," for women. Some of the advice for women focused on health remedies, such as advice for "obstructions of the liver" or for how "to increase a womans milk." "The Table," the major section of the book, provided recipes for "simple sallads" and "excellent way to boil chickens." English colonists adapted old country recipes to new country foods, but they also learned from Native Americans how to prepare corn, which became a staple menu item north and south.

In addition to practical advice, Markham begins his treatise with a statement prescribing the ideal English housewife. As you read this prescription, look for the qualities of a good housewife that Markham thinks important.

GERVASE MARKHAM
Countrey Contentments (1615)

Having already in a summary of briefness passed through those outward parts of husbandry, which belong unto the perfect Husband-man, who is the father and master of the family, and whose offices and employments are ever for the most part abroad or removed from the house as in the field or yard: It is now meete that we defend in as orderly a method as we can to the office of our english Housewife, who is the mother and mistress of the family, and has her most general employments within the house; where from the general example of her virtues, and the most approved skilled of her knowledge, those of her family may both learn to serve God, and sustain man in that godly and profitable sort which is required at the hands of every true Christian.

First then to speak of the inward virtues of her mind; she ought, above all things, to be of an upright and sincere religion, and in the same both zealous and constant; giving, by her example, an incitement and spur unto all her family to pursue the same steps, and to utter forth by the instruction of her life those virtuous fruits of good living, which shall be pleasing both to God and his creatures; I do not mean that herein she should utter forth that violence of spirit which many of our (vainly accounted pure) women do, drawing a contempt upon the ordinary Ministry, and thinking nothing lawful but the fantasies of their own inventions, usurping to themselves a power of preaching and interpreting the holy word, to which only they ought to be but hearers and believers, or at the most but modest persuaders, this is not the office either of good Housewife or good woman. But let our english Housewife be a godly, constant, and religious woman, learning from the worthy Preacher and her Husband those good examples which she shall with all careful diligence see exercised amongst her servants.

Next unto this sanctity and holiness of life, it is meete that our english Housewife be a woman of great modesty and temperance as well inwardly as outwardly; inwardly as in her behavior and carriage towards her Husband, wherein she shall shun all violence of rage, passion and humor, coveting less to direct than to be directed, appearing ever unto him pleasant, amiable, and delightful; and though occasion, mishaps or the misgovernance of his will may induce her to contrary thoughts, yet virtuously to suppress them, and with a mild sufferance rather to call him home from his error, then with the strength of anger to abate the least spark of evil, calling into her mind that evil and uncomely language is deformed though uttered even to servants, but most monstrous and ugly when it appears before the presence of a husband. . . .

To conclude, our english Housewife must be of chaste thought, stout courage, patient, untired, watchful, diligent, witty, pleasant, constant in friendship, full of good neighbor-hood, wise in discourse but not frequent therein, sharp and quick of speech, but not bitter or talkative, secret in her affairs, . . . and generally skillful in all the worthy knowledges which do belong to her vocation, of all, or most parts whereof I now intend to speak more largely.

SOURCE: Gervase Markham, *Countrey Contentments* (Amsterdam, 1615; repr., New York: De Capo Press, 1973), 1–4.

POETRY

ONE MAJOR BODY OF WORK written by a woman that historians can draw on is the poetry of Anne Dudley Bradstreet (1612–1672). Bradstreet came to Massachusetts in 1630 and eventually settled in Ipswich and later Andover. Well educated, she was an elite woman whose husband served as governor of the colony. Her first volume of verse, *The Tenth Muse, Lately Sprung Up in America* (1650), was also the first poetry volume produced by a colonist, and a highly successful one at that. Bradstreet's influential brother-in-law, John Woolbridge, arranged the London publication and explained in the introduction that it was "the work of a woman, honoured and esteemed where she lives, for . . . her exact diligence in her place, and discreet managing of her family occasions, and . . . these poems are but the fruit of some few hours, curtailed from her sleep and other refreshments."[34] This not-so-subtle assertion that Bradstreet's writing did not interfere with her wifely duties was to some extent borne out in the poetry itself. Bradstreet's many poems on daily life and family reveal a pious woman who enjoyed her role as wife and mother. But Bradstreet had a rebellious side as well. The very fact that she wrote and published her work set her outside the realm of women's proper sphere. And the content of much of her poetry criticized men who would limit women's intellectual endeavors.

The following extract of a poem about the late Queen Elizabeth of England (1533–1603) suggests Bradstreet's thoughts on women's capabilities.

ANNE BRADSTREET
In Honour of That High and Mighty Princess Queen Elizabeth of Happy Memory

Now say, have women worth? or have they none?
Or had they some, but with our Queen is't gone?
Nay masculines, you have thus taxed us long,
But she, though dead, will vindicate our wrong.
Let such as say our sex is void of reason
Know 'tis a slander now but once was treason.

But happy England which had such a queen;
Yea happy, happy, had those days still been.
But happiness lies in the higher sphere,
Then wonder not Eliza moves not here.
Full fraught with honour, riches and with days
She set, she set, like Titan in his rays.
No more shall rise or set so glorious sun
Until the heaven's great revolution,
If then new things their old forms shall retain,
Eliza shall rule Albion [Britain] once again.

SOURCE: Sandra M. Gilbert and Susan Gubar, comps., *The Norton Anthology of Literature by Women: The Tradition in English* (New York: Norton, 1985), 63–68.

LETTERS

L ETTERS, THOUGH RELATIVELY RARE, are another source for exploring early colonial women's experiences. The following examples offer insight into very diverse southern women's lives, that of the prosperous Eliza Lucas Pinckney and a desperate indentured servant, Elizabeth Sprig.

Eliza Lucas Pinckney (1722–1793), a South Carolinian woman, left numerous records detailing her life among her colony's elite. Daughter of a wealthy planter and invalid mother, Eliza Lucas ran the large household, supervised her father's estates in his lengthy absences, experimented with new crops, and was instrumental in introducing indigo to the region. She made good use of her father's legal library and not only represented her family in court but neighbors as well. Lucas married a much older man, the recently widowed Charles Pinckney, and became a devoted wife and energetic mother. At her husband's death, she again employed her business skills to run the complex estate of her family. Pinckney's letters and diaries reflect on the privileged life of an elite woman in the mid-eighteenth-century South, with slaves and servants at her disposal. As you read these letters, consider the factors in early South Carolinian life that shaped her opportunities and limits.

In the following passage from a letter to a Miss Bartlett, Pinckney is unusual in her concern for teaching her slaves to read, but typical of wealthy plantation women in how she spends her time.

ELIZA LUCAS PINCKNEY
To Miss Bartlett

In general then I rise at five o'Clock in the morning, read till Seven, then take a walk in the garden or field, see that the Servants are at their respective business, then to breakfast. The first hour after breakfast is spent at my musick, the next is constantly employed in recolecting something I have learned least for want of practise it should be quite lost, such as French and short hand. After that I devote the rest of the time till I dress for dinner to our little Polly and two black girls who I teach to read, and if I have my paps's approbation (my Mams I have got) I intend [them] for school mistres's for the rest of the Negroe children — another scheme you see. But to proceed, the first hour after dinner

as the first after breakfast at musick, the rest of the afternoon in Needle work till candle light, and from that time to bed time read or write. 'Tis the fashion here to carry our work abroad with us so that having company, without they are great strangers, is no interruption to that affair; but I have particular matters for particular days, which is an interruption to mine. Mondays my musick Master is here. Tuesdays my friend Mrs. Chardon (about 3 mile distant) and I are constantly engaged to each other, she at our house one Tuesday — I at hers the next and this is one of the happiest days I spend at Woppoe. Thursday the whole day except what the necessary affairs of the family take up is spent in writing, either on the business of the plantations, or letters to my friends. Every other Fryday, if no company, we go a vizeting so that I go abroad once a week and no oftener.

SOURCE: *The Letterbook of Eliza Lucas Pinckney 1739–1762*, ed. Elise Pinckney (Columbia: University of South Carolina Press, 1997), 34, 35, 38.

OTHER LETTERS OF PINCKNEY show the energetic businesswoman at work. In the following excerpt from a 1740 letter to a friend, she explains her plans for one of her father's plantations, which she clearly considers her property.

Wont you laugh at me if I tell you I am so busey in providing for Posterity I hardly allow my self time to Eat or sleep and can but just snatch a minnet to write to you and a friend or two now. I am making a large plantation of Oaks which I look upon as my own property, whether my father gives me the land or not; and therefore I design many years hence when oaks are more valueable than they are now—which you know they will be when we come to build fleets. I intend, I say, 2 thirds of the produce of my oaks for a charity (I'll let you know my scheme another time) and other 3rd for those that shall have the trouble of putting my design in Execution. I sopose according to custom you will show this to your Uncle and Aunt. 'She is [a] good girls, says Mrs. Pinckney. 'She is never Idle and always means well.' 'Tell the little Visionary,' says your uncle, 'come to town and partake of some of the amusements suitable to her time of life.' Pray tell him I think these so, and what he may not think whims and projects may turn out well by and by. Out of many surely one may hitt.

IN STARK CONTRAST TO THE LIVES of elite southern women like Pinckney were the lives of their servants. Details about the thousands of European women who came to the colonies as indentured servants in the seventeenth century are largely lost to historians because such women left few written records.

The following is a rare document, a letter written by a distressed servant in Maryland to her father. We cannot know what she had done to so displease her parent, but what does her letter indicate about the hardships facing indentured servants in America?

ELIZABETH SPRIGS
To Mr. John Sprigs White Smith in White Cross Street Near Cripple Gate London

Maryland Sept'r 22'd 1756.

Honred Father

My being for ever banished from your sight, will I hope pardon the Boldness I now take of troubling you with these, my long silence has been purely owing to my undutifullness to you, and well knowing I had offended in the highest Degree, put a tie to my tongue and pen, for fear I should be extinct from your good Graces and add a further Trouble to you, but too well knowing your care and tenderness for me so long as I retain my Duty to you, induced me once again to endeavour if possible, to kindle up that flame again. O Dear Father, belive what I am going to relate the words of truth and sincerity, and Ballance my former bad Conduct [to] my sufferings here, and then I am sure you'll pitty your Destress[ed] Daughter, What we unfortunat English People suffer here is beyond the probability of you in England to Conceive, let it suffice that I one of the unhappy Number, am toiling almost Day and Night, and very often in the Horses druggery, with only this comfort that you Bitch you do not halfe enough, and then tied up and whipp'd to that Degree that you'd not serve an Annimal, scarce any thing but Indian Corn and Salt to eat and that even begrudged nay many Negroes are better used, almost naked no shoes nor stockings to wear, and the comfort after slaving dureing Masters pleasure, what rest we can get is to rap ourselves up in a Blanket and ly upon the Ground,; this is the deplorable Condition your poor Betty endures, and now I beg you have any Bowels of Compassion left show it by sending me some Relief, C[l]othing is the principal thing wanting, which if you should condiscend to, may easely send them to me by any of the ships bound to Baltimore Town Patapsco River Maryland, and give me leave to conclude in Duty to you and Uncles and Aunts, and Respect to all Friends

    Honred Father

    Your undutifull and Disobedient Child

Source: Nancy Cott, ed., *Root of Bitterness: Documents of the Social History of American Women* (New York: E. P. Dutton, 1972), 89–90. Original Source: Isabel Calder, ed., *Colonial Captivities, Marches, and Journeys* (New York: Macmillan, 1935), 151–52. Reprinted by permission of Mrs. Alfred Howe Terry for the National Society of Colonial Dames of America in the State of Connecticut. Copyright 1935 by The Macmillan Co.

NEWSPAPER ADVERTISEMENTS

A NOTHER SOURCE THAT ALLOWS US to recapture women's voices are newspaper ads appearing in colonial publications. While men predominate among those offering services and goods for sale, as the eighteenth century wore on, women's names appeared with greater frequency.

What do the following ads suggest about the expansion of women's economic roles in urban colonial America?

Philadelphia Gazette, April 15, 1731

Elizabeth Gray, in Wallace's Alley, in Front Street near the sign of the Pewter Platter, in Philadelphia, washes and calendars [for?] any sort of linen cloth which hath received damage by salt water or otherwise and also table l*inens of damask and diaper, at a very reasonable rate.*

Philadelphia Gazette, June 24, 1731

At Mary Gordon's shopkeeper in Front Street, is sold good Bohen Tea at 14 s. per pound by the single pound, and good Jamaican (?) pepper at 18 d.

August, 19, 1731. The widow Read, removed for the upper end of high street to the new printing office near the Market, continue to make and sell her well known ointment for the itch, with which she has cured abundance of people in and about this city for many years past. It is always effectual for that purpose, and never fails to perform the cure speedily. It also kills or drives away all sorts of Lice in once or twice using. It has no offensive smell; but rather a pleasant one; and may be used with the least apprehension of danger, even to a sucking infant, being perfectly innocent and safe. Price 2 s. a gallypot containing an ounce, which is sufficient to remove the most intolerable Itch, and render the skin clear and smooth. She also continues to make and sell her excellent family salve and ointment, for burns or scalds, (Price 15 an ounce) and several other sorts of ointments and salves as usual. At the same place may be had Lockyer's Pills at 3 d. a pill.

South Carolina Gazette, Charleston, October 22, 1744

This is to give Notice, to all Persons inclinable to put their Children to board, under the Care of the Subscriber [illegible], that she has noow Vacancies; where there is taught, as usual, Writing, and all sorts of fine Needle work. Masters likewise attend to teach Writing, Arithmetick, Dancing, and Musick, if required. Mary Hext.

ADVERTISEMENTS CONCERNING SERVANTS AND SLAVES called for the return of runaways or offered slaves for sale or slaves or servants for hire. What clues do the following ads give about slave women's experiences?

Virginia Gazette, Williamsburg, April 28 to May 5, 1738

RAN away on the 22d of February last, from Col. Richard Randolph's Quarter, in Amelia County, Four Negroes, viz. Sancho, a tall lusty fellow, about 25 Years of Age, cloathed with a Manx Cloth Wastecoat, white Plains Breeches, died Yellow, Plad Hose, and Hobb-nailed Shoes. Warwick, a middle-siz'd Fellow, thin Face, small Eyes, and a sneaking Look, cloathed as the other. Bella, a lusty likely Woman. Phebe, a small Woman, with Marks in her Face, cloathed as the other. Whoever takes up and secures the said Negroes, so that their Owner above mention'd may have them again, shall have Five Pistoles Reward, besides what the Law allows.

SOURCE: Thomas Costa, University of Virginia's College at Wise, "Virginia Runaways," http://etext.lib.virginia.edu/subjects/runaways/1730s.html (accessed May 31, 2004).

South Carolina Gazette, Charleston, December 23, 1745

To be hired out a home born Negro girl about thirteen or fourteen years of age who has been for some years past kept employed at her needle and is a handy waiting maid. Enquire at the Printer [illegible].

Boston Gazette, April 28, 1755

A likely Negro woman, about 25 years of age, has had the smallpox, and been in the country ten or twelve years, understands all household work, and will do either for town or country.

Source: Susan Dion, "Women in the *Boston Gazette*," *Historical Journal of Massachusetts* 14 (1986): 98.

Boston Gazette, July 11, 1757

To be sold a strong, hearty Negro girl; and her son about a week old.

Source: Susan Dion, "Women in the *Boston Gazette*," *Historical Journal of Massachusetts* 14 (1986): 98.

Boston Gazette, June 20, 1735

A white Servant Maids Time to be disposed of for about four years and a half; she is a Scotch woman that can do all sorts of Household Business and Knit, and thoroughly honest. Enquire of The Publisher.

LEGAL PROCEEDINGS

ALTHOUGH IN ENGLISH AND BRITISH COLONIAL LAW, married women as *femes covert* had no legal identity, women appear frequently in legal documents. Unmarried women and widows could act for themselves, and even some married women successfully petitioned the courts for *feme sole* rights in order to conduct a business—usually in the absence of their husbands. They sued and were sued, sold and bought property. Women appeared as beneficiaries or as servants and slaves in men's wills. Women were also brought to court as defendants, on trial for sexual offenses, slander, theft, infanticide, and witchcraft. With one exception, the will of Elizabeth Howland, the documents offered here are from courts in the Chesapeake region, but they have many similarities to those from other British colonies.

SLANDER AND THE COURTS

Slander cases were common throughout the colonies, revealing the way in which individuals in small communities placed great store on their reputations; when their neighbors engaged in gossip accusing them of inappropriate behavior, many victims turned to the court for satisfaction. In analyzing defamation cases from seventeenth-century Maryland, historian Mary Beth Norton has discovered that while women participated in only 19 percent of the colonies' civil cases, they appeared in over 50 percent of the slander cases.[35] Cases that men brought against their defamers tended to concern questions of business and honesty, while those by women focused on sexual irregularities, although witchcraft was another common accusation. While some women came to court to protect their reputations, others were summoned for having spread rumors. The repetition of names in the following cases testifies to how closely connected the settlers in Maryland were in the seventeenth century, but also suggests that some people had an affinity for both gossip and the courts.

What does women's gossiping indicate about their role in the community? What do the court cases suggest about privacy in colonial towns?

Michael Baisey's Wife (1654)

Richard Manship Sworne Saith that the wife of Peter Godson related . . . that Michael Baiseys wifes Eldest Son was not the Son of Anthony Rawlins her former husband, but She knew one at Maryland that was the father of him, but Named not the man, and that the Said Michael Baisey's wife was a whore and a Strumpett up and Down the Countrey, and Said that Thomas Ward of Kent tould her Soe.

Elizabeth Manship Sworne Saith the Same.

Margaret Herring Sworne Saith that the wife of Peter Godson affirmed that Anthony Rawlins

Source: *Archives of Maryland Judicial and Testamentary Business of the Provincial Court, 1649/50–1675,* ed. William Hand Browne (Baltimore, 1887), 10:399, 10:402, 10:403, 10:409.

Son was not his Son but the Son of another man at Maryland. . . .

Whereas Peter Godsons wife hath Slandered the wife of Michael Baisey & Saying She was a whore & a Strumpet up and Down the Countrey, It is ordered that the Said Godson's wife Shall be Committed into the Sheriffs hand untill She Shall find Security for the behaviour which the plft [plaintiff] is Satisfied with as he hath declared in Court. . . .

Whereas Mrs Godson was bound in a bond of Good behaviour from the 21st of October till the 5th of December towards the wife of Michael Baisey, and none appearing to renew the Said Bond, It is ordered that she be remitted from her Bond of Good behaviour.

Richard Manship's Wife (1654)

Bartho: Herringe aged forty yeares or thereabouts Sworne Saith, That Peter Godson and Richard

Manship meeting in Yor Pettrs plantation, Richard Manship asked the Said Peter Godson whether he would prove his wife a Witch, Peter Godson replyed take notice what I Say, I came to your house where your wife layd two Straws and the woman in a Jesting way Said they Say I am a witch, if I am a witch they Say I have not power to Skip over these two Strawes and bid the Said Peter Godson to Skip over them and about a day after the Said Godson Said he was Lame, and, thereupon would Maintaine his wife to be a witch

Bartho: Herringe . . .

John Killy aged twenty five yeares or thereabouts Sworne Sayth. That at the house of Phillip Hide, Richard Manship Said to Peter Godson you Said you would prove my wife a Witch, Peter Godson answered Gentlemen take Notice what I Say I will prove her a witch beare Witness you that Stand by.

John Killey

Margarett Herringe aged twenty three or thereabouts Sworne Saith, That Rich: Manship asked Peter Godson if he would prove his wife a witch, and Peter desired them that were present to take Notice what he Said your wife tooke four Strawes and Said in the Name of Jesus Come over these Strawes, and upon this your wife is a witch and I will prove her one.

Whereas Peter Godson and his wife had defamed Richard Manship's wife in Saying She was a witch and Uttered other Slanderous Speeches agst her, which was Composed and Determined by the plft and defendant before mr Richard Preston, Soe as Peter Godson Should pay Charges of Warrants and Subpoenas in these Actions which Richard Manship desired may be Manifested in Court that the Said Peter Godson & his wife have acknowledged themselves Sorry for their Speeches & pay Charges.

WOMEN "JURORS"

Other court cases reveal the ways in which women could expand their limited public power. When women were accused of witchcraft, the court might ask a group of women, which usually included a midwife, to examine the defendant's body for telltale signs of witchcraft. They might also be called to duty in cases in which it was crucial to determine whether a woman had given birth.

In the following complex murder accusation, the court officially termed the group of women a "jury." What does the case suggest about women's access to authority in their communities?

Judith Catchpole (1656)

At a Generall Provinciall Court Held at

Putuxent September 22th

Present Capt William ffuller, mr John Pott Present

    mr Richard Preston: mr Michael Brooke

    mr Edward Lloyd

Whereas Judith Catchpole being brought before the Court upon Suspicion of Murdering a Child which She is accused to have brought forth, and denying the fact or that She ever had Child the Court hath ordered that a jury of able women be Impannelled and to give in their Verdict to the best of their judgment whether She the Said Judith hath ever had a Child

Or not . . .

The Names of the Jury of women Impannelled to Search the body of Judith Catchpole . . .

Rose Smith	mrs Cannady
mrs Belcher	mrs Bussey
mrs Chaplin	mrs Brooke
mrs Brooke	Elizabeth Claxton
mrs. Battin	Elizabeth Potter
	Dorothy Day

We the Jury of Women before named having according to our Charge and oath Searched the body of Judith Catchpole doe give in our Verdict that according to our best judgment that the Said Judith Catchpole hath not had any Child within the time Charged.

SOURCE: *Archives of Maryland Judicial and Testamentary Business of the Provincial Court, 1649/50–1675*, ed. William Hand Browne (Baltimore, 1887), 10:456–58.

Whereas Judith Catchpole Servant to William Dorrington of this Province of Maryland Was apprehended and brought before this Court upon Suspicion of Murthering a Child in her Voyage at Sea bound for this Province in the Ship Mary and ffrancis who Set forth of England upon her intended Voyage in or about october Last 1655 and arrived in this Province in or about January following, and her accuser being deceased and no murther appearing upon her Examination denying the fact; was Ordered that her body Should be Searcht by a Jury of able women, which being done the Said Jury returning their Verdict to this Court that they found that the Said Judith had not had any Child within the time Chargd And also it appearing to this Court by Severall Testimonies that the party accusing was not in Sound Mind, whereby it is Conceived the Said Judith Catchpole is not Inditable, The Court doth therefore order that upon the reasons aforesaid, that She the Said Judith Catchpole be acquitted of that Charge unless further Evidence appeare.

WIVES AND WIDOWS: PROPERTY SETTLEMENTS AND WILLS

Court records are a vital source of information about property holding. Through wills and property settlement documents, we can determine the range of goods that people owned and make distinctions between rich and poor; we can discover patterns of slave ownership and servant holding; and we can acquire some information about women's economic circumstances.

The following is a prenuptial settlement by Ralph Wormley, a wealthy man, on a widow, Mrs. Agatha Stubbings, whose first husband had been a successful merchant. How does it shed light on the economic advantages widows in early Virginia might have experienced? What clues does the reference to black "servaunts" give us about African Americans' circumstances in early Virginia?

Mrs. Agatha Stubbings (1645)

To All to whom these presents shall come I Ralph Warmley [sic] of the Parrish and County of Yorke in Virginia gentleman send Greeting etc. Knowe Yee, That I the sayde Ralph Wormley For and in consideration of the unfayned love and affection That I beare unto Mrs. Agatha Stubbings late the wife of Luke Stubbings of the County of Northampton gentleman deceased, And especially in Consideration of Matrimony intended presently (by gods grace) to bee solemnized betweene the sayde Ralph and the sayde Agatha doe by these presents give graunt confirme and endow, And by these presents have given graunted and in nature of a Free Joynture endowed unto Nathaniell Littleton Esquire and Phillip Taylor gentlemen . . . in trust For and on the behalfe of the sayde Agatha six Negro servaunts . . . Fower Negro men, and Two women, To say Sanio, and Susan his wife, and greate Tony, and his wife Dorothis, Tony the younger, and Will, Tenn Cowes, six Draught Oxen, two young Mares, two Feather Bedds and Furniture, sixe paire of sheetes of Holland, two Dyaper table cloathes, two dozen of Napkins and Cubboard Cloath to it, two dozen of Napkins, Twelve pewter dishes, one dammaske table cloath, one Dozen of Napkins and cubboard Cloath to it, To have and to hold, the said Recited promisses and every parte thereof, unto her the sayde Agatha, and the heyres [heirs] Lawfully ingendered between mee the said Ralph Wormley and shee the sayde Agatha whether Male or Female or both to bee equally devided after his decease Provided always that the same and every parte thereof graunted as afore-

said shalbe and Remayne to the only use benifitt and behoofe of mee the said Ralph Wormley during my naturall Life, And in case I the said Ralph shall happen to depart this lyfe without issue begotten betweene mee the said Ralph and shee the said Agatha as aforesayde, Then the said demised promisses and every parte thereof with the proceeds and increase thereof shalbe and Remayne to the only use benifitt and behoofe of the sayde Agatha her heyres Executors or Administrators And For the true and reall performance of this deede and every parte and parcel thereof in manner and Forme aforesaid I the said Ralph Wormley doe bynde over unto the said Nathaniell Littleton Esquire and Phillip Taylor gentlemen the said Six Negroes and Six other Negroes, the sayde Tenn Cowes and other tenn Cowes, the sixe Oxen and other sixe Oxen, one plantation and houses whereon I now live scituate at Yorke aforesaid Conteyning Five hundred Acres more or lesse according to the purchase lately made by mee of Jefery Power to bee all Lyable and Responsable For the full Assurance of making good the abovesaid Joynture for the use of the said Agatha her heyres Executors or Administrators as aforesaid In Witnes whereof I the sayde Ralph Wormley have hereunto sett my hand and Scale the second day of this instant July Annoque Domini 1645.

Ralph Wormeley
The Seale

Source: Susie M. Ames, ed., *County Court Records of Accomack-Northampton, Virginia 1640–1645* (Charlottesville: University Press of Virginia, 1973) 433–34.

Like agatha stubbings, Elizabeth (Tilley) Howland of Plymouth, Massachusetts, was also a widow. She died in the home of her daughter Lydia in December 1687. The 1672 will of her late husband, John Howland, left plots of land to his three sons, and to Elizabeth, "the use and benifitt of my now Dwelling house in Rockey nooke in the Township of Plymouth aforsaid, with the outhousing lands, . . . During her naturall life to Injoy make use of and Improve for her benifitt and Comfort."[36] He also made Elizabeth the executrix of his estate. His six daughters received 20 shillings each. Elizabeth's 1686 will, reproduced here, offers many insights into her life, both spiritual and economic.

What kinds of goods does Howland leave to her descendants? What do they suggest about her class status? Is it significant that the only money she specifies is given to her eldest son? And that the only property she lists goes to the son of her eldest son? She itemizes a number of books in this document, yet she signs with her "mark," not a signature. What does this suggest about her education? Whom does she choose as her executors and why? Finally, why does Howland dedicate so much space to religious concerns in this will?

Elizabeth (Tilley) Howland (1686)

In ye Name of God Amen I Elizabeth Howland of Swanzey in ye County of Bristoll in ye Collony of Plymouth in New Engld being Seventy nine yeares of Age but of good & perfect memory thanks be to Allmighty God & calling to Remembrance ye uncertain Estate of this transitory Life & that all fflesh must Yeild unto Death when it shall please God to call Doe make constitute & ordaine & Declare This my last Will & Testament, in manner & forme following Revoking and Anulling by these prsents all & every Testamt & Testamts Will & Wills heretofore by me made & declared either by Word or Writing And this to be taken only for my last Will & Testament & none other. And first being penitent & sorry from ye bottom of my heart for all my sinns past most humbly desiring forgivenesse for ye same I give & Committ my soule unto Allmighty God my Savior & redeemer in whome & by ye meritts of Jesus Christ I trust & believe assuredly to be saved & to have full remission & forgivenesse of all my sins & that my Soule wt my Body at the generall Day of Resurrection shall rise againe wt Joy & through ye meritts of Christs Death & passion possesse & inheritt ye Kingdome of heaven prepared for his Elect & Chosen & my Body to be buryed in such place where it shall please my Executrs hereafter named to appoint And now for ye settling my temporall Estate & such goodes Chattells & Debts as it hath pleased God far above my Deserts to be-

stow upon me I Do Dispose order & give ye same in manner & forme following (That is to say) First that after my funerall Expences & Debts paid wc I owe either of right or in Conscience to any manner of person or persons whatsoever in Convenient tyme after my Decease by my Execrs hereafter named I Give & bequeath unto my Eldest Son John Howland ye sum of five pounds to be paid out of my Estate & my Booke called Mr Tindale's Workes & also one pair of sheetes & one pr of pillowbeeres & one pr of Bedblanketts, Item I give unto my son Joseph Howland my Stillyards° & also one pr of sheetes & one pr of pillobeeres Item I give unto my son Jabez Howland my ffetherbed & boulster yt is in his Custody & also one Rugg & two Blanketts yt belongeth to ye said Bed & also my great Iron pott & potthookes Item I give unto my son Isaack Howland my Booke called Willson on ye Romanes & one pr of sheetes & one paire of pillowbeeres & also my great Brasse Kettle already in his possession Item I give unto my Son in Law Mr James Browne my great Bible Item I give & bequeath unto my Daughter Lidia Browne my best ffeatherbed & Boulster two pillowes & three Blanketts & a green Rugg & my small Cupboard one pr of AndyIrons & my lesser brasse Kettle & my small Bible & my booke of mr Robbinsons Workes called Observations Divine & Morrall & allso my finest pr of Sheetes & my holland pillowbeeres, Item I give unto my Daughter Elisabeth Dickenson one pr of Sheetes & one pr of pillowbeeres & one Chest Item I give unto my

Source: The Plymouth Colony Archive at the University of Virginia, http://etext.lib.virginia.edu/users/deetz/Plymouth/howlandwill.html (accessed April 2, 2004).

°Probably a weighing device.

Daughter Hannah Bosworth one pr of sheets & one pr of pillowbeeres, Item I give unto my Grand Daughter Elizabeth Bursley one paire of sheets and one paire of Pillowbeeres Item I give & bequeath unto my Grandson Nathaniel Howland (the son of Joseph Howland) and to the heires of his owne Body lawfully begotten for ever all that my Lott of Land with ye Meadow thereunto adjoyning & belonging lying in the Township of Duxbury neare Jones River bridge, Item I give unto my Grandson James Browne One Iron barr and on Iron Trammell now in his possession, Item I give unto my Grandson Jabez Browne one Chest Item I give unto my Grand Daughter Dorothy Browne my best Chest & my Warming pan Item I give unto my Grand Daughter Desire Cushman four Sheep, Item I give & bequeath my wearing clothes linnen and Woollen and all the rest of my Estate in mony Debts linnen or of what kind or nature or sort soever it may be unto my three Daughters Elisabeth Dickenson, Lidia Browne and Hannah Bosworth to be equally Devided amongst them, Item I make constitute and ordaine my loving Son in Law James Browne and my loving son Jabez Howland Executors of this my last Will and Testament, Item it is my Will & Charge to all my Children that they walke in ye Feare of ye Lord, and in Love and peace towards each other and endeavour the true performance of this my last Will & Testament In Witnesse whereof I the said Elizabeth Howland have hereunto sett my hand & seale this seventeenth Day of December Anno Dm one thousand six hundred Eighty & six.

The mark of Elisabeth **E H** Howland
Signed Sealed & Delivd
in ye prsence of us Wittnesses
Hugh Cole
Samuel Vyall
John Browne

LAWS ON WOMEN AND SLAVERY

ALTHOUGH SLAVE WOMEN OF THIS PERIOD left behind no written documents, references to them do appear in newspapers and in their owners' letters and diaries (see pp. 53–54). As the prenuptial settlement of Agatha Stubbings suggests, property inventories are another clue that historians use to determine something of slave women's environment. More impersonal, but vital to understanding slaves' experiences, are the laws that, taken together, created the system of perpetual slavery.

In the southern colonies, the laws that created boundaries between slave and free and black and white were added in a piecemeal fashion. One of the first legal distinctions between blacks and whites concerned the labor of women. Instead of taxing land, Virginia taxed planters according to the numbers of the laborers who worked in their tobacco fields.

In this first sentence of a 1643 statute designed to support the colony's ministers, the assembly refers specifically to taxing ("tithing") the labor of "negro women." Although white women worked in the tobacco fields, they are not mentioned here. What does the presence of black women and the absence of white women in this law suggest about the distinctions being made between the two?

Laws of Virginia (1643)

Be it further enacted and confirmed That there be tenn pounds of tob'o. per poll & a bushell of corne per poll paid to the ministers within the severall parishes of the collony for all tithable persons, that is to say, as well for all youths of sixteen years of age as upwards, as also for all negro women at the age of sixteen years.

SOURCE: William Waller Hening, ed., *The Statutes at Large, Being a Collection of All the Laws of Virginia* (Charlottesville: University Press of Virginia, 1969), I:242.

AN EVEN MORE DRAMATIC INDICATION of the hardening of lines between black and white is the short 1662 law that assigned the child of a black woman and a white man to the status of the mother. The statute also assigned penalties for interracial sex. The use of the term "christian" was common, to distinguish English people from Africans, who were considered heathens. What are the implications of this act for the institutionalization of slavery?

Laws of Virginia (1662)

WHEREAS some doubts have arrisen whether children got by any Englishman upon a negro woman should be slave or free, Be it therefore enacted and declared by this present grand assembly, that all children borne in this country shalbe held bond or free only according to the condition of the mother. And that if any christian shall committ fornication with a negro man or woman, hee or shee soe offending shall pay double the fines imposed by the former act.

SOURCE: William Waller Hening, ed., *The Statutes at Large, Being a Collection of All the Laws of Virginia* (Charlottesville: University Press of Virginia, 1969), I:242. II:170.

QUESTIONS FOR ANALYSIS

1. What evidence do these documents offer about the diversity of women's experiences in colonial America? What are some of the hardships or challenges that women encountered? In what ways did women of this period seek control over their lives?

2. What do these documents suggest about societal expectations for white elite women's roles? About the roles of servants and slave women?

3. How do legal documents allow us to understand the experiences of women who left no personal writings behind? What insights can descriptions of property give about the social circumstances of colonial women? How do the court cases concerning slander and witchcraft portray women and expectations about their behavior?

NOTES

1. William Wood, *New Englands Prospect* (1634; Amsterdam: Theatrum Orbis Terrarum; New York: Da Capo Press, 1968), 96.

2. Judith K. Brown, "Economic Organization and the Position of Women among the Iroquois," *Ethnohistory* 17, no. 3-4 (Summer-Fall 1970): 159.

3. Ibid., 153.

4. Ibid.

5. Richard White, *The Middle Ground: Indians, Empires, and Republics in the Great Lakes Region, 1650–1815* (Cambridge: Cambridge University Press, 1991), 63.

6. James Axtell, ed., *The Indian Peoples of Eastern America: A Documentary History of the Sexes* (New York: Oxford University Press, 1981), 142.

7. Clara Sue Kidwell, "India Women as Cultural Mediators," *Ethnohistory* 39, no. 2 (Spring 1992): 97.

8. *Proceedings of the General Assembly,* vol. 1 (Jan. 1637/8–Sept. 1664), 239. Archives of Maryland Online, http://www.mdarchives.state.md.us/megafile/msa/speccol/sc2900/sc2908/000001/000001/html/am1--239.html (accessed 8/5/2004).

9. Paula A. Treckel, *To Comfort the Heart: Women in Seventeenth-Century America* (New York: Twayne, 1996), 37.

10. Carol Berkin and Leslie Horowitz, eds., *Women's Voices, Women's Lives: Documents in Early American History* (Boston: Northeastern University Press, 1998), 16.

11. Cynthia A. Kierner, *Beyond the Household: Women's Place in the Early South, 1700–1835* (Ithaca, NY: Cornell University Press, 1998), 44.

12. Peter Kolchin, *American Slavery, 1619–1877* (New York: Hill and Wang, 1993), 51.

13. Kathleen M. Brown, *Good Wives, Nasty Wenches, and Anxious Patriarchs* (Chapel Hill: University of North Carolina Press, 1996), 118.

14. Brown, *Good Wives,* 132.

15. Cornelia Hughes Dayton, *Women before the Bar: Gender, Law, and Society in Connecticut, 1639–1789* (Chapel Hill: University of North Carolina Press, 1995), 115.

16. Treckel, *To Comfort the Heart,* 145.

17. Mary Beth Norton, *Founding Mothers and Fathers: Gendered Power and the Forming of American Society* (New York: Knopf, 1996), 351.

18. Lyle Koehler, *A Search for Power: The "Weaker Sex" in Seventeenth-Century New England* (Urbana: University of Illinois Press, 1980), 31.

19. Treckel, *To Comfort the Heart,* 105.

20. Nancy Wooloch, *Women and the American Experience* (New York: Knopf, 1984), 14.

21. Norton, *Founding Mothers and Fathers,* 281.

22. Vivian Bruce Conger, " 'If Widow, Both Housewife and Husband May Be': Widows' Testamentary Freedom in Colonial Massachusetts and Maryland," in Larry D. Eldridge, ed., *Women and Freedom in Early America* (New York: New York University Press, 1997), 249.

23. Treckel, *To Comfort the Heart*, 68.

24. Wulf, *Not All Wives*, 58.

25. Ibid., 57.

26. Treckel, *To Comfort the Heart*, 175.

27. Neal Salisbury, "The Indians' Old World: Native Americans and the Coming of Europeans," in Peter C. Mancall and James H. Merrell, eds., *American Encounters: Natives and Newcomers from European Contact to Indian Removal, 1500–1850* (New York: Routledge, 2000), 7.

28. Father Joseph-François Lafitau, *Customs of the American Indians Compared with the Customs of Primitive Times*, ed. and trans. William N. Fenton and Elizabeth L. Moore (1724; Toronto: Champlain Society, 1977), 2:8.

29. Paul Hulton, *America, 1585: The Complete Drawings of John White* (Chapel Hill: University of North Carolina Press, 1984), 114.

30. John Demos, *The Tried and the True: Native American Women Confronting Colonization* (New York: Oxford University Press, 1995), 56.

31. K. I. Koppedrayer, "The Making of the First Iroquois Virgin: Early Jesuit Biographies of the Blessed Kateri Tekakwitha," *Ethnohistory* 40, no. 2 (Spring 1993): 287.

32. Captain John Smith, *The Generall Historie of Virginia, New England & the Summer Isles, Together with the True Travels, Adventures and Observations, and a Sea Grammar—Volume 1* (1607), Library of Congress, American Memory, "The Capital and the Bay: Narratives of Washington and the Chesapeake Bay Region, ca. 1600–1925," http://memory.loc.gov/cgi-bin/query/r?ammem/lhbcb:@field(DOCID+@lit(lhbcb0262adiv12)) (accessed April 18, 2004).

33. Karen Ordahl Kupperman, *Indians and English: Facing Off in Early America* (Ithaca, NY: Cornell University Press, 2000), 199.

34. Sandra M. Gilbert and Susan Gubar, comps., *The Norton Anthology of Literature by Women: The Tradition in English* (New York: Norton, 1985), 60.

35. Mary Beth Norton, "Gender and Defamation in Seventeenth-Century Maryland," *William and Mary Quarterly*, 3rd ser., 44 (January 1987): 4–5.

36. "The last will and testament of John Howland," Pilgrim Hall Museum, http://www.pilgrimhall.org/willjhowland.htm (accessed June 9, 2004).

SUGGESTED REFERENCES

General Works   General accounts of women during the early colonial era include Carol Berkin, *First Generations: Women in Colonial America* (1996); Jane Kamensky, *Colonial Mosaic: American Women 1600–1760* (1995); Mary Beth Norton, *Founding Mothers and Fathers: Gendered Power and the Forming of American Society* (1996); and Paula T. Treckel, *To Comfort the Heart: Women in Seventeenth-Century America* (1996). For a valuable collection of documents, see Carol Berkin and Leslie Horowitz, eds., *Women's Voices, Women's Lives: Documents in Early American History* (1998).

Native Americans (General) Important general studies of Native Americans are James F. Brooks, *Captives and Cousins: Slavery, Kinship, and Community in the Southwest Borderlands* (2002); Colin G. Calloway, *New Worlds for All: Indians, Europeans, and the Remaking of Early America* (1997); Colin G. Calloway, *One Vast Winter Count: The Native American West before Lewis and Clark* (2003); Andrew C. Isenberg, *The Destruction of the Bison: An Environmental History, 1750–1920* (2000); Karen Ordahl Kupperman, *Indians and English: Facing Off in Early America* (2000); David J. Weber, *The Spanish Frontier in North America* (1992); Peter H. Wood et al., eds., *Powhatan's Mantle: Indians in the Colonial Southeast* (1989).

Native American Women There is a growing literature on Native American women and gender specifically. For a gendered approach to archaeology, see Karen Olsen Bruhns and Karen E. Stothert, *Women in Ancient America* (1999). In *The Indian Peoples of Eastern America: A Documentary History of the Sexes* (1981), James Axtell offers primary documents with introductions. John Demos, *The Tried and the True: Native American Women Confronting Colonization* (1995), is a short synthesis. Larry D. Eldridge, ed., *Women and Freedom in Early America* (1997), has essays on Native American women. For Pueblo women, see Rámon A. Gutiérrez, *When Jesus Came, the Corn Mothers Went Away: Marriage, Sexuality, and Power in New Mexico, 1500–1846* (1991). On the Iroquois, see Judith K. Brown, "Economic Organization and the Position of Women among the Iroquois," *Ethnohistory* 17, no. 3-4 (Summer-Fall 1970): 151–67, and Daniel K. Richter, *The Ordeal of the Longhouse: The Peoples of the Iroquois League in the Era of European Colonization* (1992). For the Great Lakes area, see Karen Anderson, "Commodity Exchange and Subordination: Montagnais-Naskapi and Huron Women, 1600–1650," *Journal of Women in Culture and Society* 11 (1985): 48–62; Lucy Murphy, *A Gathering of Rivers: Indians, Métis, and Mining in the Western Great Lakes, 1737–1832* (2000); Richard White, *The Middle Ground: Indians, Empires, and Republics in the Great Lakes Region, 1650–1815* (1991). For southeastern women, see Kathryn E. Holland Braund, "Guardians of Tradition and Handmaidens to Change: Women's Roles in Creek Economic and Social Life during the Eighteenth Century," *American Indian Quarterly* 14 (Summer 1990): 239–58, and Theda Perdue, *Cherokee Women: Gender and Culture Change, 1700–1835* (1998).

Women in the Southern Colonies An overview of women of the early South is Cynthia A. Kierner, *Beyond the Household: Women's Place in the Early South, 1700–1835* (1998). An important study that addresses a wide range of women is Kathleen M. Brown, *Good Wives, Nasty Wenches, and Anxious Patriarchs* (1996). Specialized studies that focus primarily on white women include Stephen Innes, ed., *Work and Labor in Early America* (1988); Gloria L. Main, *Tobacco Colony: Life in Early Maryland, 1650–1720* (1982); Mary Beth Norton, "Gender and Defamation in Seventeenth-Century Maryland," *William and Mary Quarterly*, 3rd ser., 44 (January 1987); Darrett B. and Anita H. Rutman, *A Place in Time: Middlesex County, Virginia, 1650–1750* (1984); Terri L. Snyder, *Brabbling Women: Disorderly Speech and the Law in Early Virginia* (2003); Lorena S. Walsh, "'Till Death Us Do Part': Marriage and Family in Seventeenth-Century Maryland," in Thad W. Tate and David L. Ammerman, eds., *The Chesapeake in the Seventeenth Century: Essays on Anglo-American Society* (1979). On African women and slavery, see Ira Berlin, *Many Thousands Gone: The First Two Centuries of Slavery in North America* (1998); David Barry Gaspar and Darlene Clark Hine, eds., *More Than Chattel: Black Women and Slavery in the Americas* (1996); Darlene Clark Hine, ed., *Black Women in American History: From Colonial Times through the Nineteenth Century* (1990); Allan Kulikoff, "The Beginnings of the Afro-American Family in Maryland," in Aubrey Land, Lois Green Carr, and Edward C. Papenfuse, eds., *Law, Society, and Politics in Early Maryland* (1977); Carole Shammas, "Black Women's Work and the Evolution of Plantation Society in Virginia," *Labor History* 26 (1985): 5–28; Peter H. Wood, *Black Majority: Negroes in Colonial South Carolina: From 1670 through the Stono Rebellion* (1974). For background on the slave trade, see David Eltis, *The Rise of African Slavery in the Americas* (2000).

Women in the Northern Colonies   Older works but still valuable starting points for the New England colonies are John Demos, *A Little Commonwealth: Family Life in Plymouth Colony* (1970), and Lyle Koehler, *A Search for Power: The "Weaker Sex" in Seventeenth-Century New England* (1980). For a comparative study of New England and the Chesapeake, see Mary Beth Norton, *Founding Mothers and Fathers: Gendered Power and the Forming of American Society* (1996). On women and the law, see Cornelia Hughes Dayton, *Women before the Bar: Gender, Law, and Society in Connecticut, 1639–1789* (1995), and Marylynn Salmon, *Women and the Law of Property in Early America* (1986). The two major works on witchcraft are Carol F. Karlsen, *The Devil in the Shape of a Woman: Witchcraft in Colonial New England* (1987), and Mary Beth Norton, *In the Devil's Snare: The Salem Witchcraft Crisis of 1692* (2002). A study of women's household production is Laurel Thatcher Ulrich, *The Age of Homespun: Objects and Stories in the Creation of an American Myth* (2002). See also Laurel Thatcher Ulrich's *Goodwives: Image and Reality in the Lives of Women in Northern New England* (1982). Midwifery is addressed in Rebecca Tannenbaum, *A Healer's Calling: Women and Medicine in Early New England* (2002), and the experiences of an urban tradeswoman are analyzed in Patricia Cleary, *Elizabeth Murray: A Woman's Pursuit of Independence in Eighteenth-Century America* (2000).

Women in the Middle Colonies   For the middle colonies, see Linda Briggs Biemer, *Women and Property in Colonial New York: The Transition from Dutch to English Law, 1643–1727* (1983); Joan M. Jensen, *Loosening the Bonds: Mid-Atlantic Farm Women, 1750–1850* (1986); Rebecca Larson, *Daughters of Light: Quaker Women, Preaching and Prosphesying in the Colonies and Abroad* (1999); Karin Wulf, *Not All Wives: Women of Colonial Philadelphia* (2000). Valuable articles include David E. Narrett, "Men's Wills and Women's Property Rights in Colonial New York," in Ronald Hoffman and Peter J. Albert, eds., *Women in the Age of the American Revolution* (1989); Jean R. Soderlund, "Black Women in Colonial Pennsylvania," *Pennsylvania Magazine of History and Biography* 107 (January 1983): 49–68; Jean R. Soderlund, "Women in

Eighteenth-Century Pennsylvania: Toward a Model of Diversity," *Pennsylvania Magazine of History and Biography* 115 (April 1991): 163–83.

Selected Web Sites

The Salem Witch Trials Documentary Archive and Transcription Project is a collaboration of Professor Benjamin C. Ray, University of Virginia, and Professor Bernard Rosenthal, University of Binghamton. See the Web site at <**etext.virginia.edu/salem/witchcraft/home.html**> for transcriptions of the Salem Witch Trials, as well as other documents and historical analysis.

Virtual Jamestown, at <**virtualjamestown.org**>, is a project of the University of Virginia and Virginia Tech. It offers a variety of resources of colonial Virginia, including reproductions of the watercolors John White made of Native Americans and the prints produced by Theodor de Bry.

Slave Advertisements, compiled by Professor Thomas Costa, appears on the University of Virginia's Web site at <**etext.lib.virginia.edu/subjects/runaways/1730s.html**>. It provides a searchable database of advertisements in eighteenth-century Virginia newspapers for runaway servants and slaves.

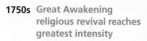
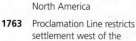

2

Mothers and Daughters of the Revolution

1750–1800

YEARS AFTER THE AMERICAN REVOLUTION ENDED British colonial rule in 1783, Sarah Osborn applied for a widow's pension from the U.S. government. In her 1837 deposition, she described not only her husband's service as a soldier but also her contributions to the war effort. During one battle, her testimony reveals, she took "her stand just back of the American tents, say about a mile from the town, and busied herself washing, mending, and cooking for the soldiers, in which she was assisted by the other females. . . . She heard the roar of the artillery for a number of days."[1] Osborn's account of life close to the fighting suggests a significant break from notions of women's traditional place at the hearth. But that she performed domestic work for her husband and his fellow soldiers also reveals that, even in the disruptive context of war, women's customary domestic roles prevailed. Osborn's experiences were hardly universal, yet her deposition underscores a crucial point. Even though the dramatic events of the second half of the eighteenth century centered on political and international concerns, which were customarily viewed as exclusively male terrain, women actively participated — although usually in distinctly gendered ways — in the American Revolution and the founding of the new nation.

Historians vigorously debate the long-term impact of the revolutionary crisis on women's lives. Some scholars argue that as white men enjoyed expanded legal and political rights during the postrevolutionary period, women's relative status declined. Others contend that women developed a new consciousness that led to their improved education and increased their opportunities to influence public life. These historians also point out that the religious revival of the period, the Great Awakening, similarly offered women a greater voice in the world beyond their homes. Neither scenario, however, neatly fits the experience of all women. This chapter emphasizes the ways in which women participated in the Revolution and traces the complex changes the revolutionary era brought to their lives. Although traditional expectations about women's roles were challenged, they were rarely overturned.

BACKGROUND TO REVOLUTION, 1754–1775

Native American women and white women settlers on the frontier experienced the events leading up to the Revolution as part of an ongoing struggle over land rights that intensified in the mid-eighteenth century. During the early settlement years, colonists enjoyed a high degree of freedom from British intrusion in their domestic affairs. But the French and Indian War of 1754–1763, in which British and colonial troops conquered New France, opened up more land for British settlement. The war also drew various Native American peoples into the conflict as they sided and fought with whichever colonial power they thought most likely to honor Native American claims to territory—usually the French who, unlike the British, had not encroached on Native American lands. By the terms of the Treaty of Paris that ended the war, the French yielded their vast lands in North America to the British, who now claimed all the territory east of the Mississippi River (see Map 2.1).

Streams of Irish, Scots, Ulster Scots, Germans, and English peoples swelled the population of the British colonies, which counted almost 2 million settlers by 1765. Cities grew, but so too did the population of the backcountry regions. Pressured for years by a scarcity of good, affordable land, settlers as well as land speculators eagerly

1778	Mary Hays McCauley tends a cannon in the Battle of Monmouth, New Jersey
1780	General Washington orders strict control over women army followers
1780	Esther DeBerdt Reed and Sarah Franklin Bache organize Philadelphia women to support the troops
1780	Reed writes the broadside "Sentiments of an American Woman"
1780s–1807	Property-owning women allowed to vote in New Jersey
1781	British surrender at Yorktown, Virginia
1781	Articles of Confederation ratified
1781	Elizabeth Freeman ("Mum Bett") sues for her freedom in Massachusetts

1783	Treaty of Paris officially ends war
1783	Slavery banned in Massachusetts
1785	Jemima Wilkinson establishes a religious colony in New York
1787	Benjamin Rush's *Thoughts on Female Education* published
1788	U.S. Constitution adopted
1789	George Washington becomes first U.S. president
1790	Republican Motherhood ideal emerges
1790	Women's educational opportunities begin to expand outside the South
1790s	Second Great Awakening begins
1792	Mary Wollstonecraft's *A Vindication of the Rights of Woman* published in the United States
1793	The cotton gin invented
1793	Judith Sargent Murray's *Observations on Female Abilities* published
1796	John Adams elected president
1800	Thomas Jefferson elected president

◆ **Map 2.1 British Colonies in America, 1763**
Following the French and Indian War, the Treaty of Paris gave Britain control over all of New France east of the Mississippi and all of Spanish Florida. At the same time, Britain imposed the Proclamation Line of 1763, which prohibited white settlement west of the Appalachian Mountains. Subsequent legislation designated most of the western lands reserved for Indians. This western policy angered settlers hungry for land and land speculators eager to make a profit, and it contributed to the crisis in the British colonies that eventually led to the American Revolution.

eyed the Native American lands along the frontier. The British, hoping to put an end to the recurring Indian wars, issued the Proclamation of 1763, which temporarily closed the land west of the Appalachians to settlement. Expansion-minded colonists resented (and often ignored) the British policy, thus establishing a major bone of contention between the colonists and the mother country.

The Growing Confrontation

Other examples of British efforts to exert more control over its American empire included a series of fiscal and administrative reforms, which affected women primarily in their roles as household producers and consumers. The Revenue or Sugar Act of 1764 lowered duties on sugar but firmly established the means of enforcing their collection. It was followed by the Stamp Act of 1765, which required stamps on legal documents, playing cards, newspapers, and other printed matter, and was designed to defray the cost of keeping British troops in North America. These taxes on items of household consumption heightened women's political consciousness. Vigorous colonial resistance, especially in the seaport cities, forced the British to back down temporarily, but in the Townshend Act of 1767 they introduced new duties, including the tax on imported tea that became a famous symbol of British control and colonial resistance. The British increased their bureaucratic presence in the colonies—the number of Crown officials doubled during this period—and sought to limit the autonomy of the colonies' governing assemblies.

As tensions between Britain and the colonists took center stage in the years after the French and Indian War, deep social and economic problems roiled through the colonies, affecting both men and women. Seaport towns and cities suffered an economic downturn after the war boom, and the colonists, especially those indebted to English creditors, became all the more resentful of British taxation. Hard times widened the gap between rich and poor in the colonies, deepening dissatisfaction. Extraordinary unrest in the backcountry regions of the southern and middle colonies—where poorer farmers went on rampages against Native Americans and resisted the authority of colonial elites on the seaboard—also promoted the desire for change. While poor people might resent the wealthy colonial merchants and landed gentry who controlled so much of the economic and political life of the colonies, in some areas, especially the mid-Atlantic colonies, they diverted much of their anger toward British authority and its efforts to bring the American colonies more tightly into the imperial fold. Yet another social factor that paved the way for challenging imperial power was the religious ferment of the Great Awakening, discussed later in the chapter (see p. 96). These evangelical religious revivals, in which women were prominent participants, challenged traditional religion and promoted an egalitarianism that many scholars think fostered political unrest as well.

The onrushing crisis with England led some colonists to examine closely not only their relationship to the Crown but also their conceptions of the existing social order and government itself. Among educated elites, the ideas of the Enlightenment, especially of political philosophers such as John Locke, had a powerful impact. This European intellectual movement emphasized the rights of individuals, the role of reason, the promise of social progress, and the importance of the scientific method. In America, it contributed to the questioning of the British Crown's authority and to an appreciation for the rights of the individual.

The public debates occasioned by the British efforts to control the colonies more tightly were conducted almost exclusively by men. Although many addressed the questions of hierarchical structures within the British Empire and within the colonial governments, few questioned the hierarchy embedded in their gender system. Despite societal assumptions that the weighty considerations of government, diplomacy, and the economy were outside the realm of women's concerns, many women from diverse groups actively participated in the events surrounding the revolutionary conflict. But while many women found themselves acting in novel ways, for the most part their activities followed the traditional lines of household production and family obligation.

Liberty's Daughters: Women and the Emerging Crisis

When the colonists resisted the new taxes by boycotting British goods, women were necessarily involved as consumers and producers. Where formerly colonists relied on imported cloth, now they proposed to do without to send a potent message to British leaders. Despite the fact that cloth-making was women's work, initial reports of the substitution of homespun cloth for imported fabric often ignored women's contribution. In 1768, the *Providence Gazette* commended one man for the large quantities of cloth and yarn "spun in his own house," without reference to the women who were doing the work. But male patriots, as colonials who protested British domination were called, quickly realized that "after all our efforts depend greatly upon the female sex for the introduction of economy upon us," and northern newspaper reports of patriotic women's production of homespun cloth escalated.[2] In New England, spinning bees for manufacturing the yarn for homemade cloth were particularly popular. A group of twenty to forty young women, dressed in homespun and often observed by hundreds of spectators, would gather at a minister's home and there set to work spinning. These communal exercises included lively conversations, "American" refreshments, which were "more agreeable to them than any foreign Dainties and Delicacies," and usually a minister's speech commending the women on their industriousness.[3]

Southern white women also did their part, but because they lived on farms and plantations often widely separated from one another, they rarely did so in the large groups typical in the North. Nor was there much publicity for their work, and indeed the southern press tended to criticize women for their extravagant taste in clothes and to suggest that men would have to make efforts to "persuade our wives to give us their assistence, without which tis impossible to succeed."[4] Although free white women did provide "assistence," on large plantations masters bought equipment and set groups of slave women to the task of spinning. Robert Carter of Virginia had his overseer "sett a part, Ten black Females the most Expert spinners belonging to me—they to be Employed in Spinning, solely."[5] This method of slave production of cloth continued through the Revolutionary War, initiating a change in the organization of some slave women's work that gave them the chance to acquire new skills.

While black slave women had little choice in the matter of assisting their masters in their boycotts against the British, free white women could and did see themselves as acting in a patriotic cause, and many called themselves "Liberty's Daughters." Their spinning bees may not have resulted in a large amount of cloth, but their efforts took on symbolic importance and reinforced their importance as consumers—or nonconsumers—in the boycott. The spinning bees were, says one historian, "ideological showcases" that demonstrated women's contribution to the colonial struggle.[6]

Beyond the production of homespun, women practiced all sorts of economies as they spurned a wide variety of British goods. Tea became the focus of the boycotting in the early 1770s, especially after 1773 when the British instituted new regulations designed to undercut the colonials' illegal importation of non-British tea and force them to buy British tea instead. Women substituted herbal teas and coffee and engaged in collective efforts to encourage others to do the same. In Edenton, North Carolina, fifty-one women acknowledged their "duty" to support the nonimportation resolutions passed by the First Continental Congress in 1774. (See Figure 2.6, p. 110.) Women boycotters were roundly applauded in the press for their sacrifice. Presbyterian leader William Tennent III told women that "you have it in your power more than all your committees and Congresses, to strike the Stroke, and make the Hills and Plains of America clap their hands."[7] And, in contrast to the earlier homespun activity, even southern papers celebrated women's role in making the tea boycott successful. The *South Carolina Gazette* reported that in Charleston eminent women "engaged in a Promise . . . to reject, and totally renounce the baneful Herb," and proposed to "obtain the Assent of every Mistress of a Family" in the city, for "the Complexion of the Times is truly alarming, and calls aloud to every Inhabitant of America, whether Male or Female, to exert themselves in Defence of those Rights which God and Nature has bestowed on us."[8]

Both northern and southern newspapers printed articles written either by women or by men using female pseudonyms. Either way, they helped to legitimate the idea of women as authors with valuable insights to impart. Some women wrote poems denouncing tea drinking, as it "will *fasten Slavish Chains upon my Country.*"[9] A 1768 poem, "The female Patriots, Address'd to the Daughters of Liberty in America," acknowledged that "tho' we've no voice, but a negative here," yet announced that "Rather than Freedom, we'll part with our Tea / And well as we love the dear Draught when adry, As American Patriots,— our Taste we deny."[10]

WILLIAM JACKSON,

an *IMPORTER*; at the

BRAZEN HEAD,

North Side of the TOWN-HOUSE,

and *Opposite the Town-Pump, in*

Corn-hill, B O S T O N.

It is defired that the Sons and Daughters of *LIBERTY,* would not buy any one thing of him, for in fo doing they will bring Difgrace upon *themfelves,* and their *Pofterity,* for *ever* and *ever,* AMEN.

◆ **Don't Buy British Goods**
In reaction to the Townshend Act, which imposed taxes on glass, paper, paint, and imported tea to pay for the salaries of British royal officials in the colonies, outraged colonists in the major seaports began a boycott of British imports in 1768. This broadside, which would have been posted in public places, was aimed at merchants who refused to honor the boycott. The reference to "Daughters of Liberty" conveys how important women as consumers were to colonial resistance in the crisis years preceding the American Revolution. *Courtesy of the Massachusetts Historical Society.*

Other women produced thoughtful essays, such as the one in the *Virginia Gazette* (published by Clementina Rind) in 1774 explaining to women that "Much, very much, depends on the public virtue the ladies will exert at this critical juncture," and concluded that American women "will be so far instrumental in bringing about a redress of the evils complained of, that history may be hereafter filled with their praises, and teach posterity to venerate their virtues."[11]

Despite the widespread sense that politics was not a woman's affair, participation in the boycotts and in the production of homespun did bring women to the margins of political action. Even someone as young as thirteen-year-old Anna Green Winslow wrote in her diary in 1771, "As I Am (as we say) a daughter of liberty, I chuse to wear as much of our own manufactory as possible."[12] The political ferment in the years leading to the Revolution encouraged colonial women to see themselves as part of a larger American whole. Another young girl, Betsy Foote, recorded her daily labor at spinning and carding, and reported that she "felt Nationly into the bargain."[13] Women wrote of duty, of civic virtues, of freedom, and of sacrifice. Through the process of protesting British taxation and colonial intervention, women entered into the public arena, but they were still heavily constrained by gender assumptions. Despite the centrality of women's contributions to the success of the Americans' resistance, their efforts were extensions of their roles within the home—as good wives and consumers—and, as such, the potential challenge to the gender order was minimized.

WOMEN AND THE FACE OF WAR, 1775–1783

Colonial resistance escalated from boycotts and protests to armed conflict in April 1775, when British troops marched on Lexington and Concord, Massachusetts, in an effort to put down the growing rebellion. Although colonial leaders did not issue the Declaration of Independence until July 1776 (see the Appendix, p. A-1), the Revolution had begun. An imperial struggle between Great Britain and its colonies, the American Revolution was also a civil war in which British subjects fought one another and former friends and neighbors became enemies. While many colonists tried to avoid taking sides, historians estimate about one-fifth of the white population opposed the Revolution and were loyalists, also called Tories by their enemies. Probably two-fifths were patriots, supporters of the Revolution. Native Americans and African Americans, too, became embroiled in the conflict on both sides of the fence. A wide spectrum of Americans, both male and female, thus faced profound disruptions and complex decisions.

Choosing Sides: Native American and African American Women

Native American communities confronted particularly weighty choices. In part because their experiences with land-grabbing settlers had been so negative, many nations opted to side with the British—who had made some efforts to control the colonists' encroachment into Indian territory—and they waged war against the

◆ **"First Blow for Liberty"**
The April 1775 battle of Concord and Lexington marked the beginning of the Revolutionary War. Although this nineteenth-century engraving is a romanticized rendering of the conflict, its depiction of women assisting fallen soldiers appropriately acknowledges women's presence on the battlefields of the American Revolution, battlefields that were often in their own towns and villages. *Culver Pictures.*

patriots and their Indian allies throughout the backcountry. In many of the Indian nations, including the Iroquois and the Cherokee, women traditionally exerted significant influence over the decision to go to war; the causes were often linked to the desire to avenge deaths of loved ones killed by enemies. As Native Americans became enmeshed in European and American conflicts, the rationale for warfare shifted from kinship issues, and women's role may have diminished. Nonetheless, when some of the Iroquois peoples (Mohawk, Cayuga, Seneca, and Onondaga, but not the Oneidas and Tuscarosas) decided to ally with the British, they announced that the "mothers also consented to it," and some well-known Native American women were highly visible in the war effort. Molly Brant, a Mohawk woman who for many years had been the consort of Sir William Johnson, a British official on the frontier, followed the path of many Native American women who had married white men and then mediated between the two cultures (see Chapter 1). After Johnson died, Brant returned to her people and enjoyed unusual wealth and status. She so actively engaged in revolutionary era diplomacy on the side of the British that one officer claimed that her influence among her tribe was "far superior to that of all their Chiefs put together."[14]

Black women's choices in the Revolution were of a completely different nature. Although small free black communities existed throughout the colonies, the Revolution affected slaves far more profoundly. The disruptions produced by war offered unusual opportunities. Scarcities of food stuffs and clothing bore particularly hard on slaves, whose owners gave their needs a low priority, but wartime labor shortages and political circumstances gave slaves more room for maneuvering in their relations with their masters. Southern whites repeatedly complained about slaves' insolence and intractability. Thomas Pinckney's mother complained of the slaves on her South Carolina plantation that "they all do now as they please everywhere."[15]

Slaveowners were particularly worried about the prospect of insurrection and flight, especially after November 1775 when Virginia's royal governor offered freedom to rebels' slaves who agreed to fight for the British. His goal was not just to acquire troops and laborers but to pressure white slaveholders to stay within the loyalist fold. His offer led to a massive flight of slaves, not just men expecting to serve as soldiers, but women and children as well.

Throughout the war, slave men and women pondered their choice: Could they make it safely to the British lines? Would the British be true protectors? Would they or the rebels win? An estimated 55,000 southern slaves escaped during the Revolution. Some made their way to the British, or, as was the case of Mary Willing Byrd's slaves in Virginia, had the British come to them. When the British left after occupying Byrd's home, forty-nine slaves went with them. Many other slaves simply escaped their owners, looking for freedom independent of the British. Those who went over to the British often did so in groups, frequently with family members. Historians estimate that one-third of those who fled were women, a much higher proportion of runaways than before the Revolution. With nearby British troops offering sanctuary, women with children were willing to take the risk.

Escape from their owners, however, did not mean escape from danger and hardships. Former slaves were forced to work for the British, often at the most disagreeable tasks. When the British occupied Philadelphia, for example, they formed a "Company of Black Pioneers." This group of seventy-two men, fifteen women, and eight children were to "assist in Cleaning the Streets and Removing all Newsiances being thrown into the Streets."[16] Living conditions were harsh. In the British camps, many former slaves succumbed to smallpox and other diseases. In 1781, the British general Alexander Leslie reported that "about 700 Negroes are come down the River in the Small Pox." In an eighteenth-century version of germ warfare, he decided to "distribute them about the Rebell Plantations."[17] This callous attitude toward the black men and women under his care underlines the fact that most British officers viewed the slaves seeking freedom as pawns in the imperial struggle. Despite the unsettled conditions of wartime, black men and women fought an uphill battle to escape and survive to freedom.

White Women: Pacifists, Tories, and Patriots

White women also had to make decisions about the war, but of a very different sort than those of black slave women. The war created a painful situation for Quaker women, whose pacifism made them abhor war of all sorts. Maintaining a neutral stance was difficult. Patriots were often suspicious of Quakers' loyalty, and Quakers themselves clearly struggled with their political identity. Margaret Morris of New Jersey was concerned about the welfare of soldiers on both sides. Yet she was critical of the patriots' rowdy and aggressive efforts to capture loyalists and proudly recounted her success in hiding a friend from a group of armed men who appeared at her door. At the same time, she described General George Washington's troops as "our side." Her account suggests that despite her hatred of war and her personal sympathy for individual loyalists, on some levels she understood herself to be American, not British.

American or British, patriot or Tory: Did a woman's political identity follow her husband's? What was the allegiance of the wife of a Tory man? Women whose loyalist husbands had been exiled or who had gone to fight with the British were subject to ostracism. They sometimes found their land and personal goods plundered. State laws permitting the confiscation of land of known Tories differed slightly regarding the rights of the wife or widow of an "absentee." Massachusetts, for example, acknowledged her dower rights in the estate only if she had remained in the state and not followed her husband. Most generally states assumed a woman's allegiance followed her husband's, in accordance with the assumptions of *feme covert* practices (see Chapter 1). Significantly, most states did not require the loyalty oaths of women that they required of men, an indication that women were not viewed as political actors.

Not all women followed the allegiance of their husbands. A few took up the patriot cause despite their husband's loyalty to the British Crown. Florence Cook of Charleston, South Carolina, attempted to regain her family's dispossessed property after the war. In her petition, she described herself as a "Sincere friend to her Country," who taught her daughter "the love of Liberty and this her Native Country." Jane Moffit of Albany, New York, was protected from expulsion despite her husband's political sentiments because, said city leaders, she "has always been esteemed a Friend to the American Cause."[18] In New Jersey, Sally Medlis swore that she would "never hold any correspondence whatsoever with her Husband or in any Manner of Way injure the State." Nonetheless, the New Jersey Council of Safety exiled her to the enemy lines.[19] In case after case, decisions about the fate of wives were based on the assumption that wives could not act independently of their husbands, but they also reflected the reality that some women did directly aid the loyalist cause.

Many women who remained behind when their loyalist husbands left served as couriers and spies or in other ways assisted the British. In Albany, thirty-two women were brought to the attention of the New York State Commissioners for Detecting and Defeating Conspiracies in 1780. Some, like Lidia Currey or Rachael Ferguson, were jailed for hiding loyalists in their homes. Others smuggled messages to British troops. In Philadelphia, Margaret Hutchinson carried "Verbal Intelligence, of what, she had seen of their [the Rebels] different Movements" to British spies. While in absolute numbers such daring women were not numerous, they were considered so serious a threat that patriot committees of safety sought the help of "discreet Women, of Known attachment to the American Cause" to search for contraband and hidden letters on the persons of suspected female Tory couriers.[20]

Maintaining the Troops: The Women Who Served

Service to one's country during wartime often becomes a defining moment of citizenship. Sacrifices become emblems of civic virtue and worthiness. Since the ultimate sign of service is bearing arms and risking death, women's contributions are frequently less valued than men's. During the Revolution, few women actually fought in combat. But the exceptions are notable. In South Carolina, one woman joined her son-in-law to resist 150 British soldiers who were trying to destroy a cache of ammunition. Pennsylvanian Mary Hays McCauley, perhaps the inspiration for the legendary Molly Pitcher, routinely carried water to troops in battle. When her husband fell at the Battle of Monmouth, New Jersey, in 1778, she took his place, keeping a cannon loaded in the face of enemy fire, for which she later received a pension from the state of Pennsylvania "for services rendered in the revolutionary war." Deborah Sampson, later Gannett, was one of a handful of female cross-dressers in the Revolution. Donning men's clothing and enlisting as Robert Shurtleff in the Fourth Massachusetts Regiment, she served eighteen months from 1782 to 1783 and was wounded twice before her sex was discovered and she was discharged. Congress later granted her a modest pension, and she also generated income by lecturing. Less fortunate was the woman who attempted to enlist in 1778 at Elizabethtown, New Jersey. A suspicious officer required that she submit to a physical exam, and the following day, "ordered the Drums to beat her . . . Threw the Town with the whores march."[21]

More generally women's role in the military was the auxiliary role that women had historically played in warfare: the so-called camp follower. Some who attached themselves to the patriots' Continental Army under George Washington's command were prostitutes, but more were soldiers' wives. While officers' wives did make protracted visits to encourage their husbands and participate in entertainments, most women who followed the army were poor men's wives. Their presence may have signaled a patriotic fervor to aid the cause, but more probably indicated their desire to attend to their husbands' welfare as well as their inability to function on their own financially. Camp followers, often with their children in tow, faced extraordinary challenges, risking disease, injury, and death. Living under primitive conditions with scanty provisions, some even gave birth in army camps.

◆ **Deborah Sampson**

This genteel image painted in 1797 of Deborah Sampson, later Gannett, gives no hint of the reason for her
fame. For eighteen months (1782–1783), Sampson assumed men's clothing and the name Robert Shurtleff
while she served as a soldier in the Fourth Massachusetts
Regiment. She was wounded twice before being discovered and honorably discharged. Although some sources
claim that Gannett was African American, scholars generally agree that she was white and descended from
Mayflower families on both sides. *Courtesy of the Rhode
Island Historical Society. Joseph Stone, Portrait of Deborah
Sampson Gannett, 1797. Oil on panel. 1900.6.1. Rhix3 2513.*

But camp followers did provide valuable services. Some were "sutlers," merchants who sold provisions to the troops. More commonly women such as Sarah
Osborn, whose story opens this chapter, did laundry or worked as cooks (see box,
"Remembering the Revolution"). Women served as nurses, both in the fields and
at the general hospitals for the sick and wounded where conditions were primitive.
While male doctors and their assistants performed the skilled work, females were
assigned "to see that the close-stools or pots are emptied as soon as possible after
they are used . . . they are to see that every patient, upon his admission into the
Hospital is immediately washed with warm water, and that his face and hands are
washed and head combed every morning."[22] The sexual division of labor relegated
women to menial tasks, and no matter how important this work was, women's
compensation was small.

Even though he recognized that these women were crucial to the maintenance
of the army, Washington found them exasperating nuisances. He viewed them as
"a clog upon every movement" and worried that the cost of their subsistence cut
into the provisions of his soldiers. In 1780, at West Point, officers were required to
"make the Strictest inspection into the Carractor of the women who Draw [ra-
tions] in their Corps and report on their honour and Artificers." Unmarried
women would be sent away; married women could stay but would be required to
work as laundresses at minimal wages. Women's ragtag presence with the troops
also undercut the public image of a victorious army. In addition, Washington was

SARAH OSBORN
Remembering the Revolution

In 1837, Sarah Osborn (1756–1858) submitted a deposition to obtain a pension based on her husband's Revolutionary War service as a commissary guard. The statement provides evidence that her husband had indeed served and that she had firsthand knowledge of the course of the war. At the same time, her deposition reveals her own active participation on the battlefield. Osborn received her pension. This passage describes her activities in the battle of Yorktown.

Deponent [Osborn] took her stand just back of the American tents, say about a mile from the town, and busied herself washing, mending, and cooking for the soldiers, in which she was assisted by the other females; some men washed their own clothing. She heard the roar of the artillery for a number of days, and the last night the Americans threw up entrenchments, it was a misty, foggy night, rather wet but not rainy. Every soldier threw up for himself, as she understood, and she afterwards saw and went into the entrenchments. Deponent's said husband was there throwing up entrenchments, and deponent cooked and carried in beef, and bread, and coffee (in a gallon pot) to the soldiers in the entrenchment.

On one occasion when deponent was thus employed carrying in provisions, she met General Washington, who asked her if she "was not afraid of the cannonballs?"

She replied, "No, the bullets would not cheat the gallows," that "It would not do for the men to fight and starve too."

offended by poor women's lack of gentility, their failure to be ladylike. When he prepared to lead the troops through the city of Philadelphia after the battle of Germantown, he issued orders that "not a woman belonging to the army is to been seen with the troops on their march."[23]

Thus although camp followers lived and worked in the very midst of war, drawing on a physical fortitude associated with male activities, they did not break down traditional expectations about women's proper role. Their presence with the army was for the most part a reflection of their dependence. Women continued to be controlled not only by their husbands but also by what one historian terms "that most male of institutions, the military."[24] Their activities were extensions of women's traditional household work. Although many undoubtedly took pride in their patriotic contributions, they did not exhibit a new sense of independence.

They dug entrenchments nearer and nearer to Yorktown every night or two till the last. While digging that, the enemy fired very heavy till about nine o'clock next morning, then stopped, and the drums from the enemy beat excessively. . . .

The drums continued beating, and all at once the officers hurrahed and swung their hats, and deponent asked them, "What is the matter now?"

One of them replied, "Are not you soldier enough to know what it means?"

Deponent replied, "No."

Then they replied, "The British have surrendered."

Deponent, having provisions ready, carried the same down to the entrenchments that morning, and four of the soldiers whom she was in the habit of cooking for at their breakfasts.

Deponent stood on one side of the road and the American officers upon the other side when the British officers came out of the town and rode up to the American officers and delivered up [their swords, which the deponent] thinks were returned again and the British officers rode right on before the army who marched out beating and playing a melancholy tune, their drums covered with black handkerchiefs and their fifes with black ribbons tied around them, into an old field and there grounded their arms and then returned into town again to await their destiny. Deponent recollects seeing a great many American officers, some on horseback and some on foot, but cannot call them all by name. Washington, Lafayette, and Clinton were among the number.

SOURCE: John C. Dann, ed., *The Revolution Remembered: Eyewitness Accounts of the War for Independence* (Chicago: University of Chicago Press, 1980), 244–45.

Some women did not follow the armies but had the fighting come to them. Occupying armies commandeered homes for quartering soldiers, and women frequently bore the brunt of their demands for food and firewood. In September 1777, Elizabeth Drinker, alone with her children in Philadelphia, found herself the unwilling hostess to a British officer. "Our officer mov'd his lodging from the bleu Chamber to the little front parlor, so that he has the two front parlors, a chamber up two pair of stairs for his bagge, and the Stable wholly to himself, besides the use of the kitchen."[25] Catherine Van Cortlandt, a Tory woman, wrote disparagingly to her husband about the patriot troops who commandeered her house in New Jersey: "They were the most disorderly of their species and their officers were from the dregs of the people." She complained that "the farmers are forbid to sell me provisions, and the millers to grind our grain. Our woods are cut down for the use of their army, and that which you bought and left corded near the river my

ESTHER DeBERDT REED
Sentiments of an American Woman

In 1780, Esther DeBerdt Reed (1746–1780) and Sarah Franklin Bache (1743–1808) created the Ladies Association of Philadelphia. As Reed explained it in a broadside, "Sentiments of an American Woman," the purpose was to organize women to be "really useful" in supporting the revolutionary effort, especially in regard to the raising of funds for the army.

On the commencement of actual war, the Women of America manifested a firm resolution to contribute as much as could depend on them, to the deliverance of their country. Animated by the purest patriotism, they are sensible of sorrow at this day, in not offering more than barren wishes for the success of so glorious a Revolution. They aspire to render themselves more really useful; and this sentiment is universal from the north to the south of the Thirteen United States. Our ambition is kindled by the same of those heroines of antiquity, who have rendered their sex illustrious, and have proved to the universe, that, if the weakness of our Constitution, if opinion and manners did not forbid us to march to glory by the same paths as the Men, we should at least equal, and sometimes surpass them in our love for the public good. I glory in all that which my sex has done great and commendable. I call to mind with enthusiasm and with admiration, all those acts of courage, of constancy and patriotism, which history has transmitted to us. . . . So many famous sieges where the Women have been seen forgetting the weakness of their sex, building new walls, digging trenches with their feeble hands, furnishing arms to their defenders, they themselves darting the missile weapons on the enemy, resigning the ornaments of their apparel, and their fortune, to fill the public treasury, and to hasten the deliverance of their country; burying themselves under its ruins, throwing themselves

servants are forbid to touch, though we are in the greatest distress for the want of it."[26] Women caught in the crossfire worried about their personal safety and that of their children. While reported rapes were infrequent, British soldiers were brutal on occasion. More commonly, women had to adjust to being alone and to handling the day-to-day affairs of running a farm or managing a business in a husband's prolonged absence. Their independent management proved to be one of their most significant roles in the revolutionary era.

A small group of patriot women carved out more public ways of participating in the war effort by raising funds for the beleaguered continental army. Following a discouraging defeat at Charleston in 1780, Esther DeBerdt Reed, the wife of the

into the flames rather than submit to the disgrace of humiliation before a proud enemy.

Brave Americans, your disinterestedness, your courage, and your constancy will always be dear to America, as long as she shall preserve her virtue. . . . And shall we hesitate to evidence to you our gratitude? Shall we hesitate to wear a cloathing more simple; hair dressed less elegant, while at the price of this small privation, we shall deserve your benedictions. Who, amongst us, will not renounce with the highest pleasure, those vain ornaments, when she shall consider that the valiant defenders of America will be able to draw some advantage from the money which she may have laid out in these; that they will be better defended from the rigours of the seasons, that after their painful toils, they will receive some extraordinary and unexpected relief; that these presents will perhaps be valued by them at a greater price, when they will have it in their power to say: *This is the offering of the Ladies.* The time is arrived to display the same sentiments which animated us at the beginning of the Revolution, when we renounced the use of teas, however agreeable to our taste, rather than receive them from our persecutors; when we made it appear to them that we placed former necessaries in the rank of superfluities, when our liberty was interested; when our republican and laborious hands spun the flax, prepared the linen intended for the use of our soldiers; when exiles and fugitives we supported with courage all the evils which are the concomitants of war. Let us not lose a moment; let us be engaged to offer the homage of our gratitude at the altar of military valour, and you, our brave deliverers, while mercenary slaves combat to cause you to share with them, the irons with which they are loaded, receive with a free hand our offering, the purest which can be presented to your virtue,

By An AMERICAN WOMAN.

SOURCE: *Pennsylvania Magazine of History and Biography* XVIII (1894): 361–63.

governor of Pennsylvania, and Sarah Franklin Bache, the daughter of Benjamin Franklin, organized the Ladies Association of Philadelphia to raise money for the troops. They urged prosperous women to go without luxuries to aid the cause and asked poorer women to offer what they could. Reminiscent of the Daughters of Liberty who had organized spinning bees in the early stages of the Revolution, women once again acted collectively. In a powerfully worded broadside (see box, "Sentiments of an American Woman"), Reed outlined the rationale for the fundraising and answered any challenge to the appropriateness of women's fundraising: "he cannot be a good citizen who will not applaud our efforts for the relief of the armies which defend our lives, our possessions, our liberty."[27]

◆ **Sarah Franklin Bache**
Together with Esther DeBerdt Reed, Sarah Franklin Bache, the daughter of Benjamin Franklin, organized the Ladies Association of Philadelphia to raise money for General George Washington's troops. This group of elite women raised $300,000, which was used to provide 2,200 shirts to the soldiers. Like many of her female peers, Bache actively supported the colonial cause, but in ways that did not sharply challenge conventional expectations about appropriate feminine behavior. *The Metropolitan Museum of Art, Catharine Lorillard Wolfe Collection, Wolfe Fund, 1901. (01.20)*

The Pennsylvania women publicized their efforts and sent letters to women in other states, urging them to raise funds as well. In Virginia, the scattered nature of settlement made an exact duplication of Pennsylvania's door-to-door effort impossible, but Martha Wayles Jefferson, wife of governor Thomas Jefferson, did encourage other Virginian women (Martha was not in good health) to raise funds, describing it as an "opportunity of proving that they also participate on those virtuous feelings."[28] In most cases, the sums raised were modest. In New Jersey, women collected $15,488 in paper dollars, but because of high inflation, the money purchased only 380 pairs of stockings for the state's soldiers.

The distribution of the $300,000 that the Philadelphia women collected offers a revealing insight into perceptions of women's supporting role. Writing to Washington, Reed explained that the women did not want the money to go into a general fund that would provide soldiers "an article to which they are entitled from the public." Rather the women hoped that their money—approximately $2 per soldier in hard currency—might be given directly to the soldiers. Washington demurred: the men might waste it on liquor, and having hard currency, when they were generally paid in paper money, might create discontent and exacerbate inflation. He declared that their "benevolent donation" should be used to provide men with shirts and requested further that the women make the shirts themselves. In the midst of the exchange, Reed died of dysentery, but Bache followed through with the project, eventually sending Washington 2,220 shirts. A French visitor to

Bache's home reported that "on each shirt was the name of the married or unmarried lady who made it."[29]

For the most part, these women's efforts received favorable attention from men. The editor of the *Pennsylvania Packet* grandiosely proclaimed that "the women of every part of the globe are under obligations to those of America, for having shown that females are capable of the highest political virtue."[30] Yet however novel the Philadelphia women's plan may have been, Washington's response placed their efforts firmly in the realm of woman's more traditional sphere—of sewing for her family. The Philadelphia women's efforts may have been more overtly political than the service of poor women following the army, but in both cases women's contributions were constrained by traditional notions of women's roles. The link between women's patriotism and the domestic sphere was to be one of the principal ideological legacies of the Revolution.

REVOLUTIONARY LEGACIES

The patriots emerged victorious in 1781 when the British surrendered at Yorktown, Virginia. In that same year, the colonies, now states, ratified the Articles of Confederation, their first attempt at national governance. Weaknesses in that body led eventually to adoption of the U.S. Constitution in 1788 (see the Appendix, p. A-4) and the inauguration of George Washington as the new nation's first president in 1789. As a national government was being framed, the various states also wrote constitutions. The period was rich with debates about the nature of government and the rights of citizens, as Americans pondered the implications of their Revolution. What were the legacies of the Revolution for women? For many, war and revolution translated into hardship and poverty; for others, new opportunities emerged, but these were always constrained by prevailing assumptions about women's marginal role in public life.

A Changing World for Native American Women

How the Revolution affected the lives of Native American women is difficult to gauge, in part because historians have so little evidence about these women's experiences. Many nations, especially those that sided with Britain, suffered devastating losses in the war. American forces in New York invaded Iroquois territory in 1779, burning forty towns and destroying crops. The Cherokees to the south in the Appalachian region suffered a similar destruction. Native American men's preoccupation with warfare and their role in diplomacy may have heightened their power within their own communities, but it also increased women's responsibilities in maintaining their communities in the men's prolonged absences, and in the face of destruction, disease, and starvation.

In the postwar period, as the weakened Native Americans started to come under the power of the new federal government, challenges to traditional gender roles arose. Men acted as primary mediators between their nations and the newly created American government. As men's roles took on magnified importance, women may have correspondingly lost influence in their communities. The government's efforts to encourage Native Americans' assimilation to white norms also disturbed traditional patterns. American leaders insisted that men give up hunting and become farmers and that Native American women become farmer's wives. In a letter to the Cherokees in 1796, President George Washington was explicit about his expectations. "You will easily add flax and cotton which you may dispose of to the White people; or have it made up by your own women into clothing for yourselves. Your wives and daughters can soon learn to spin and weave."[31] But if white Americans envisioned a family order in which women were subordinate, Cherokee women adapted to the new expectations in ways that maintained their traditional roles in the community. They continued their customary farming work, tended livestock, and took on the responsibilities of spinning and weaving. In contrast, men found it far more difficult to adjust to their changed circumstances. Deprived of hunting by the loss of their lands and depletion of furs, they were often idle and despairing. Overuse of alcohol also contributed to the exploitation of Native Americans and to unhappy domestic situations in which women were abused.

After the Revolution, Native Americans became the objects of missionary activity, especially during the Second Great Awakening of the early nineteenth century (see Chapter 3). White missionaries sought not only to bring Christianity to the natives but to "civilize" them, in part by urging them to adopt European notions of proper male and female behavior. Calls for change also came from within Indian nations. Handsome Lake, a Seneca religious prophet who had been influenced by the Quakers, called for major reforms for his people. He promoted a return to some of the old ways, especially in regard to religion. He condemned the abuse of alcohol and criticized men's physical mistreatment of their wives. At the same time, however, he urged that they follow the family patterns of whites: men should take up farming and women limit themselves to spinning and weaving. Privileging the nuclear family and the husband-wife relationship, he downplayed the older emphasis on kinship relations and was especially critical of older women, the tribes' matrons. In the long run, assimilative pressures and a changed economic and political order undermined women's position among many Native American peoples, especially where men took on economic roles of increased importance to the community and their families. But that process was neither immediate nor universal.

African American Women: Freedom and Slavery

For African American women, the Revolution also left a complex, but completely different, legacy. At the end of the war, many slaves who had fled to the British to achieve their freedom were evacuated by ship from New York, Charleston, and Savannah. Of those who left from New York and whose sex is known, 42.3 percent were women, and apparently many had their children with them. Once on board, their problems were not over, however. Some of these African Americans were sold again into slavery in the West Indies; others were shipped to Nova Scotia where

◆ **Redefining Gender Roles among the Creeks**
This early nineteenth-century painting features Creek Indians as U.S. agent Benjamin Hawkins introduces them to plows as a first step in Americanizing them. Hawkins focuses his attention on the men, placing his back to a woman who stands amidst the foodstuffs she has produced. This stance represents white officials' and missionaries' goal of redefining gender roles among the Creek so that men would abandon hunting in exchange for farming, while women would give up their traditional role of raising crops to undertake domestic roles in the home. *Greenville County Museum of Art, Greenville, South Carolina. Gift of the Museum Association, Inc.*

they eked out an existence in harsh conditions; and some ended up in another marginal environment, a new colony in Sierra Leone, West Africa.

For some African Americans who had not joined the British, the most important legacy of the Revolution was freedom. Even before the conflict, a small movement had supported manumission (owners granting slaves their freedom), primarily the result of the Quakers' growing revulsion against slavery. The ideological issues at the center of the Revolution, especially those concerning the natural rights of man and liberty, encouraged some white Americans to examine the institution of slavery. Even for those with little humanitarian interest in slaves themselves, the inconsistencies of building a nation based on notions of liberty while maintaining chattel slavery were troublesome. Antislavery sentiment was also promoted by more mundane concerns—white immigrant workers who were increasingly available and who were easily hired and fired became more attractive in the urban commercial culture of the North. Anxieties about slave insurrections during the war also raised questions about the slave system.

African Americans were active participants in the emancipation process, especially in Massachusetts. Elizabeth Freeman, also known as Mum Bett, was the slave of Colonel John Ashley in Sheffield, Massachusetts. (See Visual Sources: Portraits of Revolutionary Women, pp. 102–9.) In 1781 she petitioned a Massachusetts county court for her freedom. Freeman's suit, combined with several others, led to the state court's 1783 decision that "there can be no such thing as perpetual servitude of a rational creature."[32] In other northern states, manumission came through legislation. Only Vermont provided for immediate emancipation (1777). Elsewhere, the process was protracted. In Pennsylvania, unborn children of slaves would not be free until they were 28 years old. Although each year more slaves became free in the North, one-fourth of northern blacks were still enslaved as late as 1810. This gradualism meant that slave women would continue to bear children who would be slaves until they were adults, but they could take some comfort in their children's future freedom.

The emancipation laws, as well as individual manumissions in the North and the Upper South and the migration of southern free blacks, created growing free black populations in the last years of the eighteenth century, especially in cities such as Philadelphia, Boston, and New York. Although a small number of these African Americans were able to carve out a modest success, constrained education and pervasive discrimination limited their opportunities. Most women worked at jobs similar to those that had occupied them when they were slaves—domestic work, washing, cooking, and child care. Some black women were proprietors, especially of boarding houses, where they would have been important resources for the freed blacks migrating to the cities during this period. A handful of women were prominent enough to make a mark in the historical record. Lydia York, for example, petitioned the Philadelphia Abolition Society to assist her in indenturing her niece Hetty. Catherine Ferguson, an ex-slave who had purchased her own freedom, established a school for poor black and white children in New York in 1793. Another former slave, Eleanor Harris, became the first black teacher in Philadelphia.

As they worked at their jobs and cared for their families, many free black women participated in building up the network of black institutions, including churches and benevolent societies devoted to self-help efforts that had emerged by the turn of the century. Their role in these organizations, however, has remained largely obscured in the historical record. These free black institutions were a source of strength and pride for the community, but they also exemplified the segregated lives that African Americans lived in the North. Emancipation brought freedom for some black women and men, but they enjoyed that freedom within the constraints of a racial and economic hierarchy. The egalitarian promises implicit in revolutionary ideology were closed to African Americans.

In the South, these promises were even less in evidence. In the Upper South, there was a spate of individual manumissions, especially through the wills of slaveholders, and the free black population did expand significantly. But there was no widespread sentiment for dispensing with the institution altogether. Most slaveowners were not unduly troubled by the implications of a rhetoric of individual freedom and natural rights for their system of chattel laborers. Indeed, slaveowners became more deeply entrenched in the institution after the war, especially in the Deep South, where the 1793 invention of the cotton gin, which mechanically removed the seed and hull from the cotton fiber, made the crop highly profitable. This gave new impetus to the slave system, which was also reinforced by increased importation of African slaves, a trade explicitly permitted by the U.S. Constitution until 1808. The regional differences in patterns of slavery grew after the Revolution, with slaves in the Deep South more likely to maintain a more distinct African-based culture and to live in more isolation from whites.

In the Chesapeake region, tobacco declined in importance and the region's economy diversified, creating more varied jobs for slave populations. While some women had developed textile skills during the revolutionary period, for the most part males were the skilled slaves in the Upper South, trained as wagon makers or mill workers or in the building trades. As some male slaves became artisans, women inherited more of the disagreeable labor such as breaking new ground and

◆ **Women Slaves in the Tobacco Fields**

In 1798, architect Benjamin Henry Latrobe produced this image entitled "An overseer doing his duty. Sketched from life near Fredricsburg." Latrobe apparently recognized the irony presented by the overseer, a white male in the employ of the plantation owner, standing idly on a tree stump, his duty merely to watch the two women slaves hard at work hoeing in a tobacco field. *The Maryland Historical Society, Baltimore, Maryland.*

collecting manure. Slaves also became extremely important to the growing urban areas of the region, and women in particular were used in the tobacco factories of Petersburg and Richmond, Virginia. Women also served as domestic workers and participated in city markets, selling wares such as cakes, oysters, and garden produce, an occupation that gave them an unusual amount of liberty to move about the city.

Most slaves, however, enjoyed little personal freedom. This was particularly evident in the way in which slaveholders in the Upper South increasingly sought to reproduce the slave population, forcing some black women into sexual relations with men not of their own choosing. Others encouraged slave family formation. Thomas Jefferson provided gifts for at least one couple on his Virginia plantation and explicitly commented on the value of a fertile female slave: "I consider a woman who brings a child every two years as more profitable than the best man on the farm."[33]

Despite the slaveowners' appreciation of female slaves as breeders, slaveowners throughout the South expected pregnant women to work well into their pregnancy and to return to their labors almost immediately after delivery. The hardships of being a mother under these conditions were magnified by the constant threat of separation. A white observer in Wilmington, North Carolina, in 1778 described the trauma he witnessed: "A wench clung to a little daughter, and implored, with the most agonizing supplication, that they might not be separated."[34] Children could be sold from their parents, and husbands from their wives, even in the households of paternalistic owners. The effects of financial reversals or the death of the master often rippled through the slave quarters, undercutting slaves' efforts to create a stable family life.

White Women: An Ambiguous Legacy

Just as the Revolution had mixed results for black women, its meaning for white women eludes easy generalizations. Many women faced enormous hardships. Petitions from widows and soldiers' wives provide eloquent evidence for the personal tragedies that came with war. Sarah Welsh's husband had died in 1780, but "being a destress widow not knowing how to or whom aplication was to be made . . . untill it was too late," she waited until 1791 to ask the government for his back pay.[35] Many wives of Tory men, too, found themselves in dire straits. After the war, they waged lengthy, and only rarely successful, legal battles to regain property seized when their husbands left to fight with the British. While some impoverished women could turn to friends, many others worked in the few avenues of employment offered to women, as shopkeepers, teachers, innkeepers, servants, seamstresses, or milliners. By 1800, as the nation moved toward the first stages of industrialization and the "putting-out" industries, such as textiles, shoes, and straw bonnets, expanded, poorer women increasingly turned to doing piecework in their homes (see Chapter 3).

For more privileged educated women, war and revolution contributed to a changed conception of self, as many expanded their horizons beyond the narrow sphere of the hearth. Women whose husbands served in the army or the new governments, were left alone for extended periods. As women had been doing since the early colonial period, they became "deputy husbands," managing farms and businesses and often rising impressively to the new challenges. The *Norwich Packet* (Connecticut) reported in 1776 that "in this distressing Time of gathering in the Harvest, the Men being universally gone . . . a Number of Young Women, willing to support the Cause which the Men are engag'd in . . . assembled together at the House of Captain Stephen Johnson and husked out near two Hundred Bushels of corn, partook of an elegant Supper and returned to their respective dwellings by Day Light." The *Packet* hoped that "this laudable Example may be followed."[36]

In the extant correspondence and diaries from this period, primarily from the wives of officers and politicians, a distinct pattern concerning women's roles as deputy husbands emerges. Men originally left detailed instructions, urging their wives to consult male kin or neighbors. Through time, many men began to trust their wives' judgment, as indicated by New Yorker James Clinton's comment to his wife Mary that "I Can't give any Other Directions About Home more than what I have done but must Leave all to your good Management."[37] Women themselves often made pointed reference to their own competence, and some even ignored their husband's directions. The letters of the Bartletts of New Hampshire are particularly revealing of the transformation in consciousness the war brought to one woman. When Josiah Bartlett wrote his wife with instructions about "my out Door affairs," or "my farming business," she initially replied in kind, referring to "Your farming business." But eventually she began to use the word "our." Even more explicit in pointing out that male and female roles had become less sharply defined was Lucy Flucker Knox in New York, who wrote to her husband Henry Knox that she was "quite a woman of business," and hoped that in the future "you will not consider yourself as commander in chief of your own house—but be convinced that there is such a thing as equal command."[38]

Although few women challenged their subordinate position as overtly as Lucy Knox, the postwar years did see a significant questioning of white women's status in the home and, to some extent, in politics. Early in the revolutionary crisis women speaking about politics often made apologies, almost ritualistically accepting women's inferiority. In a June 1776 letter to a female friend, Elizabeth Feilde followed her comments on contemporary politics with the self-deprecating remark, "No; I assure you it's a subject for which I have not either Talents or Inclination to enter upon."[39] But in the turmoil of rebellion and war, the apologies became less evident, as astute women got caught up in the dramatic events unfolding before them. Eliza Wilkinson of South Carolina frankly resented men's claim that women had no business with politics, writing to a friend in 1782 that "I won't have it thought that because we are the weaker sex as to *bodily* strength, my dear, we are capable of nothing more than minding the dairy, visiting the poultry-house, and all such domestic concerns. . . . They won't even allow us the liberty of thought, and that is all I want. . . ."[40]

As Wilkinson's term "liberty of thought" suggests, many women made overt connections between the ideology of the Revolution concerning natural rights, liberty, and equality and the position of women. Abigail Adams's admonition to her husband, John Adams, that the men drawing up the new government and its code of laws should "remember the ladies" is probably the most famous expression of the handful of elite women who hoped to see at least modest changes in women's status (see Figure 2.2, p. 104). The issue attracted a significant amount of attention in the decade after the Revolution. Following publication in the United States in 1792 of *A Vindication of the Rights of Women* by the English activist Mary Wollstonecraft, American magazines debated women's rights and roles. Some articles referred to marriage as a form of slavery. Others blamed women's limited education for women's vanity and superficiality.

Did the flurry of attention to women's rights in the postrevolutionary era lead to an improvement in white women's status? The states in the new nation were now free of British legal statutes and could theoretically construct laws in keeping with the new emphasis on protecting individual rights. Divorce law was one area in which women did benefit. British common law did not allow divorce, but now all states except South Carolina permitted it. Still, the procedure was difficult. In most states, divorce petitions required action by the state assembly. Courts in Pennsylvania and the four New England states could decree divorce. Causes offered for divorce changed over time, hinting at a slight shift in marital expectations. During most of the colonial period, women were far more likely than men to seek a divorce, usually doing so on the grounds of desertion. After the Revolution, the grounds women used expanded to include adultery, and more men began to seek divorce, usually for desertion. The changes were subtle ones, as one historian concedes: "All one can say, and perhaps it is enough, is that after the war women were physically moving out of their unhappy households, an action that, judging from the divorce literature, had been relatively uncommon before the war."[41]

In other legal matters, white women gained little. In many states, widows' rights to their dower was, if anything, eroded in the years after the Revolution. In addition, states maintained the British system of coverture, a major impediment to married women's autonomy. Women continued to be excluded from juries and from legal training and thus were excluded from the male political culture that centered at the courthouse.

Most significantly, women were denied the vote. Despite the revolutionary rhetoric of equality, the majority of the founding fathers believed that in a democratic republic only independent people should be permitted to vote, and independent people, by definition, owned property. Thus propertyless men and all women were excluded. In the case of women, however, exclusion was less a matter of property than of sex. Married or not, women were assumed to be dependent creatures by nature. The fleeting exception to this assumption was New Jersey, whose 1776 state constitution did not explicitly define the qualifications for voters, declaring only that "all inhabitants" who met certain property and residence requirements "shall be entitled to vote," thus technically permitting both white women and blacks to vote. In the 1780s, some property-holding women seized the initiative and voted in local elections. A 1796 statute specifically excluded black men and women, but reaffirmed white women's right to vote.[42]

By 1800, however, criticism of women as voters in New Jersey had mounted. That wives and daughters living at home, who were thus not independent, and men without property sometimes voted increased concern. When an 1807 referendum election revealed extensive fraud, the legislature moved to tighten suffrage requirements. All women were excluded on the grounds that they were easily manipulated by men and were thus not independent. But at the same time the state expanded suffrage to include propertyless white men and sons living at home, further emphasizing the different political stature of men and women.

The results in New Jersey lend credence to the conclusion that while men gained as a result of the Revolution, white women actually lost ground. After 1800, as states granted universal white male suffrage, women's exclusion from suffrage more sharply defined their political dependence and inequality than ever before. But to define women's experience solely in terms of their formal political and legal roles obscures other significant factors that shaped their lives. For many women, the revolutionary years sparked a political consciousness, one that encouraged women to move outside their preoccupations of home and family. At the same time, improvements in white women's education—the substantial number of revolutionary women's diaries and letters indicate that more women had become fully literate—helped to broaden women's vision and open some opportunities.

The move for improved education for both men and women accelerated after the war—for practical as well as ideological reasons. As the new nation began the long process of industrialization, its more complex economy required literacy and other skills. Formal education became more necessary as print replaced oral tradition as the means of communication. Americans also believed that the new republic needed an educated, enlightened citizenry. Thomas Jefferson understood that schools were now needed to "instruct the mass of our citizens in these their rights, interests and duties, as men and citizens."[43] For women, the interest in educational reform was linked to the civic good. Observers roundly criticized the type of education elite white women most often received. Beyond basic literacy, women were taught domestic skills and refinements meant to enhance their position in the marriage market. But what sort of wife and mother could such a poorly educated woman become? The image of flighty women concerned primarily with fashion and sentimental novels seemed especially out of step with the expectations of the new nation.

A number of critics addressed the issue of women's education at length, including Mercy Otis Warren (see Figure 2.1, p. 103), Judith Sargent Murray, and Dr. Benjamin Rush. Although they challenged conventional assumptions that more fully educating women would make them less feminine and more discontented with their lot, these critics rarely recommended that women be educated primarily to move beyond the domestic sphere. Most of the proponents of improved education for women articulated an ideology that historians have called Republican Motherhood, the idea that women had vital roles in educating their children for their duties as citizens. One notable advocate, Abigail Adams, wrote, "If we mean to have heroes, statesmen, and philosophers, we should have learned women. If as much depends as it is allowed upon the early education of youth and the first principles which are instilled take the deepest root great benefit must arise from the literary accomplishments in women."[44] In addition to this emphasis on children, the ideology of the postrevolutionary years stressed that women's enlightened and virtuous influence on their husbands could contribute mightily to civic culture and order. (See Documents: Education and Republican Motherhood, pp. 124–30.)

The new thinking about women's education bore some fruit. Not only did some states, like Massachusetts in 1789, institute free elementary public schooling for all children, but academies and boarding schools specifically designed for middle-class and elite women proliferated in the North and eventually appeared in the South. Parents and educators expected that this enhanced education would, according to one historian, "allow women to instruct their sons in the principles of patriotism, to make their homes well-run havens of efficiency, to converse knowledgeably with their husbands on a variety of subjects, and to understand family finance."[45] Rather than discouraging women from domestic pursuits, education was expected to improve their chances for a suitable and happy marriage. But many of the women educated at the new academies apparently were inspired to move beyond the household sphere. Some became famous as writers, missionaries, or reformers, and a substantial number became teachers themselves, pursuing jobs that offered the earliest form of professional opportunity for American women. The ideology of Republican Motherhood and the educational reforms it inspired began a long process of expanded opportunities for women. Eventually women would demand opportunities to learn as much as, and even alongside, men.

WOMEN AND RELIGION: THE GREAT AWAKENING

In addition to education, religion was crucial in the new conception of white womanhood arising in the last half of the eighteenth century. Waves of religious revivalism had begun as early as the 1730s and 1740s, inspired by English minister George Whitefield's preaching tours throughout the English colonies. Known as the Great Awakening, these outpourings of evangelical fervor reached their greatest intensity between the 1750s and the 1770s, especially in the South where revivalism touched both blacks and whites. Complex theological issues were involved, but the one essential ingredient was conversion—an immediate and ecstatic religious experience. This experience of conversion challenged the Puritan emphasis on salvation as demonstrated by good works and right behavior and the Anglican emphasis on formal worship and priestly hierarchy. The Great Awakening split established churches and created increasing numbers of converts to new denominations, such as the Baptists and the Methodists, whose evangelicalism emphasized an emotional spiritual rebirth. Evangelical worshipers gathered outside, in fields and pastures, where their religious joy could have physical expression; the converted were likely to shout and jump about. Evangelicalism validated the religious experience of ordinary people. In challenging religious authority and church hierarchy, it promoted a new egalitarianism with an appeal that cut across gender, class, race, and slave status.

White Women's Religious Fervor

For much of the eighteenth century, women in New England churches, for which we have the most information, outnumbered men. Historians suggest that as men became increasingly involved in the region's thriving trade and business, they lost interest in a religion that required submission and restraint. Women, in contrast, were accustomed to subordination. Moreover, repeated experiences with the dangers of childbirth heightened their concern with salvation and spiritual matters. The Great Awakening temporarily brought many men back to the churches. But even as it slightly diminished women's numerical majority in their congregations, its egalitarianism and challenge to traditional orthodoxy nonetheless offered women a greater voice in religious worship and church affairs than had been available to women previously, with the exception of Quaker meetings (see Chapter 1).

Most commonly, women's voices were heard as they offered their dramatic conversion narrative, accounts of how they came to experience Jesus Christ in their souls. They also made their presence known by their physical manifestations of the spirit—they wept and cried out, they moved and flailed around. A Massachusetts woman, Sarah Sparhawk, was so physically affected that she seemed "unbounded, and like one deprived of her reason."[46] While some ministers welcomed this display as evidence for their power as preachers, others resented what they saw as a distraction from their religious message. Some also worried about the unseemliness of women's physical display.

Two radical religious groups centered around charismatic women who broke dramatically with tradition. Jemima Wilkinson, a former Quaker, believed that she was the female incarnation of Christ and attracted a host of devoted followers, primarily in Rhode Island and Connecticut (see Figure 2.5, p. 108). Mother Ann Lee, a founder of the "Shaking Quakers" (so named for the ecstatic dances that were part of their worship) or more simply, "Shakers" (see Chapter 4), styled herself as a preacher and prophet. In different ways both these remarkable women denied their femaleness. Wilkinson dressed in male-style clothing and refused to answer to her female name, insisting that she be called the Public Universal Friend. Lee required celibacy, not only for herself but for her followers. This adamant denial of sexuality minimized her femaleness and blocked the issue of gender from undercutting her religious leadership.

In newer congregations, such as northern Baptist churches, women could vote to elect deacons and even "exhort," or act as a lay preacher. One of the more radical groups, the Separates, or Strict Congregationalists, explicitly affirmed women in their "just *Right* . . . to speak openly in the Church."[47] In the South, only one group, the Separate Baptists, permitted women official roles, appointing them as deaconesses and eldresses. A Baptist minister traveling in Virginia and the Carolinas in the early 1770s described the duties of the eldresses as "praying, and teaching at their [women's] separate assemblies; presiding there for maintenance of

◆ The Great Awakening

English evangelical preacher George Whitefield traveled between the colonies and Britain in the 1740s and 1750s, helping to ignite the Great Awakening. This mid-eighteenth-century painting depicts Whitefield's charismatic effect on his audience. Given how deeply engaged women were in the Great Awakening, it is appropriate that the image highlights a young woman. Her transfixed gaze and the light that shines on her reinforce the sense that she is experiencing spiritual illumination. *National Portrait Gallery, London.*

rules and government; consulting with sisters about matters of the church which concern them, and representing their sense thereof to the elders; attending at the unction of sick sisters; and at the baptism of women, that all may be done orderly."[48]

But none of the larger denominations accepted women as preachers, equal to male ministers. In backcountry regions, some women may have been traveling preachers, but generally their roles, even in evangelical churches, were unofficial. Typically, they served as counselors. Women created informal religious groups, encouraging friends and families along the road to conversion. Sarah Osborn of Newport, Rhode Island (not the same Sarah Osborn who participated in the Revolutionary War), organized a young women's religious society in 1737 that met more or less continuously for fifty years. In the 1760s, she expanded her focus and on Sunday evenings taught a group of African Americans in her home. Osborn had to tread carefully, however. Like Anne Hutchinson a century earlier, she was criticized for usurping the role of male ministers. So she was careful to explain that "to avoid Moving beyond my Line" she did not "instruct" married men or teenaged boys. She even justified her outreach to black men and women by characterizing both as "no otherwise now then children tho for Stature Men and Women."[49] Despite her willingness to picture herself as staying within the confines of traditional women's roles—of teaching other women, black men, and children—Osborn resisted suggestions that she halt her activities, sharply asking one critic if he would "advise me to shut up my Mouth and doors and creep into obscurity?"[50] Throughout her life, she continued to exert considerable influence within her congregation, an experience shared by many women in evangelical churches throughout the country.

By 1800, the ability of white women to be active in doctrinal disputes and matters of church discipline and procedures diminished. In northern Baptist churches, for example, women's public voices were increasingly silenced after the Revolution. As the Baptists matured as a religious denomination, the growth of church bureaucracy and a new emphasis on an educated ministry eroded women's position in favor of men. Establishing respectability for the church often meant controlling what were now viewed as "disorderly" women. This shift in women's influence was accomplished despite the fact that women outnumbered men in the congregation almost two to one, yet another indication that the egalitarian spirit of the postrevolutionary era did not encompass white women.

This suppression of women's voices was not long-lived, however. Beginning around 1795, another series of revivals, loosely categorized as the Second Great Awakening, swept the nation in periodic waves, lasting through the 1830s (see Chapter 3). In the eighteenth century, women's role in evangelical religion paralleled their course in the public sphere, where the ideas formulated around Republican Motherhood articulated a civic role for patriotic women that was only partially realized. Yet both evangelical religion and Republican Motherhood formed an important rationale for women's expanding roles in a wide range of benevolent and reform associations, other areas of informal public space that white women claimed as their own in the nineteenth century.

African American Women's Religious Lives

The religious ferment that so powerfully affected white women also touched the lives of many African American women. Too little is known about early African American women's spiritual world to make many generalizations. But we do know that the Africans herded aboard the slave ships brought with them diverse religions, including Islam. Most West African groups emphasized a belief in a supreme being, as well as a series of lesser divinities, and venerated their ancestors. They had a rich variety of rituals, especially those connected to birth and death. Women played significant roles in religious expression, often serving as healers, mediums, or priestesses.

Only slowly did slaves convert to Christianity. The missionary efforts of the Society for the Propagation of the Gospel founded in 1701 in London, with a major goal to convert enslaved Africans throughout the British American empire, made little headway. Masters resisted efforts to proselytize among their slaves, in part because slavery was rationalized by the immense difference perceived between civilized Christians and "savage pagans." Slaves themselves apparently showed little interest in the religion of their masters. There were notable exceptions, such as Phillis Wheatley, a New England slave who became a noted poet. (See Documents: Phillis Wheatley, Poet and Slave, pp. 119–23, and Figure 2.3, p. 105.)

Yet during and after the Revolution, the Great Awakening had a broad impact on slave women's lives. A few evangelical churches explicitly condemned the institution of slavery, and some slaveholders, moved by the evangelical message, freed their slaves or, at the least, encouraged their slaves to become Christians. Evangelicals within the Methodist and Baptist churches, especially the Separate Baptists in the South, reached out to the poor and uneducated, generally welcoming black converts. Scholars suggest other factors that made the evangelical Protestantism attractive to black Americans. The evangelical emphasis on spontaneous conversion harmonized with West African beliefs that "the deity entered the body of the devotee and displaced his or her personality."[51] Southern slaves synchretized this new form of Protestantism with their traditional religion to create a distinctive religious style. In turn African influences—especially dances and shouts typical of West African religious rituals—influenced the shape of white evangelicalism.

Like white women, black women were highly visible in revivals. A 1741 account told of a "Moorish" woman on a South Carolina plantation "singing a spiritual at the waters edge." This same "heathen woman," according to her sympathetic owner, had a few days earlier "attained a certain assurance of the forgiveness of sins and the mercy of God in Christ, and that she, along with others who love Christ, was shouting and jubilating because of this treasure." Another observer described a black Virginia woman in 1776 who "clapped her hands in an ecstasy of joy."[52] Historians suggest that since many small southern revivals started in the household, slave women's role in bringing others to the conversion experience may have been significant, replicating the white women's role of counselor. "Within this setting, women became the principal creators of an affective style of worship and of revival culture more generally."[53] Although black women were rarely permitted to be preachers in eighteenth-century evangelical churches, they were able to create a sphere of influence and power for themselves, roles that would assume even greater importance in the nineteenth century, when the majority of slaves had adopted Christianity.

CONCLUSION: To the Margins of Political Action

Whatever their social or racial group, women living on the eastern part of the continent in the late eighteenth century were affected by the imperial conflicts that eventually resulted in the founding of a new nation. Most women's activities were filtered through traditional expectations about their female roles: slave women tried to protect their children; Native Americans maintained villages while men were at war; elite ladies sewed shirts for George Washington's army; poor women cooked for soldiers. Yet despite these traditional trajectories, and despite the fundamentally male character of eighteenth-century diplomacy, politics, and warfare, women did exercise some choice in the revolutionary era. They acted politically when they decided to escape slavery by fleeing to the British, when they participated in their native councils' deliberations over alliances, or when they chose to be loyalists or patriots.

The impact on women of the dramatic events of the revolutionary era varied considerably. Slave women in the North benefited from gradual emancipation, while many in the South suffered from their owners' deepening commitment to the institution of slavery. Many Native American women saw their traditional roles erode under the pressures of assimilation, yet most scholars marvel at their resilience and adaptability. White women's positions became more limited in some respects, as white men's political rights expanded while women's remained static.

But if the Revolution did not prompt a deep-seated questioning of women's rights and roles, it did embody harbingers of change, especially for white women. The economic expansion of the new nation would lead to industrial development and an expanded presence of women in the paid workforce. The U.S. territorial expansion would not only promote western migration of white women and their families, but also significantly affect Native Americans and slaves. In addition, revolutionary ideology, educational advancements, and the egalitarianism of the Great Awakening sowed the seeds for greater participation of middle-class and elite women in public life, not in politics per se, but in informal spheres of public spaces—churches, benevolent societies, and reform movements—which were to be such an important part of nineteenth-century American culture.

Portraits of Revolutionary Women

B Y THE MIDDLE OF THE EIGHTEENTH CENTURY, portraiture flourished in America. Its success was in part a product of prosperous colonials' enthusiasm for consumer goods. Imported items—textiles, furniture, china, and books—filled their homes and served as marks of refinement. Paintings also were signs of status and taste. While artists like Charles Willson Peale, John Singleton Copley, and Benjamin West were fine painters, they owed some of their success to their ability to produce images that pleased their subjects' self-images. These men, as well as a large number of lesser painters, turned out portraits that adorned their owners' homes much like fine furnishings. This enthusiasm for portraiture produced a sizeable number of images of women, many of whom were prominent in the revolutionary era.

The 1763 portrait by John Singleton Copley shown in Figure 2.1 makes Mercy Otis Warren's high status quite clear. She is dressed in a rich fabric with elegant trimmings. The picture also emphasizes her femininity. Contemporaries understood the nasturtiums entwined in her hands as symbols of fertility, and indeed she had given birth the year before she sat for this portrait and would have another child the following year.

Warren and her husband James, a politician and prosperous merchant, lived with their five children in Boston. Through her brother James Otis, also a political leader, her husband, and her friends John and Abigail Adams, she had close ties to her colony's revolutionary leadership and was active in politics. In private letters, she ruminated about the propriety of women's participation in politics, writing to one friend in 1774 that she understood that the topic was "a subject . . . much out of the road of female attention." Yet, she continued, "as every domestic enjoyment depends on the decision of the mighty contest, who can be an unconcerned and silent spectator? not surely the fond mother, or the affectionate wife who trembles lest her dearest connections should fall victims of lawless power, or at least pour out the warm blood as a libation at the shrine of liberty."[54]

But Warren went far beyond the role of concerned and informed mother and wife, becoming famous for her pamphlets, poems, and plays, many of which are social satires or political commentaries. In plays such as *The Defeat* (1773) and *The Affrighted Officers* (1776), she castigated the pro-British local officials and loyalists. She also produced widely circulated poems celebrating revolutionary exploits such as the Boston Tea Party and exhorting women to uphold the boycotts against British goods. After the war, she published two major works. With *Poems, Dramatic and Miscellaneous* (1790), she became one of three American women to have published a book of poems, joining Anne Bradstreet and Phillis Wheatley.

◆ Figure 2.1 **John Singleton Copley, *Mercy Otis Warren* (1763)**
John Singleton Copley, American, 1738–1815. Mrs. James Warren (Mercy Otis), about 1763. Oil on canvas. 126.05 × 100 cm (49⅝ × 39½ in.). Museum of Fine Arts, Boston. Bequest of Winslow Warren, 31.212. Photograph © 2004 Museum of Fine Arts, Boston.

Her 1805 *History of the Rise, Progress and Termination of the American Revolution,* a monumental three-volume work, reflected Warren's deep commitment to the cause of the Revolution and her hope for America's future as a repository of republican virtue.

Consider Warren's bearing and pose in this portrait. What sort of personality do they suggest? How does Copley reveal Warren as a woman of many accomplishments?

◆ **Figure 2.2** *Abigail Adams* **(1785, artist unknown)**
Fenimore Art Museum, Cooperstown, New York.

The portrait shown in Figure 2.2 gives us a visual record of one of the most admired of American first ladies, Abigail Adams. Dating from 1785, it was painted in London, where her husband and future president of the United States John Adams was serving in a diplomatic capacity. Abigail Adams's charm and brilliance comes down to us through her extensive correspondence. Her letters from the revolutionary era reveal the able way in which she managed her family's farm in Braintree, Massachusetts, while her husband attended to politics in Boston and Philadelphia. But Adams was more than an impressive "deputy husband." Like other women of her day, she had not been formally schooled, but she had access to an excellent library and acquired a sophisticated education. In her extensive correspondence to John and to friends like Mercy Otis Warren, Adams commented extensively on pressing political questions of the day.

In contrast to Warren, Adams did not write for publication: she made her mark on public life through informal channels. She offered advice freely to her husband John. In 1776, as John participated in the Continental Congress, Abigail urged the assembled men, "Remember the Ladies, and be more generous and favourable to them than your ancestors. Do not put such unlimited power into the

◆ Figure 2.3 *Phillis Wheatley* (1773)
Courtesy of the Massachusetts Historical Society.

hands of the Husbands. Remember all Men would be tyrants if they could. If perticuliar care and attention is not paid to the Ladies we are determined to foment a Rebelion, and will not hold ourselves bound by any Laws in which we have no voice, or Representation."[55] While some historians have used this passage to portray Abigail Adams as a staunch feminist, most agree that the comment was made partly in jest and that she did not envision radical challenges to the prevailing sexual hierarchy and, in particular, was not advocating women's political equality. However, Adams did feel that women should be given more protections in law and strongly advocated for women's improved education so as to meet the prevailing goals of Republican Motherhood.

How does this portrait indicate Adams's status as an elite woman? If the artist were portraying an elite man involved in the politics of the era, how might the portrait be different? Might he be shown writing? Or posed with revolutionary symbols?

Figure 2.3, a portrait of Phillis Wheatley (see Documents: Phillis Wheatley, Poet and Slave, pp. 119–23), was not intended as an ornament for her home or that of her masters. Rather, it was commissioned as the frontispiece for her book,

Poems on Various Subjects, Religious and Moral (1773). Wheatley's owner had sent the poems to London bookseller Archibald Bell, who in turn had taken them to an antislavery noblewoman, the Countess of Huntington, to receive permission for Wheatley to dedicate the book to her, a common practice designed to enhance a book's prestige. Huntington, enthusiastic about the poems, apparently asked for reassurance that the author was *"real,* without a deception." Perhaps to offer proof to future readers that Wheatley was indeed a black slave, the countess requested a picture of Wheatley for the frontispiece. The painting was executed by another slave, Scipio Moorhead, owned by a Boston minister, and sent to England for engraving. Wheatley appreciated Moorhead's talents as an artist and wrote the following poem to "SM. a young *African* painter":

> To show the lab'ring bosom's deep intent,
> and though in living characters to paint,
> When first they pencil did those beauties give,
> And breathing figures learnt from thee to live,
> How did those prospects give my soul delight,
> A new creation rushing on my sight?
> Still, wond'rous youth! each noble path pursue,
> On deathless glories fix thine ardent view:
> Still may the painter's and the poet's fire
> To aid thy pencil, and thy verse conspire![56]

Why do you think Wheatley was so pleased by the portrait? Why do you suppose the painting includes the information that Wheatley was "servant to Mr. John Wheatley"?

Mum Bett, later Elizabeth Freeman, was born a slave, either in New York or Massachusetts, and eventually became the property of Colonel John Ashley of Sheffield, Massachusetts. In 1781, Mum Bett sued her master for her freedom. Her case, *Brom and Bett v. Ashley,* was one of several cases in Massachusetts that in 1783 led to that state's Supreme Court's ruling that slavery was invalid in the state. Historians are not certain what circumstances led Mum Bett to her unusual course of action. One story, possibly apocryphal, indicates that she ran away from Ashley's home after receiving a blow from a heated shovel. A later account by novelist Catherine Sedgwick, the daughter of Freeman's lawyer Theodor Sedgwick, claimed that Freeman made her decision after hearing the Declaration of Independence (see the Appendix, p. A-1). It is also possible that she and her fellow slave, Brom, were chosen by prominent men interested in testing the constitutionality of slavery in Massachusetts. After her freedom, Mum Bett adopted the name Elizabeth Freeman and spent the rest of her life as a beloved paid servant to the Sedgwick family. When she died in 1829, Catherine Sedgwick's brother, Charles, wrote the following epitaph for her tombstone: "She was born a slave and remained a slave for nearly thirty years. She could neither read nor write, yet in her own sphere she had no superior nor equal. She neither wasted time nor property. She never violated a trust, nor failed to perform a duty. In every situation of domestic trial, she was the most efficient helper, and the tenderest friend. Good Mother, farewell."[57]

◆ Figure 2.4 **Susan Anne Livingston Ridley Sedgwick,** *Elizabeth Freeman* **("***Mum Bett***") (1811)**
Courtesy of the Massachusetts Historical Society.

The watercolor portrait in Figure 2.4 was painted in 1811 by Susan Sedgwick. Freeman's dress is vivid blue, and she wears what is apparently a gold necklace around her neck. Why do you suppose the Sedgwick family made the effort (through the portrait and the poem) to document Freeman's life? What is the artist hoping to convey about Freeman in this portrait?

The turning point in Jemima Wilkinson's life came in October 1776 when she fell ill from a fever. When she recovered, she announced that she had died and been resurrected. She renamed herself "Public Universal Friend" and, as the text notes (see p. 97), became a charismatic evangelical preacher who emphasized the golden rule of treating others as one wishes to be treated. Her followers had numerous congregations in Rhode Island and Connecticut; in 1785 they established a Friend's community in the frontier region of New York, where Wilkinson hoped they might be free from the worldly evils.

The portrait of Wilkinson at the age of sixty-three in Figure 2.5 was painted in 1816 by John L. D. Mathies, a self-taught artist living in the Guyanoga valley of New York where Wilkinson lived at the end of her life. It gives us a glimpse of the

◆ Figure 2.5 **John L. D. Mathies, *Jemima Wilkinson* (1816)**
Village of Penn Yan, New York, and the Yates County Genealogical and Historical Society, Inc.

self-styled prophetess. Wilkinson's insistence on obliterating her sex went beyond her refusal to answer to her name and her insistence that her followers avoid the feminine pronouns of "she" and "her" when referring to their leader. Her clothing style was more similar to men's of the times than women's. After hearing her preach in New Haven, Connecticut, one critical observer described her in 1787 as wearing "a light cloth Cloke with a Cape like a Man's—Purple Gown, long' sleeves to Wristbands—Mans shirt down to the Hands with neckband—purple hand-kerchief or Neckcloth tied around the neck like a man's—No Cap—Hair combed turned over & not long—wears a Watch—Man's Hat."[58]

Has Mathies attempted to present Wilkinson as sexless in this portrait? Al-though Wilkinson's style of dress may have stemmed from her religious belief that she had died and been resurrected and thereby transcended her sex, why else might she have preferred male attire?

QUESTIONS FOR ANALYSIS

1. How do the portraits presented here differ from one another? What factors might account for those differences?

2. How realistic are the portrayals of the women in these portraits? Are portray-als by professional artists more or less accurate, do you think, than the por-trayals by amateur artists?

3. What roles do dress, props, and background play in defining the characteris-tics of the sitter?

VISUAL SOURCES

Gendering Images of the Revolution

I N ADDITION TO THE REPRESENTATIONS OF American women contained in the portraits of the late eighteenth century are a variety of other images specifically connected to the American Revolution. Many of these—whether paintings or cartoons—had propagandistic purposes. Few portray actual women and instead render females as abstractions, often as icons of "liberty."

Englishmen on both sides of the Atlantic often ridiculed women's interest in fashion and represented them as weak-minded and frivolous. These negative

◆ Figure 2.6 **"A Society of Patriotic Ladies" (1774)**
Library of Congress LC-USZ62-12711.

stereotypes about women took on propagandistic value in Figure 2.6, a British cartoon, "A Society of Patriotic Ladies," created as a response to the fifty-one women of Edenton, North Carolina, who signed a pledge in 1774 to uphold the boycotts against British goods. By depicting fashionable women neglecting their children (note the child on the floor being licked by a dog) and acting in unfeminine ways (note the grotesque woman with the gavel), the cartoon devalues the boycott and American women at the same time.

Consider the choices of the cartoonist. Why do you think he decided to include a black servant in his drawing? Why did he depict the woman in the center being fondled by a man?

A powerful piece of propaganda on the patriot side was this engraving (Figure 2.7) by Paul Revere of the 1770 Boston Massacre, an episode in which British troops, quartered in the city to enforce the unpopular customs laws, fired on a mob of unruly citizens, killing five. It was a riot more than a massacre, but

◆ Figure 2.7 **Paul Revere, *The Boston Massacre* (1770)**
Library of Congress LC-USZ62-35522.

◆ Figure 2.8 *Miss Fanny's Maid* (1770)
Courtesy, American Antiquarian Society.

Revere's rendering of the event helped to galvanize support for the patriot cause. There are a number of inaccuracies in the engraving, the most important of which is Revere's depiction of Crispus Attucks, one of the dead men, as white instead of black. The female figure, garbed in widow's black, does not appear to portray an actual person, but rather to represent, in abstract form, the female victim of the British soldiers. The engraving fails to reveal that working-class women were often active participants in demonstrations that erupted to protest the British taxes and the presence of troops. In addition to sharing their menfolk's resentment of the British, some women may have had gender-specific grievances against the soldiers. At one point, when four thousand troops were quartered in the city, twenty-one allegations of rape and assault were lodged against the soldiers, charges that may have helped to politicize women during the pre-revolutionary period. What is the significance of Revere's decision to depict the lone woman as a passive bystander of the riot/massacre?

A number of images of women holding muskets circulated during the revolutionary era. Scholars think that the 1770 drawing in Figure 2.8 was modeled after a 1750 woodcut of Hannah Snell, an English woman who had joined the British navy in 1745. Though *Miss Fanny's Maid* predates the outbreak of fighting, it coincides with the disruptive atmosphere of Boston in the 1770s. The American illustration was probably not intended to refer to a specific woman bearing arms; the story of cross-dressing Deborah Sampson (see pp. 80–81) was not made public until 1781, for example. What do you think might have been the purpose of this image for revolutionary propagandists?

The tendency to depict women as abstractions was most evident in the widespread popularity of images of "Liberty." The convention of using a stylized woman to represent political virtues such as liberty or justice was a long-standing one in western European art, though, as one historian explains, "the female form [of liberty] does not refer to particular women, does not describe

◆ Figure 2.9 **"Banner of Washington's Life Guard" (date unknown)**
Special Collections, John D. Rockefeller Jr. Library, Colonial Williamsburg Foundation.

women as a group, and often does not even presume to evoke their natures."[59] Instead, this idealized image was intended to embody the principles for which men were fighting.

Figure 2.9, a "Banner of Washington's Life Guard," was used to represent a group of military men attached to General Washington. How do we know that this image is not of a real woman but is rather a symbol? What other symbols of the Revolution can you identify?

A more complex rendering of a female version of liberty appeared in the well-known painter Edward Savage's engraving, "Liberty in the Form of the Goddess of Youth Giving Support to the Bald Eagle," created in 1796. In Figure 2.10, the youthful Liberty, clad in white with a garland of flowers, nourishes an eagle, who symbolizes the Republic. In the background is the flag of the union with a liberty cap. At the bottom right, lightning rains down on the British fleet in the Boston harbor. Crushed under Liberty's feet are symbols of the British monarchy: a key, a broken scepter, and the garter of a royal order. This version of Liberty was so popular that it was reproduced in many forms—including needlework—well into the nineteenth century. Why do you think Savage depicts Liberty as a "goddess of youth"? Why was the image so popular with Americans?

This type of image also appeared in commercial usage, as indicated in Figure 2.11, the signpost for a tavern in Bissell's Ferry, East Windsor, Connecticut. The sign was made originally in 1777 and then repainted in 1781 and 1801. Why would

◆ Figure 2.10 **Edward Savage, "Liberty in the Form of the Goddess of Youth Giving Support to the Bald Eagle" (1796)**
Worcester Art Museum, Worcester, Massachusetts, gift of Mrs. Kingsmill Marrs.

◆ Figure 2.11 **Signpost for a Tavern (1777)**
Wadsworth Atheneum, Hartford. Bequest of Emma Bell King.

◆ Figure 2.12 **Frontispiece from** *Lady's Magazine* **(1792)**
The Library Company of Philadelphia.

◆ Figure 2.13 **Samuel Jennings, *Liberty Displaying the Arts and Sciences* (1792)**
The Library Company of Philadelphia.

a tavern choose to feature a female icon of liberty? When the sign became worn, why do you think the tavern owners decided to repaint the original rather than create a new sign?

Two somewhat unusual depictions of a female Liberty had more radical political meaning than most versions. Figures 2.12 and 2.13 suggest the way in which revolutionary ideology ignited questions about women's and slaves' freedom. In

Figure 2.12, the frontispiece from *Lady's Magazine* (1792), "The Genius of the Ladies Magazine, accompanied by the Genius of Emulation, who carries in her hand a laurel crown, approaches Liberty, and kneeling, presents her with a copy of the Rights of Woman." This issue contained segments of Mary Wollstonescraft's *Vindication of the Rights of Woman*. Wollstonecraft's work did not originate interest in the question of women's rights in America but rather coincided with a flurry of interest in the question in the postrevolutionary years.

Why does this illustration feature a woman representing "the Ladies Magazine"? In this image, Liberty is given a statement on the rights of women. Why has the artist chosen to depict the exchange as a gift to Liberty, instead of depicting Liberty as bestowing the rights of women?

Figure 2.13, *Liberty Displaying the Arts and Sciences* by Samuel Jennings (1792), was initially suggested by the artist himself to the Library Company of Philadelphia, an institution founded by Benjamin Franklin and others in 1731. The directors specifically asked Jennings to portray a tableau of "Liberty (with her Cap and proper Insignia) displaying the arts by some of the most striking Symbols of Painting, Architecture, Mechanics, Astronomy, &ca. whilst She appears in the attitude of placing on the top of a Pedestal, a pile of Books, lettered with, *Agriculture, Commerce, Philosophy & Catalogue* of *Philadelphia Library*."[60] The directors, many of whom were active antislavery advocates, also requested the inclusion of African Americans and the symbolic broken chains. In the image, Liberty is offering a book to the grateful African Americans.

Examine the images associated with Liberty. What do they suggest? What did the library directors hope to convey in combining a depiction of Liberty, books, and freed slaves?

QUESTIONS FOR ANALYSIS

1. How do these diverse images of women contribute to our understanding of how gender shaped the experience of the American Revolution?

2. The images presented here have propagandistic purposes. If images of men had been used instead, how would they be different?

3. How can historians analyze these propagandistic images in the effort to reconstruct the actual experiences of women in the revolutionary era?

DOCUMENTS

Phillis Wheatley, Poet and Slave

EIGHTEENTH-CENTURY AMERICAN WOMEN left behind far more written material than those in the seventeenth century; we have diaries, letters, essays, and books to help us flesh out the lives of many women, especially educated white women. The experiences of individual black women are far more obscure in the historical record, with the important exception of poet Phillis Wheatley (c. 1753–1784). At age seven or eight, Wheatley, who was probably from the Gambia area of the West Coast of Africa, was brought to Boston as a slave. Her owners, John and Susannah Wheatley, were immediately impressed with her precociousness. "Without any Assistance from School Education, and by only what she was taught in the Family, she, in sixteen Months Times from her Arrival, attained the English Language, to which she was an utter Stranger before, to such a Degree, as to read any, the most difficult Parts of the Sacred Writings, to be the great Astonishment of all who heard her."[61] The Wheatleys, especially Susannah and her daughter Mary, took pride in their slave's learning but also in her quick and deeply felt conversion to Protestantism. Their own evangelical beliefs made them open to the notion of blacks' spiritual equality and led them to encourage Wheatley's religious and intellectual gifts.

Wheatley began writing poetry as early as 1765 and apparently published her first poem in 1767. By 1772, she had attempted, with the help of Susannah Wheatley and other sponsors, to publish a book of collected works in Boston. When that venture failed, she found a publisher in London and had the opportunity to accompany the son of her owner to London where she was able to complete the arrangements for *Poems on Various Subjects, Religious and Moral* (1773). At about the same time, her owners granted her freedom.

After the publication of her book, Wheatley continued to write, undeterred by her sadness at the deaths of her former owners, Susannah Wheatley in 1774, and John Wheatley in 1778, or by her own marriage in 1778 to a free black, John Peters. Her poems, such as one in honor of General George Washington, were published individually, but she failed to gain backing for her proposal, printed in the *Evening Post* and *General Advertiser* (1779), in which she described herself as a "female African" who sought subscriptions to print a second book of poems and letters to be dedicated to Benjamin Franklin. Other disappointments followed. Toward the end of her life she worked as a scrubwoman in a boarding house. Two of her children died, and she and her third baby died of complications in childbirth on December 8, 1784.

Because of the profoundly religious content of much of her work, Wheatley's poetry was warmly received by evangelical Protestants, both in England and in America. Apparently some slaveowners read Wheatley's poems to their slaves to encourage their conversion. Opponents of slavery also welcomed the poet's work, viewing her as proof of the humanity and capabilities of Africans.

LETTERS

TWENTY-TWO OF WHEATLEY'S LETTERS have survived. The first one, printed below, is to a black friend, Arbour Tanner, a servant to James Tanner in Newport, Rhode Island, who shared Wheatley's religious ardor. The letter refers to a frequent theme in the poet's work: the conversion of her fellow Africans. What is the purpose of Wheatley's letter to Tanner?

To Arbour Tanner

Boston May 19th 1772

Dear Sister

I rec'd your favour of February 6th for which I give you my sincere thanks, I greatly rejoice with you in that realizing view, and I hope experience, of the Saving change which you So emphatically describe. Happy were it for us if we could arrive to that evangelical Repentance, and the true holiness of heart which you mention. Inexpressibly happy Should we be could we have a due Sense of the Beauties and excellence of the Crucified Saviour. In his Crucifixion may be seen marvellous displays of Grace and Love, Sufficient to draw and invite us to the rich and endless treasures of his mercy, let us rejoice in and adore the wonders of God's infinite Love in bringing us from a land Semblant of darkness itself, and where the divine light of revelation (being obscur'd) is as darkness. Here, the knowledge of the true God and eternal life are made manifest; But there, profound ignorance overshadows the Land, Your observation is true, namely that there was nothing in us to recommend us to God. Many of our fellow creatures are pass'd by, when the bowels of divine love expanded towards us. May this goodness & long Suffering of God lead us to unfeign'd repentance

It gives me very great pleasure to hear of so many of my Nation, Seeking with eagerness the way to true felicity, O may we all meet at length in that happy mansion. I hope the correspondence between us will continue, (my being much indispos'd this winter past was the reason of my not answering yours before now) which correspondence I hope may have the happy effect of improving our mutual friendship. Till we meet in the regions of consummate blessedness, let us endeavor by the assistance of divine grace, to live the life, and we Shall die the death of the Righteous. May this be our happy case and of those who are travelling to the region of Felicity is the earnest request of your affectionate

Friend & hum. Sert. Phillis Wheatley

SOURCE: Julian D. Mason Jr., ed., *The Poems of Phillis Wheatley* (Chapel Hill: University of North Carolina, 1989), 190.

THE FOLLOWING LETTER, to Rev. Samson Occom, a Mohegan Indian and Presbyterian minister, was published in the *Connecticut Gazette; and the Universal Intelligencer,* March 11, 1774, and widely reprinted. Written after Wheatley had gained freedom, it is her most critical statement about slavery. What is the essence of her criticism?

To Rev. Samson Occom

Rev'd and honor'd Sir,

I have this Day received your obliging kind Epistle, and am greatly satisfied with your Reasons respecting the Negroes, and think highly reasonable what you offer in Vindication of their natural Rights: Those that invade them cannot be insensible that the divine Light is chasing away the thick Darkness which broods over the Land of Africa; and the Chaos which has reign'd long, is converting into beautiful Order, and [r]eveals more and more clearly the glorious Dispensation of civil and religious Liberty, which are so insep[a]rably united, that there is little or no Enjoyment of one without the other. Otherwise, perhaps, the Israelites had been less solicitous for their Freedom from Egyptian slavery; I do not say they would have been contented without it, by no means, for in every human Breast, God has implanted a Principle which we call Love of Freedom; it is impatient of Oppression and pants for Deliverance; and by the Leave of our modern Egyptians I will assert, that the same Principle lives in us. God grant Deliverance in his own Way and Time and get him honour upon all those whose Avarice impels them to countenance and help forward the Calamities of their fellow Creatures. This desire not for their Hurt, but to convince them of the strange Absurdity of their Conduct whose Words and Actions are so diametrically opposite. How well the Cry for Liberty, and the reverse Disposition for the exercise of oppressive Power over others agree,—I humbly think it does not require the Penetration of a Philosopher to determine.

SOURCE: Mason, *Poems of Phillis Wheatley,* 203–4.

POEMS

OVER FIFTY OF WHEATLEY'S POEMS have survived. They encompass a wide range of topics, from elegies to thoughts "On Virtue," from religious commentaries to a patriotic ode to George Washington. Her references to Africa, Africans, and slavery are particularly interesting for the ways in which her poetry insists on the humanity of Africans and makes criticisms—sometimes veiled—of slavery.

On the surface, this 1772 poem seems to adopt white Christians' condescension toward pagan Africans, but what does the final line suggest?

On Being Brought from Africa to America

'Twas mercy brought me from my *Pagan* land,
Taught my benighted soul to understand
That there's a God, that there's a *Saviour* too:

SOURCE: Mason, *Poems of Phillis Wheatley*, 53.

Once I redemption neither sought nor knew.
Some view our sable race with scornful eye,
"Their colour is a diabolic die."
Remember, *Christians*, Negroes, black as Cain,
May be refin'd, and join th' angelic train.

THE FOLLOWING POEM, addressed to the British secretary of state for North America, was written in a period when tensions had eased—temporarily—between the colonies and the mother country, hence Wheatley's statement in the second stanza about grievances being addressed. The poem reveals not only her sensitivity to the political turmoil of the period but also her understanding of the parallels between the colonists' desire to resist British "enslavement" and her own people's experience of slavery. What does she seem to be asking Lord Dartmouth for in the final stanza?

To the Right Honourable William, Earl of Dartmouth, His Majesty's Principal Secretary of State for North America, &c.

HAIL, happy day when, smiling like the morn,
Fair *Freedom* rose *New-England* to adorn:
The northern clime beneath her genial ray,
Dartmouth, congratulates thy blissful sway:
Elate with hope her race no longer mourns,
Each soul expands, each grateful bosom burns,
While in thine hand with pleasure we behold
The silken reins, and *Freedom's* charms unfold.
Long lost to realms beneath the northern skies

She shines supreme, while hated *faction* dies:
Soon as appear'd the *Goddess* long desir'd,
Sick at the view, she lanquish'd and expir'd;
Thus from the splendors of the morning light
The owl in sadness seeks the caves of night.

No more, *America,* in mournful strain
Of wrongs, and grievance unredress'd complain,

SOURCE: Mason, *Poems of Phillis Wheatley*, 82–83.

No longer shalt thou dread the iron chain,
Which wanton *Tyranny* with lawless hand
Had made, and with it meant t' enslave the land.

Should you, my lord, while you peruse my song,
Wonder from whence my love of Freedom
    sprung,
Whence flow these wishes for the common good,
By feeling hearts alone best understood,
I, young in life, by seeming cruel fate
Was snatch'd from *Afric's* fancy'd happy seat:
What pangs excruciating must molest,
What sorrows labour in my parent's breast?
Steel'd was that soul and by no misery mov'd
That from a father seiz'd his babe belov'd:
Such, such my case. And can I then but pray
Others may never feel tyrannic sway?

For favours past, great Sir, our thanks are due,
And thee we ask thy favours to renew,

Since in thy pow'r, as in thy will before,
To sooth the griefs, which thou did'st once
    deplore.
May heav'nly grace the sacred sanction give
To all thy works, and thou for ever live
Not only on the wings of fleeting *Fame,*

Though praise immortal crowns the patriot's
    name,
But to conduct to heav'ns refulgent fane,
May fiery coursers sweep th' ethereal plain,
And bear thee upwards to that blest abode,
Where, like the prophet, thou shalt find thy God.

QUESTIONS FOR ANALYSIS

1. What do these selections of Wheatley's poems and letters reveal about the importance and role of religion in her life?

2. What are the grounds for her criticism of slavery?

3. How might opponents of slavery have used her poetry to criticize the institution?

D O C U M E N T S

Education and Republican Motherhood

F OR MUCH OF THE COLONIAL PERIOD, women's opportunities for education were quite limited. A small number of slave women were instructed by benevolent owners, and some Native American women had access to missionary schools where the emphasis was on assimilation rather than education. White women had little formal schooling, and their training usually emphasized domestic skills with a smattering of reading and sums. By the time of the Revolution in New England, 90 percent of white men could write, while fewer than half of white women could.

The Revolution and its aftermath ushered in significant changes. Outside the South, where public schools were rare, primary public education for white women and men became more common. Women's opportunities for higher education—while not universally endorsed—also expanded. While some of the most famous schools, like Philadelphia's Young Ladies Academy, were in urban areas, educational entrepreneurs also established them in small towns such as Litchfield, Connecticut, where Sarah Pierce's school attracted young women from throughout the region, as well as from other states. The Bethlehem, Pennsylvania, Moravian Seminary had special appeal for parents eager to give their daughters a rigorous education; in addition to academic subjects, the school encouraged its students' industry and moral development. While the new schools still offered ornamental skills such as needlework and dancing, they emphasized academic subjects such as history, grammar, geography, logic, and philosophy.

The post-Revolution improvement in white women's education was in part a product of the efforts of reformers, who eagerly promoted the idea that in a republic, all citizens needed education to contribute to the general public good. In keeping with the ideas associated with Republican Motherhood (see pp. 95–96), supporters of women's education argued that mothers needed to be well educated to prepare their children, especially their sons, for their duties as citizens. Advocates also emphasized the importance of women's influence on their husbands. While a number of people participated in the call for expanded opportunities, including Mercy Otis Warren and Sarah Pierce, two of the most significant, whose writings are reproduced here, were Dr. Benjamin Rush and Judith Sargent Murray.

"A PECULIAR MODE OF EDUCATION"

B ENJAMIN RUSH SIGNED the Declaration of Independence and was the preeminent physician and medical teacher of the revolutionary era. His essay, *Thoughts upon Female Education*, reflects both increased expectations as well as the limits to new ideas about women's education. The curriculum he promoted included geography, bookkeeping, reading, and arithmetic and omitted the traditional female accomplishment of needlework. But he did not recommend that women study advanced mathematics, natural philosophy, or Latin or Greek, subjects that remained hallmarks of educated men. Rush and most other reformers emphasized the utilitarian potential of an academic curriculum for women. Although Rush lectured to both men at the College of Philadelphia and women at the Philadelphia Young Ladies Academy on natural philosophy, his presentation for the latter — "Lectures, Containing the Application of the Principles of Natural Philosophy, and Chemistry to Domestic and Culinary Purposes" —was tailored to their perceived future roles. Still, Rush's views were progressive for his time, when many people felt that too much learning might "unsex" a woman and make her unfeminine.

The following selection is from an essay based on a speech Rush gave to the Board of Visitors of the Young Ladies Academy of Philadelphia in 1787. As you read, take note of Rush's major justifications for educating women.

BENJAMIN RUSH
Thoughts upon Female Education (1787)

There are several circumstances in the situation, employments and duties of women in America which require a peculiar mode of education.

I. The early marriages of our women, by contracting the time allowed for education, renders it necessary to contract its plan and to confine it chiefly to the more useful branches of literature.

II. The state of property in America renders it necessary for the greatest part of our citizens to employ themselves in different occupations for the advancement of their fortunes. This cannot be done without the assistance of the female members of the community. They must be the stewards and guardians of their husbands' property. That education, therefore, will be most proper for our women which teaches them to discharge the duties of those offices with the most success and reputation.

III. From the numerous avocations to which a professional life exposes gentlemen in America from their families, a principal share of the instruction of children naturally devolves upon the women. It becomes us therefore to prepare them, by a suitable education, for the discharge of this most important duty of mothers.

IV. The equal share that every citizen has in the liberty and the possible share he may have in the government of our country make it necessary that our ladies should be qualified to a certain degree, by a peculiar and suitable education, to concur in instructing their sons in the principles of liberty and government.

V. In Great Britain the business of servants is a regular occupation, but in America this humble station is the usual retreat of unexpected indigence; hence the servants in this country possess less knowledge and subordination than are required from them; and hence our ladies are

SOURCE: Frederick Rudolph, ed., *Essays on Education in the Early Republic* (Cambridge: Belknap Press of Harvard University Press, 1965), 27–40.

obliged to attend more to the private affairs of their families than ladies generally do of the same rank in Great Britain. "They are good servants," said an American lady of distinguished merit . . . in a letter to a favorite daughter, "who will do well with good looking after." This circumstance should have great influence upon the nature and extent of female education in America.

[Rush proceeds to discuss the most important "branches of literature most essential for a young lady in this country," in which he emphasizes "a knowledge of the English language," "the writing of a fair and legible hand," "some knowledge of figures and bookkeeping," so that she "may assist her husband with this knowledge," "an acquaintance with geography and some instruction in chronology [history]," vocal music and dancing, "the reading of history, travels, poetry, and moral essays," and the "regular instruction in the Christian religion."]

A philosopher once said, "let me make all the ballads of a country and I care not who makes its laws." He might with more propriety have said, let the ladies of a country be educated properly, and they will not only make and administer its laws, but form its manners and character. It would require a lively imagination to describe, or even to comprehend the happiness of a country where knowledge and virtue were generally diffused among the female sex. . . .

The influence of female education would be still more extensive and useful in domestic life. The obligations of gentlemen to qualify themselves by knowledge and industry to discharge the duties of benevolence would be increased by marriage; and the patriot—the hero—and the legislator would find the sweetest reward of their toils in the approbation and applause of their wives. Children would discover the marks of maternal prudence and wisdom in every station of life, for it has been remarked that there have been few great or good men who have not been blessed with wife and prudent mothers.

"ALL THAT INDEPENDENCE WHICH IS PROPER TO HUMANITY"

ALTHOUGH JUDITH SARGENT MURRAY (1751–1820), the daughter of a distinguished and wealthy Gloucester, Massachusetts, family, also believed in the tenets of Republican Motherhood, she was far more radical than Rush in her approach to women's capabilities and needs. Murray's parents denied her the opportunity for the extensive education that they provided for her brother, but she was a voracious reader of both American and European writers. A contemporary of the Englishwomen historian Catharine Macaulay and women's rights activist Mary Wollstonecraft, Murray was an early American proponent of women's rights and an accomplished writer. Intensely religious, she had left the Puritan fold for Universalism, a far more egalitarian faith that encouraged her to challenge traditional authority. Already influenced by her religion, as well as her frustration over her limited schooling, Murray was further energized by the ideas swirling around the American Revolution that led her to articulate her belief in men's and women's mental and spiritual equality. As she contemplated the themes of liberty, equality, and independence, she struggled with her own dependence.

After she was widowed in 1787, her second marriage in 1788, like her first, provided little financial security, and she was highly conscious of the legal and financial constraints on women. It is not surprising, then, that many of her essays call for an education that would help women to be self-reliant and even self-supporting. She pointed out that she would want her daughters to be taught "industry and order." They "should be enabled to procure for themselves the necessaries of life; independence should be placed within their grasp."[62] Unlike reformers such as Rush who saw women's education primarily as a tool for promoting the family and the public good, Murray understood it as something contributing to women's independence, to a reverence of self. But she shared with more conventional reformers the assumption that most women would marry and have children and that women's improved education would make them better wives and virtuous Republican Mothers.

The essay excerpted here contains Murray's most radical statements concerning women's capabilities. It is the final installment of a four-part series, "Observations on Female Abilities," and highlights the accomplishments of two women. Why do you think Murray chose those women? How do you account for the seeming shift in tone and argument in the last two paragraphs?

Judith Sargent Murray
Observations of Female Abilities (1798)

We take leave to repeat, that we are not desirous to array THE SEX in martial habiliments°; we do not wish to enlist our women as soldiers; and we request it may be remembered, that we only contend for the *capabilities* of the female mind to become possessed of any attainment within the reach of *masculine exertion*. We have produced our witnesses; their depositions have been heard: the cause is before the public; we await their verdict; and, as we entertain all possible veneration for the respectable jury, we shall not dare to appeal from their decision.

But while we do homage to the women of other times, we feel happy that nature is no less bountiful to the females of the present day. We

°Characteristic garments or furnishings.

SOURCE: Sheila L. Skemp, ed., *Judith Sargent Murray: A Brief Biography with Documents* (Boston: Bedford, 1998), 145–49.

cannot, indeed, obtain a list of the names that have done honour to their Sex, and to humanity during the period now under observation: The lustre of those minds, still enveloped in a veil of mortality, is necessarily muffled and obscure: but the curtain will be thrown back, and posterity will contemplate, with admiration, their manifold perfections. . . . Nor is America destitute of females, whose abilities and improvements give them an indisputable claim to immortality. It is a fact, established beyond all controversy, that we are indebted for the discovery of our country, to female enterprize, decision and generosity. The great Columbus, after having in vain solicited the aid of Genoa, France, England, Portugal, and Spain—after having combated, for a period of eight years, with every objection that a want of knowledge could propose, found, at last, his only resource in the penetration and magnanimity of Isabella of Spain, who furnished the equipment, and raised the sums necessary to defray the expenses on the sale of her own jewels; and while we conceive an action, so honourable to THE SEX, hath not been sufficiently applauded, we trust, that the equality of the female intellect to that of their brethren, who have so long usurped an unmanly and unfounded superiority, will never, in this younger world, be left without a witness. We cannot ascertain the number of ingenious women, who at present adorn our country. In the shade of solitude they perhaps cultivate their own minds, and superintend the education of their children. Our day, we know, is only dawning—But when we contemplate a Warren [Mercy Otis Warren—see Figure 2.1, p. 103], a Philenia [Sarah Wentworth Morton, poet and novelist], &c. &c. we gratefully acknowledge, that genius and application, even in the female line, already gild, with effulgent radiance, our blest Aurora.

But women are calculated to shine in other characters than those adverted to, in the preceding Essays; and with proper attention to their education and subsequent habits, they might easily attain that independence, for which a [Mary] Wollstonecraft hath so energetically contended; the term, *helpless widow,* might be rendered as unfrequent and inapplicable as that of *helpless widower;* and although we should undoubtedly continue to mourn the dissolution of wedded amity, yet we should derive consolation from the knowledge, that the infant train had still a remaining prop, and that a mother could assist as well as weep over her offspring.

That women have a talent—a talent which, duly cultivated, would confer that independence, which is demonstrably of incalculable utility, every attentive observer will confess. THE SEX should be taught to depend on their own efforts, for the procurement of an establishment in life. The chance of a matrimonial coadjutor, is no more than a probable contingency; and if they were early accustomed to regard this *uncertain* event with suitable *indifference* they would make elections with that deliberation, which would be calculated to give a more rational prospect of

tranquility. All this we have repeatedly asserted, and all this we do invariably believe. To neglect polishing a gem, or obstinately to refuse bringing into action a treasure in our possession, when we might thus accumulate a handsome interest, is surely egregiously absurd, and the height of folly. *The united efforts of male and female* might rescue many a family from destruction, which, notwithstanding the efforts of its *individual* head, is now involved in all the calamities attendant on a dissipated fortune and augmenting debts. It is not possible to educate children in a manner which will render them *too beneficial* to society; and the more we multiply aids to a family, the greater will be the security, that its individuals will not be thrown a burden on the public.

An instance of *female capability* this moment occurs to memory. In the State of Massachusetts, in a small town, some miles from the metropolis, resides a woman, who hath made astonishing improvements in agriculture. Her mind, in the early part of her life, was but penuriously cultivated, and she grew up almost wholly uneducated: But being suffered, during her childhood, to rove at large among her native fields, her limbs expanded, and she acquired a height of stature above the common size; her mind also became invigorated; and her understanding snatched sufficient information to produce a consciousness of the injury she sustained in the want of those aids, which should have been furnished in the beginning of her years. She however applied herself diligently to remedy the evil, and soon made great proficiency in writing, and in arithmetic. She reads every thing she could procure; but the impressions adventitiously made on her infant mind still obtained the ascendancy. A few rough acres constituted her patrimonial inheritance; these she has brought into a state of high cultivation; their productions are every year both useful and ornamental; she is mistress of agricolation, and is at once a botanist and a florist. The most approved authors in the English language, on these subjects, are in her hands, and she studies them with industry and success.

She has obtained such considerable knowledge in the nature of soils, the precise manure which they require and their particular adaptation to the various fruits of the earth, that she is become the oracle of all the farmers in her vicinity and when laying out, or appropriating their grounds they uniformly submit them to her inspection. Her gardens are the resort of all strangers who happen to visit her village; and she is particularly remarkable for a growth of trees, from which, gentlemen, solicitous to enrich their fruitgardens, or ornament their parterres, are in the habit of supplying themselves; and those trees are, to their ingenious cultivator, a considerable income. Carefully attentive to her nursery, she knows when to transplant and when to prune; and she perfectly understands the various methods of inoculating and ingrafting. In short, she is a complete *husbandwoman,* and she has, besides, acquired a vast stock of general knowledge while her judgment has attained such a degree of maturity, as to justify the confidence of the villagers, who are accustomed to consult her on every perplexing emergency.

In the constant use of exercise, she is not corpulent, and she is extremely active, and wonderfully athletic. Instances almost incredible, are produced of her strength. Indeed, it is not surprising that she is the idol and standing theme of the village, since, with all her uncommon qualifications, she combines a tenderness of disposition not to be exceeded. Her extensive acquaintance with herbs, contributes to render her a skilful and truly valuable nurse; and the world never produced a more affectionate attentive or faithful woman: Yet, while she feelingly sympathizes with every invalid, she is not herself subject to imaginary complaints; nor does she easily yield to real illness. . . .

Although far advanced in years, without a matrimonial connexion, yet, constantly engaged in useful and interesting pursuits, she manifests not that peevishness and discontent, so frequently attendant on *old maids;* she realizes all that independence which is proper to humanity; and she knows how to set a just value on the blessings she enjoys.

From my treasury of facts, I produce a second instance, equally in point. I have seen letters, written by a lady, an inhabitant of St. Sebastian (a Spanish emporium), that breathed the true spirit of commerce, and evinced the writer to possess all the integrity, punctuality and dispatch, which are such capital requisites in the mercantile career. This lady is at the head of a firm, of which herself and daughters make up the individuals—Her name is *Birmingham.* She is, I imagine, well known to the commercial part of the United States. She was left a widow in the infancy of her children, who were numerous: and she immediately adopted the most vigorous measures for their emolument. Being a woman of a magnanimous mind, she devoted her sons to the profession of arms; and they were expeditiously disposed of, in a way the best calculated to bring them acquainted with the art of war. Her daughters were educated for business; and, arriving at womanhood, they have long since established themselves into a capital trading-house, of which, as has been observed, their respectable mother is the head. She is, in the hours of business, invariably to be found in her counting-house; there she takes her morning repast; her daughters act as clerks (and they are adepts in their office), regularly preparing the papers and letters, which pass in order under her inspection. She signs herself, in all accounts and letters, *Widow Birmingham;* and this is the address by which she is designated. I have conversed with one of our captains, who has often negociated with her the disposal of large and valuable cargoes. Her consignments, I am told, are to a great amount; and one of the principal merchants in the town of Boston asserts, that he receives from no house in Europe more satisfactory returns. Upright in their dealings, and unwearied in their application, these ladies possess a right to prosperity; and we trust that their circumstances are as easy, as their conduct is meritorious.

"Would you, good Mr. Gleaner, station us in the counting-house?" No, my fair countrywomen, except circumstances unavoidably pointed the way. Again I say, I do but hold up to your view, the *capability* of your Sex; thus stimulating you to cultivate your talents, to endeavour to acquire general knowledge, and to aim at making yourselves so far acquainted with some particular branch of business, as that it may, if occasion requires, assist in establishing you above that kind of dependence, against which the freeborn mind so naturally revolts. Far be it from me, to wish to unsex you—I am desirous of preserving, by all means, those amiable traits that are considered as characteristic—I reverence the modesty and gentleness of your dispositions—I would not annihilate a single virtue; but I would assiduously augment the faithfulness and affection of your bosoms. An elegant panegyrist of your Sex, hath assigned you the superiority in the feelings of the heart; and I cannot more emphatically conclude my subject, than in his beautifully pathetic language:

"The pleasures of women must arise from their virtues. It is by the cradle of their children, and in viewing the smiles of their daughters, or the sports of their sons, that mothers find their happiness. Where are the powerful emotions of nature? Where is the sentiment, at once sublime and pathetic, that carries every feeling to excess? Is it to be found in the frosty indifference, and the sour severity of some fathers? No—but in the warm and affectionate bosom of a *mother*. It is she, who, by an impulse as quick as involuntary, rushes into the flood to preserve a boy, whose imprudence had betrayed him into the waves—It is she, who, in the middle of a conflagration, throws herself across the flames to save a sleeping infant—It is she, who, with dishevelled locks, pale and distracted, embraces with transport, the body of a dead child, pressing its cold lips to her's, as if she would reanimate, by her tears and her caresses, the insensible clay. These great expressions of nature—these heart-rending emotions, which fill us at once with wonder, compassion and terror, always have belonged, and always will belong, only to Women. They possess, in those moments, an inexpressible something, which carries them beyond themselves; and they seem to discover to us new souls, above the standard of humanity."

QUESTIONS FOR ANALYSIS

1. What do Rush and Murray see as the benefits of female education? How does the proper education of females differ from that of males?

2. What do Rush and Murray assume about the abilities of females?

3. How do Rush's and Murray's ideas accord with the ideas associated with Republican Motherhood?

NOTES

1. Mary Beth Norton and Ruth M. Alexander, eds., *Major Problems in American Women's History,* 2nd ed. (Lexington, MA: D.C. Heath, 1996), 81.

2. Mary Beth Norton, *Liberty's Daughters: The Revolutionary Experience of American Women, 1750–1800* (Boston: Little, Brown, 1980), 166.

3. Norton, *Liberty's Daughters,* 167.

4. Cynthia Kierner, *Beyond the Household: Women's Place in the Early South, 1700–1835* (Ithaca, NY: Cornell University Press, 1998), 75.

5. Norton, *Liberty's Daughters,* 164.

6. Ibid., 168.

7. Ibid., 159.

8. Kierner, *Beyond the Household,* 80–81.

9. Norton, *Liberty's Daughters,* 159.

10. "Trivia," *William and Mary Quarterly* 34 (April 1977): 307–8.

11. *Virginia Gazette,* September 15, 1774.

12. Marylynn Salmon, *The Limits of Independence: American Women, 1760–1800* (New York: Oxford University Press, 1994), 58.

13. Norton, *Liberty's Daughters,* 169.

14. Colin G. Calloway, *First Peoples: A Documentary Survey of American Indian History* (Boston: Bedford, 2004), 159.

15. Jeffrey J. Crow and Larry E. Tise, eds., *The Southern Experience in the American Revolution* (Chapel Hill: University of North Carolina Press, 1978), 214.

16. Benjamin Quarles, *The Negro in the American Revolution* (Chapel Hill: University of North Carolina Press, 1961), 135.

17. Ibid., 142.

18. Linda K. Kerber, *Women of the Republic: Intellect and Ideology in Revolutionary America* (Chapel Hill: University of North Carolina Press, 1980) 52.

19. Ibid., 51.

20. Ibid., 54.

21. Holly A. Mayer, *Belonging to the Army: Camp Followers and Community during the American Revolution* (Columbia: University of South Carolina Press, 1996), 20.

22. Kerber, *Women of the Republic,* 59.

23. Ibid., 57.

24. Mayer, *Belonging to the Army,* 124.

25. Kerber, *Women of the Republic,* 64.

26. "Secret Correspondence of a Loyalist Wife," in Marcus and David Burner, eds., *America Firsthand,* 4th ed. (Boston: Bedford, 1997), 2:109–11.

27. Norton, *Liberty's Daughters,* 80.

28. Ibid., 184.

29. Ibid., 187.

30. Ibid., 194.

31. Theda Perdue, *Cherokee Women: Gender and Culture Change, 1700–1835* (Lincoln: University of Nebraska Press, 1998), 111.

32. Peter Kolchin, *American Slavery, 1619–1877* (New York: Hill and Wang, 1993), 78.

33. Salmon, *Limits of Independence,* 111.

34. Jeffrey J. Crow, *The Black Experience in Revolutionary North Carolina* (Raleigh: North Carolina Department of Cultural Resources, 1977), 17.

35. Kierner, *Beyond the Household,* 99.

36. Barbara E. Lacey, "Women in the Era of the American Revolution: The Case of Norwich, Connecticut," *The New England Quarterly* 53 (December 1980): 539.

37. Norton, *Liberty's Daughters,* 216.

38. Ibid., 223–24.

39. Ibid., 171.

40. Ibid., 188–89.

41. Kerber, *Women of the Republic,* 163–64.

42. Linda Grant De Pauw, *Founding Mothers: Women in America in the Revolutionary Era* (Boston: Houghton Mifflin, 1975), 100.

43. Salmon, *Limits of Independence,* 82.

44. De Pauw, *Founding Mothers,* 211.

45. Norton, *Liberty's Daughters,* 287.

46. Catherine A. Brekus, *Strangers and Pilgrims: Female Preaching America, 1740–1845* (Chapel Hill: University of North Carolina Press, 1998), 47.

47. Ibid., 49.

48. Ibid., 63–64.

49. Norton, *Liberty's Daughters,* 130.

50. Ibid., 130.

51. Sylvia R. Frey and Betty Wood, *Come Shouting to Zion: African-American Protestantism in the American South and British Caribbean to 1830* (Chapel Hill: University of North Carolina Press, 1998), 13.

52. Ibid., 110–11.

53. Ibid., 109.

54. Kerber, *Women of the Republic,* 83–84.

55. Nancy Neims Parks, "Abigail Adams," in John A. Garraty and Mark C. Carnes, eds., *American National Biography* (New York: Oxford University Press, 1999), 1:64.

56. Sidney Kaplan and Emma Nogrady Kaplan, *The Black Presence in the Era of the American Revolution,* rev. ed. (Amherst: University of Massachusetts Press, 1989), 181.

57. Bethany K. Dumas, "Elizabeth Freeman," in Garraty and Carnes, *American National Biography,* 8:440.

58. Brekus, *Strangers and Pilgrims,* 87.

59. Marina Warner, *Monuments and Maidens: The Allegory of the Female Form* (New York: Atheneum, 1985), 12.

60. Edwin Wolf II and Marie Elena Korey, *Quarter of a Millennium: The Library Company of Philadelphia 1731–1981* (Philadelphia: The Company, 1981), 79.

61. Daniel C. Littlefield, *Revolutionary Citizens: African Americans, 1776–1804* (New York: Oxford University Press, 1997), 14.

62. Kerber, *Women of the Republic,* 205.

SUGGESTED REFERENCES

General Works   In *The Limits of Independence: American Women, 1760–1800* (1994), Marylynn Salmon provides a brief overview of the revolutionary era. Crucial scholarly works are Linda K. Kerber, *Women of the Republic: Intellect and Ideology in Revolutionary America* (1980), and Mary Beth Norton, *Liberty's Daughters: The Revolutionary Experience of American Women, 1750–1800* (1980). For a review essay, see Jan E. Lewis, "A Revolution for Whom? Women in the Era of the American Revolution," in Nancy A. Hewitt, ed., *A Companion to Women's History* (2002), 83–99.

Women and the American Revolution   Analyses of women's contributions to the colonists' efforts to resist British expanded control over the colonies are found in Linda Grant De Pauw, *Four Traditions: Women of New York during the American Revolution* (1974), and Cynthia Kierner, *Beyond the Household: Women's Place in the Early South, 1700–1835* (1998), as well as in the Norton and Salmon studies. The best sources on Native Americans are Colin G. Calloway, *The American Revolution in Indian Country* (1995) and "New England Algonquins in the American Revolution," in *Algonkians of New England: Past and Present,* Dublin Seminar for New England Folklife Annual Proceedings 1991, 51–165. On African American women and the Revolution, see Jeffrey J. Crow, *The Black Experience in Revolutionary North Carolina* (1977); Jeffrey J. Crow and Larry E. Tise, eds., *The Southern Experience in the American Revolution* (1978); Jacqueline Jones, *Labor of Love, Labor of Sorrow: Black Women, Work and the Family, from Slavery to the Present* (1985); Sidney Kaplan and Emma Nogrady Kaplan, *The Black Presence in the Era of the American Revolution* (1989); Cynthia Kierner, *Beyond the Household: Women's Place in the Early South, 1700–1835* (1998); Mary Beth Norton, "The Fate of Some Black Loyalists of the American Revolution," *Journal of Negro History* 58 (1973): 402–26; and Benjamin Quarles, *The Negro in the American Revolution* (1996). On Phillis Wheatley, see Charles W. Akers, "'Our Modern Egyptians': Phillis Wheatley and the Whig Campaign against Slavery in Revolutionary Boston," *Journal of Negro History* 60 (1975): 397–410, and Sondra O'Neale, "Slave's Subtle War: Phillis Wheatley's Use of Biblical Myth and Symbol," *Early American Literature* 21 (1986), 144–59.

Studies that focus primarily on white women's experience in the Revolution include Sally Smith Booth, *The Women of '76* (1973); Linda Grant De Pauw and Conover Hunt, *"Remember the Ladies": Women in America, 1750–1815* (1976); Mary Beth Norton, "What an Alarming Crisis Is This: Southern Women and the American Revolution," in Jeffrey J. Crow and Larry E. Tise, eds., *The Southern Experience in the American Revolution* (1978); and Alfred F. Young, "The Women of Boston: 'Persons of Consequence' in the Making of the American Revolution, 1765–76," in Harriet B. Applewhite and Darline G. Levy, eds., *Women and Politics in the Age of the Democratic Revolution* (1990). Two accounts of individual women provide insight into the problems conflicting loyalties created. See Patricia Cleary, *Elizabeth Murray: A Woman's Pursuit of Independence in Eighteenth-Century America* (2000), and John W. Jackson, *Margaret Morris: Her Journal with Biographical Sketch and Notes* (1949). On camp followers, see Holly A. Mayer, *Belonging to the Army: Camp Followers and Community during the American Revolution* (1996).

Revolutionary Legacies for Women   On revolutionary legacies for Native Americans, see Colin G. Calloway, *The American Revolution in Indian Country* (1995), and Theda Perdue, *Cherokee Women: Gender and Culture Change, 1700–1835* (1998). Other studies that do not address the Revolution specifically but provide valuable insights are Daniel R. Mandell, "Shifting Boundaries of Race and Ethnicity: Indian-Black Intermarriage in Southern New England, 1760–1880," *Journal of American History* 85 (Sept. 1998): 466–501, and Margaret Connell Szasz, " 'Poor Richard' Meets the Native American: Schooling for Young Indian Women in Eighteenth-Century Connecticut," *Pacific Historical Review* 49 (1980): 215–35. For African Americans, see Ira Berlin, *Many Thousands Gone: The First Two Centuries of Slavery in North America* (1998); Ira Berlin and Ronald Hoffman, eds., *Slavery and Freedom in the Age of the American Revolution* (1983); Gary B. Nash and Jean R. Soderlund, *Freedom by Degrees: Emancipation in Pennsylvania and Its Aftermath* (1991); Shane White, *Somewhat More Independent: The End of Slavery in New York City, 1770–1810* (1991); T. Stephen Whitman, *The Price of Freedom: Slavery and Manumission in Baltimore and Early National Maryland* (1997); Betty Wood, *Gender, Race, and Rank in a Revolutionary Age* (2000); and Arthur Zilversmith, "Quok Walker, Mumbet, and the Abolition of Slavery in Massachusetts," *William and Mary Quarterly* 25 (1968): 614–24.

There is an extensive literature that addresses the impact of revolutionary ideology on American women. See essays in Madelon Cheek, " 'An Inestimable Prize,' Educating Women in the New Republic: The Writings of Judith Sargent Murray," *Journal of Thought* 20 (1985): 250–62; Joan R. Gundersen, "Independence, Citizenship, and the American Revolution," *Signs* 13 (1987): 59–77; R. M. Janes, "On the Reception of Mary Wollstonecraft's *A Vindication of the Rights of Woman,*" *Journal of the History of Ideas* 39 (1978): 293–302; Mark E. Kann, *The Gendering of American Politics: Founding Mothers, Founding Fathers, and Political Patriarchy* (1997); Mary Kelley, " 'Vindicating the Equality of Female Intellect': Women and Authority in the Early Republic," *Prospects* 17 (1992): 1–28; Linda K. Kerber, *No Constitutional Right to Be Ladies: Women and the Obligation of Citizenship* (1998);

Jan Lewis, "The Republican Wife: Virtue and Seduction in the Early Republic," *William and Mary Quarterly,* 3rd ser., 44 (1987): 689–721; Margaret A. Nash, "Rethinking Republican Motherhood: Benjamin Rush and the Young Ladies' Academy of Philadelphia," *Journal of the Early Republic* 17 (1997): 171–91; Sheila L. Skemp, ed., *Judith Sargent Murray: A Brief Biography with Documents* (1998); and Rosemarie Zagarri, "Morals, Manners, and the Republican Woman," *American Quarterly* 44 (June 1992): 192–215. On women and divorce, see Norma Basch, *Framing American Divorce: From the Revolutionary Generation to the Victorians* (1999), and for New Jersey suffrage, see Judith Apter Klinghoffer and Lois Elkis, " 'The Petticoat Electors': Women's Suffrage in New Jersey, 1776–1807," *Journal of the Early Republic* 12 (1992): 159–93.

Women in the Great Awakening On women in the Great Awakening, see Catherine A. Brekus, *Strangers and Pilgrims: Female Preaching America, 1740–1845* (1998); Susan Juster, *Disorderly Women: Sexual Politics and Evangelicism in Revolutionary New England* (1994); and Stephen J. Stein, *The Shaker Experience in America: A History of the United Society of Believers* (1992). On African American women in particular, see Sylvia R. Frey and Betty Wood, *Come Shouting to Zion: African-American Protestantism in the American South and British Caribbean to 1830* (1998); Albert G. Raboteau, *Slave Religion: The "Invisible Institution" in the Antebellum South* (1978); and Mechal Sobel, *The World They Made Together: Black and White Values in Eighteenth-Century Virginia* (1987).

Selected Web Sites

An exceptionally valuable Web page for studying women during the Revolution, How Did the Ladies Association of Philadelphia Shape New Forms of Women's Activism during the American Revolution, 1780–1781?, is available through subscription at <**womhist.binghamton.edu/index.html**>. This site, produced by the Center for the Historical Study of Women and Gender at the State University of New York at Binghamton, is part of the Women and Social Movements in the United States, 1600–2000, project. It links to twenty-eight primary documents and offers detailed information on Esther DeBerdt Reed, author of "Sentiments of an American Woman," and Sarah Franklin Bache.

The Colonial Williamsburg site, <**history.org**>, is maintained by the Colonial Williamsburg Foundation and is associated with that well-known "living museum." The site provides excellent insight into life in this Virginia city during the 1770s. It is fully searchable; entering the keyword "women" takes the user to a variety of primary documents.

3

Pedestal, Loom, and Auction Block

1800–1860

L UCY LARCOM'S TEENAGE YEARS WERE SPENT AS A mill worker in the new factory town on the Merrimack River, Lowell, Massachusetts. In 1835, at the age of eleven, she moved to Lowell with her widowed mother, who had taken a job as manager of one of the company-owned boarding houses to support herself and her children. For Lucy, life and work in the textile factory, a "rather select industrial school for young people," was the formative experience of her life, the memory of which she carried into her future career as a poet and writer.[1] She loved both the experience of doing work that was significant to the larger society and "the pleasure we found in making new acquaintances among our workmates." But in later years she became uneasy with the condescension of those who called themselves "ladies" toward her humble past as a "factory girl." "It is the first duty of every woman to recognize the mutual bond of universal womanhood," Larcom wrote in her memoirs. "Let her ask herself whether she would like to hear herself or her sister spoken of as a shopgirl or a factory-girl or a servant-girl, if necessity had compelled her for a time to be employed. . . ."[2]

Larcom's experiences embodied two of the three crucial processes shaping the lives of women in the United States during the first half of the nineteenth century. First, she was responding to an influential nineteenth-century ideology of womanhood, home life, and gender relations that treated women as fundamentally different from men; this ideology placed women on a pedestal, simultaneously elevated and isolated by their special domestic role. At the same time, Larcom was participating in the first wave of American industrialization, a process that dramatically redirected the young nation's economy and created new dimensions of wealth and poverty, levels of production and consumption, and ways of life for many Americans. Historians tend to identify these two phenomena with two different and emerging classes—domestic ideology with the middle class, industrialization with the working class—but through the eyes of women like Lucy Larcom, it is possible to see that they were mutually influential.

The very cotton fibers that mill girls like Larcom spun and wove indicate the third major development considered in this chapter: slavery. By the nineteenth century, slavery was a regional social and economic system but one with profound national implications. Slavery was of incomparable importance in the antebellum (or pre–Civil War) years, not only to those American women who lived as or by unfree labor, but to those who dedicated themselves to ending the commerce in human beings and, ultimately, to all who would endure the devastating conflict fought over slavery's very existence.

THE IDEOLOGY OF TRUE WOMANHOOD

Lucy Larcom's concern with the implications of her factory years for her character as a woman reflects a powerful ideology of gender roles that historians have variously labeled "the cult of true womanhood," "the ideology of separate spheres," or simply "domesticity." This system of ideas, which took hold in the early years of the nineteenth century just as the United States was coming into its own as an independent nation, treated men and women as complete and absolute opposites, with almost no common human traits that transcended the differences of gender. The ideology of true womanhood also saw the larger society as carved into complementary but mutually exclusive "spheres" of public and private concerns, work and home life, politics and family. "In no country has such constant care been taken as in America to trace two clearly distinct

1834	**First Female Moral Reform Society formed**
1835-1842	**Runaway slave Harriet Jacobs hides in her grandmother's attic**
1837	Panic touches off major industrial depression
1837	**Sarah Josepha Hale becomes editor of *Godey's Lady's Book***
1837	Samuel Morse patents the Morse code for the telegraph
1841	**Catharine Beecher's *A Treatise on Domestic Economy* published**
1844	Gradual economic recovery evident
1845	Potato blight in Ireland prompts a huge wave of immigration to the United States
1845	**New England Female Labor Reform Association formed**
1845	*The Narrative of the Life of Frederick Douglass* published
1848	**Ellen and William Craft escape from South Carolina slavery**
1848	**New York State passes Married Women's Property Act**
1848	**Seneca Falls women's rights convention held**
1850	Compromise of 1850 includes an oppressive federal Fugitive Slave Law
1850s	**Commercial sewing machine developed**
1851	Harriet Beecher Stowe's *Uncle Tom's Cabin* published
1860	Ellen and William Craft's *Running a Thousand Miles for Freedom* published
1860	Republican Abraham Lincoln elected president
1860	Southern states begin to secede from the Union
1861	Harriet Jacobs's *Incidents in the Life of a Slave Girl* published

137

lines of action for the two sexes," declared Alexis de Tocqueville, the great French observer of American culture in the 1830s. "American women never manage the outward concerns of the family, or conduct a business, or take a part in political life; nor are they, on the other hand, ever compelled to perform the rough labor of the fields, or to make any of those laborious exertions, which demand the exertion of physical strength. No families are so poor, as to form an exception to this rule."[3]

The experience of innumerable women in antebellum America—the slave women of the South, the mill girls of the North, the impoverished widows of the new cities, the rising number of female immigrants, even the hardworking farm wives—contradicted these assertions. Yet no aspect of this complex reality seemed to interfere with the widespread conviction that this gender ideology was "true." The challenge of understanding American women's history in the first half of the nineteenth century is to reconcile the extraordinary breadth and power, or hegemony, of the ideology of separate spheres with the wide variety of American women's lives in these years, many of which tell a very different story.

Christian Motherhood

An ideology as culturally widespread as that of true womanhood is difficult to reduce to a set of beliefs, but several basic concepts do stand out. First and foremost, proponents situated true women in an exclusively domestic realm of home, family, childrearing, and caretaking. They did not consider what women did as wives and mothers as work but as an effortless expression of their feminine natures. Action and leadership were reserved for man; inspiration and assistance were woman's province. The home over which women presided was not merely a residence or a collection of people but, to use a popular phrase, "a haven in a heartless world," where men could fine solace from a grueling public existence. "The perfection of womanhood . . . is the wife and mother, the center of the family, that magnet that draws man to the domestic altar, that makes him a civilized being, a social Christian," proclaimed the popular women's magazine, *Godey's Lady's Book,* in 1860. "The wife is truly the light of the home."[4]

At the core of woman's domesticity and of her being was motherhood. The basic elements of this argument were present in late eighteenth-century rhetoric about the importance of Republican Motherhood to the success of the American democratic experiment (see Chapter 2). In stark contrast to the self-serving individualism expected of men and rewarded by economic advancement in the world outside the home, proponents of true womanhood described motherhood as a wholly selfless activity built around service to others. Oddly enough, given the importance that American political culture placed on independence of character, women's selfless mothering was seen as the very source of national well-being and constituted the way that citizens of the new nation could be trained to be virtuous, concerned with the larger good, and yet industrious and self-disciplined. Maternal nurturance was a vocation theoretically open even to women without children of their own who could bestow their motherly instincts on society's unloved and ignored unfortunates. "Woman's great mission is to train immature, weak and ignorant creatures, to obey the laws of God," preached author and domestic ideologue Catharine Beecher in one of her many treatises on true womanhood, "first in the family, then in the school, then in the neighborhood, then in the nation, then in the world."[5] Beecher herself was unmarried and childless (see box, "The Peculiar Responsibilities of the American Woman").

Women's expansive maternity was thought to make them natural teachers and underlay the feminization of this profession in the early nineteenth century. Whereas in the eighteenth century, teaching was seen as a fundamentally male vocation, in these years, women were increasingly regarded as best suited to instruct the young, and primary school teaching became an overwhelmingly female occupation. Especially in New England, public education was becoming widespread, and young Yankee women, literate but less expensive to hire than men, supplied the teachers. By one estimate, one-quarter of all native-born New England women in the years between 1825 and 1860 were schoolteachers at some point in their lives.[6]

Women's motherly vocation had a deeply religious dimension. True womanhood was a fervently Protestant notion, which gave to female devotion and selfless sacrifice a redemptive power. The true woman functioned as Christ's representative in daily life, and the domestic environment over which she presided served as a sort of sacred territory, where evil and worldly influences could be cleansed away. As Beecher insisted, "the preparation of young ministers for the duties of the church does not surpass in importance the training of the minister of the nursery and school-room."[7]

The special identification of women with Christian piety was firmly established by a new wave of religious revivals that swept through American society in the late eighteenth and early nineteenth centuries. Beginning in the frontier communities of Ohio, Kentucky, and Indiana, the "Second Great Awakening"° moved east by the 1810s and 1820s. Western New York was known as the "burned-over district" because of the zealous religiosity that swept through it in these years. Conveyed by preachers inspired by personal spiritual conviction rather than theological training, religious fervor especially thrived outside large cities. In the South, blacks and whites were drawn together in similar extended revivals. A cultural phenomenon with many different sources, this intense return to religious conviction was a reaction both to the political preoccupations of the revolutionary period and to swift changes in the American economic system. This religious revivalism also had a populist element, as it bypassed established clerical authority in favor of more direct spiritual experience among the broad mass of the American people. The evangelical nature of new forms of Protestant worship, especially in Baptist and Methodist congregations, stressed personal conversion and commitment to rooting out sin in this world.

Religious enthusiasm and activism gave women, who were the majority of converts in these revivals, an arena for individual expression and social recognition that they were denied in secular politics. Popular evangelical preachers relied

°As discussed in Chapter 2, the original Great Awakening occurred in the 1730s–1770s.

CATHARINE BEECHER

The Peculiar Responsibilities
of the American Woman

In the first chapter of A Treatise on Domestic Economy *(1841), a book de-voted to the details of childrearing and homemaking, author and domestic ideologue Catharine Beecher (1800–1878) elaborates her theory of Ameri-can democracy and women's place in it. She insists that women's inclusion in the American promise of equality is completely compatible with the subordi-nation that she believes is divinely ordained in wives' relations to their hus-bands. More than a half century after the American Revolution, she shifted the grand political purposes served by women's special domestic role from the establishment of a stable nation to the spread of American Protestant ideals to the entire world.*

In this Country, it is established, both by opinion and by practice, that woman has an equal interest in all social and civil concerns; and that no domestic, civil, or political, institution, is right, which sacrifices her inter-est to promote that of the other sex. But in order to secure her the more firmly in all these privileges, it is decided, that, in the domestic relation, she take a subordinate station, and that, in civil and political concerns, her interests be intrusted to the other sex, without her taking any part in voting, or in making and administering laws. . . . In matters pertaining to the education of their children, in the selection and support of a, clergy-

on their female followers to establish their reputations as effective religious lead-ers. Catharine Beecher's father, Lyman, and her brother, Henry Ward, were two such evangelical ministers. Catharine's own religious experience was frustrating and incomplete; try as she might, she was never able to experience a full personal conversion and always doubted the depth of her religious conviction. Nonetheless, the career she was able to build for herself as an authority on proper Christian womanhood was much assisted by the association of the Beecher name with evan-gelical piety.

Women's reputation for deeper religious sentiment was closely related to the assumption that the true woman was inherently uninterested in sexual expression, that she was "pure." The notion of woman's natural sexual innocence was a rela-tively modern concept. For many centuries in European Christian culture, women were considered more dangerously sexual than men. What one historian labels the belief in women's basic "passionlessness" was a new idea, and one that in the con-text of the time served to raise women's stature.[8] In the hierarchical worldview of

man, in all benevolent enterprises, and in all questions relating to morals or manners, they have a superior influence. In such concerns, it would be impossible to carry a point, contrary to their judgement and feelings; while an enterprise, sustained by them, will seldom fail of success.

If those who are bewailing themselves over the fancied wrongs and injuries of women in this Nation, could only see things as they are, they would know, that, . . . there is nothing reasonable, which American women would unite in asking, that would not readily be bestowed. . . . To us [Americans] is committed the grand, the responsible privilege, of exhibiting to the world, the beneficent influences of Christianity. . . . But the part to be enacted by American women, in this great moral enterprise, is the point to which special attention should here be directed. . . . The proper education of a man decides the welfare of an individual; but educate a woman, and the interests of the whole family are secured. . . .

The woman, who is rearing a family of children; the woman, who labors in the schoolroom; the woman, who, in her retired chamber, earns, with her needle, the mite, which contributes to the intellectual and moral elevation of her Country; even the humble domestic, whose example and influence may be moulding and forming young minds, while her faithful services sustain a prosperous domestic state; — each and all may be animated by the consciousness, that they are agents in accomplishing the greatest work that ever was committed to human responsibility.

Source: Catharine Beecher, *A Treatise on Domestic Economy* (New York: Marsh, Capen, Lyon, and Webb, 1841), ch. 1.

---

nineteenth-century Protestant values, woman was less tied to humanity's animal nature than man, and this lifted her closer to the divine. Sexual appetite in the female was virtually unimaginable.[9] These assumptions made the presence of prostitutes profoundly disturbing to nineteenth-century moralists. If women were as lustful as men, there would be no one to control and contain sexual desire. As Dr. William Sanger wrote in his pathbreaking 1860 study of prostitution in New York City, "Were it otherwise, and the passions in both sexes equal, illegitimacy and prostitution would be far more rife in our midst than at present."[10] (See Documents: Prostitution in New York City, 1858, pp. 169–74.)

Starting in the 1820s, pious women expanded their religious expression beyond churchgoing to participation in a wide variety of voluntary organizations that promoted the spiritual and moral uplift of the poor and unenlightened. Some of these female benevolent associations sponsored missionary efforts to bring the blessings of Christianity to unbelievers at home and abroad. By the 1830s, an extensive network of Protestant women's organizations was sending money to

Time, Midnight.   *Place*, not very far from the Academy of Music.
SERIOUS YOUNG LADY. "Ah! Fanny, *you* coming from the Opera! How long have you been *gay?*"

◆ **New York City Prostitutes**
Whether the number of prostitutes rose dramatically in the mid-nineteenth century, as many observers charged, in large cities they were certainly more visible and thus more disturbing to the middle-class public. Prostitutes and their clients commonly frequented the "third tier" of theaters, which was informally reserved for them. As this contemporary cartoon indicates, they could even be found at the most elegant theaters. The joke in this cartoon refers to the difficulty of distinguishing between prostitutes and reputable women of fashion. The term "gay" referred to prostitution, not homosexuality, in the nineteenth century. *Culver Pictures.*

church missions throughout Asia and Africa. A handful of adventuresome women went to preach the gospel abroad, mostly as wives of male missionaries. Ann Hasseltine Judson, who served with her husband in the 1820s in Rangoon, Burma, was the first American woman missionary in Asia. Closer to home, female missionaries brought Christian solace to the American urban poor. Pious middle-class women joined their ministers in "friendly visiting" to preach the word of Christ to society's downtrodden and outcast.

A Middle-Class Ideology

Despite the wide range of those who subscribed to its tenets, the ideology of true womanhood was a thoroughly middle-class social ethic. Certainly, the assumption that a woman should be insulated from the economic demands of the outside world so as to concentrate on creating a stable and peaceful home environment presumed she was married to a man willing and able to support her as a dependent wife. The middle-class wife in turn was responsible for what Beecher characterized as "the regular and correct apportionment of expenses that makes a family truly comfortable."[11] The idealized true woman, presiding over a virtuous family life, was a crucial staple of the way Americans contrasted themselves with European aristocratic society. Adherence to the ideology of true womanhood also helped people of the middle classes to distinguish themselves from those they regarded as their social and economic inferiors. In their charitable activities among the poor, true women preached their own beliefs in separate sexual spheres and female domesticity, convinced that the absence of these family values, rather than economic forces, was what made the poor poor.

These ideas reflected changing conditions in middle-class American women's lives. The birthrate for the average American-born white woman fell from 6 in 1800 to 4.9 in 1850, as economic modernization meant that children were less important as extra hands to help support the family and more likely to be a financial drain. Also, technological developments were just beginning to ease women's household burden, for example, the new cast-iron stove, which was easier and safer than open-hearth cooking. As the industrial production of cloth accelerated, women no longer had to spin and weave at home, although they still cut and sewed their family's clothes. Depending on their husbands' incomes, middle-class women might be able to hire one or more servants to help with their labors. Even so, the middle-class housewife did plenty of work herself. Despite technological developments, leisure time was a privilege for only the very richest women.

◆ **Lilly Martin Spencer,** *Washerwoman* **(1854)**
Lilly Martin Spencer, an immigrant from France, was virtually the only woman in antebellum America to make a living as a painter. Despite efforts at painting grander historical subjects, her domestic paintings were so popular that she concentrated on this genre. Her subjects included both domestic sentiments and domestic labor. She used her own servant as a model, and her paintings demonstrate an intimate knowledge of the actual labor involved in maintaining a household, as in this unusual painting of laundering. The same servant-model appears in other Spencer paintings, always robust and smiling. Spencer's own domestic life was unconventional: she had thirteen children, of whom seven survived; but with her husband's assent, she served as the family breadwinner while he tended to the household duties. *Hood Museum of Art, Dartmouth College, Hanover, New Hampshire; purchased through a gift from Florence B. Moore in memory of her husband, Lansing P. Moore, Class of 1937.*

Laundry, the most burdensome of domestic obligations, remained a difficult weekly chore for housewives.

The doctrine of domesticity was elaborated by ministers in sermons and physicians in popular health books. Women, however, did much of the work of spreading these ideas. The half century in which this rigid ideology of gender flourished was also the period in which writing by women first found a mass audience among middle-class women. Lydia Sigourney, a beloved woman's poet, Mrs. E. D. E. N. Southworth, popular author of numerous sentimental novels, and Sarah Josepha Hale, editor of the influential women's magazine, *Godey's Lady's Book* (150,000 subscribers in 1860), built successful careers elaborating the ideology of true womanhood. (See Visual Sources: *Godey's Lady's Book,* pp. 182–89.) Catharine Beecher taught that woman's sphere was a noble "profession," equal in importance and challenge to any of the tasks assigned to men, in her influential and much reprinted *A Treatise on Domestic Economy* (1841). Her younger half sister, Harriet Beecher Stowe, relied heavily on the ideas of woman's sphere in her book, *Uncle Tom's Cabin* (1851), which became the most widely read American novel ever written.

In the judgment of such women, the tremendous respect paid to woman's lofty state was one of the distinguishing glories of nineteenth-century America. While proponents of true womanhood insisted that woman's sphere differed from man's, they certainly did not regard it as of less importance to society or less worthy of respect. Lucy Larcom put it this way: "God made no mistake in her [woman's] creation. He sent her into the world full of power and will to be a *helper.* . . . She is here to make this great house of humanity a habitable and a beautiful place, without and within, a true home for every one of his children."[12]

The many women of the nineteenth century who energetically subscribed to the ideas of true womanhood were not brainwashed victims of a male ideological conspiracy. Private writings of middle-class women that come down to us from this period, letters and diaries notably, show women embracing these ideas and using them to give purpose to their lives. Not only could the true woman claim authority over the household and childrearing, but the widespread belief in her special moral vocation legitimated a certain amount of activity outside the domestic sphere. Despite its middle-class character, it is striking how widespread was belief in the doctrine of true womanhood throughout antebellum American society. Almost the only women during this period who openly challenged its tenets were the women's rights radicals (see Chapter 4).

Domesticity in a Market Age

By fervently insisting that women had to be insulated from the striving and bustle of the outside world, the advocates of true womanhood were implicitly responding to the impact of larger economic pressures on women's lives. The ideology of separate spheres and women's protected domesticity notwithstanding, women's history during this period can be understood only in the context of the burgeoning market economy. The development and growth of a cash-based, market-oriented economy—as opposed to one in which people mostly produced for their own immediate use—reaches back to the very beginnings of American history and forward into the twentieth century. But early nineteenth-century America is rightly seen as the time in which the fundamental shift towards market-oriented production took place.

The triumph of the market economy had particular implications for women. In preindustrial society, men's work as well as women's was considered fundamentally "domestic." Although what each did was different, both sexes worked within and for the household, and their labor was oriented for their own family's use, not for trade on the open market. Already by the eighteenth century, this was changing as commercial transactions were growing in significance (see Chapter 2). Especially within urban areas, various household goods—soap and candles for example, or processed foods like flour and spices—were available for purchase. By the early nineteenth century, households needed to acquire more and more cash to meet the needs of daily life with the market goods that fulfilled those needs.

With the rise of the market economy, much of men's work moved outside the home, and women alone did work at home for direct use. Because work was increasingly regarded as what happened outside of the home, done by men and compensated for by money, what women did in the home was becoming invisible as productive labor. From this perspective, the lavish attention paid by the ideology of true womanhood to the moral significance of woman's domestic sphere might be seen as a measure of the decline in its economic value, as if in compensation.

Industrial depressions, the repercussions of which affected the entire society and not just the lower rungs of wage earners, were becoming a regular, seemingly inescapable characteristic of industrial society, the bust that inevitably followed the boom. In 1837, the economy, which had been growing by leaps and bounds, violently contracted, and prices dropped precipitously, banks collapsed, and wages fell by as much as a third. The Panic of 1837, as it was called for the response of investor and wage earner alike, was an early and formative experience in the life of the future women's rights leader Susan B. Anthony, whose father lost his grain mill business in that year.

Despite waning recognition of women's role in economic production, popular nineteenth-century ideology assumed that in the household women could counter some of the more disturbing aspects of economic growth and change in this period. Contemporary writings on woman's sphere contended that a woman's household management skills and emotional steadiness were crucial in helping her family survive the dramatic and unexpected shifts in financial position that were such an unnerving aspect of the new economy. "When we observe the frequent revolutions from poverty to affluence and then from extravagance to ruin, that are continually taking place around us," wrote Mrs. A. J. Graves in her popular handbook *Woman in America* (1841), "and their calamitous effects upon families brought up in luxury and idleness, have we not reason to fear that our 'homes of order and peace' are rapidly disappearing?"[13] Seen this way, the proper conduct of woman's sphere virtually became a matter of economic survival.

WOMEN AND WAGE EARNING

As Mrs. Graves's admonition indicates, the depiction of woman's sphere as opposed to the striving and bustle of the outside world is misleading. Indeed, the pressures of a cash-based, market economy were felt by women in many ways. Women found methods to gain cash remuneration for their labors. They also found ways to make money from within their households—for instance, by selling extra butter or eggs. Barely visible to a society focused on its own capacity for productive prosperity, impoverished urban women, widowed or deserted by men, scrounged or begged for pennies to buy shelter, food, and warmth.

Of all the ways that women intersected with the cash economy and the forces of the market revolution, none was more important for women's history than the employment of young New England women like Lucy Larcom as factory operatives at the power-driven spindles and looms of the newly established American textile industry. Though their numbers were small, these young women constituted the first emergence of the female wage labor force (see the Appendix, p. A-37).

From Market Revolution to Industrial Revolution

To understand the experiences of early nineteenth-century women factory workers, we must place them in the setting of the industrial transformations of the early nineteenth century. The growth of a market economy encouraged the centralization and acceleration of production in fewer, larger locales. This industrializing process was gradual and uneven, a fact that becomes especially clear when the distinct contribution of women workers becomes the focus. For a long time after the industrialization process began, much production continued to take place in producers' homes, even as their control over what they made and their share of its value was seriously eroded. In this transitional form of manufacture for market, a separate class of men, called *factors*, purchased the raw materials for production and distributed them to workers in their homes, then collected the finished goods and sold them. The cash that workers received in exchange was no longer the full value of what they had produced since the factor also made money from the production and distribution process. In essence, the workers were receiving a wage for their labor instead of being paid for their products, which were no longer theirs to dispose of. Their labor was increasingly considered only an element, not the entirety, of the production process.

Shoemaking is a particularly interesting example, both because its transition to full industrialization was very prolonged and because women and men underwent this transition at very different rates. Shoemaking for sale was already well underway by the early nineteenth century, especially in cities north of Boston, notably Lynn, Massachusetts. At first, shoes were manufactured in home-based workshops in which the male head of the household was the master artisan and his wife, children, and apprentices worked under his direction. Starting in the 1820s and 1830s, a new class of shoemaking entrepreneurs brought male workmen, who specialized in cutting and sewing soles, to a centralized site, while women continued to do their part of the work, handsewing the shoes' uppers and linings, from their homes. By the 1840s and 1850s, women's labor was being directed and paid for by the factors. It was not until later in the nineteenth century, after the Civil War, that women's part in shoe production moved into factories.

Clothing manufacture remained in a similar "outwork" phase for a long time. Most of the clothing manufactured for sale in the antebellum period was produced by women working within their homes. By 1860, there were 16,000 female "tailoresses" and seamstresses in New York City alone.[14] The impoverished lives of these women reveal the ravages dealt to mid-nineteenth-century poor women and families by the processes of industrialization. The manufacture of clothing did not begin to shift into factories until after the Civil War, and well into the twentieth century the workshop form of production continued to thrive as what came to be called sweatshops (see Chapter 5). Other industries that relied on women outworkers included straw hatmaking and bookbinding. Held to their homes by childrearing responsibilities, married women remained home-based industrial outworkers much longer than men or unmarried women. The more exclusively female that outwork became, the more poorly it was paid.

Manufacturing could be said to be fully industrialized only on its shift to a separate centralized physical location of labor, the factory, at which point home and work would be fully separated. There the entrepreneurs could introduce more expensive machinery and supervise producers' labor more closely, both intended to maximize their profits. This factory building and the machines within it were the manufacturer's contribution to the process, his "capital," and gave him the control and ownership that the actual workers had now lost. Male artisans, no longer the masters of their family workshops, experienced the shift to the factory as absolute decline, whereas for women the shift of manufacturing to outside the home offered a more mixed experience. The ownership of the factories was entirely in the hands of men, and women, whose secondary status had already been established in home manufacturing, earned a much lower wage than men for tasks that were inevitably considered less skilled. Yet, women's turn to factory labor also gave them the chance to escape their family-based subordination, to earn wages as individuals, and at times to experience a taste of personal freedom. As Larcom explained, young women like herself "were clearing away a few weeds from the overgrown track of independent labor for other women."[15]

The Mill Girls of Lowell

Textile production, one of the most important of America's early industries—and certainly the most female dominated—began as home-based outwork, but by the 1820s it was decisively shifting in the direction of factory labor. Here could be found America's first female factory workers. If the impoverished "tailoresses" working out of their dark urban garrets stood for the depredations of industrial capital toward women, the factory girls of the textile industry came to represent the better possibilities that wage labor might offer women. And "girls" they were—unmarried, many in their teens. (See Visual Sources: Early Photographs of Factory Operatives and Slave Women, pp. 190–97.) Though they were only a tiny percentage of women—as of 1840, only 2.25 percent[16]—these first female factory workers understood themselves, and were understood by others in their society, as opening up new possibilities of personal independence and economic contribution for their sex.

The story of the first women factory workers, and of the American textile industry within which they worked, began in the years during and immediately after the War of 1812. At the beginning of the nineteenth century, when Americans bought industrially manufactured wool, linen, and cotton cloth, they did so from the textile factories of Great Britain. The war with England interrupted the transatlantic trade in factory-made cloth, creating an irresistible opportunity for wealthy New England merchants, who had heretofore made their money by importing these British manufactured goods, to invest in American-based industry. In 1814 in Waltham, Massachusetts, a group of local merchants opened the first American factory to house all aspects of textile production under one roof. They had spirited out of England designs for water-driven machinery for both spinning and weaving, in an early and daring example of industrial espionage. Investors enjoyed quick and substantial profits, and in 1823, the same group of venture capitalists opened a much larger operation twenty-three miles away, on Merrimack River farmland north of Boston. The new factory town, named after the leading figure in the merchant capital group, Francis Cabot Lowell, soon became synonymous with the energetic American textile industry and especially with the young women who provided its labor force.

Previously, in England and in earlier, unsuccessful efforts at factory textile production in the United States, whole families who would otherwise be destitute were the workers. Many children worked the spinning machines and looms. This impoverished working population gave factory production a bad name, best captured by British poet William Blake's terrifying 1804 image of the "dark satanic mills" soiling "England's green and pleasant land."[17] Textile factories were regarded as little more than poorhouses to keep indigent people from disrupting society. Given the predominance of farming in the United States, this type of labor force was not as available to aspiring American textile industrialists. But an alternative had been identified as early as the 1790s by President Washington's secretary of the treasury, Alexander Hamilton, an early promoter of American industrial production. Hamilton advocated hiring the unmarried daughters of farming families, who could move in and out of industrial production without becoming a permanent and impoverished wage labor force, like that which haunted England. These would be factory workers who worked more from choice than necessity. Theoretically, by laboring for wages in textile factories, these young women could help provide their families with the cash that they increasingly required. The fact that the spinning of fiber for cloth had been the traditional work of women in the preindustrial household (especially unmarried women, hence the term "spinster") provided an additional argument for turning to a female labor force.

To the delight of New England textile capitalists, girls from Yankee farm families took to factory labor in the 1820s and early 1830s with great enthusiasm. Working as individual wage earners offered a degree of personal independence that was entirely new and very attractive to these young women. Many were eager to work in the factories, despite thirteen-hour days, six-day work weeks, and wages of $1 to $2 per week.[18] "I regard it as one of the privileges of my youth that I was permitted to grow up among these active, interesting girls," Lucy Larcom wrote in her memoirs, "whose lives were not mere echoes of other lives, but had principles and purposes distinctly their own."[19] Even though they saved their wages and sent as much as possible to their families, the mill girls occasionally spent some of their earnings on themselves; for this they were regarded by contemporaries as spoiled and self-indulgent. And although their workdays were extraordinarily long and the labor much more unrelenting than that to which they were accustomed, they reveled in the small amounts of time they had for themselves in the evenings. Larcom's reminiscences detail the lessons she and her sister attended, the writing they did, and the friendships they made. Factory girls at Lowell and elsewhere even formed female benevolent societies, as did their more middle-class counterparts.

One problem, however, stood in the way of the success of the Waltham/Lowell solution to the problem of factory labor: where were the young women workers to live? Given the scale of the labor force required by the large new factories and the decentralized character of the New England population, young women would have to be brought from their homes far away to the new factories. Parents were reluctant to allow their daughters to be so far from home and away from family supervision. Factory work for women, probably because it had been so dreadfully underpaid, was suspected of being an avenue to prostitution. The capitalists' solution to both the housing and moral supervision dilemmas was to build boarding houses for their young workers and to link work and living arrangements in a paternalistic approach to industrial production. Four to six young women shared each bedroom, and their behavior was closely supervised. The boarding houses, and the camaraderie among young women that flourished there, added to the allure of factory labor. To the farm girls of New England, this was greater cosmopolitanism than they had ever known.

For about a decade, the city of Lowell and the Lowell system (as the employment of young farm girls as factory workers was called) were among the glories of the new American nation. Visitors came from Europe to see and sing the praises of the moral rectitude and industry of the women workers in this new type of factory production, free of the corruptions of the old world. "They were healthy in appearance, many of them remarkably so," Charles Dickens wrote on the basis of a visit in 1842, "and had the manners and deportment of young women; not of degraded brutes of burden."[20] The dignity and probity of the Lowell girls were crucial elements in the optimistic vision that temporarily thrived about the possibilities of a genuinely democratic American version of industrial factory production, in which all could share in and profit by the new levels of wealth. "The experiment at Lowell had shown that independent and intelligent workers invariably give their own character to their occupation," Larcom proudly wrote.[21] One of the most

REGULATIONS

TO BE OBSERVED BY ALL PERSONS EMPLOYED IN THE FACTORIES OF THE

MIDDLESEX COMPANY.

The overseers are to be punctually in their rooms at the starting of the mill, and not to be absent unnecessarily during working hours. They are to see that all those employed in their rooms are in their places in due season. They may grant leave of absence to those employed under them, when there are spare hands in the room to supply their places; otherwise they are not to grant leave of absence, except in cases of absolute necessity. Every overseer must be the last to leave the room at night, and must see that the lights are all properly extinguished, and that there is no fire in the room. No overseer should leave his room in the evening while the mill is running, except in case of absolute necessity.

All persons in the employ of the Middlesex Company are required to observe the regulations of the overseer of the room where they are employed. They are not to be absent from their work, without his consent, except in case of sickness, and then they are to send him word of the cause of their absence.

They are to board in one of the boarding-houses belonging to the Company, unless otherwise permitted by the agent or superintendent, and conform to the regulations of the house where they board. They are to give information at the counting-room of the place where they board when they begin; and also give notice whenever they change their boarding place.

The Company will not employ any one who is habitually absent from public worship on the Sabbath, or whose habits are not regular and correct.

All persons entering into the employment of the Company are considered as engaged for twelve months; and those who leave sooner will not receive a regular discharge.

All persons intending to leave the employment of the Company are to give two weeks' notice of their intention to their overseer; and their engagement is not considered as fulfilled unless they comply with this regulation.

Smoking within the factory yards will in no case be permitted.

The pay-roll will be made up to the end of every month, and the payment made in the course of the following week.

These regulations are considered a part of the contract with persons entering into the employment of the MIDDLESEX COMPANY.

Samuel Lawrence, *Agent.*

Lowell, July 1, 1846.

Joel Taylor, Printer, Courier Office.

◆ **Regulations, Middlesex Company (1846)**

All of the Lowell companies required their young women workers to observe rules governing not only their activities in the factories but also their lives outside the mills. Most striking are the requirements that workers live in company-run boarding houses and regularly attend church. No doubt the smoking prohibition applies to the male workers, mostly weavers, in the factory. *Center for Lowell History, Lowell, Massachusetts.*

unusual aspects of life in Lowell was the literary output of the workers themselves. Young women workers wrote stories, essays, and poems, usually about their experience at the factories, for their own literary journal, the *Lowell Offering,* to put their uprightness and their intelligence on display. Larcom began her career as a writer this way. Factory owners, not insensitive to the propaganda value of such efforts, underwrote the magazine, paid the editor's salary, and distributed issues widely.

The End of the Lowell Idyll

Eventually, however, economic pressures took their toll on Lowell's great promise, at least for the workers. Declining prices for cotton and wool and investors' expectations of high returns led factory owners to slash wages to reduce costs. Within the first decade, wages were cut twice. The gender of the Lowell labor force again played an important role: the factory owners counted on the womanly demeanor of their employees to lead them to accept the cuts. But they were wrong. In 1834 and 1836, in response to lower wages, Lowell girls "turned out"—conducted spontaneous strikes—and in the process began to question notions of womanhood that forbade such demonstrations of self- and group-assertion. They repudiated the deference and subordination expected of them on the grounds of their sex and championed, instead, their dignity and independence as proud "daughters of freemen." One young striker, Harriet Hanson, who went on to become a leader in the woman suffrage movement, remembered that the strike "was the first time a woman had spoken in public in Lowell, and the event caused surprise and consternation among her audience."[22] But the Panic of 1837, which triggered contraction of the entire industrial economy, doomed the efforts of the women operatives to act collectively, defend their jobs, and preserve the level of their wages. Workers were laid off and mills shut down. Young girls went back to their farm families to wait out the economic downturn.

When the economy revived and the mills resumed full production, workers were expected to work faster, tend more machines, and produce more cloth. Production levels rose, but wages did not. Moral concerns were giving way to the bottom line. In the 1840s, Lowell's women workers tried once again to organize, this time in a more consistent and determined way. Joining with male workers in other Massachusetts factories, the women of Lowell petitioned the state legislature to establish a ten-hour legal limit to their workdays as a way to resist work pressure and keep up levels of employment. This turn to the political system to redress group grievance was part of the larger democratic spirit of the period, but what is striking is to find women engaged in these methods at a time when politics was regarded as thoroughly outside of woman's sphere. Indeed, the legislative petitions of the women textile workers of the 1840s are an important indicator that women were beginning to imagine themselves part of the political process. But for precisely this reason, because women lacked whatever power of the franchise male workers could muster, they were unable to secure any gains by their legislative petitions.

Conditions of factory labor were changing in other ways as well, most notably in the composition of the labor force. The Lowell system had been devised in the context of a shortage of workers willing to take factory jobs. By the 1840s, however, immigrants were providing an ever growing labor pool for industrial employment. Coming to the United States in large numbers, they poured into the wage labor force. This, America's first major immigrant wave, included Germans, French, Canadians, and British, but the Irish were both the largest and the most economically desperate of all the immigrant groups. Starting in 1845, a terrible blight on the potato crop that was the staple of the Irish diet, exacerbated by the harsh policies of England toward its oldest colony, threw the population into starvation conditions and compelled well over a million Irish men and women to emigrate to the United States. The textile capitalists, no longer pressured by labor shortages to make factory employment seem morally uplifting, paid lower wages and enforced harsher working conditions on these new immigrant workers, who soon constituted the majority of mill laborers.

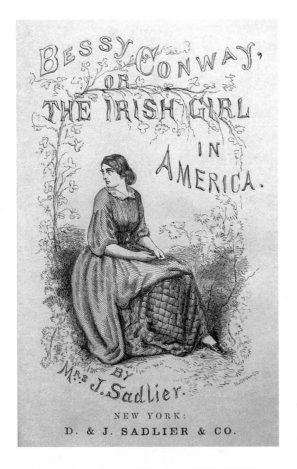

◆ **Irish Immigration**
Mary Anne Madden Sadlier, the author of the first American-written novel about an Irish immigrant woman, herself left Ireland in 1844. Living first in Montreal, she and her husband, James Sadlier, a book and magazine publisher, moved to New York City in 1860. Her novel, *Bessy Conway, or The Irish Girl in America* (1861), modified the domestic focus of true womanhood ideology for a Catholic audience and blamed instead Protestant values and prejudices for the poverty and social ills that the Irish experienced in the United States. *Courtesy of the Burns Library, Boston College.*

Part of the initial attraction that native-born farm girls had for capitalists was the expectation that they would eventually marry and return to their families and farms, and therefore their factory labor would be only a brief episode in their lives. (And many did, although their time in Lowell seems to have subtly altered their prospects: they tended to choose husbands closer to their own ages than did similar young women who had not been away to the factory.) The dreaded, old-world fate of becoming a permanently degraded and dependent wage labor class went instead to the Irish Catholic immigrants, who by 1860 were well over half of the workers in the industry. Immigrant men now worked the looms and immigrant women the spindles. The image of the high moral character of the factory operatives—their womanly demeanor and hunger for self-improvement that were once the boast of the industry—was no more. Wage earning was increasingly seen as undermining respectable femininity. Working women and true women were going their separate ways.

At the Bottom of the Wage Economy

Tremendous prejudice was directed at the Irish in the early years of industrialization, in no small part because they were becoming so thoroughly identified with wage labor. The Irish were one of the very few immigrant groups in American history in which women outnumbered men. Those who did not work in factories labored as domestic servants, in ways that were quite different from the traditional means by which housewives had arranged for assistance in their domestic tasks. In preindustrial America, the housewife had turned to young neighbors or kin as "helps" in her domestic obligations. Lucy Larcom worked for her sister in this traditional capacity whenever the downturns in factory conditions were too much for her. But in industrializing America, especially as the numbers of Irish immigrants grew, mistress and maid were becoming separated by a much greater cultural and economic gap and losing their sense of common task and purpose. In 1852, Elizabeth Cady Stanton, founding mother of the American women's rights movement (see Chapter 4), complained of the "two undeveloped Hibernians in my kitchen" whose ignorance of modern household procedures she felt powerless to remedy.[23] To the industrious, Protestant, Yankee middle-class housewife, the Irish "girls" who she hired to cook and clean and do laundry seemed like nothing more than dirty, ignorant, and immoral Catholics.

In the relationship between mistress and maid, the path of the native-born, middle-class, true woman crossed that of the immigrant, wage-earning woman, and more often than not the relation was troubled. The divide between mistress and maid could almost be said to define the class distinction among women. Complaints about the difficulty of finding or keeping "good help" was a staple of middle-class female culture (see Figure 3.5, p. 187). Female benevolent societies formed to protect young working girls from the threat of poverty did so by arranging for their employment, not in factories, but in their benefactors' kitchens. However, the objects of their charity rarely regarded domestic service as a privilege. Domestic servants' habits of working erratically, changing employers often,

and presenting a sullen demeanor were means of protesting a form of employment they did not like and that was not respected in democratic America, where
the deference expected in personal service already had given it a bad name. Their
employers could never understand why, even when wages were competitive, their
domestic servants did their best to switch to factory employment. There, though
the workday was long and the labor hard, the job ended with the dismissal bell and
a young woman's time became her own; she could go out with her friends, away
from her boss's watchful eye.

At the very bottom of the economic ladder, beneath even the lower rungs of
domestic service, were the urban poor. Often the newest immigrants, these people
could scarcely find enough work to pay for basic food and shelter. America had
long had its poor people, but this destitute class was new, as it included able-
bodied people willing but unable to find work that would support themselves and
their families The most desperate of the urban poor were the women with children but without men (or, more precisely, without access to the higher wages a
man could earn). Such women were seen on the streets of the cities, begging for
pennies or scavenging for wood or coal. These poor urban women were the absolute antithesis of the true woman. The rooms in which they lived could hardly
be called homes: they were not furnished, clean, or private. Their children were
not sheltered and watched over but went into the streets or worked for a pittance
to help support their families. Their housework was especially difficult: they carried water for laundry or coal for warmth or small amounts of food for dinner or
raw materials for home manufacture up steps into tiny tenement apartments or
down into cellar spaces (where 29,000 lived in New York City as of 1850).[24] After
each downturn of the industrial economy, the numbers of urban poor swelled.

About the only positive function respectable Americans attributed to the poor
was to serve as the objects of benevolence for middle-class women. A Society for
the Relief of Poor Widows, formed in New York City in 1799, was the first charity
organized by women for women.[25] The charitable ladies did not provide outright
cash or employment, instead dispensing spiritual and moral ministrations along
with occasional food, coal, and clothing. In such exchanges, just as in the relationship between mistress and maid, middle-class and poor women met each other
across the class divide, probably struck more with what separated them than with
what they allegedly shared by virtue of their common gender (see Chapter 4).

WOMEN AND SLAVERY

Perhaps the greatest irony embedded in the dynamic beginnings of industrial capitalism is the degree to which it rested on a very different social and economic system that also thrived in early nineteenth-century America: chattel slavery. By 1800,
as states from New England to Pennsylvania and Delaware abolished slavery, the
institution had become identified exclusively with the South. Even so, a great deal
linked the North with the South. The gigantic cotton crop grown by slave labor literally fueled the textile industry of New England. Among the greatest advocates of

American democracy were numerous southern slaveholders, including four of this country's first five presidents. And at many levels, the regions shared a national culture. Their citizens read the same books and magazines, worshipped in the same Protestant denominations, and voted for the same political parties. Southern white women followed many essentials of the cult of domesticity. But underlying these similarities were fundamental differences, signifying a conflict between regions that eventually led to civil war.

The absence in the South of the wage relationship between producer and capitalist lay at the heart of these sectional differences. There were great profits accumulated in the South, and much of what was produced there was intended for sale. But the workers of the system were not paid any wages for their labor. They were *chattel* slaves, not only owned but the value of whose current and future labor, along with the land they worked, constituted the wealth of their owners. Like the factory buildings and machines that produced wealth in the Northeast, they were capital; but they were also human beings.

Far more than even the most impoverished, degraded wage worker in the North, slaves were forbidden the basic elements of personal freedom—to live with their own families, to move about, to be educated, to marry and raise children—not to mention the loftier rights of citizenship. The slaves were traded as valuable commodities, objects of a legal commerce that was recognized by the laws of all the southern states and protected by the careful wording of the U.S. Constitution. Indeed, the Constitution, in permitting legislation ending the transatlantic slave trade after 1808 and relegating the institution of slavery entirely to the states, laid the foundation for an enormous commerce in slaves within this country. The profitable, vigorous internal market in slaves touched the lives of virtually all persons of African descent in the United States, for each man and woman experienced either being sold, the fear of being sold, or the heartrending knowledge of a loved one being sold. The auction block loomed over all.

Plantation Patriarchy

Slaveowning was by no means evenly distributed in the South. Although percentages varied across regions, slave ownership in the nineteenth century was being concentrated in the hands of fewer and fewer whites. Only an estimated 25 percent of southern white families owned any slaves as of 1860; of these, only a small minority owned enough to qualify for elite status and significant political and economic power. These were the great slave plantations, the large concentrations of land and labor that formed the core of southern slave society (see Map 3.1). On plantations, slaves were organized into large work gangs in which they worked to produce the cotton, rice, sugar, and tobacco that made the South wealthy. These plantations were not only the economic core but the social, political, and cultural center of slave society. In general, the nineteenth-century slave South did not develop the dynamic civil society that flourished in this period in the North. The growth of an industrial economy and a wage labor class were limited to a few urban centers, such as Richmond and Atlanta. With the sole exception of party

◆ **Map 3.1 Distribution of the Slave Population in 1860**
The cotton boom shifted enslaved African Americans to the Old Southwest. In 1790, most slaves lived and worked on the tobacco plantations of the Chesapeake and in the rice and indigo areas of South Carolina. By 1860, the centers of slavery lay along the Mississippi River and in an arc of fertile cotton land sweeping from Mississippi through Georgia.

politics, which wealthy men dominated, public life did not thrive. As a result, plantation women's lives varied dramatically from those of northern women.

To begin with, family life was different. On the great plantations, the ideological distinction between public and private, work and family—much touted in the North—did not really exist. The plantation was residence and factory simultaneously, and the white male head of household presided over both. Instead of the mutually exclusive but allegedly equal gender roles dictated by the northern culture of domesticity, slave society was proudly patriarchal, with men's social and political power derived from their leadership in the home. Wealthy white southern men were fiercely jealous of the honor of their women and their families and were notorious for their willingness to resort to violence to avenge any perceived slights against them. Female deference to male authority was considered a virtue, and any moral superiority that women could claim gave them no social or political authority. Inasmuch as wealthy women left their childrearing to their slaves, maternity was neither revered nor sentimentalized.

Slave men and women were crucial to this plantation patriarchy: they were regarded by their owners not just as workers but as permanent children—amusing, guileless, but lacking in judgment and authority. By this obfuscating ideology, the plantation community was treated as a single, large family, with master-parents and slave-children, bound by devotion and reciprocal obligations of service and protection. One white woman, writing about her father's plantation, truly believed that "the family servants, inherited for generations, had come to be regarded with great affection. . . . The bond between master and servant was, in many cases, felt to be as sacred and close as the tie of blood."[26] When slavery was abolished, masters and mistresses were often astounded to discover the degree of hostility their slaves felt toward them.

Plantation patriarchy was a gender and family system, but one organized around racial difference and inequality. The structures and inequalities of race, much like those of gender, were so omnipresent as to seem natural and god-given. Black equaled slave and was understood as the opposite not only of white but of free. For this reason, it is important to recognize that although black was equated with slavery and white with freedom, by 1830 there were a third of a million black people who were not slaves, half of them living in the South. The lives of these people and their claims to free status were deeply compromised by the power of slavery and racial inequality. In the South they were required to have passes to travel from county to county, kept out of certain occupations, forbidden to carry firearms, and denied the right to assembly. Even in the North, where a small black urban middle class emerged in Philadelphia, New York, and Boston, most free blacks occupied the lowest ranks of wage labor as common laborers, dock workers, and, among women, domestic servants.

Despite slave society's insistence that the racial divide was absolute, the line that separated "black" from "white" was constantly being breached. White masters could—and certainly did—compel black slave women to have sexual relations. When a slave gave birth to a master's child, how was the racial divide on which slave patriarchy was premised to be maintained? The legal answer was that the child followed the status of the mother, slave if she was slave, free if (far more rarely) she was free. This simple legal answer to a complex set of social relations hidden within slave society had enormous implications for the lives of southern women, black and white. While slavery is usually considered a system for organizing labor and producing profit, it was also a way of organizing and restraining sexual and reproductive relations, of controlling who could have sex—and legitimate children—with whom. In other words, managing race necessitated managing gender and sexuality.

Plantation Mistresses

This linkage between racial inequality and gender ideals is seen in the effusive literary and rhetorical praise devoted to the southern white feminine ideal. Elite white women in plantation society were elevated to a lofty pedestal that was the ideological inverse of the auction block on which slave women's fate was sealed. As

◆ **Charlotte Forten Grimké**
As a member of the tiny antebellum black middle class, Charlotte Forten (later Grimké) combined belief in the ideals of true womanhood and political and social activism on behalf of her race. She was born in 1837 into a relatively prosperous and politically active family in Philadelphia and was educated in Salem, Massachusetts. During the Civil War, she traveled to Union-controlled islands off the coast of South Carolina to teach emancipated slaves and kept a fascinating diary of her experience there. She married Francis Grimké, whose father and former owner was the brother of white abolitionists Sarah and Angelina Grimké. *Photographs and Prints Division, Schomburg Center for Research in Black Culture, The New York Public Library, Astor, Lenox, and Tilden Foundations.*

in the North, the idealized white woman was supposed to be selfless, pure, pious, and possessed of great, if subtle, influence over husband and sons. But the difference in the South was that white women's purity was defined by its contrast to the condition of black slave women.

As slavery came under more and more open criticism from northern opponents during the nineteenth century, rhetorical devotion to elite white women's leisure and culture, to the preservation of their beauty and their sexual innocence, and to their protection from all distress and labor intensified. The message seemed to be that the purity of elite white womanhood, rather than the enslavement of black people, was the core value of southern society. "We behold," proclaimed southern writer Thomas Dew, "the marked efficiency of slavery on the conditions of woman—we find her at once elevated, clothed with all her charms, mingling with and directing the society to which she belongs, no longer the slave, but the equal and the idol of man."[27] For the most part, women of the slaveholding class also held to the opinion that a lady's life on a southern plantation was a great privilege. Greater political and economic rights for white women were "but a piece of negro emancipation," declared Louisa McCord, daughter of an important South

Carolina slaveholder and politician, in 1852.[28] She was sure that women like herself wanted no part of such a movement.

Whereas in the North, womanly virtues were meant to be universal, in the South, they were proudly exclusionary, applicable only to the few, a mark of the natural superiority of the elite and their right to own and command the labor of others. While the northern true woman was praised for her industrious domesticity, in the South a real lady was not allowed to sully herself or risk her charms with any actual labor, which was the mark of the slave. Leisure was especially the privilege of the unmarried young woman of the slaveholding class, who was not only spared any household obligations but was relieved of even the most intimate of responsibilities—dressing herself, for instance—by the presence of personal slaves. "Surrounded with them ["Negroes"] from infancy, they form a part of the landscape of a Southern woman's life," one woman recalled long after slavery had ended. "They watch our cradles; they are the companions of our sports; it is they who aid our bridal decorations; and they wrap us in our shrouds."[29]

Once a woman married, however, she took on managerial responsibility for the household. Unlike their husbands, who hired overseers to manage slaves in the fields, plantation mistresses themselves oversaw the labor of the household slaves and the feeding, clothing, and doctoring of the entire labor force. One admittedly unusual plantation mistress, who insisted that she was more put upon than privileged by the ownership of slaves, recalled that when she heard the news of the Emancipation Proclamation, she exclaimed, "Thank heaven! I too shall be free at last!"[30]

Because slavery was a labor system in which there were no positive incentives for hard work, the management of workers relied almost entirely on threats, punishment, and beating. Within the household, the discipline of slaves was the responsibility of the mistress. The association of allegedly delicate womanhood with brutal violence was a disturbing aspect of the slave system, even to its most passionate adherents. Opponents of slavery played endlessly on this theme to indicate the fundamental corruption of the system, which reached even to the women of slaveholding families. "There are *female tyrants* too, who are prompt to lay their complaints of misconduct before their husbands, brothers, and sons, and to urge them to commit acts of violence against their helpless slaves," wrote Angelina Grimké, daughter of a powerful southern slaveowner, who left the South in 1829 to fight against the system (see Chapter 4). "Other mistresses who cannot bear that their delicate ears should be pained by the screams of the poor sufferers, write an order to the master of the Charleston workhouse . . . to render the stroke of the whip or the blow of the paddle more certain to produce cuts and wounds."[31]

In the South, as in the North, free married women were legally prohibited from the privileges of property ownership. Changing this practice was one of the initial goals of the American women's rights movement, within which southern white women, committed to the plantation patriarchy, were notoriously absent (see Chapter 4). Thus there is considerable irony in the fact that the first states to liberalize property ownership for married women were in the South and were motivated by concern for the protection of slave property. Far more than middle-class northern women, elite southern women were expected to bring dowries—wealth packages—into their marriages, and it was not uncommon for a young woman to bring into her new home slaves from her parents' plantation. This was one of the many ways in which slaves were separated from their own families. To protect their daughters—and the family property that had been transferred with them—against spendthrift husbands, southern patriarchs modified married women's property laws to allow wives to retain title to inherited property. Mississippi was the first state to do so in 1823, twenty-five years before married women's property laws were reformed in response to pressure from women's rights activists in New York State.

In all other ways, however, the slave system made for more severe constraints on free women than in the North. The rhetorical weight that rested on elite white women's purity meant that women's independent public activities were far more limited than outside of the South. In contrast to northern factory operatives and teachers in this period, there was no form of money earning available to respectable southern white women. Marriage was literally the only option available to leave the parental home, and women who remained unmarried faced futures as marginal members of the households of their married kin. Slaveholding men were free to come and go from their plantations, but their wives could travel only in their company. Whatever education existed for young women was oriented to the ornamental graces rather than more serious subjects. The sorts of benevolent societies that northern middle-class women formed to care for the indigent and poor did not exist in the South, although plantation mistresses, defensive about whether they were sufficiently benevolent, frequently claimed that the care and feeding of their own slaves constituted an equivalent moral responsibility.

For the most part, slaveholding women and men did not regard themselves as heading up a brutal and inhumane system. On the contrary, they were convinced that the society over which they presided, which elevated them to lives of such enviable grace and culture, was the best of all possible worlds, certainly better than the lives led by money-grubbing capitalists and degraded wage workers in the North. They regarded their slaves as well treated compared to the northern wage earners, whom they believed were ignored and eventually abandoned, their welfare of no concern to bosses who wanted only to exploit their labor and then dispose of them. "How enviable were our solidarity as a people, our prosperity and the moral qualities that are characteristic of the South," one southern matron mourned many years after the Civil War. Even in retrospect, white southerners' "love of home, their chivalrous respect for women, their courage, their delicate sense of honour, their constancy . . . [all] are things by which the more mercurial people of the North may take a lesson."[32]

Non-Elite White Women

While the power of southern society lay in the hands of the plantation elite, the majority of whites were not large slaveholders. Indeed, something like three-quarters of all white families owned no slaves and relied on their own labor to farm, occasionally hiring a slave or two from a neighbor. Even the great majority of those who did own slaves were working farmers themselves, living and laboring alongside the few slaves they owned. These small, self-sufficient farmers are often called yeomen, a British term signifying the nonnoble agricultural classes. The slave system would not have worked without the active support of the many white people who did not directly profit from it. Non-elite white men patrolled the roads for runaway slaves, voted in favor of aggressively proslavery state governments, and served as overseers and skilled craftsmen on the great plantations.

Women on the small farms and modest households of the South had much less interaction with planter culture than did their husbands. About the only role they played on the great plantations was occasionally as midwives and nurses for slave women. There was no common women's culture that linked them to plantation mistresses—another difference with the North. Indeed, the class gap between elite and non-elite whites was clearest when it came to women's roles. While elite women lived lives of leisure in their grand plantation houses, women of the yeoman class worked very hard both outside and inside their small homes. They continued to produce mainly for their own family's consumption, for instance, spinning and wearing homespun long after northern farm women were purchasing factory-made cloth. They sold a smaller portion of their produce for cash than in the North. About the only thing that took such non-elite southern women away from their homes and farms was church. And even there, they lacked the numerous voluntary activities and associations that Protestant women formed in the North in pursuit of moral uplift.

Men of the southern yeoman class had few or no slaves over whom to establish the patriarchal authority that was so crucial to masculinity in slave society. But they did have wives, and female subordination was prized in this sector of southern society. If the difference between the lives of non-elite and elite women was one of the most pronounced markers of class distinction among southern whites, the ethic of male headship bonded white men of both classes, despite their economic differences. "As masters of dependents, even if only, or perhaps if especially, of wives and children," one historian observes, "every freeman was bound to defend his household, his property, against invasion."[33]

Slave Women

When we recall de Tocqueville's confident assertion in 1830 that American women were so privileged and honored that they "never labor in the fields," we begin to see the degree to which the slave women of the South were not only ignored in all the sweeping generalizations of true womanhood but conceptually were excluded from the category of "woman" altogether. Ninety percent of the slave women of the South labored in the cotton, sugar, tobacco, and rice fields that generated the region's wealth. Plantation patriarchy extolled an image of slaves who provided personal and domestic service in their own households (see Figures 3.11 and 3.12, pp. 194 and 195), but these were a small minority. It was the giant mass of agricultural slaves on whom the power of the planter class rested.

Nowhere in early nineteenth-century America was labor less separated by gender than in the fields of the plantation South. Slave women and men hoed and planted and reaped alongside each other in gangs that worked, as the saying went, "from sunup to sundown." For purposes of accounting and sale, women were regarded as partial hands, but the lore of the plantation is full of stories of individual women famous for their strength and ability to work as hard as any man. A former slave remembered that her mother "could do anything. She cooked, washed, ironed, spun, nursed, and labored in the field. She made as good a field hand as she did a cook." Her daughter recalled, with some pride, that her master said about her that "she can outwork any nigger in the country. I'd bet my life on that."[34] On the larger plantations, where some specialization of labor was possible, slave men practiced skills such as blacksmithing and carpentering while individual women might gain reputations as slave midwives, but overall, the demands of slave labor made little distinction by sex. Even among household slaves, estimated at about 10 percent of the labor force of the South, gender lines were not strong: men served as personal valets, as butlers, and occasionally even as nursemaids for their owners' young sons.

In other ways, however, slave women's lives were distinguished from those of slave men's. Considerable evidence suggests that the vulnerabilities of their sex were exploited when they were beaten. Numerous stories record that slave women's skirts were raised over their heads before whippings, presumably to humiliate them and perhaps to make their physical sufferings greater. Only at the very end of a slave woman's pregnancy might she be spared the worst whippings, and only then to protect her baby who, when born, would be worth a great deal to the slave owner. Similarly, field labor was suspended just briefly after childbirth. Northern visitors commented frequently on the sight of a slave woman too old to labor bringing infants to the fields so that their young mothers could nurse them quickly and return to work. When beatings failed to discipline female slaves who resisted yielding to their masters' control, sale was an even greater threat, especially if it meant separating a woman from her child. A runaway slave told the story of a Maryland woman who was punished for resisting her master in all these ways: after beating her, the master controlled her by "taking away her clothes and locking them up. . . . He kept her at work with only what she could pick up to tie on her for decency. He took away her child which had just begun to walk. . . . He waited [to whip her] until she was confined [pregnant]."[35]

As chattels rather than persons with legal rights, slaves were not permitted binding marriage contracts, which might interfere with the master's right to buy and sell them away from their husbands or wives. Nonetheless, men and women under slavery went to great lengths to sustain conjugal and parental relationships. Frequently, such bonds extended between plantations, linking women and men who belonged to different masters. In these so-called abroad marriages, it usually fell to the man to visit his wife and children. Often traveling at night without his master's knowledge or permission, the abroad husband risked punishment, whipping, and even being sold away to maintain links to his family. (See Documents:

Two Slave Love Stories, pp. 175–81). Slaves had their own ritual for solemnizing their marriages, by together "jumping the broom." Masters might attend such ceremonies and even amuse themselves by providing for elaborate slave weddings that mimicked their own. But everyone understood that the bottom line was the slave's status as property, not her emotional attachment to another slave. When the Civil War ended slavery in the South, many African Americans showed extraordinary determination in traveling great distances to find spouses long lost to sale (see Chapter 5).

Motherhood also distinguished the lives of slave women from those of slave men. For slave women, childbearing was simultaneously the source of their greatest personal satisfaction and their greatest misery, the latter because their children ultimately belonged to the master. This was the tragic irony of the system's perversely matrilineal rule that a child followed the condition of its mother into slavery. Slave mothers had the immensely difficult task of teaching their children to survive their owners' power and at the same time to know their own worth as human beings. From many decades later, one woman remembered how her mother spoke to her daily about the cruelties of slavery. Still young enough to be treated as her owners' pet, the child did not believe her mother until the master announced that her mother was to be sold away. "I felt for the first time in my life that I had been abused," the child recalled. "My mother had been right. Slavery was cruel, so very cruel."[36]

Most of the direct testimony about the power of the auction block to sever the relation between slave mothers and children comes from the perspective of the child, but there are other sorts of evidence that some women did whatever they could to terminate their pregnancies or even kill their infants rather than give birth for slaveowners. We can never know the number of such women, but individual examples tell much. Margaret Garner, a Kentucky slave woman who escaped to Ohio in 1856, became the most notorious of these avenging mothers in the nineteenth century when she slit the throat of her youngest child in anticipation of their being recaptured and sent back South. Known at the time as the Black Medea, her story became the core of Toni Morrison's great modern slave tragedy, *Beloved* (1987).

There was much suspicion at the time that Garner's master was also the father of her children. Sexual relations between male masters and slave women were an open secret in the South, heartily denied by slaveowners and yet virtually endemic to the society. The light complexions and white features of numerous nineteenth-century slaves were eloquent testimony to this intimate connection between slave and master. Mary Boykin Chesnut, a member of the South Carolina slaveholding aristocracy whose diaries are much quoted by historians for what they reveal about slave society's contradictions, understood and wrote of this hidden reality (see box, "Slavery a Curse to Any Land").

While running afoul of Christian morality, the sexual exploitation of slave women by their masters was encouraged by everything else about the slave system: that the master was the legal owner of the slave woman's sexuality and

◆ **Mary Boykin Chesnut**

Mary Boykin Chesnut is one of the few individual women of the plantation class who is known to historians. This rare, early photograph was taken in 1847, soon after she married James Chesnut, an up-and-coming South Carolina politician. Mary was only seventeen at the time. Both she and James came from families that owned numerous slaves. Living in her mother-in-law's home, Mary had much time for observation, conversation, and writing. Perhaps it is possible to see in her face the unflinching intelligence that made her the most important chronicler of domestic relations in the slave South. *Mulberry Plantation, Camden, South Carolina.*

reproductive capacity along with her labor; that any child born of a slave woman was also a slave, thus benefiting the master financially as well as sexually; and that a slave woman could occasionally gain small favors for herself or her children through sexual relations with her master. In one of the best-known accounts of a master's assaults on a female slave, Harriet Jacobs described how, when she was only fifteen, her master began to insist that she have sexual relations with him (see box, "Trials of Girlhood"). In the end, she thwarted her master's intentions but only by finding another older white man to become her lover, a moral compromise for which she remained deeply ashamed the rest of her life. Modern DNA analysis has strengthened suspicion that even Thomas Jefferson, author of the Declaration of Independence and fourth president of the United States, was implicated in the sexual and reproductive underside of slavery. The likelihood that he began a long sexual relationship with his slave Sally Hemings when she was only fourteen and had several children with her suggests how commonplace were masters' appropriation of their female slaves' bodies. Modern efforts to render the Hemings-Jefferson relationship as a great interracial love story ignore the absolutely unrestrained white male power around which such associations were structured.

The issue of deliberate breeding was an explosive one in the slave South. Opponents of slavery accused owners of encouraging and arranging pregnancies among their female slaves so as to produce more slaves to sell on the lucrative internal slave market. Evidence suggests that they were right. "Marsa used to sometimes pick our wives fo' us," former slave Charles Grandy recalled. "Marsa would stop de old nigger-trader and buy you a woman. . . . All he wanted was a young healthy one who looked

MARY BOYKIN CHESNUT
Slavery a Curse to Any Land

The diary kept by the South Carolina slave mistress Mary Boykin Chesnut (1823–1886) has long been regarded as a major source for insight into the minds of southern slaveholders. More recently, historians have explored Chesnut's views on the position of the women of this class. In writing about the hidden but extensive sexual relations between slaveholding men and their female slaves, she is far more resentful than sympathetic to slave women.

March 14, 1861: I wonder if it be a sin to think slavery a curse to any land. . . . we live surrounded by prostitutes. An abandoned woman is sent out of any decent house elsewhere. Who thinks any worse of a Negro or Mulatto woman for being a thing we can't name. God forgive us, but ours is a monstrous system & wrong & iniquity. Perhaps the rest of the world is as bad. This is only what I see: like the patriarchs of old, our men live all in one house with their wives & their concubines, & the Mulattos one sees in every family exactly resemble the white children—& every lady tells you who is the father of all the Mulatto children in everybody's household, but those in her own, she seems to think drop from the clouds or pretends so to think—. . . . My disgust sometimes is boiling over—. . . . Thank God for my countrywomen—alas for the men! No worse than men everywhere, but the lower their mistresses, the more degraded they must be.

SOURCE: Mary Boykin Chesnut, *A Diary from Dixie* (Boston: Houghton Mifflin, 1949), 21.

like she could have children, whether she was purty or ugly as sin."[37] The southern elite understandably resented the charges that they deliberately bred the slaves whom they claimed to protect, but the economic development of slavery in its last decades certainly points in this direction. In the nineteenth century, slavery expanded south and west into what was called the "new" or "lower" South (western Georgia, Florida, Alabama, Arkansas, Mississippi, Louisiana, and Texas). Meanwhile, in the older southern states such as Virginia, Maryland, and the Carolinas, as exhausted soils and changing agricultural practices decreased the need for slave labor, slaves themselves became a surplus to be sold. Women of childbearing age who were described as "good breeders" brought a higher price on the auction block.

HARRIET JACOBS
Trials of Girlhood

Harriet Jacobs (1813–1897) was born a slave in North Carolina. From the age of twelve, she was sexually harassed by an older white man who wanted her as his concubine. After a decade, she escaped from his home, but because of her attachment to her children, she stayed nearby, hidden in the cramped attic room of relatives. There she remained for seven years until she and her daughter finally fled the South. So extraordinary was Jacobs's story that its legitimacy was long doubted, but recent historians have substantiated virtually everything about her story, including her authorship.

I now entered on my fifteenth year—a sad epoch in the life of a slave girl. My master began to whisper foul words in my ear. Young as I was, I could not remain ignorant of their import. I tried to treat them with indifference or contempt. . . . He was a crafty man, and resorted to many means to accomplish his purposes. Sometimes he had stormy, terrific ways, that made his victims tremble; sometimes he assumed a gentleness that he thought must surely subdue. Of the two, I preferred his stormy moods, although they left me trembling. He tried his utmost to corrupt the pure principles my grandmother had instilled. He peopled my young mind with unclean images, such as only a vile monster could think of. I turned from him with disgust and hatred. But he was my master. I was compelled to live under the same roof with him—where I saw a man forty

Any hope that the bonds of gender might have crossed the boundaries of race and class was crushed by the burden that slave concubinage laid on southern society. Jealous or suspicious mistresses took out on their slaves the anger and rage they dared not express to their husbands. Harriet Jacobs feared her mistress every bit as much as she did her master. Female slaves who worked in the plantation house were at the greatest risk, exposed day in and day out to the mistress's moods. Slave narratives frequently describe an impatient or intolerant mistress striking out at a cook or a nursemaid or even a slave child unable to handle an assigned task. In their diaries and letters, slaveowning white women recorded their secret fears of violent retribution from slaves. As Civil War was breaking out, Mary Boykin Chesnut wrote anxiously about the death of a cousin who, it was suspected, had been "murdered by her own people."[38]

Although both black and white women suffered in the slave system, slave women knew they could expect no sympathy from their mistresses. The luxury and culture of the white southern woman were premised on the forced labor and

years my senior daily violating the most sacred commandments of nature. He told me I was his property; that I must be subject to his will in all things. My soul revolted against the mean tyranny. But where could I turn for protection? No matter whether the slave girl be as black as ebony or as fair as her mistress. In either case, there is no shadow of law to protect her from insult, from violence, or even from death; all these are inflicted by fiends who bear the shape of men. The mistress, who ought to protect the helpless victim, has no other feelings towards her but those of jealousy and rage. The degradation, the wrongs, the vices, that grow out of slavery, are more than I can describe. They are greater than you would willingly believe. . . .

Even the little child, who is accustomed to wait on her mistress and her children, will learn, before she is twelve years old, why it is that her mistress hates such and such a one among the slaves. Perhaps the child's own mother is among those hated ones. She listens to violent outbreaks of jealous passion, and cannot help understanding what is the cause. She will become prematurely knowing in evil things. Soon she will learn to tremble when she hears her master's footfall. She will be compelled to realize that she is no longer a child. If God has bestowed beauty upon her, it will prove her greatest curse. That which commands admiration in the white woman only hastens the degradation of the female slave. . . .

SOURCE: Harriet Jacobs, *Incidents in the Life of a Slave Girl: Seven Years Concealed* (Boston: published for the author, 1861), ch. 5.

sexual oppression of her slaves. Violence against and violations of slave women mocked southern deference to womanhood and female sexual purity. With only the rarest of exceptions, slavery turned black and white women against each other and set their interests and their perspectives in direct opposition.

CONCLUSION: True Womanhood and the Reality of Women's Lives

Perhaps at no other time in American history were the prescriptions for a properly domestic role for women more precise and widely agreed upon than during antebellum America. Much of the young country's hope for stability and prosperity rested on the belief in a universally achievable middle-class family order, with the devoted, selfless wife and mother at the center.

As we shall see, some women were able to use the ideas of true womanhood to expand their sphere in subtle ways, but even so, this ideology was exceedingly rigid and limiting, ignoring the reality of women who led very different sorts of lives in antebellum America. Factory operatives were outside the boundaries of acceptable womanhood because they lived and worked in what *Godey's Lady's Book* editor Sarah Josepha Hale called "the accursed bank note world" that only men were supposed to occupy.[39] And slave women were deprived—absolutely—of the protection and privileges that were meant to compensate true women for their limited sphere. While the rhetoric of true womanhood seemed to place domestic women at the heart of American society, in reality the giant processes in which these other women were caught up—industrialization and slavery—were the dynamic forces shaping the young American nation and foreshadowing the trends and crises of its future.

DOCUMENTS

Prostitution in New York City, 1858

As chief physician in the 1850s for the "lock hospital" to which New York City prostitutes were sent when they ran afoul of the law or were suspected of spreading venereal disease, Dr. William Sanger had both knowledge of and compassion for the women he attended. Hopeful that more accurate information about prostitution would help to eradicate it, he interviewed two thousand prostitutes, using a carefully drawn up set of questions. He was determined to bring the facts of prostitution into the light of day and to convey the prostitutes' experiences and ideas by including numerous individual accounts. The originals of Sanger's interviews were destroyed in a fire the year after he gathered them, so his report to the trustees of the New York Alms House provides the closest we have to firsthand accounts from the prostitutes themselves. Interestingly, he did no research into the men who were the prostitutes' clientele.

Sanger's sample, although not chosen by random selection, was large enough to allow for statistical generalizations as well. These, too, are rare historical sources; they are among the first statistics available to us about nineteenth-century women's lives. Even the federal census taken every ten years, a method of numerical fact gathering required by the U.S. Constitution, was still very primitive in form in the mid-nineteenth century, first recording the individual occupations of women only in 1850. Among the generalizations Sanger's data allowed him to make were the following: most prostitutes were from fifteen to twenty years old; three-fifths were native born; among the immigrants, 60 percent were Irish; one-fifth were married; half had children; half were or had been domestic servants; half were afflicted with syphilis; the average length of life after entering prostitution was four years.

Sanger estimated that six thousand women were engaged in commercial sex in New York City, a number based on his careful survey of police records, lock hospitals, and known brothels. Prostitution disturbed middle-class observers so much that they saw it everywhere, and extraordinarily inflated numbers, as high as one-tenth of all New York women, were common. Despite his restraint, the numbers Sanger presented were still distressing. As Sanger repeatedly insisted, they reflected not the inherent lack of virtue of the prostitutes themselves but rather the relentless financial pressure on poor urban women. The effects of a sharp economic depression in 1857 are detected everywhere in the prostitutes' descriptions of their situations.

Despite Sanger's best efforts, his own middle-class attitudes to prostitution occasionally overtook the experience and voices of the prostitutes themselves. Sanger believed that women were too often blamed for prostitution; he wanted to show that they were the victims, both of men's callousness and their own lack of economic opportunity. Despite these reformist sentiments, however, Sanger held conventional notions of femininity. Indeed, he championed prostitutes because he was certain that most women would never of their own accord undertake a life of casual, public, nonmarital sex. Rather, he believed, they must have been deserted, seduced, driven by destitution, or forced into prostitution by some other extraordinary event over which they had no control. Underlying his compassion for those who were remorseful, the traces of a harsher set of judgments can be found. Women who were openly, straightforwardly sexual remained in his judgment a moral blight. Thus Sanger's report can be read as evidence of middle-class attitudes toward sexuality, poverty, and gender as well as of prostitutes' own experience.

What follows is Sanger's summary and analysis of the answers given to one of his most revealing questions, "What are the causes of your becoming a prostitute?" He begins with aggregate numbers and then moves on to more individual responses. As you read, think about how Sanger arrived at the categories into which he grouped his respondents' answers and what he means by each of them. Looking beyond Sanger's own assumptions, consider how the elaborate personal stories that he relates and the words that he quotes indicate a more complicated set of explanations for individual women's entry into prostitution.

WILLIAM W. SANGER
The History of Prostitution: Its Extent, Causes, and Effects throughout the World (1858)

[Question:] *What are the causes of your becoming a prostitute? . . .*

Causes	Numbers
Inclination	513
Destitution	525
Seduced and abandoned	258
Drink, and the desire to drink	181
Ill-treatment of parents, relatives, or husbands	164
As an easy life	124
Bad company	84
Persuaded by prostitutes	71
Too idle to work	29
Violated	27
Seduced on board emigrant ships	16
Seduced in emigrant boarding houses	8
Total	2000

SOURCE: William W. Sanger, *The History of Prostitution: Its Extent, Causes, and Effects throughout the World* (New York: Medical Publishing, 1921), 488–522.

This question is probably the most important of the series, as the replies lay open to a considerable extent those hidden springs of evil which have hitherto been known only from their results. First in order stands the reply *"Inclination,"* which can only be understood as meaning a voluntary resort to prostitution in order to gratify the sexual passions. . . . The force of desire can neither be denied nor disputed, but still in the bosoms of most females that force exists in a slumbering state until aroused by some outside influences. . . . In the male sex nature has provided a more susceptible organization than in females, apparently with the beneficent design of repressing those evils which must result from mutual appetite equally felt by both. In other words, man is the *aggressive* animal, so far as sexual desire is involved. Were it otherwise, and the passions in both sexes equal, illegitimacy and prostitution would be far more rife in our midst than at present.

Some few of the cases in which the reply *"Inclination"* was given are herewith submitted, with the explanation which accompanied each return. C. M.: while virtuous, this girl had visited dance-houses, where she became acquainted with prostitutes, who persuaded her that they led an easy, merry life; her inclination was the result of female persuasion. E. C. left her husband, and became a prostitute willingly, in order to obtain intoxicating liquors which had been refused her at home. E. R. was deserted by her husband because she drank to excess and became a prostitute in order to obtain liquor.... Enough has been quoted to prove that, in many of the cases, what is called willing prostitution is the sequel of some communication or circumstances which undermine the principles of virtue and arouse the latent passions.

Destitution is assigned as a reason in five hundred and twenty-five cases. In many of these it is unquestionably true that positive, actual want, the apparent and dreaded approach of starvation, was the real cause of degradation....

During the progress of this investigation in one of the lower wards of the city, attention was drawn to a pale but interesting-looking girl, about seventeen years of age, from whose replies the following narrative, is condensed, retaining her own words as nearly as possible.

"I have been leading this life from about the middle of last January (1856). It was absolute want that drove me to it. My sister, who was about three years older than I am, lived with me. She was deformed and crippled from a fall she had while a child, and could not do any hard work.... One very cold morning, just after I had been to the store, the landlord's agent called for some rent we owed, and told us that, if we could not pay it, we should have to move. The agent was a kind man, and gave us a little money to buy some coals. We did not know what we were to do, and were both crying about it, when the woman who keeps this house (where she was then living) came in and brought some sewing for us to do that day. She said that she had been recommended to us by a woman who lived in the same house, but I found out since that she had watched me, and only said this for an excuse. When the

work was done I brought it home here. I had heard of such places before, but had never been inside one. I was very cold, and she made me sit down by the fire, and began to talk to me, saying how much better off I should be if I would come and live with her.... When I got home and saw my sister so sick as she was and wanting many little things that we had no money to buy, and no friends to help us to, my heart almost broke. However, I said nothing to her then. I laid awake all night thinking, and in the morning I made up my mind to come here.... I thought that, if I had been alone, I would sooner have starved, but I could not bear to see her suffering. She only lived a few weeks after I came here. I broke her heart. I do not like the life. I would do almost any thing to get out of it; but, now that I have once done *wrong*, I can not get any one to give me work, and I must stop here unless I wish to be starved to death."

These details give some insight into the under-current of city life. The most prominent fact is that a large number of females, both operatives and domestics, earn so small wages that a temporary cessation of their business, or being a short time out of a situation, is sufficient to reduce them to absolute distress. Provident habits are useless in their cases; for, much as they may feel the necessity, *they have nothing to save,* and the very day that they encounter a reverse sees them penniless. The struggle a virtuous girl will wage against fate in such circumstances may be conceived: it is a literal battle for life, and in the result life is too often preserved only by the sacrifice of virtue....

Moralists say that all human passions should be held in check by reason and virtue, and none can deny the truthfulness of the assertion. But while they apply the sentiment to the weaker party, who is the sufferer, would it not be advisable to recommend the same restraining influences to him who is the inflictor? No woman possessed of the smallest share of decency or the slightest appreciation of virtue would voluntarily surrender herself without some powerful motive, not pre-existent in herself, but imparted by her destroyer. Well aware of the world's opinion, she would not recklessly defy it, and precipitate herself into an abyss of degradation and shame unless some overruling influence had urged her forward. This motive and this influence, it is believed, may be uniformly traced to her weak but truly feminine dependence upon another's vows. . . . Thus there can be little doubt that, in most cases of seduction, female virtue is trustingly surrendered to the specious arguments and false promises of dishonorable men.

Men who, in the ordinary relations of life, would scruple to defraud their neighbors of a dollar, do not hesitate to rob a confiding woman of her chastity. They who, in a business point of view, would regard obtaining goods under false pretenses as an act to be visited with all the severity of the law, hesitate not to obtain by even viler fraud the surrender of woman's virtue to their fiendish lust. Is there no inconsistency in the social laws which condemn a swindler to the state prison *for his offenses,* and condemn a woman to perpetual infamy *for her wrongs?* Undoubtedly there are cases where the woman is the seducer, but these are so rare as to be hardly worth mentioning.

Seduction is a social wrong. Its entire consequences are not comprised in the injury inflicted on the woman, or the sense of perfidy oppressing the conscience of the man. Beyond the fact that she is, in the ordinary language of the day, ruined, the victim has endured an attack upon her principles which must materially affect her future life. The world may not know of her transgression, and, in consequence, public obloquy may not be added to her burden; but she is too painfully conscious of her fall, and every thought of her lacerated and bleeding heart is embittered with a sense of man's wrong and outrage. . . . It can not be a matter of surprise that, with this feeling of injustice and insult burning at her heart, her career should be one in which she becomes the aggressor, and man the victim; for it is certain that in

this desire of revenge upon the sex for the falsehood of one will be found a cause of the increase of prostitution. . . .

In one of the most aristocratic houses of prostitution in New York was found the daughter of a merchant, a man of large property, residing in one of the Southern states. She was a beautiful girl, had received a superior education, spoke several languages fluently, and seemed keenly sensible of her degradation. Two years before this time she had been on a visit to some relations in Europe, and on her return voyage in one of her father's vessels, she was seduced by the captain, and became pregnant. He solemnly asserted that he would marry her as soon as they reached their port, but the ship had no sooner arrived than he left her. The poor girl's parents would not receive her back into their family, and she came to New York and prostituted herself for support. . . .

"Drink and the desire to drink." . . . It will be conceded that the habit of intoxication in woman, if not an indication of the existence of actual depravity or vice, is a sure precursor of it, for drunkenness and debauchery are inseparable companions, one almost invariably following the other. In some cases a woman living in service becomes a drunkard; she forms acquaintances among the depraved of her own sex, and willingly joins their ranks. Married women acquire the habit of drinking, and forsake their husbands and families to gratify not so much their sexual appetite as their passion for liquor. Young women are often persuaded to take one or two glasses of liquor, and then their ruin may be soon expected. Others are induced to drink spirits in which a narcotic has been infused to render them insensitive to their ruin. In short, it is scarcely possible to enumerate the many temptations which can be employed when intoxicating drinks are used as the agent.

"Ill-treatment of parents, husbands, or relatives" is a prolific cause of prostitution, one hundred and sixty-four women assigning it as a reason for their fall. . . .

J. C.: "My father accused me of being a Prostitute when I was innocent. He would give me no clothes to wear. My mother was a confirmed drunkard and used to be away from home most of the time." Here we have a combination of horrors scarcely equaled in the field of romance. The unjust accusations of the father, and his conduct in not supplying his child with the actual necessaries of life, joined with the drunkenness of the mother, present such an accumulation of cruelty and vice that it would have been a miracle had the girl remained virtuous. It is to be presumed that no one will claim for this couple the performance of any one of the duties enjoined by their position. . . .

Great as are the duties and responsibilities of a father, they are equaled by those devolving upon a husband. He has to provide for the welfare of his wife besides caring for the interests of his children. . . . All married prostitutes can not be exonerated from the charge of guilt, yet the facts which will be hereafter quoted prove that many were driven to a life of shame by those who had solemnly sworn to protect and cherish them. . . .

C. H.: "I was married when I was seventeen years old, and have had three children. The two boys are living now; the girl is dead. My oldest boy is nearly five years old, and the other one is eighteen months. My husband is a sailor. We lived very comfortably till my last child was born, and then he began to drink very hard, and did not support me and I have not seen him or heard any thing about him for six months. After he left me I tried to keep my children by washing or going out to day's work, but I could not earn enough. I never could earn more than two or three dollars a week when I had work, which was not always. My father and mother died when I was a child. I had nobody to help me, and could not support my children, so I came to this place. My boys are now living in the city, and I support them with what I earn by prostitution. It was only to keep them that I came here." . . . In order to feed her helpless offspring she was forced to yield her honor; to prevent them suffering from the pains of hunger, she voluntarily chose to endure the pangs of a guilty conscience; to prolong their lives she periled her own. And at the time when this alternative was forced upon her, the husband was lavishing his money for intoxicating liquor. If she smiled— and this fact can not be denied, however charity may view it—it was the non-performance of his duty that urged, nay, positively forced her to sin. She must endure the punishment of her offenses, but, after reading her simple, heart-rending statement, let casuists decide what amount of condemnation will rest upon the man whose desertion compelled her to violate the law of chastity in order to support his children. . . .

Seventy-one women were persuaded by prostitutes to embrace a life of depravity. One of the most common modes by which this end is accomplished is to inveigle a girl into some house of prostitution as a servant, and this is frequently done through the medium of an *intelligence office*. . . . [At such establishments] servants who wish to obtain situations register their wants and pay a fee. If there are no places likely to suit them on the list of employers, they have permission to remain in the waiting-room until an applicant appears. In these waiting-rooms may be found a crowd of expectants varying from twenty to one hundred, according to the business transacted by the office. . . .

Keepers of houses sometimes visit these offices themselves, but generally some unknown agent is employed, or, at times, one of the prostitutes is plainly dressed, and sent to register her name as wishing a situation, so as to be able to obtain admission into the waiting-room. There she enters into conversation with the other women, whom she uses all the art she possesses to induce to visit her employer.

Some of the sources of prostitution have been thus examined. To expose them all would require a volume; but it is hoped that sufficient has been developed to induce observation and inquiry, and prompt action in the premises. . . .

QUESTIONS FOR ANALYSIS

1. What is Sanger's view of the moral nature of women? How does he view the strength of their character, or their lack of it?

2. What does Sanger think are the causes and consequences of prostitution for women? What use could temperance reformers have made of Sanger's document?

3. How do Sanger's conclusions about prostitution reflect the values of his own day? What conclusions from his data do you draw?

DOCUMENTS

Two Slave Love Stories

M OST OF THE HISTORICAL TESTIMONY ABOUT SLAVERY comes from the writings of slaveowners, who understood little about the interior emotional lives of their slaves. By and large, they considered emotional bonds between slaves as insignificant, except when they hampered the master's power and control. Formal marriage was not possible between slaves, who could not make legally binding agreements between themselves that interfered with their masters' rights of ownership. And as Polly Shine, whose testimony appears here, explains, slaveowners actively interfered in the creation of such bonds: "They did not let us know very much about our people . . . they took us away from our parents when we was real young so that when they got ready to trade us we would not put on too much demonstration or holler and take on so much."

But two kinds of sources, both represented here, reveal the slaves' own perspective on their condition: slave narratives and oral histories. In the decades leading up to the Civil War, people who had escaped from slavery wrote personal accounts of their experiences. Since slaves were forbidden to learn to read and write, some of these fugitives needed the help of sympathetic white listeners to record their stories and secure publication. Others had been secretly taught, either by compassionate owners or by other slaves, and were literate enough to write their own accounts. Rather than disinterested reports on slavery, these slave narratives were intended to provide northern white audiences with evidence of the system's fundamental inhumanity.

The most famous slave narrative was *The Narrative of the Life of Frederick Douglass,* first published in 1845 but subsequently revised and republished in many versions. Modern audiences are also familiar with Harriet Jacobs's *Incidents in the Life of a Slave Girl,* first published in 1861 (see box, "Trials of Girlhood," pp. 166–67). Douglass's account of slavery contributed to the antislavery cause by its heart-wrenching account of the young Frederick's forcible separation from his mother and his heroic path to freedom. Douglass's exceptionally articulate writing was itself powerful propaganda against the slave system, which denied the humanity, capacity, and individuality of slaves. Jacobs's narrative concentrated on the sexual assaults of her master and the cruelty and indifference to her suffering of her mistress. The themes of these two accounts—motherhood and chastity violated—were popular and effective in antebellum antislavery literature.

Interviews taken from former slaves, long after the system's eradication, provide a second kind of source for the direct experience of black people under slavery. In the 1930s, as part of the New Deal Works Project Administration (see Chapter 8), federally funded interviewers were sent throughout the South to record the memories of the last generation of black people to have lived under slavery, all of whom had been children at the time and were now almost eighty or older. Preserved only as typescripts (and in a few cases, as primitive tape recordings) for many years, the WPA oral histories were made available in published form in the 1960s.

As do the written slave narratives of the nineteenth century, these twentieth-century sources have many limitations. Most of the interviewers were white and many of the interviewees were probably deferential to or intimidated by them. Perhaps that is why Polly Shine begins her account with assurances that her masters were such "plumb good" owners. Certainly the details of her account tell a different story. In addition, in most cases interviewers wrote down the words of their informants after the interview was concluded, a process that introduced many errors and omissions. Furthermore, interviewers were expected to render the testimony in dialect, and the result probably reflects their expectations of how black people talked as much as the actual speech of the narrators.

Nonetheless, despite the problems of memory, transcription, and interviewer bias, the slave oral histories of the 1930s are extraordinary and crucial resources. The sheer number of people included—2,300 separate interviews in over 40 volumes—constitutes a massive archive of insights into slavery as slaves experienced it; and the narrators, unlike the exceptional few who escaped and then rendered their tales into slave narratives before the Civil War, bring us much closer to the common experience of slavery.

WILLIAM AND ELLEN CRAFT

WILLIAM CRAFT'S ACCOUNT of his and his wife Ellen's escape differs from Douglass's and Jacobs's narratives in several respects. Refugees usually escaped slavery as individuals (like Douglass) or, more rarely, as a single parent with a child (like Jacobs). The Crafts, however, fled together—Ellen posing as a young white slaveowner and William as "his" slave valet. The narrative itself focuses our attention on the deep marital attachment of these two people, as they together stole their way out of the South. The cooperation and trust between them and their sense that their fates must always be joined carried them through to freedom. Moreover, this narrative was produced without white assistance. William Craft waited twelve years after his escape before publishing his story in order to learn to write it on his own.

Although William narrates their tale, Ellen emerges as a clear and strong character. Her light complexion—both her father and grandfather were white (indeed, the owners of her mother and grandmother)—was the crucial factor that underlay their entire incredible plan. Ellen not only passed through the color line as white; she passed through the gender line as male. Indeed, each transgression necessitated the other: inasmuch as a white female lacked sufficient authority to travel across the South with a male slave, Ellen had to turn herself into a man. And feeling that as a black slave she was deprived of the protections and privileges of white womanhood, she was willing to cross the line into manhood. William's decision to refer to Ellen as "he" and "my master" after the deception began makes the Crafts' narrative even more compelling. At the crucial moment in their escape, Ellen found within herself an unexpected boldness, as if she had become in truth that which she was masquerading as: someone with white male self-confidence and assertiveness.

As you read, consider what aspects of the slave system and assumptions about race and gender allowed the Crafts to thwart the system. What about the Crafts' story made it useful to the antislavery cause?

Running a Thousand Miles for Freedom; or, The Escape of William and Ellen Craft from Slavery (1860)

My wife's first master was her father, and her mother his slave, and the latter is still the slave of his widow.

Notwithstanding my wife being of African extraction on her mother's side, she is almost white—in fact, she is so nearly so that the tyrannical old lady to whom she first belonged became so annoyed, at finding her frequently mistaken for a child of the family, that she gave her when eleven years of age to a daughter, as a wedding present. This separated my wife from her mother, and also from several other dear friends. But the incessant cruelty of her old mistress made the change of owners or treatment so desirable, that she did not grumble much. . . . After puzzling our brains for years, we were reluctantly driven to the sad conclusion that it was almost impossible to escape slavery in Georgia, and travel 1,000 miles across the slave States. . . .

We were married, and prayed and toiled on till December, 1848, at which time (as I have stated) a plan suggested itself. . . .

Knowing that slaveholders have the privilege of taking their slaves to any part of the country they think proper, it occurred to me that, as my wife was nearly white, I might get her to disguise herself as an invalid gentleman, and assume to be my master, while I could attend as his slave, and that in this manner we might effect our escape. After I thought of the plan, I suggested it to my wife, but at first she shrank from the idea. She thought it was almost impossible for her to assume that disguise, and travel a distance of 1,000 miles across the slave States. However, on the other hand, she also thought of her condition. She saw that the laws under which we lived did not recognize her to be a woman, but a mere chattel, to be bought and sold, or otherwise dealt with as her owner might see fit. Therefore the more she contemplated her helpless condition, the more anxious she was to escape from it. . . .

Some of the best slaveholders will sometimes give their favourite slaves a few days' holiday at Christmas time; so, after no little amount of perseverance on my wife's part, she obtained a pass from her mistress, allowing her to be away for a few days. The cabinet-maker with whom I worked gave me a similar paper, but said that he needed my services very much, and wished me to return as soon as the time granted was up. . . .

On reaching my wife's cottage she handed me her pass, and I showed mine, but at that time neither of us were able to read them. . . .

SOURCE: William Craft, *Running a Thousand Miles for Freedom; or, The Escape of William and Ellen Craft from Slavery* (London: W. Tweedie, 1860).

However, at first, we were highly delighted at the idea of having gained permission to be absent for a few days; but when the thought flashed across my wife's mind that it was customary for travellers to register their names in the visitors' book at hotels, as well as in the clearance or Custom-house book at Charleston, South Carolina . . . our spirits droop[ed] within us.

So, while sitting in our little room upon the verge of despair, all at once my wife raised her head, and with a smile upon her face, which was a moment before bathed in tears, said, "I think I have it!" I asked what it was. She said, "I think I can make a poultice and bind up my right hand in a sling, and with propriety ask the officers to register my name for me." I thought that would do.

It then occurred to her that the smoothness of her face might betray her; so she decided to make another poultice, and put it in a white handkerchief to be worn under the chin, up the cheeks, and to tie over the head. This nearly hid the expression of the countenance, as well as the beardless chin. . . .

We sat up all night discussing the plan and making preparations. Just before the time arrived, in the morning, for us to leave, I cut off my wife's hair square at the back of the head, and got her to dress in the disguise and stand out on the floor. I found that she made a most respectable looking gentleman.

My wife had no ambition whatever to assume this disguise, and would not have done so had it been possible to have obtained our liberty by more simple means; but we knew it was not customary in the South for ladies to travel with male servants; and therefore, notwithstanding my wife's fair complexion, it would have been a very difficult task for her to have come off as a free white lady, with me as her slave; in fact, her not being able to write would have made this quite impossible. We knew that no public conveyance would take us, or any other slave, as a passenger, without our master's consent. . . .

We shook hands, said farewell, and started in different directions for the railway station. I took the nearest possible way to the train, for fear I should be recognized by someone, and got into the negro car in which I knew I should have to ride; but my *master* (as I will now call my wife) took a longer way round, and only arrived there with the bulk of the passengers. He obtained a ticket for himself and one for his slave to Savannah, the first port, which was about two hundred miles off. My master then had the luggage stowed away, and stepped into one of the best carriages. . . . [From Savannah they took train and boat to Baltimore.]

They are particularly watchful at Baltimore to prevent slaves from escaping into Pennsylvania, which is a free State. After I had seen my master into one of the best carriages, and was just about to step into mine, an officer, a full-blooded Yankee of the lower order, saw me. He came quickly up, and, tapping me on the shoulder, said in his unmistakable native twang, together with no little display of his authority, "Where are you going, boy?" "To Philadelphia, sir," I humbly replied. "Well, what are you going there for?" "I am travelling with my master, who is in the next carriage, sir." "Well, I calculate you had better get him out; and be mighty quick about it because the train will soon be starting. It is against my rules to let any man take a slave past here, unless he can satisfy them in the office that he has a right to take him along."

The officer then passed on and left me standing upon the platform, with my anxious heart apparently palpitating in the throat. At first I scarcely knew which way to turn. But it soon occurred to me that the good God, who had been with us thus far, would not forsake us at the eleventh hour. So with renewed hope I stepped into my master's carriage, to inform him of the difficulty. I found him sitting at the farther end, quite alone. As soon as he looked up and saw me, he smiled. I also tried to wear a cheerful countenance, in order to break the shock of the sad news. . . . [A]s there was no time to lose, I went up to him and asked him how he felt. He said "Much better," and that he thanked God we were getting on so nicely. I then said we were not getting on quite so well as we had anticipated. He anxiously and quickly asked what was the matter. I told him. He started as if struck by lightning, and exclaimed, "Good Heavens! William, is it possible that we are, after all, doomed to hopeless bondage?" I could say nothing, my heart was too full to speak, for at first I did not know what to do. However we knew it would never do to turn back. . . . So, after a few moments, I did all I could to encourage my companion, and we stepped out and made for the office: but how or where my master obtained sufficient courage to face the tyrants who had power to blast all we held dear, heaven only knows! . . . We felt that our very existence was at stake, and that we must either sink or swim. But, as God was our present and mighty helper in this as well as in all former trials, we were able to keep our heads up and press forwards.

On entering the room we found the principal man, to whom my master said, "Do you wish to see me, sir?" "Yes," said this eagle-eyed officer; and he added, "It is against our rules, sir, to allow any person to take a slave out of Baltimore into Philadelphia, unless he can satisfy us that he has a right to take him along." "Why is that?" asked my master, with more firmness than could be expected. "Because, sir," continued he, in a voice and manner that almost chilled our blood, "if we should suffer any gentleman to take a slave past here into Philadelphia; and should the gentleman with whom the slave might be travelling turn out not to be his rightful owner; and should the proper master come and prove that his slave escaped on our road, we shall have him to pay for; and, therefore, we cannot let any slave pass here without receiving security to show, and to satisfy us, that it is all right."

This conversation attracted the attention of the large number of bustling passengers . . . not because they thought we were slaves endeavouring to escape, but merely because they thought my master was a slaveholder and invalid gentleman, and therefore it was wrong to detain him. The officer, observing that the passengers sympathised with my master, asked him if he was not acquainted with some gentleman in Baltimore that he could get to endorse for him, to show that I was his property, and that he had a right to take me off. He said, "No"; and added, "I bought tickets in Charleston to pass us through to Philadelphia, and therefore you have no right to detain us here." "Well, sir," said the man, indignantly, "right or no right, we shan' let you go." These sharp words fell upon our anxious hearts like the crack of doom, and made us feel that hope only smiles to deceive.

For a few moments perfect silence prevailed. My master looked at me, and I at him, but neither of us dared to speak a word, for fear of making some blunder that would tend to our detection. . . .

We felt as though we had come into deep waters and were about being overwhelmed, and that the slightest mistake would clip asunder the last brittle thread of hope by which we were suspended, and let us down for ever into the dark and horrible pit of misery and degradation from which we were straining every nerve to escape. While our hearts were crying lustily unto Him who is ever ready and able to save, the conductor of the train that we had just left stepped in. The officer asked if we came by the train with him from Washington; he said we did, and left the room. Just then the bell rang for the train to leave; and had it been the sudden shock of an earthquake it could not have given us a greater thrill. The sound of the bell caused every eye to flash with apparent interest, and to be more steadily fixed upon us than before. But, as God would have it, the officer all at once thrust his fingers through his hair, and in a state of great agitation said, "I really don't know what to do; I calculate it is a right." He then told the clerk to run and tell the conductor to "let this gentleman and slave pass"; adding, "As he is not well, it is a pity to stop him here. We will let him go." My master thanked him, and stepped out and hobbled across the platform as quickly as possible. I tumbled him unceremoniously into one of the best carriages, and leaped into mine just as the train was gliding off towards our happy destination.

POLLY SHINE

W HEN POLLY SHINE WAS NINETY YEARS OLD, WPA interviewer B. E. Davis took down her story in Madisonville, Texas. Hers is one of the fuller WPA narratives. She was an only child, she explains, as her parents "had been put together or married when they was in their middle life." Most of her account, like that of the majority of the WPA narratives, is about the nature of the work slaves did and the conditions under which they lived. But as she dutifully answered the questions Davis most likely asked (they were omitted from the transcript) — Did you see slaves sold? How were slaves punished? Could you read? Did you go to church? — she also recalled a dramatic story of love between a man and a woman that almost thwarted the master's control over them. Shine was a teenager when slavery was abolished. This story, which may have been told to her by her parents, obviously made a powerful impression on her. It is a tale of both heroic and tragic passion. As you read, try to imagine the original interview. What can you tell of Shine and Davis's attitudes toward each other and to the story that she told?

WPA Interview (1938)

I was born in Shreveport, La. in 1848. My father's name was Jim Shine and mother's name was Jessie Shine. . . .

Well, Maser he was a jolly good man but strict. Mistress was a plum angel and their 3 children they was plum good. They were real good to their black people. Yes Maser he would whip the negro if he had to but not beat them up like some Masers would. . . .

Maser had about 100 acres in his plantation and about 35 or 40 slaves. He planted it all in cotton, corn and sugar cane. . . . Maser woke us every morning about 4 o'clock with a big bell, so'es we could get our morning work done, eat and be in the field at daylight or before and be ready to work. Well, no he never had no overseer, he done all that himself and he worked us till plum dark every day, we just quit long enough to eat our dinner at noon then right back to work.

SOURCE: Interview by B. E. Davis, February 1, 1938, in George P. Rawick, ed., *The American Slave: A Composite Autobiography,* ser. 2 (Texas Narratives Part 8) (Westport, CT: Greenwood Press, 1977), 9:3511–17.

That is we worked from sun to sun as we called it then. . . .

Yes, I have seen slaves sold and auctioned off. They made us wash and clean up real good first, then grease our hands and feet also our legs up to our knees and greased our neck, face and ears good so we would look real fat and slick. Then they would trot us out to and fro before our buyers and let them look us over real good. They felt of our legs, arms and so on before they would offer a price for us. We would be awful sad because we did not know what kind of Maser we were going to have, did'nt know but what he would be real mean to us or would take us plum out of the state where we never would see or hear of our people any more. . . .

Yes, I have seen a few slaves in chains because they would be so unruly that their Maser would have to put them in chains. We have one slave there on our plantation that Maser could not do anything with in the way of keeping him at home. When night come — he had him a girl that lived over on another plantation joining ours and that negro would go over there when Maser told him to go to bed in his quarters, and just as soon as Maser got to bed he would get up and slip off over to see his girl and he would not come back to his quarters until just before daylight, then he would not be any account at all that day. So Maser he tried ever way to get along with that negro without putting him in chains, he whipped him and the patterrollers° they got hold of him several times but that did not do any good so he finely got him some chains, and put around that negroes legs and then he would get him a pole and hop around on, he would get over there some way to see his girl. They got to where they could get them chains off that negro and Maser he would not be out done so he fixed that negro a shed and bed close to a tree there on the plantation and chained his hands and feet to that tree so he could not slip off to see his girl. Of course that fixed the negro slave so he could not travel at night to see his girl, but still that did not do any good but Maser finely did put a stop to the negro

° Slang for "patrollers," white men who stopped slaves off their plantations to make sure that they were not escapees.

man running around at night, then his girl started. She would come over there to his shed and bed and they would lay around there, talk and go on all night, so that negro he would lose so much sleep that he still was not any account. Still they could not out do Maser. He put that negro up for sale and not one that lived there close by would not [sic] offer to buy him as they knew how he was, but there was a man that came in there from another state offered to buy him from Maser and he sold him, and when that negro found out that his Maser had sold him he began to beg him not to. He promised Maser if he would not sell him and take him away from his girl and would let him go . . . to see his girl once a week, he would stay at home and be a real good negro, as him and this girl had one child by now. But Maser would not listen to that negro as he had done had too much trouble with him and let the man have him. The man told him he could not go to see any girl where he was carrying him as there was not any girls there for him to slip off to see. That like to have killed that negro but it did not do any good. . . .

QUESTIONS FOR ANALYSIS

1. How did the characters in these two accounts reject and resist the assumptions about black people fundamental to the slave system? On what personal resources did they draw to make their challenges?

2. Both of these stories were written after the fact: the Crafts' ten years following emancipation and Polly Shine's after about seven decades. Evaluate the role memory plays in these accounts, and consider the ways in which it distorts or possibly authenticates the narrators' experiences.

3. What do these stories tell about the forces shaping love and other intimate relations among black people under slavery?

Godey's Lady's Book

By the year 1850 *Godey's Lady's Book,* with forty thousand subscribers, was the most widely circulated "ladies magazine" in the United States. For $3 a year, readers from all over the country enjoyed a rich monthly collection of fiction, history (specializing in heroes and heroines of the American Revolution), poetry, and illustrations. Contributors to the magazine included well-known men and women writers, such as Nathaniel Hawthorne, who elsewhere bitterly castigated women writers as "that damned mob of scribbling women."[40] Lavish pictorial "embellishments," printed from full-page, specially commissioned steel engravings and hand colored by the magazine's special staff of 150 female colorists (wage laborers, unlike most of the magazine's readers), lifted *Godey's* above the run-of-the-mill periodicals published for the literate female public. Subscribers treasured their issues, circulated them among friends, and preserved them in leather bindings. The magazine's large readership was testimony to the degree to which *Godey's* both reflected and affected the sympathies and values of its subscribers.

Godey's Lady's Book was edited by a woman and published by a man. Sarah Josepha Hale, a schoolteacher, mother, and widow from Boston, had turned to magazine editing to support herself and her children after the death of her husband in 1828. Like Catharine Beecher, she had very pronounced views on the dignity and power of woman's distinct domestic sphere. In the aftermath of the Panic of 1837, she joined forces with a commercially minded publisher, Louis Godey, to become the editor of *Godey's Lady's Book.* Her concerns for feminine values were now combined with his eye for women's possibilities as consumers. The magazine's illustrations thus combined advertisements for the latest fashions (which readers took to their seamstresses to duplicate) with illustrations promoting the feminine ideal of selflessness, purity, and subtle maternal influence. Although editor Hale was consistent in preaching this notion of women's redemptive, domestic influence throughout her career, her position became more defensive in the 1840s in reaction to the rising tide of the women's rights movement, which she thought dangerous both to women and to the nation (see Chapter 4). "The elevation of the [female] sex will not consist in becoming like man, in doing man's work, or striving for the dominion of the world. The true woman . . . has a higher and holier vocation. She works in the elements of human nature."[41]

Through stories and images, *Godey's Lady's Book* preached a compelling if conservative doctrine of women's importance to the nation. In a society rapidly being transformed by economic growth and political upheaval, domestic women were expected to provide emotional and spiritual stability. They were to function,

◆ Figure 3.1 *The Constant, or the Anniversary Present,* 1851
Courtesy of the Houghton Library at Harvard University.

as Figure 3.1 advocates, as "the constant" to middle-class American family life. This drawing illustrated a story of a young wife whose quiet, steady love wordlessly convinced her wandering husband to join with her in embracing the healing "close communion of home life."[42] Note the woman's pose, at once submissive to her husband and protective of her children. In a subsequent issue, this image of woman was juxtaposed against an illustration warning women against being a flirtatious "coquette."

The ideology of true womanhood imbued motherhood with both a secular and a spiritual role. *Godey's Lady's Book* considered mothers as crucial to preserving the memory of the American Revolution and to securing its legacy within a stable, peaceful, and permanent American nation. Mothers accomplished this task by raising the next generation of citizens. As Figure 3.2 suggests, the citizen-child was often figured as male. "How Can an American Woman Serve Her Country?" *Godey's* asked: "By early teaching her sons to consider a republic as the best form of government in the world."[43] Motherhood was also a religious obligation, as the

◆ Figure 3.2 *The Christian Mother,* 1850
General Research Division, The New York Public Library, Astor, Lenox, and Tilden Foundations.

visual reference to the Madonna and Child in this illustration makes quite clear. This equation—of American mother and the mother of Christ—became more problematic as the midcentury influx of European Catholic immigrants (see p. 152) put images of Mary off limits to the overwhelmingly Protestant middle class. Consider how the spiritual and secular dimensions of nineteenth-century motherhood are reconciled in this image.

While preaching the virtues of motherhood and domesticity, female ideologues of middle-class femininity protrayed teaching as a natural profession for women, drawing as it did on the maternal virtues and emotions. Hale wrote that "the reports of common school education show that women are the *best* teachers,"

◆ Figure 3.3 *The Teacher*, 1844
Culver Pictures.

in response to which she sponsored a petition to Congress urging public support for women's teacher training.[44] Teaching, at least of boys, had previously been the province of men and began changing into a woman's occupation only during the 1820s and 1830s. The reasons for the shift were economic as well as ideological. Outside of the South, public education, long considered essential to a virtuous citizenry, was expanding at a rapid rate. Also, female teachers were usually paid a third or less of what men were paid. Consider the similarity between the representation of woman as teacher (Figure 3.3) and as mother (Figure 3.2).

Barbara Welter, the first modern historian to examine the ideology of true womanhood, identified its four basic elements as domesticity, piety, submission,

◆ Figure 3.4 *Purity,* 1850
Picture Collection, The Branch Libraries, The New York Public Library, Astor, Lenox, and Tilden Foundations.

and purity.[45] Purity of course referred to sexuality—not just experience but also desire—of which the true woman was expected to be innocent. In Figure 3.4, the feminine virtue of purity is illustrated at the same time it is used to advertise designs for fashionable wedding dresses. How do ideological and economic concerns come together in this image?

The middle-class character of the doctrine of domesticity was revealed in the frequent illustrations of the difficulties that the true woman had in hiring and supervising household servants. Although—or because—the relation between mistress and maid was one of the more distressing of the middle-class housewife's

◆ **Figure 3.5 *Cooks,* 1852**
General Research Division, The New York Public Library, Astor, Lenox, and Tilden Foundations.

domestic obligations, the stories and drawings about this dilemma were invariably humorous, with the incompetent and stupid housemaid or cook as the sure butt of the joke. The very face and figure of the cook in Figure 3.5 indicate a female very different from the mistress (see Figure 6.7 on p. 395 for a late nineteenth-century parallel). How is the mistress designated as a true woman while the cook is not? What does the illustration suggest about the relationship of husband and wife, as well as that of mistress and maid?

Although *Godey's Lady's Book* insisted on the distinction between woman's domestic sphere and man's worldly obligations, the writing and illustrations hint

◆ **Figure 3.6** *Shoe Shopping,* **1848**
General Research Division, The New York Public Library, Astor, Lenox, and Tilden Foundations.

at the ways that economic realities and the larger society impinged on middle-class women's efforts to practice their home-based ideals. While Hale preached women's special virtues as an antidote to the distressingly materialistic world outside the home, *Godey's* itself was implicated in those same worldly values. The true woman was a frequent shopper, and in 1852, the magazine instituted a shopping service to assist its readers in the purchase of accessories and jewelry. Figure 3.6 portrays middle-class women leaving their cloistered homes for the pleasures and luxury of an elegant shoe emporium, presided over by a male clerk. Looking at this mid-nineteenth-century illustration, keep in mind the women workers far away who manufactured these shoes. Note also how shopping is portrayed as a recreational activity already at this early stage in market society.

Similarly, Figure 3.7 portrays some of the fashionable dresses that the magazine advised its readers to request of their seamstresses; they are pictured against a distant background of the hurrying, ambitious world, symbolized by a railroad, just beginning to appear in the New England countryside. Why do you think the illustrator juxtaposed the well-dressed women against this background? What does the image suggest about the relationship of the fashions and the women who wear them to the steam train behind?

◆ **Figure 3.7** *The Train Is Coming,* **1850**
General Research Division, The New York Public Library, Astor,
Lenox, and Tilden Foundations.

QUESTIONS FOR ANALYSIS

1. Examine the expressions, demeanor, and dress of all the women from *Godey's*. What do they have in common? Why do they show so little variety? How might women readers have regarded these images and tried to imitate them?

2. Look at the profiles of the true women from *Godey's*. Notice their tiny waists, the composure of their hands, the elegance of their bearing. How do these and other details reinforce the message that women are unfit for the public sphere?

3. Consider *Godey's* in light of fashion magazines you are familiar with today. What is the appeal of fashion magazines for women? How seriously do you take the lifestyle and the profiles modeled in the magazines you read? How can such sources be read critically to reveal something about contemporary times?

Early Photographs of Factory Operatives and Slave Women

PHOTOGRAPHY, INVENTED IN FRANCE in the 1830s, came to the United States in the 1840s. By 1850, commercial photographers were working in all the major cities. Compared to portrait painting, photography was quick and relatively inexpensive, exactly the modern form of artistic representation appropriate to a young, democratic nation. Perhaps also because so many Americans were on the move, they wanted these small, portable pictures of themselves to send to loved ones. In Massachusetts alone, there were four hundred photographic studios by 1855.[46] Nationwide the estimate is three thousand by 1860.[47] Pocket-size portraits could be had for a few dollars, and common folks, not just the well-to-do, were eager to purchase their likenesses. In 1853, the *New York Tribune* estimated that 3 million photographs were being made annually. Unfortunately, only a very few have survived.[48]

The earliest of these photographs are known as daguerreotypes, named for Louis Jacques Daguerre, the Frenchman who discovered the technology in 1837. The daguerreotypist created a positive image on a metal plate treated with mercury and exposed to light. The finished product was enclosed in a case to protect it from the light. In the United States, the technology gave way in the mid-1850s to simpler and less expensive processes: the tintype (which shortened the sitting time and reduced the cost) and the ambrotype (which used glass instead of metal for the photographic plate and produced a negative rather than a positive image).[49] By the early 1860s, photographers were learning how to make multiple positive prints on paper from negative glass plates. In the early studio photographs, sitters had to remain still for minutes, sometimes with their heads in braces to keep them still; not surprisingly, few smiled. The images that resulted were extremely fragile but also often stunning in their intimacy and delicacy. The sitters seem to look out at us, over a century or more, inviting us to study them and detect their sentiments.

For modern students of history, who rely on images for a great deal of information, photographs are particularly satisfying as a source of historical documentation. In our eagerness to see precise, seemingly objective images of the past, however, it is important to realize that the objects of these early historical photographs are selective: some things—and people—were photographed relatively frequently and others not at all. To put it another way, we cannot see photos of everything about which we are curious, only of what previous generations wanted to be seen. Thus, in addition to the obvious visible information that these early photographs convey about the American past, they also document what versions and aspects of themselves nineteenth-century Americans wanted to preserve.

The images that follow—of female factory workers and of slaves—represent women living and working outside the dominant, middle-class ethic of mid-nineteenth-century true womanhood. Their existence prompts us to ask: who took care to preserve these images and why?

FACTORY OPERATIVES

Female textile factory operatives arranged to have their own photographs taken. They posed in their work clothes and held shuttles as symbols of their work as spinners and weavers of cloth. The tools signified that the sitter was a skilled worker, with valuable knowledge, experience, and ability. As these images indicate, the women were proud of their presence in and contribution to the burgeoning industrial economy of those years.

Workers often posed for these portraits in groups, which suggests that they thought of their labor as collective and of their coworkers as friends. For women, coworkers were often relatives as well; sisters and cousins followed their kin into the mills, took jobs that had been secured for them, and worked in the same room at the same task. Factory work was a new experience for most of these young women, and the presence of familiar faces may have eased their transition into a strange environment. Family relations were still crucial elements of their lives, even in the impersonal environment of the textile factory.

By 1860, textile factories and the women who worked in them were found throughout much of New England. The four young women shown in Figure 3.8

◆ Figure 3.8 **Four Women Mill Workers, 1860**
American Textile History Museum, Lowell, Massachusetts.

◆ Figure 3.9 **Two Women Mill Workers, 1860**
American Textile History Museum, Lowell, Massachusetts.
(Special thanks to Claire Sheridan for her help in researching this
photograph.)

were photographed near Winthrop, Maine. The two Lowell weavers pictured in Figure 3.9 look enough alike to be sisters. By 1860, when both of these tintypes were taken, Irish newcomers were beginning to take over from Yankee workers in the textile industry, and these women may have been Irish-born. As you study the photographs presented in Figures 3.8 and 3.9, examine the poses, settings, and props. What do they suggest about these women's identities and perhaps even their thoughts? What do the photographs capture about these women's relationships?

The very unusual collection of ambrotypes in Figure 3.10 was taken in 1854 in Manchester, New Hampshire, by a group of male and female employees of the Amoskeag Manufacturing Company and presented to the foreman who oversaw their labor. Although the men and women worked together in the carding room, preparing the raw cotton for the spinning process, they did different work. The men worked the carding machines, which began the process, while the women tended the drawing frames and double speeders, which turned the raw fibers into crude strands in preparation for spinning. Despite earning lower wages than the men, women who worked in the carding room were among the best paid of their sex. These subjects posed themselves as dignified, upstanding individuals, dressed in their best clothes for the camera's eye. What does the fact that men and women allowed themselves to be photographed together suggest about gender relations in factories? How do Figures 3.8, 3.9, and 3.10 represent the pride that early factory workers took in their position?

◆ Figure 3.10 **Amoskeag Manufacturing Company Workers, 1854**
Courtesy of the Manchester (N.H.) Historic Association.

SLAVE WOMEN

◆ **Figure 3.11 The Hayward Family's Slave Louisa with Her Legal Owner, c. 1858**
Missouri Historical Society, St. Louis.

Unlike factory operatives, slaves did not choose to have their photographs taken. The following photographs of slave women come from two different sources. The first group is that of slave baby nurses, portrayed with their white charges or as part of a larger family group. The slaveholders who arranged for these photographs meant to convey that these black women, the "mammies" of southern nostalgic memory, were beloved, trusted servants to their families. Dissenting from opponents' portrayal of slaveholders as a violent, inhumane class, many regarded themselves as benevolent masters and mistresses who lived in harmony and intimacy with the slaves entrusted to their care.

From the perspective of the twenty-first century, nearly 150 years after the abolition of slavery, such photographs can tell a different story. These nineteenth-century black women look out at us with a humanity and individuality that slavery denied they had. Their expressions and poses suggest the complex, if controlled, meanings that their responsibilities to care for white children may have had for them. What appeared to be maternal love was actually unpaid labor. These photographs did not belong to them but to their masters. Where were their own children as they attended to those of their owners?

Of the numerous photographs of slave mammies, we know more about the individuals in Figure 3.11 than most. The slave woman, Louisa, had been bought in 1858 at age twenty-two at a slave auction in New Orleans to serve as nursemaid for the Hayward family. The tiny child in the photograph was her legal owner. Many decades later, after he had grown up, he gave the ambrotype to the Missouri Historical Society.[50] What does the fact that he so treasured this photograph tell you about the relations between slaves and masters? As you look into Louisa's eyes, try to recover what she was feeling when the photograph was taken.

By contrast, nothing is known about the family portrayed in Figure 3.12, although the photographer, Thomas Easterly of St. Louis, was well known. What is most striking about this 1850 family photograph is the absence of a white woman. We have to wonder what happened to her and what her absence means for the

◆ **Figure 3.12 Thomas Easterly, *Family with Their Slave Nurse*, c. 1850**
Thomas Martin Easterly, Father, Daughters, and Nurse, *about 1850, daguerreotype. © The J. Paul Getty Museum, Los Angeles.*

black woman who is included. The slave mistress may have died, leaving the black woman to take over her domestic and childrearing duties. Could the man, like so many slave masters, have had his own sort of intimate relationship with the unnamed black woman whom he includes in his family portrait? Consider the affectionate grouping of the father and daughters and the physical isolation of the black woman. What does this composition suggest about this family? Again, what do you see in the face of the slave nurse?

In a different category from the photographs of domestic slaves are the images of slave women that northern photographers made in the context of the Civil War (see Chapter 4). Like the famous photographs that Mathew Brady took of

◆ **Figure 3.13 Timothy O'Sullivan, *Plantation in Beaufort, South Carolina, 1862***
Library of Congress, LC-B8171-152-A.

battlefields and male soldiers, these images were meant to document the North's purposes in the war and the Union army's military conduct. Figure 3.13 shows a photograph taken in 1862 by Timothy O'Sullivan, a colleague of Brady, on a plantation in Beaufort, South Carolina. O'Sullivan was traveling with the Union army, which had seized and occupied the coastal Sea Islands of eastern Georgia and

South Carolina early in the war. Their masters and overseers having fled, these black people continued to work the plantations where they lived but now under the supervision of northern officers, in anticipation of the relationship later formalized within the U.S. Army's Freedmen's Bureau (see Chapter 5). O'Sullivan posed this picture of an entirely black, multigenerational family just freed from slavery. Contrast this image with Figures 3.11 and 3.12, the photographs taken by slaveholders to document their notions of the sentiments that bound slaves to white families. How does O'Sullivan's photograph give evidence to the bonds of love and kinship among black people that the cruelties of the plantation system ignored and threatened? Do you see anything different in the faces and postures of these black people?

QUESTIONS FOR ANALYSIS

1. Compare the attitudes and expressions of the factory operatives and the slave women, especially the slave "mammies." How does the fact that one group chose to photograph themselves while the others were photographed by their masters change the meaning of the photographs?

2. All of these early photographs show women defined by their labor. Does work, in any way, offer common ground between factory operatives and slaves? How are the women in these photographs different from the images in *Godey's Lady's Book* (Visual Sources, pp. 182–89) of leisured, middle-class, "true women"? What do you think of the fact that the former were more likely to come down to us in photographs, while the images of the latter were preserved in illustrations and paintings?

3. Consider what photographs add to historical documentation. What can photographs, even at this early stage, tell us about women's history that other sorts of images cannot? Conversely, how should we analyze photographs to avoid the temptation of regarding them as transparent mirrors of a lost historical reality?

NOTES

1. Lucy Larcom, *A New England Girlhood: Outlined from Memory* (Boston: Houghton Mifflin, 1889), 222.

2. Ibid., 200.

3. Alexis de Tocqueville, *Democracy in America*, quoted in Catherine Beecher, *Treatise on Domestic Economy* (1841; repr., New York: Schocken Books, 1977), 6.

4. Quoted in Harvey Green, *The Light of the Home: An Intimate View of the Lives of Women in Victorian America* (New York: Pantheon, 1983), 56.

5. Catharine Beecher, *Woman Suffrage and Woman's Profession* (Hartford: Brown & Gross, 1871), 175.

6. Nancy Cott, *The Bonds of Womanhood: "Woman's Sphere" in New England, 1780–1835* (New Haven: Yale University Press, 1977), 28.

7. Beecher, *Woman Suffrage and Woman's Profession*, 28.

8. Nancy Cott, "Passionlessness: An Interpretation of Victorian Sexual Ideology, 1790–1850," *Signs* 4 (1978): 219–36.

9. Ibid.

10. William Sanger, *The History of Prostitution: Its Extent, Causes, and Effects throughout the World* (New York: Medical Publishing, 1921), 488.

11. Beecher, *Treatise on Domestic Economy*, 178.

12. Larcom, *New England Girlhood*, 198.

13. Mrs. A. J. Graves, *Woman in America: Being an Examination into the Moral and Intellectual Condition of American Female Society* (New York: Harper and Brothers, 1841), 58.

14. American Social History Project, *Who Built America? Working People and the Nation's Economy, Politics, Culture and Society* (New York: Pantheon Books, 1989), 1:249.

15. Larcom, *New England Girlhood*, 196.

16. Alice Kessler-Harris, *Out to Work: A History of Wage-Earning Women in the United States* (New York: Oxford University Press, 1982), 47.

17. William Blake, "Jerusalem," 1804.

18. Cott, *Bonds of Womanhood*, 38.

19. Larcom, *New England Girlhood*, 196.

20. Charles Dickens, *American Notes* (London: Chapman and Hall, 1842), ch. 4.

21. Larcom, *New England Girlhood*, 146.

22. Harriet Hanson Robinson, *Loom and Spindle: Or Life among the Early Mill Girls* (New York: T. Y. Crowell, 1889), 83.

23. Elizabeth Cady Stanton to Paulina Wright Davis, December 6, 1852, in Ann D. Gordon, ed., *The Selected Papers of Elizabeth Cady Stanton and Susan B. Anthony* (New Brunswick: Rutgers University Press, 1997), 214.

24. Christine Stansell, *City of Women: Sex and Class in New York, 1789–1860* (New York: Alfred A. Knopf, 1986), 47.

25. Ibid., 14.

26. Susan Smedes, *Memorials of a Southern Planter* (Baltimore: Cushings and Bailey, 1887), 48.

27. Quoted in Brenda E. Stevenson, *Life in Black and White: Family and Community in the Slave South* (New York: Oxford University Press, 1996), 42.

28. Quoted in Stephanie McCurry, *Masters of Small Worlds: Yeoman Households, Gender Relations, and the Political Culture of the Antebellum South Carolina Low Country* (New York: Oxford University Press, 1995), 223.

29. Caroline Howard Gilman, *Recollections of a Southern Matron* (New York: Harper and Brothers, 1838), 94.

30. Caroline Elizabeth Merrick, *Old Times in Dixie Land: A Southern Matron's Memories* (New York: Grafton Press, 1901), 18.

31. Angelina Grimké, *An Appeal to the Women of the Nominally Free States* (1838), quoted in Nancy Cott, ed., *Root of Bitterness: Documents of the Social History of American Women* (Boston: Northeastern University Press, 1986), 197.

32. Virginia Clay-Clopton, *A Belle of the Fifties: Memories of Mrs. Clay of Alabama: Covering Social and Political Life in Washington and the South* (New York: Doubleday, 1905), 212.

33. McCurry, *Masters of Small Worlds,* 260.

34. Ophelia Settle Egypt, quoted in Gerda Lerner, ed., *Black Women in White America: A Documentary History* (New York: Vintage Books, 1992), 34–35.

35. Mrs. James Stewart, from Benjamin Drew, ed., *A North-side View of Slavery: The Refugee; or, The Narratives of Fugitive Slaves in Canada Related by Themselves* (1856), quoted in Cott, *Root of Bitterness,* 187.

36. Ophelia Settle Egypt, quoted in Lerner, ed., *Black Women in White America,* 38.

37. Quoted in Stevenson, *Life in Black and White,* 232.

38. Mary Boykin Chesnut, *A Diary from Dixie* (1949), quoted in Cott, *Root of Bitterness,* 212.

39. Sarah Josepha Hale, quoted in Cott, *Bonds of Womanhood,* 68.

40. As cited in Susan Conrad, *Perish the Thought: Intellectual Women in Romantic America, 1830–1860* (Secaucus, NJ: Citadel Press, 1978), 20. See Nathaniel Hawthorne, "Witches: A Scene from Main Street," *Godey's Lady's Book* 42, no. 17 (1851): 192.

41. "Editors' Table," *Godey's Lady's Book* 42 (1851): 65.

42. Alice B. Neal, "The Constant, or the Anniversary Present," *Godey's Lady's Book* 42 (1851): 5.

43. Kate Berry, "How Can an American Woman Serve Her Country?" *Godey's Lady's Book* 43 (1851): 362.

44. "Editor's Table," *Godey's Lady's Book* 47 (1853): 554.

45. Barbara Welter, "The Cult of True Womanhood, 1820–1860," *American Quarterly* 18 (1966): 151–74.

46. John Wood, ed., *America and the Daguerreotype* (Iowa City: University of Iowa Press, 1991), 95.

47. Oliver Jensen et al., *An American Album* (New York: American Heritage Publishers, 1968), 21.

48. Ibid.

49. Kenneth E. Nelson, "A Thumbnail History of the Daguerreotype," Daguerreian Society, http://www.daguerre.org (accessed June 8, 2004).

50. Information from Duane Sneddeker, photographic curator, Missouri Historical Society.

SUGGESTED REFERENCES

True Womanhood   The term "true womanhood" was first introduced into historical studies by Barbara Welter in "The Cult of True Womanhood, 1820–1860," *American Quarterly* 18 (1966): 151–74. The two most important full-length studies of the cult of domesticity are Nancy Cott's study of New England middle-class women's lives and ideas, *The Bonds of Womanhood: "Woman's Sphere" in New England, 1780–1835,* 2nd ed. (1997), and Kathryn Kish Sklar's intellectual biography of Catharine Beecher, *Catharine Beecher: A Study in American Domesticity* (1976). An original and revealing local study is Mary Ryan's *Cradle of the Middle Class: The Family in Oneida County, 1780–1835* (1983). On the important editor of *Godey's Lady's Book,* see Ruth Finley, *The Lady of* Godey's: *Sarah Josepha Hale* (1974). Catharine Beecher's *A Treatise on Domestic Economy,* first published in 1841 and subsequently reissued numerous times, eventually in an 1869 version coauthored with Harriet Beecher Stowe and titled *The American Woman's Home* (2002), is invaluable for ideas on femininity and domesticity in this period. On the sexual dimension of true womanhood ideology, see Nancy Cott's article, "Passionlessness: An Interpretation of Victorian Sexual Ideology, 1790–1850," *Signs* 4 (1978): 219–36.

Early Industrial Women Workers   The most comprehensive modern research into female mill workers at Lowell is found in the work of Thomas Dublin: *Women at Work: The Transformation of Work and Community in Lowell, Massachusetts, 1826–1860,* 2nd ed. (1993), and *Farm to Factory: Women's Letters, 1830–1860,* 2nd ed. (1993). An earlier but still very valuable study is Hannah Josephson, *The Golden Threads: New England's Mill Girls and Magnates* (1949). Jeanne Boydston examines the impact of early industrialization on women's household labor and family roles in *Home and Work: Housework, Wages, and the Ideology of Labor in the Early Republic* (1990). There is no full-length biography of Lucy Larcom, but Bernice Selden's *The Mill Girls: Lucy Larcom, Harriet Hansen Robinson, Sarah G. Bagley* (1983) considers the three best known of the Lowell writers and activists. Larcom's autobiography, *A New England Girlhood: Outlined from Memory* (1889), remains well worth reading. Mary Blewett concentrates on the shoe industry, where home work continued to play a major role for a long time, in *Men, Women, and Work: Class, Gender, and Protest in the New England Shoe Industry, 1780–1910* (1988) and *We Will Rise in Our*

Might: Workingwomen's Voices from Nineteenth-Century New England (1991). Carol Turbin considers a uniquely female industry, collar making and laundering, in *Working Women of Collar City: Gender, Class, and Community in Troy, New York, 1864–1886* (1992). Christine Stansell investigates the lives of impoverished urban women and children in *City of Women: Sex and Class in New York, 1789–1860* (1987). Regarding prostitution in this early period, see Barbara Meil Hobson, *Uneasy Virtue: The Politics of Prostitution and the American Reform Tradition* (1990).

Women in Slave Society   To understand women in the slave South, various sources must be consulted. For women of the plantation class, the best study is Elizabeth Fox-Genovese, *Within the Plantation Household: Black and White Women of the Old South* (1988). Stephanie McCurry has written about the lives of poor white women in *Masters of Small Worlds: Yeoman Households, Gender Relations, and the Political Culture of the Antebellum South Carolina Low Country* (1995). Deborah Gray White has authored the first comprehensive study of slave women in *Ar'n't I a Woman: Female Slaves in the Plantation South*, rev. ed. (1999). Also see the relevant chapters in Jacqueline Jones, *Labor of Love, Labor of Sorrow: Black Women, Work, and the Family from Slavery to the Present* (1986). Brenda Stevenson considers all these groups in one Virginia county in *Life in Black and White: Family and Community in the Slave South* (1996). Suzanne Lebsock's *The Free Women of Petersburg: Status and Culture in a Southern Town, 1784–1860* (1984) investigates the understudied subject of property holding among women, white and black, in the slave South.

Selected Web Sites

Because *Godey's Lady's Book* is such a rich source for the nineteenth-century ideology of femininity and domesticity, several Web sites make available entire issues, including stories, poems, and illustrations. These include <**www.history.rochester .edu/godeys/**> and <**jefferson.village.virginia.edu/utc/sentimnt/gallgodyf.html**>.

To learn about the Lowell mill girls, consult the Web site associated with the Lowell National Historical Park, <**nps.gov/lowe/millgirls.htm**>. Lucy Larcom's entire autobiography is available online in a Project Gutenberg edition, <**digital .library.upenn.edu/webbin/gutbook/lookup?num=2293**>.

Harriet Jacobs is the subject of a Web site assembled by Trudy Mercer, <**drizzle .com/~tmercer/Jacobs**>, which includes primary sources that enrich Jacobs's own account. The site even has an excellent guide for students on how to properly cite and avoid plagiarism in papers that they write on Jacobs. Also on slavery, the Library of Congress American Memory Project includes an entire section on slave narratives gathered by the Works Projects Administration, <**lcweb2.loc.gov/ammem/ snhtml**>. Born in Slavery includes photographs and rare tape recordings made in the 1930s of aged ex-slaves. The American Memory Project also has a section on early American daguerreotypes, <**lcweb2.loc.gov/ammem/daghtml/**>.

4

Shifting Boundaries

EXPANSION, REFORM, AND CIVIL WAR, 1840–1865

T HE YEAR 1848 WAS A DECISIVE ONE IN THE HISTORY of the nation and of its women. Mexico, on the losing side of a grueling border war with the United States, had just signed the Treaty of Guadalupe Hidalgo and transferred 1.5 million square miles of land and many thousand human beings to U.S. sovereignty. The term "Manifest Destiny," coined a few years before, described the young nation's ambition to wrest much of the continent from its resident peoples, who, U.S. expansionists claimed, could not be trusted to exploit its potential riches. Responding to this crusade, tens of thousands of land-hungry American° women and men crossed the central plains to settle on the Pacific Coast. Less than a year after the end of the Mexican War, the discovery of gold in California dramatically accelerated this migration.

The beginning of the American women's rights movement also dates from 1848. Female reformers had been engaged for several decades in efforts to reshape and perfect

---

° The term "American" can be problematic, especially in a chapter that emphasizes the distinction between the North American continent and the United States, which had not yet gained control over its eventual fifty states. Nonetheless, by the 1840s the term "American" was being used to describe those who lived in the United States, and it is used that way in our narrative.

American society, their goals in part fostered by the excitement and opportunities of western expansion. As proponents of temperance and opponents of slavery, they pushed at the boundaries of woman's designated sphere and moved into more public roles. With the inauguration of the women's rights movement at the Seneca Falls Convention of 1848, they openly breached these boundaries, directing their utopian hopes and activist energies toward the freedom of women themselves.

Finally in 1848, the issue of slavery began to move into American party politics. Although Congress had been eluding the issue of slavery for decades, in that year the first political party to oppose the expansion of slavery, the Free-Soil Party, was established, followed by the formation of the Republican Party six years later. On the basis of its antislavery platform, the Republican Party captured the presidency in 1860, prompting eleven southern slave states to secede and fracturing the nation. The resulting Civil War threw the lives of all women, Union and Confederate, white and black, into upheaval for four deadly years.

In different ways, each of these historical processes was a kind of "movement." In this dynamic period in American history, when traditional social arrangements were being challenged and reformulated, when politics were confronting fundamental questions about the nature of American democracy and the future of the American nation, when the physical nation itself was breaking and remaking its borders, and when these vital sources of growth gave way to war and destruction and death, American women were on the move as well. Despite cultural conventions about their rootedness at home, American women struck out in all sorts of directions, playing a distinctive part in the nation's history and transforming themselves in the process.

AN EXPANDING NATION, 1843–1861

For a century before and a half century after 1848, continental expansion was a defining aspect of the American experience. Starting in the 1840s, however, the westward movement of American settlers entered a distinctive phase. In 1843, the overland passage through the Rockies called the Oregon Trail was mapped, and over the next two decades approximately 350,000 Americans crossed the

1848	**First New York State Married Women's Property Act passed**
1848	**Seneca Falls Convention initiates women's rights movement**
1848	Free-Soil Party founded
1850	Compromise of 1850, including Fugitive Slave Law, passed
1850	California becomes a state
1850	**First National Women's Rights Convention held in Worcester, Massachusetts**
1851	**Susan B. Anthony and Elizabeth Cady Stanton's partnership begins**
1852	**New York Women's Temperance Society formed**
1852	Harriet Beecher Stowe's *Uncle Tom's Cabin* published
1854	Republican Party formed
1854	Congress passes Kansas-Nebraska Act; guerrilla war between pro- and antislavery advocates follows
1854	**Elizabeth Cady Stanton addresses New York legislature on women's rights**
1857	Supreme Court decides *Dred Scott v. Sandford,* rejecting possibility of black citizenship
1860	**Second New York State Married Women's Property Act passed**
1860	Republican candidate Abraham Lincoln elected president
1860–1861	Southern states secede
1861	Civil War begins
1863	Emancipation Proclamation declares slaves in rebel territory free
1863	**Women's National Loyal League established**
1863	Battle of Gettysburg proves turning point in war
1863	Food riots in Richmond, Virginia, and draft riots in New York City erupt
1865	Robert E. Lee surrenders
1865	Lincoln assassinated
1865	Thirteenth Amendment ratified

continent, moving through the Indian lands of mid-America to reach the Pacific Coast. The migrants were mostly young American families: men charged with economic obligation, and women with childbearing and childrearing responsibilities. Except for slaves brought by southerners, they were white and, given the costs of the trek, from the middle ranks of society. When gold was discovered in California in 1848, the character and purposes of American migration changed. With permanent settlement no longer their objective, hordes of eager, ambitious men—and a few women—rushed to California to realize their dreams of quick wealth. The outbreak of the Civil War effectively ended the overland migration, and when expansion resumed, it took a different form, following the nation's new railroad system to concentrate on the great expanse of the trans-Mississippi plains (see Chapter 6 and the map at the end of the book).

Throughout the period of the Oregon Trail, women from the diverse cultures that met in the West came into conflict. Mexican women who lived in the Southwest looked askance as American women moved into their land. Respectable women settlers shunned prostitutes and female adventurers. Through it all, Indian women were relegated to the status of domestic servants for Mexican women, and by the outbreak of the Civil War, Mexican women were beginning to labor for American women in the same capacity. The conflicts between different groups of women were sometimes overt, sometimes implicit, but always more significant than the commonalities that the ideology of true womanhood claimed they shared.

Overland by Trail

Selfless wives and pioneer mothers have been celebrated for their role on the Oregon Trail, and it is undoubtedly true that men alone could not have made the new claims of continental nationhood a reality. But what of the actual experience of the individual women who pulled up stakes, cooked and laundered out of their primitive wagons for half a year or longer, gave birth and tended children across more than two thousand miles? Men usually made the decision to move. In 1852, Martha Read wrote to her sister of her reluctance to emigrate from New York with her husband. "It looks like a great undertaking to me but Clifton was bound to go and I thought I would go rather than stay here alone with the children."[1] Other women undertook the crossing with much the same eagerness as did their men. Looking west from the banks of the Missouri River that same year, Lydia Rudd wrote in her diary, "With good courage and not one sign of regret . . . [I] mounted my pony."[2] Individual families joined together in long lines ("trains") of thirty to two hundred covered wagons to share the effort and the danger of the trip. Single men made the overland crossing but rarely did unmarried women.

Occasionally, documents left by the migrants provide glimpses of the domestic tension that accompanied the difficult decision to uproot and migrate. A month into her 1848 trip to Oregon Territory, Keturah Belknap recorded a quarrel she overheard in a nearby wagon between a husband and wife. "She wants to turn back and he won't, so she says she will go and leave him . . . with that crying baby."

Then Belknap heard a "muffled cry and a heavy thud as if something was thrown against the wagon box." "Oh you've killed it," she heard the wife say, to which the husband responded "he would give her more of the same."[3] In another one of these rarely recorded incidents of desperate female resistance, a woman on the trail was so determined to turn back that she set the family's wagon on fire.[4]

Throughout the crossing, each sex held to its own distinctive responsibilities. Men drove the wagons and tended the animals. Women fed their families, cared for their children, and did their best to "keep house" in a cramped wagon bumping its way across the country. As the months wore on and the horses and oxen weakened, women walked more often than they rode. Men's tasks were concentrated during the day: after the wagons stopped and the animals were tended, they could snatch a bit of time to relax. If decisions about direction or pace had to be made, the men met alone and made them. The women's workdays were effectively the reverse. They woke up earlier to prepare breakfast, cared for children as the train moved forward, and worked for many hours after the wagons stopped to prepare for the next day. On the Oregon Trail, everyone worked to the full limit of her or his capacities. Even so, the average woman's workday was several hours longer than that of a man.

Overlanders took care to bring some of the few household improvements American women had gained in settled areas by the mid-nineteenth century, such as industrially spun cloth, prepared flour, and soap, on the trek west. Other modern inventions—iron stoves, for example—could not be carried westward, returning women to the domestic conditions of their mothers' and grandmothers' generations. On the rare days when the wagon train stopped, many women did laundry, pounding the dirt out of clothes in cold running streams. Often women begged men to stop the train to observe the Sabbath, but instead of resting, women caught up on their work.

In certain situations, women had to help the men drive the wagons or tend the stock. Rather than seize the chance to show that they could do a man's job, they were frequently reluctant to undertake new and difficult obligations on top of their regular work, clinging to the ideas of true womanhood as a way to preserve dignity on the trail. As Catherine Haun's party crossed the daunting mountain range to Oregon, she described how she joined in to keep the wagons from plunging uncontrollably back or forth. She complained bitterly, not so much that the work was difficult as that it was "unladylike." Whatever the conditions, however, she always had time for "tatting, knitting, crocheting, exchanging recepes [sic] . . . or swapping food," activities that "kept us in practice of feminine occupations and diversions."[5]

Women had exclusive responsibility for children on the trip. Since the average period between births for white women in 1850 was twenty-nine months, it is reasonable to assume that many, perhaps most, women were either pregnant or nursing and caring for infants in the wagons. Pregnancy was not discussed publicly, although domestic "confinement" was not possible on a wagon train. Often, the only way that the historian can detect a pregnancy is through a woman's references in letters or diary to "getting sick," followed soon afterwards by mention of a new child. "Still in camp, washing and overhauling the wagons . . . ," Amelia Stewart Knight wrote in her 1853 trail diary. "Got my washing and cooking done and started on again . . . (here I was sick all night, caused by my washing and working too hard)."[6] Within two weeks, just as their trip ended, she gave birth to her eighth child. She had been pregnant but had not referred directly to it for the entire six-month trip west.

In contrast to the infrequent references to birth, deaths, especially of children, were amply described. On her way to Oregon in 1862, Jane Gould Tortillott wrote

◆ **An American Family Arrives in California**
This painting commemorates the 1846 arrival of the Andrew Jackson Grayson family of Missouri to "the promised land" of California, as artist William S. Jewett titled the painting he completed in 1850. Jewett, also a newcomer to California, discovered that he could make a better living by painting than by panning for gold. Each of the family members indicates a different aspect of American settlement of the Far West. Mr. Grayson wears the buckskin clothes, adapted from Indian dress, that mark him as a pioneering westerner. His son wears a fanciful robe to signify his future rule over all that his father surveys. And what of Mrs. Grayson? How has the artist used her to represent not the danger and hard work of the over-land crossing but the middle-class domestic family culture by which the migrants sought to Americanize the West? By picturing a time before the upheaval unleashed by the 1848 gold rush, this painting reminds us of another kind of dream that California embodied for emigrating Americans. *William S. Jewett,* The Promised Land—The Grayson Family, *1850, oil on canvas, 50¾ × 64 inches, Terra Foundation for the Arts, Daniel J. Terra Collection, 1999.70; photograph courtesy of Terra Foundation for the Arts Chicago.*

about overtaking a particularly ill-fated wagon train. "There was a woman died in this train yesterday," she wrote. "She left six children, one of them only two day's old." Three days later, they passed the train. "They had just buried the babe of the woman who died days ago, and were just digging a grave for another woman who was run over. . . . She lived twenty-four hours, she gave birth to a child a short time before she died. The child was buried with her."[7] Older children were also at risk since their busy mothers could not always supervise them. There are numerous stories of children falling under and being crushed by the wheels of a moving wagon. While her mother was caring for a new baby, according to Catherine Sager, "[I got] the hem of my dress caught on an axle-handle, precipitating me under the wheels both of which passed over me, badly crushing my left leg."[8]

As the number of overlanders rose, more and more graves marked the trail. Lydia Rudd, who had begun her trip west so optimistically, within weeks was counting the graves she passed. Many migrants died of cholera, a swift-moving infectious disease that killed by severe dehydration. The disease had come with European immigrants in the mid-nineteenth century, and the overland migrants brought it with them as they traveled west. Sarah Royce wrote in her diary about the death of a man in her group. "Soon terrible spasms convulsed him. . . . Medicine was administered which afforded some relief . . . but nothing availed and in two or three hours the man expired." After the body was buried and the wagons were cleansed, Royce could only wait. "The destroyer seemed let loose upon our camp. Who would go next?"[9]

Women's relief at having arrived at their destination in Oregon or Washington or California was quickly replaced by the realization that they still had to build homes and establish communities. Cultivating the land took first priority, and it was years before a thriving family life could be realized. Long after they had moved west, many still missed the lives and families they had left behind. Still, the numerous memoirs written about the trail experience and the diaries handed down to children and grandchildren attest to the pride that overlanders, women as much as men, took in pioneering American society in the Far West. These records speak of the sense of accomplishment that such settlers felt for their endurance and determination.

The Underside of Expansion: Native and Mexican Californiana Women

The mid-nineteenth-century ideologies of Manifest Destiny and of true womanhood came together to designate the women emigrants as agents of civilization, responsible for reestablishing a settled, propertied, American family existence in the Far West. While individual women suffered during the crossing, their way of life, culture, and standards for womanhood eventually triumphed, and over time their willingness to move west was vindicated. The native women and the resident Mexican citizens who were pushed violently out of the way as the United States overtook the continent experienced conquest and displacement instead. The process of American expansion set women against each other on the grounds of culture, race, and ethnicity.

Earlier, the Indian peoples of the Southeast—the Creek, Chickasaw, Choctaw, and especially the Cherokee—had tried to adapt to American society (see Chapter 2). Women had learned the domestic tasks of housewifery. Cherokee leader Sequoyah had devised a written language, enabling the translation of the Christian Bible and the drafting of a political constitution. Some Cherokee even became slaveholders. But all of these efforts failed in the face of whites pressing for economic advantage. President Andrew Jackson, an old "Indian fighter" himself, pushed the Indian Removal Act of 1830 through Congress and then sent federal troops to Georgia to execute it. In 1838, the Cherokee were forcibly driven into the newly established Indian Territory west of the Mississippi, across what the Cherokee called the "Trail of Tears." The justification for this brutal relocation was that only when native peoples had been moved to the barren lands of the southern plains would they and their cultures be safe from the irresistible pressures of white American expansion. There, amid other Indian peoples who already lived in the area, they reestablished their society. They continued as farmers, traders, and housewives and built new community institutions. Among these was the Cherokee Female Seminary, where the tribe continued its policy of assimilation to white American norms by educating its daughters in the virtues of Christian womanhood.

Within a decade after the relocation of the Cherokee, migrating overlanders were crossing through Indian Territory in large numbers. Rather than appreciating the disruption and threat that they posed to native peoples, emigrant women were sure that they were at risk from the "red man." "Some of the women were very alarmed to night," Catharine Washburn recorded in her 1853 trail diary. "They thought they herd the Indians coming to attack us which turned out to be the ferry rope splashing in the water."[10] Over and over, trail accounts speak of Indian "attacks" that turn out to be something quite different. Hunger and illness were spreading among the Plains Indians, a consequence of encroaching American settlement. To alleviate their poverty, Indians requested or demanded food and money from the emigrants as they passed through their lands. In 1849, Sarah Royce's wagon train was stopped outside of Council Bluffs, Iowa, by Sioux who wanted payment of a toll. A tense encounter ensued, in which the American men brandished their weapons and declared that "the country we were traveling over belonged to the United States and that these red men had no right to stop us."[11] Royce recorded "the expression of sullen disappointment, mingled with a half-defiant scowl" on the Indians' faces as the emigrants moved on.

Living in and around the U.S. Army forts and trading posts that dotted the trail were Indian women who had left their own people to live with white men in informal sexual and domestic unions but who had been abandoned when the men married white women. Not allowed by their native communities to return, many ended up instead on the edges of white culture, as domestic servants to women settlers or prostitutes to men, where they were met with scorn as "black dirty squaws."[12] The term "squaw" had originally been used by white people simply to mean "Indian woman," but it had come to hold exclusively negative connotations of sexual degradation and unrelenting, unrewarded, and unskilled female labor.

◆ **Sarah Winnemucca, c. 1883–1890**
Sarah Winnemucca was born in 1844 to the Piute tribe on the Nevada–California border. A champion for the rights of her people, she wrote the first autobiography of a Native American woman, *Life among the Piutes* (1883). At about the same time, she lectured to white audiences on the lives and sufferings of Native Americans. To satisfy her audiences' desire to see a "real" Indian, she wore this elaborately beaded deerskin dress over red leather leggings and Indian moccasins. Like Master Grayson in the picture shown on page 206, she appears in regal dress. She was the daughter and granddaughter of Piute leaders, and her crown was meant to reinforce her billing as "Princess" Winnemucca. She died in 1891, exhausted and frustrated in her efforts to get white America to treat her people fairly. *Nevada Historical Society.*

Compared to the numerous accounts that white women left of their fears of Indians, little is known about how Indian women felt about white people. In her autobiography, Sarah Winnemucca, a Piute from the eastern side of the Sierra Nevada mountain range, related her encounter with American emigrants who crossed into her people's lands when she was a small child. (See Documents: Cross-Cultural Encounters in California, 1848–1850, pp. 236–44.) The Piute had their own rumors and fears that the white people "were killing everybody and eating them." The men of her father's band were away from camp and the women and children were gathering seeds when they realized that whites were approaching. The terrified women buried their children in mud and then hid their faces with bushes. "Can any one imagine my feelings buried alive . . . ?" Winnemucca recalled. "With my heart throbbing and not daring to breathe, we lay there all day." Her parents rescued her later that night. Soon after, the band's winter supplies were burned by a party of white men, and their impoverishment began.[13]

Native peoples on the Pacific Coast suffered severe losses as Americans poured into their lands. California Indians were particularly devastated. Their traditional sources of food were destroyed by American settlement and agriculture. Outright violence cost the lives of many. In 1850 at Clear Lake in northern California, 130

Pomo Indians, including women and children, were massacred by a U.S. Army detachment. Frequently, young native girls were kidnapped into servitude, and some were undoubtedly raped by white settlers. Sarah Winnemucca remembered that her mother feared that her "young and very good-looking" sister was unsafe among white men, even those whom her grandfather considered friends. These assaults, along with the syphilis that American men brought with them, dramatically reduced Indian women's fertility. The California Indian population, which had already been cut in half by disease and poverty in the years of Mexican rule, declined even more precipitously, from 150,000 to 30,000 between 1850 and 1860.

When they reached California, Americans also encountered the Californios, descendents of the original Mexican colonists. Most of the first Mexican women who had come to California were the wives of soldiers and banished convicts, but far less is known about them than about the women of the small class of Mexican landholders, who were celebrated in both Mexican and American legend. Starting in the 1830s, American men who went to California made their way into Mexican society by marrying the women of these elite families. In 1841 Abel Stearns, an ambitious merchant from Massachusetts, married Arcadia Bandini, daughter of one of the largest landholders in California. Abel was forty and Arcadia was fourteen, so she outlived him. When she died in 1912, she was the richest woman in southern California.

Mexican law gave married women more control over their property than did U.S. law. This helped to account for the phenomenon of the Californiana *ranchera,* the older woman or widow who controlled her own property with strength and savvy. Maria Angustias de la Guerra was such a woman. The daughter of the most prominent Californio in Santa Barbara, she presided over the elaborate home she shared with her husband Manuel Cesarin. (See Documents: Cross-Cultural Encounters in California, 1848–1850, pp. 236–44.) Helen Hunt Jackson's popular 1880 novel, *Ramona: A Romance of the Old Southwest,* offered a fictional portrait of such a woman in Senora Morena, a Mexican widow who was consumed with hatred for the Americans for seizing her land and despoiling her culture. Allegedly she was modeled after Arcadia Bandini's sister, Ysadora.

In the early years after statehood, California legislators sought to preserve some of the advantages that Mexican law provided married women, but gradually state courts and legislatures began to rewrite and reinterpret the laws of marital property to conform to the American standard, which favored husbands over wives. These legal shifts may have helped to accelerate the rapid transfer of California lands from Mexican to American hands in the 1850s and 1860s. As they did, Mexican women in California followed the path of Indian women into landlessness, domestic service, and poverty.

The Gold Rush

The combination of the discovery of gold in 1848 with the end of the Mexican War and the achievement of statehood in 1850 greatly accelerated the Americanization of California. The year before the discovery of gold there were four thousand overland migrants; the year after there were thirty thousand. Overlanders were joined by other gold-seekers who sailed around the southern tip of South America or crossed the wild Panamanian isthmus. Large numbers of miners came from Chile, Sonora Province in Mexico, and China. At the end of the war with Mexico, California had been populated by 100,000 Indians, perhaps a tenth as many Mexicans, and only a few thousand Americans. After the discovery of gold, it became one of the most cosmopolitan places on earth. Based on almost unlimited hopes for the quick achievement of fortune, California was a thoroughly cash-dependent society; anything could be bought, and everything cost dearly.

Most of the gold-seekers were men. By one estimate, for every one hundred men in gold country, there were three women.[14] Some of these women came with their husbands, either to share in the adventure or to fulfill a sense of duty to their husbands. But some women went west on their own, moved by the same adventurous dreams as men. In a letter to her mother soon after news broke of the discovery of gold, Susan B. Anthony, later one of the founders of the women's rights movement, wrote, "I wish I had about $100,000 of the precious dust. I would no longer be [a] School marm."[15] Although Anthony was too bound to her family to go, other women did join the rush, some to work close to the mines and others to set up businesses in San Francisco or Sacramento and make their fortunes at a distance. One of the few African American women in gold-rush San Francisco was Mary Ellen Pleasant, who ran a boarding house and a restaurant from 1849 through 1855. "A smart woman can do very well in this country . . . ," one woman wrote to a friend back East. "It is the only country that I ever was in where a woman recev'd anything like a just compensation for work."[16]

Despite the economic unpredictability of gold-rush California, women continued to maintain class differences among themselves. Middle-class women tended to remain in San Francisco, where furniture, solid houses, and the labor of servants could be purchased, albeit for enormous sums. Louise Clapp was the rare example of a middle-class woman who lived in the gold fields. She came with her physician husband and set up housekeeping in a tiny cabin furnished with three chairs, several rough tables, a bed, and a trunk. Of the three other white women who made up female society there, one was Irish-born and earned the enormous sum of $100 a week doing laundry. Clapp, who missed having servants as much as she did the company of women of her own class, became one of her customers. "Since all women cannot be manglers," she wittily observed of the woman's work washing and pressing her clothes, "the majority of the sex must be satisfied with simply being mangled."[17]

Most white women at the diggings were probably more like the unnamed laundress. While their husbands sought their fortunes at the mines, these women supported their families by feeding, housing, sewing, and laundering for the hordes of unmarried men who were willing to pay well for such services. When Luzena Wilson arrived in the boom town of Nevada City with her husband, she realized that women could make good money tending to the miners. She charged two hundred men $25 each a week for meals.[18] Mary Ballou, who ran a similar establishment, was astounded at the money she could make in California compared to how little women's labor was worth in the East. Even so, she concluded that "I would not advise any Lady to come out here and suffer the toil and fatigue that I have suffered for the sake of a little gold."[19]

Of all the women in gold-rush California, prostitutes have drawn the most attention from historians, much of it either romantic or salacious. "The first females to come were the vicious and unchaste," wrote Hubert Howe Bancroft, the state's first historian. "Flaunting in their gay attire, they were civilly treated by the men, few of whom, even the most respectable and sedate, disdained to visit their houses."[20] This image of the gold-rush prostitute accorded the respectability in California denied to her elsewhere in American society is inaccurate. So too is the claim that sexual labor provided these women with wealth and independence. The glamorous whores of California legend were few and limited to San Francisco. Closer to the minefields, the majority of prostitutes worked in seedy "crib hotels," where they had sex with many men for $1 or $2 per customer. All were at great risk for venereal disease and beatings and likely to die young.

The hierarchy of sex service in midcentury California reflected sharp racial and national distinctions, with white American and French women in the highest strata, and Mexicans, South Americans, and African Americans much lower. At the very bottom were the Chinese. By the late 1850s, approximately 35,000 Chinese men had come as miners but had been forced by discriminatory laws into low-paid, unskilled mining and railroad labor. The much smaller numbers of immigrant Chinese women were found almost exclusively in prostitution, a situation that did not change until federal measures restricted Chinese immigration in 1882 (see Chapter 6). By 1860, approximately two thousand women had been kidnapped or purchased in China and sent to the United States, where they were resold for tremendous profits. Chinese prostitutes were held in virtual slave conditions. Their terms of indenture were repeatedly extended for all sorts of spurious reasons, and many did not outlive their terms. Should they somehow elude their captors and the Chinese syndicates that organized the trade, they had no place to turn. U.S. courts ruled that prostitutes who had run away were guilty of the crime of property theft (of themselves) and returned them to their masters. A few survived to marry Chinese laborers; marriage to American men was legally prohibited.

Middle-class American women settlers expended little compassion on prostitutes. They were intent on distinguishing themselves from what they saw as the debased standards of womanhood brought in by the gold rush. Author and reformer Eliza Farnham, who had left New York for Santa Cruz to become an independent woman farmer just before gold was discovered, was a fervent advocate of the ideas of true womanhood and one of the "missionar[ies] of virtue, morality, happiness and peace" to the golden land of California. She could barely bring herself to describe the very different sorts of women who were rushing in to live "a false life, derelict from noble self-respect and divine purity."[21] When a vigilante movement sprang up in the 1850s to drive out the gambling and prostitution that had become endemic in San Francisco, Farnham championed its goals and violent methods, all in the name of establishing the morality that she identified with women like herself. (See Documents: Cross-Cultural Encounters in California, 1848–1850, pp. 236–44.)

ANTEBELLUM REFORM

The physical expansion of the United States along with the economic transformation of early industrialization generated a thriving spirit of moral and social activism from 1840 to the Civil War. Antebellum reformers pushed beyond established social and cultural norms to improve, even perfect, both the individual and the society. The centers of this reform ferment were in New York and New England, as if the era's impatience with established boundaries took a metaphoric rather than physical form in that region. Initially rooted in deeply religious conviction, antebellum reformers eventually followed the lodestar of moral virtue to arrive at the deeply political issues of abolition and women's rights. Accordingly, reform activism was virtually nonexistent in the slave South.

Women played a notable role in antebellum reform. By one estimate, at any given time as many as 10 percent of adult women in the Northeast were active in benevolent and reforming societies in these years.[22] The influential ideology of true womanhood credited women with the selflessness necessary to counterbalance male individualism. Their modest efforts on behalf of the community's welfare were thus compatible with domesticity and female respectability. But over time, women's dedication to moral and social causes led them beyond their homebound roles and to the edges of woman's allotted sphere. In the case of women's rights, some crossed over into new gender territory altogether.

Expanding Woman's Sphere: Maternal, Moral, and Temperance Reform

Following the intense wave of revivals in the late 1820s known as the Second Great Awakening (see Chapter 3), women from an ever wider swath of American society became involved in efforts to deepen and broaden the Protestant faith. Initially their role was to support male missionaries in bringing Christianity to the unconverted at home and abroad. For the most part, they deferred to male clergy and kept to their place, but the fervor of their faith inspired some to venture into new territory, figuratively and literally. In 1836, for instance, Narcissa Whitman and Eliza Spaulding traveled with their minister husbands to Oregon Territory by wagon, probably the first American women to do so, to convert the Nez Perce and Cayuse Indians.

Even in these supportive roles, however, pious women began to form their own organizations dedicated to aspects of their religious duty. They formed mothers' societies to protect the virtue of their children from the rampant immorality they perceived in a society in social and economic flux. These organizations published magazines to advise mothers and established and administered orphanages and Sunday religious schools. By emphasizing the Christian exercise of maternal responsibility, their members reconceptualized their maternal role as a basis for expanded social authority for their sex. Pious women also formed moral reform societies to combat the upsurge of drink, prostitution, and other forms of what they called "vice." By the early 1840s there were four hundred female moral reform societies in New England and New York. Moral reform enthusiasm was expansive enough to cross boundaries of race and class. Women of the tiny African American middle class formed their own societies to encourage standards of sexual decorum and family respectability in the free black community. The Lynn, Massachusetts, branch brought together artisans' wives and unmarried seamstresses to guard against the prostitution that they feared would take root in factory towns.

Moral reform societies were particularly concerned with the increase in casual sexuality among young women impoverished by the economic forces of rapid industrialization. Female moral reformers raised money to send ministers to save the souls of those women who had already "fallen" and campaigned to exclude "persons of either sex known to be licentious" from upstanding society.[23] Eventually they became bolder and reached out directly to prostitutes, despite the threat that such actions posed to their womanly reputations. Because they considered sexual excess as fundamentally male and regarded all women, even prostitutes, as its victims, they felt that sexual immorality represented sin in its most distinctly male form. To be sure, if prostitutes were not sufficiently penitent, they lost their claim to Christian women's sympathy. Nonetheless, women's moral reform activism deepened many middle-class women's gender consciousness and expanded their sense of common womanhood, thus helping to lay the foundations for the later women's rights movement.

Women's religiously motivated social activism in the mid-nineteenth century reached its height in the temperance movement. Americans were heavy drinkers in these years, but the temperance fervor focused on more than alcohol abuse. In an era of rapid and disorienting economic growth, the lack of self-restraint expressed through drunkenness provided a convenient explanation for why so many people suffered dramatic downward social mobility. The gospel of temperance promised that if a man could just control his impulses, subdue his appetites, and redirect his energies, his family might survive and even prosper through economic shifts. No reform movement was more widely supported in the 1840s and 1850s.

Although drunkenness was considered (not quite accurately) to be an exclusively male vice, images of its female victims—the suffering wives and children of irresponsible drunkards—figured prominently in antialcohol propaganda. Not content to remain mere symbols for the tragedies that "King Alcohol" wreaked, women became active proponents of temperate living. They began to form their own Daughters of Temperance societies to challenge both the morality and the legality of commerce in alcohol. When New York women activists created a State Women's Temperance Society in 1852, five hundred women attended the convention.

Much like the moral reform associations, women's temperance organizations incubated the expression of female discontent with middle-class family life and marital practices. Temperance activism allowed women to criticize men for their failure to live up to the marital bargain, by which wives would subordinate them-

◆ **Frances Ellen Watkins Harper**

Frances Ellen Watkins Harper was a teacher, lecturer, social activist, and poet. Although a free person from birth, she and her family fled their southern hometown of Baltimore after the 1850 passage of the Fugitive Slave Law, which put even free African Americans at risk for seizure as runaway slaves. She was the first African American woman to work for the American Anti-Slavery Society founded by William Lloyd Garrison (see p. 219). Following the Civil War, she worked on behalf of the southern freedpeople and continued her political and literary efforts through the end of the century. *Library of Congress, LC-USZ62-118946.*

selves to their husbands so long as the men were reliable breadwinners and even-handed patriarchs. Numerous female activists began their reform careers within the temperance movement, among them Susan B. Anthony and Frances Ellen Watkins Harper, the most prominent midcentury African American woman writer and speaker. After the Civil War, women's temperance activism continued to grow until it led to the most important women's organization of the Gilded Age, the Woman's Christian Temperance Union (see Chapter 5).

Exploring New Territory: Radical Reform in Family and Sexual Life

As women's enthusiasm for moral reform and temperance suggests, family and sexual life were important concerns of antebellum female reformers. The private nuclear family that was so central to the middle-class cult of domesticity was also a locale for domestic violence, sexual abuse, and female disempowerment. Some antebellum reformers called for more radical change in women's sexual and reproductive lives and for the establishment of alternative social systems not based on the private family.

Women's menstrual, reproductive, and sexual complaints made them eager advocates and consumers of health reform. Unwilling to rely on the questionable diagnoses of regular physicians, health activists developed alternative therapeutic regimes to increase bodily vitality. They made use of natural, uninvasive methods and urged avoidance of too much sensual stimulation as unhealthy. The "water cure," a system that emphasized cold water baths and loose clothing, offered comfort to women worn out from too many and too frequent pregnancies. The Graham system, which stressed the benefits of cold, unspiced foods (and left us the Graham cracker), promised to remedy sexual as well as digestive complaints.

Mary Gove Nichols, an outspoken critic of the sexual abuses hidden within marital life, advocated both the Graham and water-cure systems. Through the 1840s, she spoke forcefully and wrote explicitly about women's physical frustrations and sufferings in marriage. Insistent that "a healthy and loving woman is impelled to material union"—this was her term for sexual intercourse—"as surely, often as strongly as man," she declared that "the apathy of the sexual instinct in woman is caused by the enslaved and unhealthy condition in which she lives."[24] Very few nineteenth-century women ever heard such direct speech about female sexuality as did Nichols's readers and audiences. Paulina Wright, who went on to be a leader in the women's rights movement as Paulina Wright Davis, was also a women's health lecturer. She used a female manikin to teach women about their sexual and reproductive anatomy.

Radical reformers of sexuality and the family could be found as residents of the many communitarian experiments that sprang up in the 1830s and 1840s. From the viewpoint of women's history, what is interesting about these intentional communities was their challenge to conventional notions of marriage and the family. The Shakers occupied one end of the continuum; they prohibited all sexual relations, even within marriage. Men and women lived and worshiped in separate but conjoined communities, coming together to dance and sing their religious ecstasies. Obviously unable to enlarge their numbers by biological reproduction, Shakers took in orphans, apprentices, and individuals in flight from unhappy families, including destitute widows. In the 1830s, an estimated six thousand Shakers lived in nineteen communities throughout the country. Their celibate way of life and the alternative they offered to the private, patriarchal family strongly appealed to women, particularly inasmuch as their founder and chief saint was a woman. "Mother" Ann Lee had emigrated in the 1770s from England, where she had been the victim of marital rape and domestic abuse. She taught that God was both male and female, and that marriage was based on the subjugation of women and thus violated divine law.

Although it was as hostile to conventional marriage as the Shakers, the Oneida community took the opposite approach and sanctified extramarital sexuality. Moved by deep dissatisfaction with his own marriage, in 1848 John Humphrey Noyes founded a community in Oneida near Syracuse, New York. There, property was owned collectively, and children were raised communally, but the collectivization of sexual relations was the source of the community's greatest notoriety. Both men and women were sexually active but foreswore monogamy, lest they substitute attachment to an individual for the exclusive love of God. They also practiced a strict contraceptive regime, which required men to withhold ejaculation through prolonged sexual intercourse. Despite the Oneidans' sexual radicalism, they were deeply Christian and justified all their practices in biblical terms. The collectivization of housework, the availability of different sexual partners, male responsibility for contraception, and what might fairly be called the institutionalization of foreplay offered women at Oneida alternatives available nowhere else. Yet Noyes's insistence on retaining authority over all community life (including assigning sexual partners) also gave Oneida a deeply patriarchal air. Nonetheless, the Oneida community survived into the 1880s.

The Church of Jesus Christ of Latter-Day Saints, commonly known as Mormonism, was the most historically significant of these intentional antebellum communities but is the most difficult to assess through the eyes of women, because the estimations of insiders and outsiders were so different with respect to women's status in it. Founded in 1830 in Palmyra, New York, nine years later Mormons numbered 15,000 and migrated to form a cooperative community in Nauvoo, Illinois. Responding to rumors that church leaders had multiple wives, non-Mormons drove them out, and starting in 1847, the community trekked further west to Utah. There, polygamy became an open practice, a sign of special divinity. In response to federal pressure against polygamy, Utah Territory enfranchised its women to indicate their power and stature. When Elizabeth Cady Stanton, the great philosopher of nineteenth-century women's rights who had her own critique of marriage, traveled to Salt Lake City in 1871, she reported that "the Mormon women, like all others, stoutly defended their religion, yet they are no more satisfied [with their marriage practices] than any other sect."[25] The Mormons held to the practice of polygamy until 1896, when they formally rejected it in order for Utah to be admitted as a state.

While the Shakers, the Oneidans, and the Mormons were inspired by radical Christian notions of human perfectibility, there were other communal experiments based on more secular, indeed socialist, ideas. The most famous was Brook Farm, founded in Roxbury, Massachusetts, in 1841 by members of the Boston-based intellectual circle known as the Transcendentalists. For its brief existence, Brook Farm combined high culture and cooperative labor. Although young Georgiana Kirby, recently arrived from England, was not one of the luminaries of the experiment, she enthused that "the very air seemed to hold more exhilarating qualities than any I had breathed before."[26] The most prominent woman associated with Brook Farm was Margaret Fuller. During the period that she was a frequent visitor, Fuller wrote the first full-length feminist treatise in American history, *Woman in the Nineteenth Century* (see box, "What Woman Needs").

Crossing Political Boundaries: Abolitionism

Of all the forms of antebellum social activism, the movement to abolish chattel slavery had the most profound impact on American history, contributing significantly to the social and political tensions leading to the Civil War. Like temperance and moral reform, abolitionism arose out of a deep religious conviction that slaveholding was a sin that the truly God-fearing had the obligation to eliminate. "Let but each *woman* in the land do a Christian woman's duty," implored the Boston

MARGARET FULLER
What Woman Needs

Margaret Fuller (1810–1850) was the most prominent woman intellectual in antebellum America. In 1844, she wrote an article on the conflict between women's possibilities and their assigned roles. A year later she published a longer version as Woman in the Nineteenth Century. *Less overtly political than other women's rights activists, she was nonetheless widely admired by them for her ideas and teachings.*

Without attaching importance, in themselves, to the changes demanded by the champions of woman, we hail them as signs of the times. We would have every path laid open to woman as freely as to man. Were this done and a slight temporary fermentation allowed to subside, we should see crystallizations more pure and of more various beauty. . . .

[T]hen and only then will mankind be ripe for this, when inward and outward freedom for woman as much as for man shall be acknowledged as a right, not yielded as a concession. . . . If the negro be a soul, if the woman be a soul, apparelled in flesh, to one Master only are they accountable. There is but one law for souls, and if there is to be an interpreter of it, he must come not as man, or son of man, but as son of God.

Were thought and feeling once so far elevated that man should esteem himself the brother and friend, but nowise the lord and tutor of woman, were he really bound with her in equal worship, arrangements as to function and employment would be of no consequence. What woman needs is not as woman to act or rule, but as nature to grow, as an intellect to discern, as a soul to live freely and unimpeded, to unfold such powers as were given her when we left our common home.

SOURCE: Bell Gale Chevigny, *The Woman and the Myth: Margaret Fuller's Life and Writings,* rev. ed. (Boston: Northeastern UP, 1997), 248.

Female Anti-Slavery Society in 1836, "and the result cannot fail to be [the slave's] instant, peaceful, unconditional deliverance."[27] But unlike these other reforms, abolitionism brought its proponents, women along with men, into open conflict with America's basic political and religious institutions.

The call for immediate, uncompensated abolition of slavery and full civil rights for black people first came from the free black community, which by 1820 numbered over a quarter of a million. Many free blacks were kin to enslaved people, whom they struggled to purchase or smuggle into freedom through the Underground Railroad, the elaborate system of escape routes they developed to aid fleeing slaves. African American women aided the cause of abolitionism in other ways as well. In 1831, Maria Stewart, a black domestic servant from Connecticut, became the first American woman to criticize slavery publicly before mixed audiences of women and men. Speaking in Boston in September 1832, she boldly insisted, "The whites have so long and so loudly proclaimed the theme of equal rights and privileges, that our souls have caught the flame also, ragged as we are."[28]

Black men and women who had experienced slavery directly also challenged the institution. Frederick Douglass escaped slavery in Maryland in 1838 to become an internationally renowned advocate of freedom for his people. Sojourner Truth was born in 1797 as Isabella Baumfree, a slave in New York before the practice was abolished there. After her emancipation, she spent several years in a religious community in New York City, dropped her slave name, and rechristened herself Sojourner Truth to become an itinerant preacher and prophet. Starting in 1846, she became an abolitionist lecturer, traveling as far west as Kansas. Unlike most other black abolitionists, Truth did not present a respectable, middle-class face to the world. She spoke and acted like the woman she was—unlettered, emotionally intense, opinionated, and forthright. In her dialect and style, she made a tremendous impact, especially on white audiences. Author Harriet Beecher Stowe praised "her wonderful physical vigor, her great heaving sea of emotion, her power of spiritual conception, her quick penetration, and her boundless energy," and wondered what such a woman might have been and done had she not been born into slavery.[29]

Knowing that their numbers and influence were insufficient to uproot slavery, African American abolitionists sought sympathetic white allies, beginning with William Lloyd Garrison. From 1831 until 1865, Garrison edited the leading abolitionist newspaper, the *Liberator*. Women were always a substantial proportion of Garrison's followers. His radical principles, universalist notions of human dignity, and personal appreciation for women's discontent with their sphere made him a trusted leader. Elizabeth Cady Stanton—not one to bestow praise on men lightly—wrote of him: "I have always regarded Garrison as the great missionary of the gospel of Jesus to this guilty nation, for he has waged uncompromising warfare with the deadly sins of both Church and State. My own experience is, no doubt, that of many others. . . . I met Garrison . . . a few bold strokes from the hammer of his truth and I was free!"[30]

In 1833 Garrison founded the American Anti-Slavery Society, which was committed to the immediate, uncompensated abolition of slavery. Its membership was racially integrated, although the great majority of its members were white. At first, men led the organization and women supported them. Lucretia Mott, an influential Quaker who went on to become the dean of female abolitionists, attended the founding meeting of the American Anti-Slavery Society, but neither she nor any other women were listed as members. "I do not think it occurred to any one of us at the time, that there should be propriety in our signing the [founding] document," she later wrote.[31]

Accordingly, women abolitionists, white and black, organized separate auxiliary female societies. In the Philadelphia Female Anti-Slavery Society, formed also

◆ **Am I Not a Woman and a Sister?**

This image, widely used in antislavery literature, expresses the complex sentiments that underlay women's abolitionist activism. The phrase "Am I Not a Woman and a Sister?" challenges the fundamental premise of chattel slavery that the slave woman was mere property. Instead, she is portrayed as sister to the free woman, a member of the same human family. At the same time, the image emphasizes the inequality of the two, as the female slave is pictured as a powerless supplicant, waiting on the actions of the abolitionist woman to reach down and lift her up from her chains. This version appeared on the special pages for women in William Lloyd Garrison's abolitionist newspaper, the *Liberator*.
By permission of the Houghton Library, Harvard University.

in 1833, black women were 10 percent of its members and an even higher proportion of its officers.[32] Among the most prominent were Charlotte Forten (grandmother of the better-known Charlotte Forten Grimké) and her daughters Margaretta, Sarah Louise, and Harriet, and Grace and Sarah Douglass (not related to Frederick). Despite greater wealth and education than the overwhelming majority of African Americans, these women were no strangers to racial prejudice. In 1838, when a nationwide meeting of women abolitionists was held in Philadelphia, a mob, infuriated by witnessing black and white women meeting together, attacked them and burned down Pennsylvania Hall, the building they had just dedicated to the abolitionist movement.

Female abolitionists' willingness to go beyond the limits of female propriety to defeat slavery, combined with their increasing realization that free women, white as well as black, experienced barriers to full personhood like those faced by slaves, pushed many of them in the direction of women's rights. Sarah and Angelina Grimké led the way. Born into a wealthy and politically prominent slaveholding family in South Carolina, in 1829 the sisters fled to Philadelphia, where they became Quakers and abolitionists. Driven by their deep conviction of slavery's profound sinfulness, in 1836 they followed Maria Stewart's lead and preached against slavery to "promiscuous" (mixed) audiences of men and women, providing shockingly detailed descriptions of the sexual corruptions of slavery. The Massachusetts General Association of Congregationalist clergy publicly reprimanded them: "We appreciate the unostentatious prayers and efforts of woman in advancing the cause of religion at home and abroad . . . but when she assumes the place and tone of man as a public reformer, . . . her character becomes unnatural. . . . We especially deplore the intimate acquaintance and promiscuous

Sarah Grimké
On the Traditions of Men

Sarah Grimké (1792–1873) and her sister Angelina were slaveowners turned abolitionists. Their attacks on slavery brought them tremendous criticism from the organized clergy of Massachusetts, which issued a "Pastoral Letter" accusing the sisters of stepping outside of the sphere God had assigned their sex. Sarah's defense of women's equal right (and obligation) to uproot slavery was published in 1838 in a series of abolitionist and feminist essays entitled Letters on the Equality of the Sexes and the Condition of Women.

The Lord Jesus defines the duties of his follower in his Sermon on the Mount. . . . I follow him through all his precepts, and find him giving the same directions to women as to men, never even referring to the distinction now so strenuously insisted upon between masculine and feminine virtues: this is one of the anti-christian "traditions of men" which are taught instead of the "commandments of God." Men and women were CREATED EQUAL; they are both moral and accountable beings; and whatever is *right* for man to do, is *right* for woman.

SOURCE: Elizabeth Ann Bartlett et al., eds., *Sarah Grimké: Letters on the Equality of the Sexes and Other Essays* (New Haven: Yale UP, 1988), 38.

conversation of females with regard to things 'which ought not to be named.' "[33] The sisters neither admitted error nor retreated. Instead, they insisted that it was not man's place but God's to assign woman's sphere (see box, "On the Traditions of Men").

The Grimkés' courageous defense of their equal rights as moral beings and social activists produced a split in the abolitionist movement over the role of women. One wing, led by Garrison, moved to include women as full and equal participants in the work of converting white Americans to realize the moral necessity of abolishing slavery. After 1840, women served as officers and paid organizers of the American Anti-Slavery Society. A second wing, which included among its leaders Frederick Douglass, insisted that the issue of women's equality needed to be kept separate from that of abolition. The non-Garrisonians moved in the direction of more pragmatic, political methods, including the formation of political parties against slavery. These two issues—separating abolition from women's rights and moving beyond moral to political methods—were connected. Women, who were identified with moral purity and who lacked political rights, had little to offer a more political approach to abolitionism, at least until they began to make claims for suffrage rights.

The surfacing of political methods within abolitionism reflected the dramatic democratization of electoral politics in this period. By 1840, virtually all adult white men, regardless of wealth, had the right to vote. White men of all ranks followed elections closely, boasted proudly of their partisan inclinations, and contended openly for the candidates of their choice. Historians have labeled this expansion of political involvement "Jacksonianism" because the Democratic Party, formed in 1828 to nominate Andrew Jackson for the presidency, was its first institutional embodiment, followed in 1834 by the formation of the Whig Party. While only 30 percent of adult white men went to the polls in 1824, by 1840, 80 percent did so. Free black men were not included in this enfranchisement; indeed, they lost political rights in these years.

Nor were women included in the Jacksonian expansion of the franchise. On the contrary, the right to vote was becoming the distinguishing characteristic of white American manhood. And yet as the reformist spirit of the age began to spill over into politics, women were drawn into the excitement of electoral contests. They participated in political discussions and championed candidates and parties. When they felt compelled to register formally their political opinion on an issue, they turned to the only mechanism allowed to them, petitioning their legislators. As early as 1830, non-Indian women petitioned the federal government to halt the violent removal of the Cherokee from their own lands. Women also petitioned their state legislatures to ban the sale of alcohol and to make men's seduction of women a punishable crime.

Women abolitionists conducted the most ambitious and controversial of these petition campaigns. Starting in the 1830s, they began to gather thousands of signatures on petitions to Congress to ban slavery in the territories and in Washington, D.C., and to end the internal slave trade between the states. "Let us know no rest til we have done our utmost to . . . obtain the testimony of every woman . . . against the horrible Slave-traffic . . . ," they declared.[34] In 1836, Congress passed a "gag rule" to table all petitions on slavery without discussion, but abolitionist women only intensified their efforts (see Map 4.1). Their congressional champion, John Quincy Adams (who had become a Massachusetts congressman after a single term as president) defended the movement of women beyond the boundaries of woman's sphere into the male world of politics: "Every thing which relates to peace and relates to war, or to any other of the great interests of society, is a political subject," he declared. "Are women to have no opinions or actions on subjects relating to the general welfare?"[35]

Entering New Territory: Women's Rights

Starting in the 1840s, all of these developments—moral reform and temperance, circulating petitions against slavery, the Grimkés' defense of their equal right to champion the slave—led many women reformers into women's rights. But unlike other activist efforts, women's rights openly challenged the basic premise of true

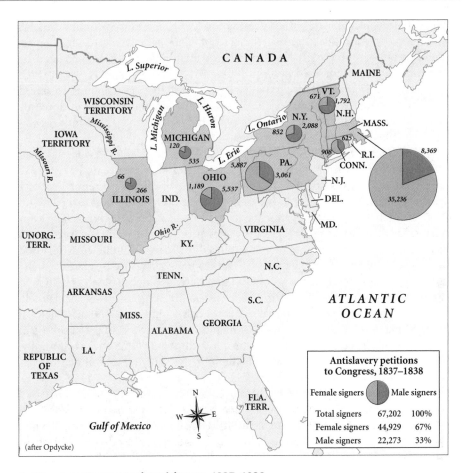

◆ Map 4.1 **Women and Antislavery, 1837–1838**

In the late eighteenth and early nineteenth centuries, most legislative petitions from women came from individuals, for instance to legally dissolve their marriages. In the 1830s, when women began to petition collectively on behalf of pressing political issues, the tone of their petitions became less supplicating, more assertive. Men and women usually submitted separate petitions on behalf of common goals. This map indicates the geographically concentrated character of women's antislavery activism. Their petitions to the U.S. Congress accelerated the interregional tensions and national crisis over slavery, leading twenty-three years later to the Civil War.

womanhood—that women were fundamentally selfless. Women's rights advocacy led women to insist that they had the same claim on individual rights to life, liberty, property, and happiness as men.

First articulated in 1793 by the English radical Mary Wollstonecraft, the doctrine of women's rights was brought to the United States in the 1820s by Frances

Wright, a Scotswoman who gained great notoriety by her radical pronouncements on democracy, education, marriage, and labor. The threat Wright's ideas represented to notions of respectable, Christian womanhood can be appreciated by Catharine Beecher's horrified description of her: "There she stands, with brazen front and brawny arms, attacking the safeguards of all that is venerable and sacred in religion, all that is safe and wise in law, all that is pure and lovely in domestic virtue."[36] For several years, any woman who publicly advocated radical ideas was derisively called a "Fanny Wright" woman.

For women's rights to grow from a set of ideas associated with one maligned individual into a reform movement took several decades. Changes to the extensive body of state laws that deprived married women of all independent property rights was an early goal. These laws treated wives as nonpersons before the law, on the grounds that they were dependents on and subordinates to their husband's authority. This pervasive Anglo-American legal principle was called "coverture," a term signifying the notion that marriage buried (or "covered") the wife's selfhood in that of the husband (see Chapter 1). A law to undo coverture by granting married women the same right to earnings and property as single women and all men was introduced into the New York State legislature in 1836 by Elisha Hertell. Hertell was assisted by Ernestine Rose, a Jewish immigrant who had fled an arranged marriage in Poland, married a man of her own choosing, and settled in New York City to become a leader in the "free-thinking" (atheistic) community. Despite great effort, however, she was able to gather only a handful of women's names to a petition on behalf of Hertell's bill.

By the 1840s, two other women joined Rose to work on behalf of married women's economic rights. One was Paulina Wright (later Davis), the activist who had started her career as a women's health educator. (See Documents: Paulina Wright Davis, the *Una*, and Women's Rights, pp. 245–50.) The other was Elizabeth Cady Stanton, destined to become the greatest women's rights thinker of the nineteenth century. Born into a wealthy and politically conservative New York family, her great intelligence and high spirits consistently led her afoul of the boundaries of woman's sphere. Her father, Daniel Cady, was a prominent lawyer and a judge, and although she could never hope to follow in his footsteps, she studied law informally in his office. As a young woman, she was deeply influenced by her kinsman, the abolitionist Gerrit Smith. In his home, a stop on the Underground Railroad, she met fugitive slaves. She also met her future husband, the charismatic abolitionist orator Henry Stanton. In 1840, despite her father's opposition, they married. When Henry introduced his new bride to Sarah and Angelina Grimké, they noted that they "were very much pleased" with Elizabeth but wished "that Henry was better calculated to help mould such a mind."[37]

Cady Stanton soon found her mentor in Quaker and abolitionist leader Lucretia Mott. On her honeymoon in London in 1840, she met Mott at an international antislavery convention at which female delegates were confined behind an opaque curtain and barred from participating in formal discussion. Both women were incensed, but the thrill of meeting each other outweighed the insult. "The acquaintance of Mrs. Mott, who was a broad, liberal thinker on politics, religion, and all questions of reform, opened to me a new world of thought," Cady Stanton later recalled.[38] For the next several years, Mott instructed her young protégé in the principles of women's rights. Soon Cady Stanton was lobbying in the New York legislature for reform of married women's economic rights. In April 1848, the legislature passed a bill that gave wives control over inherited (but not earned) wealth.

By this time Cady Stanton was the mother of four boys and living in the small industrial town of Seneca Falls, New York. Her husband was often away working for the abolitionist cause. With Lucretia Mott as her teacher and Henry Stanton as her husband, Elizabeth Cady Stanton was perfectly situated to bridge the gap between the moral activist tradition of women reformers and the increasingly political focus within abolitionism. She was also eager for a dramatic change in her own life. "The general discontent I felt with woman's portion as wife, mother, housekeeper, physician, and spiritual guide," she wrote, "the wearied, anxious look of the majority of women impressed me with a strong feeling that some active measures should be taken to right the wrongs of society in general, and of women in particular."[39] In July 1848, Cady Stanton, Mott, Mott's sister Martha Coffin Wright, and two other local female abolitionists called a public meeting in a local church to discuss "the social, civil and religious condition of Woman." Of the approximately three hundred women and men who attended, one-third, including a large contingent of Quakers, endorsed a manifesto that rewrote the Preamble of the Declaration of Independence to declare that "all men *and women* are equal."[40]

The Seneca Falls Declaration of Sentiments went on to list eighteen instances of "repeated injuries and usurpations on the part of man toward woman." (See the Appendix for the complete text.) Women were denied access to professions, trades, and education, their rights in marriage and motherhood, their self-confidence and their moral equality before God. The most controversial resolution asserted women's equal right to vote. To abolitionist purists, however, resort to the ballot represented participation in a fundamentally corrupt system. Yet, more and more issues about which women cared—notably abolition—were being debated and resolved within the electoral arena. And, as Cady Stanton repeatedly insisted, all the other changes needed in women's condition would ultimately require women's ability to affect the law. Frederick Douglass, living nearby in Rochester, was the only man in the room who could not vote, and he supported the suffrage resolution eloquently. After debate, the delegates passed it.

In the years after the Seneca Falls Convention, the women's rights movement grew energetically but haphazardly. Lucy Stone, the first U.S. woman to receive a bachelor's degree and a traveling lecturer on abolition and women's rights, inspired many women to join the ranks. Women learned about the new movement from friends and relatives. In 1851, on the advice of her sisters, Susan B. Anthony traveled from nearby Rochester to meet Cady Stanton and the two women immediately formed a working friendship that lasted sixty years. Women brought women's rights ideas with them as they migrated west. In 1850 California emigrants Eliza Farnham and Georgiana Bruce debated women's rights as they plowed the land side by side. Throughout the 1850s, women's rights advocates convened to share ideas, recruit new adherents, and fortify themselves for future efforts. At one such meeting, in

SOJOURNER TRUTH
I Am as Strong as Any Man

The most oft-cited version of Sojourner Truth's eloquent 1851 women's rights speech was published by a white activist, Frances D. Gage, twelve years after it was delivered. Recently, historian Nell Painter has drawn attention to a version of the speech published in the Anti-Slavery Bugle *at the time Truth made her remarks. In this presumably more accurate version, Truth (c. 1797–1883) makes her important argument for women's rights on the basis of her own experience of black womanhood without the southern dialect, the "Ain't I a woman" refrain, or the lament for her children lost to slavery, all of which Gage attributed to her.*

I am a woman's rights [woman]. I have as much muscle as any man, and can do as much work as any man. I have plowed and reaped and husked and chopped and mowed, and can any man do more than that? I have heard much about the sexes being equal; I can carry as much as any man, and can eat as much too, if I can get it. I am as strong as any man that is now. . . .

I can't read, but I can hear. I have heard the Bible and have learned that Eve caused man to sin. Well, if woman upset the world, do give her a chance to set it right side up again. The Lady has spoken about Jesus, how he never spurned woman from him, and she was right. When Lazarus died, Mary and Martha came to him with faith and love and besought him to raise their brother. And Jesus wept and Lazarus came forth. And how came Jesus into the world? Through God who created him and the woman who bore him. Man, where was your part?

SOURCE: Marius Robinson, *Anti-Slavery Bugle,* June 21, 1851, reprinted in Nell Irvin Painter, *Sojourner Truth: A Life, a Symbol* (New York: Norton, 1996).

1851 in Akron, Ohio, abolitionist Sojourner Truth delivered a women's rights speech that has come down through the years as a forceful case for a new standard of womanhood expansive enough to include women like her (see box, "I Am as Strong as Any Man").

Gradually, these pioneering activists began to reform the laws that denied women, especially wives, their rights, especially their economic rights. The most successful of these campaigns was conducted by Cady Stanton and Anthony in New York State. Cady Stanton, confined by her growing brood of children, wrote the speeches and petitions from her Seneca Falls home. In these years, she spoke in public only once, in 1854, before the members of the New York legislature (see box, "On Behalf of All Women"). Anthony, freer as an unmarried woman, traveled

◆ "Bloomer Costumes or Woman's Emancipation"

The heavy skirts worn by middle-class women in the mid-nineteenth century were awkward and confining. In the 1850s, women's rights advocates adopted an alternative costume, which featured loose trousers under a shortened skirt. Named after Amelia Bloomer, a Seneca Falls neighbor of Elizabeth Cady Stanton who championed the outfit in the pages of a temperance journal she edited, the "reform dress" was actually first developed by the women of the Oneida community. Bloomers were widely lampooned, as in this cartoon, which links them to male accessories and behaviors. Those who tried the bloomer costume reluctantly gave it up as it brought them so much unwanted attention that they were more rather than less restricted in their freedom of movement. *National Museum of American History, Smithsonian Institution, neg. #49741-B.*

through the state to collect signed petitions on behalf of women's civil and political rights. Women's rights reformers also confronted cultural practices that, along with laws, constrained women.

In 1860, the New York State legislature finally passed a bill that gave wives the rights to own and sell their own property, to control their own wages, and to claim rights over their children upon separation or divorce. Cady Stanton was ready to

ELIZABETH CADY STANTON
On Behalf of All Women

On February 14, 1854, Elizabeth Cady Stanton (1815–1902) became the first woman to speak before the legislature of New York State. She spoke on behalf of a law granting married women full property rights, but it took another six years to pass. Here, she ably refuted the claim that only a few unrepresentative middle-class women supported the demands of the women's rights movement.

In behalf of the women of this State, we ask for all that you have asked for yourselves . . . simply on the ground that the rights of every being are the same and identical. You may say that the mass of the women of this State do not make the demand; it comes from a few sour, disappointed old maids and childless women. You are mistaken; the mass speak through us. A very large majority of the women of this State support themselves and their children, and many their husbands too. . . . The drunkards' wives speak through us, and they number 50,000. . . . For all these, then, we speak. If to this long list you add the laboring women who are loudly demanding remuneration for their unending toil; those women who teach in our seminaries, academies, and public schools for a miserable pittance; the widows who are taxed without mercy; the unfortunate ones in our work-houses, poor-houses, and prisons; who are they that we do not now represent?

SOURCE: Ellen Carol DuBois, ed., *The Elizabeth Cady Stanton–Susan B. Anthony Reader* (Boston: Northeastern UP, 1992), 51–52.

move onto a campaign to liberalize divorce laws, but this was too much even for women's rights radicals. Moreover, by this point political conflicts over slavery between North and South had reached such a level of intensity that, like other Americans, women's rights activists were thoroughly preoccupied with the fate of the Union.

CIVIL WAR, 1861–1865

Ever since the northern states had ended slavery early in the nineteenth century, national political leaders had tried to render the practice an exclusively southern problem. In 1821, Congress had crafted the Missouri Compromise, which drew a line across the territories of the Louisiana Purchase at the southern border of the new slave state of Missouri and declared that no further slave states could be established north of it. The goal was to keep the number of slave and nonslave states equal so as to give neither side an advantage in the Senate. Despite the petitions of abolitionist women, the two major parties, the Democrats and the Whigs, cooperated in keeping debate over slavery out of national politics. But continuing western expansion, especially the acquisition of lands from Mexico which lay outside the Louisana Territory, eroded this fragile political balance.

In 1850, congressional leaders crafted a second compromise. California would enter the Union as a nonslave state, in exchange for which special federal commissioners would be appointed with the power to return people charged with being runaway slaves to those who claimed to be their masters. Escaping to the North would no longer mean freedom, as it had for Frederick Douglass or Ellen and William Craft. With slave catching now federalized under the Fugitive Slave Law, nowhere was safe. What southerners regarded as proper federal protection of their property rights, northerners regarded as evidence that an ambitious slave power was taking over the country. From this point forward, the expansion of slavery became an inescapable national crisis.

In 1861, political crisis became military conflict. Just as the Civil War pit brother against brother, women too were intensely divided in their loyalties. The difference, of course, is that women were barred by their sex from the two forms of direct participation in the war—the ballot box and the battlefield. But as in all civil wars, the home front was impossible to separate from the battle front. Many women actively supported their causes and their armies. A small but surprising number participated directly, either on the battlefield or in the politics that shaped the changing purposes for which the war was fought. All women were affected by the war—its passions, devastations, and deaths.

Women and the Impending Crisis

As the political conflict over slavery intensified, women were drawn into the growing crisis. Most famously, Harriet Beecher Stowe wrote *Uncle Tom's Cabin* to dramatize the dangers facing the escaping slave under the new federal law (see box, "Reflections on *Uncle Tom's Cabin*"). By far the most popular American novel ever written, the story of the slave Eliza fleeing slave catchers to save her child was avidly read when it first appeared in installments in an antislavery newspaper in 1851 to 1852. Inspired by Stowe's book, Harriet Jacobs, who had escaped from slavery twelve years before, determined to write her own story. *Incidents in the Life of a Slave Girl: Written by Herself* was published in 1861, with the help of white abolitionist Lydia Maria Child.

Throughout the political events of the 1850s, women's involvement was everywhere. In 1854, the Republican Party was founded to oppose the expansion (though not the existence) of slavery and succeeded in bringing the issue squarely into the center of national politics. The party's 1856 presidential nominee was U.S. Senator John Frémont of California, the man who had originally surveyed the

HARRIET BEECHER STOWE
Reflections on Uncle Tom's Cabin

Harriet Beecher Stowe (1811–1896) was the daughter, sister, and wife of influential Protestant ministers. Like her sister Catharine Beecher, she was a highly successful author, whose books elaborated the ideas of true womanhood. In 1849, her eighteen-month-old son died, an experience that informed her powerful antislavery novel, Uncle Tom's Cabin, *published in 1851–1852. In it, the slave heroine Eliza is threatened with the loss of her own child, through sale rather than death. Stowe's novel is widely credited with building popular antislavery sentiment, especially among women, in the North.*

For many years of her life, the author avoided all reading upon or allusion to the subject of slavery, considering it as too painful to be inquired into . . . But, since the legislative act of 1850, when she heard, with perfect surprise and consternation, Christian and humane people actually recommending the remanding of escaped fugitives into slavery, as a duty binding on good citizens, . . . she could only think, These men and Christians cannot know what slavery is; if they did, such a question could never be open for discussion. . . . You, mothers of America,—you who have learned, by the cradles of your own children, to love and feel for all mankind,—by the sacred love you bear your child; . . .—I beseech you, pity the mother who has all your affections, and not one legal right to protect, guide, or educate, the child of her bosom! . . . If the mothers of the free states had all felt as they should, . . . the sons of the free states would not have connived at the extension of slavery, in our national body; the sons of the free states would not, as they do, trade the souls and bodies of men as an equivalent to money, in their mercantile dealings. There are multitudes of slaves temporarily owned, and sold again, by merchants in northern cities; and shall the whole guilt or obloquy of slavery fall only on the South?

SOURCE: Harriet Beecher Stowe, *Uncle Tom's Cabin* (New York: Bantam Classics, 1982), 437–38.

Oregon Trail. His wife, Jessie Benton Frémont, was the first wife of a presidential candidate to figure significantly in a national campaign. Daughter of U.S. Senator Thomas Hart Benton of Missouri, she was young, attractive, vivacious, and considered a liberal influence on her husband. Campaign paraphernalia advertised Jessie as much as her husband. Other women were Republican activists and contributed to the party's extraordinarily rapid rise. In Minnesota, Jane Grey Swisshelm earned herself the title "Mother of the Republican Party" for publishing the only pro-Republican newspaper in her part of the state. Although Frémont was defeated by the Democratic candidate, James Buchanan, the Republicans succeeded in displacing the Whigs to become one of the two major national parties.

Then, in 1857, the Supreme Court ruled in favor of slavery in the momentous case *Dred Scott v. Sandford.* The case might more appropriately be called the Dred and Harriet Scott case since it involved not only Missouri slave Dred Scott but also his wife Harriet. Together they sued their owner for their freedom and that of their two daughters. (Indeed, some modern legal scholars think that Harriet's case may have been the stronger.) By being brought in 1834 into federal territory where slavery was not lawful, the Scotts argued that they had become free persons. A majority of the Supreme Court ruled against the Scotts. In addition, Chief Justice Roger B. Taney wrote an opinion that the entire legal framework dating back to the Missouri Compromise was unconstitutional because it violated slaveowners' property rights. The Scotts eventually bought their own freedom, but the larger battle between pro- and antislavery forces for control of the federal government had been profoundly intensified by the decision.

The election of 1860 took place against the background of John Brown's abortive guerilla raid on the federal armory in Harper's Ferry, Virginia, which was intended (but failed) to start a general slave uprising. To southerners, the handful of black and white antislavery warriors under Brown's command constituted exactly the violent threat that they long had feared from abolitionists. Many northerners regarded Brown quite differently, as a martyr. "I thank you that you have been brave enough to reach out your hands to the crushed and blighted of my race . . . ," Frances Ellen Watkins Harper wrote to Brown as he awaited execution after his capture by federal forces. "I hope from your sad fate great good may arise to the cause of freedom."[41]

For president, the Republicans nominated former Illinois Congressman Abraham Lincoln, a moderate critic of slavery, hardly an abolitionist, and no great friend of the slave. Despite his moderation, because he was a Republican his election was intolerable to the South. But to many northerners, Lincoln's election was cause to celebrate. Twenty-one-year-old Frances Willard, who would go on to head the Woman's Christian Temperance Union in the 1870s, observed events from her Illinois home. "Under the present system I am not allowed to vote for [Lincoln], but I am as glad on account of this Republican triumph as any man who has exercised the elective franchise can be."[42]

By April 1861, eleven southern slave states had seceded from the Union to form the Confederate States of America. On April 13, South Carolinian slaveholder Mary Chesnut watched as southern gunboats fired upon U.S. ships that Lincoln had sent to provision the lightly garrisoned federal Fort Sumter in Charleston harbor in an effort to reject Confederate claims to independent national sovereignty. When she learned that federal forces had surrendered to the Confederates, she "sprang out of bed and on my knees—prostrate—I prayed as I never prayed before."[43]

Chesnut understood that war had begun in earnest. North and South, men and boys, rushed to enroll in their local regiments, and wives and mothers prepared to say good-bye. "Love for the old flag became a passion," wrote Mary Livermore from Illinois, "and women crocheted it prettily in silk, and wore it as a decoration on their bonnets and in their bosoms."[44] Both sides hoped for a brief war and a glorious victory but got instead a four-year conflict, the most deadly war in American history.

Women's Involvement in the War

Although formally excluded from enlistment and armed service, both Union and Confederate women were nonetheless deeply involved in the war. Eager and patriotic, a minority found their way to the battlefield, as nurses, spies and strategists, and, disguised as men, even as soldiers. (See Visual Sources: Women on the Civil War Battlefields, pp. 251–63.) Far more women participated at a distance. Because both armies were decentralized and almost entirely unprovisioned—except for munitions—by their respective governments, women volunteers were responsible for much of the clothing, feeding, and nursing of the soldiers. In the South this was done at a local level. Within a few months after the conflict had begun, Mary Ann Cobb, wife of a Confederate officer in Georgia, found herself charged with rounding up provisions for a company of eighty men. By going door to door among her neighbors, she accumulated 300 pounds of meat and 500 pounds of biscuits.

In the North, where women had greater experience in running their own voluntary associations, soldiers' relief was better organized. Local societies were drawn together in a giant national organization known as the United States Sanitary Commission. Mary Livermore spent the war directing the Chicago branch. Her duties were manifold: "I . . . delivered public addresses to stimulate supplies and donations of money; . . . wrote letters by the thousand . . . ; made trips to the front with sanitary stores . . . ; brought back large numbers of invalid soldiers . . . ; assisted to plan, organize, and conduct colossal [fund-raising] fairs . . . ; detailed women nurses . . . and accompanied them to their posts."[45] The experience turned Livermore and others like her into skilled, confident organization women, and after the war they used these experiences to build similarly ambitious, centralized women's federations. On the basis of her experience organizing relief supplies for northern soldiers, Clara Barton went on to found the American division of the International Red Cross.

The labors of such women earned them elaborate praise. But for the average woman on either side of the conflict, these were not years of uplifting service or patriotic heroism so much as of prolonged suffering. Women struggled to support their families without the aid of husbands, sons, and brothers. Anna Howard Shaw, who later became one of America's leading suffragists, was a young woman living in rural Michigan in 1861: "I remember seeing a man ride up on horseback, shouting out Lincoln's demand for troops. . . . Before he had finished speaking the men on the [threshing] machine had leaped to the ground and rushed off to enlist, my brother Jack . . . among them. . . . The work in our community, if it was done at all, was done by despairing women whose hearts were with their men."[46]

The South, which relied on slave workers, initially had the advantage over the North, which lost much of its labor force to the fighting. Even so, most white southerners were small-scale subsistence farmers who relied almost entirely on their own labor rather than on that of slaves. With or without official leaves from the Confederate army, numerous southern soldiers responded to the entreaties of their wives to leave their posts, come home, and bring in the harvest. "Since your connection with the Confederate army, I have been prouder of you than ever before . . . ," one such woman wrote to her husband, "but before God, Edward, unless you come home we must die."[47] By the middle of the war, such seasonal desertions, conservatively estimated at more than 100,000, as much as 10 percent of the Confederate forces, were a major strain on the South's capacity to fight.

As the conflict wore on, patriotism and optimism gave way to discontent on both sides. In the South, the situation was exacerbated by a Union naval blockade that led to terrible shortages and triple-digit inflation. In the spring of 1863, the women of Richmond rampaged through the streets protesting the high cost of food and demanding that they be able to buy bread and meat at the same prices as the Confederate armies. Three months later, New York City was paralyzed by mobs protesting passage of a federal Conscription Act that allowed wealthy men to buy themselves out of the draft for $300. Elizabeth Cady Stanton, who had just moved to the city with her three youngest children, found herself in the middle of the upheaval. She watched as one of her older sons was recognized by the rioters as "one of those three-hundred-dollar fellows." "You may imagine what I suffered in seeing him dragged off," she wrote to her cousin. "I was alone with the children expecting every moment to hear the wretches thundering at the front door. . . . I then prepared a speech, determined, if necessary, to go down at once, open the door and make an appeal to them as Americans and citizens of the Republic."[48] The mob changed direction, and she fled the city.

Emancipation

While the South was fighting to preserve slavery and defend its sovereignty, the war aims of the North remained muddled. For more than a year, Lincoln insisted that his only goal was to end secession and restore the Union. Despite the fact that the southern states had seceded because they believed slavery was imperiled, the president was unwilling to declare opposition to slavery for fear that the border states of Kentucky, Missouri, Maryland, and Delaware, where slavery was legal, would leave the Union and join the Confederacy. The abolition of slavery became the Union's goal only when slaves themselves took action through a massive, prolonged process of what might well be characterized as "self-emancipation." Like the slaves who for decades had run away, men and women in large numbers began to flee into the arms of the Union army, buoyed by news of northern victories and hoping that they would be freed. One woman described her escape onto a Union gunboat sailing down the Mississippi River. "We all give three times three cheers for the gunboat boys and three times three cheers for big Yankee sojers an three times three cheers for gov'ment," she recalled; "an I tell you every one of us, big and little, cheered loud and long and strong, an' made the old river just ring ag'in."[49] Union officers disagreed on how to respond to the masses of refugees. Those unsympathetic to the antislavery cause wanted to return them to their owners, but the army eventually decided on a policy of accepting them under the category of confiscated enemy property. Thousands of these human "contraband" provided crucial aid to the Union army as laborers, cooks, and servants. As many as forty thousand gathered in Washington, D.C., where Sojourner Truth, Harriet Jacobs, and others organized a freedmen's village for them.

As their numbers increased, Lincoln realized that the steady flight of the southern labor force out of slavery offered an irresistible military advantage to the Union. Accordingly, he issued an Emancipation Proclamation, to take effect on January 1, 1863, which declared all slaves in rebel territory "forever free" and instructed the Union army and navy to "recognize and maintain the freedom of such persons." The status of slaves living in the Union border states, however, was left untouched. Since the Union could not actually emancipate slaves in lands it did not control, the Proclamation was meant only to encourage slaves in the renegade states to abandon their masters and free themselves. Despite its limits, however, the Emancipation Proclamation finally made the Civil War a war against slavery.

Women's rights leaders Elizabeth Cady Stanton and Susan B. Anthony were determined to push Lincoln to enact a more comprehensive abolition policy. "If it be true that at this hour, the women of the South are more devoted to their cause than we to ours, the fact lies here," wrote Cady Stanton. "The women of the South know what their sons are fighting for. The women of the North do not."[50] Along with Lucy Stone and other women's rights activists, they formed the Women's National Loyal League to force Lincoln to adopt a broader emancipation policy. As abolitionist women had done thirty years before, they gathered signatures on petitions to Congress to "pass at the earliest practicable day an act emancipating all persons of African descent."[51] Working closely with U.S. Senator Charles Sumner of Massachusetts, the League collected and submitted to Congress 260,000 signatures, two-thirds of them from women. The first popular campaign ever conducted on behalf of a constitutional amendment, these efforts contributed significantly to the 1865 passage and ratification of the Thirteenth Amendment, which permanently abolished slavery throughout the United States.

In 1863, after two years of grueling warfare, the military tide began to turn in the Union's favor. An important factor was the Union army's decision, in the wake of the Emancipation Proclamation, to permit African American men to fight. Close to 200,000 enlisted, providing a final burst of military energy as well as a manly model of black freedom. On July 4, 1863, the Union won two decisive battles, one at Gettysburg, Pennsylvania, and the other at Vicksburg, Mississippi. Still, the war lasted two more years. In the autumn of 1864, General William Sherman marched the western division of the Union army across Georgia, determined to break the spirit of the rebellion by destroying everything of value as he went. At her plantation, Mary Chesnut found "every window was broken, every bell torn down, every piece of furniture destroyed, every door smashed in."[52]

Finally, on April 9, 1865, almost four years to the day after the attack on Fort Sumter, General Robert E. Lee, head of the Confederate army, surrendered. An ex-slave woman from South Carolina remembered that on "de fust day of freedom we was all sittin' roun' restin' an' tryin' to think what freedom meant an ev'ybody was quiet an' peaceful."[53] "The people poured into the streets, frenzied with gladness," wrote Mary Livermore, "until there seemed to be no men and women in Chicago,—only crazy, grown-up boys and girls." Then, five days later, "from the height of this exultation the nation was swiftly precipitated to the very depths of despair": Lincoln was assassinated. "Never was a month so crowded," Livermore wrote, "with the conflicting emotions of exultation and despair, as was the month of April 1865."[54] "Thank God, the wretch has gotten his just deserts," exulted a Confederate woman.[55]

CONCLUSION: Reshaping Boundaries, Redefining Womanhood

In the years from 1840 to 1865, the women of the United States had traveled a tremendous distance. They had taken a country across a continent. They had joined in a series of social movements to remake and reform American society. They had challenged slavery and undertaken systematic reform in their own status as women. They had begun to demand their inclusion in the democratization of American politics. And, along with men but in their own ways, they had joined in the fight over the character and existence of the Union, participating in the Civil War both on and off the battlefield.

Their experiences through these changes had by no means been the same. Some women had taken possession of new land, in the process displacing others from their homes of long standing. Some had challenged crucial elements of American society and culture and ended up challenging conventional notions of womanhood itself. And while some had defended and lost their right to own slaves, those who had been slaves became free women. Through all of this, however, American women had been deeply involved in these years of momentous national change and had themselves been changed in the process. In the decades after the Civil War, in the victorious North and the struggling South, they began to enter more fully into public life, as workers and socially engaged citizens, in civic organizations and in colleges. Like 1848, 1865 was a decisive year in the history of the nation and of its women.

DOCUMENTS

Cross-Cultural Encounters in California, 1848–1850

Each of these selections focuses on the cross-cultural experience of women in California at the moment of statehood. Three groups of people—the Indians, the Californios (Mexican citizens who lived in California prior to American statehood), and the emigrants from the East (called Americans or Yankees by all concerned)—came upon each other with various combinations of curiosity, hospitality, alliance, exploitation, and violence. Starting in the late eighteenth century, the Californios thinly populated the Pacific Coast up to the San Francisco Bay. Coastal Indians became their laborers and servants. Inland and to the north, larger numbers of Indian peoples still lived the nomadic lives of their ancestors. The arrival of Yankee emigrants beginning in the mid-1840s brought rapid change. Within a very few years, the Californios had lost control of the coastal lands, the lives of the Indians had been profoundly disrupted by illness and warfare, and California had become the thirty-first state of the United States.

SARAH WINNEMUCCA

Our first eyewitness to these encounters, Sarah Winnemucca, was born in 1844. Her name was then Thocmetony. Her people, later called Piutes (she thought as a corruption of "pine nuts," a crucial part of the tribe's diet), had for centuries moved back and forth between the area near what is now Reno, Nevada, and the eastern part of Oregon. Later, she adopted the English name Sarah, and Winnemucca was the name of her paternal grandfather and father. Despite a fearful and violent initial exposure to white people, she lived among, married into, and cooperated with them for much of her adult life. She used her knowledge of American culture, her connections to influential U.S. figures, and her exceptional language skills to speak on behalf of her people as their conditions worsened. When she was forty years old, she wrote her autobiography, here excerpted.

Sarah's account is addressed to an American audience and is meant to give the native side of the encounter between the two peoples. In this selection she describes her first meeting, at age six, with white people and the strong interest that her maternal grandfather, Captain Truckee, took in the Americans, alongside whom he fought during the Mexican War. At first she was frightened of the strange people, but she gradually accommodated to them. Her account reveals how the American newcomers, like the Californios before them, were able to extract labor from the Piutes. Hiram Scott and Jacob Bonsal, Americans who are featured prominently in her story, ran a business ferrying people over the San Joaquin River near Stockton, California. In this episode, Sarah's mother goes with her father to live and work with the Americans, while her husband, who is hostile to them, stays away. In the end, her mother's pleading with the Americans wins Sarah and her family permission to return to their band.

As you read, consider what this selection reveals about Piute family dynamics. Given the disagreements in Sarah's family about whether to trust the Americans, who prevails and why? How are those family dynamics extended to include the Yankee newcomers, to whom Sarah's grandfather is so devoted, and with what consequences? Why is her mother so frightened for Sarah's sister, and what resources does she have to protect her? Finally, as a young child, what frightens Sarah about these strange people, and what attracts her to them?

I was born somewhere near 1844, but am not sure of the precise time. I was a very small child when the first white people came into our country. They came like a lion, yes, like a roaring lion, and have continued so ever since, and I have never forgotten their first coming. My people were scattered at that time over nearly all the territory now known as Nevada. My grandfather was chief of the entire Piute nation, and was camped near Humboldt Lake, with a small portion of his tribe, when a party . . . was seen coming. When the news was brought to my grandfather, he asked what they looked like? When told that they had hair on their faces, and were white, he jumped up and clasped his hands together, and cried aloud,

"My white brothers, my long-looked-for white brothers have come at last!". . . [T]he next spring the emigrants came as usual, and my father and grandfather and uncles, and many more went down on the Humboldt River on fishing excursions. While they were thus fishing, their white brothers came upon them and fired on them, and

killed one of my uncles, and wounded another. Nine more were wounded, and five died afterwards. My other uncle got well again, and is living yet. Oh, that was a fearful thing, indeed!

After all these things had happened, my grandfather still stood up for his white brothers. . . .

It was late that fall when my grandfather prevailed with his people to go with him to California. It was this time when my mother accompanied him. Everything had been got ready to start on our journey. My dear father [who was not friendly to the Americans] was to be left behind. How my poor mother begged to stay with her husband! . . .

At last we came to a very large encampment of white people, and they ran out of their wagons, or wood-houses, as we called them, and gathered round us. I was riding behind my brother. I was so afraid, I told him to put his robe over me, but he did not do so. I scratched him and bit him on his back, and then my poor grandfather rode up to the tents where they were, and he was asked to stay there all night with them. After grandpa had talked awhile, he said to his people that he would camp with his brothers. So he did. Oh, what nice things we all got from my grandpa's white brothers! Our men got

SOURCE: Sarah Winnemucca Hopkins, *Life among the Piutes: Their Wrongs and Claims,* ed. Mrs. Horace Mann (Reno: U Nevada P, 1994), 5–38.

red shirts, and our women got calico for dresses. Oh, what a pretty dress my sister got. I did not get anything, because I hid all the time. I was hiding under some robes. . . .

So I kept thinking over what [my grandfather] said to me about the good white people, and saying to myself, "I will make friends with them when we come into California." . . .

One of my grandpa's friends was named Scott, and the other Bonsal. . . . We stayed there some time. Then grandpa told us that he had taken charge of Mr. Scott's cattle and horses, and he was going to take them all up to the mountains to take care of them for his brothers. He . . . told his dear daughter that he wanted her two sons to take care of a few horses and cows that would be left. My mother began to cry, and said, "Oh, father, don't leave us here! My children might get sick, and there would be no one to speak for us; or something else might happen." He again said, "I don't think my brothers will do anything that is wrong to you and your children." Then my mother asked my grandfather if he would take my sister with him. My poor mother felt that her daughter was unsafe, for she was young and very good-looking. . . .

So my brothers took care of their horses and cows all winter, and they paid them well for their work. But oh, what trouble we had for a while! The men whom my grandpa called his brothers would come into our camp and ask my mother to give our sister to them. They would come in at night, and we would all scream and cry; but that would not stop them. My sister, and mother, and my uncles all cried and said, "Oh, why did we come? Oh, we shall surely all be killed some night." My uncles and brothers would not dare to say a word, for fear they would be shot down. So we used to go away every night after dark and hide, and come back to our camp every morning. One night we were getting ready to [leave the Scott house], and there came five men. . . . My uncles and my brothers made such a noise I don't know what happened; . . . I asked my mother if they had killed my sister. She said, "We are all safe

here. Don't cry." . . . My poor sister! I ran to her, I saw tears in her eyes. I heard someone speak close to my mother. I looked round and saw Mr. Scott holding the door open [to escape]. Mother said, "Children, come."

He went with us and pointed to our camp, and shook his head ["no"], and motioned to mother to go into a [separate] little house where they were cooking. He took my hand in his, and said the same words that I had learned, "Poor little girl." . . . Oh, what pretty things met my eyes. I was looking all over and I saw beautiful white cups, and every beautiful thing on something high and long, and around it some things that were red.

I said to my sister, "Do you know what those are?" for she had been to the house before with my brothers. She said, "That high thing is what they use when eating, and the white cups are what they drink hot water from, and the red thing you see is what they sit upon when they are eating." There was one now near us, and I thought if I could sit upon it I should be so happy! I said to my mother, "Can I sit on that one?" She said, "No, they would whip you." . . .

So I said no more. . . . Then the woman fixed five places and the men went out and brought in my brothers, and kept talking to them. . . . Brother said, "Mother, Mr. Scott wants us all to stay here. He says you and sister are to wash dishes, and learn all kinds of work. We are to stay here all the time and sleep upstairs, and the white woman is going to teach my sister how to sew. I think, dear mother, we had better stay, because grandpa said so, and our father Scott will take good care of us. . . ." All the time brother was talking, my mother and sister were crying. I did not cry for I wanted to stay so that I could sit in the beautiful red chairs. . . .

[My mother said to her sons] "Oh, how can that bad man keep you from going [with me back to your father]? . . . Oh, if your father only knew how his children were suffering, I know he would kill that white man who tried to take your sister. I cannot see for my life why my father calls them his white brothers. They are not people. They have no thought, no mind, no love. They are beasts, or they would know I, a lone woman, am here with them. They tried to take my girl from me and abuse her before my eyes and yours too, and oh, you must go too."

"Oh, mother, here [Mr. Scott] comes!"

My mother got up. She held out her two hands to him, and cried out, —

"Oh, good father, don't keep my children from me. If you have a heart in you, give them back to me. Let me take them to their good father, where they can be cared for."

We all cried to see our poor mother pleading for us. Mother held on to him until he gave some signs of letting her sons go with her; then he nodded his head, — they might go.

ELIZA FARNHAM

T HE SECOND SELECTION was written by the New York–born author Eliza Farnham. Farnham arrived in California from Boston in 1849, just after the discovery of gold and right before statehood, about the same time that Sarah Winnemucca was encountering her first white people farther east. A thirty-two-year-old mother of two sons, Farnham had inherited land in the area of the Santa Cruz Mission from her recently deceased husband, who had been one of the first U.S. citizens in the area and had bought land there from the local Californio families.

Farnham's childhood was impoverished, but she succeeded in gaining an education and became a writer. Because her husband was away on the West Coast for much of their married life, she had the responsibility of supporting herself and her children, and she found ways to take advantage of the opportunities that were just beginning to open to women. She wrote *Life in Prairie Land* (1846), a popular account of her years on the Illinois frontier. Then she was employed as the first matron of women for the New York State prison at Sing Sing (now Ossining). There she gained a reputation for the courage to make humane reforms in the treatment of prisoners, but she was dismissed in 1848. At this point, she decided to go to California to take possession of the lands inherited from her husband. By the time she arrived in California, she was already something of a public figure.

Farnham held a distinctive set of ideas about womanhood, an idiosyncratic and crusading version of the doctrine of sexual spheres quite different from that of the women's rights movement emerging at just this time. She did not advocate equality of the sexes or for women to join men in the public sphere, but she firmly rejected the idea that women should subordinate themselves to men. Her own life was marked by repeated acts of boldness and independence. In the context of American expansion, she contended that women had a special role to play in national life, based on their unique claim to moral leadership. Women could help the United States fulfill its national mission, its 'Manifest Destiny,' but only if they were allowed a broader scope for their distinctive talents. In California, she hoped that woman's superior moral influence could counter the rapacious, masculine spirit of the gold rush. "Believing that the presence of women would be one of the surest checks upon many of the evils that are apprehended," she determined to go

there and help claim the area for the best—not the worst—of American nationhood.[56]

Farnham's first grand plan was to import Yankee women to serve as wives for
the American men rushing into California. But when no other women took up her
invitation, she went to California herself, traveling by ship around the tip of South
America. Arriving in Santa Cruz, she moved into a crude one-room ranch house,
which she optimistically renamed *El Rancho La Libertad* (Freedom Ranch). She
began to farm potatoes and onions and plant fruit trees. Despite her best efforts,
her experiment in self-sufficient agriculture failed. She needed to hire male laborers, but most of the able-bodied men had left for the gold fields. Within a few
years, she had married an abusive Irish immigrant, had secured one of the first divorces in the county, and had left the state.

Farnham's final plan was to write about her experiences in California, and in
this, at last, she was successful. The following selection is from her memoir, *California, In-doors and Out* (1856). In this episode, she is returning from a trip to San
Francisco and stays overnight at the *rancho* home of a Californio family near San
Juan Bautista. There, the Castro family, an extended network that includes the
"senior senor," his wife, his children, their cousins, and Indian servants, offers her
hospitality.

As you read, consider how the Californios' way of life offends the "Yankee
housewife" in Farnham. What about it does she appreciate? On what basis do she
and the women of the household communicate and connect? What do you think
she means by the sentence, "No ungratified want or cankering ambition, shorn of
the power to achieve, consumes them"? Does she mean to criticize the Americans
as well as the Californios? How can the sense of Manifest Destiny that brought
Americans to California be detected in Farnham's account?

Our weary horses did not get so well over the
ground to-day. . . . An American had told us that
we could find comfortable quarters at Castro's
rancho, about eighteen miles further on, and
thither we bent our way. It was nightfall before we
reached the neighborhood he had indicated, and
after dragging wearily on till it seemed as if neither of the animals could possible get over another mile, we descried a light which appeared
to be twice that distance away and quite off the
road. . . . [W]e learned that Castro's ranch was still

two miles away, but that we could stay there for
the night.

On the ground, under the corridor that ran
along the old adobe building, two immense fires
were blazing, around which were gathered twenty
or thirty men and women, and several mules and
horses. . . .

The Yankee housewife thinks, now, I ought to
have been very comfortable; for the kitchen, in her
land, is a bright, cheerful place to enter from the
chilliness of a dark night. But this was not a Yankee
kitchen. The apartment might have been eighteen
by twenty-four feet, lighted only by a door in day
time, and, at this hour, by the fitful blaze of the
wood-fires, built upon a sort of brick range that
ran across the end of the room. In the corner, at one

SOURCE: Eliza Farnham, *California, In-doors and Out, or
How We Farm, Mine, and Live Generally in the Golden State*
(New York: Dix, Edwards, 1856), 123–31.

end of this range, a dirty Indian girl was making tortillas—the bread of the country. She was kneading a large lump of dough upon a stone bench, slightly hollowed toward the centre, beside which stood a very ill-favored basin of water, into which she occasionally thrust her hands. . . .

At the other end of the range, a buxom merry-faced girl was superintending a pot of *caldo* [a heavy, hot soup], and another of *frijoles* [beans], with an apron before her so excessively dirty, that I involuntarily reached my hand out to stay it when it fell too near the cooking. Five or six other young [Californio] women were sitting or standing about, and several more were passing in and out to other parts of the *casa* [house]. A merrier set could nowhere be found; they chatted to me in Spanish, and laughed if I failed to understand them. They laughed when they could not understand my English. They examined my riding-hat, habit, whip, rings, watch, pin—every thing, in short, their eyes could see, and put on whatever they could detach from my person, trying its effect with a critical and generally an approving eye. . . .

After what seemed an interminable delay, I was called to supper in a long, spacious room or hall, at the upper end of which stood two beds. The long table occupied one entire side near the wall. . . . When we were seated, the senior senor threw each a tortilla from a stack that was piled on the cloth near his plate, and, helping himself, signed to us to do likewise. The supper was delicious. The mercy of Providence, in the shape of a fasting stomach, enabled me to forget the filthy apron, and the long hair and suspicious-looking arms of the Indian girl, and I made ample amends for the fast that I had observed since morning. . . .

The supper was a far more palatable one than I believed it could be. The *caldo* was deliciously flavored; the tortillas very sweet and crisp; and everybody knows the *frijole* so well that praise of it would be quite superfluous. When we had supped, I retired again to the kitchen, and here I found all the young people taking their evening meal, quite informally, seated upon the earthen

floor about the room. Two or three large toilet basins, placed in various parts, contained the food, from which each supplied his or her plate at will; and my cook, with the formidable apron, washing the dishes as they were handed to her; an operation which she performed in a very summary manner, by dashing a handful or two of water over the plate, tilted on the edge of the kettle, and, shocking to tell, wiping them on the very apron! . . .

The sleeping-apartment was in the second story, to which I mounted by a sort of ladder, constructed by tying bits of wood, upon two poles, with thongs of green hide, and placed against the sill of the door. The chamber was the entire size of the building, and was used as clothes, store-room, and granary. Two beds occupied the nearer end; wheat and barley the remote one, and sides of leather, old barrels, boxes, broken chairs, etc., the intermediate space. Zarapas [probably *serapes,* decorative blankets] of all styles were pendant from the roof, rafters, and walls. I objected to the door, as lacking all means of fastening, but my solicitude was promptly removed by the intelligence that six or eight persons were to share the apartment with me. I certainly did wish for a curtain of some sort; but my extreme weariness suggested that the curtain of irresistible sleep would divide me from all the world in a very few moments. The bed was not of the freshest, though everything upon it was snowy white; but my sleep was unbroken till the words, "the horses are ready, ma'am," sounded loudly in my ears next morning. With infinite difficulty, a pint bowl of water was obtained for my ablutions, and I soon descended equipped for departure. . . .

This, then, was a Spanish rancho and the manner of life in it. These people were the owners of a great estate here, and another up the coast, on which were hundreds, if not thousands, of horned cattle and horses. Not a drop of milk nor an ounce of butter could be had in their house. Their chief articles of food are beef and beans. Of the wheat grown on their lands they make a kind of coarse flour which they use in porridge. The tortilla can only be made of fine flour, which they have always imported, though occupying one of the finest wheat countries in the world. The simplicity of their external lives is quite in harmony with that of their natures. No ungratified want or cankering ambition, shorn of the power to achieve, consumes them, and though the same lack of material refinement in almost any other people would argue a positive coarseness which could not fail to distress a stranger, their whole manner, though familiar to a degree, is so evincive of kindness and respect, that there is nothing left to read or doubt as to their motives. They are a simple-hearted people, whose contentment flowed out in acts of continual hospitality and kindness to all who came to them before their peaceful dream of life was broken in upon by the frightful selfishness of the late emigration. It is difficult for us to imagine contentment in the idle, aimless life of these rancheros, or cheerfulness in the dark, dirty, naked houses they inhabit; but they have sufficed for them. . . .

MARIA ANGUSTIAS DE LA GUERRA ORD

In the 1870s and 1880s, Hubert Howe Bancroft, California's first major historian, recorded the memories, or *testimonios*, of the remaining prestatehood Californios. Most of his aged narrators were men, but among the women he interviewed was Maria Angustias de la Guerra Ord. Through her father, she had been closely attached to the mission at San Juan Bautista, and the events described took place in that vicinity. This excerpt from her reminiscence describes her role in that part of the Mexican War that took place in California in the area between Los Angeles and Monterey.

Angustias de la Guerra Ord's *testimonio* has become a source of controversy among historians. As originally recorded in 1878, she declared that "*la toma del pais no nos gusto nada a los californios, y menos a las mujeres.*" In 1956, this important sentence was mistranslated as "The conquest of California did not bother the Californios, least of all the women," and this mistranslation was subsequently much quoted. But later scholars corrected the translation to clarify that her actual opinion was in fact the opposite: "The conquest of California wasn't liked by the Californians, least of all the women."[57]

Angustias de la Guerra Ord's tale concerns an attempt by the Californio army to kidnap the U.S. consul, Thomas Larkin. In the ensuing fray, José Antonio Chavez, one of the erstwhile kidnappers, was wounded. Ord's story involves Chavez's efforts to elude pursuit by the U.S army. The first person to give Chavez refuge was the Californiana wife of a Yankee, who disobeyed her husband to harbor her fugitive countryman. Then he fled to the house of a fellow soldier, and this man brought Chavez to the home of de la Guerra Ord.

As you read, consider how de la Guerra Ord exerts her domestic authority to the Yankees and how the U.S. officer indicates his military authority in response. Why is de la Guerra Ord motivated to help Chavez, and who do you think, she or the Americans, gets the better of the encounter? Who is living in the de la Guerra Ord residence and why? How does this account illuminate the family relations in Rancho Castro that Eliza Farnham found so confusing?

I was in bed, having given birth to a baby girl a few days before. I was very astonished by what the soldier told me. He reported what had happened to Chavez, and for the love of God, to take him out of his house and hide him in mine. The words, "love of God," had great force and made me think. My husband was away at our Pajaro ranch. I decided to dress and though it was raining hard, to go to see my brothers, Pablo and Miguel, who were prisoners, to ask them what they thought I should do. Not having my husband there to consult with, I wanted to know their opinion. . . .

I was very angry with the Americans, because they had mistreated my brothers, holding them prisoners without cause or reason. I angrily told [Pablo] that if he thought that the Yankees believed they could find a person at will, I would hide him.

Finally I went to the soldier's house myself and consulted with Chavez about the means of getting him to my house as he couldn't walk because of the dislocation of his ankle. The son-in-law of the soldier was a Portuguese of small stature, and as Chavez was also small, the two together would make one man of large stature. The Portuguese carried Chavez sitting on his shoulders covered with a Spanish shawl and a felt hat which I had provided. Thus they passed through the guards of my Yankees and arrived at my house without being discovered. I had already returned to my house and gotten into bed, . . . I told no one my plan and nobody suspected anything.

During my husband's absence, Capt. Mariano Silva and his wife, Maria de la Torre, were living at my house. I informed them of the situation about Chavez. When he arrived he was confined in a room. No one but Capt. Silva and his wife, my daughter, Manuela, and I saw him. . . .

During the night, with a full moon, I heard a noise in my little garden. Some sheep I owned had gotten in. I sent an Indian girl to tell the cook to get the sheep out. The girl only opened the door and saw the armed soldiers. She closed it and came to tell me. Then I spoke to Silva, telling him that I believed the Americans had surrounded my house. Then we heard a rap on the door, and I told Silva to go and see what they wanted. Then they told my servants that Chavez was hiding in a room because they were going to kill him. Silva's wife went to get [Chavez]. Meanwhile the Indian maids took off the blankets from the couch which had been put in my room. We put Chavez there by the garden so he could breathe easily, and as he was very slender, the whole space was stuffed with blankets so that it would be smooth. We put my baby, Carolina, to bed on top of him. Silva's wife got into my bed with me. . . .

[T]he Lieutenant and his people came into my bedroom without saying a word. He had a pistol in one hand and a candle in the other. He looked under my bed but found nothing. Then he came near me holding the pistol and candle to my face and said that he was hunting for a man who was said to be hidden in my house. I asked him if he had found him, and he said he had not. It pleased me greatly because I had not told them any lies. Then he said he was rather tired and that he regretted having had to bother me, because he supposed that I was rather frightened, and would like a chair to sit down. I answered that I was not frightened by anything and that he could go to his house to rest, because no one could rest in my room who was not a member of my family or a friend. He said good night and nothing more. . . .

This military search and occupation of my house lasted from 10:00 P.M. until 2 or 3 in the morning.

Chavez came out of hiding and Silva's wife applied remedies to his foot. He said to me, "Madam, I am alive today because of you." To which I replied, "What I have done for you today, I would do tomorrow for an American if you unjustly attempted to do him wrong."

Chavez left 2 days later. He went from my house dressed as a woman. In the pines he mounted a horse and went to Santa Barbara.

SOURCE: Angustias de la Guerra Ord, *Occurrences in Hispanic California,* trans. and ed. Francis Price and William Ellison (Washington, DC: Academic Press of American Franciscan History, 1956), 61–64.

QUESTIONS FOR ANALYSIS

1. Each of these three women responds to the strangers she encounters with both fear and curiosity. About what is each curious? What are the different sources of their fear, and how does each woman exhibit or conceal her reaction?

2. What are the sources of strength on which Farnham, de la Guerra Ord, and the mother of Sarah Winnemucca each draw? How does the absence of men affect the way that they act?

3. What role does the preparation and consumption of food play in these various cultural encounters? How is intercultural hospitality expressed? How important were manufactured goods from the East in the cross-cultural encounters of California in the late 1840s?

4. The Farnham and de la Guerra Ord episodes occurred quite close geographically at about the same time, in 1850. Can you imagine how de la Guerra Ord would have reacted to Farnham as a guest in her home and what Farnham might have thought of her?

DOCUMENTS

Paulina Wright Davis, the *Una,*
and Women's Rights

T HE ANTEBELLUM WOMEN'S RIGHTS MOVEMENT had diverse origins. Deep religious conviction coexisted with free-thinking criticism of Protestant moralism. Veteran abolitionist and temperance activists were joined by novelists and editors of women's journals in support of economic rights for wives, expanded occupational opportunities for working women, and political equality with men. In the years after the first women's rights convention at Seneca Falls in 1848, women's rights advocates considered numerous issues and debated various perspectives. They were concerned not only with formal legal and political equality but with the many forms that women's inequality took—customary as well as legal—and with its connection to the basic structures of American society.

The first periodical dedicated exclusively to this movement was the *Una.* Its editor and primary author, Paulina Wright Davis, had been a middle-class white woman married to a wealthy merchant in economically booming Utica, New York. Childless, she threw herself into religious and moral causes, one of which, abolitionism, was the source of her growing radicalism. After the death of her first husband, she became a health educator for women and an early proponent of reform of the laws prohibiting wives from independent property ownership. In 1850, she was the chief organizer for the first National Women's Rights Convention in Worcester, Massachusetts.

After marrying again and moving to Rhode Island, she decided that the women's rights movement needed its own journal and published the first issue at her own expense in February 1853. She named it the *Una,* after a character in Edmund Spenser's sixteenth-century epic poem *The Faerie Queene* who represented faith and purity in an ideal female form. The monthly journal considered a wide range of concerns from a women's rights point of view. By this time, Wright (now Davis) had shed her previous religious convictions and was, like her friend Elizabeth Cady Stanton, a free-thinker who found conventional Protestantism intellectually indefensible and politically conservative.

Davis especially dissented from the common notion that women's allegedly greater religiosity and higher morality was a satisfactory basis for their place in American society. She was a sharp-eyed critic of the sentimental conservatism that appeared to revere femininity but actually denied women their basic liberties. Her vision for women's emancipation incorporated the principle of equal rights for women, but her ultimate goal was more than equality: it was liberty. After two and a half years, unable to find a copublisher who shared her high literary standards and women's rights radicalism, and unable to maintain the expense of the undertaking, Davis ceased publishing the *Una*. But if short-lived, the *Una* was influential at the time, and in retrospect, it illuminates the breadth and radicalism of the early women's rights movement.

WOMEN AND WORK

Central to the *Una*'s concerns was the issue of paid labor for women. In these years, traditional Jeffersonian notions that liberty was based on subsistence farming and independent proprietorship were being reconceived to apply to the growing ranks of those who worked for others. In contrast to the slave system, northerners proclaimed the glory of "free labor," meaning labor that was not only compensated but allowed workers untrammeled choice of employment, decent wages, personal autonomy, and social respect. Working women, the *Una* argued, were largely shut out of these free-labor rights. Domestic servants, for instance, had little control over their own lives. Lacking basic personal liberties, they were vulnerable to sexual harassment, which Davis called "libertine insult." Those women who were employed as teachers or as factory operatives were paid so poorly that they lacked the means to support themselves and live with dignity. Working women would never be the equals of working men, the *Una* contended, until they were free to select the work that most suited them as individuals.

As you read the following selection, notice the many forms of personal freedom and public respectability available to working men that are denied to working women. What about women's jobs create these unequal conditions? How would greater economic opportunity lead to larger freedoms for women?

Whether Women should or should not be permitted to Vote, to hold Office, to serve on Juries, and to officiate as Lawyers, Doctors or Divines, are questions about which a diversity of opinion is likely long to exist. But that the current rates of remuneration for Woman's Work are entirely, unjustly inadequate, is a proposition which needs only to be considered to insure its hearty acceptance....

Every able bodied Man, inured to Labor, though of the rudest sort, who steps on shore in America from Europe, is worth a dollar per day, and can readily command it....

SOURCE: "Woman and Work," *Una* 2, no. 1 (January 1854): 203–4.

But the sister of this same faithful worker, equally careful, intelligent, and willing to do anything honest and reputable for a living, finds no such chances proffered *her*.... She may think herself fortunate if a week's search opens to her a place where by the devotion of all her waking hours she can earn five or six dollars per month, with a chance of its increase, after several years' faithful service, to seven or eight dollars at most.

The brother is in many respects the equal of his employer; may sit down beside him at the hotel where they both stop for dinner; their votes may balance each other at any election; the laborer lives with those whose company suits him, and needs no character [reference] from his last place to secure him employment or a new job when he gets tired of the old one. But the sister never passes out of the atmosphere of caste—of conscious and galling inferiority to those with whom her days must be spent. There is no election-day in *her* year, and but the ghost of a Fourth of July. She must live, not with those she likes, but with those who want her; she is not always safe from libertine insult in what serves her for a home; she knows no Ten-Hour Rule, and would not dare to claims its protection if one were enacted. Though not a slave by law, she is too often as near it in practice as one legally free can be.

Now this disparity between the rewards of Man's and Woman's labor at the base of the social edifice is carried up to its very pinnacle. . . . The mistress who conducts the rural district school in summer, usually receives less than half the monthly stipend that her brother does for teaching that same school in the winter. . . . Between male and female workers in the factories and mills, the same difference is enforced. . . .

What then is the appropriate remedy?

Primarily and mainly, a more rational and healthful Public Sentiment with regard to woman's work—a sentiment which shall welcome her to every employment wherein she may be useful and efficient without necessarily compromising her purity or overtasking her strength. Let her be encouraged to open a Store, to work a Garden, plant and tend an Orchard, to learn any of the lighter mechanical Trades, to study for a Profession, whenever her circumstances and her tastes shall render any of these desirable. . . . Let the ablest of the sex be called to the lecture-room, to the Temperance rostrum, &c, and whenever a Post-office falls vacant and a deserving woman is competent to fill and willing to take it, let her be appointed, as a very few have already been. . . . With a larger field and more decided usefulness will come a truer and deeper respect; and Woman, no longer constrained to marry for a position, may always wait to marry worthily and in obedience to the dictates of sincere affection. Hence constancy, purity, mutual respect, a just independence and a life of happiness, may be reasonably anticipated.

SLAVERY AND MARRIAGE

An analogy between the condition of free women and that of slaves ran throughout the Una's discussion of women's rights. Davis pressed the parallels in calling for labor freedoms, the right to vote, and reforms in the laws and practice of marriage. An abolitionist, fully conscious of the extreme deprivation of rights suffered by African Americans, she wielded this rhetorical device with great skill. By equating the condition of northern white women with chattel slaves, she meant to break through the omnipresent, flowery discourse of true womanhood and shock her women readers into seeing their own condition in a radically different way. At the same time, the equation challenged the stubborn refusal of northern middle-class audiences to acknowledge that black Americans shared a common humanity with them.

As you read the following selection, identify the aspects of married women's lives that the *Una* characterizes as servile. In what ways is the status of the married woman *not* like that of the slave? Does Davis take these into account?

The words which describe the wrongs of men, are strangely enough, exact definitions of the positions in society, prescribed for women. . . . The civil and criminal laws under which they [women] are governed, are made without their participation or consent; their property interests and the fair proceeds of their industry during marriage, are administered and disposed of by those whom they took for husbands, but the laws change into masters; in the household they are at best but upper servants, under life-long engagements; and in all the business avocations by which pecuniary independence might be secured, they are restricted by the rules of custom and opinion, to those which are most servile in character and least profitable in returns.

In fact, the analogy that exists between the conditions of women, and of the negro race in the United States, is so close, that slavery and caste apply to the one as well as the other. In the Southern States "all that a slave possesses belongs to his master. . . . The earnings of slaves and the price of their services belong to their owners." . . .

Those provisions of the Louisiana code relating to slaves, are to the letter descriptive of the condition of wives under our common law. . . . The wife indeed, cannot be sold for the debts of her husband, or bartered for his pecuniary benefit, but her services and their proceeds may be. . . . And how are widowhood and maidenhood treated? They are released from the bondage of domestic masterdom, but like the free negro they suffer still, all the disqualifications and oppressions of caste. . . . Sex, as absolutely as color, denies them all the political rights of citizenship, and they are as sternly barred out of lucrative official stations, liberal professions and profitable employments. Their labor is mainly confined to domestic service and needle-work, which at best, but poorly feed and clothe them, and never affords . . . position and power in society.

Truly, the correspondence is more exact than we are accustomed to admit. . . . This subject is not nearly exhausted, but the comparisons we have drawn, the analogy between the most hated and despised race on earth, may startle some who sleep, into earnestness, and compel them to feel their own false, unnatural, and despicable position. If it does this, if it rouse one woman to feel her degradation, its suggestions will have accomplished their mission.

SOURCE: "Pecuniary Independence of Women," *Una* 1, no. 12 (December 1853): 184.

INEQUALITY OF WOMEN IN MARRIAGE

Nowhere was the analogy between slaves and free white women deployed by Davis to more critical effect than with respect to marriage. Legally, if not experientially, free women's condition within marriage was similar to that of chattel slaves: both groups were nonpersons before the law, obligated to obey those who had formal authority over them. Certainly with respect to sexuality, wives were regarded as their husbands' property. The women's rights agenda of the 1850s paid special attention to the elimination of wives' subordination by securing full economic rights for women regardless of marital status.

The *Una* sought to challenge not only the legal framework of marriage but also its blighted emotional character. When it came to marriage, Davis was both a romantic and a critic. "True" marriage, she believed, offered the possibility of knowing oneself more deeply by profound revelation to another, but the "enforced inferiority" of women made this impossible. Denied full freedom and self-expression, wives could only worship, never understand, their husbands. Davis married twice, apparently happily, to men who shared her reform convictions. Her hopes for a fundamental transformation in the nature of marriage perhaps best reveal the utopian nature of her women's rights beliefs and of the movement to which she contributed.

Davis addresses the following argument more to men than to women. How, according to Davis, does women's subordination interfere with love between the sexes? To what degree does this argument remain true 150 years later?

We have already more than hinted at the inequality of women in the marriage relation; it is a common theme, but those things which are most familiar are not always the best understood. . . . Polygamy in Paris and slavery in Virginia, despotism in Russia and barbarism in the wilds of America, do not exhibit their special enormities to the observation of the people among whom they prevail. . . .

In like manner the conditions of the marriage relation among us may be a grave departure from the true economy [system] of the institution, and yet challenge no especial wonder among its custom-trained subjects. We are creatures of habit, and are skilful [sic] in discovering reasons for things that we habitually do, not only without reason, but against all reason, right and expediency. . . .

We believe that woman's enforced inferiority in the marriage relation, not only wrongs her out of the best uses of her existence, but also cheats her master of the richest and noblest blessings of the nuptial union. Let us see. A man may derive such happiness as gratified vanity is capable of from political or literary fame; he may enjoy the reputation of wealth, of wit, of taste in art . . . but in marriage, if he is wise and noble, he will seek something that he can find in none of these, nor in them all combined. His real want is to be

known, to be understood, as the soul knows and is known. . . .

How mean and meagre then must be the marriage, that narrows his heart to a miniature of humanity, a dwarfed womanhood, a modest apology for a match that must not meet the measure of his demands, for fear of overreaching that measure of meanness that idolises [sic] because it cannot comprehend his majesty! . . . He still seeks the worship of one created in his own likeness and image, and he is robbed of the honors due him till he finds it—Nay he needs as much to give as to receive, such exalted regards. . . . His loves must go out and return to him on the plane of a level reciprocity, or he is dragged down by the descent of his affections. . . . He mingles contempt with his affections, and suffers the reflected degradation, and all the infinite loss of adequate worthiness in the object of his love. . . . Men and women are one in their natures, and marriage is eminently that relation in which they become one flesh and one blood. . . .

Men and women are in fact and effect, just what their accidental developments make of them. Deny the unfolding, the growth and excellence, that the faculties receive from all the functions of civil life—restrict the social liberties within the narrow compass assigned by custom to womanhood—train her in youth to the restraints of semi-annihilation, and in marriage bar her out from all the larger and higher interests and offices, the trusts, sympathies and experiences of the

SOURCE: "Inequality of Women in Marriage," *Una* 2, no. 2 (February 1854): 214–15.

common life of the world around her, and what chance for the reciprocities of equality are left to him who looks to such a mutilated existence for the reflex [reflection] of his own? . . .

The man that shuts his wife out . . . must not rely upon the sentiments of duty merely, to secure to him what alone can come from conformity to truth, nature, and right. Indeed, we doubt not that the religiousness of women, by which they are distinguished from men, is, in a majority of instances, only a substitute for the denied happiness of domestic life, and a sanctuary of retreat from the vice and wretchedness which the in-

equality of marriage engenders. . . . The worship given in church, is often that which is unavailable at home. It has much of the nature of death-bed piety in it; it springs from the mourning of the soul over a lost world, a celibacy of the heart that drives it. . . .

We may content ourselves now with the plain proposition, that womanhood can never come up to its full worth, nor manhood derive the resulting blessings, until every faculty and every function of her nature is drawn out in unrestrained liberty to the utmost measure of which it is in any wise capable.

QUESTIONS FOR ANALYSIS

1. To what degree did the antebellum women's rights movement challenge the middle-class gender ideology of a domestic sphere for women that was separate from the public world of men?

2. How do you think Davis's women's rights ideas would have been received by devout Protestant women, mill workers, or slaves (if they had read them)? In the context of mid-nineteenth-century America, do you think that Davis succeeded in creating an inclusive vision of women's freedom?

3. What were the obstacles that women's rights advocates faced in convincing women that their position in the family and society needed radical change? What sorts of arguments did Davis use to appeal to her audience?

4. Examine Davis's analogy between the status of women and the status of slaves. Does her argument pertain to slave women in any way?

Women on the Civil War Battlefields

THE BATTLEFIELD has not always been an exclusively male space. Wives and mothers of common soldiers came to cook, launder, and nurse the men of their families, while officers' wives were permitted social visits with their husbands. But women went to the scene of fighting for other reasons too. Political passions are no respecter of gender, and patriotism, dedication to cause, eagerness to be a part of historic events, and the simple desire for adventure brought women to the bloody heart of the Civil War.

The most common battlefield role of women was nurse—the "angel" of the battlefield who comforted wounded and dying soldiers, representing domestic tranquility in the midst of armed conflict. Despite the desperate need for medical personnel to care for the enormous number of casualties, female nurses had to fight their own kinds of battles with male medical officers for the opportunity to serve. A much smaller number of women also served the Union and Confederate armies in less conventionally "womanly" ways, as spies, strategists, and even soldiers.

While the Civil War had a tremendous impact on women overall, generating aspirations for greater public responsibilities and equal rights, those who had had direct battlefield experience found it difficult to have their particular contributions fully appreciated. Northern male veterans could count on an old-age army pension in recognition for their services, but only some of the women who served received anything, and even then they received less than men. African American women, whose dedication and need were particularly great, were especially undercompensated. Many of the images in this essay are taken from memoirs written by women who served on and around battlefields, who wrote to make sure that the historical record included their stories. They permit us to see the Civil War through women's eyes.

THE NURSES

An estimated ten thousand women served as nurses during the Civil War.[58] Nursing was not yet a profession requiring special training and would not become so until the turn of the century (see Chapter 7). At first, both military hospitals and battlefield infirmaries were run by male surgeons who had little to offer the wounded other than the removal of a limb and whiskey to blunt the pain. Their assistants were also men, themselves often recuperating from battlefield injuries.

Nursing under wartime conditions seemed too brutal for women, an unacceptable offense against their modesty.

Nonetheless, care of the sick and injured was traditionally a female skill, and women began to offer their services as soon as the first call for troops was issued. In the North, Dorothea Dix, already well known for her work to improve the treatment of the insane, persuaded Edwin Stanton, U.S. secretary of war, to appoint her as superintendent of nursing for the Union army. "All nurses are required to be plain looking women," Dix declared. "Their dresses must be brown or black with no bows, no curls, no jewelry and no hoop skirts."[59] Clothing had to be not only respectable but functional in the gory environment of the military hospitals. Louisa May Alcott, unmarried and struggling to become a writer, was one of those Dix recruited. "I love nursing and *must* let out my pent-up energy in some new way," she wrote in the journal that became her first published book, *Hospital Sketches*. "I want new experiences and am sure to get 'em if I go."[60] In 1861 Congress authorized $12 a month for the female nurses under Dix's supervision, about a third of what male nurses received.

In the regimental hospitals away from Washington, D.C., women whose relatives had been wounded or who just felt moved to care for the troops convinced local medical staff to allow them to serve without army commission or pay. One of the most famous was Mary Ann Bickerdyke of Illinois, who became a legend for her battlefield stamina and disregard for military hierarchy. A mother and widow in her mid-forties, Bickerdyke offered her services for the length of the war. She was a dedicated caregiver, moving from battlefield to battlefield, cooking and laundering as well as tending to the Union army wounded. Eventually, she was appointed field agent for the United States Sanitary Commission, which, despite its name, was not part of the government but rather a massive, volunteer, largely female organization that provided clothing and medical supplies to the Union army.

Like other nineteenth-century women with commanding personalities, Bickerdyke assumed the powerful female appellation of "Mother." In an environment that reserved official control for men, "Mother" was a role that could be translated into informal public authority. Bickerdyke insisted that she had the right to be near the action and to tend to the troops as she saw fit, on the basis of selfless concern for "her" boys. Indeed Mother Bickerdyke seems to have treated most of the military men with whom she came into contact, including surgeons and generals, as overgrown boys for whom she knew best. Like other such female figures with unusual public standing who called themselves "Mother"—such as the late nineteenth-century labor organizer Mother Jones—Bickerdyke used the maternal ideal as a framework for venturing beyond the genteel middle-class role of true womanhood.

Bickerdyke saw an extraordinary amount of military action. She arrived in Vicksburg, Mississippi, in time for the city's surrender to General Ulysses S. Grant, and escorted home Union soldiers released from the Confederate prison at Andersonville, Georgia. In 1864, she joined General William T. Sherman, with whom she claimed a special bond, for his devastating march across the heart of the South. At the end of the war, when Sherman and his troops paraded through Washington,

◆ **Figure 4.1 F. O. C. Darley, *Midnight at the Battlefield***
General Research Division, The New York Public Library, Astor, Lenox, and Tilden Foundations.

D.C., to celebrate victory, Mother Bickerdyke rode in a place of honor. Then, she slipped back into private life. In 1886, the army awarded her an army pension of $25 a month.

Figure 4.1 depicts the initial episode of the Bickerdyke legend, her role at the battle of Fort Donelson, Tennessee, site of an early Union victory. Bickerdyke achieved renown for her courage in remaining at the killing fields late at night, until she was absolutely sure that she had found all survivors. The illustration, a steel engraving, was commissioned for *My Story of the War*, an account of the wartime contribution of the women of the Sanitary Commission, written in 1889 by Mary Livermore. It pictures Bickerdyke as a female savior, moving alone among the dead in search of life. How did the artist choose to idealize her? How does the use of light (and dark) suggest women's role on the battlefield?

In the Confederate army hospitals in Richmond, elite women of the slave-holding class considered it their patriotic duty to visit the wounded, while women drawn from the poor white and slave classes did the dirtier jobs. In the second year of the war, the Confederate government authorized funds to hire matrons for

◆ Figure 4.2 **Phoebe Yates Pember**
Milstein Division of United States History, Local History and Genealogy, The New York Public Library, Astor, Lenox, and Tilden Foundations.

these larger military hospitals, charging them with securing and distributing provisions and seeing to it that the wounded were decently and regularly fed.

Phoebe Yates Pember was appointed head matron of Chimborazo Hospital in Richmond; with eight thousand beds, it was reputed to be one of the largest in the world. Born into a prosperous Charleston Jewish family, she had nursed her husband until he died of tuberculosis. The matron positions were being filled, Pember later wrote, by "inefficient and uneducated women, hardly above the laboring classes."[61] Although the matron's salary was hardly sufficient for her needs, Pember agreed to take the job. It was a difficult and unconventional decision for a "woman of delicacy and refinement," as she described herself, "used to all the comforts of luxurious life."° At Chimborazo, she struggled with the surgeons for control over the hospital whiskey, which they wanted to drink and she wanted to dispense to the wounded men to alleviate their pain. Her other concern was to improve the quality of hospital food, which was so unpalatable that patients were dying of starvation. After the war, she too returned to private life.

In the immediate aftermath and humiliation of Confederate defeat, women's wartime service in the South was not as widely celebrated as in the North. But fifteen years later, white southern defense of the slave system was being recalled with increasing nostalgia. White women played a major role in this historical recuperation of the white southern memory and meaning of the Civil War. In this context in 1879, Pember published her memoirs. Figure 4.2, a photograph of Phoebe Yates Pember, is one of the few images available of women serving as Confederate nurses. What do the determined set of Pember's jaw and the straight line of her mouth suggest about the characteristics that she brought to her job as hospital

°Hospital matrons were authorized $30 to $40 a month, but the Confederate currency was so hyperinflated that the actual value was insufficient for their basic needs.

◆ Figure 4.3 **Sisters of Charity with Doctors and Soldiers, Satterlee Hospital, Philadelphia, c. 1863**
Courtesy, Archives Daughters of Charity, Emmitsburg, Maryland.

matron? How might Pember's portrait of her service to the "lost cause," as southern nationalism was called, have contributed to its historical recuperation?

Catholic nuns were the only group of women on the battlefield with any prior experience in caring for the wounded. Their selflessness and virtue were unassailable. For these reasons, they were more welcomed than other Civil War nurses by the male military establishment, an attitude that is particularly remarkable given the rampant anti-Catholic prejudice of the era. Civil War chronicler Mary Livermore, no admirer of "the monastic institutions of that [Catholic] church," nonetheless praised the Catholic nurses. "They gave themselves no airs of superiority or holiness, shirked no duty, sought no easy place, bred no mischief."[62] Livermore thought the sisters represented a model of organized public service that Protestant women would do well to follow. Dorothea Dix, on the other hand, resented the Catholic women, who were not under her supervision.

◆ Figure 4.4 **Susie King Taylor**

Dedicated to the service of God and humanity rather than the victory of North or South, the sisters attended both Confederate and Union wounded. During the long Union siege of Vicksburg, the Sisters of Charity cared for Confederate soldiers and civilians alike. The same order provided nurses for the giant Satterlee Hospital in Philadelphia, which received many of the Union wounded from the war's deadliest battle, Gettysburg. Figure 4.3 shows most of the forty nuns who served at Satterlee. How did the nuns' religious habits solve the problems of uniform and functional clothing for nurses? While other Civil War nurses were portrayed individually, why and with what effect did these women appear as a group?

Most of the women valorized for their contributions to the war effort were white. Yet African American women, for whom the outcome was of the greatest importance, found their own way to the battlefields. Some were free black women from the North who went south to attend to the welfare of freed slaves living in areas occupied by the Union army. But others were themselves fugitives from slavery, who provided an important source of support labor for the northern war effort. These women served as cooks and laundresses for the Union troops and as servants for the officers. Although much of their labor was subservient, they were participating in an enterprise that would bring their people freedom, and this gave their labor new meaning.

Susie King Taylor is the rare example of a refugee from slavery whose name and wartime story we know. She was born near Savannah, Georgia, in 1848 to a fourteen-year-old slave mother. Her grandmother, who lived nearby, was free and taught Susie to read and write. In the spring of 1863, she fled with relatives to a South Carolina coastal island that was Union-occupied, where she secured her own freedom. There the Union army encouraged the refugees to undertake formal marriages, and Susie, fourteen at the time, wed Edward King.

Like other eager ex-slaves, her husband enlisted in one of the special "colored" divisions of the Union army, and King went to the battlefield with him. She worked as a laundress but was also entrusted with cleaning and caring for the musketry. The privilege of holding and handling guns was one of the markers of freedom for freed male slaves and for Susie King as well: "I learned to handle a musket very well while in the regiment, and could shoot straight and often hit the target."[63] Primarily, however, she was a nurse and served in a segregated military hospital for black soldiers. She and the other black nurses received $10 a month, $2 less than white women.

After the war, King worked as a teacher and a domestic servant in Georgia, until she was widowed and moved to Boston. There, in 1879, she married Russell Taylor. In 1902 she published *A Black Woman's Civil War Memoirs.* Of the more than one hundred Civil War reminiscences by women, hers is the only account by a former slave woman. Part of the impulse to publish her story may have been to clarify that her wartime service—and perhaps that of other freedwomen as well—went beyond that of a laundress. Figure 4.4 is the image she chose as the frontispiece for her book. Compare it to the Sisters of Charity photograph shown in Figure 4.3. How does King convey her sense of dignity and historic contribution to the war effort?

THE SPIES

By far, the most well-known African American woman on the battlefield was Harriet Tubman, renowned for her role as conductor on the Underground Railroad. Born a slave in Maryland about 1821, she ran away from her master in 1849 and returned between ten and thirteen times, often disguised as a man, to rescue as many as seventy relatives and friends still enslaved. When the war began, she came back from Canada, where she had gone to evade the Fugitive Slave Law, and made her way to the Union-occupied South Carolina coastal islands to offer her services. There, she functioned in virtually every role available to women in and around the fighting. She was a nurse, a liaison between the Union army and the many refugees from slavery (such as Susie King Taylor), a spy, and a military strategist for Union coastal invasions into Georgia and South Carolina.

Tubman began her military service in the way that most women did, as a nurse, first to the former slaves and then to black troops along the Carolina coast. There is some indication that cures she learned as a slave made her especially valuable in this role. But it soon became clear that, as a black woman who appeared to be merely a common slave, she could move easily about the South gathering information for the Union army. Union officers asked her to organize a corps from among the black male refugees to serve with her as military spies and scouts.

In 1863, on the basis of Tubman's reports, a regiment of 150 black Union soldiers sailed up South Carolina's Combahee River to cut the enemy's supply lines, seize or destroy foodstuffs, and encourage the desertion of the slave labor force of the plantations along the banks. Eight hundred black men and women—"thousands of dollars worth of property," according to a contemporary newspaper account—fled to the Union gunboats and were transferred to the freedmen's encampments on the occupied Sea Islands.[64] The raid was commemorated more than a century later when a group of black feminists from Massachusetts took as their name the Combahee River Collective (see Chapter 10).

Despite influential supporters, after the war Tubman was never able to secure the back pay or army pension that some white women, such as Mother Bickerdyke, received. In 1867, her husband, John Tubman, was murdered by a white man, who was acquitted of the crime. She spent the rest of her life in Auburn, New York, struggling to raise money to support herself and an old-age home for freedmen that she established. Proceeds from her memoir, *Scenes in the Life of Harriet Tubman,* were her major source of income. Tubman was not literate, and so her oral reminiscences were recorded in book form by a neighbor and friend, Sarah H. Bradford. Figure 4.5, the book's frontispiece, is described as a woodcut likeness of Tubman in her "costume as scout." Like other women on the battlefield (see Figure 4.7), Tubman wore a combination of men's and women's clothing. The jacket may have been military issue. What about this outfit reconciles her femaleness with the largely male nature of the battlefield? What might have been the impact on her readers of showing this former slave woman posed in front of a military camp, carrying an ammunition pouch and a gun?

◆ **Figure 4.5 Harriet Tubman**
© *Bettmann/Corbis.*

If Tubman's race allowed her to spy for the North, white southerner Rose O'Neal Greenhow's sex allowed her to spy for the South. In the Union capital of Washington, D.C., nearby southern sympathizers were able to conduct a brisk trade in military information. Some of these spies were women who made use of their sexual attractiveness to serve their cause. Greenhow, one of the best known, was described by a contemporary as possessed of "almost irresistible seductive powers."[65]

When the war broke out, Greenhow was a widow and mother in her mid-thirties. She was prominent in Washington, D.C., social circles and well connected to important congressmen, including her nephew Senator Stephen A. Douglas of Illinois. Committed to the Confederate cause and opposed to freedom for black people, she gathered political and military information helpful to the South from her numerous admirers and lovers, allegedly information that helped the Confederates win the first battle of Bull Run. Although constantly under suspicion, she avoided arrest by appealing to principles of gentlemanly chivalry shared by North and South alike.

◆ **Figure 4.6 Rose O'Neal Greenhow in the Old Capitol Prison with Her Daughter**
Library of Congress LC-DIG-cwpbh-04849.

Eventually, however, Greenhow was arrested and sent to a special Washington prison reserved for enemy agents, many of them women. (One of the other Confederate women imprisoned there was the sister of Phoebe Yates Pember, Figure 4.2.) She was subsequently released to Virginia. The circumstances of her death, soon after, were as extraordinary as those of her life. In 1864 she was a passenger on a British boat running the Union naval blockade off the Carolina coast. Northern gunships fired, and Greenhow's lifeboat capsized. She was close to shore and would have made it to land except that she held on to her purse, which was heavy with gold, and therefore drowned.

The photograph in Figure 4.6 was taken by a member of the studio of renowned Civil War photographer Mathew Brady, when Greenhow was imprisoned. What comment does the photographer's artful posing make on Greenhow's career as a Confederate spy? What do Greenhow's dress, pose, and the presence of her daughter suggest about her imprisonment at Union hands?

THE SOLDIERS

Although we will never know their numbers, the evidence is incontrovertible that hundreds of women, possibly more, fought on the battlefields of the Civil War. These women warriors fall into two categories: those who were known to be women at the time and those who passed themselves off as men. In the first category were the so-called daughters of the regiment. Often arriving in camp with their newly enlisted husbands, a few may have also been as motivated by the desire to see military action as by marital sentiment. After performing such womanly tasks as nursing, cooking, and laundering, occasionally these women took on the all-important job of carrying the regiment's flag (or standard) into battle. Soldiers, who were recruited at the local and state level, fought as much out of loyalty to their regiment as to the army or the nation, and the way their regimental colors were displayed represented their comradeship and military fervor. The standard bearer's job was to lead and encourage the troops, and women who undertook this role inspired tremendous devotion from their comrades.

Bridget Divers, known as "Michigan Bridget," was one of these regimental "daughters." She was an Irish immigrant and came to the First Michigan Calvary with her husband. Early in the war, her regiment was the object of a surprise attack, and the troops panicked. One of Divers's comrades remembered how she leaped to her feet, grabbed the flag, and yelled (note the accent), "Go in Boys and bate Hell out of them."[66] Divers found army life so much to her liking that, after the war, she continued to serve with her husband in the western Indian conflicts.

As with other such women, the legends that accrued around Michigan Bridget emphasized her combination of manly bravery and female sympathy. Figure 4.7, a steel engraving commissioned, like that of Mary Ann Bickerdyke (Figure 4.1), by Mary Livermore for *My Story of the War,* portrays Divers bearing the U.S. flag in the midst of battle. Divers knew how to shoot, and Livermore approvingly wrote of her, "When a soldier fell she took his place, fighting in his stead with unquailing

◆ Figure 4.7 **F. O. C. Darley,** *A Woman in Battle — "Michigan Bridget"*
Carrying the Flag
General Research Division, The New York Public Library, Astor, Lenox, and Tilden Foundations.

courage."[67] How and with what purpose does the artist position Divers with respect to the battle? Why might she have been pictured with a flag instead of the
gun that she allegedly knew how to use? And why might the artist have chosen to
show her carrying not the regimental colors but the U.S. flag?

"Of the three hundred and twenty-eight thousand Union soldiers who lie
buried in national cemeteries," the editors of the *History of Woman Suffrage* (1881)
wrote, ". . . hundreds are . . . women obliged by army regulation to fight in
disguise."[68] "Passing women," as historians have come to label such women, fought
in many wars, but they seem to have been particularly numerous in the U.S. Civil
War. The Union army discovered and dismissed many women among its recruits,
and the sex of others was not discovered until they were wounded or killed. During the war, authorities' greatest fear was that women who had sneaked into the
ranks would engage in immoral sexual activities with male soldiers. Stories of
women who disguised themselves as men in order to fight continued to surface for

◆ **Figure 4.8 Madam Velazquez in Female Attire** *(left)* **and Harry T. Buford, 1st Lieutenant, Independent Scouts, Confederate States Army** *(right)*
Documenting the American South (http://docsouth.unc.edu), The University of North Carolina at Chapel Hill Libraries. From Loreta Janeta Velazquez, The Woman in Battle: A Narrative of the Exploits, Adventures, and Travels of Madame Loreta Janeta Velazquez, Otherwise Known as Lieutenant Harry T. Buford, Confederate States Army *(Richmond: Dustin, Gilman & Co., 1876).*

many decades. In 1910, an Illinois Civil War pensioner named Albert Cashier was discovered to be a woman, declared insane, sentenced to an asylum, and forced to dress as a woman.[69] For a long time after the war, some passing women, like Cashier, lived as men. They worked in men's occupations and even married women, who invariably claimed to have believed their husbands to be men, which is hard to believe but impossible to dismiss.

With one exception, all of the well-known "passing women" of the Civil War era were Union soldiers. Loreta Velazquez, a Cuban immigrant, began her career in the Confederate army with her husband's support but maintained her masquerade even after he was killed. Using the name of Harry T. Buford, Velazquez fought as an officer with several regiments and participated in the Confederate victory at the first battle of Bull Run. Although she was wounded, she escaped detection and continued to live a life of high adventure after the war.

In 1876, Velazquez wrote a popular and controversial memoir, *The Woman in Battle,* in which she described her lifelong habit of wearing men's clothes and the attraction that being able to make money like a man held for her. She included the illustrations shown in Figure 4.8 of her female and male personas. How did she depict herself as a woman, and what designated her visually as a man? Above all, what point might she have been seeking to make by demonstrating through illustrations that she could shift from role to role? How does her story begin to suggest what today is called the social construction of gender?

QUESTIONS FOR ANALYSIS

1. What are the similarities in the images of the quite different women who served as Civil War nurses? What attitudes toward women help explain these similarities?

2. Male soldiers are issued official uniforms to designate their rank and military affiliation. What similarities do you notice in Divers's and Tubman's outfits? How might this clothing have constituted a kind of informal uniform for women on the battlefield?

3. The Civil War was fought between two cultures as much as between two economic and political systems. Do you detect patterns in the images of northern versus southern women? What do these differences tell you about the gender dimensions of the North–South divide?

4. Taken as a group, do these images indicate that the women who participated directly in the war did more to maintain or to undermine their standard gender roles?

NOTES

1. Martha S. Read to Lorinda Shelton, April 6, 1852, Norwich, New York, http://xroads.virginia.edu/~HYPER/HNS/domwest/read.html (accessed June 16, 2004).

2. Lillian Schlissel, ed., *Women's Diaries of the Westward Journey* (New York: Schocken Books, 1982), 188.

3. Cathy Luchetti, ed., *Women of the West* (St. George, Utah: Antelope Island Press, 1982), 145.

4. John Mack Faragher, *Women and Men on the Overland Trail* (New Haven: Yale University Press, 1979), 172.

5. Schlissel, *Women's Diaries of the Westward Journey,* 179-80.

6. Ibid., 214.

7. Ibid., 223.

8. Ibid., 39.

9. Sarah Royce, *A Frontier Lady,* excerpted in *No Rooms of Their Own: Women Writers of Early California,* ed. Ida Rae Egli (Berkeley: Heyday Books, 1992), 15.

10. Catharine Washburn, quoted in *A Place to Grow: Women in the American West,* ed. Glenda Riley (Arlington Heights, IL: Harlan Davidson, 1992), 113.

11. Royce, *A Frontier Lady,* in *No Rooms of Their Own,* 13.

12. Quoted in Riley, *A Place to Grow,* 127.

13. Sarah Winnemucca Hopkins, *Life among the Piutes: Their Wrongs and Claims* (1883; repr., Bishop, CA: Sierra Media, 1969), 11.

14. J. S. Holliday, *The World Rushed In: The California Gold Rush Experience* (New York: Simon and Schuster, 1981), 164.

15. Susan B. Anthony to Mary Anthony, February 7, 1848, in *The Selected Papers of Elizabeth Cady Stanton and Susan B. Anthony: In the School of Anti-Slavery, 1840–1866,* ed. Ann D. Gordon (New Brunswick: Rutgers University Press, 1996), 134.

16. Anonymous to Catherine D. Oliver, 1850, cited in Edith Sparks, "Capital Instincts: The Economics of Female Proprietorship in San Francisco, 1850–1920" (PhD diss., UCLA, 1999).

17. Louise Clappe, *The Shirley Letters, Being Letters Written in 1851–1852 from the California Mines* (1922; repr., Santa Barbara: Peregrine, 1970), 36.

18. Schlissel, *Women's Diaries of the Westward Journey,* 6.

19. Christiane Fischer, ed., *Let Them Speak for Themselves: Women in the American West* (New York: E. P. Dutton, 1978), 43–45.

20. Hubert Howe Bancroft, quoted in J. S. Holliday, *The World Rushed In,* 165.

21. Eliza W. Farnham, *California, In-doors and Out, or How We Farm, Mine, and Live Generally in the Golden State* (New York: Dix, Edwards, 1856), 384.

22. Nancy Hewitt, *Women's Activism and Social Change: Rochester, New York, 1822–1872* (Ithaca: Cornell University Press, 1984), 40.

23. Constitution of the New-York Female Moral Reform Society, 1836, reprinted in *Public Women, Public Words: A Documentary History of American Feminism,* vol. 1, *Begin-*

nings to 1900, ed. Dawn Keetley and John Pettegrew (Madison, WI: Madison House, 1997), 129.

24. T. L. Nichols, M.D., and Mrs. Mary S. Gove Nichols, *Marriage: Its History, Character and Results; Its Sanctities and Its Profanities; Its Science and Its Facts* (New York: T. L. Nichols, 1854), 202.

25. Elizabeth Cady Stanton, *Eighty Years and More: Reminiscences, 1815–1897* (1898; repr., Boston: Northeastern University Press, 1993), 284.

26. Georgiana Bruce Kirby, "On Brook Farm," in *Years of Experience: An Autobiographical Narrative* (New York: G. P. Putnam's Sons, 1887), 99.

27. Boston Female Anti-Slavery Address, July 13, 1836, reprinted in *Our Mothers Before Us: Women and Democracy, 1789–1920* (Washington, DC: Foundation for the National Archives, 1998), 11–23.

28. Maria Stewart, Lecture Delivered at the Franklin Hall, Boston, September 21, 1832, reprinted in *Maria Stewart, America's First Black Woman Political Writer: Essays and Speeches,* ed. Marilyn Richardson (Bloomington: Indiana University Press, 1987), 47.

29. Harriet Beecher Stowe, "Sojourner Truth: The Libyan Sibyl," *Atlantic Monthly,* April 1863, 473–481.

30. Elizabeth Cady Stanton, "Speech to the Anniversary of the American Anti-Slavery Society," *Liberator,* May 18, 1860, 78.

31. Carolyn Williams, "The Female Antislavery Movement: Fighting Against Racial Prejudice and Promoting Women's Rights in Antebellum America," in *The Abolitionist Sisterhood: Women's Political Culture in Antebellum America,* ed. Jean Fagan Yellin and John C. Van Horne (Ithaca: Cornell University Press, 1994), 162.

32. Jean R. Soderlund, "Priorities and Power: The Philadelphia Female Anti-Slavery Society," in Yellin and Van Horne, *The Abolitionist Sisterhood,* 73.

33. "Pastoral Letter of the Massachusetts Congregationalist Clergy," 1837, reprinted in *Up from the Pedestal: Selected Writings in the History of American Feminism,* ed. Aileen Kraditor (Chicago: Quadrangle Books, 1968), 51.

34. Boston Female Anti-Slavery Address, July 13, 1836, reprinted in *Our Mothers Before Us,* 11–23.

35. Quoted in Lori D. Ginzberg, *Women and the Work of Benevolence: Morality, Politics, and Class in the Nineteenth-Century United States* (New Haven: Yale University Press, 1990), 93.

36. Ibid., 26.

37. Angelina Grimké Weld to Gerrit and Anne Smith, June 18, 1840, *Letters of Theodore Dwight Weld, Angelina Grimké Weld, and Sarah Grimké, 1822–1844,* eds. Gilbert Barnes and Dwight Dumond (New York: Appleton-Century, 1934), 2: 842.

38. Stanton, *Eighty Years and More,* 83.

39. Ibid., 147–48.

40. "Declarations of Sentiments and Resolutions, Seneca Falls Convention," 1848, reprinted in Kraditor, *Up from the Pedestal,* 183–89.

41. Frances Ellen Watkins Harper, letter to John Brown, November 25, 1859; reprinted in James Redpath, *Echoes of Harper's Ferry* (Boston: Thayer and Eldridge, 1860), 418–19.

42. Frances Willard, *Glimpses of Fifty Years: The Autobiography of an American Woman,* (Chicago: H. J. Smith, 1889), 155.

43. Mary Chesnut, April 12, 1861, in *Mary Chesnut's Civil War,* ed. C. Vann Woodward (New Haven: Yale University Press, 1981), 46.

44. Mary Livermore, *My Story of the War* (Hartford: A. D. Worthington, 1898), 465.

45. Ibid., 472.

46. Anna Howard Shaw, with the collaboration of Elizabeth Jordan, *The Story of a Pioneer* (New York: Harpers Bros., 1915), 51.

47. Quoted in Bell Irvin Wiley, *Confederate Women* (Westford, CT: Greenwood Press, 1975), 177.

48. Elizabeth Cady Stanton to Nancy Smith, July 20, 1863, *Elizabeth Cady Stanton as Revealed in Her Letters, Diary, and Reminiscences,* eds. Theodore Stanton and Harriot Stanton Blatch (New York: Harper & Brothers, 1922), 95.

49. Quoted in *We Are Your Sisters: Black Women in the Nineteenth Century,* ed. Dorothy Sterling (New York: W. W. Norton, 1984), 239.

50. Elizabeth Cady Stanton, "To the Women of the Republic," April 24, 1863, reprinted in *The Selected Papers of Elizabeth Cady Stanton and Susan B. Anthony: In the School of Anti-Slavery,* ed. Ann D. Gordon (New Brunswick, NJ: Rutgers University Press), 483.

51. Elizabeth Cady Stanton, Susan B. Anthony, and Matilda J. Gage, eds., *History of Woman Suffrage* (Rochester, NY: Susan B. Anthony, 1881), 79.

52. Mary Chesnut, May 7, 1865, in Woodward, *Mary Chesnut's Civil War,* 802.

53. Quoted in Sterling, *We Are Your Sisters,* 244.

54. Livermore, *My Story of the War,* 469.

55. Cited in Marilyn Mayer Culpepper, *All Things Altered: Women in the Wake of Civil War and Reconstruction* (Jefferson, NC: McFarland, 2002), 23.

56. Circular, "California Association of American Women," February 28, 1848, republished with Farnham, *California, In-doors and Out* (originally 1856) (Amsterdam: F. De Graaf, 1972).

57. Angustias de la Guerra Ord, *Occurrences in Hispanic California,* trans. and ed. Francis Price and William Ellison (Washington, DC: Academic Press of American Franciscan History, 1956), 59. For the correction, see Rosaura Sanchez, *Telling Identities: The Californio "Testimonios"* (Minneapolis: University of Minnesota Press, 1995), 324.

58. Mary Denis Maher, *To Bind Up the Wounds: Catholic Sister Nurses in the U.S. Civil War* (New York: Greenwood Press, 1989), 51.

59. Bulletin issued by Dorothea Dix, quoted in Maher, *To Bind Up the Wounds,* 53.

60. Louisa May Alcott, *The Journals of Louisa May Alcott,* ed. Joel Myerson, Daniel Sheahy, and Madeleine B. Stern (Boston: Little, Brown, 1989), 110.

61. Phoebe Yates Pember, *A Southern Woman's Story* (1879; repr., Jackson, TN: McCowat-Mercer Press, 1959), ch. 1.

62. Mary Livermore, *What Shall We Tell Our Daughters: Superfluous Women and Other Lectures* (Boston: Less and Shepard, 1883), 177–78, quoted in Maher, *To Bind Up the Wounds,* 39.

63. Susie King Taylor, *A Black Woman's Civil War Memoirs: Reminiscences of My Life in Camp with the 33rd U.S. Colored Troops, Late 1st South Carolina Volunteers,* excerpted in *Growing Up Female in America: Ten Lives,* ed. Eve Merriam (New York: Dell, 1971), 195.

64. *Commonwealth,* July 10, 1863, cited in Earl Conrad, *Harriet Tubman* (Washington, DC: The Associated Publishers, 1943), 169.

65. Quoted in Elizabeth Leonard, *All the Daring of the Soldier: Women of the Civil War Armies* (New York: W. W. Norton, 1999), 94.

66. Quoted in Leonard, *All the Daring of the Soldier,* 123.

67. Livermore, *My Story of the War,* 116.

68. Stanton, Anthony, and Gage, *History of Woman Suffrage,* 2:23.

69. Leonard, *All the Daring of a Soldier,* 188–89.

SUGGESTED REFERENCES

Women and the West   For general overviews on women and the West in this period, see Julie Roy Jeffrey, *Frontier Women: The Trans-Mississippi West, 1840–1880* (1979); and Glenda Riley, *Women and Indians on the Frontier* (1984). On the overland trail experience, see John Mack Faragher, *Women and Men on the Overland Trail* (1979). Lillian Schlissel has edited a major collection of overland trail diaries in *Women's Diaries of the Western Journey* (1992). For the impact of American migration on the California Indians, see Albert Hurtado, *Indian Survival on the California Frontier* (1987), and *Sex, Gender and Culture in California* (1999). On the Cherokee experience through women's eyes, see Theda Perdue, *Cherokee Women: Gender and Culture Change, 1700–1835* (1998). Gae Canfield has written a biography of Sarah Winnemucca, *Sarah Winnemucca of the Northern Paiutes* (1983). On Mexican California, see Ramón A. Gutiérrez and Richard J. Orsi, eds., *Contested Eden: California before the Gold Rush* (1997); and Rosaura Sanchez, *Telling Identities: The Californio "Testimonios"* (1995). On women and the California gold rush, see Joanne Levy, *They Saw the Elephant: Women in the California Gold Rush* (1990). Susan Lee Johnson offers a gendered history in *Roaring Camp: The Social World of the California Gold Rush* (2000). Important book-length primary sources concerning women in the West in this period include Louise Clappe, *The Shirley Letters from the California Mines, 1851–1852* (1998); Eliza Farnham, *California, In-doors and Out* (1972); and Sarah Winnemucca Hopkins, *Life among the Piutes: Their Wrongs and Claims* (1994).

Women and Reform Movements   For the roots of women's reform activism, see Ann Boylan, *The Origins of Women's Activism, New York, and Boston, 1797–1840* (2002); Keith Melder, *Beginnings of Sisterhood: The American Woman's Rights Movement, 1800–1850* (1977); Mary Ryan, *Cradle of the Middle Class: The Family in Oneida County, New York, 1790–1865* (1981); and Anne F. Scott, *Natural Allies: Women's Associations in American History* (1993). On female moral reform, see

Barbara J. Berg, *The Remembered Gate: Origins of American Feminism, the Woman, and the City, 1800–1860* (1978); and Carroll Smith-Rosenberg, "Beauty, the Beast and the Militant Woman: A Case Study of Sex Roles and Social Stress in Jacksonian America," *American Quarterly* 23 (1971), 562–84. On temperance, see Barbara Epstein, *The Politics of Domesticity: Women, Evangelism, and Temperance in Nineteenth-Century America* (1981). Two studies on women and health reform are Susan Cayleff, *Wash and Be Healed: The Water Cure Movement and Women's Health* (1987); and Jean L. Silver-Isenstadt, *Shameless: The Visionary Life of Mary Gove Nichols* (2002). On women and utopian communities, see Lawrence Foster, *Women, Family and Utopia: Communal Experiments of the Shakers, the Oneida Community, and the Mormons* (1991); and Louis J. Kern, *An Ordered Love: Sex Roles and Sexuality in Victorian Utopias — The Shakers, the Mormons, and the Oneida Community* (1981). On Margaret Fuller, see Charles Capper, *Margaret Fuller: An American Romantic Life* (1992); and Bell Gale Chevigny, ed., *The Woman and the Myth: Margaret Fuller's Life and Writings* (1997).

Women and Abolitionism   There is much written on women and abolitionism, including Blanche Hersh, *The Slavery of Sex: Female Abolitionists in Nineteenth-Century America* (1978); Nancy Hewitt, *Women's Activism and Social Change, Rochester, New York, 1822–1872* (2001); Julie Roy Jeffrey, *The Great Silent Army of Abolitionism: Ordinary Women in the Antislavery Movement* (1998); Gerda Lerner, *The Grimké Sisters from South Carolina* (1967); Shirley Yee, *Black Women Abolitionists: A Study in Activitism, 1828–1860* (1992); Jean Baker Yellin and John C. Van Horne, eds., *The Abolitionist Sisterhood: Women's Political Culture in Antebellum America* (1994); and Susan Zaeske, *Signatures of Citizenship: Petitioning, Antislavery, and Women's Political Identity* (2003). On Sojourner Truth, see Nell Painter, *Sojourner Truth: A Life, a Symbol* (1996). On women's rights, see Ellen Carol DuBois, *Feminism and Suffrage: The Emergence of an Independent Women's Movement in America, 1848–1869* (2003), and *Woman Suffrage, Women's Rights* (1998); and Nancy Isenberg, *Sex and Citizenship in Antebellum America* (1998). An important collection of hitherto unpublished sources for the period can be found in Ann D. Gordon, ed., *The Papers of Elizabeth Cady Stanton and Susan B. Anthony*, vol. 1, *In the School of Anti-Slavery* (1997). Elizabeth Cady Stanton's engaging autobiography, *Eighty Years and More: Reminiscences, 1815–1897* (2002), should also be consulted. Bonnie Anderson situates American women's rights in an international context in *Joyous Greetings: The First International Women's Movement, 1830–1860* (2000).

Women and the Civil War   On women's roles leading up to the Civil War, see Jean Baker, *Mary Todd Lincoln: A Biography* (1987); and Melanie Gustafson, *Women and the Republican Party, 1854–1900* (2001). On Harriet Beecher Stowe and *Uncle Tom's Cabin*, see Joan Hedrick, *Harriet Beecher Stowe: A Life* (1994); and Barbara Ann White, *The Beecher Sisters* (2003). On southern women during the war, see Laura Edwards, *Scarlett Doesn't Live Here Anymore: Southern Women in the Civil War Era* (2000); Drew Gilpin Faust, *Mothers of Invention: Women of the Slaveholding South in the American Civil War* (1998); and George Rable, *Civil Wars: Women and the Crisis* *of Southern Nationalism* (1989). For women in the North, important studies include Jeanie Attie, *Patriotic Toil: Northern Women and the American Civil War* (1998); and Lori Ginzberg, *Women and the Work of Benevolence: Morality, Politics, and Class in the Nineteenth-Century United States* (1990). Elizabeth Leonard, *All the Daring of the Soldier: Women of the Civil War Armies* (1999), covers both sides, including women as soldiers. Sister Mary Denis Maher examines an understudied topic in *To Bind Up the Wounds: Catholic Sister Nurses in the U.S. Civil War* (1989). Two new biographies of Harriet Tubman are Catherine Clinton, *Harriet Tubman, The Road to Freedom* (2004); and Kate Clifford Larson, *Bound for the Promised Land: Harriet Tubman, Portrait of an American Hero* (2003).

Selected Web Sites

The Women of the West Museum, an entirely online site, has now been absorbed by the Autry Museum of the American West and can be accessed at <**museumoftheamericanwest.org**>. In addition to the groups of documents at this site, the Autry site has other online exhibitions of use, notably a history of the Chinese in California entitled On Gold Mountain, <**apa.si.edu/ongoldmountain**>.

The major online source for materials on women's antebellum reform is the extremely important women's history site Women and Social Movements in the United States, 1600–2000, originally created by the Center for the Historical Study of Women and Gender at the State University of New York at Binghamton. Some of these materials are available at <**womhist.binghamton.edu**>; a fuller set can be accessed, with subscription, at <**alexanderstreet6.com/wasm/index.html**>. For Chapter 4, the relevant document sets include Internationalizing Feminism in the Nineteenth Century; Oberlin Women and Antebellum Social Movements; The Appeal of Female Moral Reform, 1835–1841; The Nineteenth-Century Dress Reform Movement, 1838–1881; Lucretia Mott's Reform Networks, 1840–1860; Bible Communism and the Women of the Oneida Community, 1848–1879; Male Supporters of Women's Rights in the 1850s; and Relations Between Abolitionist Women and Slaveholding Relatives.

For the history of the antebellum women's rights movement, see the Web site for the Elizabeth Cady Stanton and Susan B. Anthony Papers at Rutgers University, which includes an online "mini-edition" on Stanton's and Anthony's travels for women's rights in the 1850s, <**adh.sc.edu/sa/sa-table.html**>. Another excellent Web site covers the many different sorts of women's reform activities in upstate New York, a center of reform activism, <**lib.rochester.edu/rbk/women/women.htm**>. The Lucretia Mott Papers Web site includes material on both antislavery and women's rights, <**lucidcafe.com/lucidcafe/library/96jan/mott.html**>. And Duke University Library, which has many sources relating to women's history on its Web pages, has a special collection focusing on women in the Civil War and including sources for both the Union and the Confederacy. Among these are the diaries of Rose O'Neal Greenhow, <**scriptorium.lib.duke.edu/collections/civil-war-women.html**>.

5

Reconstructing Women's Lives North and South

1865–1900

IDA B. WELLS, MARY KENNEY, AND M. CAREY THOMAS were all daughters of the Civil War era. Wells was born in 1862 to Mississippi slaves, Kenney in 1864 to Irish immigrants in Hannibal, Missouri, and Thomas in 1857 to a wealthy, pro-abolitionist Baltimore Quaker family. Despite these great differences in background, the unfolding of each woman's life illustrates something of the forces that affected American women's history in the years after the Civil War and of women's capacity to be forces in the making of American history.

Wells (later Wells-Barnett) was shaped by the violent struggles between former slaves seeking to realize the emancipation promised to them and white southerners seeking to retain racial dominance over their society. As a journalist, Wells exposed new, brutal methods of white supremacy, and her work sparked an organized women's movement among African Americans. Kenney (later O'Sullivan) was a bookbinder and a lifelong wage earner who recognized that workers needed to act collectively rather than individually to improve their lives. A pathbreaking female labor organizer, she helped form the Women's Trade Union League in 1903 (see Chapter 7). Thomas, a self-proclaimed tomboy who had no interest in marriage or a conventional domestic life, became a pioneer of higher education for women. She was one of the first women to graduate from Cornell University and to receive a PhD (in Switzerland), and she was the founding dean of Bryn Mawr College. In the post–Civil War (or postbellum) years, these women and others like them laid the basis for an era of extraordinary achievement by American women.

"Reconstruction" is the term used to describe American history immediately after the Civil War, in particular the revision of the U.S. Constitution to deal with the consequences of emancipation, the rebuilding of the South after the devastations of war, and the reconstitution of national unity after the trauma of sectional division. The formal period of Reconstruction lasted twelve years. It ended in 1877 when U.S. troops withdrew from their occupation of the former Confederacy, leaving the South to work out its own troubled racial destiny without federal oversight and the North to concentrate on industrial development and economic growth.

The term "reconstruction" can also be used to cover a longer period, during which the United States was reconstituted around the sole remaining economic system, industrial capitalism. The free labor ethic on which the Republican Party was founded evolved into a commitment to unbridled industrialization, the wealth, optimism, and productivity of which were not shared equally. On the contrary, the gap between rich and poor grew enormously during the postbellum years, producing great tension and violence between owners and workers. With chattel slavery eliminated, industrial society could no longer ignore its internal class divisions, and by the end of the century, conflict between labor and capital overtook the inequalities of race as the most overt challenge to America's national unity.

Women were reconstructing their lives in these years as well. In the defeated South, women emancipated from slavery grappled with the challenges and dangers of their tentative freedom, while their former mistresses sought to maintain their privileges of racial superiority despite the end of slavery. In the triumphant North, a determined group of women sought equal political rights with men, and the woman suffrage movement came into its own. Industrial capitalism generated both a rapidly expanding female labor force and new leisure and wealth for middle- and upper-class women. In the years during and after Reconstruction, women's labor, the terms of appropriate

271

womanhood within which women lived, and their scope for public action all changed and grew. By the opening of the twentieth century, the basis had been laid for an epoch to come of female assertion and accomplishment unparalleled in American history.

GENDER AND THE POSTWAR CONSTITUTIONAL AMENDMENTS

American history's first presidential assassination (Abraham Lincoln), followed quickly by its first presidential impeachment (Andrew Johnson), left the executive branch in shambles and the legislative branch in charge of national Reconstruction. Republicans controlled Congress, and former abolitionists, known as Radicals, controlled the Republican Party. To protect the North's victory and their party's control over Congress, the Radicals were determined to enfranchise the only population on whom the Republicans could depend in the defeated Confederacy—former slaves. In 1866, Radicals proposed a Fourteenth Amendment to the U.S. Constitution to establish the citizenship of ex-slaves. It began with the simple, inclusive sentence: "All persons born or naturalized in the United States, and subject to the jurisdiction thereof, are citizens of the United States and of the State wherein they reside."

Leaders of the women's rights movement hoped to revise the Constitution and reconstruct democracy without distinction of either race *or* gender. Despite their best efforts, however, the ratification of the Fourteenth Amendment in 1868, followed by the Fifteenth Amendment in 1870, established black suffrage without reference to woman suffrage. Thwarted in Congress, these women turned to the Supreme Court to argue a novel interpretation of the new amendments, contending that women's political rights were included within the new constitutional definitions of national citizenship and political rights.

Their efforts failed. The only actual enfranchisement of women in the Reconstruction era occurred in the territories of Wyoming (1869) and Utah (1870), where a handful of legislators accorded women the vote in territorial and local elections. Even so, the campaign for women's enfranchisement changed and expanded from its northeastern base, drawing new adherents from the Midwest and the Pacific Coast. The old alliance with abolitionists was shattered, and most efforts for women's equality were no longer linked to those for racial equality. The advocates of woman suffrage had undertaken a campaign that would require an additional half-century and another constitutional amendment—the Nineteenth, ratified in 1920—to complete. (See Chapter 7 and, for the complete text of all amendments to the U.S. Constitution, the Appendix, pp. A-12–A-17.)

Constitutionalizing Women's Rights

In 1865–1866, as Congress was considering how to word the Fourteenth Amendment, women's rights activists called for woman suffrage to be joined with black suffrage in a single constitutional act of universal adult enfranchisement. Many northern women had fought for the end of slavery, and so, in the memorable words of Elizabeth Cady Stanton, "Would it not be advisable, when the constitutional door is open, [for women to] avail ourselves of the strong arm and blue uniform of the black soldier to walk in by his side?"[1] To pursue this goal, they formed the American Equal Rights Association, dedicated to both black and woman suffrage. "We resolved to make common cause with the colored class—the only other disfranchised class," observed Lucy Stone, "and strike for equal rights for all."[2]

But Radicals in Congress contended that pursuing woman suffrage and black suffrage simultaneously would doom the latter, which was their priority. To clarify that women were not to be included, they wrote the second section of the Fourteenth Amendment, meant to encourage states to grant voting rights to former slaves, to apply only to "male inhabitants . . . twenty-one years of age and citizens of the United States." This was the first reference to gender in the U.S. Constitution. Stanton predicted, "If that word 'male' be inserted it will take us a century at least to get it out."[3] Suffragists petitioned Congress to get the wording changed, but they were told by Wendell Phillips, Frederick Douglass, and other former male allies, "This hour belongs to the Negro," leaving Stanton to wonder impatiently if "the African race is composed entirely of males."[4]

Two years after the 1868 ratification of the Fourteenth Amendment, congressional Radicals wrote the Fifteenth Amendment to advance black suffrage more forcefully, explicitly forbidding disfranchisement on the grounds of "race, color or previous condition of servitude." Gender was not included, leading Stanton to charge that Congress intended to reform the electorate as "an aristocracy of sex." "All mankind will vote not because of intelligence, patriotism, property or white skin," she denounced, "but because it is male, not female."[5] The American Equal Rights Association collapsed amid accusations that those who opposed the amendments were racist.

In its wake, woman suffragists divided over whether to endorse the Fifteenth Amendment. To reconcile woman suffrage advocacy with the Radical Republican agenda, in 1869 Lucy Stone and her husband Henry Ward Blackwell organized the American Woman Suffrage Association. They focused on campaigns for suffrage at the state level and in 1870 inaugurated *The Woman's Journal,* a weekly newspaper that was continually published for the next fifty years. Elizabeth Cady Stanton and Susan B. Anthony took a different route. They broke with their former Radical Republican allies and formed the rival National Woman Suffrage Association (NWSA).

Of the two societies, the NWSA pursued the more aggressive, independent path. As Stanton proudly recalled, "Standing alone we learned our power; . . . [W]oman must lead the way to her own enfranchisement, and work out her own salvation with a hopeful course and determination that knows no fear nor trembling."[6] The organization's newspaper, defiantly named *The Revolution,* lasted only two years. It proclaimed on its masthead: "Women their rights and nothing less; men their rights and nothing more." NWSA gained political autonomy for the suffrage movement but lost an important part of the women's rights legacy: attention to the interrelation of the hierarchies of race and gender. As the larger society left

◆ **Elizabeth Cady Stanton and Susan B. Anthony**
Taken in 1870, this is the earliest photograph of the most
important partnership in the U.S. woman suffrage movement. Stanton and Anthony had already been collaborat-
ing for two decades, and would do so for another three.
Stanton's rambunctious curls and Anthony's severe bun
give some indication of their quite different yet compatible personalities. Despite their bond, there was a hint
of inequality between them. Although Anthony was only
five years younger, she addressed her friend as "Mrs. Stanton," while Stanton called her "Susan." © *Bettmann/ Corbis.*

behind the concerns of the ex-slaves and of Radical Reconstruction, much of the
woman suffrage movement did too, envisioning women's emancipation largely in
terms of white women.

A New Departure for Woman Suffrage

One final episode of Reconstruction-era woman suffrage activism deserves attention. Once the new constitutional amendments had been ratified, NWSA proposed an inventive, bold interpretation of them. Their argument was both simple
and profound: first, women were "persons" whose rights as national citizens were
established by the first sentence of the Fourteenth Amendment; second, the right
to vote was central to and inherent in national citizenship. Thus, women's right to
vote was already established and did not require any additional constitutional
change.

This argument, which was called the "New Departure," brought to prominence one of the most unusual advocates in the history of woman suffrage, Victoria Claflin Woodhull. Born into poverty, she made her way into the highest ranks
of New York society, in large part by cultivating powerful men. Aided by a congressman friend and without the knowledge of other suffragists, in 1871 she pre-

sented the case for the New Departure before the Judiciary Committee of the U.S. House of Representatives. NWSA leaders were thrilled. Within a year, however, Woodhull had become involved in a scandal over the alleged adultery of Henry Ward Beecher, powerful Brooklyn minister and brother of Catharine Beecher and Harriet Beecher Stowe (see Chapter 3). Under a new federal anti-obscenity law known as the Comstock Act (named for the "social purity" crusader who drafted the legislation, Anthony Comstock), Woodhull was jailed for sending accounts of the scandal through the federal mails. Stanton, one of the few suffragists who steadfastly defended Woodhull, insisted, "We have already women enough sacrificed to this sentimental, hypocritical prating about purity. If this present woman be crucified, let men drive the spikes."[7] Woodhull avoided jail but dropped out of public life; she eventually moved to England, where she married a wealthy man, remade her reputation, and lived until 1927.

Independent of Woodhull, suffragists around the country pursued their voting rights on the basis of the New Departure theory that they were already enfranchised. During the elections of 1871 and 1872, groups of women went to their local polling places, put forth their constitutional understanding to stunned election officials, and stepped forward to submit their votes. In Washington, D.C., the African American journalist Mary Ann Shadd Cary was able to register but not to vote. Susan B. Anthony was more successful. She convinced polling officials in her hometown of Rochester, New York, to let her vote. "Well I have been & gone & done it!!," she wrote exuberantly. "Positively voted the Republican ticket."[8] Two weeks later, she was arrested for violating a federal law meant to disfranchise former confederates. Her trial was a spectacle from start to finish. The judge ordered the jury to find Anthony guilty. During the sentencing, he futilely tried to silence her: "The Court cannot allow the prisoner to go on . . . the prisoner must sit down . . . the prisoner has been tried according to the established forms of law."[9] Anthony was found guilty, and the judge's final insult was to refuse to jail Anthony so as to keep her from appealing her verdict (see box, "Not One Is My Peer, All Are My Political Sovereigns").

The U.S. Supreme Court finally considered the New Departure argument in 1875, in the case of Virginia Minor, a St. Louis, Missouri, suffragist who sued the official who had not allowed her to vote. In *Minor v. Happersett,* one of the most important rulings in the history of women's rights (see the Appendix, p. A-25), the Supreme Court ruled unanimously that, while Minor was indeed a citizen, voting was not a right but a privilege bestowed by the federal government on those who could be trusted to use it wisely. Not only did this decision strike the New Departure theory dead, but the ruling also indicated that the Court was bent on narrowing the meaning of the Fourteenth and Fifteenth Amendments in general. Subsequently, the freedpeople of the South got virtually no protection from the federal government for their constitutional rights, as the Court permitted more and more devices to deprive black men of their franchise.

After the *Minor* decision, NWSA began to advocate a separate constitutional amendment, modeled on the Fifteenth, to bar disfranchisement explicitly "on the grounds of sex." This was the wording that would eventually go into the

SUSAN B. ANTHONY
Not One Is My Peer, All Are My Political Sovereigns

Soon after voting in the 1872 presidential election, Susan B. Anthony (1820–1906) was arrested for violating federal law. She approached her trial, held in June 1873, as an opportunity to argue the injustice of denying women political equality. For weeks before, she lectured extensively on the constitutional basis of her decision to cast her ballot. At the trial, after being declared guilty, Anthony made a statement that her right to a jury trial was meaningless so long as she was tried by men who did not share her disfranchised condition.

All of my prosecutors, from the 8th ward corner grocery politician, who entered the complaint, to the United States Marshal, Commissioner, District Attorney, District Judge, your honor on the bench, not one is my peer, but each and all are my political sovereigns; . . . [I have been tried] by forms of law all made by men, interpreted by men, administered by men, in favor of men, and against women; . . . But, yesterday, the same man-made forms of law, declared it a crime . . . for you, or me, or any of us, to give a cup of cold water, a crust of bread, or a night's shelter to a panting fugitive as he was tracking his way to Canada. And every man or woman in whose veins coursed a drop of human sympathy violated that wicked law, reckless of consequences, and was justified in so doing. As then, the slaves who got their freedom must take it over, or under, or through the unjust forms of law, precisely so, now, must women, to get their right to a voice in this government, take it; and I have taken mine, and mean to take it at every possible opportunity.

SOURCE: Susan B. Anthony's response to Judge Hunt at her June 1873 trial, "Stanton and Anthony Papers Online Project," Rutgers University, http://ecssba.rutgers.edu/docs/sbatrial.html (accessed June 19, 2004).

Nineteenth Amendment (1920), but for the time being, the proposed amendment made little headway. Uninvited, in 1876 NWSA leaders forced their way into the national celebration in Philadelphia of the hundredth anniversary of the Declaration of Independence. "Our faith is firm and unwavering in the broad principles of human rights proclaimed in 1776, not only as abstract truths, but as the corner stones of a republic," they declared. "Yet we cannot forget, even in this glad hour, that while all men of every race, and clime, and condition, have been invested with the full rights of citizenship under our hospitable flag, all women still suffer the degradation of disfranchisement."[10]

WOMEN'S LIVES IN SOUTHERN RECONSTRUCTION AND REDEMPTION

Meanwhile, life in the defeated South was being dramatically reconstructed. No element of freedom came easily or automatically for the former slaves, and southern whites changed their lives and expectations only reluctantly. Black women fought for control over their labor, their children, and their bodies. Elite white women sought new capacities and strengths to accommodate the loss of the labor and wealth of slaveowning. White women from the middle and lower ranks remained poised between loyalties of race and the resentments of class.

By 1870, all the southern states had met the terms Congress mandated for readmission to the union. After the removal of federal troops in 1877, white southerners, in a process known as "Redemption," moved to reclaim the political control they had lost during occupation and to reassert white superiority and control. The region's economy, still largely agricultural, developed pockets of industrialization. The complex result of these post-Reconstruction social, political, and economic changes was known as "the New South."

Black Women in the New South

After the defeat of the Confederacy, many freedwomen and freedmen stayed on with their masters for months because they did not know they had been freed or had nowhere to go. Some took to the road to find long-lost spouses and family members. Those who could not travel posted advertisements, such as this one in the *Anglo-African Magazine*: "Martha Ward Wishes information concerning her sister, Rosetta McQuillan, who was sold from Norfolk, Va. About thirty years ago to a Frenchman in Mobile, Ala."[11]

The hard-won family reunions of the freed slaves did not always end happily. Some spouses had formed new unions. Laura Spicer, sold away from a Virginia plantation, was contacted by her husband three years after the war ended. He had since become attached to another woman and was deeply conflicted. "I do not know which I love best, you or Anna," he wrote to Laura. "[T]ry and marry some good, smart man . . . ; and do it because you love me, and not because I think more of the wife I have got than I do of you. The woman is not born that feels as near to me as you do."[12] Nor were parents always recognized by the children they had been forced to leave behind. "At firs' I was scared of her, 'cause I didn't know who she was," one child remembered of her mother. "She put me in her lap an' she most' nigh cried when she seen de back o' my head . . . where de lice had been an' I had scratched 'em."[13]

In 1865, the U.S. army, charged with occupying and governing the defeated Confederacy, organized a special division to deal with the former slaves that provided temporary relief, oversaw their labor, and adjudicated disputes with former masters. The Freedmen's Bureau was the first systematic welfare effort of the U.S. government for an oppressed racial minority. One of its tasks was to ensure that freedpeople had rights over and to their own children. On returning to the Union,

◆ The Right to Marry

As disregard of slave marriages had been considered one of the fundamental immoralities of slavery, immediately after the Civil War the Freedmen's Bureau rushed to legalize marriages among freedpeople, who were eager to have their unions recognized. To indicate that slaves had been married in fact if not in law, bureau officials "solemnized" rather than authorized these marriages. In this engraving, an African American Bureau chaplain presides at a ceremony for two former slaves; the husband was serving in the U.S. Army. © *Corbis*.

southern states had passed laws known as black codes to limit the freedoms of newly emancipated slaves. Apprenticeship laws, for example, provided for the indenture of black children into servitude regardless of the wishes of their parents. Black mothers and grandmothers fought especially hard against the black codes. "We were delighted when we heard that the Constitution set us free," Lucy Lee of Baltimore explained, "but God help us, our condition is bettered but little; free ourselves, [but] deprived of our children. . . . Give us our children and don't let them be raised in the ignorance we have."[14]

By all accounts, the deepest desire of the freedpeople was to have their own family farms. However, Congress was unwilling to reapportion southern lands, and so the longed-for "forty acres and a mule" that would have established genuine black self-sufficiency never materialized. A few former slaves became homesteaders on public lands in Florida, Kansas, Texas, and Alabama, and a handful were able to acquire substantial property. But the overwhelming majority found that they had to continue to work for others, largely as agricultural labor. The fundamental questions of Reconstruction for most ex-slaves were on what terms, with what degree of personal freedom, and for what compensation would they resume working for white people.

One of the most subtle and complex aspects of this dilemma concerned the disposition of black women's labor. During slavery, working alongside men in the fields had placed African American women outside the boundaries of acceptable femininity. Black women began to leave fieldwork immediately after emancipation, much to the dismay of white landowners who appreciated their importance to the agricultural labor force. Some observers reported that black men, eager to assert the rights of manhood over their own families, were especially determined that their wives not work for whites and wanted them to assume instead a properly domestic role as wife and mother. Black women, who discovered that any assertion of autonomy towards white employers might be punished as unacceptable "cheekiness," had their own reasons for withdrawing their labor. In Nashville, Tennessee, Eliza Jane Ellison was shot to death by her employer during an argument over a labor contract.[15]

To achieve even a small degree of independence from direct white oversight, three out of four black families ended up accepting an arrangement known as sharecropping. Black families worked small farms, carved out of the holdings of white landowners, and were allowed to keep a "share" of the crops they grew. There were no foremen to drive and beat them, and they could work together as families. But in bad times, the value of their yield did not equal the credit that white landowners had extended them to cover their expenses, and over time, most slipped into a situation of permanent indebtedness, their hopes for economic independence fading into nothingness.

The ex-slaves were more successful in realizing their desire for education than for land. Even before the war ended, black and white women from the North had gone south to areas captured and occupied by the Union army to begin teaching the black population. Throughout Reconstruction, freedpeople built their own schools, funded by the Freedmen's Bureau and northern missionary societies, to gain the basics of literacy. Edmonia Highgate, the daughter of fugitive slaves, was one of the many sympathetic women who taught in these schools. She was motivated by a sense of racial solidarity to return to the South, and she worked among former slaves for six years, until sheer exhaustion forced her to retire.[16]

Many of the colleges and universities that are now termed "historically black" began during the era of Reconstruction. A number of these schools—unlike prestigious white institutions—were opened to women as well as to men. Howard University, established in Washington, D.C., in 1867, trained both women and men, white or black. In 1881, white multimillionaire John D. Rockefeller founded the Atlanta Baptist Female Seminary, an all-female school that developed into Spelman College. Until the late nineteenth century, most of these institutions provided little more than a high school education. They nonetheless played a major role in educating leaders of the race. Many African American women educated at these schools went on to become teachers, carrying the commitment to education to the rest of their people. This fragile educational infrastructure helped to create a small southern black middle class in cities like Atlanta, Richmond, and New Orleans.

The right to vote awarded to ex-slave men by the Fourteenth and Fifteenth Amendments lay at the very core of ex-slaves' hopes for the future. During Reconstruction, protected by occupying federal troops, freedmen elected approximately two thousand black men to local, state, and national political office. Black and white women disagreed on this expansion of the suffrage, from which they both were excluded. Black women understood the political franchise as a community rather than an individual right. They regularly attended political meetings and told men who had the vote how to use it. Southern white women, by contrast, regarded the enfranchisement of black men as yet another insult to their sex and their race.

White Women in the New South

At the end of the war, white women faced loss and defeat, not emancipation and hope for the future. Food shortages were compounded by the collapse of the economy. Paper money went from hyperinflated to worthless, and many people relied on primitive barter. More than a quarter million southern white men died on Civil War battlefields, leaving one generation of widows and another that would never marry. The occupation by federal troops after the war deepened white southerners' feelings of humiliation. One historian argues that southern white women, who did not share men's sheer relief of being off the battlefield, harbored greater resentment than southern white men toward the North.[17]

Elite white women felt the emancipation of the slaves acutely. "We were reduced from a state of affluence to comparative poverty," recalled Gertrude Thomas, "so far as I am individually concerned to utter beggary for the thirty thousand dollars Pa gave me when I was married was invested in Negroes alone."[18] If they wanted black men in their fields and black women in their kitchens, they had to concede some of the freedpeople's new expectations for wages, personal autonomy, and respect. Elite white women began for the first time to cook and launder for themselves and their families. "We have most of the housework to do all the time," complained Amanda Worthington of Mississippi, "and . . . it does not make me like the Yankees any better."[19]

Non-elite white southerners had depended less on slave labor and were therefore less affected by its withdrawal. But because they lived much closer to the edge of subsistence, they suffered far more from the collapse of the economy and the physical devastation of the South. Over time, economic pressures drove many into the same sharecropping arrangement and permanent indebtedness as ex-slaves. Poor southern white women and their children also provided the labor force for the textile mills that northerners and a new class of southern industrialists began building in the 1880s. Inasmuch as black people were not allowed to work in the mills, white women experienced underpaid textile work as a kind of racial privilege, rewarded by feelings of racial superiority rather than adequate wages. Poor women, whose white skin sometimes seemed the only thing of value they had, believed as fervently as former plantation mistresses in the inviolability of racial hierarchies.

Even so, the collapse of the overtly patriarchal slave system provided new opportunities for public life for those white women who chose to take them. Elite women became involved in the memorialization of the Confederacy. Coming together in 1894 as the Daughters of the Confederacy, they raised funds, built monuments, and heroicized the men who had fought for southern independence, all the while creating an expanded civic role for their sex. Poor farm women found their opportunities in the Grange, a social and educational movement that later fed into the rise of Populism (see Chapter 6). With a very few exceptions, however, southern white women kept their distance from any woman suffrage efforts, which reminded them all too much of the federal intervention to enfranchise their former slaves.

Racial Conflict in Slavery's Aftermath

Changes in gender and racial relations together generated considerable violence in the postwar South. Whites experienced African American autonomy as a profound threat. The Ku Klux Klan, founded in 1866 in Pulaski, Tennessee, terrorized freedpeople for asserting their new freedoms. Klan members sexually humiliated, raped, and murdered many freedwomen. In Henry County, Georgia, two Klansmen pinned down Rhoda Ann Childs and, as she told a congressional investigation in 1871, "stretched my limbs as far apart as they could . . . [and] applied the Strap to my Private parts until fatigued into stopping, and I was more dead than alive." She was then raped with the barrel of a gun.[20] Harriet Postle reported to the congressmen how, when she was seven months pregnant, Klansmen broke into her home, called her a "lying bitch," and threatened to crush her children and beat her senseless unless she told them where her husband was; she refused.[21]

Through such actions, white men were not only punishing black men but also attempting to reassert their slave-era control over black women's bodies. Nevertheless black women were determined to defend themselves. An African American woman recalled that after the war her father vowed "never to allow his wife and daughters to be thrown in contact with Southern white men in their homes." Decades later, she felt the same. "There is no sacrifice I would not make . . . rather than allow my daughters to go in service where they would be thrown constantly in contact with Southern white men, for they consider the colored girl their special prey."[22] In an age when sexual propriety was the essence of true womanhood, black women were deeply concerned with challenging the notion that they and the men of their race were sexually immoral.

Eventually, the region's hidden history of cross-racial sex took an even more deadly form. Whites charged that black men had become sexual predators seeking access to white women. The irony, of course, was that under slavery, it was

◆ **Ida B. Wells with the Family of Thomas Moss**
In 1893, the date of this photograph, Ida B. Wells (standing left) was already an important figure for her courageous journalistic expose of the lynchings of southern black men. She organized African American clubwomen to join her and challenged white reformers to speak out against this barbaric practice. With her are the widow and orphans of Thomas Moss, the Memphis shopkeeper whose murder inspired Wells's crusade. In 1895, Wells married Frederick Barnett, a Chicago newspaper publisher, and they raised four children. She remained a lifelong activist. *The University of Chicago Library, Special Collections Research Center, Ida B. Wells Papers.*

white men who had unrestricted sexual access to black women. Southern white women of all classes supported these charges against black men, and most northerners assumed that they were true. At the slightest suspicion of the merest disrespect to a white woman, black men could be accused of sexual aggression and then lynched—killed (often hanged) by mobs who ignored due process of law to execute their own form of crude justice. Lynchings, often involving gruesome mutilation as well as murder, were popular events in the post-Reconstruction South, with women and children attending amid a carnival-like atmosphere. In 1892, the high point of this practice, 160 Africans Americans were lynched.[23]

Toward the end of the century, Ida B. Wells, an African American journalist from Memphis, inaugurated a campaign, eventually international in scope, to investigate and expose the false charges behind the lynching epidemic and to get leading white figures to condemn it. She recognized that allegations of black men's lewd behavior toward white women were closely related to assumptions of black women's sexual disreputability, and contended that black women had a major role to play in challenging the system of which lynching was the consequence. Her efforts helped to catalyze the organization of an African American women's reform movement. (See Documents: Ida B. Wells, "Race Woman," pp. 306–10.)

Southern blacks' efforts to claim their rights suffered many major setbacks in the last decades of the century. One by one, all-white Democratic parties "redeemed" state governments from Republicanism and "black rule," instituting devices to disfranchise black men, such as requiring voters to demonstrate literacy or prove that their grandfathers had been voters. By the beginning of the twentieth century, black voting had been virtually obliterated throughout the South.

Simultaneously, a new legal system of rigid racial separation in social relations was put in place. Called Jim Crow after a foolish minstrel character played by whites in black face, these laws and practices were a way to humiliate black people and intimidate them from claiming common humanity with whites. Segregation of the races had not been necessary under slavery, where black people had no rights, but now it became a way to reassert white domination. Recalling what enforced segregation felt like, a southern black woman wrote, "I never get used to it; it is new each time and stings and hurts more and more. It does not matter how good or wise my children may be; they are colored. . . . Everything is forgiven in the South but color."[24]

Segregation affected many things including education, public services, and public accommodations, but black women particularly resented Jim Crow regulations in public transportation. Wells began her career as a defender of her race in 1884 by suing a Tennessee railroad company that ejected her from a special "ladies" car and sent her instead to the "colored" car. The point of course was that because she was "colored," she was not a "lady." Twelve years later, the Supreme Court considered a similar suit by Homer Plessy against a Louisiana railroad for its segregation policy. In *Plessy v. Ferguson* (1896), the Court characterized the entire Jim Crow regime as "separate but equal" and thus compatible with the Fourteenth Amendment's requirement of equality before the law. This constitutional defense of slavery survived for nearly sixty years. (See the Appendix, p. A-26.)

FEMALE WAGE LABOR AND THE TRIUMPH OF INDUSTRIAL CAPITALISM

Industrial growth accelerated tremendously after the defeat of the slave system and the northern victory in the Civil War. Intense competition between industrialists and financial magnates gradually gave way to economic consolidation, and by the end of the century, industries such as steel, railroads, coal mining, and meat production were dominated by a handful of large, powerful corporate entities. Paralleling the growth of capital, the American working class also came into its own and organized to find ways to offset the power of its employers.

The growth of the female labor force was an important part of this development, and flew in the face of the still-strong presumption that women belonged exclusively in their homes. Domestic service was the largest sector but manufacturing labor by women, especially the industrial production of garments, with its distinctive and highly exploitative form of production, the "sweat shop," was growing faster. Important technological developments accelerated the division of labor in clothing production and introduced women into the new field of office work.

The dynamic growth of industrial society produced a level of class conflict in the last quarter of the nineteenth century as intense as any in American history. Starting in 1877, as the federal army retreated from the South and the first major postwar depression receded, waves of protests by disgruntled workers shook the economy and drew a powerful and violent response from big business and government. Coming so soon after the Civil War, escalating class antagonism seemed to threaten another collapse of national unity, this time along economic rather than sectional lines. Women played a significant role in these labor upheavals and, in doing so, laid the groundwork for a female labor movement in the early twentieth century.

Women's Occupations after the Civil War

Between 1865 and 1900, the percentage of the nonagricultural wage labor force that was female increased from 14 to 18 percent (see Chart 5.1). Since the size of the population in these years increased enormously, the change in absolute numbers was even more dramatic: by 1900, 5.7 million women were working for pay in nonagricultural labor, three times the number in 1870. The average pay for women remained a third to a half of that of men. The great majority of working women were young and unmarried girls. It is important to clarify that this portrait

◆ Chart 5.1 **Women and the Labor Force, 1800–1900**

Year	Percent of All Women in the Labor Force	Percent of the Labor Force That Is Female
1800	4.6	4.6
1810	7.9	9.4
1820	6.2	7.3
1830	6.4	7.4
1840	8.4	9.6
1850	10.1	10.8
1860	9.7	10.2
1870	13.7	14.8
1880	14.7	15.2
1890	18.2	17.0
1900	21.2	18.1

Sources: W. Elliot Brownlee and Mary M. Brownlee, *Women in the American Economy: A Documentary History* (New Haven: Yale University Press, 1976). *Historical Statistics of the United States: Colonial Times to 1970,* Part 1, Bicentennial Edition, Bureau of the Census, U.S. Department of Commerce, 1975. "Marital and Family Characteristics of Workers," March 1983, U.S. Department of Labor. *Statistical Abstract of the United States,* Bureau of the Census, U.S. Department of Commerce, 1983 and 1992; Daphne Spain and Suzanne Bianchi, *Balancing Act* (New York: Russell Sage, 1996).

applies primarily to white women workers. The labor of southern black women remained largely agricultural and often was not compensated for by wages. Black women also were much more likely to work outside the home after marriage, constituting the single greatest exception to the characterization of the nineteenth-century working woman as young and single.

Beyond these generalizations, much about the working women of the nineteenth century, especially the numbers and statistics on which historians rely, must remain guesswork. Although women had been working for wages since the 1830s, the centrality and permanence of female wage earners were slow to be recognized. Not until 1890 did the U.S. census identify or count working women with any precision. After the Civil War, some states began to collect detailed labor statistics on female wage labor, but these labor bureaus often framed their inquiries in moralistic terms. A great deal of attention was paid, for instance, to disproving that working women were inclined to prostitution. These statistical portraits were fleshed out by investigative reporting, usually by middle- or upper-class women, who went among the working classes to report on their conditions. (See Documents: The Woman Who Toils, pp. 311–16.)

Nonetheless, it is clear that for white women paid domestic work was on the decline. Domestic servants, who before the war were the majority of the white female labor force, constituted less than 30 percent by the end of the century. From the beginnings of industrialization, working women had been impatient with domestic service and left it whenever they could, usually for factory labor. After the Civil War, the end of slavery gave personal service an even greater taint. Investigator Helen Campbell took testimony in the mid-1880s in New York City from women who had abandoned domestic service. "It's freedom we want when the day's work is done," one young working woman explained. "You're never sure that your soul's your own except when you are out of the house and I couldn't stand that a day."[25] "I hate the very words 'service' and 'servant,'" another renegade from domestic labor, an Irish immigrant, explained. "We came to this country to better ourselves, and it's not bettering to have anybody ordering you around."[26]

As white women workers shifted out of domestic service, the percentage in manufacturing increased to 25 percent as of 1900. Women continued to work in the textile industry, and in the shoe industry women organized their own trade union, the Daughters of St. Crispin (named after the patron saint of their trade). One of the first female trade unions, it survived only a few years. The biggest change in women's manufacturing labor was the rise of the garment industry, as the pre–Civil War outwork system began to give way to a more fully industrialized system. During the war, Union soldiers' uniforms were the first form of clothing to be factory produced. The takeoff decade for the industrial production of women's clothing came in the 1890s.

The industrial manufacture of clothing depended on the invention of the sewing machine, one of the most consequential technological developments in U.S. women's history. The introduction of the sewing machine made it possible to subdivide the production of clothing into discrete tasks that were assigned to different workers. Thus a single worker no longer made an entire piece of clothing but instead spent her long days sewing sleeves or seams, incurring the further physical and spiritual toll of endless, repetitive motion. Unlike the power looms and spindles of the textile mills, sewing machines were foot-powered and small; they did not need to be housed in massive factories where water power was available but could be placed in small shops that cost little to set up in urban areas. As sewing machines were also comparatively inexpensive, the cost of buying and maintaining them could be shifted to the workers themselves, who were charged rent or made to pay installments for them.

Profits in the garment industry came primarily from pushing the women workers to produce more for less pay. This system became designated as the "sweating" system, meaning that it required women workers to drive (or sweat) themselves to work ever harder. Workers were paid not for the time at work but by the "piece" completed. Women workers were much more likely to be paid by the piece than men, who tended to be paid by the day or week. Employers set the "piece rate" low, and as women produced more, the bosses lowered the rate even further so that workers had to accelerate the pace of their own work just to maintain their earnings level. In addition, workers were charged for thread and fined for sewing errors. The work was highly seasonal, and periods of twelve-hour workdays alternated with unemployment. At the beginning of the Civil War, the average earnings of sewing women were $10 per week; by 1865, they were $5 per week. Despite working long hours, these women could not make a living wage.

Regardless of their ability or speed, women in the garment, textile, and shoe industries were generally considered unskilled workers, in part because they worked in a female-dominated industry, in part because they were easily replaced by other women, in part because they learned their work on the job rather than through an apprenticeship. The term "skilled labor" and the pay associated with it were reserved for trades that men dominated. A few women gained entrance to male-dominated skilled trades, such as typesetting and printing, where they earned up to $15 per week. Initially, women made their way into print shops by replacing male workers who were out on strike, but they were let go when the men came back to work. In 1869, after a newspaper strike in New York City, Augusta Lewis protested on behalf of women printers: "It is their general opinion . . . that we are most justly treated by what is termed 'rat' [anti-union] foremen, printers and employers than they are by union men."[27] After this strike, the printers' union voted to admit women as equal members, thus becoming only the second male trade union to do so.

In the 1870s, a new field began to open up for female wage earners: office work. Before 1860, the office environment had been totally male, and young men aspiring to careers in business or law apprenticed as clerks or secretaries. During the Civil War, young women began to replace men as government copyists and stenographers. The shift to female labor was accelerated by another crucial technological development, the typewriter, mass production of which built on wartime advances in the manufacture of guns. Women, with their smaller hands, were thought to be especially suited to typing. Moreover, as a relatively new occupation, there were fewer men to displace. Office work required education and a

◆ **The Invention of the Typewriter**
A practical machine for mechanical writings — the type-writer — was devised just after the Civil War. Further changes were later made in the size of the machine and placement of the keyboard as well as the arrangement of the letters. This illustration from a manual on typewriting originally appeared with the caption, "Operator sitting in correct position for rapid writing." From the beginning, women were envisioned as the major operators of this new technology. © *Corbis.*

command of the English language, adding to its prestige as an occupation for women. It also paid more than textile mills or garment sweatshops. Yet from the employers' perspective, hiring women rather than men to meet the growing demand for clerical labor constituted a considerable savings. By 1900, office work was still only 9 percent of the female labor force, but it was the fastest growing sector, a harbinger of things to come in the twentieth-century female labor force (see the Appendix, p. A-39).

Who Were the Women Wage Earners?

Age and marital status were crucial elements in the structure of the female labor force. In 1890, three-quarters of white working women were unmarried. As a leading historian of working women puts it, "In the history of women's labor market experience in the United States the half century from about 1870 to 1920 was the era of single women."[28] Looked at from the perspective of young women, working for wages was a common experience. In 1900, an estimated one-third of all single, urban women worked for wages outside the home.[29] For employers, these characteristics provided an excuse, and for the society as a whole an explanation, for women's limited job opportunities and low wages. Unlike working men, whose wages were supposed to provide for an entire family, these young women allegedly had no one but themselves to support. "Working girls" were expected to work for pay for only a few years, then marry and become dependent on the earnings of their husbands. This was the principle of the so-called family wage, which justified men's greater wages as much as it did women's lesser. Wage labor for women was to be only an interlude between childhood and domestic dependence, while men expected to work this way throughout their adult lives.

The reality of working women's lives was considerably more complex. Approximately 10 to 15 percent of urban families were headed by single mothers and were acutely disadvantaged by the family wage system.[30] More generally, contrary to the ideal of the single male breadwinner, most wage earning families depended on more than one income, with teenage sons and daughters providing supplementary earnings. Approximately two-thirds of unmarried wage earning women lived in their parents' homes and contributed significantly to the support of their families. Carroll Wright, first director of the Massachusetts Labor Bureau, reported in 1888 that the other third "have been obliged to leave their homes on account of bad treatment or conduct of [a] dissipated father or because they felt the need of work and not finding it at home, have come to [a large city] and are dependent on themselves for maintenance."[31] Such women workers lived in commercial lodging or charity boarding homes established by middle-class philanthropists, who feared that "women adrift" were morally vulnerable without parents or husbands to protect them. The Young Women's Christian Association, formed soon after the Civil War, also provided supervised housing for working women in many large cities.

The minority of working women who were wives, mothers, or both were considered at best an anomaly and at worst an indicator of family and social crisis. If the male breadwinner was hurt or killed on the job or if he abandoned his family, the wife had to work and try to support her children on a woman's wage. African American women wage earners were three times as likely as white women to be married, partly because their husbands' pay was so low and partly because many chose to work rather than send their daughters into work situations where they would be vulnerable to sexual harassment from white men. In retrospect, it appears that African American women were pioneering a pattern of combining wage labor and domestic responsibilities that would eventually characterize all working women, but at the time, the high number of black working mothers was taken as yet another index of their marginal social status.

Responses to Working Women

Contemporaries' attempts to grapple with the growing female labor force contained a revealing contradiction. On the one hand, social observers contended that only women driven by sheer desperation should work outside the home. Women who worked merely "by choice" were taking work away from truly needy women and—even more disturbing—from male breadwinners. Wives who had wage earning husbands and unmarried women who lived with their parents were especially subjected to this criticism. If young working women used any part of their pay to buy attractive clothing or go out with men, they were castigated for frivolity. Working girls "who want pin-money do work at a price impossible for the self-supporting worker, many married women coming under this head," observed journalist Helen Campbell.[32]

On the other hand, those women who were driven into wage labor by absolute necessity were so ill-paid, so unrelentingly exploited, as to constitute a major social tragedy. "All alike are starved, half clothed, overworked to a frightful degree," wrote the same Helen Campbell, "with neither time to learn some better method of earning a living, nor hope enough to spur them in any new path."[33] Sympathetic observers concluded that the only humane response was to remove young women from the labor force altogether. Wage earning women were therefore criticized if they worked out of choice or pitied if they worked out of need. In either case, they seemed to be trespassing where they did not belong: in the wage labor force.

Set against middle-class social observers' steady chorus of criticism or lament, the lives and choices of working women hint at a different picture. Working girls were often reluctant to take charity. They objected to the constant supervision at philanthropic working girls' homes, stubbornly spent their wages as they pleased, occasionally continued to work even after they got married, and preferred their morally questionable factory jobs to the presumed safety of domestic service. Though they were criticized for taking jobs away from the truly deserving, many regarded themselves simply as women who liked to earn money, preferred the sociability of sharing work with others, chose the experience of manufacturing something new over endless domestic routine, and enjoyed their occasional moments of hard-earned personal freedom.

Class Conflict and Labor Organization

Women were part of all the dramatic strikes and labor conflicts of the late nineteenth century. In 1877, during the nationwide rail strikes protesting layoffs and wage cuts, women were among the mobs that burned roundhouses and destroyed railroad cars. Women's involvement in such violent acts underlined the full fury of working-class resentment at the inequalities of wealth in postbellum America. "Women who are the wives and mothers of the [railroad] firemen," reported a Baltimore newspaper, "look famished and wild and declare for starvation rather than have their people work for the reduced wages."[34] To end the conflict, President Rutherford B. Hayes sent federal forces, recently withdrawn from occupying the South, to suppress the riots. More than a hundred strikers were killed nationwide.

In the late 1870s, angry workers joined the Knights of Labor, originally a secret society that became the largest labor organization of the nineteenth century. The Knights aimed to unite and elevate working people and to protect the country's democratic heritage from unrestrained capitalist growth. In 1881, women were admitted (housewives as well as wage earners), and they soon became a significant part of the organization. At its peak, the Knights had 750,000 members, of whom perhaps 10 percent were women. Unlike most trade unions, the Knights welcomed women, as their goal was to unite "the producing classes," irrespective of industry or occupation or gender. Race was more complicated. In the South, the Knights admitted black workers, albeit into segregated local chapters, but in the West, Chinese men were excluded, regarded as economic competitors rather than as fellow workers.

The Knights played a major role in the nationwide campaign to shorten the workday for wage earners to eight hours, a movement of obvious interest to women. On May 1, 1886, hundreds of thousands of workers from all over the country struck on behalf of the eight-hour day. A few days later, at a protest in Chicago's Haymarket Square, a bomb exploded, killing seven policemen. Although the bomb thrower was never identified, eight male labor leaders were charged with conspiracy to murder. Lucy Parsons, the wife of one of the accused, helped to conduct their defense. An African American woman, Lucy had met her husband in Texas, where he had gone after the war to organize black voters for the Republican Party. Defense efforts eventually won gubernatorial pardons for three of the accused men, although not in time to save Albert Parsons and the others. The violence and repression unleashed by the Haymarket incident devastated the Knights of Labor. By 1890, it had ceased to play a significant role in American labor relations. The eight-hour workday would not be won for many decades (see Chapter 7).

After the collapse of the Knights, the future of organized labor was left to male-dominated trade unions and their umbrella organization, the American Federation of Labor (AFL), founded in 1886 by Samuel Gompers, a cigar maker from New York City. While the goal of the Knights was inclusive, to unify the producing classes, the purpose of AFL unions was exclusive, to protect the jobs of skilled and relatively well-paid labor from less skilled, lower paid workers. Most members of AFL unions regarded women workers as exactly this sort of threat: unskilled, underpaid workers who "ratted" against men during strikes. Furthermore, the AFL subscribed to the notion that women belonged in the home and that the standard of decent pay for a male worker was a wage sufficient to keep a wife out of the labor force and at home. No longer was the domestic ideal of true womanhood confined to the middle class. In answer to the question, "Should the Wife Help to Support the Family?," Samuel Gompers explained, "In our country, . . . producing wealth in such prodigious proportions, the wife as a wage-earner is a disadvantage economically considered, and socially unnecessary."[35]

Although overwhelmingly male and generally biased against women workers, the late nineteenth-century labor movement did provide a few exceptional working women with the chance to begin speaking and acting on behalf of female wage earners. In this period, Leonora Barry and Mary Kenney were among the first women appointed by unions to organize other women workers. In 1886, the Knights of Labor designated Barry, a widowed Irish-born garment worker, to head its Woman's Department (see box, "Women in the Knights of Labor"). Although just meeting with her might mean being fired, women workers around the country shared with Barry their complaints about wages and working conditions. Barry was their devoted advocate, but after two years, frustrated with the timidity of many working women and perhaps also with the limits of her support from the male leadership of the organization, she resigned her position.

Kenney's trade was bookbinding. She joined an AFL union in Chicago and in 1891 was appointed the AFL's first paid organizer for working women. She believed that working women should organize themselves but that they also needed

◆ **Mary Kenney O'Sullivan and Children**

Kenney left school at fourth grade, "as far," she said, "as any children of wage earners . . . was expected to go,"[36] and became a skilled bookbinder. A natural labor organizer, she was encouraged and supported by both clubwomen and male unionists. In 1894, she married labor activist John F. O'Sullivan and had four children, one of whom died, but within a decade she was widowed. She played a major role in the founding of the Women's Trade Union League in 1903 and, like Ida B. Wells-Barnett, remained an activist throughout her life. *Schlesinger Library, Harvard University; c. 1900–1905.*

the moral and financial support of middle- and upper-class women. The AFL was less committed to working women than the Knights, and Kenney was dismissed from her post after only six months. In the decades to come, many more female labor activists followed Barry and Kenney to play important roles in shaping women's history.

LEONORA BARRY
Women in the Knights of Labor

Leonora Barry (1849–1930) was one of the first female labor organizers. Her final report to the Knights of Labor expresses the ambivalence toward wage earning women that was so common in the late nineteenth century: they belonged at home but deserved equality in the labor force. In 1890, Barry, a widow when she began her assignment, resigned when she remarried.

I believe it was intended that man should be the breadwinner. But as that is impossible under present conditions, I believe women should have every opportunity to become proficient in whatever vocation they choose or find themselves best fitted for. When I took a position at [the Woman's Department's] head, I fondly hoped to weld together in organization a number of women as would be a power for good in the present, . . . I was too sanguine, . . . and I believe we now should . . . put more women in the field as Lecturers to tell women why they should organize as part of the industrial hive, rather than because they are women. There can be no separation or distinction of wage-workers on account of sex, and separate departments for their interests is a direct contradiction of this. . . . Therefore I recommend the abolition of the Woman's Department, believing as I now do that women should be Knights of Labor without distinction, and should have all the benefits that can be given to men — no more, no less. . . .

SOURCE: Leonora Barry, Woman's Department, Knights of Labor, 1889, Report of the General Investigator, Proceedings of the General Assembly of the Knights of Labor, 1888.

WOMEN OF THE LEISURED CLASSES

Paralleling the expansion of the American working class was the dramatic growth, both in numbers and wealth, of the middle and upper classes. For this reason, one of several terms used for the post-Reconstruction years is the Gilded Age. The term, first used by Mark Twain for a novel about economic and political corruption after the Civil War, captured both the riches and superficiality of the wealthier classes in the late nineteenth century. In the United States, with its proud middle-class ethic, the distinction between upper and middle class has always been hard to draw with precision, but in these years what was more important was the enormous and growing gap between those who lived comfortable, leisured lives and those who struggled with poverty. While the poor labored unceasingly, the upper class enjoyed unprecedented new wealth and influence, and the middle class imitated their values of material accumulation and display. For women of the leisured classes, the Gilded Age meant both new affluence and growing discontent with an exclusively domestic sphere.

New Sources of Wealth and Leisure

The tremendous economic growth of the post–Civil War era emanated from the railroads that wove together the nation and carried raw materials to factories and finished goods to customers. The great fortunes of the age were made especially in the mining of iron, the manufacture of steel, the laying of railroads, and the financing of these endeavors. New technologies, government subsidies, cut-throat competition resulting in a few corporate giants, and always the pressure on workers to work faster and produce more contributed to this development. All this wealth was distributed very unevenly. It is estimated that in 1890 the wealthiest 1 percent of the population controlled fully one-quarter of the country's wealth.[37]

Millionaires proliferated after the Civil War. In New York City alone, the number went from a few dozen in 1860 to several hundred in 1865. Many of the great American family fortunes were begun in the Gilded Age: by John D. Rockefeller in oil, Cornelius Vanderbilt in railroads, J. P. Morgan in finance, and Andrew Carnegie in steel. One of the very few women to amass spectacular wealth was Hetty Robinson Green. She began her financial career with a $10 million inheritance, which she multiplied tenfold through shrewd investment. Operating as she did in the man's world of high finance, her womanliness was constantly suspected. The popular press played up her eccentricities, dubbing her "the witch of Wall Street" rather than one of the brilliant financiers of the epoch.

Wives of wealthy men faced no such criticism. On the contrary, they were regarded as the ultimate in womanly beauty and grace. In the world of the extremely wealthy, men's obligation was to amass money, women's to display and spend it. Wealthy women were also responsible for the conduct of "society," a word that came to mean the comings and goings of the tiny upper class, as if the rest of the population faded into insignificance by contrast. In *The Theory of the Leisure Class* (1899), sociologist Thorstein Veblen astutely observed that, at the highest levels of the class structure, women not only purchased and displayed expensive commodities but were themselves their husbands' most lavish and enviable possessions. (See Visual Sources: Winslow Homer's Women, pp. 327–33.)

Shopping was a new and important role for leisure-class women in the postbellum years. In the upper class, women purchased fine furniture and European art for their giant mansions. Middle-class women also became active consumers, albeit on a more modest level. Previously, their domestic responsibilities involved a great deal of productive household labor. Now, with the dramatic increase in the country's manufacturing capacity, their obligation was to purchase rather than to make food and clothing. Middle-class women shopped for luxuries as well as necessities. They flocked to the many department stores established in this period, grand palaces of commodities such as Marshall Field's in Chicago (founded in 1865), Macy's in New York (1866), Strawbridge and Clothiers in Philadelphia

◆ **Rikes Department Store, Dayton, Ohio**
Department store counters were one place where working- and leisure-class women met.
Neat dress, good English, and middle-class manners were job requirements, even though pay
was no better than factory work. Customers like the woman being fitted for gloves in this
1893 photograph sat, but clerks stood all day, one of the conditions of their work to which
they most objected. © *Bettmann/Corbis.*

(1868), Hudson's in Detroit (1887), and May's in Denver (1888). They filled the
elaborate Victorian interiors of their homes with furniture and decorative items.
Even at a distance from the proliferating retail possibilities of the cities, mail order
catalogs allowed rural women to look at, long for, and occasionally purchase the
many commodities of the age.

Rising incomes lifted the burden of housekeeping off of urban middle- and
upper-class women in other ways. In the cities, water and sewer lines, for which
each household was charged a fee, were laid in wealthier neighborhoods. Indoor
plumbing and running water made housework easier for prosperous women. But
the most important factor in easing the load of housekeeping for leisure-class

women was undoubtedly the cheap labor of domestic servants. Despite constant complaints about the shortage of domestic help, middle-class families regarded having at least one or two paid domestic servants as a virtual necessity, while the wealthy had small armies of them. Working women's labor outside the home also relieved women of the leisure classes from domestic labor. Laundry, which required enormous energy and much time when done in an individual household, was sent out to commercial establishments, where poor and immigrant women pressed and folded sheets and linens in overheated steam rooms.

Another important factor in freeing middle- and upper-class women from domestic demands was the declining birthrate (see the Appendix, p. A-36). Between 1850 and 1900, the average number of live births for white, native-born women fell from 5.42 to 3.56. African American birthrates declined even more dramatically as freedwomen took control of their lives at the most intimate level. Ironically, birthrates declined in inverse proportion to class status: the wealthiest, with money to spare, had proportionately fewer children than the very poor, whose earnings were stretched to the limit but who relied on children for income.

The challenge is to understand the many individual decisions that went into the declining birthrate among leisure-class women. The answers are not obvious. There were no dramatic improvements in contraceptive technology or knowledge in these years. On the contrary, traditional means of controlling pregnancy—early versions of condoms and diaphragms—were banned by new laws that defined them as obscene devices, and even discussions aimed at limiting reproduction were forbidden. Following the Comstock Act of 1872, which outlawed the use of the U.S. mails for distributing information on controlling reproduction, twenty-four states criminalized the dissemination of contraceptive devices. Women still used these methods, but they were increasingly difficult to acquire.

Declining birthrates seem to have been both a cause and an effect of the expanding sphere of leisure-class women. Women's decisions to limit their pregnancies reflected a growing desire for personal satisfaction and social contribution beyond motherhood. Even though maternity remained the assumed destiny of womanhood, many individual women were coming to believe that they could choose when and how often to become pregnant. In advocating "voluntary motherhood," Harriot Stanton Blatch encouraged women to choose for themselves when to have sexual intercourse (see box, "Voluntary Motherhood"). Reformers like Blatch did not yet envision the separation of women's sexual activity from the possibility of pregnancy, but they did believe that women should have control over both. The very term "birth control" and the movement to advance it came later, in the twentieth century (see Chapter 7), but basic changes in female reproductive behavior were already under way.

As women's reproductive lives changed, so did their understanding of their sexuality. To be sure, many restrictive sexual assumptions remained in place. Some physicians regarded strong sexual desire in women as a disease, which they treated by methods ranging from a diet of bland foods to surgical removal of the clitoris (clitorectomy). But the heterosexual double standard, encompassing both the notion that men's sexual desire was uncontrollable and that women's was

HARRIOT STANTON BLATCH
Voluntary Motherhood

In this 1891 speech, Harriot Stanton Blatch (1856–1940), daughter of Eliza-beth Cady Stanton, brilliantly exploited the nineteenth-century belief that motherhood was woman's highest vocation in order to argue for women's rights to control whether and when they had children. Although she used the term "race" here to mean humanity, she was relying on the racial "science" of the period, which emphasized the biological dimension of human progress.

Men talk of the sacredness of motherhood, but judging from their acts it is the last thing that is held sacred in the human species . . . men in laws and customs have degraded the woman in her maternity. Motherhood is sacred—that is, voluntary motherhood; but the woman who bears un-welcome children is outraging every duty she owes the race. . . . Let women but understand the part unenforced maternity has played in the evolution of animal life, and their reason will guide them to the true path of race development. . . . [Women] should refuse to prostitute their cre-ative powers, and so jeopardize the progress of the human race. Upon the mothers must rest in the last instance the development of any species.

SOURCE: Harriot Stanton Blatch, "Voluntary Motherhood," 1891, in Aileen S. Kraditor, comp., *Up from the Pedestal: Selected Writings in the History of American Feminism* (Chicago: Quadrangle Books, 1968), 167–75.

nonexistent, was beginning to come under fire. Occasionally, defiant female voices openly asserted the power of female sexual feeling. "I am a Free Lover!," Victoria Woodhull declared in 1871. "I have an inalienable, constitutional and natural right to love whom I may . . . to change that love every day if I please."[38] But by the end of the century, even the conservative physician Elizabeth Blackwell was writing, al-beit in carefully chosen language, that "in healthy, loving women, uninjured by the too frequent lesions which result from childbirth, increasing physical satisfaction attaches to the ultimate physical expression of love."[39]

Lesbianism in the modern sense, of women openly and consistently express-ing sexual desire for other women, had not yet been named and is difficult to iden-tify, but in these years many women formed intense attachments with each other. Contemporaries called these intimacies "Boston marriages," while historians have renamed them "homosocial" relationships. M. Carey Thomas had a series of such romantic friendships beginning in her teenage years, through college, and as dean of Bryn Mawr College. "I think I must feel towards Anna . . . like a boy would," she

◆ "Get Thee Behind Me, (Mrs.) Satan!"
By 1872, when this cartoon appeared in *Harper's Weekly* magazine, suffragist Victoria Woodhull had gained considerable notoriety both for her dramatic pro-suffrage testimony before a congressional committee and for her bold critiques of sexual hypocrisy within the marriage relationship. Her proclamations and behavior won her the label of America's foremost "free lover." This image, created by the great nineteenth-century political cartoonist Thomas Nast, portrays her as the devil incarnate. He contrasts Woodhull to a heavily burdened drunkard's wife, who will be further weighted down by following her lead. *Library of Congress LC-USZ62-74994.*

wrote at age eighteen, "for I admire her so . . . and I like to touch her."[40] Historians cannot know for sure the intimate physical practices that may have accompanied these passions. But by the 1890s, advanced women like Thomas were beginning to read scientific writings about homosexuality and to wonder about the meaning and nature of their own feelings.

The "Woman's Era"

Before the Civil War, women had formed charitable and religious societies and had worked together on behalf of temperance, abolition, and women's rights (see Chapter 4). After the war, associational fervor among women was more widespread, diverse, secular, and independent of male oversight. Participation in Gilded Age women's societies provided numerous women with new opportunities for collective activity, intellectual growth, and public life. By the end of the nineteenth century, leisure-class women had almost totally commandeered nongovernmental civic life from men. Thus, another apt label for the post-Reconstruction years is the "Woman's Era."

Local women's societies designated themselves as "clubs." The women's club movement began in the Northeast just after the Civil War among white middle-class women. In 1868, two women's clubs were established. "Sorosis," a botanical term that suggested sisterhood, was the name chosen by New York City women writers for a group they organized to protest their exclusion from an important public event held by male writers. "The object of this association is to . . . establish a freemasonry° among women of similar pursuits, to render them useful to each other . . . ," Sorosis's constitution declared, "[and] to exert an important influence on the future of women and the welfare of society."[41] Simultaneously, a group of Boston reformers led by Julia Ward Howe (author of "The Battle Hymn of the Republic") organized the New England Women's Club, dedicated to the cultivation of intellectual discussion and public authority for leisure-class women. Despite the impeccable reputations of both groups, they were publicly lambasted for their unladylike behavior. "Woman is straying from her sphere," warned *The Boston Transcript*.[42]

Such criticisms merely helped to publicize the idea of clubs for women. Women's clubs thrived among those middle-aged married women whose childrearing years were behind them. The concerns of the women's club movement evolved from literary and cultural matters in the 1870s to local projects of social service in the 1880s to regional and national federations for political influence in the 1890s. Individual women's clubs, however, followed their own patterns. Some focused on "self-cultivation," while others concentrated on projects of community service. Many public institutions established in the Gilded Age—hospitals and orphanages as well as libraries and museums—were originally established by women's clubs. From the Northeast, the club movement spread to the West and then the South.

Clubs by their nature are exclusive institutions, and the sororal bonds of women's clubs reflected their tendency to draw together women of like background. In the larger cities, class differences distinguished elite women's clubs from those formed by wives of clerks and shopkeepers. Working women's clubs were rarely initiated by wage earning women themselves but were likely to be uplift projects of middle- and upper-class clubwomen. Race and religion were especially important principles of association. Jewish women and African American women organized separately from the mainstream women's club movement, which was largely white and Protestant. Generally, the middle-class Jewish or African American women formed their own clubs both to assist poorer women and to cultivate their own skills and self-confidence. Catholic women, still largely immigrants, did not form women's clubs until the twentieth century.

The ethic of women's clubs was particularly compelling to African American women. They formed organizations not just to enlarge their horizons as women but to play their part in the enormous project of postemancipation racial progress. "If we compare the present condition of the colored people of the South with their condition twenty-eight years ago," explained African American clubwoman Sarah J. Early in 1893, "we shall see how the organized efforts of their women have contributed to the eleva-

---

° "Freemasonry" refers to the most well-known and widespread male fraternal organization of the nineteenth century and was a synonym for collective solidarity and common purpose.

tion of the race and their marvelous achievement in so short a time."[43] By her estimate, there were five thousand "colored women's societies" with half a million members. Black women organized separately from white women because they were serving a different population with distinctive needs but also because they were usually refused admission into white women's clubs. Racism in genteel and feminine form was definitely alive and well in the women's club movement.

The relation of the Gilded Age women's club phenomenon to woman suffrage is complex. At first, white women who formed and joined clubs took care to distinguish themselves from the radicalism and notoriety associated in the 1860s and early 1870s with woman suffragists. Yet women's rights and woman suffrage were standard subjects for discussion in their clubs, and over time members came to accept the idea that women should have political tools to accomplish their public goals. Black clubwomen were less hesitant to embrace woman suffrage in light of their concerns over the disfranchisement of black men. Over time women's clubs incubated support for woman suffrage within a wide swath of the female middle class and prepared the way for the tremendous growth in the suffrage movement in the early twentieth century (see Chapter 7).

The Woman's Christian Temperance Union

The largest women's organization of the Woman's Era was the Woman's Christian Temperance Union. Following on women's temperance activities in the 1850s, the WCTU was formed in 1874 after a series of women's "crusades" in Ohio and New York convinced local saloon owners to close their doors and abandon the liquor trade. Initially focused on changing drinking behavior at the individual level, the organization soon came to challenge the liquor industry politically and to undertake a wide range of public welfare projects such as prison reform, recreation and vocational training for young people, establishment of kindergartens, labor reform, and international peace. These projects and the ability of the WCTU to cultivate both organizational loyalty and individual growth among its female members were characteristics it shared with women's clubs, but the WCTU was different in crucial ways. First and foremost, it defined itself explicitly as Christian. Racially, it was more inclusive than the club movement. The writer Frances E. W. Harper was one of several African American WCTU spokeswomen, and black women were welcomed into the organization, though in separate divisions. The WCTU's centers of strength were less urban and more western and midwestern than those of women's clubs.

Finally, unlike the women's club movement, the WCTU was to a large degree the product of a single and highly effective leader, Frances Willard. Willard was born in 1839 and raised on a farm in Ohio. She never married. Determined to serve "the class that I have always loved and that has loved me always—the girls of my native land and my times,"[44] at age thirty-four she became the first Dean of Women at Northwestern University. In 1879, she was elected president of the WCTU, rapidly increasing its membership, diversifying its purposes, and making

◆ Frances Willard Learns to Ride a Bicycle

Frances Willard, president of the WCTU, combined sympathy with conventional Protestant middle-class women and an advanced understanding of women's untapped capacities. In 1895, "sighing for new worlds to conquer," she learned to ride a bicycle, one of the signature New Woman activities of the period. "Reducing the problem to actual figures," she methodically reported, "it took me about three months, with an average of fifteen minutes' practice daily, to learn, first, to pedal; second, to turn; third, to dismount; and fourth, to mount."[45] Willard, not yet sixty, died in 1898, after which the WCTU never regained its prominence or progressive vision. *National Woman's Christian Temperance Union.*

it the most powerful women's organization in the country. Disciplined and diplomatic, she was able to take the WCTU in political and reform directions that the unwieldy mass of clubwomen could never go. Notably, this included active advocacy of woman suffrage, which the WCTU formally and enthusiastically endorsed in 1884. "If we are ever to save the State," Willard declared, "we must enfranchise the sex . . . which is much more acclimatized to self-sacrifice for others. . . . Give us the vote, in order that we may help in purifying politics."[46]

Consolidating the Gilded Age Women's Movement

The endorsement of woman suffrage by the WCTU convinced Susan B. Anthony to encourage and draw together the pro-suffrage leanings developing within so many women's organizations. "Those active in great philanthropic enterprises," she insisted, "[will] sooner or later realize that so long as women are not acknowledged to be the political equals of men, their judgment on public questions will have but little weight."[47] Accordingly, in 1888, in honor of the fortieth anniversary of the Seneca Falls Convention, the National Woman Suffrage Association (NWSA) sponsored an International Congress of Women, attended by representatives of several European countries and many U.S. women's organizations. Out of this congress came an International Council of Women and a U.S. National Council of Women, both formed in 1893. Both organizations were so broadly inclusive of women's public and civic activities as to admit anti-suffragists, much to Anthony's disappointment. Neither served as the vehicle for advancing the prospects of woman suffrage that she had hoped. In 1890, NWSA and the American Woman Suffrage Association reconciled, forming the National American Woman Suffrage Association, and this large organization led the suffrage movement for the next thirty years. On the international level, U.S. suffragists joined with European colleagues to initiate the formation of an International Woman Suffrage Association in 1902.

Other overarching organizational structures were formed. The associative impulse was constantly tending to greater and greater combination, amalgamating not only women in clubs but clubs in state federations, and state federations in national organizations. The vision shared by these federative efforts was of a unity of women so broad and ecumenical as to obliterate all differences between women. But the vision of all-inclusivity was a fantasy. For as women's social activism and public involvement grew, so did their ambitions and rivalries. Even as the National Council of Women was formed, the leaders of the venerable Sorosis club, who felt they should have been chosen to head this endeavor, set up a rival in the General Federation of Women's Clubs. Nor were federations any more inclusive than individual clubs. The General Federation of Women's Clubs refused to admit black women's clubs. In 1895, African American women's clubs federated separately as the National Association of Colored Women, and the next year Jewish women's clubs formed the National Council of Jewish Women.

The ambitious scope and unresolved divisions of "organized womanhood" were equally on display in Chicago in 1893 at the World's Columbian Exposition, America's first world's fair. A "Board of Lady Managers," led by wealthy Chicagoan Bertha Palmer, received public funds to build and furnish a special "Woman's Building." In an elaborate week-long "Congress of Representative Women," more than eighty sessions addressed "all lines of thought connected with the progress of women." The promise of the Woman's Building was that "all organizations can come together with perfect freedom and entire harmony and discuss the problems presented, even from divergent points of view, with utmost friendliness."[48] But its conception, establishment, and management were rife with disagreement, power struggles, and frustrated ambitions. The Board of Lady Managers argued with Susan B. Anthony and Frances Willard about how prominent to make woman suffrage. Despite much rhetoric about the importance of women's work, wage earning women were not invited to participate in the building's planning or to speak for themselves at the congresses. And the leadership of the Woman's Building was as white as its gleaming walls. African American women, proud of their achievements

◆ **The Woman's Building**
The Woman's Building was one of the most successful exhibits at the World's Columbian Exposition in Chicago in 1893. Everything about it demonstrated the variety and extent of women's achievements. The architect was twenty-two-year-old Sophia Hayden, and all the interior adornments were designed by women. Books written by women filled the library, and paintings by women lined the art gallery. This photograph shows the special organizational hall where the achievements of women in their various organizations and societies were on display. © *Corbis.*

since emancipation, petitioned Palmer to include them in the planning and management—but to no end. Willing as always to speak uncomfortable truths to those in power, Ida B. Wells exposed racism at the fair in a pamphlet she coauthored with Frederick Douglass, *Reasons Why the Colored American Is Not in the World's Columbian Exposition* (1893). Women from indigenous cultures, including the American Eskimo, were "on display" elsewhere as exotics on the fair's midway.

Looking to the Future

By 1890, a new, more modern culture was slowly gathering force under the complacent surface of late nineteenth-century America. The Gilded Age was organized around grand and opposing categories: home and work, black and white, capital and labor, virtue and vice, masculine and feminine. While nineteenth-century society subscribed to a rigid hierarchy of values and a firm belief in absolute truth, modernist convictions allowed for greater contingency and relativism in assessing people and ideas. The concept of morality, so crucial to nineteenth-century cultural judgment, was losing some of its coercive force, giving way to a greater emphasis on individuality, inner life, the free development of personality, and psychological variety.

An important sign of this cultural shift was the growing displacement of the ideal of the "true woman" by the image of the "new woman," both in women's rights circles and in popular representations of femininity. For modern women of the late nineteenth century, "true womanhood" no longer seemed virtuous and industrious but idle and purposeless. "New women" pushed against the boundaries of woman's sphere to participate in public life, whether by earning a wage, gaining an education, or performing community service. (See Visual Sources: The Higher Education of Women in the Postbellum Years, pp. 317–26.) Their ethic emphasized "woman's work," a term that sometimes meant paid labor, sometimes public service, but always an alternative to exclusive domesticity.

Clubwoman and author Charlotte Perkins Gilman was the first great spokeswoman for the New Woman. Gilman went so far as to criticize the single family household and the exclusive dedication of women to motherhood. "With the larger socialization of the woman of today, the fitness for and accompanying desire for wider combination, more general interest, more organized methods of work for larger ends," she wrote in her widely read *Women and Economics* (1898), "she feels more and more heavily the intensely personal limits of the more primitive home duties, interests, methods."[49] Gilman's writings emphasized a second element of the new woman ethic, the importance of female individuation, of each woman realizing her distinctive talents, capacities, and personality. Individualism was a long-standing American value, but it had been traditionally reserved for men. The classic figure of the self-reliant, self-supporting American man was contrasted with the self-*denying* woman by his side. Men were individuals with different abilities; women were members of a category with common characteristics. New womanhood challenged this vision of contrasting masculinity and femininity and claimed the legacy of individualism for women.

Nearing her eightieth year, Elizabeth Cady Stanton stressed this dimension in her 1892 speech, "The Solitude of Self," presented to a committee of the U.S. Congress and then to the National American Woman Suffrage Association. The speech was Stanton's swan song from suffrage leadership. Anthony's vision of a moderate, broad-based suffrage movement contrasted with Stanton's inclination to challenge women's conventional values relentlessly (see box, "The Solitude of Self"). For instance, a few years later, she went so far as to lambaste the Bible for its misogyny. Arguably Stanton's greatest expression of her life-long passion for women's

ELIZABETH CADY STANTON
The Solitude of Self

In 1892, at the age of seventy-six, Elizabeth Cady Stanton (1815–1902) de-livered her manifesto for the future of the new American woman. Her vision was stark because of the economic and political clouds that hung over Amer-ican society at century's end, and also because she was at odds with the movement that she had begun fifty years before. Her radical vision was not accepted by the more conventional women who were coming to suffragism from their club and WCTU experience. Stanton's unrelenting focus on indi-vidualism and on the psychological dimensions of emancipation in "The Solitude of Self" makes it a fundamentally modern statement of women's freedom.

The strongest reason for giving woman all the opportunities for higher ed-ucation, for the full development of her faculties, forces of mind and body; for giving her the most enlarged freedom of thought and action; a complete emancipation from all forms of bondage, of custom, dependence, supersti-tion; from all the crippling influences of fear, is the solitude and personal responsibility of her own individual life. The strongest reason why we ask for woman a voice in the government under which she lives; in the religion she is asked to believe; equality in social life, where she is the chief factor; a place in the trades and professions, where she must earn her bread, is be-cause of her birthright of self-sovereignty; because, as an individual, she

freedom, "The Solitude of Self" looked forward to a future of women's efforts for emancipation that would be so different from the approach of the Woman's Era, so modern in its emphasis on the self and on psychological change, as to require a new name: feminism.

CONCLUSION: Toward a New Womanhood

The end of the Civil War ushered in a period of great conflict. Reconstruction sought to restore the Union and to replace sectionalism with a single sense of nationhood, but its end in 1877 meant that true unity remained elusive for all Americans. Various terms for the post-Reconstruction era indicate its different aspects. In the South during "Redemption," black and white women regarded each other over an em-battled racial divide, altered and intensified by emancipation. Meanwhile, in the America of the "Gilded Age," a new divide had opened up between labor and capital.

must rely on herself. No matter how much women prefer to lean, to be protected and supported, nor how much men desire to have them do so, they must make the voyage of life alone, and for safety in an emergency must know something of the laws of nagivation. . . .

Nothing strengthens the judgment and quickens the conscience like individual responsibility. Nothing adds such dignity to character as the recognition of one's self-sovereignty; the right to an equal place, every where conceded; a place earned by personal merit, not an artificial attainment, by inheritance, wealth, family, and position. Seeing, then that the responsibilities of life rest equally on man and woman, that their destiny is the same, they need the same preparation for time and eternity. The talk of sheltering woman from the fierce storms of life is the sheerest mockery, for they beat on her from every point of the compass, just as they do on man, and with more fatal results, for he has been trained to protect himself. . . .

We see reason sufficient in the outer conditions of human beings for individual liberty and development, but when we consider the self-dependence of every human soul we see the need of courage, judgment and the exercise of every faculty of mind and body, strengthened and developed by use, in woman as well as man.

SOURCE: Elizabeth Cady Stanton, "The Solitude of Self," *The Woman's Column*, January 1892, 2–3.

As the American economy became increasingly industrialized, the numbers and visibility of women wage earners grew, along with their determination to join in efforts to bring democracy to American class relations. For their part, middle- and upper-class women created a kind of "Woman's Era," as they pursued new opportunities in education, civic organization, and public authority.

Two other aspects of the changing face of America in the late nineteenth century are considered in the next chapter: the massive immigration that underlay the growth, and much of the assertiveness, of the American working class and the physical consolidation of the nation through the further incorporation of western lands. Women were important actors in the multifaceted political crisis in the 1890s, which brought together all of these phenomena—racial and class conflict, woman's expanding sphere, massive ethnic change, and the nation's physical expansion up to and beyond its borders. By 1900, women were poised on the brink of one of the most active and important eras in American history through women's eyes, the Progressive years.

DOCUMENTS

Ida B. Wells, "Race Woman"

IN THE YEARS AFTER 1877, when the federal protections of Reconstruction ended and the freed black population of the South was left on its own to resist resurgent white supremacy, a generation of exceptional female African American leaders emerged. Of these, none was more extraordinary than Ida B. Wells. Born in 1862 in Mississippi, she was orphaned at the age of sixteen by a yellow fever epidemic. Determined to assume responsibility for her siblings and to keep her family together, she found work first as a teacher and then as a journalist. In 1889 in Memphis, she purchased part ownership of an African American newspaper, *The Free Speech.* Her goal was to expose and publicize the mistreatment of her people. In an age notable for its florid and euphemistic writing, Wells's style was straightforward and explicit. She was not afraid to use the word "rape" to describe the accusations against black men and the experiences of black women.

Wells was catapulted into the role that changed her life when an African American man she knew, Thomas Moss, was lynched by a Memphis mob in 1892 (see p. 282). Although the practice had a long history elsewhere, in the South during this period, the accused were black and the mobs white. Wells concluded that Moss's "crime" had been the competition that his successful grocery business posed to whites. Over a hundred years later, we take for granted the connections that she was the first to make: between the postwar political and economic gains made by freed people and the brutal violence unleashed on them by resentful whites, and between the long history of sexual exploitation of black women during slavery and the inflammatory charges made after emancipation to justify lynching—that black men were sexual predators.

Perhaps the most remarkable element of Wells's analysis was her insistence that black and white people sometimes voluntarily chose to be each other's sexual partners. She was not particularly in favor of the practice. She was what was called in this period a "race woman," meaning that her concerns were less for integration than for the happiness and progress of African Americans. "A proper self-respect is expected of races as individuals," she later wrote, "We need more race love; the tie of racehood should bind us [through] . . . a more hearty appreciation of each other."[50] Nonetheless, she appreciated the difference between willing and coerced sexuality and defended the former while criticizing the latter. She understood that so long as interracial sex was concealed as a fact of southern life, black people would pay the deadly price.

Her investigations into the practice of lynching got her driven out of Memphis in 1892. This autobiographical account details the impact that her harrowing experience had on African American women in the North, who went on to form the National Association of Colored Women and to join in the work of exposing the true nature, extent, and causes of southern lynchings. Exiled from the South, she moved to Chicago, where in 1895 she married Frederick Barnett, also a journalist and activist, and continued to battle for justice for her race by working for greater political power for black people. She played an early role in organizing African American women to secure and use the right to vote. Her autobiography remained unfinished and unpublished until brought into print by her youngest child, Alfreda Duster, more than a century after her mother's birth.

As you read, consider what led Wells to undertake an expose of lynching and how doing so challenged the expectations of race and gender that she faced. What does Wells's analysis of the causes of and attitudes toward the lynching of African Americans reveal about the dynamics between whites and blacks several decades after the end of slavery?

IDA B. WELLS
Crusade for Justice: The Autobiography of Ida B. Wells (1970)

While I was thus carrying on the work of my newspaper, . . . there came the lynching in Memphis which changed the whole course of my life. . . .

Thomas Moss, Calvin McDowell, and Henry Stewart owned and operated a grocery store in a thickly populated suburb. . . . There was already a grocery owned and operated by a white man who hitherto had had a monopoly on the trade of this thickly populated colored suburb. Thomas's grocery changed all that, and he and his associates were made to feel that they were not welcome by the white grocer. . . .

One day some colored and white boys quarreled over a game of marbles and the colored boys got the better of the fight which followed. . . . Then the challenge was issued that the vanquished whites were coming on Saturday night to clean out [Thomas's] Colored People's Grocery Company. . . . Accordingly the grocery company armed

SOURCE: Alfreda M. Duster, ed., *Crusade for Justice: The Autobiography of Ida B. Wells* (Chicago: University of Chicago Press, 1970), 47–82.

several men and stationed them in the rear of the store on that fatal Saturday night, not to attack but repel a threatened attack. . . . The men stationed there had seen several white men stealing through the rear door and fired on them without a moment's pause. Three of these men were wounded, and others fled and gave the alarm. . . . Over a hundred colored men were dragged from their homes and put in jail on suspicion.

All day long on that fateful Sunday white men were permitted in the jail to look over the imprisoned black men. . . . The mob took out of their cells Thomas Moss, Calvin McDowell, and Henry Stewart, the three officials of the People's Grocery Company. They were loaded on a switch engine of the railroad which ran back of the jail, carried a mile north of the city limits, and horribly shot to death. One of the morning papers held back its edition in order to supply its readers with the details of that lynching. . . . The mob took possession of the People's Grocery Company, helping themselves to food and drink, and destroyed what they could not eat or steal. The creditors had the place closed and a few days later what remained of the stock was sold at auction. Thus, with the aid of city and county authorities and the daily papers, that white grocer had indeed put an end to his rival Negro grocer as well as to his business. . . .

Like many another person who had read of lynchings in the South, I had accepted the idea meant to be conveyed—that although lynching was irregular and contrary to law and order, unreasoning anger over the terrible crime of rape led to the lynching; that perhaps the brute deserved death anyhow and the mob was justified in taking his life.

But Thomas Moss, Calvin McDowell and Henry Stewart had been lynched in Memphis, one of the leading cities of the South, in which no lynching had taken place before, with just as much brutality as other victims of the mob; and they had committed no crime against white women. This is what opened my eyes to what lynching really was. An excuse to get rid of Negroes who were acquiring wealth and property and thus keep the race terrorized and "keep the nigger down." I then began an investigation of every lynching I read about. I stumbled on the amazing record that every case of rape reported . . . became such only when it became public.

Many cases were like that of the lynching which happened in Tunica County, Mississippi. The Associated Press reporter said, "The big burly brute was lynched because he had raped the seven-year-old daughter of the sheriff." I visited the place afterward and saw the girl, who was a grown woman more than seventeen years old. She had been found in the lynched Negro's cabin by her father, who had led the mob against him in order to save his daughter's reputation. That Negro was a helper on the farm. . . .

It was with these and other stories in mind in that last week in May 1892 that I wrote the following editorial:

Eight Negroes lynched since last issue of the *Free Speech*. They were charged with killing white men and five with raping white women. Nobody in this section believes the old thread-bare lie that Negro men assault white women. If Southern white men are not careful they will overreach themselves and a conclusion will be drawn which will be very damaging to the moral reputation of their women.

This editorial furnished at last the excuse for doing what the white leaders of Memphis had long been wanting to do: put an end to the *Free Speech*. . . .

Having lost my paper, had a price put on my life, and been made an exile from home for hinting at the truth, I felt that I owed it to myself and to my race to tell the whole truth now that I was where I could do so freely. Accordingly, the fourth week in June, the *New York Age* had a seven-column article on the front page giving names, dates and places of many lynchings for alleged rape. This article showed conclusively that my editorial in the *Free Speech* was based on facts of illicit association between black men and white women.

Such relationships between white men and colored women were notorious, and had been as long as the two races had lived together in the South. . . . Many stories of the antebellum South were based upon such relationships. It has been frequently charged in narratives of slave times that these white fathers often sold their mulatto children into slavery. It was also well known that many other such white fathers and masters brought their mulatto and quadroon children to the North and gave them freedom and established homes for them, thus making them independent.

All my life I had known that such conditions were accepted as a matter of course. I found that this rape of helpless Negro girls and women, which began in slavery days, still continued without . . . hindrance, check or reproof from church, state, or press until there had been created this race within a race—and all designated by the inclusive term of "colored."

I also found that what the white man of the South practiced as all right for himself, he assumed to be unthinkable in white women. They could and did fall in love with the pretty mulatto and quadroon girls as well as black ones, but they professed an inability to imagine white women doing the same thing with Negro and mulatto men. Whenever they did so and were found out, the cry of rape was raised, and the lowest element of the white South was turned loose to wreak its fiendish cruelty on those too weak to help themselves. . . .

The more I studied the situation, the more I was convinced that the Southerner had never gotten over his resentment that the Negro was no longer his plaything, his servant, and his source of income. The federal laws for Negro protection passed during Reconstruction had been made a mockery by the white South where it had not secured their repeal. This same white South had secured political control of its several states, and as soon as white southerners came into power they began to make playthings of Negro lives and property. This still seemed not enough "to keep the nigger down."

Here came lynch law to stifle Negro manhood which defended itself, and the burning alive of Negroes who were weak enough to accept favors from white women. The many unspeakable and unprintable tortures to which Negro rapists (?) [here Wells inserted a parenthetical question mark to indicate her skepticism of these charges] of white women were subjected were for the purpose of striking terror into the hearts of other Negroes who might be thinking of consorting with willing white women.

I found that in order to justify these horrible atrocities to the world, the Negro was branded as a race of rapists, who were especially after white women. I found that white men who had created a race of mulattoes by raping and consorting with Negro women were still doing so wherever they could; these same white men lynched, burned and tortured Negro men for doing the same thing with white women; even when the white women were willing victims.

That the entire race should be branded as moral monsters and despoilers of white womanhood and childhood was bound to rob us of all the friends we had and silence any protests that they might make for us. For all these reasons it seemed a stern duty to give the facts I had collected to the world. . . .

About two months after my appearance in the columns in the *New York Age,* two colored women remarked on my revelations during a visit with each other and said they thought that the women of New York and Brooklyn should do something to show appreciation of my work and to protest the treatment which I had received. . . . A committee of two hundred and fifty women was appointed, and they stirred up sentiment throughout the two cities which culminated in a testimonial at Lyric Hall on 5 October 1892.

This testimonial was conceded by the oldest inhabitants to be the greatest demonstration ever attempted by race women for one of their number. . . . The leading colored women of Boston and Philadelphia had been invited to join in this demonstration, and they came, a brilliant array . . . behind a lonely, homesick girl who was an exile because she had tried to defend the manhood of her race. . . .

So many things came out of that wonderful testimonial.

First it was the beginning of the club movement among the colored women in this country. The women of New York and Brooklyn decided to continue that organization, which they called the Women's Loyal Union. These were the first strictly women's clubs organized in those cities. Mrs. Ruffin of Boston, who came over to that testimonial . . . called a meeting of the women at her home to meet me, and they organized themselves into the Woman's Era Club of that city. Mrs. Ruffin had been a member of the foremost clubs among white women in Boston for years, but this was her first effort to form one among colored women. . . .

Second, that testimonial was the beginning of public speaking for me. I have already said that I had not before made speeches, but invitations came from Philadelphia, Wilmington, Delaware, Chester, Pennsylvania, and Washington, D.C. . . .

In Philadelphia . . . Miss Catherine Impey of Street Somerset, England, was visiting Quaker relatives of hers in the city and at the same time was trying to learn what she could about the color question in this country. She was the editor of *Anti-Caste,* a magazine published in England in behalf of the natives of India, and she was there-fore interested in the treatment of darker races everywhere. . . . [Thus happened] the third great result of that wonderful testimonial in New York the previous month. Although we did not know it at the time, the interview between Miss Impey and myself resulted in an invitation to England and the beginning of the worldwide campaign against lynching.

QUESTIONS FOR ANALYSIS

1. What were the underlying tensions and larger conflicts that led to the lynching of Thomas Moss?

2. What was the prevailing opinion about lynching that Wells was determined to challenge?

3. What did Wells see as the relationship between the long history of white men raping black women and the charges raised against black men of raping white women?

4. How did Wells's campaign contribute to the consolidation of the organized African American women's movement?

DOCUMENTS

The Woman Who Toils

T HE LIVES AND LABORS of wage earning women and women of the leisure classes intersected in numerous ways in the late nineteenth century. Working women were the maids, cooks, nannies, and laundresses for women of the middle and upper classes, providing the labor that made possible their leisure, elaborate homes, and active social lives. Working women and their children were the objects of the charitable and philanthropic projects that middle- and upper-class women, aiming for a larger role in community affairs, organized in these years. Above all, working women provided the labor to manufacture the food, clothing, and luxuries that the rich bought and which distinguished them from the poor. As the authors of *The Woman Who Toils* wrote, working women stood between wealthy women "and the labour that must be done to satisfy your material demands."[51]

By the end of the century, working-class women were also the subject of professional women's journalistic and sociological investigations, of which *The Woman Who Toils: Being the Experiences of Two Ladies as Factory Girls* (1903) is a notable example. The authors, Marie and Bessie Van Vorst, were upper-class women. Marie was born a Van Vorst, and Bessie married into the family. Neither went to college. Both were educated instead in the manner preferred by the upper classes for their daughters, by private tutors and at female academies. After Bessie's husband, Marie's brother, died, the two women, both still in their thirties, undertook to live more independent lives together. They moved to Paris and cowrote a novel about an upper-class American woman abroad. Their next collaborative effort was *The Woman Who Toils*, a journalistic account of the lives of wage earning women. As upper-class "New Women" aspiring to independence, they were motivated by both their growing awareness of the lives of working-class women and their own authorial ambitions.

To research the book, they returned to the United States, assumed fictional identities, and took a series of working-class jobs. Marie worked in a New England shoe factory and a southern textile mill. Bessie became the Irishwoman "Esther Kelly" and took a job in a pickling factory in Pittsburgh, where she went from eagerness to exhaustion in a few short days. Moving from job to job in the factory, Bessie explored how different it felt to work for a preset daily wage and to work for payment by the piece—an arrangement that led workers to drive themselves to work faster. A day in the male workers' dining room allowed her to compare manufacturing to domestic service labor.

Throughout Bessie's account, the distance she maintained from the women she wrote about is evident. She and her sister-in-law chose a subtitle to clarify that they were still "ladies," despite their brief stint as factory girls. Like most reformers, they did not endorse wage labor for women with children, a point emphasized by President Theodore Roosevelt in his introduction to their book. Nonetheless, Bessie came to appreciate the generosity of her coworkers, the pleasures of collective work, and the "practical, progressive" democracy of working-class life. Above all it was the sheer physical demands of doing the job, descriptions of which are among the best parts of the Pittsburgh pickling section of *The Woman Who Toils*, that seem to have broken through her shield of gentility and brought her a measure of closeness to the women workers about whom she wrote.

As you read this account of working in the pickle factory, identify what Bessie Van Vorst finds attractive about the jobs she does and the women who do them and what she finds repellent. Consider the points at which her class prejudices emerge, and the points at which she gets beyond them.

MARIE AND BESSIE VAN VORST
The Woman Who Toils: Being the Experiences of Two Ladies as Factory Girls (1903)

"What will you do about your name?" "What will you do with your hair and your hands?" "How can you deceive people?" These are some of the questions I had been asked by my friends.

Before any one had cared or needed to know my name it was morning of the second day, and my assumed name seemed by that time the only one I had ever had. As to hair and hands, a half-day's work suffices for their undoing. And my disguise is so successful I have deceived not only others but myself. I have become with desperate reality a factory girl, alone, inexperienced, friendless. I am making $4.20 a week and spending $3 of this for board alone, and I dread not being strong enough to keep my job. I climb endless stairs, am given a white cap and an apron, and my life as a factory girl begins. I become part of the ceaseless, unrelenting mechanism kept in motion by the poor....

My first task is an easy one; anybody could do it. On the stroke of seven my fingers fly. I place a

SOURCE: Mrs. John Van Vorst and Marie Van Vorst, *The Woman Who Toils: Being the Experiences of Two Ladies as Factory Girls* (New York: Doubleday, Page & Co, 1903), 58.

lid of paper in a tin jar-top, over it a cork; this I press down with both hands, tossing the cover, when done, into a pan. In spite of myself I hurry; I cannot work fast enough—I outdo my companions. How can they be so slow? Every nerve, every muscle is offering some of its energy. Over in one corner the machinery for sealing the jars groans and roars; the mingled sounds of filling, washing, wiping, packing, comes to my eager ears as an accompaniment for the simple work assigned to me. One hour passes, two, three hours; I fit ten, twenty, fifty dozen caps, and still my energy keeps up....

When I have fitted 110 dozen tin caps the forewoman comes and changes my job. She tells me to haul and load up some heavy crates with pickle jars. I am wheeling these back and forth when the twelve o'clock whistle blows. Up to that time the room has been one big dynamo, each girl a part of it. With the first moan of the noon signal the dynamo comes to life. It is hungry; it has friends and favourites—news to tell. We herd down to a big dining room and take our places, five hundred of us in all. The newspaper bundles are unfolded. The menu varies little: bread and jam, cake and pickles, occasionally a sausage, a bit of cheese or a piece of stringy cold meat. In ten minutes the repast is over. The dynamo has been fed; there are twenty minutes of leisure spent in dancing, singing, resting, and conversing chiefly about young men and "sociables."

At 12:30 sharp the whistle draws back the life it has given. I return to my job. My shoulders are beginning to ache. My hands are stiff, my thumbs almost blistered. The enthusiasm I had felt is giving way to numbing weariness. I look at my companions now in amazement. How can they keep on so steadily, so swiftly? . . . New girls like myself who had worked briskly in the morning are beginning to loiter. Out of the washing-tins hands come up red and swollen, only to be plunged again into hot dirty water. Would the whistle never blow? . . . At last the whistle blows! In a swarm we report: we put on our things and get away into the cool night air. I have stood ten hours; I have fitted 1,300 corks; I have hauled and loaded 4,000 jars of pickles. My pay is seventy cents. . . .

For the two days following my first experience I am unable to resume work. Fatigue has swept through my body like a fever. Every bone and joint has a clamouring ache. . . .

The next day is Saturday. I feel a fresh excitement at going back to my job; the factory draws me toward it magnetically. I long to be in the hum and whir of the busy workroom. Two days of leisure without resources or amusement make clear to me how the sociability of factory life, the freedom from personal demands, the escape from self can prove a distraction to those who have no mental occupation, no money to spend on diversion. It is easier to submit to factory government which commands five hundred girls with one law valid for all, than to undergo the arbitrary discipline of parental authority. I speed across the snow-covered courtyard. In a moment my cap and apron are on and I am sent to report to the head forewoman. . . .

She wears her cap close against her head. Her front hair is rolled up in crimping-pins. She has false teeth and is a widow. Her pale, parched face shows what a great share of life has been taken by daily over-effort repeated during years. As she talks she touches my arm in a kindly fashion and looks at me with blue eyes that float about under weary lids. "You are only at the beginning," they seem to say. "Your youth and vigour are at full tide, but drop by drop they will be sapped from you, to swell the great flood of human effort that supplies the world's material needs. You will gain in experience," the weary lids flutter at me, "but you will pay *with your life* the living you make."

There is no variety in my morning's work. Next to me is a bright, pretty girl jamming chopped pickles into bottles.

"How long have you been here?" I ask, attracted by her capable appearance. She does her work easily and well.

"About five months."

"How much do you make?"

"From 90 cents to $1.05. I'm doing piecework," she explains. "I get seven-eighths of a cent for every dozen bottles I fill. I have to fill eight dozen to make seven cents. . . ."

"Do you live at home?" I ask.

"Yes; I don't have to work. I don't pay no board. My father and my brothers supports me and my mother. But," and her eyes twinkle, "I couldn't have the clothes I do if I didn't work."

"Do you spend your money all on yourself?"

"Yes."

I am amazed at the cheerfulness of my companions. They complain of fatigue, of cold, but never at any time is there a suggestion of ill-humour. The suppressed animal spirits reassert themselves when the forewoman's back is turned. Companionship is the great stimulus. I am confident that without the . . . encouragement of example, it would be impossible to obtain as much from each individual girl as is obtained from them in groups of tens, fifties, hundreds working together.

When lunch is over we are set to scrubbing. Every table and stand, every inch of the factory floor must be scrubbed in the next four hours. . . .

The grumbling is general. There is but one opinion among the girls: it is not right that they should be made to do this work. They all echo the same resentment, but their complaints are made in whispers; not one has the courage to openly rebel. What, I wonder to myself, do the men do on scrubbing day. I try to picture one of them on his hands and knees in a sea of brown mud. It is impossible. The next time I go for a supply of soft soap in a department where the men are working I take a look at the masculine interpretation of house cleaning. One man is playing a hose on the floor and the rest are scrubbing the boards down with long-handled brooms and rubber mops.

"You take it easy," I say to the boss.

"I won't have no scrubbing my place," he answers emphatically. "The first scrubbing day they says to me 'Get down on your hands and knees,' and I says—'Just pay me my money, will you; I'm goin' home. What scrubbing can't be done with mops ain't going to be done by me.' The women wouldn't have to scrub, either, if they had enough spirit all of 'em to say so."

I determined to find out if possible, during my stay in the factory, what it is that clogs this mainspring of "spirit" in the women....

After a Sunday of rest I arrive somewhat ahead of time on Monday morning, which leaves me a few moments for conversation with a piece-worker who is pasting labels on mustard jars....

"I bet you can't guess how old I am."

I look at her. Her face and throat are wrinkled, her hands broad and scrawny; she is tall and has short skirts. What shall be my clue? If I judge by pleasure, "unborn" would be my answer; if by effort, then "a thousand years."

"Twenty," I hazard as a safe medium.

"Fourteen," she laughs. "I don't like it at home, the kids bother me so. Mamma's people are well-to-do. I'm working for my own pleasure."

"Indeed, I wish I was," says a new girl with a red waist. "We three girls supports mamma and runs the house. We have $13 rent to pay and a load of coal every month and groceries. It's no joke, I can tell you."...

Monday is a hard day. There is more complaining, more shirking, more gossip than in the middle of the week. Most of the girls have been to dances on Saturday night, to church on Sunday evening with some young man. Their conversation is vulgar and prosaic; there is nothing in the language they use that suggests an ideal or any conception of the abstract.... Here in the land of freedom, where no class line is rigid, the precious chance is not to serve but to live for oneself; not to watch a superior, but to find out by experience. The ideal plays no part, stern realities alone count, and thus we have a progressive, practical, independent people, the expression of whose personality is interesting not through their words but by their deeds.

When the Monday noon whistle blows I follow the hundreds down into the dining-room.... I am beginning to understand why the meager lunches of preserve-sandwiches and pickles more than satisfy the girls whom I was prepared to accuse of spending their money on gewgaws rather than on nourishment. It is fatigue that steals the appetite. I can hardly taste what I put in my mouth; the food sticks in my throat.... I did not want wholesome food, exhausted as I was. I craved sours and sweets, pickles, cakes, anything to excite my numbed taste....

Accumulated weariness forces me to take a day off. When I return I am sent for in the corking-room. The forewoman lends me a blue gingham dress and tells me I am to do 'piece'-work. There are three who work together at every corking-table. My two companions are a woman with goggles and a one-eyed boy. We are not a brilliant trio. The job consists in evening the vinegar in the bottles, driving the cork in, first with a machine, then with a hammer, letting out the air with a knife stuck under the cork, capping the corks, sealing the caps, counting and distributing the bottles. These operations are paid for at the rate of one-half a cent for the dozen bottles, which sum is divided among us. My two companions are earning a living, so I must work in dead earnest or take bread out of their mouths....

There is a stimulus unsuspected in working to get a job done. Before this I had worked to make the time pass. Then no one took account of how much I did; the factory clock had a weighted pendulum; now ambition outdoes physical strength. The hours and my purpose are running a race together. But, hurry as I may, as we do, when twelve blows its signal we have corked only 210 dozen bottles! This is no more than day-work at seventy cents. With an ache in every muscle, I redouble my energy after lunch. The girl with the goggles looks at me blindly and says: "Ain't it just awful hard work? You can make good money, but you've got to hustle."

She is a forlorn specimen of humanity, ugly, old, dirty, condemned to the slow death of the over-worked. I am a green hand. I make mistakes; I have no experience in the fierce sustained effort of the bread-winners. Over and over I turn to her, over and over she is obliged to correct me. During the ten hours we work side by side not one murmur of impatience escapes her. When she sees that I am getting discouraged she calls out across the deafening din, "That's all right; you can't expect to learn in a day; just keep on steady." . . .

The oppressive monotony is one day varied by a summons to the men's dining-room. I go eagerly, glad of any change. . . . The dinner under preparation is for the men of the factory. There are two hundred of them. They are paid from $1.35 to $3 a day. Their wages begin upon the highest limit given to women. The dinner costs each man ten cents. The $20 paid in daily cover the expenses of the cook, two kitchen maids, and the dinner, which consists of meat, bread and butter, vegetables and coffee, sometimes soup, sometimes dessert. If this can pay for two hundred there is no reason why for five cents a hot meal of some kind could not be given to the women. They don't demand it, so they are left to make themselves ill on pickles and preserves. . . .

[In the dining room] I had ample opportunity to compare domestic service with factory work. We set the table for two hundred, and do a thousand miserable slavish tasks that must be begun again the following day. At twelve the two hundred troop in, toil-worn and begrimed. They pass like locusts, leaving us sixteen hundred dirty dishes to wash up and wipe. This takes us four hours, and when we have finished the work stands ready to be done over the next morning with peculiar monotony. In the factory there is stimulus in feeling that the material which passes through one's hands will never be seen or heard of again. . . .

My first experience is drawing to a close. I have surmounted the discomforts of insufficient food, of dirt, a bed without sheets, the strain of hard manual labor. . . . In the factory where I worked men and women were employed for ten-hour days. The women's highest wages were lower than the men's lowest. Both were working as hard as they possibly could. The women were doing menial work, such as scrubbing, which the men refused to do. The men were properly fed at noon; the women satisfied themselves with cake and pickles. Why was this? It is of course impossible to generalize on a single factory. I can only relate the conclusions I drew from what I saw myself. The wages paid by employers, economists tell us, are fixed at the level of bare subsistence. This level and its accompanying conditions are determined by competition, by the nature and number of labourers taking part in the competition. In the masculine category I met but one class of competitor: the bread-winner. In the feminine category I found a variety of classes: the bread-winner, the semi-bread-winner, the woman who works for luxuries. This inevitably drags the wage level. The self-supporting girl is in competition with the child, with the girl who lives at home and makes a small contribution to the household expenses, and with the girl who is supported and who spends all her money on her clothes. It is this division of purpose which takes the "spirit" out of them as a class. There will be no strikes among them so long as the question of wages is not equally vital to them all. . . .

On the evening when I left the factory for the last time, I heard in the streets the usual cry of murders, accidents and suicides; the mental food of the overworked. It is Saturday night. I mingle with a crowd of labourers homeward bound, and with women and girls returning from a Saturday sale in the big shops. They hurry along delighted at the cheapness of a bargain, little dreaming of the human effort that has produced it, the cost of life and energy it represents. As they pass, they draw their skirts aside from us, the cooperators who enable them to have the luxuries they do; from us, the multitude who stand between them and the monster Toil that must be fed with human lives. Think of us, as we herd in the winter dawn; think of us as we bend over our task all the daylight without rest; think of us at the end of the day as we resume suffering and anxiety in homes of squalour and ugliness; think of us as we make our wretched try for merriment; think of us as we stand protectors between you and the labour that must be done to satisfy your material demands; think of us—be merciful.

QUESTIONS FOR ANALYSIS

1. What different sorts of women does Bessie Van Vorst meet in the factory, and how and why do their responses to their work vary?

2. Why does Van Vorst conclude that working women are passive in accepting their working conditions and unwilling to stand up for themselves in the way of working men? Do you think she is right?

3. How might the working women described in *The Woman Who Toils* have responded on reading the book? What accounts for your view?

4. In light of Van Vorst's final comments, how do you think her life and attitudes were changed by her experience as a factory girl?

The Higher Education of Women in the Postbellum Years

WHENEVER WOMEN HAVE SOUGHT to improve their lives, almost invariably they have begun by aspiring to better education. "The neglected education of my fellow-creatures is the grand source of the misery I deplore," announced the eighteenth-century British feminist Mary Wollstonecraft.[52] In the revolutionary era, grateful political leaders praised educated women as American patriots for their role in mothering an enlightened (male) citizenry. Within fifty years, women were teachers in America's burgeoning system of public education. But even so, women continued to have far less access to education than men. Before the Civil War, women could rise no further than high-school level, all-female "seminaries." Only Ohio's Oberlin College, an evangelical Protestant institution founded in 1833, admitted a few women to its regular baccalaureate course, most famously women's rights advocate Lucy Stone, who graduated in 1847. Even at Oberlin, however, most women students were educated in a special "ladies' program," with easier language and mathematics requirements than the baccalaureate course.

Two developments in the 1860s made higher education much more available to women. In 1862, the Morrill Act provided grants of federal land to the states and territories for the support of public institutions of higher education. While the act did not explicitly mention women, as one historian has explained, "taxpayers demanded that their daughters, as well as their sons, be admitted."[53] As coeducation spread, long-standing concerns that such easy association between the sexes would coarsen women students and distract men began to give way. The great land-grant universities established in the 1860s and early 1870s in Illinois, Nebraska, Kansas, Arkansas, Ohio, and California accepted women students along with men. Public universities founded earlier—in Michigan, Indiana, Iowa, Missouri, and Wisconsin—changed their policies to admit women. Private universities such as Northwestern and University of Chicago in Illinois, Stanford in California, and Tulane in Louisiana, and colleges such as Whitman in California, Colorado College, and Grinnell in Iowa, also followed the trend. By the end of the century, coeducational institutions granted college degrees to approximately four thousand women each year.

Because the great land-grant universities were primarily in the Midwest and West, most coeducation occurred in these regions. The most important exception in the East was New York's Cornell University, which opened in 1868. Cornell, like virtually all coeducational colleges and universities, nonetheless remained an institution shaped largely by the needs of men. Female students had to struggle to establish their own place, starting with where to live since dormitories housed male students only. The establishment of sororities solved the problem in many state universities. At Cornell, benefactor Russell Sage donated a special women's building. Figure 5.1 is a 1904 photograph of Cornell women at a get-together called a "chafing dish party" in one of their rooms in Sage Hall. What do the activities, dress, and furnishings in the photograph indicate about these women's lives as college students? Consider also what the photograph suggests about the relations among women at a largely male institution.

After the Civil War, the establishment of all-women's colleges also increased women's opportunities for higher education. In 1865, Vassar College, the first of these, opened, funded by a wealthy brewer from Poughkeepsie, New York, who wanted to create an educational institution "for young women which shall be to them, what Yale and Harvard are to young men."[54] Philanthropists endowed other all-female institutions, and by 1891 Smith and Wellesley Colleges in Massachusetts, Bryn Mawr College outside Philadelphia, and Goucher College near Baltimore were graduating women with bachelor's degrees. (Mount Holyoke in Massachusetts, begun many years before as a female seminary, upgraded to college level in 1890.) These all-women institutions produced about sixteen hundred college graduates each year. Combining all-female and coeducational institutions, public and private, by 1890 women were approximately 40 percent of the total of college graduates — an extraordinary development in less than four decades.

There was much debate about whether women students received a better education and had a better collegiate experience at an all-women's college or at a co-

◆ Figure 5.1 **A Chafing Dish Party, Cornell University (1904)**

educational institution. To strengthen their claims, the top women's colleges were dedicated to providing a first-class education in the sciences, which were becoming increasingly important in modern higher education. The Wellesley College class pictured in Figure 5.2 is studying zoology. The students are examining a fish skeleton and a piece of coral to learn about animal physiology. This photograph, like so many of late nineteenth-century college women, is carefully posed. How does the deliberate positioning of the students convey the intellectual seriousness, intensity, and engagement of the scientific learning going on in this all-female classroom? Consider the simple and functional character of the students' clothes, especially compared to the elaborate and costly appearance of elite women engaged in less serious pursuits (see picture on p. 294).

Figure 5.2 also underscores the opportunities that all-female colleges in this period provided for the employment of educated women. Here, unlike in most coeducational schools, women could be professors and administrators. The zoology professor, the young woman seated at the center, is Mary Alice Wilcox, a graduate of Newnham College, the women's college of Britain's Cambridge University. Standing behind her and slightly to the right is Alice Freeman, the twenty-eight-year-old Wellesley College president. Freeman, an early graduate of the University of Michigan, was the first woman to head an institution of higher education in the United States. In 1886, she married Harvard professor George Herbert Palmer and resigned her position as college president. Why might women professors have been employed only at all-women's colleges? What difference do you think they made to women's experience of higher education? How might the youth of

◆ Figure 5.2 **A Class in Zoology, Wellesley College (1883–1884)**
Courtesy of Wellesley College Archives, photo by Seaver.

professors such as Wilcox and administrators such as Freeman have influenced the learning of these women students?

Anxiety that higher education would have a negative impact on women's health, in particular on their reproductive capacities, haunted the early years of women's higher education. In 1873 Dr. Edward Clarke published a controversial book, *Sex and Education,* in which he argued that higher education for women drained vital physical energy—literally blood—from the reproductive organs to the brain. Defenders of women's education rushed to challenge Clarke's argument that higher education endangered women's reproductive and maternal vocation. They undertook scientific studies of women college students to demonstrate that physical health and intellectual growth were not incompatible. Proponents of women's education were particularly anxious to prove that the menstruation of college girls was not disrupted by disciplined study.

To further counter the charge that higher education weakened women physically, but also to strengthen women's bodies as well as their minds, colleges added women's athletics and physical education to their curricula. Competition, however, was prohibited as unladylike, certainly between the sexes in coeducational institutions but even among the women themselves. Nonetheless, in the 1890s, soon after basketball was introduced among young men, a modified version of the game became the rage among college women. Figure 5.3 is a photograph of the team of the class of 1904 from Wells College, an all-women's college in Aurora, New York. In addition to their white tie blouses the players are wearing loose, divided

◆ Figure 5.3 **Basketball Team, Wells College (1904)**
Wells College Archives, Louis Jefferson Long Library, Aurora, New York.

"bloomer" skirts. What in the photograph gives evidence of the physical freedom that sports brought to women's college experience? Why might the photographer have posed the team members with their hands folded, rather than in a more forceful representation of young women in action?

Black women faced extraordinary educational challenges. In the first years of emancipation, the overwhelming task for ex-slaves was the achievement of basic literacy. During Reconstruction, black educational institutions were founded, virtually all of them opened to women as well as men, but these schools provided secondary and vocational rather than baccalaureate education. Even the nation's premiere all-black college, Howard University, founded in Washington, D.C., in 1867, did not open its collegiate program until 1897 and did not graduate its first woman BA until 1901. In the same year, Atlanta's all-female Spelman College also granted its first BA degree (see p. 279).

By 1900, an estimated 252 African American women held bachelor's degrees, but almost all had been granted by predominantly white institutions, one-quarter from Oberlin College alone. Committed to equal education by both race and gender, Oberlin had produced the very first black woman college graduate—Mary Jane Patterson—in 1862. Many of its black female graduates, including Mary Church Terrell and Anna Julia Cooper, went on to become leading spokeswomen for their race and their sex.

In southern black educational institutions, the dramatic downturn in race relations in the 1880s and 1890s had a discouraging impact on higher education for African Americans. Instead of striving for academic equality with white colleges, they concentrated on preparing their students for skilled trades and manual vocations. This approach to higher education was preached by Booker T. Washington, the era's premiere African American educator.

Figure 5.4 is a photograph of a history class at Hampton Institute, a freedmen's school founded in 1868 in Virginia where Washington began his career, and a model for many similar institutions throughout the South. In a controversial experiment in interracial education, Hampton also began enrolling Native American students in 1878. Freedpeople regarded the educational opportunities that Hampton and other such schools provided them as immense privileges. Speaking at the 1873 graduation, Alice P. Davis, born a slave in North Carolina in 1852, praised Hampton Institute as her "Alma Mater": "a mother indeed she has been to us, for she has given us more instruction in these three years than our dear but illiterate mothers ever could."[55] Nonetheless, such institutions, which were often overseen by white benefactors, maintained strict controls over their black students to train them in the virtues of industriousness and self-discipline. The young women were prepared for jobs as teachers, but also as domestic servants and industrial workers.

In 1899, Hampton's white trustees hired America's first important female documentary photographer, Frances Benjamin Johnston, who was white, to portray the students' educational progress. Her photographs were displayed at the Paris Exposition of 1900, where they were much praised for both their artistic achievement and

◆ Figure 5.4 **Class in American History, Hampton Institute (1899–1900)**
Library of Congress LC-USZ62-38149.

their depiction of racial harmony. Figure 5.4, entitled "Class in American History," is an exceptionally rich image for the diversity of its subjects and the complexity of its content. A white female teacher stands in the center among her female and male, African American and Native American, students. All are contemplating a Native American man in ceremonial dress. He can be likened in some way to the scientific specimens in Figure 5.2. Consider what the man himself might have been thinking as he was exhibited to the gaze of both the photographer and the history class. Historian Laura Wexler has unearthed the name of one of the students, the young Indian woman standing at the far right: she is Adele Quinney, a member of the Stockbridge tribe.[56] What lessons were she and the other students being taught about American history by the living exhibit of traditional Indian ways placed before them? What does their precise posing and uniform dress suggest about the dis-

◆ Figure 5.5 **Science Class, Washington, D.C., Normal College (1899)**
Library of Congress LC-USZ62-14684.

cipline expected of Hampton students? Above all, what does this single image capture about the forces at work in late nineteenth-century American society?

During the post–Civil War years, many "normal colleges" were established to concentrate exclusively on the training of teachers. Such schools provided a briefer, less demanding program of study than baccalaureate courses. With less competitive standards for admission and lower costs, they educated a much larger number of women students. The first teacher training institution supported with public funds was founded in 1839 in Framingham, Massachusetts. After the Civil War, normal colleges, which benefited from public land grants under the 1862 Morrill Act, proliferated. Normal colleges were an important avenue of upward mobility for working-class immigrants, African Americans, and other people of color.

Many of these institutions survived into the twentieth century and became full-fledged colleges and universities. Figure 5.5 is a photograph of a class at Washington, D.C.'s Normal College, established in 1873. Because Washington was a southern town, public education there was racially segregated, and the Normal College enrolled only white students. Washington's Myrtilla Miner Normal School, founded in 1851 and named after a heroic white woman educator of African American girls, enrolled only African American students. The two schools remained separate and segregated until 1955, one year after the Supreme Court found segregated education unconstitutional in the case of *Brown v. Board of Education* (see Chapter 9). Then they were merged into the District of Columbia Teachers College, now named the University of the District of Columbia.

As in Figure 5.2, the students in Figure 5.5 are studying science, once again illustrating the importance of this subject in meeting the ambitions of the leaders of women's higher education to offer young women a modern and intellectually challenging education. And yet the kind of teaching and learning that went on in an elite college such as Wellesley and a teacher training institution such as the Normal School were very different. The former had a far more educated faculty and resources of equipment and specimens that the latter lacked. Consider what other differences can be detected by comparing this photograph with Figure 5.2. Figure 5.5 also invites comparison with Figure 5.4 because both photographs were taken by Frances Johnston. How has Johnston positioned her subjects in this picture, compared to those at Hampton Institute? What educational message is this very different staging meant to communicate?

Like teachers, doctors were trained in specialized medical colleges. For most of the nineteenth century, a bachelor's degree was not a prerequisite to study medicine in the United States. Instead, students studied medicine at special medical schools and in undergraduate medical departments of large universities. The first major obstacle that women faced was gaining admission into these all-male programs of medical education. Anxieties about coeducation were particularly intense over the prospect of women sitting beside men at lectures about the human body. But women's desire for medical education was strong. Medicine, unlike other professions such as law or the ministry, fit comfortably with women's traditional role as healers. In 1849, after applying to a dozen major medical schools, Elizabeth Blackwell broke this educational barrier by graduating from Geneva Medical College in rural upstate New York.

One remedy was the establishment of all-female medical colleges. The Boston Female Medical College was established in 1849 by Dr. Samuel Gregory, who wanted to train women to attend their own sex in childbirth. Dr. Elizabeth Blackwell founded the Women's Medical College of New York in 1868 to help other women follow her into the profession. Such all-female schools played a major role in educating women physicians, but as they lacked adequate clinical resources and opportunities, women continued to demand admission to men's medical colleges, where they were eventually accepted.

By 1890, women represented between 15 and 20 percent of all medical students. After 1890, the number of medical colleges shrank, even as their standards rose. Educationally, the crucial change came in 1893 when the Johns Hopkins University in Baltimore established the first postgraduate medical course in the United States. A

◆ **Figure 5.6 Graduating Class, Medical College of Syracuse University (1876)**
Prints & Photographs Department/Moorland-Spingarn Research Center, Howard University.

group of women, led by Mary Garrett, close friend of Bryn Mawr College dean M. Carey Thomas, donated $500,000 to the new postgraduate medical college on the condition that women be admitted along with men. Overall, however, women began to lose access to medical education after 1890, and the percentage of women in most medical schools dropped by half or more by the turn of the century.

Figure 5.6 is a photograph of the 1876 class of the Medical College of Syracuse University, which in 1872 absorbed the resources of Geneva Medical College,

Elizabeth Blackwell's alma mater. This medical class was impressively diverse, not only because four of the students were women but because one of them was African American. Sarah Loguen (after marriage, Fraser) was the daughter of a fugitive slave who became an abolitionist. After graduation, she practiced medicine in Washington, D.C. Notice that the men look much more directly at the photographer than the women, several of whom look down or away. Does this photograph provide any hints about how the male students regarded their female colleagues or how the women felt about their presence in the medical classroom?

QUESTIONS FOR ANALYSIS

1. Nineteenth-century women's higher education proceeded along two parallel lines: the struggle for coeducation and the establishment of all-women's institutions. What were the advantages and disadvantages of each approach?

2. In what way did the motivations for and rewards of higher education differ for white and African American women?

3. How did the growth of higher education for women relate to other major postbellum developments in women's history discussed in this chapter?

VISUAL SOURCES

Winslow Homer's Women

BOSTON-BORN Winslow Homer (1836–1910) was one of America's most important and popular American painters during and after the Civil War. His paintings of women from all classes offer insights into women's lives during these years. Homer's images do more than offer simple visual portraits; each painting or print is infused with meaning, embodying an interpretation as well as a representation of its subject.

Encouraged by his mother, a talented amateur watercolorist, Homer began his long career in 1856 as a lithographer for the illustrated weekly magazines that Americans were so fond of in the mid-nineteenth century. The most important of these was *Harper's Weekly,* a magazine of politics and culture subtitled *A Journal of Civilization.* It was here that Homer encountered the wide range of concerns that became the subjects of his art. He also worked in oils (later in watercolor), and his most famous images were rendered both as paintings for private collectors and as magazine illustrations that were mass-produced and widely enjoyed. An avid supporter of the Union cause, Homer was sent by *Harper's Weekly* to Virginia during the Civil War. There he won acclaim for his drawings of northern soldiers. His subsequent illustrations and paintings conveyed his hopefulness and confidence about the direction being taken by postbellum American society.

Homer's portrayal of American society and culture encompassed women's lives and concerns. Gilded Age women, in all their variety, self-confidence, and activity, embodied for Homer the modern, forward-looking character of American life. He did not portray women in conventional domestic or sentimental ways. Instead, he worked from his own observations and perceptions, picturing not only wealthy and leisured women but women hard at work, not only white women but (most unusual for an artist of this period) black women. As for his personal relations with women, he never married, although he was rumored to have had great passion for one woman, the artist Helena de Kay (portrayed in Figure 5.11, p. 332). His artistic interest in female subjects dropped off in the late 1870s.

For historians of U.S. women, Homer's most important subject has been the textile mill girls of his home region of New England in the 1830s (see Chapter 3). In these representations, Homer, born in 1836, worked from imagination rather than memory. The images recall an industrial past in which textile mills were small and set in the countryside, along streams still rural but strong enough to power the early machines. Homer produced various portraits of these early women wage workers, many of which share with Figure 5.7 the title *The Morning Bell.* The reference is to the factory bell, here tolling just above the factory roof to announce

◆ **Figure 5.7 Winslow Homer, *The Morning Bell* (1873)**
© *Corbis.*

the beginning of the workday. The image in *Harper's* accompanied a poem of the same name, which contrasted the "sweet bell" of the church with the "heavy factory bell" and described those whose "weary feet obey its call."

Homer created this illustration for the December 13, 1873, issue of *Harper's,* in the midst of America's first great post–Civil War industrial depression, a time of unprecedented suffering for wage workers. What does the image tell us about Homer's attitude toward an earlier period in American history, before industry dominated the American economy? What do the details of dress and of light in the image suggest about the mill girls and the nature of their factory work? What range of emotions has Homer depicted in their faces and postures? In the context of the 1870s, how can this drawing be read as a criticism of the direction that the factory system had taken over nearly half a century? "Slowly in those well worn toilsome paths / go those whose paths seem ever past in shade," the accompanying poem laments, "while others reap the sunshine of their toil / by these the factory bell must be obeyed." Interpret these lines in light of Homer's drawing.

In addition to factory workers, Homer often depicted female teachers, usually picturing them in the one-room rural schoolhouses that had once characterized New England but after the Civil War were more likely found in the West and South. Teaching was, along with factory work and domestic service (which Homer never portrayed), a major category of nineteenth-century women's work (see Chapter 3). Women teachers had begun to enter the classroom at about the same

◆ Figure 5.8 **Winslow Homer, *The Country School* (1871)**
Winslow Homer, The Country School. *Oil on canvas, 1871. The Saint Louis Art Museum. Museum Purchase.*

time as the textile mills, and by the conclusion of the Civil War, their numerical dominance of the teaching profession was complete.

In Figure 5.8, *The Country School*, the schoolroom is sparsely furnished, although it does include a blackboard, a relatively new addition to the American classroom. Other images in Homer's school series include a map of the American continent on the classroom wall, which may have been Homer's way of suggesting the important role the public school played in American nation building, especially in the reconstructed South. Homer proudly displayed this painting at an 1878 international exposition in Paris as a portrait of American democratic culture. Why do you think he chose a painting featuring a woman in a schoolroom for this honor? How does the teacher dominate the picture and the classroom? Notice the boy and girl students on separate sides of the room. What are the subtle differences in and implications of the way they are grouped and sitting?

Winslow Homer is best known as a painter of the sea. His most famous sea paintings are of men wrestling with the elements. A series of paintings done in England highlighted fisherwomen—strong, hardworking women hauling in nets and carrying fish. But in the United States, he approached the same challenge using women of a different class, walking along the shore or bathing in more tranquil seas. The painting in Figure 5.9 is known either as *Eagle Head, Manchester, Massachusetts* or *High Tide: The Bathers*. Women engaging in physical activity were a frequent subject for Homer. In addition to his seashore paintings, he pictured them playing croquet and riding horses. These paintings concern women's recreational sports activity, whereas the image in Figure 5.3 (p. 320) emphasizes the educational side of sports. However, Figures 5.3 and 5.9 both underline the growing importance of athletics to women of the post–Civil War generation.

This painting was very bold for its time. Like his French contemporary Edgar Degas, Homer used the activity of bathing as a chance to explore the female figure in motion. Modern viewers might be struck by how much clothing women wore in the 1870s when they went swimming, but at the time, Homer was considered risqué for showing women's legs and the shape of their bodies through the wet bathing outfits. The painting was chosen in 1870 for exhibit at the National Academy of Design in New York, but critics derided the work, describing the bathers as "grotesque" and "saucy." What do you think accounts for the intensity of the negative reaction to Homer's painting? How do the setting, light, and poses of the women suggest Homer's more positive attitude to his subjects? What does the painting and its reception tell us about postwar attitudes toward women's bodies and how they were supposed to display and use them?

Homer's many paintings of African American women were an unusual and important part of his body of artistic work. His sympathy with African Americans was already clear in the wartime images he published in *Harper's* of African American soldiers fighting in the Union army. While most other magazine illustrators portrayed black people through exaggerated and insulting stereotypes,

◆ Figure 5.9 **Winslow Homer, *Eagle Head, Manchester, Massachusetts* or *High Tide: The Bathers* (1870)**
The Metropolitan Museum of Art, gift of Mrs. William F. Milton, 1923. (23.77.2)

◆ **Figure 5.10** **Winslow Homer,** *The Cotton Pickers* **(1876)**

Winslow Homer, The Cotton Pickers, *1876. Los Angeles County Museum of Art. Acquisition made possible through Museum Trustees: Robert O. Anderson, R. Stanton Avery, B. Gerald Cantor, Edward W. Carter, Justin Dart, Charles E. Ducommun, Camilla Chandler Frost, Julian Ganz Jr., Dr. Armand Hammer, Harry Lenart, Dr. Franklin D. Murphy, Joan Palevsky, Richard E. Sherwood, Maynard J. Toll, and Hal B. Wallis. Photograph © 2004 Museum Associates/LACMA.*

often looking more like animals than human beings, Homer allowed his subjects the full attention of his expert brush and artist's eye. He continued to give African American subjects his attention through the Reconstruction years, and was the only major American artist to do so.

In 1876, just as federal troops were being withdrawn from the South and ex-slaves were left to find their own way against their former masters, Homer went to Petersburg, Virginia, to draw African American women and children. He was condemned by local whites as a "nigger painter" and threatened with violence if he did not leave.[57] The sketches he brought back, later turned into a set of monumental paintings, focused on two of his most cherished themes—labor and education—which were the primary concerns of southern freedmen and women as well.

Figure 5.10, *The Cotton Pickers,* portrays African American women doing the agricultural labor that was, along with domestic service, their major occupation throughout the late nineteenth and early twentieth centuries. White employers wanted to keep black women working on their large landholdings, but the freed people wanted their own small farms in which families could create independent lives. Which version of agricultural labor does this painting depict? Art historians have concluded that this was a scene Homer saw and sketched, not something he invented. What details in the painting testify to its authenticity?

◆ Figure 5.11 **Winslow Homer, *Portrait of Helena de Kay* (1871–1872)**
Art Resource, New York. Fundacion Coleccion Thyssen-Bornemisza, Madrid, Spain.

Interestingly, *The Cotton Pickers* was among the most acclaimed of Homer's paintings when it was first shown in 1877. It is difficult to assess whether his contemporaries saw in Homer's painting the longing of the ex-slaves for still greater freedom or their contentment with their limited lot. There is, however, no questioning the painting's beauty and emotional power and the monumentality of the two central figures. Ironically, it was a British cotton manufacturer who bought the painting for his private collection. Do you see hope, disillusionment, or both in Homer's painting? What might the woman on the right, looking out past the field, be thinking?

Most of Homer's female subjects are anonymous. Figure 5.11 is an exception. Helena de Kay was an aspiring artist who studied briefly with Homer, and her name has been connected romantically with his. At the time of this painting, in 1871, she was engaged in a passionate friendship with her friend, the writer and artist Mary Hallock Foote. Historian Carroll Smith Rosenberg has studied their attachment as a model of nineteenth-century women's romantic friendships.[58] In

1874, de Kay married Richard Gilder, artist and editor of the *Century Monthly Magazine,* and their home became a center of Gilded Age New York City artistic life. In a poem about the painting, Gilder hinted of romantic feelings between de Kay and Homer: "She sitteth in thought-trouble, maidenwise. / And how her lover waiting wondereth / Whether the joy of joys is drawing near."[59] Do you think the painting gives any evidence of a personal attachment between artist and subject?

Helena de Kay Gilder showed only a few of her own paintings publicly. She was, however, one of the first women to paint nude figures from life and was a founder of the New York City Art Students League, an institution that helped to produce the next generation of women artists. What do you think the details of the open book, her downcast eyes, and the discarded rose suggest?

QUESTIONS FOR ANALYSIS

1. Homer portrayed a diverse range of female subjects. Do they have anything in common? If so, what characteristics do they suggest Homer most admired about women in the postwar era?

2. This essay reveals women through Homer's eyes. There were few, if any, women painters of Homer's stature working in his period. How might a woman artist of Homer's class and background have treated similar topics differently? What other subjects might she have selected to portray?

3. Considering this chapter as a whole, are there other aspects of women's history from this era that you wish Homer had painted?

NOTES

1. "This Is the Negro's Hour," *Standard,* November 26, 1865, reprinted in Elizabeth Cady Stanton, Susan B. Anthony, and Matilda J. Gage, eds., *History of Woman Suffrage* (Rochester, NY: Susan B. Anthony, 1881), 2:94.

2. Ellen Carol DuBois, *Feminism and Suffrage: The Emergence of an Independent Women's Movement in America, 1848–1869* (Ithaca: Cornell University Press, 1999), 63.

3. Ibid., 61.

4. DuBois, *Feminism and Suffrage,* 60; Wendell Phillips, "American Anti-Slavery Anniversary," *Standard,* May 13, 1865, p. 2.

5. DuBois, *Feminism and Suffrage,* 175.

6. *History of Woman Suffrage,* 2:267.

7. Elizabeth Cady Stanton to Lucretia Mott, April 1, 1872, Theodore Stanton and Harriot Stanton Blatch, eds., *Elizabeth Cady Stanton as Revealed in Her Letters, Diary and Reminiscences* (New York: Harper and Brothers, 1922), 137.

8. Susan B. Anthony to Elizabeth Cady Stanton, November 5, 1872, Ida H. Harper Collection, Huntington Library, San Marino, CA.

9. *History of Woman Suffrage,* 2:687–89.

10. Ibid., 3:31.

11. Quoted in Dorothy Sterling, ed., *We Are Your Sisters: Black Women in the Nineteenth Century* (New York: Norton, 1984), 313.

12. Lucy Chase to unknown correspondent, 1868, American Antiquarian Society, Worcester, Massachusetts, excerpted in Nancy Woloch, ed., *Early American Women: A Documentary History, 1600–1900* (Belmont, CA: Wadsworth, 1992), 401.

13. Quoted in *We Are Your Sisters,* 311.

14. Ibid., 314.

15. Tera Hunter, *To 'joy My Freedom: Southern Black Women's Lives and Labors after the Civil War* (Cambridge: Harvard University Press, 1997), 31.

16. *We Are Your Sisters,* 293–305.

17. Marilyn Mayer Culpepper, *All Things Altered: Women in the Wake of Civil War and Reconstruction* (Jefferson, NC: McFarland, 2002), 135.

18. Quoted in Laura Edwards, *Scarlett Doesn't Live Here Anymore* (Urbana: University of Illinois Press, 2000), 175.

19. Cited in *All Things Altered,* 123.

20. Hunter, *To 'joy My Freedom,* 33.

21. *KKK Hearings, South Carolina, 1871,* vol. 9, in Gerda Lerner, ed., *Black Women in White America* (New York: Vintage Books, 1973), 187–88.

22. "The Race Problem: An Autobiography: A Southern Colored Woman," *The Independent* 56 (1904): 586–89.

23. A. Arthur Raper, *The Tragedy of Lynching* (Chapel Hill: University of North Carolina Press, 1933), 13–14.

24. "The Race Problem," 191–94.

25. Helen Campbell, *Prisoners of Poverty* (1887), cited in Nancy Cott et al., eds., *Root of Bitterness: Documents of the Social History of American Women,* 2nd ed. (Boston: Northeastern University Press, 1996), 359.

26. Cott et al., *Root of Bitterness,* 360.

27. Eleanor Flexner, *A Century of Struggle: The Woman's Rights Movement in the United States* (New York: Atheneum, 1968), 38.

28. Claudia Goldin, "The Work and Wages of Single Women: 1870 to 1920," National Bureau of Economic Research Working Paper Series, 1979, p. 1.

29. Ibid., 3.

30. Linda Gordon, *The Great Arizona Orphan Abduction* (Cambridge, MA: Harvard University Press, 1999), 8.

31. Carroll Wright, *The Working Girls of Boston* (1884), quoted in Nancy Cott et al., eds., *Root of Bitterness: Documents of the Social History of American Women* (Boston: Northeastern University Press, 1986), 319.

32. Helen Campbell, *Women Wage-Earners: Their Past, Their Present, and Their Future* (Boston: Roberts Brothers, 1893), 190.

33. Ibid., 191.

34. Quoted in Barbara Wertheim, *We Were There: The Story of Working Women in America* (New York: Pantheon Books, 1977), 178.

35. Samuel Gompers, "Should the Wife Help to Support the Family?" *American Federationist,* January 13, 1906, p. 36.

36. Mary Kenney O'Sullivan, unpublished autobiography, Schlesinger Library, Harvard University, Cambridge, MA.

37. Gary B. Nash et al., *The American People: Creating a Nation and a Society,* brief 5th ed. (New York: Addison Wesley Longman, 2000), 481.

38. Victoria Woodhull, *A Speech on the Principles of Social Freedom Delivered in New York City, November 20, 1871* (London, 1894), 23–24.

39. Elizabeth Blackwell, "On Sexual Passion in Men and Women," 1894, reprinted in Cott et al., *Root of Bitterness* (1986), 302.

40. Helen Lefkowitz Horowitz, *The Power and Passion of M. Carey Thomas* (New York: Alfred A. Knopf, 1994), 30.

41. Quoted in Karen Blair, *The Clubwoman as Feminist: True Womanhood Redefined, 1868–1914* (New York: Holmes and Meier, 1980), 23.

42. Ibid., 34.

43. "The Organized Efforts of the Colored Women of the South to Improve Their Condition," 1893, reprinted in Dawn Keetley and John Pettegrew, eds., *Public Women, Public Words,* vol. 1 (Madison, WI: Madison House, 1997), 316.

44. Quoted in Mary Earhart, *Frances Willard: From Prayers to Politics* (Chicago: University of Chicago Press, 1944), 93.

45. Frances E. Willard, *How I Learned to Ride the Bicycle: Reflections of an Influential 19th Century Woman,* ed. Carol O'Hare (Sunnyvale, CA: Fair Oaks, 1991), 17, 75.

46. Suzanne Marilley, *Woman Suffrage and the Origins of Liberal Feminism in the United States, 1820–1920* (Cambridge, MA: Harvard University Press, 1996), 128–29.

47. Quoted in Ellen Carol DuBois, ed., *The Stanton/Anthony Reader,* 2nd ed. (Boston: Northeastern University Press, 1992), 176.

48. Ellen Henrotin to May Wright Sewall, quoted in Jeanne Madeline Weimann, *The Fair Women* (Chicago: Academy Chicago, 1981), 529.

49. Charlotte Perkins Gilman, *Women and Economics* (1898), quoted in Cott et al., *Root of Bitterness* (1986), 369.

50. Quoted in Patricia Schechter, *Ida B. Wells-Barnett and American Reform, 1880–1930* (Chapel Hill: University of North Carolina Press, 2001), 62–63.

51. Mrs. John Van Vorst and Marie Van Vorst, *The Woman Who Toils: Being the Experiences of Two Ladies as Factory Girls* (New York: Doubleday, Page & Co., 1903), 58.

52. Quoted in Alice Rossi, ed., *The Feminist Papers from Adams to de Beauvoir* (Boston: Northeastern University Press, 1988), 40.

53. Rosalind Rosenberg, "The Limits of Access," in John Mack Faragher and Florence Howe, eds., *Women and Higher Education: Essays from the Mount Holyoke College Sesquicentennial Symposia* (New York: Norton, 1988), 110.

54. Quoted in Helen Lefkowitz Horowitz, *Alma Mater: Design and Experience in Women's Colleges from Their Nineteenth-Century Beginnings to the 1930s* (New York: Knopf, 1984), 29.

55. M. F. (Mary Frances) Armstrong, *Hampton and Its Students, by Two of Its Teachers, Mrs. M. F. Armstrong and Helen W. Ludlow* (New York: G. P. Putnam, 1874), 89–90.

56. Laura Wexler, *Tender Violence: Domestic Visions in an Age of U.S. Imperialism* (Chapel Hill: University of North Carolina Press, 2000), 168.

57. William Howe Downes, *The Life and Works of Winslow Homer* (New York: B. Franklin, 1974), 87.

58. Carroll Smith Rosenberg, "The Female World of Love and Ritual," *Signs: A Journal of Women and Culture* 1 (1976): 1–29.

59. Quoted in Nicolai Cikovsky Jr. and Franklin Kelly, *Winslow Homer* (Washington: National Gallery of Art, 1996), 123.

SUGGESTED REFERENCES

General Works   A general introduction to women's history in the period from 1865 to 1900 is Eleanor Flexner, *Century of Struggle: The Woman's Rights Movement in the United States* (1975), which is still the best overall history of women's rights in the United States. The equivalent work on black women's history is Paula Giddings, *When and Where I Enter: The Impact of Black Women on Race and Sex in America* (1984), a pioneering synthesis of black women's history after slavery. Alice Kessler Harris's magisterial history of working women, *Out to Work: A History of Wage-Earning Women in the United States* (1982), gives excellent coverage to this period. A general history of sexuality that treats the nineteenth century is Estelle B. Freedman and John D'Emilio, *Intimate Matters: A History of Sexuality* (1997).

Woman Suffrage   For more on the woman suffrage movement in the postbellum era, Ellen Carol DuBois, *Feminism and Suffrage: The Emergence of an Independent Women's Movement in the United States, 1848–1869* (1978), focuses on the struggle over the Fourteenth and Fifteenth Amendments; DuBois, *Women's Rights, Woman Suffrage* (1998), considers the New Departure period. Ann D. Gordon, ed., *The Selected Papers of Elizabeth Cady Stanton and Susan B. Anthony, Vol. II, Against an Aristocracy of Sex, 1866–1873* (2000), is a compilation of the important writings of the two suffrage leaders over this period. A recent biography of Victoria Woodhull is Barbara Goldsmith, *Other Powers: The Age of Suffrage, Spiritualism, and the Scandalous Victoria Woodhull* (1998). A somewhat different perspective is found in Helen L. Horowitz, *Rereading Sex: Battles over Sexual Knowledge and Suppression in Nineteenth-Century America* (2002).

Black Women in the South   For further research on African American women in the era of Reconstruction and Redemption, Tera Hunter's *To 'joy My Freedom: Southern Black Women's Lives and Labors after the Civil War* (1997) focuses on black women in Atlanta. Evelyn Brooks Higginbotham, *Righteous Discontent: The Women's Movement in the Black Baptist Church, 1880–1920* (1993), examines the roots of the southern black middle class. Deborah G. White, *Too Heavy a Load: Black Women in Defense of Themselves, 1894–1994* (1994), analyzes the black women's club movement. Two recent biographies of antilynching crusader Ida B. Wells are Patricia Schechter, *Ida B. Wells-Barnett and American Reform, 1880–1930* (2001), and Linda McMurry, *To Keep the Waters Troubled: The Life of Ida B. Wells* (1998).

White Women in the South   The pioneering work on white women in the postbellum South is Anne Firor Scott, *The Southern Lady from Pedestal to Politics, 1830–1930* (1970). Marilyn Mayer Culpepper, *All Things Altered: Women in the Wake of Civil War and Reconstruction* (2002), provides many firsthand accounts of white women in the period. Dolores Janiewski, *Sisterhood Denied: Race, Gender, and Class in a New South Community* (1985), examines non-elite southern white women, especially as they moved into industrial labor. Laura Edwards, *Gendered Strife and Confusion: The Political Culture of Reconstruction* (1992), examines challenges raised to southern patriarchy by black and white women after the Civil War. Martha Hodes, *Black Men, White Women* (1994), examines the history of interracial sex in the South. Glenda E. Gilmore, *Gender and Jim Crow: Women and the Politics of White Supremacy in North Carolina, 1896–1920* (1996), focuses on late nineteenth-century insurgent racism.

Working Women in the North   For additional reading on women and work, Barbara Wertheimer, *We Were There: The Story of Working Women in America* (1977), provides a survey of women's work and labor activism, emphasizing but not limited to wage earners. Mary Blewett, *We Will Rise in Our Might: Workingwomen's*

Voices from Nineteenth-Century New England (1991), weaves together primary sources into a historical overview of women workers, as does Rosalyn Baxandall and Linda Gordon, eds., *America's Working Women: A Documentary History, 1600 to the Present* (1995). Mary Blewett, *Men, Women, and Work: Class, Gender, and Protest in the New England Shoe Industry, 1780–1910* (1988), examines nineteenth-century working women in a single industry. So does Susan Levine, *Labor's True Woman: Carpet Weavers, Industrialization, and Labor Reform in the Gilded Age* (1984), which also examines women in the Knights of Labor. Marjorie Davies, *Woman's Place Is at the Typewriter: Office Work and Office Workers, 1870–1930* (1981), examines the shift from male to female office workers. Joanne Meyerowitz, *Women Adrift: Independent Wage Earners in Chicago, 1880–1930* (1988), concerns the lives of working women who did not live in families. Alice Henry, *The Trade Union Woman* (1915), remains a basic resource for the history of women in the labor movement, as does Philip Foner, *Women and the American Labor Movement: From Colonial Times to the Eve of World War I* (1971). Kathleen Nutter, *The Necessity of Organization: Mary Kenney O'Sullivan and Trade Unionism for Women, 1892–1912* (2000), is a biography of the first woman organizer in the AFL.

Leisure-Class Women in the North   Upper-class women in the Gilded Age are discussed in Maureen Montgomery, *Displaying Women: Spectacles of Leisure in Edith Wharton's New York* (1998). The pathologies of shopping are analyzed in Elaine Abelson, *When Ladies Go A-Thieving: Middle-Class Shoplifters in the Victorian Department Store* (1989). Barbara Solomon, *In the Company of Educated Women: A History of Women and Higher Education in America* (1985), is a comprehensive history of women's higher education; Helen Horowitz, *Alma Mater: Design and Experience in the Women's Colleges from Their Nineteenth-Century Beginnings to the 1930s* (1984), focuses on the all-female colleges. Sarah Deutsch, *Women and the City: Gender, Space, and Power in Boston, 1870–1940* (2000), examines women's activism and class relations in Boston, and Maureen Flanagan, *Seeing with Their Hearts: Chicago Women and the Vision of the Good City, 1871–1933* (2002), covers similar territory in Chicago. Anne Firor Scott, *Natural Allies: Women's Associations in American History* (1991), is a comprehensive study of women's associations. Karen Blair, *The Clubwoman as Feminist: True Womanhood Redefined, 1868–1914* (1980), is the first scholarly study of the women's club movement. The WCTU is the subject of Ruth Bordin, *Women and Temperance: The Quest for Power and Liberty, 1873–1900* (1990). The starting point for the history of women's romantic friendships is Lillian Faderman's *Surpassing the Love of Men: Romantic Friendship and Love between Women from the Renaissance to the Present* (1994).

Selected Web Sites

On the postwar woman suffrage movement, begin with the material assembled on the excellent women's history pages on the About.com Web site: <**womenshistory .about.com/od/suffrage1865/**>. For more on Victoria Woodhull in particular, consult the Learning Center of the National Women's History Project and follow the various links listed there: <**nwhp.org/tlp/biographies/woodhull/woodhullbio .html**>.

On freedwomen in the South, the Library of Congress American Memory Project offers a fine collection of resources in its African American History: From Slavery to Freedom collection, <**memory.loc.gov/ammem/aapchtml/aapchome.html**>.

For the history of working women, About.com is also useful: <**womenshistory .about.com/library/weekly/aa010228a.htm**>. Harvard University Libraries have begun an ambitious online project for digitalizing primary sources documenting the history of working women in the United States—see <**ocp.hul.harvard.edu/ww/**>. For a more focused resource, North Country Public Radio has produced an excellent radio documentary on the late nineteenth-century female labor movement emphasizing the biography and words of Leonora Barry. It can be heard at <**northcountrypublicradio.net/news/barry.html**>.

On the history of leisure-class women in the late nineteenth century, resources on the WCTU are found on the History of Religious Movements site at the University of Virginia, <**religiousmovements.lib.virginia.edu/nrms/wctu.html**>. The WCTU also has its own history page: <**wctu.com/history.html**>. It is difficult to identify a single site for the history of women's clubs because the clubs remained largely local, but they can be approached individually. As one example, see the page on the La Jolla, California, club formed in 1892, at <**lajollawomansclub.com/ history.htm**>.

On romantic friendships, the following site focuses on the theme in English and American literary history: <**glbtq.com/literature/romantic_friendship_f.html**>. On the Columbian Exposition of 1893, the University of Virginia is again a good source: <**xroads.virginia.edu/~MA96/WCE/title.html**>.

6

Women in an Expanding Nation

CONSOLIDATION OF THE WEST, MASS IMMIGRATION, AND THE CRISIS OF THE 1890S

TWENTY-THREE-YEAR-OLD SHIGE KUSHIDA ARRIVED in San Francisco in 1892. American influences had already reached her in Japan. She was Protestant, western-oriented, and one of the first woman to speak in Japan before a mixed audience of men and women. Her plan was to get an education in the United States and return to her home country, but her experience turned out differently—as it did for so many immigrants. Instead of studying, she married another Japanese Christian and settled in Oakland. There she raised her children and became a leader of the Issei (first-generation Japanese American) community. She saw to it that her daughters got the education she did not.[1]

The life of Shige Kushida Togasaki illustrates two grand historical processes that were reshaping American society at the end of the nineteenth century. First, the United States was in the midst of an unprecedented wave of immigration, which brought with it tremendous social challenges and national transformations. Second, the western part of the continent was being consolidated into the American nation. The frontier—in the sense of a westward moving line of American settlement—was entering its final stages and, according to the 1890 census, coming to a close. Western settlement, which seems like a quintessentially American phenomenon, and mass immigration, which brought the nation into greater interaction with the rest of the world, shared important links. Both involved enormous movements of people across oceans and continents, bringing individuals from different cultures into contact and sometimes into conflict. Both involved efforts to "Americanize," sometimes violently, different cultures into the national mainstream. Both developments were motivated at the individual level by hopes for better lives, greater prosperity, and more personal freedom. And yet both processes dashed hopes as much as they realized them among the immigrant poor and especially among the Native Americans pushed aside by continuing westward expansion.

Mass immigration and the consolidation of the West together helped to set the stage for a major economic and political crisis in the 1890s, as discontented immigrants, farmers, and wage workers found ways to challenge what they saw as a failure of America's democratic promise, notably the unequal distribution of America's new wealth and the unwillingness of the two established political parties to offer any vision of a better social and political path. The resolution of the crisis in favor of corporate power and the established political parties prepared the way for America's first forays abroad as an imperial power.

In all these developments—western consolidation, mass immigration, the political crisis of the 1890s, and the beginnings of American imperialism—women were involved, active, influential, and as a result, changed. In the great movements of people into and through American society in the late nineteenth century, men initially predominated, but women soon followed. When they did, families were formed and temporary population shifts became permanent new communities. By the early twentieth century, women's involvement in the grand historical processes of absorbing western lands and foreign peoples, their participation in the radical challenges of the 1890s, and their support or criticism of their country's ventures abroad had made them a significant new force in U.S. political life.

CONSOLIDATING THE WEST

American settlement reached the Pacific Coast before the Civil War, but the continent's broad heartland, through which American pioneers had crossed starting in the

1890	Jacob Riis's *How the Other Half Lives* published	
1890	Federal census declares that frontier line is "closed"	
1891	**Queen Liliuokalani becomes monarch of nation of Hawaii**	
1892	Immigrant receiving station established at Ellis Island in New York City harbor	
1892	People's Party formed in St. Louis	
1893	Illinois Factory and Workshop Inspection Act passed	
1893	Frederick Jackson Turner delivers paper, "The Significance of the Frontier in American History"	
1893	**Colorado women win equal voting rights with men**	
1893-1894	National economic depression	
1894	Pullman strike and national railroad disruption	
1896	**Idaho women enfranchised**	
1896	Populist Party collapses as William McKinley defeats William Jennings Bryan for president	
1896	**Mary (Mother) Jones's fame as labor agitator begins**	
1898	United States goes to war against Spain in Cuba	
1898	United States annexes Hawaii	
1899-1902	United States fights Filipino independence movement	
1900	L. Frank Baum's *The Wonderful Wizard of Oz* published 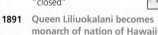	
1903	President Theodore Roosevelt speaks out against "race suicide"	
1907	U.S. and Japanese governments issue "Gentlemen's Agreement" to limit Japanese immigration	
1910	Mexican Revolution spurs immigration to the United States	
1910	Angel Island immigrant receiving station established in San Francisco Bay	

341

1840s, remained largely Indian territory. This changed in the last decades of the nineteenth century as white settlement and expansion overtook the Great Plains. The tremendous postbellum growth in industrial capitalism traced in Chapter 5 had as one of its major consequences the steady integration of the entire continent into the national economy. The growth of the cross-continental railroad system constituted the framework for a booming national market to provide eager consumers throughout the country with the beef and wheat and lumber produced in abundance in the broad expanse of the trans-Mississippi West.

These western lands were consolidated as part of the American nation through two main processes, which were distinguished as much by their gender practices as by anything else. Large numbers of single men and a few women went west to realize quick profits or find jobs in the region's mines and on its cattle ranges. This form of American expansion has long been celebrated as the "Wild West" in national legend and popular culture. But there was also a "Family West" in which settlers domesticated the prairies of America's heartland. Women and women's labor were as fundamental to this West as men and men's labor were to the other.

Native Women in the West

Despite their differences, both kinds of westerners shared a basic premise: Indians would have to be removed to make way for the new settlers, for their economic ambitions, and for what they regarded as their superior civilization. Here, the U.S. army, fresh from its victory over the Confederacy, was crucial. After 1865, federal forces moved full force against the western tribes to wrest control of the Great Plains and open these huge interior expanses to white settlement. Native American raids against encroaching white settlers provoked military retaliation in an escalating series of wars that wore away at native unity and resources. There were occasional Indian victories, most famously the 1876 Battle of the Little Big Horn in Montana, in which assembled Lakota Sioux warriors annihilated the U.S. Seventh Cavalry commanded by George A. Custer. But these only delayed the elimination of armed Indian resistance.

Bands of Native Americans who resisted pacification were regarded as "hostiles." Made up not only of male warriors but also of women and children, they were constantly on the move to elude pursuing troops. One of the last such groups was Geronimo's band of Warm Springs Apache. His female lieutenant, Lozen, exemplified the Native American practice of allowing exceptional individuals to cross the gender divide. Lozen never married, was skilled in locating the enemy, and performed the spiritual and military duties of a true warrior. Her brother called her "strong as a man, braver than most, and cunning in strategy."[2] For almost a decade, she helped her people evade and attack the U.S. army, until the Apaches' final surrender in southern New Mexico in 1886.

The massacre at Wounded Knee Creek in South Dakota in the winter of 1890 is often cited as the tragic end to the so-called Indian Wars. Following its defeat at the Little Big Horn, army troops had relentlessly pursued the Lakota Sioux. Deeply dispirited, the Lakota began to practice a new religion, the Ghost Dance, which promised restoration of their traditional lands and lives. Male and female dancers alike wore a special robe, said to be designed by a woman, that they believed would protect them against bullets fired by white people. "The woman's dress was . . . a loose robe with side, flowing sleeves, painted blue in the neck," observed a white woman. "I found they discarded everything they could which was made by white men."[3] Believing that the Ghost Dance signaled a new organized insurgency, skittish soldiers fired on a camp of mostly unarmed native people, killing many hundred. "Women with little children on their backs" were gunned down, one white witness to the Wounded Knee massacre recalled, and it was many days before their frozen bodies could be retrieved and buried.[4]

Assaults against the Plains Indians took forms other than outright military conflict. By the 1880s, hunters and soldiers with new high-powered rifles had decimated the buffalo herds that were the material basis of Plains Indians' traditional way of life. The Plains peoples were thus vulnerable to forced relocations on government reservations of the sort that had been pioneered in the 1850s among Pacific Coast tribes (see Map 6.1). Allegedly designed to protect Indians from aggressive white settlers, these reservations instead became "virtual prisons."[5] Unable to support themselves either by farming or hunting, reservation Indians were dependent on food and clothing doled out by federal agents, who often embezzled as much as they dispensed. Instead of their traditional role in gathering and preparing food, Indian women were relegated to standing in long lines, waiting for rations that frequently did not come.

After serving the U.S. army as translator and scout, Sarah Winnemucca became a crusader against the reservation system (see p. 236). Her people, the Piute, had been grossly exploited by the government agent who administered their Nevada reservation and who refused to dispense stores allocated to them. They were then relocated to a reservation in Washington Territory, where they lived uneasily among other native peoples. Winnemucca described the sufferings of her people to white audiences from California to Massachusetts and even met with President Rutherford B. Hayes, but to no avail.

In conjunction with reservation life, U.S. policy forced native children into government-run boarding schools to be forcibly "civilized," reeducated in the values and ways of dominant American culture. By the 1890s, several thousand children per year were removed from their parents' control and sent to schools where they were made to stop dressing, speaking, thinking, and believing "like Indians." Half the students were girls, whose forcible reeducation was regarded as crucial to the cultural transformation of the native population. All too frequently, their assimilation into American culture consisted of training in menial occupations and in American standards of domesticity, which they learned as servants in the homes of nearby white families.

The goal of such programs was to save the child by destroying the Indian, but the transformations sought were elusive. Evidence of repeated and harsh punishments testifies to the refusal of girls as well as boys to give up their Indian ways. One elderly Indian woman recalled later, "Two of our girls ran away . . . but they

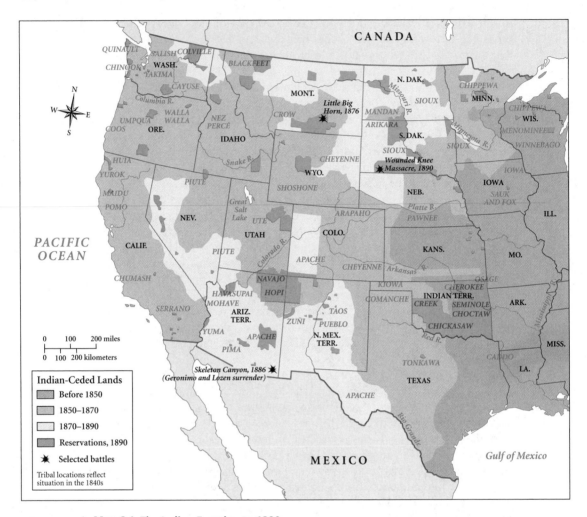

◆ **Map 6.1 The Indian Frontier, to 1890**

As settlers pushed westward after the Civil War, Native Americans put up bitter resistance but ultimately to no avail. Over a period of decades, they ceded most of their lands to the federal government. By 1890, they were confined to scattered reservations where the most they could expect was an impoverished and alien way of life.

got caught. They tied their legs up, tied their hands behind their backs, put them in the middle of the hallway so that if they fell, fell asleep or something, the matron would hear them and she'd get out there and whip them and make them stand up again."[6] Parents and tribal leaders protested the brutality of this coercive Americanization, but they could not stop it.

Some Native American women, however, were able to acquire English literacy and other useful skills in the boarding school system. They worked in reservation

◆ **Before and After Americanization**
These "before-and-after" pictures of Indian children at government-run boarding schools were common in the late nineteenth century and were sometimes sent to philanthropic donors to illustrate the schools' success in Americanizing Indians (see also Figure 5.4, p. 322). Within a little more than a year, these three girls sat on chairs, not the floor, and had lost their blankets and braids, but they retained their sad faces. The book on the lap of Sarah Walker, the girl on the right in the "after" photograph, was meant to indicate her literacy, but we cannot know whether she had really learned how to read. *Peabody Museum, Harvard University, Photos N30439A and N30440A.*

agencies and became teachers. A few, such as the Yankton Sioux writer Gertrude Simmons Bonnin and the Omaha sisters Susan and Susette La Flesche, became public advocates for their people. Susette was a writer and speaker on behalf of Indian causes. (See Documents: Susette La Flesche: The Life of an Indian Girl, pp. 373–78.) Susan was sponsored by the white women of the Woman's National Indian Association to attend the Women's Medical College of Pennsylvania and became the first white-trained native woman physician. She served her people for many years, both as a doctor and as a political leader.

Protests against the corruptions of the reservation system led in 1887 to congressional passage of the Dawes Severalty Act, which divided reservation lands into allotments for individual native families, the remaining acreage to be sold to non-Indians. Assimilationist leaders like the La Flesche sisters and white champions of native rights like the author Helen Hunt Jackson advocated allotments as an alternative to demeaning reservation existence (see box, "A Century of Dishonor"). But the way the system played out by no means ended native peoples' misery. Where land was not very fertile, Native American families could not

HELEN HUNT JACKSON
A Century of Dishonor

Published five years after the nation's centennial, Helen Hunt Jackson's A Century of Dishonor (1881) documents how U.S. Native American policy violated America's promise of liberty and freedom. The book helped catalyze public awareness of the corruptions and cruelties of the reservation system. Three years later, Jackson (1830–1885) drew on some of the same material for her popular California novel, Ramona (see p. 210).

We may hold nations to standards of justice and good faith as we hold men . . . a nation that steals and lies and breaks promises will be no more respected or unpunished than a man who steals and lies and breaks promises. . . . The history of the United States Government's repeated violations of faith with the Indians thus convicts us, as a nation, not only of having outraged the principles of justice, which are the basis of international law; and of having laid ourselves open to the accusation of both cruelty and perfidy; but of having made ourselves liable to all punishments which follow upon such sins—to arbitrary punishment at the hands of any civilized nation who might see fit to call us to account, and to that more certain natural punishment which, sooner or later, as surely comes from evil-doing as harvests come from sown seed.

To prove all this it is only necessary to study the history of any one of the Indian tribes. I propose to give in the following chapters merely outline sketches of the history of a few of them, not entering more into details than is necessary to show the repeated broken faith of the United States Government toward them. A full history of the wrongs they have suffered at the hands of the authorities, military and civil, and also of the citizens of this country, it would take years to write and volumes to hold. . . .

So long as there remains on our frontier one square mile of land occupied by a weak and helpless owner, there will be a strong and unscrupulous frontiersman ready to seize it, and a weak and unscrupulous politician, who can be hired for a vote or for money, to back him.

The only thing that can stay this is a mighty outspoken sentiment and purpose of the great body of the people. Right sentiment and right purpose in a Senator here and there, and a Representative here and there, are little more than straws which make momentary eddies, but do not obstruct the tide.

SOURCE: Helen Hunt Jackson, *A Century of Dishonor: A Sketch of the United States Government's Dealings with Some of the Indian Tribes* (New York: Harper and Brothers, 1881), 29–31.

support themselves; and where the land could be productively farmed, whites managed to gain control. The allotment program also deepened the dependency of Indian women on their men, following the pattern of white society. In contrast to communal land holding and farming practices, the allotment program meant that women who chose to divorce their husbands risked the loss of economic resources under the control of male heads of household. A group of Hopi women vainly protested to the Bureau of Indian Affairs in 1894. "The family, the dwelling house and the field are inseparable" they wrote, "because the woman is the heart of these, and they rest with her."[7]

The Family West

As Native American control over the West weakened, U.S. expansion across the vast continent continued apace. The passage of the Homestead Act in 1862 granted 160 acres to individuals willing to cultivate and "improve" the land. The railroads, themselves beneficiaries of federal largesse, also sold land to settlers to establish towns along their routes. Through this uneven process, the broad central plains—from Minnesota to Montana to Oklahoma—were settled and Americanized. By the early twentieth century, one-quarter of the U.S. population lived west of the Mississippi.

This population was surprisingly diverse. After Reconstruction, a small but steady stream of African American families were drawn west by the hope of independent farming. In all-black towns, such as Nicodemus, Kansas, and Langston, Oklahoma, African American women found ways to support their families that were less demeaning than domestic service for white people. In Boley, Oklahoma, Lulu Smith started a dressmaking business, and other women ran boarding houses, catering services, and general stores.[8] European immigrants also played a significant role in western settlement, especially in the northern territories. The Homestead Act allowed land grants to immigrants who were not yet citizens but who intended to become so. They, too, formed their own communities where they could live and speak and farm as they had in their home countries. In the late nineteenth century, in the period of mass immigration, one out of two western settlers was foreign-born.

Meanwhile, in villages throughout New Mexico, Arizona, and southern California, Spanish-speaking women continued to live much as their mothers and grandmothers had. They maintained adobe homes and cultivated small plots, while the men in their families were drawn away to work in the mines, on the railroads, or on the commercial farms and ranches run by incoming whites (known as Anglos). Ironically, while these Mexican American women were regarded by Anglo society as backward, they enjoyed considerable authority in their own communities. Local practices favored female property owning, and these Mexican American enclaves were notable for a relatively high proportion of widows who headed their own households. As the extension of the railroads brought national market pressures and a cash economy closer, however, the need for money became greater. Many Spanish-speaking women lost their distinctive advantages and followed

◆ **San Juan Fiesta**

Many Spanish-speaking residents of the Southwest maintained their traditional village life into the late nineteenth century, even as their land and economic position were being lost to Anglo incursion. Religious holidays and life passages such as baptisms and marriages were extremely important, not just for the family but for the entire community. Women did the work of putting on these lavish events — the cooking and the making of fine clothes and also the fund-raising that made the occasions possible. This family fiesta in San Juan, a southern California town centered on its thriving mission-era church, took place about 1880. *Courtesy of the Autry National Center/Southwest Museum, Los Angeles. Photo N. 30590.*

their husbands into paid labor, as domestics in Anglo towns or agricultural wage laborers in Anglo fields.

Common to all these different communities throughout the family-based West was a reliance on women's unpaid labor, in striking contrast to the emphasis on middle-class female leisure and working-class female wage labor in the more urbanized parts of American society. Western women cooked, did laundry, and made clothes without benefit of the technological improvements available in more industrialized areas. While their husbands cultivated specialized commercial crops, the wives cared for animals and grew food for the family table. One Arizona woman described her morning chores: "get up, turn out my chickens, draw a pail of water, . . . make a fire, put potatoes to cook, then brush and sweep half inch of dust off floor, feed three litters of chickens, then mix biscuits, get breakfast, milk, besides work in the house, and this morning had to go half mile after calves." She also contributed to her family's unending need for cash by churning twenty-four pounds of butter in four days. "Quit with a headache," she wrote in her diary. "Done too much work."[9]

Some women were inspired to try homesteading on their own. Perhaps as many as 15 percent of late nineteenth-century homesteads were at some point controlled by women. Romanticized accounts of these female homesteaders suggest a West so expansive that even a woman could enjoy the freedom and opportunity it offered, but the reality was more complex. Only women without husbands could be granted homesteads. Some were widows who ran their farms after their husbands died, while others may have secured their grants as a device for the men in their families to acquire additional land. Unmarried women who controlled their own homesteads combined two of the most irresistible resources for male settlers, land and female labor, and were besieged by marriage proposals. As one young Oklahoma woman wrote, as soon as she was awarded a claim, men started to court her. "The letters began pouring in—men wanting to marry me, men all the way from twenty-one to seventy-five."[10]

Whether single or married, western farm women did their homemaking in an environment where homes had to be built from scratch. On the Plains, after spending the first few months living in temporary shelters, settler families would move into huts made of sod, the top layer of soil so dense with the roots of prairie grass that it could be cut like bricks. Women sprinkled their dirt walls and floors with water to keep down the dust, and decorated their unlikely homes as lavishly as they could, eager to banish the discomfort of being surrounded by dirt. Westering was an ongoing process; as families frequently moved and resettled on more promising land, it was left to the women to repeat over and over the work of creating—both physically and emotionally—new home environments.

Of all the burdens for women settlers on the Great Plains, drudgery and loneliness seem to have been the worst, especially in the years when towns were still being established. Unlike their husbands, women rarely left the homestead—slaves, as some put it, to the cook-stove and the washtub. Ignored when she complained that "I never got to go nowhere, or see anybody . . . or [do] anything but work," one Oklahoma woman packed up the children and fled. Overtaken by a wind and ice storm, she almost froze to death and ended up back at the homestead, disabled for life.[11]

The 1867 organization of the National Grange (the full title was the Order of the Patrons of Husbandry) helped to overcome women's isolation on the prairies. By the mid-1870s, three-quarters of the farmers of Kansas had joined.[12] Based on the premise that farm families had to cooperate to succeed against the growing power of railroad and other corporate monopolies, the Grange established

◆ Immigrants in the Great Plains

As with the growth of American industry, the settling of the Great Plains required immigrant labor and determination. The Homestead Act of 1862 made immigrants intending to become citizens eligible for federal land grants. Scandinavians were particularly drawn to homesteading. This Norwegian immigrant to Minnesota, Beret Olesdater Hagebak, sits alone in front of a small house made of sod, the most common building material available on the treeless plains. Her picture captures the difficult experience of immigrant farm women, who suffered both the cultural disorientation of immigration and the isolation of Plains farm life. *Photo by H. J. Chalmers, Minnesota Historical Society.*

farmer-run stores and grain elevators and promoted laws against unfair railroad rates. It also sponsored social and cultural events that enriched local community life and were of special importance to women, who played a prominent role in the Grange. Local chapters were required to have nine female members for every thirteen male members, and women served as officers and delegates to the national meetings. The sense of community that the Grange created prepared the way for more overtly political expressions of agricultural discontent, including the Farmers' Alliance in the late 1880s and the Populist movement of the 1890s.

The "Wild West"

Alongside the families drawn by the promise of land and economic self-sufficiency were other westerners pursuing riskier, more modern schemes for getting rich. Both groups Americanized the West, but in different ways. While family settlement imported the American social and cultural values of industriousness and domesticity, these other westerners brought with them American economic practices, in particular industrial capitalism, wage labor, and subordination to growing corporate power. Despite their status as icons of individual freedom, the colorful cowboys of the cattle range and the grizzled miners of the gold and silver strikes were being drawn into paid labor and experiencing wage dependence much like the industrial workers in New York and Chicago. This was the historical context for what has come down to us through popular culture as the "Wild West."

The contrasts between the Wild West and the Family West are particularly clear if we look at the radically different gender practices on which they rested. The workers in the western industries of mining and ranching were virtually all male. Cowgirls were a staple only in the Wild West of popular culture. As early as the 1890s, the riding and roping skills of Annie Oakley were featured in Buffalo Bill Cody's Wild West Show. But in the actual mines and cattle ranges, women wage earners were rare. The rapidly expanding female labor force found elsewhere in America existed in the West only in the largest cities, such as Denver, San Francisco, and Seattle.

There were women in the Wild West, however. At first, most were prostitutes. Like the miners and cowboys who were their customers, they were black and white, English- and Spanish-speaking, native- and foreign-born. Initially, many of these women worked for themselves, as what one historian calls "proprietor prostitutes."[13] A few were able to earn or marry their way into respectable society. Others bought or rented brothels, hired other women to do the prostituting, and became successful, if disreputable, businesswomen. In 1890, in Helena, Montana, one of the most prosperous real estate entrepreneurs was an Irish-born former prostitute, "Chicago Joe." But for most of the women involved, prostitution was a thoroughly losing proposition. Two-thirds of prostitutes died young of sexually transmitted diseases, botched abortions, alcohol abuse, suicide, or gunshots. And, as in other western businesses, the initial period of entrepreneurial exuberance was replaced by increasingly centralized ownership. By the early twentieth century, men—pimps, landlords, and police—enjoyed most of the profits from western prostitution.

More respectable women—some rich, most poor—gradually began to move to these western centers of industry. The wives of western mine owners lived in expensive, elegant homes, hired servants, and imported luxuries. Their determination to use their husbands' fortunes on behalf of their own social and philanthropic ambitions was legendary. Phoebe Appleton Hearst, whose husband got rich in the mines of California and Nevada, was a major benefactor of the University of California at Berkeley. Mary (Molly) Tobin Brown, the daughter of Irish Catholic immigrants, married one of the few individual prospectors to become wealthy off the mines. She bought and refurnished an elegant Denver mansion, hired tutors to teach her the ways of the upper class, and became a generous civic donor. In 1912, she survived the sinking of the ill-fated *Titanic,* earning herself the nickname of "unsinkable Molly Brown."

At the other end of the class scale, wage-earning miners and cowboys also formed families. The immigrant copper miners of Anaconda, Montana, married the young Irish women who worked as domestic servants for their bosses or as waitresses in the local hotels. Mexican miners in Colorado surprised their employers by bringing their wives north to live with them and settling permanently in the United States. As in the family-based West, these working-class wives rarely took jobs outside the home, although they did earn money by feeding and housing the large all-male labor force of single miners, cowboys, and lumberjacks. Keeping their homes clean despite clouds of dirt and soot and stretching money to meet their family's needs, these western housewives also lived with the constant fear of losing their husbands to violent death on the range or in the mines.

Recognizing that unions would fight to raise wages and make working conditions safer, western working-class wives were strong supporters of organized labor. They formed union auxiliaries that were very active during the militant strikes that rocked the region. In Cripple Creek, Colorado, miners' wives were involved in 1893 when the radical Western Federation of Miners won higher wages and in 1904 when the state militia drove union activists out of town. The labor radicalism of such women was embodied by the legendary Irish-born Mary Harris ("Mother") Jones, who began her career as an organizer for miners' unions in the late 1890s. Jones focused her attention on the miners—her "boys"—but she also understood the power of miners' wives and organized them into "mop and broom brigades" that were an effective tool against strikebreakers. Referring to one of the family dynasties most identified with corporate greed, Jones declared: "God Almighty made women and the Rockefeller gang of thieves made the ladies."[14]

Jones's contempt for female gentility notwithstanding, western working-class wives were as careful as women of the leisure classes to maintain a distinction between their own status as respectable women and that of the disreputable females who had preceded them. Family life was gradually displacing the world of the dance halls and brothels, of prostitutes and single male workers. Respectable women took care not to patronize the same establishments or live in the same areas as these "fast" women. "If the world of work was divided into laborers and employers," writes one historian of the western female experience, "the world of women was divided into good women and bad."[15] In contrast to the popular belief that women were freer of conventions in the West, Gilded Age prescriptions of proper behavior for women may well have been more restrictive in such environments, despite the harsh conditions of their lives.

LATE NINETEENTH-CENTURY IMMIGRATION

While Americans were moving westward in the late nineteenth century, immigrants were pouring into the country, 27 million in the half century after 1880. These numbers dwarfed pre–Civil War immigration (see Chapter 3). Five million came from Italy and an equal number from Germany, almost 2 million were Eastern European Jews, 1 million were Polish Catholics, and almost as many were Scandinavians. A small but growing number of Asians and Mexicans also came to the United States in these years. By 1910, Asians constituted 2 percent of all arriving immigrants. Numbers of Mexican immigrants are harder to determine. Until 1924, when the U.S. Border Patrol was established, the Mexican-U.S. border was virtually unregulated, and those crossing back and forth melded into already existing Spanish-speaking communities. This massive immigration turned the United States into an ethnically and religiously diverse people, no longer preponderantly English and Protestant but now broadly European, with a growing minority of resident Asians and Mexicans.

The gender patterns of these immigrations were complex. Among Slavic, Greek, and Italian immigrants, more men than women came to the United States. However, many men came as temporary workers, intending to return eventually to their homelands. As they did, and as more women came to marry those who remained, sex ratios tended to even out. Some groups, notably Eastern European Jews and the still large Irish immigration, initially came in more gender-balanced numbers. Eventually, women constituted between 30 and 40 percent of all immigrants (see the Appendix, p. A-40).

The Decision to Immigrate

Women decided to leave their homelands and come to the United States for many reasons, some of which they shared with men. Economic forces were foremost. Faced with poverty, limited opportunity, and rigid class structures at home, families dispatched members to work in the United States and send money back. The booming U.S. economy had an insatiable need for workers in its factories, mines, and kitchens, and it lured men and women alike with its irresistible promises of high wages and easy prosperity. "This was the time . . . when America was known to foreigners as the land where you'd get rich," remembered Pauline Newman, who arrived from Lithuania in 1901. "There's gold on the sidewalk! All you have to do is pick it up."[16]

Political persecution also pushed people out of their homelands. Jews began immigrating in large numbers in the 1880s to escape growing anti-Semitism in Eastern Europe, especially the violent, deadly riots called pogroms. Young Sylvia Bernstein watched as terrified Russian Jews fled into her Austrian border town. No longer able to stand "what would you call it in English—the oppression of anti-Semitism," she convinced her mother to let her join her brother in the United States.[17] Similarly, the upheavals that culminated in the Mexican Revolution of 1910 drove men and women north.

But young women also had their own distinctive reasons for emigrating. Many were drawn by the reputation that the United States was developing as a society that welcomed independence for women, allowing them to earn their own wages and to marry men of their own choosing. Southern Italian girls whose families could not provide them with cash dowries immigrated so that they could wed

EMMA GOLDMAN
Living My Life

Emma Goldman (1869–1940) was raised by an overbearing father and an uninterested stepmother. She was already interested in radical politics before she left Russia in 1885 to follow her sister Helena to become a garment worker in Rochester, New York. Within a few years she had become deeply involved with the anarchist movement. Her autobiography, Living My Life *(1931), is one of the most widely read life stories in American women's history.*

Helena also hated to leave me behind. She knew of the bitter friction that existed between Father and me. She offered to pay my fare, but Father would not consent to my going. I pleaded, begged, wept. Finally I threatened to jump into the Neva [River], whereupon he yielded. Equipped with twenty-five roubles—all that the old man would give me—I left without regrets. Since my earliest recollection, home had been stifling, my father's presence terrifying. . . . [Father] had tried desperately to marry me off at the age of fifteen. I had protested, begging to be permitted to continue my studies. In his frenzy he threw my French grammar into the fire, shouting: "Girls do not have to learn much! All a Jewish daughter needs to know is how to prepare gefüllte fish, cut noodles fine, and give the man plenty of children." I would not listen to his schemes; I wanted to study, to know life, to travel. Besides, I never would marry for anything but love, I stoutly maintained. It was really to escape my father's plans for me that I had insisted on going to America.

SOURCE: Emma Goldman, *Living My Life* (New York: A. A. Knopf, 1931), ch. 1.

without dowries. A common story for young women of all groups involved fleeing from an overbearing, patriarchal father and from the threat of an arranged marriage. This was why Emma Goldman fled Russia in 1885. Upon arriving in the United States she began a life of political activism that eventually made her the most notorious radical in the United States (see box, "Living My Life").

Other women came to the United States as wives or to become wives, to join husbands who had migrated before them or to complete marriages arranged in the old country. The Japanese government encouraged male immigrants to send to Japan for women to marry. These women in turn sent letters and photographs to their potential husbands. This was a modern version of a traditional Japanese practice, but *shaskin kekkon* (literally, "photograph marriages") were regarded by

Americans as akin to prostitution and still another indication of the allegedly low morals of Asians. Similar arrangements were common, although less stigmatized, among white immigrants. Rachel Kahn came from Ukraine to North Dakota in 1894 to marry a Russian immigrant farmer. Although they had never met, they had exchanged pictures. "I liked his looks and he wrote he was pleased with my appearance as well," she recalled.[18]

Some women undoubtedly migrated for reasons so personal and painful that they were hidden from public view. Unmarried women who had become pregnant might flee or be sent away so that the scandal could be more easily hidden. The father of Lucja Krajulis's child would not marry her but sent her instead to the United States, where she was shuttled among fellow Lithuanians who refused to house her permanently.[19] During the 1910 Mexican Revolution, women in the countryside were raped by armed marauders, and crossing the border provided them escape from their shame.

The Immigrant's Voyage

Having decided to move to the United States, immigrant women had many obstacles to negotiate. Passage in the steerage class of a transoceanic steamship in 1900 cost the modern equivalent of $400. It took ten to twenty days to cross from Italy to New York and twice as long from Japan to San Francisco, during which time passengers slept in cramped, unhealthy conditions below deck and remained confined to crowded areas above. One can only imagine the experience of pregnant women or mothers of infants. Photos of arriving immigrants show dazed women, with babies held tightly in their arms and older children clinging to their skirts.

In 1892, the first federal receiving station for immigrants was established on Ellis Island in New York City harbor. The majority of immigrants were passed through quickly, although those judged "unfit" for admission, on grounds ranging from infectious diseases to suspicion of insanity, could be isolated, confined, and eventually deported. Asian women were more likely to be kept for long periods at Angel Island, the equivalent site established in San Francisco Bay in 1910. Assumed to be sexually immoral, they were detained until they could establish their respectability by answering endless questions (for which they had carefully prepared) about themselves and the men they planned to marry. "Had I known it was like this," a thirty-year-old Chinese mother recalled, "I never would have wanted to come."[20]

Young European women were regarded not so much as sexually immoral as sexually vulnerable. Concerned American middle-class women met those who arrived alone at ship depots and railroad stations to protect them from the real and imaginary dangers that awaited them. Stories circulated of unaccompanied and disoriented immigrant girls tricked or forced into prostitution. Their procurers were assumed to be immigrants as well, with Eastern European Jews particularly suspected of this practice. This phenomenon was known at the time as "white slavery," a term meant to contrast with chattel (black) slavery but which also implied that nonwhite girls had no innocence to violate. Feared as an international conspiracy to waylay and prostitute young women, white slavery was a major focus for anxieties about women and immigration. The actual extent of the practice was undoubtedly exaggerated in these concerns.

Disembarking did not mean the end of the transoceanic immigrant's voyage. Many kept on moving beyond the port cities, following friends or family or rumors of work. By the turn of the century, the populations of large midwestern cities such as Chicago and Milwaukee were preponderantly foreign-born. Numerous mining towns of the West were dense with immigrants as well. Many immigrants, wishing to retain something of their familiar homeland, preferred to live among people from their own village or region, but this could leave them ignorant of much about their new surroundings. Reformer Jane Addams told the poignant story of an Italian woman who had never seen roses in her limited Chicago neighborhood, thought they grew only in Italy, and feared that she would never enjoy their beauty again.[21]

Reception of the Immigrants

The United States' pride in its status as a nation of immigrants is embodied in New York harbor's Statue of Liberty, a giant female figure presented to the United States by the people of France in 1885 to represent the two countries' common embrace of liberty. The poem inscribed on the statue's base was written by Emma Lazarus, a descendant of Sephardic Jews who had arrived in the mid-seventeenth century. The words she wrote welcome the world's oppressed, those "huddled masses yearning to breathe free, / The wretched refuse of your teeming shore." But Lazarus's sentiment was not the norm. In the late nineteenth century, most native-born Americans regarded the incoming masses as disturbingly different, inassimilable aliens.

Anti-immigrant legislation initially targeted Asians. The Page Law of 1875, the very first federal legislation meant to discourage immigration, was directed at Chinese women on the assumption that most were prostitutes. In 1882, Congress passed a more comprehensive law, the Chinese Exclusion Act, which banned further immigration of Chinese laborers and their families. The few women who could prove that they were the wives or daughters of Chinese merchants already living in the United States were exempted. Once Chinese immigration had virtually ceased, Japanese workers began to come to the United States, but by the 1890s, anti-Asian sentiment on the West Coast had surfaced against them as well. In 1907, in the so-called Gentlemen's Agreement, the U.S. and Japanese governments agreed to restrict further immigration.

Laws against European immigrants, who were far more central to the U.S. economy, were not passed until 1921 and 1924, when highly restrictive national quotas were established, remaining in place until the 1960s. Nonetheless, European immigrants were the targets of considerable prejudice, and as their numbers grew in the late nineteenth century, so did the resentment against them. Degrading ethnic stereotypes were widely circulated and regarded as innocently amusing. (See Visual Sources: Women in the Cartoons of *Puck* Magazine, pp. 393–99.) Southern and Eastern European immigrants were seen literally as foreign races, peoples whose strangeness and difference were fundamental, physical, and

State of California,
CITY AND COUNTY OF SAN FRANCISCO.

Chin Lung, a resident of San Francisco, being duly sworn according to law, deposes and says that he is a member of the firm of Sing Kee & Company No. 808 Sacramento Street in said City:

That his wife Leung Yee was a resident of this City for 5 6 years, and that she left this City per Steamship "*Belgec*" sailing for Hong Kong on the _____ day of October 1889.

That his daughter, Ah Kum, was born in San Francisco at No. 613 Dupont Street, in 1885, and left San Francisco with her mother in October 1889. *Chin Lung*

Subscribed and sworn to before me, this 1st day of *May* A.D. 1892
F. B. Hoyt
NOTARY PUBLIC.

◆ A Document of Chinese Immigration

Through diligent research, historian Judy Yung uncovered this sworn testimony given by her great-grandfather of her great-grandmother's emigration to the United States in 1892. She found that there were several strategic lies embedded within the document. First, his wife Leung Yee had not lived in the United States previously but was immigrating for the first time in 1892. Second, the daughter that she claimed on this document was in fact a young servant of the family. Such deceits were necessary — and common — to circumvent the prohibitions of the Chinese Exclusion Act of 1882. *File 12017/37232 for Leong Shee, Chinese Departure Application Case Files, 1912–1943, San Francisco District Office, Immigration and Naturalization Service, Record Group 85, National Archives and Records Administration — Pacific Region, San Bruno, CA.*

ineradicable. Religion was also a major concern. The hundreds of thousands of Jews who arrived from Eastern Europe after 1880 were the first major group of non-Christians to settle in the United States, and Americans were very unprepared for the strange, orthodox religious rituals that they practiced. Even Catholics were regarded by American Protestants as so emotional and superstitious as barely to be common believers in Christ. Their devotion to a foreign pope was the source of much suspicion. Anti-Semitic and anti-Catholic attitudes abounded even among otherwise liberal-minded Americans. Susan B. Anthony could not understand by what logic "these Italians come over with the idea that they must be paid as much as intelligent white men."[22]

Americans were wary of immigrant gender relations, regarding their own attitudes as modern and those of the newcomers as Old World and patriarchal. They were especially uneasy with the reproductive behavior of immigrant women. While the birth rates of native-born women had been falling for some time (see Chapter 5), immigrant families were large. In Buffalo around the turn of the century, Italian women were giving birth to an average of eleven children and Polish Catholics to between seven and eight. In 1903, President Theodore Roosevelt, concerned that immigrants' higher birthrates were overtaking those of native-born Americans, charged middle-class women who were working or going to college instead of having babies with responsibility for what he called "race suicide." "If the women do not recognize that the greatest thing for any woman is to be a good wife and mother," he declared in the introduction to *The Woman Who Toils* (see p. 311), "why, that nation has cause to be alarmed about its future."[23] After some time in the United States, however, immigrant women started to want smaller families. Margaret Sanger, herself the daughter of Irish immigrants, founded the American birth control movement in the 1910s as a response to immigrant women's pleas for reliable ways to prevent unwanted pregnancy (see Chapter 7).

Starting about 1910, settlement houses and other civic institutions initiated deliberate Americanization campaigns to assimilate immigrants into mainstream U.S. culture. While these programs no longer regarded immigrants as permanently alien to American society, they did look on their languages, religions, and cultural practices as foreign and needing to be replaced by modern American practices. Women's household routines were a particular object for reform, as were practices such as arranged marriages or live-in boarders that seemed to violate American standards of family life. Initially intended as a benign program to ease the way of immigrants into American society, Americanization programs became harsher during World War I, when nativism once again surfaced and immigrants were faced with challenges to their patriotism and national loyalty.

Immigrant Daughters

Immigrant women's experience varied by age and marital status. Mothers and daughters confronted America very differently. Low wages made it difficult for immigrant men to meet the American standard of being the sole support of their families. The secondary wage earners were usually teenage children, not wives. Just as their families needed their earnings, the expanding labor force needed immigrant daughters' labor. Young girls were plunged immediately into the booming American economy, while their mothers remained largely homebound.

Young immigrant women predominated in both of the two largest categories of female wage labor, domestic labor and factory work. Many German, Polish, and Mexican girls met the late nineteenth-century middle-class demand for servants (see Chapter 5). So common was it for young Irish women to go into service that the slang terms for Irish female immigrant and housemaid were the same: Bridget. By contrast, Italian parents did not want their daughters to work as servants in strange households and preferred that they take jobs where other family members could oversee their activities, such as in seasonal fruit picking.

Young immigrant women were also drawn into factory work. They manufactured everything from cigars to canned goods, but it was the garment industry to which they made their greatest contribution. The mass production of clothes in the United States could not have occurred without their labor. By 1890, one out of three garment workers was a woman, and most of those women were immigrants. Some—Russian Jews, Japanese, Italians—had worked in clothing factories in their home countries. In the United States, New York and Chicago were the centers of the ready-made clothing industry, but garment factories filled with immigrant workers could be found throughout the country, from El Paso to San Francisco to Baltimore. Paid by the piece and pushed to work ever more quickly, young women earned low wages and risked occupational injuries. "Sometimes in my haste I get my finger caught," one woman worker observed nonchalantly, "and the needle goes right though it. It does so quick, tho, that it does not hurt much."[24] Sexual harassment was an additional problem for young immigrant women factory workers, as it was hard not to yield to the foremen who controlled their jobs.

The great majority of these young women workers lived with parents or other relatives, but intergenerational relations in immigrant families could be very fraught. Far more than their brothers, girls were expected to turn over most of their wages to their parents. Mothers needed the money for household expenses, but daughters longed to spend some of their earnings on themselves. Disagreements did not end there. Daughters wanted to dress in the modern style, while mothers wanted them to look and behave like respectable girls in the old country. Battles could be even more intense with fathers. No one resisted Old World patriarchy more intensely than its daughters. The Russian Jewish novelist Anzia Yezierska wrote often of this theme. "Should I let him crush me as he crushed [my sisters]?," a character in her 1925 novel, *The Bread Givers,* said of her father. "No. This is America. Where children are people. . . . It's a new life now. In America, women don't need men to boss them."[25]

Immigrant Wives and Mothers

While unmarried immigrant women were more likely to be wage earners than native-born women, the opposite was true of their mothers, very few of whom worked outside their homes. This behavior was not simply a carryover of Old World standards; Eastern European Jewish wives, for instance, had traditionally been shop-keepers or market vendors. Given the family wage system in the United States, how-ever, adult immigrant women had difficulty finding paid work. Immigrant wives were nonetheless expected to contribute to the family economy. Because of the numbers of single male immigrants and the preference of many groups for living among people from their own country, boarding was very common among immi-grants. The work of cooking and doing laundry fell to the wife, while the income generated was under the control of the husband. Middle-class observers, who re-garded familial privacy as sacred, roundly condemned the immigrant practice of boarders living within families. Immigrants recognized the tensions but regarded them more tolerantly, and stories of liaisons between amorous boarders and discon-tented housewives were a source of much amusement in immigrant culture.

Women's housekeeping and childrearing tasks were daunting, both because of poverty and the surrounding alien culture. In densely populated cities, apartments were crowded and residents still relied on backyard wells and outdoor privies, aug-mented by public baths. Children playing on busy city streets required added su-pervision. Women hauled water up flights of stairs, purchased coal and wood for fuel, and fought a constant battle against ash and soot. Photographer Jacob Riis, himself a Danish immigrant, did pioneering work documenting these conditions. (See Visual Sources: Jacob Riis's Photographs of Immigrant Girls and Women, pp. 386–92.) Even so, American observers were frequently astonished at the levels of cleanliness immigrant women were able to maintain. While middle-class women dealt with their domestic obligations by hiring immigrant servants, immi-grant women had no choice but to do their own scrubbing and ironing.

Immigrant mothers had responsibility for preserving customary ways against the tremendous forces working to Americanize them and their families. They con-tinued to cook traditional foods and observe religious obligations, while their hus-bands and children entered into the American economic mainstream to make the family's living. As practices that were ancient and reflexive became deliberate and problematic, it fell to these women to defend and perpetuate the old ways, thus laying the basis for what would eventually become a genuinely American ethnic identity. Such practices constituted an implicit resistance to the forces of Ameri-canization and cultural homogenization. For the time being, however, such immi-grant mothers were dismissed by their children as old-fashioned and quaint, their skills and knowledge irrelevant to the new world that their daughters mastered with such verve. Once again, Jane Addams subtly captured the emotional tenor of this role reversal in her description of the dilemma of immigrant women in search of runaway children in Chicago: "It is as if they did not know how to search for their children without the assistance of the children themselves."[26]

Despite these obstacles, adult immigrant women helped to construct lasting ethnic communities. In the mining town of Anaconda, Montana, Irish women, struggling to meet their family needs, nonetheless raised money to build St. Patrick's Catholic Church in 1888. This story was repeated over and over again in the immigrant neighborhoods within which the American Catholic church devel-oped. Occasionally, immigrant wives' community activism took a political turn, as in 1902, when New York City Jewish women demonstrated against the rising cost of meat in the city's kosher markets. Like native-born middle-class women, late nineteenth-century immigrant women formed and joined associations, but for different reasons. They had been drawn to the United States by the promise of greater freedom, if not for themselves, then for their children. But they were learning that to realize that promise, they had to find ways to work together.

CENTURY'S END: CHALLENGES, CONFLICT, AND IMPERIAL VENTURES

For many of the women who immigrated to the United States or who migrated across the continent, the American dream remained elusive. Their frustrated hopes helped to fuel a dramatic crisis at century's end. The national economy, which had gone through a series of boom and bust cycles since the beginnings of industrialization in the 1830s, experienced its greatest economic collapse yet in 1893, as overextension of the railroad system, decline in gold reserves, and international collapse in agricultural prices set off a long, deep economic contraction that kept layoffs high, wages low, and economic growth stalled for four years. In the cities, the newest immigrants bore the brunt of massive unemployment and deep family disruption. In the agricultural heartland, crops could not be sold at a profit, and family farms failed. Factory workers and farmers were not natural allies; they were not even particularly sympathetic to each other. Nonetheless, the two groups were moving in the same direction—to confront the wealthy strata that ruled a complacent nation. The turmoil of the 1890s unleashed an unprecedented wave of industrial strikes and raised the prospects for a new insurgent political movement, Populism, which mounted the first systematic electoral challenge to entrenched political power since the rise of the Republican Party in the 1850s.

In the hotly contested presidential contest of 1896, the pro-business Republican candidate William McKinley defeated the Democratic-Populist nominee William Jennings Bryan, ending for the time being these challenges to entrenched power. In the wake of their victory, corporate leaders and Republican politicians brought the United States to join European nations in the race for empire and the acquisition of overseas colonies.

Women were active everywhere in the crises of the 1890s. They were the victims of desperate economic conditions, ardent supporters of strikes, spokeswomen for political challenges, and supporters and opponents of the new imperial ventures. In two especially important ways—winning the first victories for woman suffrage in the West and establishing settlement houses to assist urban immigrants—the decade brought American women to a new level of political prominence.

Rural Protest, Populism, and the Battle for Woman Suffrage

The years after Reconstruction were difficult for American farmers. The dream of economic independence and self-sufficiency was still a powerful pull, but economic realities were rapidly changing. Farming families raised their crops for distant markets and were driven into debt by the pressures of falling prices and rising costs. Culturally, rural Americans also felt that they were losing ground—and often their children—to the magnet of city life. The powerful railroad corporations that set rates for transporting their crops were a particular target of farmers' anger. "It is an undeniable fact that the condition of the farmer and their poor drudging wives is every year becoming more intolerable," Minnesotan Mary Travis complained in 1880. "We are robbed and crowded to the wall on every side, our crop [is] taken for whatever the middlemen are of a mind to give us, and we are obligated to give them whatever they have the force to ask for their goods or go without, and all this means so . . . much toil, and less help for the farmer's wife."[27]

The Grange gave way in the 1880s to the Farmers' Alliances. While continuing to encourage community life, the Alliances emphasized the formation of farmers' buying and selling cooperatives to circumvent the powers of the banks and railroads. The Southern Alliance movement, which began in Texas in 1877, was particularly strong. In it, non-elite southern white women began to take a visible, public role. "Words fail me to express . . . my appreciation of women's opportunity of being co-workers with the brethren in the movement which is stirring this great nation," proclaimed a female officer of a North Carolina chapter in 1887.[28] Southern black farmers organized separate Colored Farmers' Alliances, approximately half of whose 750,000 members were women. African American sharecroppers, who were trapped into debt because they had to acquire their supplies from their landlords at exorbitant credit rates, were particularly attracted to cooperatives. It is possible that the People's Grocery in Memphis, the lynching of whose owner in 1892 catapulted Ida B. Wells into her reform career (see p. 306), was one such cooperative enterprise.

By 1892, Farmers' Alliances in the Midwest came together with both Southern Alliances to form a new political party, ambitiously named the People's Party, also known as the Populists. Women were very active in its meteoric life. Frances Willard, an important figure at the founding convention in St. Louis, brought the large and powerful Woman's Christian Temperance Union (WCTU) with her into the new effort. Several of the Populists' most successful organizers were also women. Kansan Mary Elizabeth Lease, daughter of Irish immigrants, was the fieriest of these radical female orators. "You wonder, perhaps, at the zeal and enthusiasm of the Western women in this reform movement," Lease proclaimed at the founding convention. "We endured hardships, dangers and privations, hours of loneliness, fear and sorrow; [w]e helped our loved ones to make the prairie blossom . . . yet after all our years of toil and privations, dangers and hardship upon the Western frontier, monopoly is taking our homes from us."[29]

The Populist insurgency lasted only four years, but it left an enduring mark on the history of women's rights. In the Reconstruction years, suffragists had fought for political rights in the U.S. Constitution (see Chapter 5). During the 1890s, while national politics remained inhospitable to reform, the focus for woman suffrage, as for other democratic reforms, shifted to the state level. In many western states, the Populists endorsed woman suffrage, giving it new life. In 1893, the Populist-controlled legislature of Colorado called for a referendum to amend the state constitution to enfranchise women voters. Women in Wyoming Territory had been enfranchised by a few legislators in 1869, and when Wyoming became a state in 1890, it maintained woman suffrage. But the Colorado referendum was the first time that the issue had been put before large numbers of male voters. Colorado was a booming state, the center of the mining industry, home both to the owners of great fortunes and a large, militant working class. A woman suffrage victory there was bound to have national reverberations.

The women of Colorado's suffrage societies, labor union auxiliaries, WCTU chapters, and Knights of Labor locals joined together to convince male voters to enfranchise them. In contrast to the violent, widespread class conflict in the western mining industry, the advocates of woman suffrage were proud of their ability to "work unitedly and well" for a common goal.[30] Middle- and upper-class women contributed money to hold giant women's rallies. Their respectability offset the charge that prostitutes would use their votes to further corrupt the world of politics. Linking their cause to struggling farmers and wage earners, suffragists asked for the vote as a tool against the entrenched power of railroads and mining corporations. "The money question has power to reach into the most sheltered home and bring want and desolation," Lease proclaimed. "Women have not invaded politics; politics have invaded the home."[31] The woman suffrage referendum won with a strong majority, passing in over three-quarters of the counties. Although suffragists had appealed to all parties, Populist support had been crucial. "There is less prejudice against and a stronger belief in equal rights in the newer communities," wrote suffrage journalist Ellis Meredith of this western victory. "The pressure of hard times, culminating in the panic of 1893, undoubtedly contributed to the success of the Populist Party and to its influence the suffrage cause owes much."[32] Three years later, Idaho women won a similar victory by an even greater margin.

Campaigns were also waged in Kansas and California, but they failed because of partisan conflict. In Kansas in 1894, two out of three male voters voted against woman suffrage and, according to Populist suffragist Annie Diggs, "the grief and the disappointment of the Kansas women were indescribable."[33] In 1896, the issue was put before the men of California. Seventy-six-year-old Susan B. Anthony went to the state to stump for suffrage. At first, all three political parties endorsed the referendum, and labor, Socialist, Spanish-language, and immigrant newspapers also came out in its favor. But when national Populist leaders decided to campaign in the presidential election that year solely on the issue of currency reform ("free silver"), the political situation changed dramatically. The Democratic Party joined with the Populists to advocate basing the nation's currency on silver as well as gold, and the two parties "fused" behind the same presidential candidate, the charismatic Nebraskan orator William Jennings Bryan. Advocacy of woman suffrage became a liability, and the Populists ceased to agitate on its behalf. Republicans turned against it, and the California referendum was defeated 45 percent to 55 percent. "We feel defeated, and it doesn't feel good," Anthony told a newspaper reporter. "But we must save ourselves for other States. 'Truth crushed to earth will rise again.'"[34]

In the South, woman suffrage, which had been held back by its association with the Reconstruction-era effort to subordinate states' rights to federal

"*You ought to be ashamed of yourself.*"

◆ *The Wonderful Wizard of Oz*
This beloved children's classic was published in 1900 in the wake of the collapse of western Populism, and many have read it as a metaphor of the movement. The author, L. Frank Baum, was an advocate of Populism. He was married to Maud Gage, daughter of suffrage leader Matilda Joslyn Gage. The book centers around an adventuresome young girl from the Populist farm state of Kansas, named "Dorothy" after the Baums' recently deceased daughter. In the book, Dorothy is saved through magical shoes made of silver, echoing the Populist demand for a silver-based currency. *Library of Congress, LC-USZ62-78613.*

authority, also got its first sustained airing in the Populist era. In 1888, Texan Ann Other defended woman suffrage against its critics in the pages of the *Southern Mercury*, a Populist newspaper. "Those men who could think less of a woman because she took a judicious interest in the laws of her country would not be worth the while to mourn over," she wrote.[35] Small woman suffrage societies formed throughout the South. Eventually, however, southern Populism was felled by the racial divisions inherited from slavery and deepening racial inequality at century's end. The threat of electoral cooperation between angry black and white farmers gave the final push to the new system of segregation and disfranchisement known as Jim Crow (see Chapter 5). When southern suffrage campaigns resurfaced again in the twentieth century, they did so in the context of this aggressive racism, arguing for white women's votes as a means for countering black men's votes.

Nationally, the election of Republican William McKinley in 1896 signaled the end of the Populist movement. For women, however, the party's brief career had enormous consequences. The women of Colorado and Idaho now had full voting rights, in federal as well as state elections. Woman suffrage had become a live political issue, and its center had shifted from the Northeast, where the movement had begun, farther west, where male voters identified it with a more democratic political system. Having driven the People's Party from the electoral arena, the Republican Party absorbed some of its reform agenda. After 1896, not only did the issue of woman suffrage pass into the hands of the reform-minded wing of the Republican Party but so did other Populist concerns, such as the impact of economic growth on the poor and the need for government regulation of corporations. As with the Populists, women activists and reformers would prove to be numerous and influential among these newly designated "Progressives" (see Chapter 7).

Class Conflict and the Pullman Strike of 1894

Just as Populism was reaching its high point in 1893, the national economy collapsed, thousands of businesses failed, and nearly a quarter of wage workers lost their jobs. The nation's most severe depression to date exposed critical problems and deep social rifts. Women suffered, both as out-of-work wage earners and as wives of unemployed men. Federal and state governments, following the laissez-faire principle of nonintervention in the marketplace, offered no help. Instead, private charities provided a few paying jobs—street cleaning for men and sewing for women—but their efforts were inadequate to the need. Across much of the country, the winter of 1893–94 was one of the coldest ever recorded. Rosa Cavalleri, a recent immigrant from Italy to Chicago, recalled waiting in a line for free food: "Us poor women were frozen to death; we didn't have warm clothes."[36] The spread of disease under such conditions—smallpox and typhoid in Chicago, diphtheria in New York—showed the middle and upper classes that, in a complex, modern society, misery and want could not be confined to one class: poverty put entire communities at risk.

For a handful, the moment promised a new American revolution. Amid rising working-class discontent, twenty-four-year-old Emma Goldman found her calling as a radical agitator and orator. She was already under suspicion for her role in the attempted assassination of the chairman of the Carnegie Steel Corporation during a violent strike at its Homestead, Pennsylvania, plant in 1892. The next year she led a phalanx of unemployed women in New York City. An advocate of anarchism, the political philosophy that condemned all government as illegitimate authority, she challenged the crowd, "Do you not realize that the State is the worst enemy you have? . . . The State is the pillar of capitalism and it is ridiculous to expect any redress from it."[37] She was arrested, tried, and sentenced to a year in prison for "inciting to riot." In jail, Goldman learned the trade of midwifery and became an advocate of sexual and reproductive freedom for working-class women. The experience forged her reputation as America's most consistently radical woman and won her the nickname "Red Emma."

Many workers fought back against falling wages and massive layoffs. The most dramatic of the strikes of this period began in May 1894 at the Pullman Railroad Car Company just south of Chicago. Company founder George Pullman was proud of his paternalistic policy of providing for all his workers' needs, but now he dug in against their protests. Determined to maintain profits, Pullman refused to lower rents in the company-owned housing, where employees were expected to live despite their diminished pay packets. Jennie Curtis, who sewed upholstery in the elegant Pullman cars, protested that three-quarters of her paycheck went back to the Pullman Company in rent. "We are not just fighting for ourselves," she declared, "but for decent conditions for workers everywhere."[38] Pullman's policy drew wives as well as women workers into the conflict. "Holding their babies close for shields," the antistrike *Chicago Tribune* reported of a workers' demonstration, "the women still break past the patrol lines and go where no man dares to step."[39] As railroad workers nationwide shut down the railroad system rather than transport Pullman cars, pressure grew on the federal government to intervene. President Grover Cleveland sent six thousand federal troops to quell riots and occupy the rail yards in Chicago. By early July, the strike was broken.

The Settlement House Movement

The Pullman strike also affected the future of middle- and upper-class women by putting a new development in female social reform, the settlement house movement, on the historical map. Settlement houses were pioneered in England in the 1880s by male college graduates who chose to live among and serve the urban poor. By 1890, settlement houses were beginning to appear in the United States, with the important difference that most of their participants were middle- and upper-class women. The most influential settlement house was Hull House, established in Chicago in 1889 by Jane Addams. (See Documents: Jane Addams and the Charitable Relation, pp. 379–85.)

Soon Hull House was serving several thousand people per week. Kindergarten and after-school classes helped immigrant mothers with childcare and encouraged the spread of American values and culture. In contrast to later, more coercive forms of Americanization, however, immigrants at Hull House were valued for their home cultures as well. Creatively struggling with the gulf between immigrant mothers and their Americanized children, Jane Addams established the Hull House Labor Museum where parents could demonstrate and explain to their children their traditional craft skills and thus "build a bridge between European and American experiences in such wise as to give them both more meaning."[40] Rooms were made available for union meetings and political discussion clubs. Immigrants in the neighborhood attended concerts and enjoyed the use of a gymnasium. A separate residence, named the Jane Club in homage to Addams, provided an alternative to commercial boarding houses for young wage earning women away from their families. "Hull-House is meant to be the centre for all the work needed around it," a sympathetic observer explained, "not committed to one line of work, but open to all that leads the way to a higher life for the people."[41]

The Pullman strike gave new prominence and impetus to the women of Hull House, who suddenly found themselves in the midst of Chicago's violent class conflict. Jane Addams, who had a reputation as an effective conciliator, was appointed to a special arbitration committee that was unable to find a way to resolve the strike. Meanwhile, Florence Kelley, another Hull House member, was developing a more direct, long-term response to the frustration and demands of working-class immigrant women and children. The daughter of a Republican congressman

◆ **Jane Addams Reading to Her Nephew**
Jane Addams built her life as a reformer around the traditional womanly virtues of care, nurturance, and concern for family life, expressed on a large, public stage. Although she never married or became a mother, she was often photographed with the immigrant children served by Hull House. In her personal life, she was a devoted aunt. Buried in this tender picture of Addams with her nephew Stanley Linn, taken around 1894, is a tragedy. In the summer of 1894, with the railroads on strike, Addams's sister Mary died before family members could reach her. Jane became the legal guardian for Mary's children. Her biographer, Victoria Brown, observes that the twin tragedies of the Pullman strike and her sister's death took a considerable toll on Addams, who looks older here than her thirty-four years. *University of Illinois at Chicago, University Library Jane Addams Memorial Collection, neg. no. 1703.*

and herself a Cornell University graduate, Kelley shared Addams's privileged background but had moved further beyond the expectations of women of her class. While living in Germany, she had become a socialist and now corresponded with Karl Marx's collaborator, Friedrich Engels, about the condition of the Chicago poor. In 1892, she wrote him, "The most visible work is [being done] at the present moment by a lot of women who are organizing trade unions of men and women."[42] Kelley had come to Hull House to get away from an abusive husband and so knew something of wives' dependency. To her deserves much of the credit for moving Hull House, and with it the entire settlement movement, decisively in the direction of modern social welfare reform.

Kelley crafted a body of protective labor laws designed to shield working-class families from the worst impact of the wage labor system. In 1893, she was part of a group that submitted a bill to the Illinois state legislature to prohibit the employment of children, constrain home-based manufacturing, and establish an eight-hour workday for adult women workers. Offered as a legislative response to the growing social and economic crisis of the poor, the Factory and Workshop Inspection Act was passed about a year before the Pullman strike. Kelley was appointed chief factory inspector for the state of Illinois, empowered to search out and prosecute violations of the new laws. She and her deputy inspectors, who included the trade union activist Mary Kenney (see Chapter 5), succeeded in drawing the attention of reformers, the state government, and labor unions to the extent and abuses of the sweating system in Illinois and helped to initiate a nationwide campaign to improve conditions in the garment industry. Many states began to pass similar factory and tenement inspection laws.

Other provisions of the law were not so successful. Illinois garment manufacturers united in opposition to the eight-hour workday for women workers. In the bitter aftermath of the Pullman strike, the Illinois Supreme Court ruled in 1895 that limitations on the working hours of women were a violation of individual freedom of contract, without "due process of law." Kelley's father had helped to write the Fourteenth Amendment, which had enshrined the principle of due process in the U.S. Constitution, and she railed against the 1895 decision as a perversion of this principle, making it into "an insuperable obstacle for the protection of women and children."[43] Ending child labor also proved extremely difficult, as even immigrant parents resisted efforts to deprive their families of young wage earners. But Kelley had chosen her life's work—to find the political backing and constitutional basis for social welfare provisions that would aid working-class women and families.

Woman-based settlement houses soon appeared in other immigrant-dense cities, among them the Henry Street Settlement in New York City, led by Lillian Wald; Neighborhood House in Dallas; and the Telegraph Hill Neighborhood Association in San Francisco. While many white settlement leaders personally believed in greater racial justice, they yielded to the prejudices of the era and practiced racial segregation in the institutions they established. In the South, middle-class African American women organized their own settlements, most notably Atlanta's Neighborhood Union, organized in 1908 by clubwoman Lugenia Hope. In the North, all-black settlement houses were also organized. Ida B. Wells-Barnett set up the Negro Fellowship Association in a rented house on Chicago's south side. Hull House, which had experimented with a few black residents in the 1890s, switched in the twentieth century to encouraging and supporting a separate black settlement house, the Wendell Phillips House. Similar black-oriented settlement houses were Robert Gould Shaw House in Boston, Karamu House in Cleveland, and Lincoln House in New York City.

Epilogue to the Crisis: The Spanish American War of 1898

In an atmosphere shaped by the crisis of the 1890s, the United States embarked on its first extracontinental imperialist efforts. Imperial advocates contended that the acquisition of overseas colonies could provide both new markets to revive the American economy and a military challenge to invigorate American manhood. In an influential paper entitled "The Significance of the Frontier in American History," historian Frederick Jackson Turner considered the advantages of an imperial future for the United States. Mourning the end of an era in which the defining national purpose was to conquer the American continent, and concerned that immigrants could not be fully Americanized in the absence of the frontier experience, Turner suggested that overseas expansion might be a way for the United States to continue to pursue its Manifest Destiny and maintain its frontier spirit.

Turner made his remarks in 1893 at the World's Columbian Exposition in Chicago, the same exposition that featured the Woman's Building (see Chapter 5). Throughout the fair, America's rising imperial aspirations were on display. The spatial organization of the grounds reflected the country's new ambitions for world leadership. At the center was the Court of Honor, where the United States welcomed and joined the great nations of Europe. Meanwhile, on the riotous Midway at the fair's periphery, belly-dancing Arabs, tribal Africans, and exotic Asians drew enormous crowds, who were fascinated and amused by the unprecedented spectacle of the world's strange variety of peoples. The implication was clear: the people on the Midway were inferior, uncivilized, and backward and needed the stewardship of the United States and other advanced Christian nations.

Some of the earliest manifestations of this crusading sense of American national superiority had come from Protestant missionaries, among whom women were prominent. Since the 1830s, women with a strong religious vocation had been bringing American values and culture along with English language and Christian Bibles to the peoples of Asia and Africa (see Chapter 3). Women's overseas missionary efforts entered a new, more organized phase in 1883 when the Woman's Christian Temperance Union (WCTU) created a World division to undertake international work. Mary Clement Leavitt, a former schoolteacher from Vermont, became the first of the WCTU's "round the world missionaries," traveling around the Pacific, from Hawaii to New Zealand and Australia to Burma, Madagascar, China, and India, to spread the ideas of temperance.

Some Asian women were able to use the resources and perspective of the WCTU missionaries to address their own problems as they understood them. In Japan, for instance, the WCTU's combined message of female purity and activism became the basis for an anticoncubinage movement, while the antiliquor arguments were ignored. Nonetheless, the assumption of American superiority and world leadership constituted a kind of "soft" imperialism. Frances Willard made the link explicit when she said that "Mrs. Leavitt has been to the women of Japan what U.S. naval and economic power has been to its commerce: an opening into the civilized world."[44]

Willard wrote those words in 1898, the year that the United States entered into its first explicitly imperial overseas war and acquired its first formal colonial possessions. The so-called Spanish American War began in Cuba, which had long drawn American attention as a possible territorial acquisition. Cuban nationalists were showing signs of winning a prolonged insurgency against Spanish colonial control. In May, the United States joined the war on the side of the Cuban forces, ostensibly to avenge the destruction of the U.S.S. *Maine*, an American battleship blown up under suspicious circumstances in Havana harbor. (It was later determined that powder on the deck exploded, probably by accident.) Spain was quickly routed, but instead of supporting Cuban independence, the United States enforced a new type of foreign oversight on the island. While not making Cuba a formal colony, the Platt Amendment, passed by Congress in 1902, gave the United States a supervisory role over Cuban affairs that it retained until 1934.

As Spanish imperial power collapsed further, the United States claimed as colonies other Spanish possessions, including Puerto Rico and Guam. But U.S. forces found it difficult to consolidate control over the rich prize of the Spanish Philippines, the gateway to trade across the Pacific and throughout Asia. An indigenous Filipino independence movement fought back against the Americans, who had come in 1898 to liberate and stayed to control. The Filipinos turned what at first appeared to be a quick U.S. victory into a long and deadly conflict, which U.S. forces brought to an end only in 1902 through considerable expenditure of life (see box, "Women of the Philippines"). Unlike Cuba, the Philippines became a formal U.S. colony and remained so until 1946.

Alongside the economic justification for imperial expansion in search of new markets, a restless, insecure, and aggressive masculinity played a significant role in America's decision to go to war. Rising New York politician Theodore Roosevelt thoroughly embodied this phenomenon. With the memory of Civil War death tolls receding, men like Roosevelt were eager to demonstrate a manliness they felt was challenged by immigrant men and threatened by activist women. For them, conflict with Spain was, as John Hay, ambassador to England, put it, the chance to conduct a "splendid little war." Newspapers encouraged popular clamor for intervention. In political cartoons, Americans were portrayed as the manly protectors of the Cuban people, who were regularly depicted as suffering women (see Figure 6.12, p. 399). These eager imperialists "regarded the war as an opportunity," says one historian, "to return the nation to a political order in which strong men governed and homebound women proved their patriotism by raising heroic sons."[45]

Most American women joined the clamor and supported intervention on what they believed was the side of the Cubans. Remembering female service in the Civil War, they raised funds for military hospitals. But when it came to the unprecedented taking of overseas colonies, opinion was much more divided. By nature a pacifist, Jane Addams recognized the threat that rising militarism posed to a more general spirit of reform. On the streets around Hull House, she observed, children were "playing war." "[I]n the violence characteristic of the age, they were 'slaying Spaniards.'"[46] Susan B. Anthony also opposed the war. Her longtime friend and political partner, Elizabeth Cady Stanton, took the opposite position and believed that colonization would civilize the Filipino people.

The annexation of Hawaii during the war illustrates other aspects of the many roles women played in the U.S. move toward empire. In 1891, Queen Liliuokalani became the reigning monarch of the sovereign nation of Hawaii. She had been educated by American Protestant missionaries, was a devout Congregationalist, spoke English, and was married to a white American. Wealthy American planters already had enormous economic power in Hawaii, but U.S. tariff policies put them at a disadvantage in selling their fruit and sugar, and they pressed for a U.S. takeover of the islands. Now that its monarch was a woman, they redoubled their claims that only annexation could assure Hawaii's stability and progress. The U.S. entry into the war against Spain created a political environment favorable to their

CLEMENCIA LOPEZ
Women of the Philippines

Clemencia Lopez and her husband Sixto were leading advocates of the cause of Philippine independence to the American people. She defended her people's dignity and sovereign rights in this 1902 address to the New England Woman Suffrage Association, many members of which were active in the Boston-based Anti-Imperialist League. Subsequently she became a student at Wellesley College, one of the first Filipinas to attend a U.S. college.

You will no doubt be surprised and pleased to learn that the condition of women in the Philippines is very different from that of the women of any country in the East, and that it differs very little from the general condition of the women of this country. Mentally, socially, and in almost all the relations of life, our women are regarded as the equals of our men. . . .

. . . [I]t would seem to me an excellent idea that American women should take part in any investigation that may be made in the Philippine Islands, and I believe they would attain better results than the men. Would it not also seem to you an excellent idea, since representation by our leading men has been refused us, that a number of representative women should come to this country, so that you might become better acquainted with us?

. . . You can do much to bring about the cessation of these horrors and cruelties which are today taking place in the Philippines, and to insist upon a more humane course. I do not believe that you can understand or imagine the miserable condition of the women of my country, or how real is their suffering. . . . [Y]ou ought to understand that we are only contending for the liberty of our country, just as you once fought for the same liberty for yours.

SOURCE: Clemencia Lopez, "Women of the Philippines," address to the New England Woman Suffrage Association, published in *The Woman's Journal*, June 7, 1902.

aspirations, and in 1898 they were able to convince Congress to acquire Hawaii. Unlike the takeover of Texas in 1845 and California in 1848, however, Hawaii did not become a state but was designated a colonial territory.

The response of U.S. suffragists was not to condemn this move, even though the deposed head of state was a woman, nor to object that Congress was imposing a government on the islands instead of allowing its residents to organize one. Rather, they protested Congress's intention to write a territorial constitution for the Hawaiians that confined political rights to men only. "The declared intention of the United States in annexing the Hawaiian Islands is to give them the benefits of the most advanced civilization," the National American Woman Suffrage Association declared in a petition to Congress, "and . . . the progress of civilization in every country is measured by the approach of women toward the ideal of equal rights with men."[47] As one historian writes, suffragists "substituted a critique of imperialism with a critique of patriarchy, and in the process lent their tacit approval to America's colonial project."[48] Even when they seemed to defend the rights of women in the colonies, late nineteenth-century suffragists did so within a framework that assumed the superiority of American culture and their right, as white Americans, to play a role in the nation's expansive "civilizing" mission.

CONCLUSION: Nationhood and Womanhood on the Eve of a New Century

At the beginning of the twentieth century, most American women faced the new century with considerable optimism. Not so long before, their country had gone through a horrific Civil War, but now it had more than recovered. The settlement of the western half of the continental United States gave a sturdy new physicality to American claims of nationhood. The U.S. economy more than equaled that of England, Germany, and France combined. Many immigrants had taken great risks and come far to participate in this spectacular growth. Strong and confident, the United States, once a colony itself, ended the century by acquiring its own colonies. The country was on its way to becoming a world power.

As this new era of national development dawned, women's prospects looked especially promising. With the important exception of Native American women, most American women in 1900 were living more active, more public, more individualized, and more expansive lives than prior generations. As a group, they were prepared to make a major contribution to solving the problems that accompanied America's new prosperity and place in the world. In the coming era, they would achieve as much influence as in any period of U.S. history. Already the beneficiaries of American progress, they were about to become the mainstays of the Progressive era, in which America undertook the challenging task of both reforming and modernizing itself.

DOCUMENTS

Susette La Flesche:
The Life of an Indian Girl

S USETTE LA FLESCHE (1854–1903) was one of the most prominent Native American women to champion the path of assimilation in the aftermath of the deadly "Indian wars" and the triumph of white American power. In threading her own way between Indian traditions and white civilization, she became an advocate for her people and a pioneer in new forms of Indian womanhood.

La Flesche was the eldest daughter of Mary Gale and Joseph La Flesche, also known as Iron Eye, principal chief of the Omaha tribe. Both her parents were children of white fathers and Indian mothers. Iron Eye believed in preparing his children for a future in white American society, and Susette was formally educated, first at a mission school on the reservation and then at a private high school in Massachusetts. Although she went through a tribal initiation ceremony, her father determined that she would not receive the traditional facial tattoo of Omaha women, which would have marked her as "savage" in white society.

The La Flesche family belonged to what was called "the citizens' party" among the Omaha people. They promoted U.S. citizenship for Indians, lived in frame houses, and wore "citizens'" (white people's) clothes. As they observed the theft of reservation lands and the corruption of federal Indian agencies, they became committed to a policy of private land ownership for Indians. Susette's younger sister Susan, the first Indian woman to graduate from an American medical college, later described how "the Indian village broke up as the dawn of civilization crept nearer and nearer; and the Indians scattered their farms on the Reservation and began to cultivate the soil. My father secured a farm of 160 acres."[49]

But the La Flesches were also champions of Indian rights. In 1879, when she was twenty-five, Susette became a public figure. She was drawn into the defense of Standing Bear, a Ponca chief who had been imprisoned for resisting the government-mandated relocation of his tribe. When he was later released on the grounds that his constitutional rights had been violated, Susette served as his translator on a highly publicized speaking tour in the East. Going by the name of Bright Eyes, the English version of her tribal name Ishthatheumba, she achieved considerable celebrity because of her beauty, her combination of Indian and American ways, and her passionate protest against the wrongs done to her people. Admirers regarded her as the living embodiment of the "beautiful Indian maiden."

La Flesche had a particularly powerful impact on white women who met her on this trip. Among those whom she drew to lifelong advocacy of Indian welfare were Helen Hunt Jackson, author of the influential expose of government mistreatment of native peoples, *A Century of Dishonor* (see box, "A Century of Dishonor," p. 346), and Amelia Quinton and Mary Bonney, founders of the white Woman's National Indian Association. La Flesche's most important convert was Alice Fletcher, a New York–based clubwoman who later became a pioneering ethnographer of Native Americans. Through these white American women, who contributed to the design, drafting, and administration of the Dawes Severalty Act (see p. 345), La Flesche had an indirect but important role in setting federal Indian policy for the next half century.

Like her female ancestors, Susette La Flesche married a white man. Her husband, T. H. Tibbles, combined advocacy of Indian rights with Populist politics, which Susette shared. She contributed significantly to articles he published under his own name, including newspaper coverage of the Wounded Knee Massacre of 1890. Tibbles's overbearing ambition to be the white savior of the Omahas eventually alienated the couple from Susette's family. They lived sometimes in a sod house that they built on Susette's allotment and sometimes in the white city named after her people, Omaha. She died at age 50 in 1903.

In assessing La Flesche's advocacy of Indian assimilation, it is important not to underestimate the complexity of her life and the context of her choices. She lived on the border between white and Indian cultures and on the outskirts of female conventionality. She believed in a pluralistic America, in which Indians could be both citizens and loyal to their own ways and beliefs. Despite her American education and her white husband, she retained deep connections to her family and her people and wrote and spoke as their champion.

Few of La Flesche's writings have come down to us. The following story was published in *St. Nicholas,* the most influential young people's magazine of the late nineteenth century. Challenging the magazine to include "Savages" among their authors, La Flesche uses a simple fictional style to present traditional Indian experience from the viewpoint of a young Indian girl. Her goal was to make Indian life seem less foreign to an American audience, especially to the coming generations. Despite her assimilation into white society, La Flesche knew this world well enough to portray it in great detail. She also knew the name of her great-great-grandmother and paid homage to her by choosing that name for her young protagonist.

As you read, consider what Nedawi's childish dilemmas reveal about traditional Indian life. How do they reflect La Flesche's understanding of the expectations of her white readers?

Susette La Flesche
Nedawi: An Indian Story from Real Life (1881)

"NEDAWI!" called her mother, "take your little brother while I go with your sister for some wood." Nedawi ran into the tent, bringing back her little red blanket, but the brown-faced, roly-poly baby, who had been having a comfortable nap in spite of being all the while tied straight to his board, woke with a merry crow just as the mother was about to attach him, board and all, to Nedawi's neck. So he was taken from the board instead, and, after he had kicked in happy freedom for a moment, Nedawi stood in front of her mother, who placed Habazhu on the little girl's back, and drew the blanket over him, leaving his arms free. She next put into his hand a little hollow gourd, filled with seeds, which served as a rattle; Nedawi held both ends of the blanket tightly in front of her, and was then ready to walk around with the little man.

Where should she go? Yonder was a group of young girls playing a game of konci, or dice. The dice were five plum-seeds, scorched black, and had little stars and quarter-moons instead of numbers. She went over and stood by the group, gently rocking herself from side to side, pretty much as white children do when reciting the multiplication table. The girls would toss up the wooden bowl, letting it drop with a gentle thud on the pillow beneath, the falling dice making a pleasant clatter which the baby liked to hear. . . . Just then, the little glittering heap caught baby's eye. He tried to wriggle out of the blanket to get to it, but Nedawi held tight. Then he set up a yell. Nedawi walked away very reluctantly, because she wanted to stay and see who would win. She went to her mother's tent, but found it deserted. Her father and brothers had gone to the chase. A herd of buffalo had been seen that morning, and all the men in the tribe had gone, and would not be back till night. Her mother, her sister, and the women of the household had gone to the river for wood and water. The tent looked enticingly cool, with the sides turned up to let the breeze sweep through, and the straw mats and soft robes seemed to invite her to lie down on them and dream the afternoon away, as she was too apt to do. She did not yield to the temptation, however, for she knew Mother would not like it, but walked over to her cousin Metai's tent. She found her cousin "keeping house" with a number of little girls, and stood to watch them while they put up little tents, just large enough to hold one or two girls.

"Nedawi, come and play," said Metai. "You can make the fire and cook. I'll ask Mother for something to cook."

"But what shall I do with Habazhu?" said Nedawi.

"I'll tell you. Put him in my tent, and make believe he's our little old grandfather."

Forthwith he was transferred from Nedawi's back to the little tent. But Habazhu had a decided objection to staying in the dark little place, where he could not see anything, and crept out of the door on his hands and knees. Nedawi collected a little heap of sticks, all ready for the fire, and went off to get a fire-brand to light it with. While she was gone, Habazhu crawled up to a bowl of water which stood by the intended fire-place, and began dabbling in it with his chubby little hands, splashing the water all over the sticks prepared for the fire. Then he thought he would like a drink. He tried to lift the bowl in both hands, but only succeeded in spilling the water over himself and the fire-place.

When Nedawi returned, she stood aghast; then, throwing down the brand, she took her little brother by the shoulders and, I am sorry to say, shook him violently, jerked him up, and dumped him down by the door of the little tent from which he had crawled. "You bad little boy!" she said. "It's too bad that I have to take care of you when I want to play."

Source: *St. Nicholas* 8 (January 1881): 225–30.

You see, she was no more perfect than any little white girl who gets into a temper now and then. The baby's lip quivered, and he began to cry. Metai said to Nedawi: "I think it's real mean for you to shake him, when he doesn't know any better." Metai picked up baby and tried to comfort him. She kissed him over and over, and talked to him in baby language. Nedawi's conscience, if the little savage could be said to have any, was troubling her. She loved her baby brother dearly, even though she did get out of patience with him now and then.

"I'll put a clean little shirt on him and pack him again," said she, suddenly. Then she took off his little wet shirt, wrung it out, and spread it on the tall grass to dry in the sun. Then she went home, and, going to a pretty painted skin in which her mother kept his clothes, she selected the red shirt, which she thought was the prettiest. . . . When Baby was on her back again, she walked around with him, giving directions and overseeing the other girls at their play, determined to do that rather than nothing.

The other children were good-natured, and took her ordering as gracefully as they could. Metai made the fire in a new place, and then went to ask her mother to give her something to cook. Her mother gave her a piece of dried buffalo meat, as hard as a chip and as brittle as glass. Metai broke it up into small pieces, and put the pieces into a little tin pail of water, which she hung over the fire. "Now," she said, "when the meat is cooked and the soup is made, I will call you all to a feast, and Habazhu shall be the chief."

They all laughed. But alas for human calculations! During the last few minutes, a shy little girl, with soft, wistful black eyes, had been watching them from a little distance. She had on a faded, shabby blanket and a ragged dress.

"Metai," said Nedawi, "let's ask that girl to play with us; she looks so lonesome."

"Well," said Metai, doubtfully, "I don't care; but my mother said she didn't want me to play with ragged little girls."

"My father says we must be kind to poor little girls, and help them all we can; so I'm going to play with her if you don't," said Nedawi, loftily.

Although Metai was the hostess, Nedawi was the leading spirit, and had her own way, as usual. She walked up to the little creature and said, "Come and play with us, if you want to." The little girl's eyes brightened, and she laughed. Then she suddenly drew from under her blanket a pretty bark basket, filled with the most delicious red and yellow plums. . . .

"Let us have them for our feast," said Metai, taking them.

Little Indian children are taught to share everything with one another, so it did not seem strange to Nedawi to have her gift looked on as common property. But, while the attention of the little group had been concentrated on the matter in hand, a party of mischievous boys, passing by, caught sight of the little tents and the tin pail hanging over the fire. Simultaneously, they set up a war-whoop and, dashing into the deserted camp, they sent the tent-poles scattering right and left, and snatching up whatever they could lay hands on, including the tin pail and its contents, they retreated. The little girls, startled by the sudden raid on their property, looked up. Rage possessed their little souls. Giving shrieks of anger, they started in pursuit. What did Nedawi do? She forgot plums, baby, and everything. The ends of the blanket slipped from her grasp, and she darted forward like an arrow after her companions.

Finding the chase hopeless, the little girls came to a stand-still, and some of them began to cry. The boys had stopped, too; and seeing the tears flow, being good-hearted boys in spite of their mischief, they surrendered at discretion. They threw back the articles they had taken, not daring to come near. They did not consider it manly for big boys like themselves to strike or hurt little girls, even though they delighted in teasing them. . . .

"You have spilt all our soup. There's hardly any of it left. You bad boys!" said one of the girls.

They crowded around with lamentations over their lost dinner. The boys began to feel remorseful.

"Let's go into the woods and get them some plums to make up for it."

"Say, girls, hand us your pail, and we'll fill it up with plums for you."

So the affair was settled.

But, meanwhile, what became of the baby left so unceremoniously in the tall grass? First he opened his black eyes wide at this style of treatment. He was not used to it. Before he had time, however, to make up his mind whether to laugh or cry, his mother came to the rescue. She had just come home and thrown the wood off her back, when she caught sight of Nedawi dropping him. She ran to pick him up, and finding him unhurt, kissed him over and over. Some of the neighbors had run up to see what was the matter. She said to them:

"I never did see such a thoughtless, heedless child as my Nedawi. She really has 'no ears.' I don't know what in the world will ever become of her. When something new interests her, she forgets everything else. It was just like her to act in this way."

Then they all laughed, and one of them said:

"Never mind—she will grow wiser as she grows older," after which consoling remark they went away to their own tents.

An hour or two after, Nedawi came home.

"Mother!" she exclaimed, as she saw her mother frying bread for supper, "I am so hungry. Can I have some of that bread?"

"Where is your little brother?" was the unexpected reply.

Nedawi started. Where had she left him? She tried to think.

"Why, mother, the last I remember I was packing him, and—and, oh, Mother! you know where he is. Please tell me."

"When you find him and bring him back to me, perhaps I shall forgive you," was the cold reply.

This was dreadful. Her mother had never treated her in that way before. She burst into tears, and started out to find Habazhu, crying all the way. She knew that her mother knew where baby was, or she would not have taken it so coolly; and she knew also that her mother expected her to bring him home. As she went stumbling along through the grass, she felt herself seized and held in somebody's strong arms, and a great, round, hearty voice said:

"What's the matter with my little niece? Have all her friends deserted her that she is wailing like this? Or has her little dog died? I thought Nedawi was a brave little woman."

It was her uncle Two Crows. She managed to tell him, through her sobs, the whole story. She knew, if she told him herself, he would not laugh at her about it, for he would sympathize in her troubles, though he was a great tease. When she ceased, he said to her: "Well, your mother wants you to be more careful next time, I suppose; and, by the way, I think I saw a little boy who looked very much like Habazhu, in my tent."

Sure enough, she found him there with his nurse. When she got home with them, she found her mother,—her own dear self,—and, after giving her a big hug, she sat quietly down by the fire, resolved to be very good in the future. She did not sit long, however, for soon a neighing of horses, and the running of girls and children through the camp to meet the hunters, proclaimed their return. All was bustle and gladness throughout the camp. There had been a successful chase, and the led horses were laden with buffalo meat. These horses were led by the young girls to the tents to be unpacked, while the boys took the hunting-horses to water and tether in the grass. Fathers, as they dismounted, took their little children in their arms, tired as they were. Nedawi was as happy as any in the camp, for her seventeen-year-old brother, White Hawk, had killed his first buffalo, and had declared that the skin should become Nedawi's robe, as soon as it was tanned and painted.

What a pleasant evening that was to Nedawi, when the whole family sat around a great fire, roasting the huge buffalo ribs, and she played with her little brother Habazhu, stopping now and then to listen to the adventures of the day, which her father and brothers were relating! The scene was truly a delightful one, the camp-fires lighting up the pleasant family groups here and there, as the flames rose and fell. The bit of prairie where the tribe had camped had a clear little stream running through it, with shadowy hills around, while over all hung the clear, star-lit sky. It seemed as if nature were trying to protect the poor waifs of humanity clustered in that spot.

Nedawi felt the beauty of the scene, and was just thinking of nestling down by her father to enjoy it dreamily, when her brothers called for a dance. The little drum was brought forth, and Nedawi danced to its accompaniment and her brothers' singing. She danced gravely, as became a little maiden whose duty it was to entertain the family circle. . . . [The story ends with a peaceful scene in which Nedawi's grandmother tells her a tale of how the turkey's eyes turned red, and then croons her to sleep with a lullaby.]

QUESTIONS FOR ANALYSIS

1. What are the traditional Omaha roles for men and women, as the author portrays them for her white readers through the play of children?

2. How does La Flesche make the Indian girls and women about whom she writes seem familiar to her nonnative readers? What does this tell us about the values and concerns of American culture in the 1880s?

3. Early in the story, the author questions whether the "little savage" Nedawi could be said to have a "conscience." Is this comment straightforward or ironic? Why?

D O C U M E N T S

Jane Addams and the Charitable Relation

J ANE ADDAMS (1860–1935) was the leader of the American settlement house movement. After graduation in 1882 from Rockford Seminary in Illinois, she went to Europe in search of a larger life purpose for herself. Like other daughters of wealthy families, she was looking for an alternative to the leisured, domestic life (which she called "the family claim") that seemed to be her fate. Restless leisure-class women like Addams did not require paid labor, but they did need work of large social purpose and a place and community in which to live. Visiting London, Addams learned of a "settlement" project of male college graduates who lived among and served the urban poor. She returned to Illinois, determined to establish a similar community of female college graduates dedicated to social service. In 1889 Addams persuaded a wealthy woman to donate a Chicago mansion, originally built by the Hull family and now in the center of a crowded immigrant district, for her planned settlement.

The reform-minded women who joined Addams to live and work in Hull House combined a palpable sympathy with the urban poor and a principled commitment to finding a nonrevolutionary solution to the era's class and ethnic conflicts. In Addams's words, they were determined "to aid in the solution of the social and industrial problems which are engendered by the modern conditions of urban life."[50] Their focus was especially on the welfare of women and children. They learned that in hard times poor women suffered the consequences of a double dependency—on men who could not be breadwinners and on governments that were slow to accept public responsibility for social welfare needs.

Addams wrote the essay excerpted here, "The Subtle Problems of Charity," in 1899, only a few years after the 1893 depression and 1894 Pullman Strike, before the success of her pioneering work at Hull House was widely acknowledged. The essay demonstrates Addams's dual vocation of empirical social observer and passionate social reformer. She actively struggled with the "perplexities" that plagued the efforts of leisure-class women like herself to respond to the needs of impoverished immigrants. In a society still imbued with a rigid morality, Addams displayed an impressive ability to avoid ethical absolutes in her understanding of immigrants' lives and choices.

Addams sought to interpret the long history of what she calls "the charitable relation." In the early nineteenth century, wealthy benefactors made sure that their money went only to the "worthy" poor, so as to encourage charity recipients to become self-supporting participants in a competitive, market-driven society. But Addams believed that these philanthropists treated their clients "exclusively as factors in the industrial system." By contrast, she advocated a more humanitarian ethic of "brotherhood and equality." She approached the problem of charity in broader terms, concerned that American political democracy should develop a social dimension. Her primary concern was not whether an individual was "worthy" of charity but the creation of constructive bonds and mutual understanding between those who need aid and those in a position to give it.

Simultaneous with this shift in the charitable ethic, the gender of those who dispensed philanthropic aid was changing. The traditional philanthropic leader had been a man who had succeeded in the struggle for individual wealth and gave in accordance with the values he credited for his own rise in society. But by the late nineteenth century, charity giving had become the responsibility of leisure-class women who had no direct experience with money making. In 1899, Addams was unsettled about the contradiction between leisure-class women's ignorance of material realities and the control they exerted over the lives of the needy poor who looked to them for necessary aid.

Contradictory intellectual frameworks can be detected in Addams's thinking about her relationship to the new immigrants. The beneficiary of expanding opportunities for higher education for women, Addams subscribed to the modern principles of progress and science, which she used to make sense of the dilemmas she and other settlement house activists faced. She used Darwinian notions of evolution to characterize the inevitable and desirable development of society from the lower stages and backward cultures represented by European immigrants to the higher stages and superior cultures of the American bourgeoisie. Yet at the same time, she also regarded the "primitiveness" of these immigrant families as more natural, more basic, and in some ways more fundamentally human than the ways of her own class and culture. She felt that women of the middle and upper classes had lost touch with fundamental human needs and experiences that were instinctively understood by immigrant women.

Addams's analysis of the dilemmas of philanthropy was not limited to the problems of the charity givers but included the ethical dilemmas faced by the immigrant recipients. She resisted treating the immigrant poor as either passive or morally pure, seeing them instead as people struggling with their own contradictory values. In her view, like the larger American society into which they had come, the new immigrants quickly learned to respect economic success more than human compassion. Thus they admired but expected little from those who had achieved material wealth while they were polite to but contemptuous of the "good . . . and kind-hearted" women of wealth on whom they depended for crucial charitable aid.

Addams's concern with the relations between parents and children is also evident in this essay. She tended to see settlement house workers in the role of parents, sometimes beneficent, sometimes uncomprehending, of the childlike immigrants. This family-based model of class relations helped female settlement house activists legitimate their efforts at expanding their social authority: Addams and women like herself saw themselves as public "mothers." But as this essay makes clear, Addams also had considerable empathy for immigrant children. Within a few years, she would become a leader in the fight to ban child labor as well as to pass laws and regulations intended to move mothers out of the labor force so that they could devote themselves entirely to the rearing of their children.

By 1910 Jane Addams was the acknowledged head of the settlement movement and a leader in American philanthropy. In Hull House, she created a modern, progressive venue to which reformers from all over the world came, from British social democrat Sidney Webb to Japanese feminist Ichikawa Fusae. At times, she was misunderstood by both the poor and the rich for her determination to negotiate between the warring classes of turn-of-the-century American society, but her approach was widely influential on women and men alike. An instinctive revulsion at militarism, first evident during the Filipino-American conflict of 1899–1902, combined with the internationalism that she embraced at the neighborhood level in her Hull House work, led her to become, later in her career, a leader of the women's international peace movement (see Chapter 7).

Jane Addams
The Subtle Problems of Charity (1899)

Probably there is no relation in life which our democracy is changing more rapidly than the charitable relation, that relation which obtains between benefactor and beneficiary; at the same time, there is no point of contact in our modern experience which reveals more clearly the lack of that equality which democracy implies. We have reached the moment when democracy has made such inroads upon this relationship that the complacency of the old-fashioned charitable man is gone forever; while the very need and existence of charity deny us the consolation and freedom which democracy will at last give.

Formerly when it was believed that poverty was synonymous with vice and laziness, and that the prosperous man was the righteous man, charity was administered harshly with a good conscience; for the charitable agent really blamed the individual for his poverty, and the very fact of his own superior prosperity gave him a certain consciousness of superior morality. Since then we have learned to measure by other standards, and the money-earning capacity, while still rewarded

out of all proportion to any other, is not respected as exclusively as it was. . . .

Of the various struggles which a decade of residence in a settlement implies, none have made a more definite impression on my mind than the incredibly painful difficulties which involve both giver and recipient when one person asks charitable aid of another.

An attempt is made in this paper to show what are some of the perplexities which harass the mind of the charity worker; to trace them to ethical survivals which are held not only by the benefactor, but by the recipients of charity as well; and to suggest wherein these very perplexities may possibly be prophetic.

. . . The charity visitor, let us assume, is a young college woman, well-bred and open-minded. When she visits the family assigned to her, she is embarrassed to find herself obliged to lay all the stress of her teaching and advice upon the industrial virtues, and to treat the members of the family almost exclusively as factors in the industrial system. She insists that they must work and be self-supporting; that the most dangerous of all situations is idleness; . . . [I]t often occurs to

Source: *Atlantic Monthly,* February 1899, 163–78.

the mind of the sensitive visitor, whose conscience has been made tender by much talk of brotherhood and equality which she has heard at college, that she has no right to say these things; that she herself has never been self-supporting; that, whatever her virtues may be, they are not the industrial virtues; that her untrained hands are no more fitted to cope with actual conditions than are those of her broken-down family.

The grandmother of the charity visitor could have done the industrial preaching very well, because she did have the industrial virtues; if not skillful in weaving and spinning, she was yet mistress of other housewifely accomplishments. In a generation our experiences have changed—our views with them. . . .

A very little familiarity with the poor districts of any city is sufficient to show how primitive and frontier-like are the neighborly relations. There is the great willingness to lend or borrow anything, and each resident of a given tenement house knows the most intimate family affairs of all the others. The fact that the economic conditions of all alike is on the most precarious level makes the ready outflow of sympathy and material assistance the most natural thing in the world. There are numberless instances of heroic self-sacrifice quite unknown in the circles where greater economic advantages make that kind of intimate knowledge of one's neighbors impossible. . . .

The evolutionists tell us that the instinct to pity, the impulse to aid his fellows, served man at a very early period as a rude rule of right and wrong. There is no doubt that this rude rule still holds among many people with whom charitable agencies are brought into contact, and that their ideas of right and wrong are quite honestly outraged by the methods of these agencies. When they see the delay and caution with which relief is given, these do not appear to them conscientious scruples, but the cold and calculating action of the selfish man. This is not the aid that they are accustomed to receive from their neighbors. . . . The only man they are accustomed to see whose intellectual perceptions are stronger than his ten-

derness of heart is the selfish and avaricious man, who is frankly "on the make." If the charity visitor is such a person, why does she pretend to like the poor? Why does she not go into business at once? . . . In the minds of the poor success does not ordinarily go with charity and kind-heartedness, but rather with the opposite qualities. The rich landlord is he who collects with sternness; who accepts no excuse, and will have his own. There are moments of irritation and of real bitterness against him, but there is admiration, because he is rich and successful. . . . The charity visitor, just because she is a person who concerns herself with the poor, receives a touch of this good-natured and kindly contempt, sometimes real affection, but little genuine respect. . . .

When the agent or visitor appears among the poor, and they discover that under certain conditions food and rent and medical aid are dispensed from some unknown source, every man, woman and child is quick to learn what the conditions may be and to follow them. . . . The deception arises from a wondering inability to understand the ethical ideals which can require such impossible virtues, combined with a tradition that charity visitors do require them, and from an innocent desire to please. It is easy to trace the development of the mental suggestions thus received. The most serious effect upon the individual comes when dependence upon the charitable society is substituted for the natural outgoing of human love and sympathy, which, happily, we all possess in some degree. . . . The charity visitor has broken through the natural rule of giving, which in a primitive society is bounded only by the need of the recipient and the resources of the giver; and she gets herself into untold trouble when she is judged by the ethics of that primitive society.

The neighborhood understands the selfish rich people who stay in their own part of the town. . . . Such people do not bother themselves about the poor; they are like the rich landlords of the neighborhood experience. But this lady visitor, who pretends to be good to the poor, and certainly does talk as though she were kind-hearted, what does she come for, if she does not intend to give them things which so plainly are needed? The visitor says, sometimes, that in holding her poor family so hard to a standard of thrift she is really breaking down a rule for higher living which they formerly possessed; that saving, which seems quite commendable in a comfortable part of the town, appears almost criminal in a poorer quarter, where the next-door neighbor needs food, even if the children of the family do not. She feels the sordidness of constantly being obliged to urge the industrial view of life. . . . She says sometimes: "Why must I talk always on getting work and saving money, the things I know nothing about? . . ."

Because of this diversity in experience the visitor is continually surprised to find that the safest platitudes may be challenged. . . .

The subject of clothes, indeed, perplexes the visitor constantly, and the result of her reflections may be summed up something in this wise: The girl who has a definite social standing, who has been to a fashionable school or to a college, whose family live[s] in a house seen and known by all her friends and associates, can afford to be very simple or even shabby as to her clothes, if she likes. But the working girl, whose family lives in a tenement or moves from one small apartment to another, who has little social standing, and has to make her own place, knows full well how much habit and style of dress have to do with her position. Her income goes into her clothing out of all proportion to that which she spends upon other things. But if social advancement is her aim, it is the most sensible thing which she can do. She is judged largely by her clothes. . . .

Have we worked out our democracy in regard to clothes farther than in regard to anything else?

The charity visitor has been rightly brought up to consider it vulgar to spend much money upon clothes, to care so much for "appearances." . . . The poor naturally try to bridge the [class] difference by reproducing the street clothes which they have seen; they therefore imitate, sometimes in more showy and often in more trying colors, in cheap and flimsy material, in poor shoes and flippant hats, the extreme fashion of the well-to-do. They are striving to conform to a common standard which their democratic training presupposes belongs to us all. The charity visitor may regret that the Italian peasant woman has laid aside her picturesque kerchief, and substituted a cheap street hat. But it is easy to recognize the first attempt toward democratic expression.

The charity visitor is still more perplexed when she comes to consider such problems as those of early marriage and child labor. . . . She discovers how incorrigibly bourgeois her standards have been, and it takes but a little time to reach the conclusion that she cannot insist so strenuously upon the conventions of her own class, which fail to fit the bigger, more emotional, and freer lives of working people. . . .

The sense of prudence, the necessity for saving, can never come to a primitive, emotional man with the force of a conviction, but the necessity of providing for his children is a powerful incentive. He naturally regards his children as his savings-bank; he expects them to care for him when he gets old, and in some trades old age comes very early. . . . [A] tailor whom I know, a Socialist, always speaks of saving as a bourgeois virtue, one quite impossible to the genuine workingman. He supports a family, consisting of himself, a wife and three children, and his parents, on eight dollars a week. He insists that it would be criminal not to expend every penny of this amount upon food and shelter, and he expects his children later to take care of him. . . .

The struggle for existence, which is so much harsher among people near the edge of pauperism, sometimes leaves ugly marks on character, and the charity visitor finds the indirect results most mystifying. Parents who work hard and anticipate an old age when they can no longer earn, take care that their children shall expect to divide their wages with them from the very first. Such a parent, when successful, seizes the immature nervous system of the child and hypnotizes it, so to speak, into a habit of obedience, that the nerves and will may not depart from this control when the child is older. The charity visitor, whose family relation is lifted quite out of this, does not in the least understand the industrial foundation in this family despotism.

The head of a kindergarten training class once addressed a club of working-women, and spoke of the despotism which is often established over little children . . . one [working woman] said, "Ah, of course, she [meaning the speaker] doesn't have to depend upon her children's wages. She can afford to be lax with them, because, even if they don't give money to her, she can get along without it." . . .

It is these subtle and elusive problems which, after all, the charity visitor finds most harassing. . . . The greatest difficulty is experienced when the two [ethical] standards come sharply together, and when an attempt is made at understanding and explanation. The difficulty of defining one's own ethical standpoint is at times insurmountable. . . .

A certain charity visitor is peculiarly appealed to by the weakness and pathos of forlorn old age. One of these poor old women was injured in a fire years ago. She has but the fragment of a hand left, and is grievously crippled in her feet. Through years of pain she had become addicted to opium. . . . Five years of tender care have done wonders for her. She lives in two neat little rooms, where with a thumb and two fingers she makes innumerable quilts, which she sells and gives away with the greatest delight. Her opium is regulated to a set amount taken each day. . . . [S]he was kept for two years in a suburb where the family of the charity visitor lived, and where she was nursed through several hazardous illnesses. . . . Her neighbors are constantly shocked by the fact that she is supported and comforted by "a charity lady," while at the same time she occasionally "rushes the growler,"° scolding at the boys lest they jar her in her tottering walk. The care of her has broken through even that second standard, which the neighborhood had learned to recognize as the

standard of charitable societies, that only the "worthy poor" are to be helped. . . . In order to disarm them, and at the same time to explain what would otherwise seem loving-kindness so colossal as to be abnormal, she tells them that during her sojourn in the suburb she discovered an awful family secret, a horrible scandal connected with the long-suffering charity visitor; that it is in order to prevent the divulgence of this that the ministrations are continued. Some of her perplexed neighbors accept this explanation as simple and offering a solution of a vexed problem. . . .

Of what use is all this striving and perplexity? Has the experience any value? It is obviously genuine, for it induces an occasional charity visitor to live in a tenement house as simply as the other tenants do. It drives others to give up visiting the poor altogether, because, they claim, the situation is untenable . . . the young charity visitor who goes from a family living upon a most precarious industrial level to her own home in a prosperous part of the city, if she is sensitive at all, is never free from perplexities which our growing democracy forces upon her.

We sometimes say that our charity is too scientific, but we should doubtless be much more correct in our estimate if we said that it is not scientific enough. . . . There is no doubt that our development of charity methods has reached this pseudo-scientific and stilted stage. We have learned to condemn unthinking, ill-regulated kind-heartedness, and we take great pride in mere repression, much as the stern parent tells the visitor below how admirably he is rearing the child who is hysterically crying upstairs, and laying the foundation for future nervous disorders. The pseudo-scientific spirit, or rather the undeveloped stage of our philanthropy, is, perhaps, most clearly revealed in this tendency to lay stress on negative action. "Don't give," "don't break down self-respect," we are constantly told. We distrust the human impulse, and in its stead substitute dogmatic rules for conduct . . . we forget that the accumulation of knowledge and the holding of convictions must finally result in the application

° Drinks alcohol.

of that knowledge and those convictions to life itself, and the course which begins by activity, and an appeal to sympathies so severe that all the knowledge in the possession of the visitor is continually applied, has reasonably a greater chance for ultimate comprehension.

For most of the years during a decade of residence in a settlement, my mind was sore and depressed over the difficulties of the charitable relationship. The incessant clashing of ethical standards, which had been honestly gained from widely varying industrial experience,—the misunderstandings inevitable between people whose conventions and mode of life had been so totally unlike,—made it seem reasonable to say that nothing could be done until industrial conditions were made absolutely democratic. The position of a settlement, which attempts at one and the same time to declare its belief in this eventual, industrial democracy, and to labor toward that end, to maintain a standard of living, and to deal humanely and simply with those in actual want, often seems utterly untenable and preposterous. Recently, however, there has come to my mind the suggestion of a principle, that while the painful condition of administering charity is the inevitable discomfort of a transition into a more democratic relation, the perplexing experiences of the actual administration have a genuine value of their own. . . .

The Hebrew prophet made three requirements from those who would join the great forward-moving procession led by Jehovah. "To love mercy," and at the same time "to do justly," is the difficult task. To fulfill the first requirement alone is to fall into the error of indiscriminate giving, with all its disastrous results; to fulfill the second exclusively is to obtain the stern policy of withholding, and it results in such a dreary lack of sympathy and understanding that the establishment of justice is impossible. It may be that the combination of the two can never be attained save as we fulfill still the third requirement, "to walk humbly with God," which may mean to walk for many dreary miles beside the lowliest of his creatures, not even in peace of mind, that the companionship of the humble is popularly supposed to give, but rather with the pangs and misgivings to which the poor human understanding is subjected whenever it attempts to comprehend the meaning of life.

QUESTIONS FOR ANALYSIS

1. Early in this essay, Addams speaks of the conditions in "the poor districts of any city" as "frontier-like." What does she mean by this? What were the similarities between the "settlement" of the West and "settlement" houses?

2. What is the "diversity of experience" that Addams witnessed in her work with immigrants in the neighborhood around Hull House, and how did it contribute to the ethical complexities about which she wrote?

3. The longest incident in this article is the story of the troubled old immigrant woman who was befriended and rescued by a leisure-class woman and then lied to her neighbors about her benefactor's motives. What does the incident reveal about the ethical dilemmas faced by charity recipients and charity givers alike and about the obstacles that class inequalities posed to the creation of bonds between them?

4. How did Addams's experience as a member of the pathbreaking generation of women college graduates affect her perspective as a settlement house volunteer?

VISUAL SOURCES

Jacob Riis's Photographs of Immigrant Girls and Women

I N THE DECADE BETWEEN 1880 AND 1890, more than 5 million immigrants came through the port of New York, and many remained in the city, swelling its population by 25 percent. By 1890 nearly half of the city's dwellings were classified as "tenements," overcrowded, urban slums where vulnerable and desperately poor people were overcharged for filthy, cramped, and unsanitary lodgings.

This rise in immigration coincided with new forms of social documentation. Pioneering social scientists provided statistics on the growing industrial labor force, including the women who were entering the workplace in unprecedented numbers. Local and state health bureaus collected information on the epidemic diseases such as diphtheria, cholera, and tuberculosis that threatened family life in the burgeoning cities. And photographers created searing images of the horrific living and working conditions of newly arrived immigrants. These new methods of documentation, informed by a rising sense of public responsibility for improving social conditions and alleviating poverty, allow us to look back through the perspectives of those who did the documenting, into the lives of late nineteenth-century immigrant girls and women.

The first series of photographs of immigrant women and children in the United States was produced in the 1880s and 1890s by a man who was himself an immigrant. Jacob A. Riis arrived in New York City from Denmark in 1870. After more than a decade struggling to earn a living, he found regular work as a newspaperman. He began as a police reporter, writing in a male-oriented, journalistic genre that sensationalized the seamy side of "downtown" life. Riis's own impulses, however, were more humanitarian and allied him with urban reformers, many of whom were women. He worked closely with Josephine Shaw Lowell, who founded the Charity Organization Society of New York State in 1882. His particular focus was "the slum," by which he meant not only the dilapidated tenement homes of the poor but the larger urban environment in which they lived and worked. He was especially concerned with children, and through them the mothers of immigrant families.

Convinced that only photographs could convey the shocking reality of urban poverty, Riis included them in *How the Other Half Lives: Studies among the Tenements of New York* (1890), a pioneering work of sociology that is still mined by historians and scholars for insights it provides into urban immigrant life, nineteenth-century attitudes toward poverty and ethnicity, and the visual conventions of early documentary photography. Though the majority of the photographs deal with male subjects—homeless street boys, male vagrants, and gang members—Riis also took pictures of women and girls that give us glimpses of their lives. In its frequent resort to sensational and melodramatic conventions, *How the Other Half Lives* reflects its author's roots in mass commercial journalism, but it also skillfully adopts strategies from literary realism and the emerging field of social science to convey a probing portrait of poverty and its consequences.

Consistent with the late nineteenth-century's preoccupation with ethnic and racial characteristics, *How the Other Half Lives* is organized like a guided tour for the middle-class reader through the ethnic geography of lower New York. Not surprisingly, it freely invokes both positive and negative stereotypes in its descriptions and illustrations. Riis, as a northwestern European immigrant, had clear ethnic biases, but his prejudices were tempered by empathy and the recognition that "we are all creatures of the conditions that surround us."[51] His goal was to call attention to the plight of the poor, not to castigate them for their poverty.

Riis begins his tour with "The Italian in New York," who, as a recent arrival, "comes in at the bottom" of the economic and social hierarchy.[52] The frequently reproduced photograph shown in Figure 6.1 depicts the wife and infant child of a "ragpicker"—one who barely made a living by picking through public rubbish

◆ **Figure 6.1 In the Home of an Italian Ragpicker: Jersey Street**
Museum of the City of New York, the Jacob A. Riis Collection.

cans and dumps for rags to sell—in their subterranean home. Riis developed the innovative technology used to make this photograph, a new chemical process that produced a "flash" bright enough to light up dark and windowless areas.

The pose of the Italian mother and her tightly swaddled child, as well as her mournful, upturned gaze, is reminiscent of religious paintings of the Madonna and Child in which the Virgin Mary's sad expression foreshadows the suffering that awaits her infant son. It bears noting that in the chapter that includes this photograph, Riis offers an extended report, complete with comparative statistics, on the high mortality rates of infants and children in this Italian neighborhood. What other explanations can be offered for her upward look?

Italian families, no matter how poor, frowned on wives and mothers working outside the home. While the room in Figure 6.1 is very sparsely furnished, what do the few items we see and their arrangement tell us about this woman and her daily life? In the text accompanying this photograph, Riis describes the Italian immigrant as "picturesque, if not very tidy."[53] Does his picture support this characterization? What overall impression does it convey about Italian immigrant mothers? Also in the text relating to this image is Riis's description of Italian men as "hotheaded . . . and lighthearted" and of Italian women as "faithful wives and devoted mothers."[54] Note the man's straw hat hanging high on the wall. What are the possible explanations for the man's absence?

In Figure 6.2, Riis continues his progression through New York City's ethnic neighborhoods to "Jewtown," an area settled by large numbers of Eastern European Jews and marked by exceptional population density and industrial activity.

◆ **Figure 6.2 Knee Pants at Forty-Five Cents a Dozen—A Ludlow Street Sweater's Shop**
Museum of the City of New York, the Jacob A. Riis Collection.

As Riis notes, "Life here means the hardest kind of work almost from the cradle."[55] The "sweater" mentioned in the title of the photograph was a subcontractor who supplied garments to a larger manufacturer and hired other immigrants to do the work, often in his own tenement apartment. The ruthless competition to deliver finished goods at the lowest possible price pressured the sweater to offer impossibly low wages and push (or "sweat") workers to their physical limits during a working day that "lengthened at both ends far into the night."[56] While Riis criticizes the "sweater's . . . merciless severity"[57] in exploiting his fellow Jews, he concedes "he is no worse than the conditions that created him."[58]

Unlike the photograph shown in Figure 6.1, this photo was not posed and has no carefully arranged central figure. It catches its subjects off guard, and the blurring of some of their features suggests frantic activity and movement. The sweater is the moving figure with his back to the camera. The young teenage girls in this picture are "greenhorns," newly arrived immigrant workers. One man looks up briefly from his work, but the other seems unwilling to lose a minute's time despite the photographer's presence. Piles of boys' short pants waiting to be finished are heaped on the floor and furniture. What visual clues tell us that this workshop is also a residence? What else goes on in this room? In what ways is it different from the living space of the Italian mother in Figure 6.1?

In contrast to the serious detachment of the adults, the young girl turns to smile directly into the lens and casually touches to her lips the long-bladed scissors she is using to cut the garments. Does this suggest she has not yet been disciplined to keep up with the brutal pace of piecework? Maybe Riis regarded her direct gaze as somewhat immodest, a consequence of work conditions that placed unsupervised young girls amid grown men. Or did she simply find pleasure in having her picture taken? In his second book, *The Children of the Poor* (1892), Riis noted that in contrast to adults, who resisted and feared being photographed, children loved posing for the camera and had a "determination to be 'took' . . . in the most striking pose they could hastily devise."[59] What other possible meanings can be suggested for this unusual and striking image of a young working woman?

Employers justified the low wages paid to female workers, which were inadequate for self-support, as supplements to a family income anchored by an adult male wage. Riis was sharply aware of the special hardships facing the unmarried, poor working women who had to live on their own. In his chapter "The Working Girls of New York," he describes the exploitation and harsh conditions they endured, sprinkling his narrative with tragic stories of underpaid and exhausted women workers driven to suicide, prostitution, and premature death. Like so many other late nineteenth-century reformers, Riis thought the best solution to working women's suffering was to get them out of the labor force. If they remained in it, their lives were bound to be intolerable.

Figure 6.3 is an unusual photograph of two adult women, past the age when even poor immigrant women were expected to leave the labor force. They are not driven by a supervisor as are the workers in Figure 6.2, but neither do they enjoy the camaraderie of other workers. How does their living space compare with that in the previous two photographs? What does their dress suggest about them?

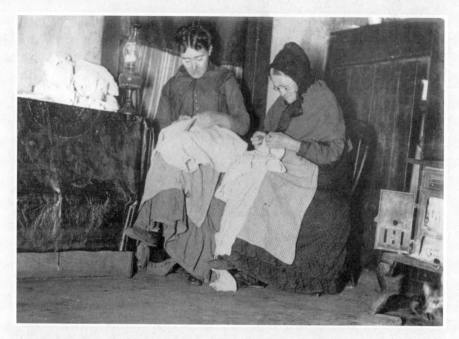

◆ Figure 6.3 **Sewing and Starving in an Elizabeth Street Attic**
Museum of the City of New York, the Jacob A. Riis Collection.

While we know little about these two women, the context of this photograph in *How the Other Half Lives* provides some help. Elsewhere in the narrative, Riis tells a heartrending story of two elderly sisters, the last of five siblings who had arrived from Ireland with their mother forty years before and who together made a scant living as lace embroiderers. When Riis encounters them, one of the sisters is crippled and the other, who had struggled to support them both, had recently been paralyzed in a fall. Now they were helpless and alone. How do the story, photograph, and title come together to reveal the conditions of women workers who had to support themselves through their own wage earning capacities?

When wages were too low or unemployment too high, poor urban workers found themselves destitute and without shelter. Those who lacked even the pennies charged by commercial lodging houses ended up in overnight shelters in police stations. Of the half-million people seeking shelter in New York City in 1889, almost one-third sought refuge in makeshift facilities in police stations, and half of those were women. Riis knew firsthand about the filthy and dangerous conditions in the police station shelters. Recalling his own experience years before as a homeless vagrant in New York, he observed, "never was parody upon Christian charity more corrupting to human mind and soul than the frightful abomination of the police lodging-house."[60] He was particularly concerned when homeless women slept in the same room as men.

The photograph in Figure 6.4 was an illustration for an article Riis wrote for the *New York Tribune* in 1892, condemning the police station shelters. The West 47th Street police station was located in the aptly named "Hell's Kitchen" area of New York, and there is no doubt that Riis intended to shock readers with a graphic, unstaged photograph of women expelled from the domestic sphere, stripped of their dignity and privacy, eating and sleeping on filthy bare floors like animals. The extent of homelessness among women pointed to the collapse of working-class family life and indicated how deeply the combination of mass immigration, rapid urbanization, and economic collapse had rent the social fabric. Nonetheless, notice the details that reveal, perhaps unintentionally, how women manage to cooperate and care for their personal needs even under the harshest of circumstances. What do these details, and the facial expressions and postures of the women, reveal about social relations in this police station lodging room?

In *The Children of the Poor*, published originally as a series of articles in *Scribner's Magazine* in 1892, Riis turned his full attention to the group with whom he was most concerned, the children whose futures were being jeopardized by life in the tenements. Figure 6.5 is a rare individual portrait of a young orphan, nine-year-old "Katie," who attended the 52nd Street Industrial School, a charitable institution for indigent children. Although Katie did not earn wages, she was not spared hard work, for she cooked and cleaned for her three older working siblings. "In her person and work, she answered the question . . . why we hear so much

◆ Figure 6.4 **Police Station Lodgers: Women's Lodging Room in the West 47th Street Station**
Museum of the City of New York, the Jacob A. Riis Collection.

◆ **Figure 6.5 "I Scrubs": Katie Who Keeps House on West 49th Street**
Museum of the City of New York, the Jacob A. Riis Collection.

about the boys and so little about the girls," wrote Riis, "because the home claims
their work earlier and to a much greater extent."[61] Consider Katie's clothing, posture, and expression. What do they suggest about her character and her prospects?
Why do you think Riis posed Katie so carefully, rather than photograph her un-
awares? In acknowledgment of Katie's contribution to her family's survival, Riis
called Katie by the nickname often given to immigrant children who cared for
younger siblings, "little mother." What does this tribute say about the economic
role that mothers and other adult women played in the lives of poor families?

QUESTIONS FOR ANALYSIS

1. Riis clearly intended to shock comfortable Americans with his images of the
   slums. What might contemporaries have found most disturbing about his
   representations of immigrant women and girls?

2. Using Riis as an example, how would you evaluate the impact of documentary
   photography on middle-class America's reaction to poverty in the late nineteenth century?

3. Drawing on both Riis and Bessie Van Voorst (see Documents: The Woman
   Who Toils, pp. 311–16) as sources, in what ways did women's experience of
   poverty and underpaid labor in this period differ from that of men?

Women in the Cartoons of *Puck* Magazine

B Y 1900 AMERICAN LITERACY was very high. About 90 percent of white Americans and 50 percent of African Americans could read and write English, and among both groups women were more literate than men. Women actively promoted literacy; their clubs organized three-quarters of the nation's circulating libraries. America's high literacy rate helped create a market for low-cost, mass-market print media, and new technologies made elaborate illustration possible.

The late nineteenth-century reading public was particularly fond of illustrated magazines that mixed words and images, political commentary and humor. Chief among these was *Puck* magazine, launched in the 1870s by German immigrant Joseph Keppler. First published in the German language, *Puck*'s circulation grew rapidly after Keppler switched to English. *Puck* and magazines like it offer useful glimpses into popular opinions and cultural attitudes of the period, including assumptions about gender.

Puck was famous for its cartoons, some of which were serious commentaries on political issues and some of which were light-hearted jokes about social and cultural matters. Political cartoons were an increasingly influential force in the shaping of public attitudes and opinions in these years, as party politics became a national preoccupation. Both political and humorous cartoons frequently portrayed women—but in quite different ways.

The changing face and place of women in American society provided rich material for *Puck*'s humor. Ridicule is a means for dealing with changes in gender patterns, and many jokes in *Puck*'s cartoons rested on stereotypes of women, from the mannish middle-class suffragist to the culturally backward female immigrant. *Puck*'s humorous treatment of late nineteenth-century women, both American and native-born, contrasted sharply with the magazine's frequent use of female figures in its didactic political cartoons. Here political abstractions in female form were as reverent and conventional as the images of immigrant and native-born women were overstated and ridiculous.

All cartoons work though caricature and exaggeration, and the 1892 cartoon strip in Figure 6.6 holds up ethnic stereotypes for ridicule. Reading beyond the humor to the assumptions on which it is based, we can draw conclusions about nativist beliefs in the alleged superiority of American gender relations. The first frame shows "Pedro," an Italian immigrant, praising America for its promise of liberty and freedom, which comes at the expense of his comically overburdened wife. In the second frame, an Irish policeman harshly berates Pedro for the treatment of his wife, who nonetheless does not seem to think she deserves better treatment. The cartoon's punch line shows the Irish policeman relaxing at home as his

PEDRO.— Dis is de greata countra,
   De landa liberty
De placea to maka de mon.
   An' evera-t'inga free !

OFFICER McSWEENEY.— Take oop thot great big boondle
   Or Oi 'll take your haythen loife.
This is a land where ivery man
   Has got t' pertect his woife.

ISABELLA.— O Pedro ! Pedro ! don'ta swear,
   It maka me cry to see !
Whena we get past de corner,
   You giva de t'ings to me.

MRS. McSWEENEY.— It does me proud to hear yez say
   Yez tuk the poor gurl's par-r-rt.
But, Dinny dear, yez always had
   A koind, considerate hear-r-rt.

◆ Figure 6.6 **The Woman of It**
Collection of the New-York Historical Society, negative #76758d.

own wife works over a washtub, surrounded by unruly children yet still praising her lazy husband. How is the reader to recognize Italian and Irish immigrants? What are the gendered dimensions of the immigrant stereotypes in this cartoon? Who, or what, is ultimately being ridiculed? What standard of marital relations is the cartoonist promoting?

The contrast between native-born and immigrant women, especially as employer and servant in the middle-class household, was made often in *Puck* cartoons, as in Figure 6.7, also published in 1892. Sometimes the joke was on the servant, who was ridiculed for her inadequate housekeeping skills. The Irish maid was such a stock cartoon figure that she was always drawn the same way. Notice the similarity to the 1852 drawing in Figure 3.5 (p. 187). In this cartoon, however, the native-born employer, while beautiful and well dressed, is the primary object of humor. How does the cartoonist make

USEFUL AS WELL AS ORNAMENTAL.

NEW GIRL.— Please, Mum, I can't make pie-crust widout a rollin' pin.

MRS. DE KORATER.— You 'll find it hanging in the parlor. Remove the ribbons and hooks, and scrape off the gold paint before you use it.

◆ Figure 6.7 **Useful as Well as Ornamental**
Collection of the New-York Historical Society, negative #76759d.

fun of this woman's place in her own household? In what ways does the contrast between mistress and maid set up the joke? What does the cartoon's title mean, about the woman as well as about the rolling pin? What does her name, "Mrs. de Korater," suggest about the role of middle-class women in America's consumer culture?

Puck also featured cartoons on women's demand for voting rights and for entry into male-dominated professions. In Figure 6.8, a cartoon published in 1898, the missing woman, away at her women's rights meeting, sets up the joke. As far back as 1848, the great French cartoonist Honoré Daumier had used a similar image of a beleaguered husband, unmanned by the demands of childrearing in the absence of his wife, to warn of the chaos that public roles for women would bring to daily life. How does the cartoon subtly mock the absent woman's concerns with rights outside the household? Yet the husband also comes in for ridicule. Is the cartoonist sympathetic with his plight—his dashed hopes for a peaceful home and supportive wife? By changing the gender of the cradle-rocker from female to male, what does the cartoon suggest about the old sentimental claim about maternal power: "The Hand That Rocks the Cradle is the Hand That Rules the World"?

In Figure 6.9, another 1898 cartoon, *Puck* once again examined the expanding sphere of women in the late nineteenth century, and once again ridiculed both men and women. As women entered higher education, they began to make gains

IRONY.

For a quiet life he got him a wife; now, with patience more than human,
He tends the children and anxiously waits, each night, for the Coming Woman:
For his wife o' nights on Woman's Rights declaims, with invectives hurled,
That "The Hand That Rocks the Cradle is the Hand That Rules the World!"

◆ Figure 6.8 **Irony**
Collection of the New-York Historical Society, negative #76760d.

WHAT WE ARE COMING TO.

THE TYPEWRITER.— Beg pardon! Did you say "My learned *sister* is mistaken —?"
THE LAWYER.— Yes; Miss Bigfee is the opposing counsel in this case.

◆ Figure 6.9 **What We Are Coming To**
Collection of the New-York Historical Society, negative #76761d.

into heretofore all-male professions. Although they were taking nearly half of all college degrees and breaking into some fields such as medicine, the legal profession remained determinedly male. Thus the notion of a woman lawyer was a good way to make fun of women's changing roles and a fine source of pictorial amusement. Many of *Puck*'s visual jokes about women's new roles used the same stereotype as the female attorney in Figure 6.9: a determined-looking woman with spectacles, a bun, and a severely tailored outfit. This caricature bears a resemblance to Susan B. Anthony, the venerable leader of the nineteenth-century women's rights movement (see p. 274 for a photograph of Anthony). How is the woman lawyer portrayed as crossing the line into mannishness? While office work continued to be a vocation held by more men than women, how is this male secretary made to look less than manly?

Middle-class women were also engaging in new leisure activities, including sports. They played tennis and golf and were avid bicyclists. In contrast to the negative way middle-class women's ambitions for political and economic equality were usually rendered, the New Woman's increasing athleticism and physical vitality were attractive to illustrators, most famously

AN IMPORTANT POINT.
" I 'm afraid we are a little slow yet."
" Possibly; but I 'm sure we don't look slow ! "

◆ **Figure 6.10** **An Important Point**
Collection of the New-York Historical Society, negative #76762d.

Charles Dana Gibson. The 1900 *Puck* cartoon in Figure 6.10 owes a great deal to the new standard of feminine beauty represented by the strapping and beautiful "Gibson girl." What elements of the illustration make for an image of womanhood that was daringly sexy for the period? How does the dialogue between the two women undercut the visual portrayal of assertion and strength?

Each issue of *Puck* also contained political cartoons that drew on common representational traditions to make their political points. Despite the growing involvement of women in politics, representations of actual women are rare in political cartoons of the period. Instead, angels, goddesses, and madonnas are used as symbols for abstract concepts, such as national sovereignty or public virtue (see Visual Sources: Gendering Images of the Revolution, pp. 110–18). There is considerable irony in the fact that cartoonists used women as symbols for the ideas and institutions of democratic political life from which they were excluded.

Figure 6.11 features the towering and powerful female figure "Columbia" to represent American democratic virtue and hope. Columbia was the female counterpart of Uncle Sam, who did not displace her as the personification of American nationhood until the 1920s. The dedication in 1885 of the Statue of Liberty

◆ Figure 6.11
**Unconscious of
Their Doom**
*Collection of the New-York
Historical Society, negative
#76763d.*

gave Columbia new heft and importance. In this 1891 image she stands on the firm ground of "human rights" and uses the lever of "education" to pry loose a precarious rock labeled "divine right," on which sit monarchs of Europe, Asia, and Africa. The message is clear: the democratic "spirit of the age" that flourishes in America will deal the final blow to a teetering and outmoded European political order and its colonial minions. Why does it benefit American democracy to be pictured as a woman? How does this image prepare the way for America to undertake its own imperial role by century's end?

Mass media played a major role in stirring up popular enthusiasm for U.S. intervention in 1898 in the war between Cuba and Spain. The political cartoon in Figure 6.12 fuses visual and verbal clichés in support of Congress's declaration of war against Spain made a few days previous. The cartoon is a visual play on the saying

◆ **Figure 6.12 The Duty of the Hour: To Save Her Not Only from Spain but from a Worse Fate**
Culver Pictures.

"out of the frying-pan, into the fire." In this image, the figure of a terrified, dark-skinned young woman carrying a tattered flag represents the national spirit of Cuba. How does this feminized national icon contrast with that of Columbia in Figure 6.11? How does the female figure emphasize what Keppler, like so many journalists, saw as America's moral obligation to intervene on Cuba's behalf?

QUESTIONS FOR ANALYSIS

1. How do the *Puck* stereotypes of immigrant women compare to Jacob Riis's photographs of immigrant girls and women in Figures 6.1–6.5?

2. How does the symbolic use of female figures in late nineteenth-century political cartoons (Figures 6.11 and 6.12) contrast with the depictions of women in cartoons meant to amuse (Figures 6.1–6.10)?

3. Do you think that the readers of *Puck* recognized the contrast between the depiction of women in the humorous and political cartoons? If so, how might they have reconciled these two different portraits?

4. How does the assumption that men should protect women function throughout these cartoons? Consider the stereotypes of immigrant women, the ridicule of native-born women entering public life, and the use of female representations to justify American imperial ambitions.

NOTES

1. Mentioned in Mei Nakano, *Japanese American Women: Three Generations, 1890–1990* (Berkeley: Mina Press, 1990). My version of her life differs on the basis of information provided by Professor Rumi Yasutake, Kobe University, author of *Transnational Women's Activism: The United States, Japan, and Japanese Immigrant Communities in California, 1859–1920* (New York: NYU Press, 2004).

2. Laura Jane Moore, "Lozen," Theda Perdue, ed., *Sifters: Native American Women's Lives* (New York: Oxford University Press, 2001), 93.

3. Mrs. A. Z. Paker, June 20, 1890, "The Ghost among the Lakota," http://www.pbs.org/weta/thewest/resources/archives/eight/gddescrp.htm (accessed June 28, 2004).

4. Nelson Miles to George Baird, November 20, 1891, Baird Collection, Western Americana Collection, Beinecke Library, Yale University.

5. The term is from Alvin M. Josephy, *500 Nations: An Illustrated History of North American Indians* (New York: Knopf, 1994), 430.

6. Carolyn J. Marr, "Assimilation through Education: Indian Boarding Schools in the Pacific Northwest," http://content.lib.washington.edu/aipnw/marr.html (accessed June 28, 2004).

7. "A Man Plants the Fields of His Wife," in Ruth Barnes Moynihan, Cynthia Russett, and Laurie Crumpacker, eds., *Second to None: A Documentary History of American Women* (Lincoln: University of Nebraska Press, 1993), 2: 82–83.

8. Linda Williams Reese, *Women of Oklahoma, 1890–1920* (Norman: University of Oklahoma Press, 1997), 152–53.

9. Diary of Lucy Hannah White Flake, excerpted in Joan M. Jensen, ed., *With These Hands: Women Working on the Land* (Old Westbury, NY: Feminist Press, 1981), 137–38.

10. Glenda Riley, *A Place to Grow: Women in the American West* (Arlington Heights: Harlan Davidson, 1992), 239.

11. Reese, *Women of Oklahoma*, 38.

12. Michael Lewis Goldberg, *An Army of Women: Gender and Politics in Gilded Age Kansas* (Baltimore: Johns Hopkins University Press, 1997), 40.

13. The term comes from Paula Petrik, *No Step Backward: Women and Family on the Rocky Mountain Mining Frontier, Helena, Montana, 1865–1900* (Helena: Montana Historical Society Press, 1987), 28.

14. Mother Mary Jones, *Autobiography of Mother Jones* (Chicago: C. H. Kerr, 1980), 204.

15. Elizabeth Jameson, "Imperfect Unions: Class and Gender in Cripple Creek, 1894–1904," in Milton Cantor and Bruce Laurie, eds., *Class, Sex, and the Woman Worker* (Westport: Greenwood Press, 1977), 171.

16. Joan Morrison and Charlotte Fox Zabusky, *American Mosaic: The Immigrant Experience in the Worlds of Those Who Lived It* (New York: E. P. Dutton, 1980), 9.

17. Ibid., 84–85.

18. Linda Mack Schloff, *"And Prairie Dogs Weren't Kosher": Jewish Women in the Upper Midwest Since 1855* (St. Paul: Minnesota Historical Society Press, 1996), 28.

19. Edith Abbott, *Immigration: Select Documents and Case Records* (Chicago: University of Chicago Press, 1924), 719.

20. Him Mark Lai, Genny Lim, and Judy Yung, *Island: Poetry and History of Chinese Immigrants on Angel Island, 1910–1940* (San Francisco: San Francisco Study Center, 1980), 74.

21. Jane Addams, *Twenty Years at Hull-House* (1910; repr., New York: New American Library, 1961), 110–11.

22. Carrie Chapman Catt, as quoted in Aileen Kraditor, *Ideas of the Woman Suffrage Movement, 1890–1920* (New York: Columbia University Press, 1965), 128.

23. Theodore Roosevelt, introduction to Mrs. John Van Vorst and Marie Van Vorst, *The Woman Who Toils: Being the Experiences of Two Ladies as Factory Girls* (New York: Doubleday, Page & Co., 1903), vii.

24. Sadie Frowne, "A Sweatshop Girl's Story," *The Independent* 54 (September 25, 1902): 2281.

25. Anzia Yezierska, *Bread Givers* (New York: George Brazillier, 1975), 135.

26. Addams, *Twenty Years at Hull-House*, ch.11, p. 182.

27. Ellen Carol Dubois, *The Elizabeth Cady Stanton–Susan B. Anthony Reader: Correspondence, Writings, Speeches*, rev. ed. (Boston: Northeastern University Press, 1992), 205.

28. Julie Roy Jeffrey, "Women in the Southern Farmers' Alliance: A Reconstruction of the Role and Status of Women in the Late Nineteenth-Century South," *Feminist Studies* 3:1/2 (1975): 72.

29. Mary Elizabeth Lease, quoted in Jensen, *With These Hands*, 157–58.

30. Susan B. Anthony and Ida H. Harper, eds., *History of Woman Suffrage* (Rochester, NY: Susan B. Anthony, 1902), 4:519.

31. Jensen, *With These Hands*, 147.

32. Ida H. Harper, ed., *History of Woman Suffrage* (New York: National American Woman Suffrage Association, 1922), 5:518.

33. Anthony and Harper, *History of Woman Suffrage*, 4:647.

34. "Women Keep Up Courage," *San Francisco Chronicle*, November 5, 1896. Thanks to Ann Gordon.

35. Marion K. Barthelme, ed., *Women in the Texas Populist Movement: Letters to the Southern Mercury* (College Station: Texas A & M Press, 1997), 111.

36. Rosa Cavalleri, in Marie Hall Ets, *Rosa: The Story of an Italian Immigrant* (Minneapolis: University of Minnesota Press, 1970), 210–12, quoted in Moynihan et al., *Second to None*, 2:81.

37. Emma Goldman, *Living My Life*, ed. Richard and Anna Maria Drinnon (New York: New American Library, 1977), 122.

38. Almont Lindsey, *The Pullman Strike: The Story of a Unique Experiment and of a Great Labor Upheaval* (Chicago: University of Chicago Press, 1942), 129.

39. Kathryn Kish Sklar, *Florence Kelley and the Nation's Work* (New Haven: Yale University Press, 1995), 272.

40. Addams, *Twenty Years at Hull-House*, 235.

41. Alice Miller, "Hull House," *The Charities* (February 1892): 167–73, clipping in *Hull House Scrapbook 1.*

42. Quoted in Sklar, *Florence Kelley,* 215.

43. Ibid., 283.

44. Frances Willard, *The Autobiography of an American Woman, Glimpses of Fifty Years* (Chicago: Woman's Temperance Publishing Association, 1892), 431.

45. Kristin Hoganson, *Fighting for American Manhood: How Gender Politics Provoked the Spanish-American and Philippine-American Wars* (New Haven: Yale University Press, 1998), 11.

46. Quoted in Allen Davis, *An American Heroine: The Life and Legend of Jane Addams* (New York: Oxford University Press, 1973), 140.

47. *The Woman's Journal,* February 11, 1899.

48. Allison Sneider, "Reconstruction, Expansion and Empire: The U.S. Woman Suffrage Movement and the Re-making of the National Political Community" (PhD diss., UCLA, 1999), 172.

49. Susan La Flesche, "My Childhood and Womanhood," *Southern Workman,* July 15, 1886, 78.

50. Quoted in Woloch, *Early American Women,* 304.

51. Jacob A. Riis, *How the Other Half Lives: Studies among the Tenements of New York,* ed. David Leviatin (Boston: Bedford/St. Martin's, 1996), 61.

52. Ibid., 92.

53. Ibid., 91.

54. Ibid., 95.

55. Ibid., 129.

56. Ibid., 141.

57. Ibid., 140.

58. Ibid., 139.

59. Jacob A. Riis, *The Children of the Poor* (New York: Scribner's Sons, 1892), 82.

60. Jacob A. Riis, *The Making of an American* (New York: Macmillan, 1929), 150.

61. Riis, *Children of the Poor,* 80.

SUGGESTED REFERENCES

Women and Western Settlement   For an overall perspective on the consolidation of the West through the eyes of diverse groups of women, see the two excellent anthologies compiled by Susan Armitage and Elizabeth Jameson: *The Woman's West* (1987) and *Writing the Range: Race, Class, and Culture in the Women's West* (1997). Among many useful other books on this subject, see Glenda Riley, *A Place to Grow: Women in the American West* (1992); Ruth B. Moynihan, Susan Armitage, and Christiane Fischer Dichamp, eds., *So Much to Be Done: Women Settlers on the Mining and*

Ranching Frontier (1990); and Julie Roy Jeffrey, *Frontier Women: The Trans-Mississippi West, 1840–1880* (1979). Linda Williams Reese, *Women of Oklahoma, 1890–1920* (1997), focuses on a single, interesting state. For two excellent, local studies of women in the Wild West, see Marion Goldman, *Gold Diggers and Silver Miners: Prostitution and Social Life on the Comstock Lode* (1968), and Elizabeth Jameson, *All That Glitters: Class Conflict and Community in Cripple Creek* (1998).

Two recent collections focus on Native American women in the West and cover a wide range of experiences: Theda Perdue, ed., *Sifters: Native American Women's Lives* (2001), and Nancy Shoemaker, ed., *Negotiators of Change: Historical Perspectives on Native American Women* (1995). On the La Flesche sisters, see Norma Kidd, *Iron Eye's Family: The Children of Joseph La Flesche* (1969), and Benson Tong, *Susan La Flesche Picotte, MD: Omaha Indian Leader and Reformer* (1994). Helen Hunt Jackson's 1881 expose, *A Century of Dishonor,* is still compelling. Valerie Mathes, *Helen Hunt Jackson and Her Indian Reform Legacy* (1997), also covers the formation of the Woman's National Indian Association.

On Mexican American women in the Southwest before the major waves of immigration in the twentieth century, see Sarah Deutsch, *No Separate Refuge: Culture, Class, and Gender on the Anglo-Hispanic Frontier in the Overland Trail* (1987), and Lisbeth Haas, *Conquests and Historical Identities in California, 1769–1836* (1995). Also, Linda Gordon's *The Great Arizona Orphan Abduction* (1999) examines ethnic and religious conflicts between Anglo and Hispanic women in southern Arizona.

Immigrant Women   The best general study on women and immigration is Donna Gabaccia, *The Other Side: Women, Gender, and Immigrant Life in the U.S., 1820–1990* (1994). Other general studies, concentrating mostly on European immigrants, include Katrina Irving, *Immigrant Mothers: Narratives of Race and Maternity, 1890–1925* (2000); Kristine Leach, *In Search of a Common Ground: Nineteenth and Twentieth Century Immigrant Women in America* (1995); and Doris Weatherford, *Foreign and Female: Immigrant Women in America, 1840–1930* (1986).

For studies of women from particular groups, see the comparison of Italians and Eastern European Jews in Elizabeth Ewen, *Immigrant Women in the Land of Dollars: Life and Culture on the Lower East Side, 1890–1925* (1985), and Judith E. Smith, *Family Connections: A History of Italian and Jewish Immigrant Lives in Providence, Rhode Island, 1900–1940* (1985). Other studies of Jews include Susan Glenn, *Daughters of the Shtetl: Life and Labor in the Immigrant Generation* (1990), and Barbara Schreier, *Becoming American Women: Clothing and the American Jewish Experience* (1994). Linda Mack Schloff offers an unusual perspective in *"And Prairie Dogs Weren't Kosher": Jewish Women in the Upper Midwest since 1855* (1996). On Italian immigrant women, see Miriam Cohen, *Workshop to Office: Two Generations of Italian Women in New York City, 1900–1950* (1992), and Virginia Yans McLaughlin, *Family Community: Italian Immigrants in Buffalo, 1880–1930* (1977). Hasia Diner considers Irish immigrant women in *Erin's Daughters in America: Irish Immigrant Women in the Nineteenth Century* (1983). Suzanne Sinke has researched an understudied group in *Dutch Immigrant Women in the United States* (2002).

For non-European immigrants, see *Chinese Women of America: A Pictorial History* (1986), *Unbound Feet: A Social History of Chinese Women in San Francisco* (1995), and *Unbound Voices: A Documentary History of Chinese Women in San Francisco* (1999), all by Judith Yung. See also Lucy Salyer, *Laws Harsh as Tigers: Chinese Immigrants and the Shaping of Modern Immigration Law* (1995). For Japanese women immigrants, see Mei Nakano, *Japanese American Women: Three Generations 1890–1990* (1990), and Evelyn Nakano Glenn, *Issei, Nisei, War Bride: Three Generations of Japanese American Women in Domestic Service* (1986). On Mexican immigrant women, see Vicki Ruiz, *From Out of the Shadows: Mexican Women in Twentieth-Century America* (1998).

Women Reformers   On the history of women and the Populist revolt, see Rebecca Edwards, *Angels in the Machinery: Gender in American Party Politics from the Civil War to the Progressive Era* (1997), and Michael Lewis Goldberg, *An Army of Women: Gender and Politics in Gilded Age Kansas* (1997). For the western suffrage movement that Populism reinvigorated, see Rebecca Mead, *How the Vote Was Won: Woman Suffrage in the Western United States, 1868–1914* (2004). For southern Populism, see Marion K. Barthelme, ed., *Women in the Texas Populist Movement: Letters to the Southern Mercury* (1997), and Julie Roy Jeffrey, "Women in the Southern Farmers' Alliance: A Reconstruction of the Role and Status of Women in the Late Nineteenth-Century South," *Feminist Studies* 3:1/2 (1975): 72–91.

On the Pullman strike from a women's perspective, see Janice Reiff, "A Modern Lear and His Daughters: Gender in the Model Town of Pullman," *Journal of Social History* 23 (1997): 316–41. For the leadership of Hull House women in this period, see Victoria Bissell Brown, *The Education of Jane Addams* (2004), and Kathryn Kish Sklar, *Florence Kelley and the Nation's Work* (1995). The best general study of settlement houses remains Allen F. Davis, *Spearheads for Reform: The Social Settlements and the Progressive Movement, 1890–1914* (1967). Kathryn Sklar, "Hull House in the 1890s: A Community of Women Reformers," *Signs* 10 (1985): 658–77, considers the personal dimension of Hull House for its women residents. Joan Waugh, *Unsentimental Reformer: The Life of Josephine Shaw Lowell* (1994), examines a leading woman reformer in New York in the 1893 depression. Elizabeth Lasch-Quinn considers racism and racial segregation in the settlement house movement in *Black Neighbors: Race and the Limits of Reform in the American Settlement House Movement, 1890–1945* (1993).

On the female missionary contribution, see Patricia Hill, *The World Their Household: The American Woman's Foreign Mission Movement and Cultural Transformation, 1870–1920* (1985); Patricia Grimshaw, *Paths of Duty: American Missionary Wives in Nineteenth-Century Hawaii* (1987); and Ian Tyrrell, *Woman's World/ Woman's Empire: The Woman's Christian Temperance Union in International Perspective, 1880–1930* (1991). On gender and late nineteenth-century imperialism, see Kristin Hoganson, *Fighting for American Manhood: How Gender Politics Provoked the Spanish American and Philippine-American Wars* (1998); Gail Bederman, *Manliness and Civilization: A Cultural History of Gender and Race in the United States, 1880–1917* (1995); Allison Sneider, "Woman Suffrage in Congress: American Expansion and the Politics of Federalism, 1870–1890," in Jean Baker, ed., *Votes for Women: The Struggle for Suffrage Revisited* (2002); and Laura Wexler, *Tender Violence: Domestic Visions in an Age of U.S. Imperialism* (2000).

Selected Web Sites

The Web site New Perspectives on the West has been assembled in connection with the Public Television documentary series *The West*: <**pbs.org/weta/thewest**>. The Smithsonian Institution provides a Web site with comprehensive sources on Native American Society and Culture: <**si.edu/resource/faq/nmai/start.htm**>. An excellent collection of images of late nineteenth-century Native American women is found at <**photoswest.org/exhib/gallery4/leadin.htm**>. For American settlers on the Great Plains, consult the megasite Midwest Women's History Sources, <**library.wisc.edu/libraries/WomensStudies/midwhist.htm**>.

The Digital History Web site includes a section on Ethnic America: <**digitalhistory.uh.edu/historyonline/ethnic_am.cfm**>. Individual immigrant groups can be studied separately: see, for instance, The Jewish Women's Archives at <**jwa.org**>, and a National Park Service site on Japanese immigration, <**cr.nps.gov/history/online_books/5views/5views4a.htm**>.

The 1890s is well represented on the Internet: <**boondocksnet.com/**>, for example, is exceptionally rich, with a focus on imperialism. The University of Illinois at Chicago Circle, which now owns the buildings of Hull House, offers an online exhibition called Hull House and Its Neighborhood at <**uic.edu/jaddams/hull/urbanexp/contents.htm**>. The Struggle for Women's Suffrage in the West is the subject of <**autry-museum.org/explore/exhibits/suffrage/**>. The 1893 Columbian World's Exposition is examined on <**chicagohs.org/history/expo.html**>. Emma Goldman is amply covered at <**sunsite.berkeley.edu/Goldman/**>.

7

Power and Politics

WOMEN IN THE
PROGRESSIVE ERA, 1900–1920

THE DAY AFTER NEW YEAR'S DAY, 1907, SEVERAL dozen women met in New York City determined to find a new way to get the drive for woman suffrage on to a winning path. Their leader, Harriot Stanton Blatch, had impeccable credentials for the task. She was the daughter of the nineteenth-century leader of the demand for political equality, Elizabeth Cady Stanton. At age fifty-one, she was also a veteran of numerous reform campaigns organized by civic-minded and politically savvy women, with goals ranging from cleaning up municipal political corruption to improving the wages and working conditions of female workers. What most distinguished these women from previous generations of suffragists was their unusual class composition. Woman suffrage had historically been a middle-class movement, but at this meeting wage earning women, most of them trade union activists, were joining with leisure-class college graduates, professionals, and social reformers. Still, no woman of color was invited to attend.

A modernized, cross-class movement for votes for women was one aspect of Progressivism, a period of intense reform activism from the late 1890s to the years just after the conclusion of the First World War in 1918. The Progressive era profoundly altered the role of government in American life. During these years, American liberalism, which had traditionally regarded government as a threat to citizens' rights, now came to embrace government as the ultimate guarantor of public welfare. Catalyzed by the devastating social consequences of industrial capitalism, the activists of this period battled for new labor laws and social welfare policies, arguing that the fate of society's most impoverished sector was linked to the general national welfare. Many socially conscious Americans, jolted by the crises of the 1890s, were ready to join in this new spirit of public stewardship.

Women played a leading role during the Progressive period. As one historian writes, "women filled the progressive landscape."[1] There is considerable irony in the public influence and power women wielded in these years, because most women would not become fully enfranchised until 1920, in the aftermath of World War I. But they were widely mobilized, organized, and ambitious. Indeed, the victory of votes for women was as much a result as a cause of women's political mobilization in the Progressive era. Earlier Gilded Age developments such as the steady increase of the female labor force, the growth of college education among women, and the spread of women's organizations laid the basis for women's dramatic rush into the public arena in the Progressive era.

Around the edges of the broad-based, mass mobilization that was Progressive era suffragism was a smaller, more daring, and more modern approach to women's emancipation for which a new name was invented, "feminism." While the achievement of the larger movement was to complete the campaign for equal political rights begun before the Civil War, early twentieth-century feminism foreshadowed the women's liberation movement of the 1960s.

THE FEMALE LABOR FORCE

A good place to start to examine dramatic changes in women's public lives in the Progressive era is a portrait of women workers. While the more obvious developments for women in this period were political, the underlying changes were economic, as the female labor force changed significantly.

The presence of large numbers of women in the workforce signaled the beginning of true modernity in the

1913	Alice Paul and Lucy Burns form the Congressional Union
1913	Ida B. Wells-Barnett organizes first all-black suffrage club, in Chicago
1914	"What Is Feminism?" mass meeting in New York City
1914	World War I begins in Europe
1914-1919	Height of African American "Great Migration"
1915	Woman's Peace Party formed
1915	Campaigns for woman suffrage fail in Massachusetts, New York, New Jersey, and Pennsylvania
1915	Jane Addams chairs International Council of Women peace meeting in The Hague
1915	Women's International League for Peace and Freedom founded
1916	Congressional Union becomes National Woman's Party (NWP)
1916	Margaret Sanger opens birth control clinic in Brooklyn
1917	Second New York referendum enfranchises women
1917	United States enters World War I; Montana congresswoman Jeannette Rankin votes against declaration of war
1917	Bolshevik Revolution ends Russian participation in war
1917	Women's Council for National Defense established
1917	NWP members begin to picket the White House
1917-1919	Urban race riots from St. Louis to Chicago
1918	Supreme Court overturns Keating-Owen Act limiting child labor
1918	Armistice ends World War I
1919	Eighteenth Amendment (Prohibition) ratified
1920	Federal Woman's Bureau established
1920	Nineteenth Amendment (woman suffrage) ratified

female role. Long a symbol of women's victimhood, the working woman came to stand in these years for women's active presence in the larger world. The visibility and forcefulness of women workers were particularly manifest through a series of spectacular strikes in the garment and textile industries, the first such sustained working women's movement since the antebellum years. Middle- and upper-class reformers in these years made the concerns of working women central to their activities.

Continuity and Change for Women Wage Earners

At the end of the nineteenth century, a minority of the labor force was female—18.3 percent in 1900—but this figure was rising and would reach 21.4 percent in 1920.[2] More than half of this female working population was foreign-born and/or nonwhite. The wage rate for women workers was very low: in 1900, the average woman worker made about half of what the average male worker earned.[3] This disparity reflected the fact that men and women largely worked in different occupations and distinct industries, a highly structured sexual division of labor that limited working women's options even as it shaped the American labor force. Domestic service was the largest category of female employment, with manufacturing steadily gaining. The average working woman was young and unmarried. Mothers and wives who worked outside the home for wages were few, although among African Americans they constituted a significant portion of women workers.

Against this general portrait, new areas of women's paid work were beginning to emerge in the early twentieth century. Clerical work, once entirely male and a form of apprenticeship in the business world, was a rapidly growing and desirable field for women. The work was clean and safe and the wages regular. The demand for clerical workers to coordinate the movement of resources, finished goods, and finances through an increasingly complex national economy was expanding. In the words of a 1929 labor survey, office work held the promise of "opportunity . . . for a rise in business success so highly and universally esteemed among us."[4] Yet just as clerical work was being feminized, it was becoming mechanized and routinized, and thus losing its capacity for upward mobility. In the offices of mail order houses, banks, insurance companies, and large corporations, the labor of secretaries and typists was beginning to look like factory labor, at times even including the use of the piece-rate form of payment.

Women were also gaining greater entry into various professional fields. The gradual opening up of professional opportunities for women constituted a partial solution to the vocational dilemma that Jane Addams's generation of college graduates had confronted (see Chapter 6). Overall, the professional sector comprised only 12 percent of the female labor force as of 1920, but it played a major role in changing society's view of paid labor for women.[5] Throughout the nineteenth century, paid labor had been regarded as an unfortunate necessity for women in the bottom strata of society. Women professional workers represented a different aspect of women's paid labor. They expected personal independence and upward mobility from their jobs, and they worked out of choice more than need. As such, they prepared the way for a new, more positive attitude toward paid labor for women.

The one male-dominated professional field in which women had made significant gains by the end of the nineteenth century was medicine, in which women were 5.5 percent of the profession by 1900. The legal profession—notoriously hostile to women—was a very different matter (compare Figures 5.6, p. 325, and 6.9, p. 396). One of the most famous Supreme Court decisions of the nineteenth century, *Bradwell v. Illinois* (1873), concerned the claim of Myra Bradwell to be admitted to the Illinois bar on the basis of the Fourteenth Amendment's guarantee of equal privilege and immunities. She had easily passed the bar examination but was disallowed from practicing law on the basis of her gender. "The harmony, not to say the identity, of interests and views which belong, or should belong, to the family institution is repugnant to the idea for a woman adopting a distinct and independent career from that of her husband," Justice Joseph B. Bradley declared in ruling against Bradwell.

But as women moved energetically into other aspects of public life, the number of women lawyers began to climb. In 1900, less than 600 women were practicing law in the United States; by 1920, this figure had tripled. Legal training was ceasing to be a form of apprenticeship, shifting instead to specialized legal colleges. Inez Milholland, one of the most glamorous figures in the American suffrage movement, applied to Harvard Law School after she graduated from Vassar in 1909 but was rejected. (Harvard Law did not admit its first woman until 1953.) Instead, she attended New York University Law School, where she specialized in labor, criminal, and divorce law.

In part because they represented a more modern generation of women than the first women doctors, in part because husbands and wives could practice law together, women lawyers were particularly interested in the issue of women balancing paid work and married life. In 1919, a group of New York City women lawyers were polled on their opinions about "the paradox of vocation and marriage" for women. The majority responded that women could continue professional life after marriage but should make family life a priority and put aside their profession while their children were small. A small minority believed that, with supportive husbands and enough paid household servants, it was possible to rear children and practice their professions simultaneously.[6] Such a solution was available only to middle-class women who could hire maids and nannies. Even so, these professional women were beginning to grapple with the problem that would affect all working women later in the twentieth century (see Chapter 10).

More women found professional opportunities in the rise of new "female professions" where they did not have to break through a male monopoly. In these years, the profession of social work began to evolve out of the volunteer labor of women reformers in settlement houses. Practitioners were eager to upgrade traditional forms of benevolence by applying new social science methods. Sophonsiba Breckinridge, a lawyer and the first American woman to receive a PhD in political science, convinced the University of Chicago to establish a Graduate School of

Social Service Administration. By 1920, there were thirty thousand trained social workers, the majority of them women.

Nursing and teaching were the largest professions dominated by women. Since the Civil War, nursing had been shifting from a form of domestic service to a profession. Between 1900 and 1910, there was a tenfold increase in the number of professionally trained nurses. Many professional nurses worked as public health missionaries, going into immigrant homes to teach sanitation methods and to investigate epidemic disease. Teaching, a woman's occupation at the primary level since the 1830s, was also undergoing changes. In the Progressive era, teachers sought to upgrade their profession, ridding it both of intrusive moral constraints and political interference in hiring. Teacher training was moving from the two-year high school level institutions of the late nineteenth century to four-year, truly collegiate institutions (see Figure 5.5, p. 323). Women pioneered the unionization of teachers, another approach to shielding the profession from external control. In Chicago, Mary Haley, a second-generation Irish American, organized a powerful teachers' union, which removed control of appointments from local politicians.

African American women were also part of this move to professionalization, although doing so in the era of Jim Crow presented obstacles. The growing practice of segregation meant that African Americans were excluded from the white-run training programs and occupational associations that structured professions. In the field of nursing, black women responded by establishing their own schools and professional association, the National Association of Colored Graduate Nurses, formed in 1908. Ironically, Jim Crow provided opportunities for African American professional women in the separate institutions that served black communities, where they worked as librarians, physicians, and especially as teachers. Largely excluded from the National Educational Association, black women teachers formed their own state-level teachers' organizations, from which they challenged racial discrimination in teachers' salaries.

Organizing Women Workers: The Women's Trade Union League

Despite the expansion of working opportunities for women in the clerical and professional strata, industrial workers, especially young immigrants, were considered the most representative working women of the Progressive era. Constituting 25 percent of the female labor force, they were a crucial factor in the tremendously productive power of the American economy and achieved an unprecedented level of public visibility. Many of the themes of the era—women's public prominence, their leadership of liberal causes, and their pursuit of independent lives—marked the women's labor movement of the Progressive period.

Working women received little assistance from the established trade union movement. Ever since the demise of the Knights of Labor in the late 1880s, the male-dominated American Federation of Labor (AFL) had provided the leadership of the trade union movement (see Chapter 5). The AFL regarded women wage earners not as potential union recruits but either as underpaid threats to their members' jobs or as pitiful victims of capitalist greed. If women were to improve their wages and working conditions through labor organization, they were going to have to find assistance from allies of gender, not of class.

The Women's Trade Union League (WTUL) was formed in 1903 to meet this need. Modeled after a British organization of the same name, the goal of the WTUL was to effect a reconciliation between women workers and the organized labor movement. It did so with the tacit permission of the AFL, the leaders of which were only too relieved to subcontract out the burden of organizing women workers. Membership was open to all committed to the labor organization of women, regardless of class or of union membership. The WTUL also aimed "to develop leadership among the women workers, inspiring them with a sense of personal responsibility for the conditions under which they work."[7]

One of the most remarkable aspects of this organization was that it was a coalition of women trade union activists and leisure-class women (known as "allies"), primarily drawn from the settlement house movement. Mary Kenney O'Sullivan, who had begun her career in Chicago as a skilled bookbinder and had served as the AFL's first official female organizer, was one of its working-class founders (see Chapter 5). Another was Leonora O'Reilly, a garment worker from New York City with connections to the Henry Street Settlement. O'Reilly recruited two wealthy sisters also from New York City, Mary Dreier and Margaret Dreier Robins, who provided most of the financial resources for the WTUL throughout the 1910s. Major chapters were formed in Boston, New York City, and Chicago, and smaller groups in Milwaukee, St. Louis, Kansas City, Philadelphia, and San Francisco.

The WTUL's interclass collaboration struck a very different note from the antagonistic class relations between leisured and wage earning women in the Gilded Age. Nonetheless, relations in the WTUL among women of different classes were

◆ **Women's Trade Union League Emblem**

The Women's Trade Union League was established at a convention of the American Federation of Labor in 1903. The two female images on its insignia represent the bond between the mother and the woman worker, the one caring, the other strong. The WTUL accepted the primacy of women's maternal obligations but recognized the reality of women's labor involvement. Thus one of the defining goals framed by their clasped hands: to guard the home. The other two objectives were a maximum of eight working hours a day for women and a wage sufficient to allow a woman to support herself. *Library of Congress, LC-DIG-ppmsca-02954.*

not smooth. Leonora O'Reilly was concerned that the WTUL would become a "charity" organization in which middle-class women approached workers with "the attitudes of a lady with something to give her sister."[8] Despite the organization's commitment to developing working-class women's leadership abilities, formal control remained in the hands of leisure-class women until 1922, when Maud Swartz, a typesetter, took over as national president. Still, the WTUL was unique in the period for its cross-class commitment to workers' empowerment.

While the WTUL worked hard on behalf of white and immigrant working-class women, its record was weak when it came to black women workers. Black workers, even more than white working women, faced hostility from the white men who led the American labor movement. They were not admitted into trade unions in this period, were hired at lower wages than white workers, and were employed as strike breakers. The WTUL's association with the organized labor movement led it to go along with the AFL's racist antagonism to black workers throughout its early years.

Initially focused on trade union organization for working women, after World War I the organization shifted its emphasis to the passage of state maximum workday hours and minimum wage laws for working women. The first director of the Women's Bureau of the Department of Labor, established in 1920, was Chicago WTUL member and shoe worker Mary Anderson. Later, Rose Schneiderman, who became the third president of the WTUL in 1927 and labored for the league throughout her career, helped to shape New Deal policy toward working women and working families (see Chapter 8).

The Rising of the Women

The WTUL came of age during a wave of early twentieth-century strikes that put the modern wage earning woman on the labor history map. The most famous of these took place over the winter of 1909–10 in New York City in the shirtwaist (blouse) industry. The strike began in late summer 1909, when Local 25 of the International Ladies Garment Workers Union (ILGWU), a small male-dominated organization, struck several manufacturers. Women walked the picket lines, protesting declining piece rates, excessive charges for materials, fines for lateness, and the practice of allowing subcontractors to hire and pay workers at dramatically different rates. Day after day, the picketers, most of them young Jewish and Italian women, were harassed by thugs hired by their bosses, arrested by police, and fined and jailed by local magistrates. Then they turned to the WTUL. When leisure-class allies joined the picket line, they were subjected to the same disrespectful treatment as the striking workers, which made the newspapers take notice. (See Visual Sources: Parades, Picketing, and Power: Women in Public Space, pp. 447–53.)

The large clothing manufacturers were able to hold out against the workers by sending their unfinished garments to smaller shops that the ILGWU was not targeting. Facing sure defeat, the union considered calling a general strike of the entire New York City shirtwaist industry. This would have been a daring strategy under any conditions, but in an industry in which the great majority of the workers were teenage immigrant girls who were not considered disciplined enough to sustain a long strike, it was even more so. Nonetheless, on November 22, 1909, more than fifteen thousand shirtwaist workers showed up at a mass meeting called by Local 25 to discuss how to proceed against the manufacturers. As male labor leaders and leisure-class WTUL members on the stage hesitated to speak, seventeen-year-old shirtwaist maker Clara Lemlich stood up from the floor and, speaking in Yiddish, galvanized the audience to walk off their jobs.

The next day, between twenty and thirty thousand workers, two-thirds of them Eastern European Jews, were on strike. The WTUL provided the resources—strike pay, publicity, legal support—to keep the strike going. Some of the wealthiest women in New York City, including Ann Morgan, daughter of banking magnate J. P. Morgan, publicly endorsed the cause of the workers. The presence and commitment of young women on the picket line during the winter of 1909–10 challenged the traditional image of women wage earners as passive victims. Even AFL president Samuel Gompers was forced to concede that the strike demonstrated "the extent to which women were taking up with industrial life, their consequent tendency to stand together in the struggle to protect their common interests as wage earners, . . . and the capacity of women as strikers to suffer, to do, and to dare in support of their rights."[9]

After almost three months, the shirtwaist strike was settled. Many, but not all, of the manufacturers agreed to a fifty-two hour work week, no more special charges or fines, more worker involvement in setting wages, and even paid holidays. But they would not allow the ILGWU to represent the workers in future negotiations. Although control remained with the manufacturers, the strike turned the ILGWU into a much more powerful labor organization. Individual working-class women, including Clara Lemlich and Rose Schneiderman, embarked on a lifetime of labor activism.

A tragic epilogue to the shirtwaist strike took place a little over a year later, highlighting why union recognition was so important to the workers. The Triangle Shirtwaist Company had begun locking the doors after the workers arrived, to keep union organizers out and workers in. On March 25, 1911, a fire broke out on the tenth floor. Workers who ran down the stairs found that they were locked inside the building. Desperately they ran up to the roof. Some were able to escape, but 146 workers, more than a quarter of Triangle's employees, fell or jumped to their deaths. At a mass funeral held a few days later, Schneiderman delivered a bitter eulogy: "This is not the first time girls have been burned alive in this city. . . . Every year thousands of us are maimed. The life of men and women is so cheap and property is so sacred. There are so many of us for one job it matters little if 143 [sic] of us are burned to death."[10]

In 1912, labor militancy broke out again in the textile factories of Lawrence, Massachusetts. Cotton, linen, and wool production was still centered in New England, as at the start of the industrial revolution. As in the garment industry, textile workers were overwhelmingly immigrant, but the textile industry employed entire families, including children. Textile workers labored long hours for very low

THE NEW YORK HERALD.

****C   NEW YORK, SUNDAY, MARCH 26, 1911.—112 PAGES.— BY THE NEW YORK HERALD COMPANY.   PRICE FIVE CENTS.

ONE HUNDRED AND FIFTY PERISH IN FACTORY FIRE; WOMEN AND GIRLS, TRAPPED IN TEN STORY BUILDING, LOST IN FLAMES OR HURL THEMSELVES TO DEATH

IDENTIFYING BODIES OF THOSE WHO JUMPED TO THE SIDEWALK.

◆ **Triangle Shirtwaist Fire**
The actual number of dead was 146. This gruesome newspaper photograph shows the broken bodies of young women who jumped to escape the fire because the doors were locked from the outside and the fire escapes pulled away from the building. A policeman leans over to identify and tag the victims. To the right is the building that housed the Triangle Shirtwaist Company, site of both the 1909–1910 strike and the 1911 fire. As Rose Schneiderman predicted, it survived long after the workers died. Currently, it is owned by New York University. No one was ever convicted of liability for the tragedy. New York Herald, *March 26, 1911.*

wages. Much of the industry was located in company towns, where employers exerted total control and workers could find no local allies. When a Massachusetts law established a maximum of fifty-four working hours per week, Lawrence manufacturers cut the wages of their workers proportionally, and the workers struck.

Because the Lawrence workers were all immigrants and mostly unskilled, the AFL was not interested in their plight. Instead, the workers turned to the Industrial Workers of the World (IWW), a radical socialist labor organization. One of the organization's most famous leaders was twenty-two-year-old Elizabeth Gurley Flynn, a single mother and an accomplished organizer and public speaker. In Lawrence, Gurley Flynn encouraged greater involvement among Italian women, whose enthusiasm for the struggle gave the lie to their reputation as cloistered and conservative peasants. A few weeks into the strike, a young Italian woman striker,

Anna Lapizza, was shot and killed. Although members of the WTUL were eager to help in the Lawrence strike, the AFL's determination to stay clear of its rival, the IWW, made that impossible. Several founding members, including Mary Kenney O'Sullivan, quit in disgust.

The turning point in the strike involved the children of the town's workers. As police and militia attacks increased, Gurley Flynn decided it was time to relocate the younger children in the homes of out-of-town sympathizers. A group of children on their way to Philadelphia were beaten by Lawrence police, and mothers were imprisoned for "neglect" by local courts. Nationwide outrage was so great that the employers were forced to agree to the strikers' demands for a fifty-four-hour week and wage increases as high as 25 percent (see Figure 7.3, p. 449). However, unlike the AFL, the IWW was not interested in a permanent presence in Lawrence and moved on to the next battle. This fact and the very magnitude of the Lawrence workers' victory contributed to the shift of much of the textile industry from New England to the South, in search of a more docile workforce.

The exceptional dedication and militancy of the women of the New York and Lawrence strikes—and other labor conflicts of this period in Paterson, New Jersey, Chicago, and Atlanta—helped to transform the popular image of working women. No longer dependent on others to defend and protect them, they were now appreciated for the ability to fight their own battles. By the beginning of World War I, the number of women in trade unions had quadrupled. Even so, women remained a minority of the labor movement and had many obstacles—male disinterest, middle-class condescension, and their own timidity—to overcome.

THE FEMALE DOMINION

The Women's Trade Union League was connected to what one historian has named the "female dominion," part of the early twentieth-century Progressive reform movement. Middle- and upper-class white women created a network of reform organizations, became active in partisan politics, and lobbied for legislation to benefit poor women and children. Largely excluded from those groups, African American women created their own institutions that promoted social welfare and self-help in their communities. Although black women faced obstacles that were unknown to white reformers, both groups demonstrated a strong commitment to women's involvement in the dramatic political changes of the early twentieth century.

Public Housekeeping

Female social reformers frequently drew on the image of public housekeeping to describe women's Progressive era activism. "City housekeeping has failed partly because women, the traditional housekeepers, have not been consulted as to its multiform activities . . . ," explained settlement house pioneer Jane Addams in

1906 of the social welfare work that women were doing in Chicago. "The very multifariousness and complexity of a city government demand the help of minds accustomed to . . . a sense of responsibility for the cleanliness and comfort of other people."[11] Women's traditional responsibilities for family and children were used to justify their dramatic move into public life and social policy. What once could be accomplished from within the home, it was argued, now required that women become leaders in the public realm.

Women's public housekeeping took many forms. Despite their disfranchisement, women organized against political corruption and for reform political candidates. In 1908–1909, women worked to drive out corrupt machine politics and install reform mayors in Los Angeles and San Francisco. They worked to improve slum housing and to establish public amenities in Boston and New York. The Civic Club of Charleston, South Carolina, established playgrounds and then convinced the city council to take them over. Many public libraries throughout the United States were founded by local women's clubs. Women were involved in the campaign to set health standards for food, especially for the notoriously impure milk supply, a particular threat to infants whose working mothers could not breast-feed. In Portland, Oregon, organized groups of women were crucial in the "pure milk war" waged by civic groups to regulate standards in the dairy industry. Women played a major role in the establishment of special juvenile and family courts, first initiated in Chicago in 1899. Activist and budding historian Mary Beard chronicled the breadth and depth of this involvement in urban politics in her 1915 book, *Woman's Work in Municipalities* (see box, "Municipal Housekeeping").

These public housekeepers worked through existing national organizations such as the Woman's Christian Temperance Union and the General Federation of Women's Clubs and its state affiliates. But they also formed new, more focused groups. Of these, the most important was the National Consumers' League (NCL), formed in 1899 in New York City by Florence Kelley, and later expanded to chapters around the country. The NCL undertook a range of reform efforts, concentrating on working conditions for women and children.

Recent historians have developed the term "maternalism" to characterize the ideological core of Progressive era women's public reform concerns.[12] Maternalist thinking had two parts. First, virtually all social and economic issues having to do with women were viewed through their maternal capacity. Every sort of program advanced on women's behalf, even those having to do with women's wage labor, was justified on the grounds that society needed to protect motherhood. Second, the women who designed and advocated for these policies conceived of their own public involvement through the lens of motherhood. These dual meanings obscured the different ways that the norm of motherhood was applied to what were essentially two different classes of women. The policy formulators legitimated themselves in terms of the power of active maternal concern, wielded from within the public arena, but viewed the beneficiaries of their policies as dependent and homebound mothers in need of protection. Thus, maternal power and maternal need were separated between two different classes, rather than understood as linked and interdependent.

MARY BEARD
Municipal Housekeeping

Mary Ritter Beard (1876–1958) was deeply involved in many aspects of the Progressive era women's movement, from the Women's Trade Union League to the New York suffrage movement to the militant National Woman's Party. In 1915, she wrote her first book on the "municipal housekeeping" of civic-minded women, from which this passage is drawn. She went on to write and edit many books on the history of women—including America Through Women's Eyes *(1933), from which the title of this book is drawn—and to coauthor, with her husband, Charles Beard, pathbreaking works in American history. Always she emphasized, as she does here, women's active role in history making.*

In this expansion of municipal functions there can be little dispute as to the influence of women. Their hearts touched in the beginning by human misery and their sentiments aroused, they have been led into manifold activities in attempts at amelioration, which have taught them the breeding places of disease, as well as of vice, crime, poverty and misery. Having learned that effectively to "swat the fly" they must swat at its nest, women have also learned that to swat disease they must swat poor housing, evil labor conditions, ignorance, and vicious interests. . . .

Middle-class and upper-class women, having more leisure than middle- and upper-class men, have had greater opportunity for social observation and the cultivation of social sympathies, for the latter accompanies the former instead of preceding it, as all active emotions are the reflexes of experience. It is these women therefore who have seen, felt, experimented, learned, agitated, constructed, advised, and pressed upon the municipal authorities the need of public prevention of the ills from which the people suffer. In their municipal demands they have often had the support of women of the working class and of working men, among others, whose own preservation is bound up with legislation and administration to an ever-increasing degree. . . .

Whatever may be the outcome of the present tendencies in social service, it is certain that women are actively engaged in every branch of it: in organized charity, in all the specialized branches of kindred work, such as care for the several types of dependents and delinquents, in organizing women workers in the industries, in making social surveys and special investigation, and in creating the literature of social service.

SOURCE: Mary Beard, *Woman's Work in Municipalities* (New York: National Municipal League, 1915), 221–22.

◆ **The Dirty Pool of Politics**
The image of civic-minded women sweeping out the dirt from the house of public life cap-
tures both the conventional and innovative nature of women's public activities in this period.
The image was widely distributed by suffragists, suggesting that the link between politics and
civic housewifery was an effective rhetorical tool with men and women alike. *Courtesy of the
Bancroft Library, University of California, Berkeley, Selina Solomons Papers, BANC MSS C-B 773:7.*

Maternalist Triumphs: Protective Labor Legislation and Mothers' Pensions

Maternalist presumptions underlay policies designed on behalf of working
women and mothers both. One of reformers' first and most important goals was
to establish a legal maximum workday for working women. However, in 1895 the
Illinois Supreme Court invalidated a state law establishing a daily maximum of ten
hours for women workers (see Chapter 6). Then, in 1905, the U.S. Supreme Court
ruled even more broadly in *Lochner v. New York* that *any* attempt to regulate the
wage labor relation for men or women was an unconstitutional infringement on
individual freedom of contract. At this point, reformers took a new approach. The
NCL designed a strategy based on the calculation that the courts might allow exceptions to the rule of *Lochner* for women workers on the grounds that their maternal capacity needed to be protected.

An opportunity came in 1908 when the constitutionality of an Oregon maximum hours law for women workers was challenged before the U.S. Supreme
Court. Josephine Goldmark, NCL secretary, arranged for Louis Brandeis, her
brother-in-law and later a member of the Supreme Court, to argue the case. The
so-called Brandeis Brief proceeded on two grounds: that "women are fundamentally weaker than men" in defending themselves against the assaults of wage labor

and must rely on the state to do so for them, and that protection of women's maternal capacity was necessary for the general welfare. In its 1908 decision, *Muller v. Oregon,* the Supreme Court accepted the argument that while men's working hours could not be regulated by law, women's could (see the Appendix, p. A-27). Within a decade, all but nine states had passed maximum hours laws for working women.

These so-called protective labor laws were widely applauded by women activists and working women alike. "Now at long last, to us who were working for the rights of working women . . . , it looked as though the long fight for the shorter working day for women could be won!" recalled glove maker and WTUL member Agnes Nestor.[13] But there were some limits to this victory. Women in domestic and agricultural labor were generally excluded, which meant that the great majority of African American women were not covered. More generally, in exchange for a desired improvement in their working conditions, working women had been formally labeled weaker than men, without the same claim on individual rights. From this perspective, the underlying principle of one of the era's great achievements for women, protective labor laws, conflicted with those of another great success, equal political rights.

The success of maximum hours laws led to additional protective labor legislation for working women, also on the basis of maternal capacity. After 1908, many states passed laws prohibiting women from working at night. Female printers and other skilled women workers whose jobs required night work protested. Laws that set minimum wages for women workers, so that any decrease in women's working hours would not result in lower earnings, were also passed, provoking controversy from a different direction. Employers such as the textile magnates at Lawrence objected strenuously to the higher labor costs that minimum wage laws would incur. In a 1923 case entitled *Adkins v. Children's Hospital,* the U.S. Supreme Court invalidated minimum wage laws for women on the grounds that women "are legally as capable of contracting for themselves as men."[14] The Court based this turnaround of perspective on the fact that the federal Constitution had just been amended to give women equal voting rights (see the Appendix, p. A-27).

The maternalist argument notwithstanding, most working women were still young, unmarried, and childless. Legislation directed at mothers themselves came with the establishment of maternal pension programs, which were intended to protect mothers who were unsupported by male breadwinners from having to go out into the workplace to earn money, allowing them to stay at home with their children instead. Thus, the two different reforms—hours legislation focused on working women and pensions for nonworking mothers—were closely linked by the maternalist ethic that it was the government's responsibility to protect motherhood from the incursions of the wage labor system and to conserve women's best energies for bearing and raising children.

The first mothers' pension program was established in 1911 in Illinois, in the aftermath of a 1909 White House Conference on the Care of Dependent Children called at the behest of settlement house leaders. The conference advocated providing all children with full-time maternal care. Although the report encouraged private charity to meet this need, two years later the Illinois legislature authorized $250,000 for this purpose. The money was to be issued in the form of monthly grants of $50 to a limited number of needy single mothers, as determined by the Juvenile Court. Almost from the beginning, the program generated tremendous concern over welfare fraud and battles over funding levels. Moreover, not all single mothers qualified. Never-married mothers were considered morally unfit, as were those who did not meet "suitable home" standards. Not surprisingly, African American mothers barely appeared on the mothers' pension rolls, kept off by institutional prejudice and their own ignorance of such programs. By 1920, thirty-eight other states had established mother's pensions programs with similar structures.

Maternalist Defeat: The Struggle to Ban Child Labor

Ironically, the least successful of the maternalist programs is the one that seems the most basic and obvious to later generations: ending child labor. In 1900, an estimated 2 million underage children were reported to be working for wages. Given the youth of the female labor force, the line between women and child workers was not sharply drawn. Was a fourteen-year-old wage earner a child or a woman? (See Figure 6.2, p. 388.)

While maximum hours laws and mothers' pensions programs were passed by state legislatures, the campaign to outlaw child labor was one of the first social welfare efforts to focus on the federal government. In 1912 Congress established a Children's Bureau in the Department of Labor, which became headquarters for the campaign to stop child labor. Hull House veteran Julia Lathrop was made head, becoming the first woman to run a federal agency. With little federal funding for her work, Lathrop turned to the female dominion and used women's clubs, especially those associated with the General Federation of Women's Clubs, to conduct surveys and to lobby for state and federal legislation regarding children's education, health, and work. One measure of their success came in 1916 when Congress passed the Keating-Owen Act prohibiting paid labor for children under sixteen, which covered 125,000 young workers.

What seemed like an amazingly quick victory in a key Progressive reform soon turned into defeat. Crucial industries such as textile manufacturing and mining relied on child workers and opposed the law. In addition, immigrant families depended heavily on the labor of their children and stubbornly resisted the perspective of middle-class social workers to eliminate it. (See Documents: Jane Addams and the Charitable Relation, pp. 379–85.) In 1918 the Supreme Court overturned the law as an unconstitutional assertion of federal authority over states' rights. Anti–child labor activists mounted a final effort to resolve the constitutionality of the issue by getting an amendment banning child labor passed through Congress in 1924. However, it failed to be ratified by the states, falling victim to an energetic campaign that labeled it as too "socialistic." By this time, growing numbers of wage earning mothers were beginning to replace working-class families' reliance on children as their secondary wage earners. This process, reinforced by the passage of anti–child labor legislation as part of the Fair Labor Standards Act of 1938, which the Supreme Court allowed to stand, ended the practice of child labor in this country.

Progressive Women and Political Parties

Despite their ideological emphasis on women's maternal attributes, many female reform activists were very drawn to the political arena. Women tended to position themselves as nonpartisan, that is, as putting issues and candidates above party loyalty, but they could be found in the ranks of all the major parties. By 1912, women in seven states were going to the polls to vote for president,° but even where women were disfranchised, they were involved in the election in anticipation that their voting rights were just over the horizon. The election featured four presidential candidates: the Democratic and Republican nominees and candidates from two upstart challengers, the Progressive and Socialist Parties.

In the aftermath of the collapse of the People's Party in 1896, the cultivation of women's support was taken up by the reform wing of the Republican Party (see Chapter 6). Here could be found many politically active women reformers, such as the Dreier sisters of the WTUL. At the 1912 Republican convention, the reformers' candidate, former president Theodore Roosevelt, lost out to incumbent William Howard Taft. As a result, the reform forces bolted the Republican Party to form the Progressive Party. The new party supported woman suffrage and integrated women into all its activities rather than relegating them to auxiliaries. Women reform activists welcomed the party enthusiastically, and at the national convention, held in August in Chicago, their de facto leader, Jane Addams, was chosen to second the nomination of Roosevelt as the Progressives' presidential candidate. As a group, African American women, devoted to the party of Lincoln and skeptical of Roosevelt's racial record, stayed loyal to the regular Republicans.

In the election, Roosevelt received more popular votes than President Taft, but the winner of the election, profiting from the split in the Republican ranks, was the Democratic candidate, Woodrow Wilson. Wilson had a reputation as a reformer from his years as governor of New Jersey, after which he served as president of Princeton University. Democrats did not have a record of cultivating female support, although this was beginning to change as full enfranchisement drew nearer. In New York State, for instance, Robert Wagner, Al Smith, and Franklin Roosevelt were beginning to connect with women labor reformers.

The fourth candidate to run in 1912 was union leader Eugene V. Debs, candidate of the Socialist Party of America, formed in 1901. The platforms of the Progressive and Socialist Parties overlapped considerably—for instance, both

---

° In addition to the women of the states of Colorado, Idaho, Utah, and Wyoming, who were enfranchised in the 1890s, the constitutions of Washington and California were amended in 1910 and 1911, respectively, to grant women full voting rights. Also, in 1911 Illinois women got partial suffrage that extended to presidential elections. (See "State Campaigns and Modern Suffrage Methods," pp. 427–31.)

advocated woman suffrage and minimum wage laws for women—but the Social-ists' ultimate goal was working-class empowerment, whereas the Progressives sought interclass harmony. Under Debs's leadership the Socialists advocated re-forms in the capitalist system and participated energetically in electoral contests. As the left wing of Progressive era politics, the Socialist Party, although small, was influential.

For women, socialism had a variety of meanings. Socialist women were strong advocates for women's emancipation. In advocating mothers' pensions, for in-stance, they called for payments not just to those without breadwinners but to all mothers, "as the first step toward an economically-free motherhood," in the words of Los Angeles Socialist Frances Noel.[15] Perhaps the most famous Socialist woman at the time came from America's heartland. Kate Richards O'Hare, who had begun her reform career in Kansas as a temperance advocate, was a nationally prominent writer, journalist, and traveling lecturer. To a younger generation, socialism also signified personal liberation and sexual freedom: birth control pioneer Margaret Sanger represented this type of Socialist.

In the 1912 election, Debs polled an impressive 6 percent, 900,000 votes. The party was able to win local and state offices and even two members of Congress, but it went into a steep decline at the end of the decade, deeply divided over the 1917 Bolshevik Revolution in Russia in which revolutionary Socialists overthrew the fragile liberal government of Russia, established a workers' state, and mur-dered the tsar and his family. Then, having opposed U.S. entry into World War I, Debs was imprisoned for treason.

Outside the Dominion: Progressivism and Race

Race was a blind spot for white reformers in the Progressive era. Anti-Asian senti-ment against Japanese immigration was strong and growing in the West. In the Southwest, newcomers from Mexico benefited from reformers' concern for immi-grants, but as the Mexican Revolution of 1910 swelled their numbers—by 1920 Mexicans constituted 12 percent of the population of California—nativist anxiety about these dark-skinned foreigners also grew stronger.

Inasmuch as the Progressive era coincided with the triumph of Jim Crow policies, however, the brunt of the era's racism fell on African Americans. In the South, white reformers advocated segregation and the disfranchisement of black men as means to improve civic life and modernize southern society. In the North, racism was also growing. Popular anti-black prejudice was reinforced by theories of racial hierarchy that claimed to be scientific. Even the most sympathetic whites saw the African American poor as less adaptable than European immigrants to in-dustrial, urban society. Given maternalist convictions about the importance of home-based childrearing, male breadwinning, and dedicated mothering, the ten-dency of black mothers to work outside the home seemed to white reformers to constitute an insurmountable barrier to their rapid improvement. Like later gen-erations of well-meaning whites, even though they blamed blacks' problems on the legacy of slavery, they had little faith in blacks' capacity for change.

Although hemmed in by the walls of segregation, African American women nonetheless shared the reform enthusiasms of the era. The small black middle class provided resources for the establishment of kindergartens for the children of working mothers and founded old age homes for ex-slaves without families to care for them. By 1900, four hundred black women's clubs and societies were affiliated with the National Association of Colored Women (NACW). In addition to the antilynching work with which it had begun, the NACW had divisions for mothers' clubs, juvenile courts, domestic science, temperance, music, literature, and votes for women. Mary Church Terrell was the association's first president. An 1884 graduate of Oberlin College, she was one of a handful of black women accepted into the white women's movement, but she put her best energies into the black women's movement. When the National Association for the Advancement of Colored People was founded in 1909, Terrell and Ida B. Wells-Barnett were the only two African American women admitted to the inner circle.

Two other important black women of the era were business entrepreneurs, a category that had no real equivalent among white women civic leaders of the period. Coincidentally, both were named Walker. Louisiana-born Sarah Breedlove Walker went from being a laundress to the founder and president of her own highly successful hair care business; Madam C. J. Walker, as she was known, provided employment to thousands of African American women who sold her products door to door. Virginia-born Maggie Lena Walker became the first woman president of a U.S bank, the St. Luke Penny Savings Bank. Both women were wealthy, philanthropic, community-minded, and deeply identified with the progress of the women of their race. Maggie Walker described her "great all absorbing interest" as "the love I bear . . . our Negro women . . . blocked and held down by the fears and prejudices of the whites, ridiculed and sneered at by intelligent blacks."[16]

During the Progressive era, Native Americans began to serve as public advocates for their people. Educated in white institutions, they had gained familiarity with the dominant culture and acquired the political skills needed to speak for themselves rather than rely on sympathetic whites. Their goal was to undo the economic and political dependency that had resulted from late nineteenth-century Indian policy (see Chapter 6). Gertrude Simmons Bonnin was the leading woman in this first generation of modern Indian activists. Known by her Yankton Sioux name Zitkala-Sa, she was a lecturer and writer who advocated both preserving native culture from destruction and securing full rights of citizenship for native peoples. Insisting that she was "as capable in serious matters and as thoroughly interested in the race" as any man, she became the secretary of the first national pan-Indian reform organization established by native peoples, the Society of American Indians.[17]

The Society of American Indians was divided over full citizenship rights for Native Americans, fearing that receiving these rights would weaken tribal communities. But in 1924, when Congress passed the 1924 Indian Citizenship Act, women were included, because by then the long battle for woman suffrage had come to a victorious end.

◆ **Madam C. J. Walker**

During the Progressive era, many wealthy women were also reformers and philanthropists, but only one earned her own fortune and was African American. Madam C. J. Walker, born Sarah Breedlove, was the daughter of ex-slaves and worked in the cotton fields before she built her immensely successful hair care and cosmetics business. Walker was active in the National Association of Colored Women and was the single largest contributor to the National Association for the Advancement of Colored People's antilynching campaign, which picked up from the earlier efforts of black club women. Walker died in 1919, and her daughter used the money her mother left her to become the most important black woman patron of the Harlem Renaissance. *Madam C. J. Walker Collection, Indiana Historical Society.*

VOTES FOR WOMEN

The labor militancy of women workers and the public involvement of Progressive women reformers together fueled a great and final drive for women's enfranchisement. Ever since the constitutional amendments of the Reconstruction years (see Chapter 5), the woman suffrage movement had been accumulating advocates and reformulating its strategy. In 1890, the two rival suffrage societies, the National Woman Suffrage Association founded by Elizabeth Cady Stanton and Susan B. Anthony and the American Woman Suffrage Association established by Lucy Stone and Henry Ward Blackwell, united as the National American Woman Suffrage Association (NAWSA). When Carrie Chapman Catt of Iowa took over the NAWSA presidency from Anthony in 1900, suffragism began to move into the modern era. Women in their clubs, colleges, unions, and temperance societies were becoming interested in the franchise. Four states, all west of the Mississippi, had granted full voting rights to women.

As the twentieth century began, a new generation of suffrage leaders was determined to expand the movement to the rest of the country and bring it into full conformity with the realities of industrial, urban, modern America. No longer rallying under the outdated nineteenth-century term "suffrage," they adopted a more contemporary-sounding slogan, "votes for women." They drew in previously uninvolved classes of women, from the wealthy to the working class, and learned to play the legislative game to their own benefit. They established small, flexible suffrage societies that could develop new tactics and strategies, and they turned to the most advanced cultural methods and artistic styles, anything to get over the old-fashioned image from which their cause suffered.

The revived movement of the Progressive era came back to life in a series of campaigns for equal political rights at the state level. But appeals to male voters in one state after another were exhausting, repetitive, and, east of the Mississippi River, impossible to win. At that point, suffrage activists shifted their focus back to an amendment to the federal constitution, the movement's original goal in the 1860s. Large but slow to change, NAWSA was challenged by a small, more aggressive group of activists, known as "militants" and "suffragettes" (the latter was a derogatory term that British suffrage activists had turned into a label of pride). By the mid-1910s, these two wings of the movement had generated the right combination of female energy, male support, and political will to effect a constitutional amendment for women's political rights.

As we examine the final stages of the suffrage movement, we ask, why did it take so very long to win votes for women? Organized opposition is a part of the answer. Ever since the 1890s, a few, mostly upper-class women actively opposed enfranchisement, either on the grounds that political rights would cost women their influence over men or that too many "unfit" women would make use of the ballot. Most "antis" were politically conservative, although a handful of left-wing radicals, including Emma Goldman and Mother Jones, thought women were spending too much time and resting too much hope on the ballot. However, suffrage leaders were less concerned with the female antis than with powerful male-led special interests—especially the liquor industry and manufacturers who exploited female and child labor—who worked against them from behind the legislative scenes.

But the really significant obstacles that had to be overcome were more elusive. Large numbers of women, who otherwise had little in common, had to unite in active pursuit of this single goal. Perhaps this was why, unlike the suffragists of Elizabeth Stanton's day, the twentieth-century movement did not emphasize abstract justice, which meant different things to different groups of adherents, but instead stressed the many concrete purposes to which organized political power could be put. With a large, diverse movement of women demanding the vote, male politicians and legislators were gradually compelled to act. That votes for women was a reform long past due did not make its final achievement any less a magnificent triumph, the most successful mass movement for the expansion of political democracy in American history.

Diversity in the Woman Suffrage Movement

In terms of diversity, the greatest achievement of the twentieth-century woman suffrage movement was its extremely broad class base. Reform collaboration between middle-class and working-class women forged in the Women's Trade Union League greatly facilitated suffrage outreach to women wage earners. "The middle class suffragist . . . has ceased to fight," asserted Socialist Josephine Conger-Kaneko. "There is another class of women, however, who . . . will give to [the suffrage cause] the earnest, intense, interesting aspect it bore at its inception. . . . The wage earning woman has an economic axe to grind. . . . Given the vote she would have an equal chance with man in this struggle."[18]

By 1910, several new suffrage organizations were focused on recruiting working women. In San Francisco, Maud Younger, a wealthy woman who organized food servers, established a Wage Earners Suffrage League; similar organizations were founded in Los Angeles, New York City, and elsewhere. More and more suffrage parades featured large divisions of working women, often marching under the banners of their trade or union. Pro-suffrage literature was printed in the languages of immigrants—Yiddish, German, Italian, Portuguese, and Spanish—and explained how votes for women would raise women's wages and improve their working conditions. Wage earning women brought with them the support of male family members and coworkers, who began to see in votes for women a tool for their own class interests. It was not uncommon in these years to see a spokeswoman for votes for women standing on a soapbox outside a factory gate and boldly preaching the cause to men at work.

Simultaneously, women from the very highest class of society became involved in the movement. Their wealth came from their husbands, but, aspiring to power of their own, they used their money to gain entrée into the world of women's politics. One of the richest was Alva Belmont, who had divorced one millionaire, William Vanderbilt, in order to marry another, August Belmont. The publicity that followed these wealthy suffragists helped to make votes for women trendy. Their money paid the salaries of organizers, rented offices, and supported the publication of newspapers and leaflets. Relations between the wealthy and the wage earning were superficially sisterly. In 1910, Belmont had joined Ann Morgan and other affluent women to support the New York City shirtwaist strikers. But under the surface, tension simmered. Wealthy suffragists expected to lead the movement, and working-class suffragists resented their condescension and were suspicious of their motives. "We want the ballot for very different reasons," explained Los Angeles working-class suffragist Minna O'Donnell in 1908. "Our idea is self protection; you want to use it [to help] some one else."[19]

The growth of suffragism among young college-educated women was also a new development. The number of college-educated women had been increasing since the 1860s (see Chapter 5), and by the end of the century, college graduates were turning toward the cause of votes for women. The College Equal Suffrage League, formed by students and young alumnae at Radcliffe College in 1898 because the administration would not permit pro-suffrage speakers on campus, became a national organization in 1908 under the leadership of Bryn Mawr president M. Carey Thomas. College graduates provided the energy of youth in many other organizations. In New York City, for example, Caroline Lexow, a 1904 Barnard College graduate, was the chief organizer for the Women's Political Union.

In contrast to such bridges across the class gap, the suffrage movement was almost completely racially segregated. NAWSA repeatedly refused to condemn discrimination against African American women and allowed southern affiliates to refuse them membership. In 1899, the last year of her presidency, Susan B. Anthony turned her back on her abolitionist past to declare that since "women are a helpless, disfranchised class," there was no point in challenging southern racism.[20] National suffrage leaders such as Kate Gordon of Louisiana and Laura Clay of Kentucky regarded the involvement of African American women as an outright threat to their plans to increase the involvement of southern white women. "The South will be compelled to look to its Anglo-Saxon women as the medium through which to retain the supremacy of the white race over the African," Belle Kearney of Mississippi hopefully predicted in 1903.[21]

Despite this discouragement, black suffragists continued to insist on their equal political rights (see box, "African Americans for Woman Suffrage"). For black women, achieving suffrage loomed very large against the background of the disfranchisement of the men of their race. Starting in the 1890s, African American women began to assert their political rights aggressively from within their own clubs and suffrage societies. "If white American women, with all their natural and acquired advantages, need the ballot," explained Adele Hunt Logan of Tuskegee, Alabama, "how much more do black Americans, male and female, need the strong defense of a vote to help secure their right to life, liberty and the pursuit of happiness?"[22] In the South, African American women advocated votes for women earlier and more aggressively than white women did. In the North, African Americans' historic links to the Republicans made black women of some interest to that party.

State Campaigns and Modern Suffrage Methods

Although the final victory of votes for women took place in the national arena, the revival of the American suffrage movement began in a series of campaigns focused on enfranchisement in particular states (see Map 7.1). In Washington State, where women had briefly voted in the 1880s only to have their suffrage revoked by the territorial legislature, they regained the vote in 1910. "The West has always been peopled by free souls," exulted Washington activist Emma DeVoe.[23] The next year,

NANNIE BURROUGHS
African Americans for Woman Suffrage

Nannie Burroughs (1879–1961), whose mother was an emancipated slave, was one of the founders of the Woman's Convention of the National Baptist Convention, an important locale for the southern black women's movement. The Crisis, the magazine of the recently formed National Association for the Advancement of Colored People, actively advocated woman suffrage. Writing in it, Burroughs made a very different sort of case than did white suffragists. Civic and political equality, she contended, would be a resource for black women to use to break free from the long history of sexual abuse they had suffered. Thus, she turned the discourse of female chastity traditionally used against black women into a tool for their defense. Note her defense of racial purity.

When the ballot is put in the hands of the American woman, the world is going to get a correct estimate of the Negro woman. It will find her a tower of strength of which poets have never sung, orators have never spoken, and scholars have never written.

Because the black man does not know the value of the ballot, and has bartered and sold his most valuable possession, it is no evidence that the Negro woman will do the same. The Negro woman therefore needs the ballot to get back, by the wise use of it, what the Negro man has lost by the misuse of it. She needs to ransom her race.... She carries the burdens of the Church, and of the school and bears a great deal more than her economic share in the home.

Another striking fact is that the Negro woman carries the moral destiny of two races in her hand. Had she not been the woman of unusual moral stamina that she is, the black race would have been made a great deal whiter, and the white race a great deal blacker during the past fifty years. She has been left a prey for the men of every race, but in spite of this, she has held the enemies of Negro female chastity at bay. The Negro woman is the white woman's as well as the white race's most needed ally in preserving an unmixed race.

The ballot, wisely used, will bring to her the respect and protection she needs. It is her weapon of moral defense. Under present conditions, when she appears in court in defense of her virtue, she is looked upon with amused contempt. She needs the ballot to reckon with men who place no value upon her virtue, and to mould healthy public sentiment in favor of her own protection.

SOURCE: Nannie Helen Burroughs, "Black Women and Reform," *Crisis*, August 1915.

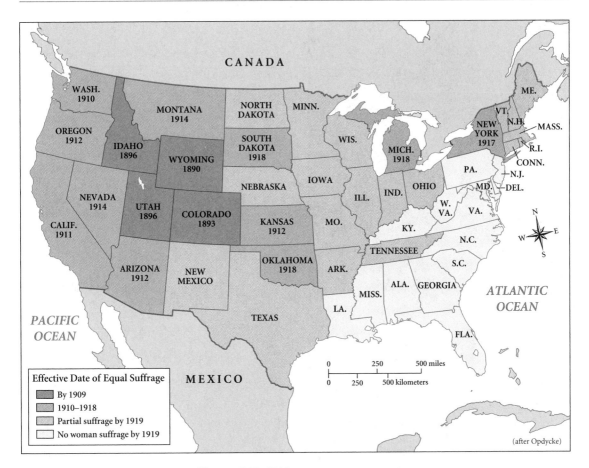

♦ Map 7.1 **Woman Suffrage, 1890–1919**

The woman suffrage movement in the United States was fought on both the state and federal levels. States traditionally defined their electorates, but starting with the Fifteenth Amendment in 1870, the Constitution prohibited particular forms of disfranchisement. In 1893, Colorado amended its state constitution to include women as voting citizens. By 1914, ten other states, all in the West, had followed suit, granting their women full voting rights, including for president and Congress. The voting power of women in these "suffrage states" became a potent political lever for moving the national parties to support what became the Nineteenth Amendment, which prohibits states from disfranchising their citizens on the basis of sex.

in 1911, fifteen years after the defeat of suffrage in California at the height of Populism (see Chapter 6), that state held its second suffrage referendum. Clubwomen, college graduates, Socialists, and trade union activists quickly came together to campaign in the state's widely divergent regions. California suffragists were great modernizers. They understood that clever advertising was more important than ponderous argument. "Although the proposition that women should vote is

◆ **Votes for Women Graphics**

To advertise the October 1911 state referendum for votes for women, California suffragists announced a contest for the most beautiful image of the cause. B. M. Boye won with her art nouveau graphic of a modern woman posed in front of the Golden Gate, the mouth of the San Francisco harbor. The sun setting in the West surrounds the woman's head, like a halo. The suffrage message is carried, not only by the banner that she holds, but by the golden yellow throughout the picture, the color chosen to designate the pro-suffrage cause for the California campaign. *The Schlesinger Library, Radcliffe Institute, Harvard University.*

seriously and profoundly true," they insisted, "it will at first be established . . . much as the virtues of a breakfast cereal are established—by affirmation."[24] The cause of votes for women was promoted through beautiful graphics, celebrity support, and department store window displays.

California suffragists were also political realists. Fearful of vote tampering, they posted poll watchers at voting places on October 10, 1911, election day. The early returns were not good, and newspapers prematurely reported that votes for women had been defeated. But then the tallies from more distant counties began to come in and, by the next day, votes for women had won by less than five thousand votes. "From then to now," suffragist Alice Park wryly remembered of that long day waiting for final numbers, "no man can be found who voted no. They must have died the next day."[25]

So far, all the state victories had been west of the Mississippi. In 1915, campaigns were mounted in Pennsylvania, New Jersey, Massachusetts, and, most important, New York. Despite extraordinary efforts, the eastern campaigns of 1915 failed. New York suffragists blamed the size of the state, the prejudices of immigrant men, and the opposition of politicians. A second state referendum campaign, scheduled for 1917, was initiated right away. But some suffrage leaders were beginning to conclude that the state-by-state approach was futile. Even if every state could be won this way—and many, certainly the entire South, could not—the time and money required were prohibitive. At this point, the momentum of the movement shifted back to an approach that would enfranchise all American women—securing an amendment to the federal constitution.

Returning to the Constitution: The National Suffrage Movement

In the Reconstruction years, the suffrage movement had concentrated on getting woman suffrage recognized in the U.S. Constitution. Congress debated a woman suffrage amendment in 1878, but soon after suffrage energies shifted to the state level. Constitutional ambiguity about where the power to determine the electorate resided—with the states or with the federal government—allowed suffragists to make this strategic change and win victories in particular states at times when amendments to the federal Constitution were not on the political agenda. This changed during the Progressive era. In 1913, two new provisions to the Constitution—one establishing a federal income tax, the other requiring the direct election of U.S. senators—were moving through the amendment process. It was time to return to the U.S. Constitution to enfranchise women.

NAWSA was slow to realize this new opportunity. Anna Howard Shaw, who had replaced Carrie Chapman Catt as NAWSA president in 1906, was unwilling to redirect organizational resources from the influential state chapters to a centralized national campaign. In 1913, two young women college graduates, Alice Paul and Lucy Burns, convinced NAWSA leaders to allow them to take over work on a federal amendment. In their very first act, they signaled their intention to jump start a national effort with the same kind of spectacular methods that had worked in state campaigns. They organized a suffrage parade in Washington, D.C. (see Figure 7.6, p. 452). They chose March 3, the day before Woodrow Wilson's inauguration, because then the nation's attention would be on the city. When the president-to-be disembarked from the train, he was told that the crowds he had expected to greet him were down on Pennsylvania Avenue, watching the suffragists. Aware that Washington, D.C., was a southern town and uninterested in challenging NAWSA's policy of segregation, Paul required black suffragists from Howard University to march at the back of the parade. Unruly crowds only added to the demonstration's publicity.

Within a few weeks, the suffrage amendment had been reintroduced and was being debated in the House of Representatives for the first time in seventeen years. Fresh off this victory, Paul and Burns formed a new national organization, smaller, more activist, and more disciplined than NAWSA. They named it the Congressional Union because its goal was to pressure Congress to pass a woman suffrage amendment. But Paul and Burns soon realized that another way to move Congress was through the political pressure generated by the votes of women who were already enfranchised in the West. This resource had never before been used in the

◆ Native Americans and Woman Suffrage

By contrast to their disregard of African American women, white suffragists found it useful to associate themselves with the "first Americans" now that they were subjugated militarily and legally. In 1902, Oregon suffragists learned of the long-forgotten figure of Sacagawea, the Shoshone woman who had accompanied the Lewis and Clark expedition, and erected a statue to her in Portland. In 1911, after California women were enfranchised, this picture was taken of a woman from the Piutes (Sarah Winnemucca's tribe; see p. 236) registering to vote. The image is meant to highlight the inclusiveness of female enfranchisement, as well as the power of citizenship to uplift women of the "lower" races. However, as the legal status of tribal Indians was highly contested, and since it is unlikely that Native American women voted after 1920 in any numbers, the event was probably staged. *Seaver Center for Western History Research.*

suffrage movement. Accordingly, in 1916 they changed the name of their organization to the National Woman's Party (NWP) to reflect the electoral focus of their strategy. That year, as President Wilson campaigned to be reelected, a corps of NWP activists fanned out through the West, urging women voters to withhold their votes from the Democrats until Wilson promised actively to back woman suffrage. They failed—Wilson won the election, including in states such as California where women voted.

Nonetheless, the activism of the NWP had a major impact. It challenged NAWSA loyalists who found the NWP's combative methods distasteful to search for an alternative way for their organization to push for federal-level enfranchisement. After the 1915 New York defeat, while other state suffragists mobilized for a second referendum to be held in 1917, Carrie Chapman Catt moved on to reassume the national presidency and reinvigorate NAWSA. She convened a secret meeting of the NAWSA Executive Board to mobilize NAWSA's enormous organizational structure in a concerted lobbying campaign for the federal amendment. Although the NWP and the NAWSA were very hostile to each other, belying the notion of a loving sisterhood on behalf of suffrage, their two approaches were complementary, the former raising the political stakes by its radical efforts, the latter negotiating with congressmen to move the amendment forward to passage. Nonetheless, it took another five years, and the upheaval of a world war, before the U.S. Constitution was amended to enfranchise women.

THE EMERGENCE OF FEMINISM

As the votes for women movement grew, a new, avante-garde approach to modernizing womanhood was surfacing on its edges. To distinguish themselves from the more conventional suffragists, these women began to use the term "feminist," borrowed from the French *feminisme*. "All feminists are suffragists," they explained, "but not all suffragists are feminists."[26] Their agenda was a broad one, moving beyond political rights and economic advancement to embrace female individuality, sexual freedom, and birth control.

The Feminist Program

Feminism was a cultural development more than an organized movement. Most of its adherents were middle-class college graduates, aspiring professionals, and artists, but female labor activists and immigrants were also in its ranks. Feminists clustered in inexpensive, often immigrant urban neighborhoods, most famously New York City's Greenwich Village. They innovated new lifestyles, living with men in "free unions," by themselves in apartments, or with other women in lesbian couples.

From the moment of its inception, the definition of feminism was imprecise. On the one hand, feminists believed that women had all the capacities and talents of men; on the other, they believed that women's distinctive intelligence and

WHAT IS FEMINISM?
COME AND FIND OUT

FIRST FEMINIST MASS MEETING
at the PEOPLE'S INSTITUTE, Cooper Union

Tuesday Evening, February 17th, 1914, at 8 o'clock, P. M.

Subject: "WHAT FEMINISM MEANS TO ME."

Ten-Minute Speeches by

ROSE YOUNG	GEORGE CREEL
JESSE LYNCH WILLIAMS	MRS. FRANK COTHREN
HENRIETTA RODMAN	FLOYD DELL
GEORGE MIDDLETON	CRYSTAL EASTMAN BENEDICT
FRANCES PERKINS	EDWIN BJORKMAN
WILL IRWIN	MAX EASTMAN

Chairman, MARIE JENNEY HOWE.

SECOND FEMINIST MASS MEETING
at the PEOPLES' INSTITUTE, Cooper Union

Friday, February 20th, 1914, at 8 o'clock, P. M.

Subject: "BREAKING INTO THE HUMAN RACE."

The Right to Work.—
 RHETA CHILDE DORR

The Right of the Mother to Her Profession.—
 BEATRICE FORBES-ROBERTSON-HALE.

The Right to Her Convictions.—
 MARY SHAW.

The Right to Her Name.—
 FOLA LA FOLLETTE.

The Right to Organize.—
 ROSE SCHNEIDERMAN.

The Right to Ignore Fashion.—
 NINA WILCOX PUTNAM.

The Right to Specialize in Home Industries.—
 CHARLOTTE PERKINS GILMAN.

Chairman, MARIE JENNEY HOWE.

ADMISSION FREE.   NO COLLECTION.

◆ **Promoting Feminism**

Feminist ideas in the early twentieth century created a fervor of excitement among young women (and some men) eager to challenge the gender order. This handbill advertised a 1914 meeting organized by the New York City feminist group, Heterodoxy (see Documents: Modernizing Womanhood, pp. 460–65). One member, radical working-class advocate Elizabeth Gurley Flynn, described the group as providing "a glimpse of women of the future, big spirited, intellectually alert, devoid of old 'femininity.' "[27] *George Middleton Papers, Library of Congress.*

powers had not yet been allowed to surface. Whether emphasizing similarities or differences with men, however, they were agreed on feminism's power to disrupt the gender order. "Feminism was something with dynamite in it," Rheta Childe Dorr wrote. "It is the state of mind of women who realize that their whole position in the social order is antiquated . . . made of old materials, worn out laws, customs, conventions, fetishes, traditions and taboos."[28] Feminists were proud individualists, impatient with the female tradition of justifying all actions (including social reform) in terms of selfless, maternal service. (See Documents: Modernizing Womanhood, pp. 460–65.)

Unlike the votes for women movement, feminism placed the cutting edge of change in women's private lives, not in their public roles. Charlotte Perkins Gilman was a feminist favorite for her conviction that the family-oriented life of the middle class was narrow and inefficient, a point she explored in her path-breaking books *Women and Economics* (1890) and *The Home* (1903). She championed collectivizing housework; and New York City feminist Henrietta Rodman organized a communal apartment house for women to realize this vision. Other feminists challenged the Gilded Age premises of female sexual restraint by insisting that women had sexual desires as well as maternal capacities. Swedish feminist Ellen Key was popular with American feminists for emphasizing the importance of freeing motherhood from subordination to and dependence on men. She envisioned a future society of state-supported, sexually active, emotionally and economically independent mothers.

In the spirit of the new feminism, younger women criticized older female activists for the "sex antagonism" they fostered toward men, believing instead that it was possible for advanced women and men to live and love together in mutual passion. A handful of women also lived openly as lesbians in partnerships with other women that clearly were sexual, in contrast to the ambiguous "Boston marriages" of the past. The sexual revolution that began among political activists and cultural radicals in the 1910s spread in subsequent decades to a wider sector of the female public (see Chapter 8).

The Birth Control Movement

The most organized and politicized manifestation of Progressive era feminism was the campaign for birth control. While the woman suffrage movement was large and public, birth control advocacy was small and surreptitious. Earlier women's rights champions had urged women only to undertake pregnancy voluntarily (see box, "Voluntary Motherhood," p. 296), but still regarding sexuality as fundamentally male, they did not think it was important—or desirable—for women to have greater amounts of sexual intercourse freed of the threat of pregnancy. They were not interested in freeing women *for* sexual activity and pleasure, only *from* unwanted pregnancy. Emma Goldman was one of the first to speak widely on women's right to contraceptive information and methods, not only so that they could avoid unwanted pregnancy but also so that they could enjoy sexual intercourse.

In 1912, Margaret Sanger, daughter of Irish immigrants, a trained nurse, and a Socialist, followed Goldman's lead to write and speak on behalf of women's right to control the frequency of their childbearing. She invented the term "birth control" to describe a practice that had long existed but had not been openly discussed or publicly advocated. Indeed, by the time Sanger began her work, birthrates among native-born, white women had already fallen significantly. From her years of nursing, Sanger knew that immigrant women, without any access to private physicians, suffered the most from the public ban on discussions of contraception (see box, "The Story of Sadie Sachs"). At first, Sanger did not have a reliable contraceptive technology to promote. She concentrated instead on teaching young girls necessary reproductive and sexual information through a series of articles entitled "What Every Girl Should Know," published first in the Socialist *Call* and then in her own magazine, *The Woman Rebel,* which started running in 1914.

In sending her writings through the U.S. mails, Sanger fell afoul of the anti-obscenity Comstock laws, which had been interfering with the spread of contra-

MARGARET SANGER
The Story of Sadie Sachs

Margaret Sanger (1879–1966), Socialist, feminist, and birth control pioneer, attributed her determination to dismantle the legal and cultural barriers keeping women from gaining access to contraceptive information to her experience as a visiting nurse among the immigrant working class in New York City. In her autobiography and elsewhere, she told the story of Sadie Sachs, who died of too many pregnancies and a self-induced abortion. Sanger did not blame individual men; she understood that the doctor and the husband in her story were trapped inside a system that regarded sexuality as a matter of morality rather than health and disregarded women's perspectives and needs.

Pregnancy was a chronic condition among women of [the immigrant working] class. Suggestions as to what to do for a girl who was "in trouble" or a married woman who was "caught" passed from mouth to mouth. . . . The doomed women implored me to reveal the "secret" rich people had, offering to pay me extra to tell them; many really believed I was holding back information for money. . . .

One stifling mid-July day of 1912 I was summoned to a Grand Street tenement. My patient was a small, slight Russian Jewess, about twenty-eight years old. . . . Jake Sachs, a truck driver scarcely older than his wife, had come home to find the three children crying and her unconscious from the effects of a self-induced abortion. He had called the nearest doctor, who in turn sent for me. . . .

After a fortnight Mrs. Sachs' recovery was in sight. . . . When the doc-

ceptive information since the 1870s (see Chapter 5). To avoid arrest, she fled to Europe, where a Dutch feminist doctor, Aletta Jacobs, taught her about the diaphragm (then known as a female pessary), an effective, female-controlled form of contraception. Smuggling these devices into the United States, in 1916 Sanger opened the first American birth control clinic, in an immigrant neighborhood in Brooklyn. Days after the clinic opened, she was arrested for promoting birth control, as she had expected. After her 1917 trial and conviction, she served thirty days in jail. She remained dedicated to the cause of birth control for the next forty years, but increasingly promoted physician-prescribed diaphragms. This approach was adopted by the organization she founded in 1921, the American Birth Control League, forerunner of the Planned Parenthood Federation of America (see Chapter 8).

tor came to make his last call, I drew him aside. "Mrs. Sachs is terribly worried about having another baby."

"She may be," replied the doctor, and then he stood before her and said, "Any more such capers, young woman, and there'll be no need to send for me."

"I know, doctor," she replied timidly, "but," and she hesitated as it took all her courage to say it, "what can I do to prevent it?" . . . "Tell Jake to sleep on the roof." . . . [She turned to Sanger,] "He can't understand. He's only a man. But you do, don't you? Please tell me the secret, and I'll never breathe it to a soul. *Please!*" . . . I did not know what to say to her or how to convince her of my own ignorance; I was helpless to avert such monstrous atrocities. . . .

The telephone rang one evening three months later, and Jake Sachs' agitated voice begged me to come at once; his wife was sick again and from the same cause. . . . [When Sanger arrived] Mrs. Sachs was in a coma and died within ten minutes. . . . I left him pacing desperately back and forth, and for hours I myself walked and walked and walked through the hushed streets. . . . [The city's] pains and griefs crowded in upon me, . . . women writhing in travail to bring forth little babies; the babies themselves naked and hungry, . . . six-year-old children with pinched, pale, and wrinkled faces. . . . I knew I could not go back merely to keeping people alive. I went to bed, knowing that no matter what it might cost, I was finished with palliatives and superficial cures; I was resolved to seek out the root of evil, to do something to change the destiny of mothers whose miseries were vast as the sky.

SOURCE: Margaret Sanger, *Margaret Sanger: An Autobiography* (1938; repr., Dover Publications, 1971), 88–92.

THE GREAT WAR, 1914–1919

At the peak of the ferment of change prompted by Progressivism, suffragism, and feminism, international events dramatically altered the American political environment. In August 1914, war broke out in Europe, as a complex set of interlocking alliances pitted the Allied powers (Britain, France, and Russia) against the Central powers (Germany, Austria-Hungary, and Italy). Even before the United States entered the war nearly three years later, the conflict had a significant impact on American women. Labor shortages benefited working women. African American men and women began a large-scale exodus out of the rural South into the industrial cities of the North. Most of these economic opportunities faded at war's end, but women's political achievements were more lasting. While the war

◆ Birth Control Clinic

The first clinic that Margaret Sanger opened up in 1916 in Brooklyn to provide birth control to Jewish and Italian immigrant women was closed down by police after only nine days. In that short time, over four hundred women, most of them mothers with young children, came to the storefront to learn how to avoid further pregnancies. As Sanger's accompanying leaflet indicates, contraception was promoted as an alternative to abortion. *Sophia Smith Collection, Smith College.*

contributed to antagonisms within the suffrage movement, it also bolstered women's claims to enfranchisement and propelled passage and ratification of the Nineteenth Amendment.

Pacifist and Anti-war Women

In the two years that the United States watched the war from the sidelines, peace advocacy among American women was widespread. NAWSA president Carrie Chapman Catt expressed the common sentiment that "when war murders the husbands and sons of women, . . . it becomes the undeniable business of women."[29] In August 1914, fifteen hundred women marched silently and solemnly down the streets of New York City to protest the violence of war. Five months later, suffragist and feminist Crystal Eastman organized the Woman's Peace Party (WPP). With over twenty thousand women members, the WPP was dedicated to resolving the conflict in Europe through peaceful, negotiated means.

In the spring of 1915, WPP members participated in an international peace conference of women, held in The Hague, Netherlands. Although transatlantic travel was dangerous, forty-seven American women sailed to Europe. Most were leisure class, but labor activist Leonora O'Reilly also attended. The Americans joined a thousand women from twelve countries to discuss a nonmilitary settlement to the war. "For the first time in all the history of the world," wrote American journalist Mary Heaton Vorse, "women of warring nations and women of neutral nations had come together to lift up their voices in protest against war, through which the women and the workers gain nothing and lose all."[30] The women's peace organization that they formed at The Hague, the Women's International League for Peace and Freedom, still exists today. The participants vowed to meet again when the war ended. For her role in this movement, Jane Addams was awarded the Nobel Peace Prize in 1931, the first American woman so honored.

President Wilson's hopes for neutrality were literally sunk by a series of conflicts with Germany, which began unrestricted submarine warfare in the Atlantic, including the United States. Wilson's position and national sentiment turned toward entering the war. On April 6, 1917, Congress declared war on Germany and its allies.

Advocating for peace when your country is not fighting is different from doing so when your country is at war. Once the United States joined the war, women who opposed it were accused of political disloyalty, and the number and prominence of women speaking against militarism plummeted. Jeanette Rankin, a suffragist from Montana and in 1914 the first woman elected to the House of Representatives, was one of fifty-six members of Congress to vote against a formal declaration of war, for which she was turned out of office. Emily Balch was fired from her job as professor of economics at Wellesley College for challenging the government's right to draft young men to fight. Ida B. Wells-Barnett was threatened with jail for her efforts to defend black soldiers who had been convicted and executed for alleged insurrection in Texas. "I'd rather go down in history as one lone Negro who dared to tell the government that it had done a

◆ American Women for Peace

Along with other members of the newly formed WPP, Jane Addams, second from the left behind the peace banner, arrives in The Hague, Netherlands, in April 1915. There she presided over an international women's peace meeting and formed a delegation to meet with the leaders of fourteen European nations to argue — in vain — for peace. Two years later, after the United States entered the war on the side of England and France, Addams remained a staunch advocate of peace, a position that then labeled her a dangerous radical. © *CORBIS*.

dastardly thing," she defiantly responded, "than to save my skin by taking back what I have said."[31]

After the 1917 Bolshevik Revolution, Russia negotiated a separate peace with Germany and left the war. This transformation of a former ally into a worker-run state intensified suspicion of American Socialists. Kate Richards O'Hare was sentenced to five years in federal prison for voicing the same kind of sentiments against mothers' being forced to sacrifice their sons to war that had been common a few years before. Emma Goldman was imprisoned for her anti-draft speeches; after the war, along with hundreds of other immigrant radicals, she was permanently deported from the United States, and she died in exile.

Within the suffrage movement, it was the militant wing that resisted the atmosphere of wartime jingoism. Prior to U.S. entry into the war, NWP members had begun picketing the White House—the first American activists ever to do so—to add to the pressure on President Wilson to supporting a federal suffrage amendment (see Figure 7.7, p. 453). Although the NWP did not formally oppose the war, it refused to halt its activities once war was declared. On the contrary, it upped the ante, carrying signs provocatively addressed to "Kaiser Wilson," declaring that "Democracy Should Begin at Home." Their peaceful protest was now perceived as the act of traitors.

From 1917 through 1919, 168 suffrage picketers were arrested, and 97 served up to six months in federal prison. Considering themselves political prisoners, many went on hunger strikes and were forcibly fed through tubes pushed down their noses into their stomachs. Rose Winslow, a Pennsylvania textile worker and veteran activist, wrote to her husband after a particularly violent forced-feeding, "I try to be less feeble-minded, . . . [but] it is hard to feel anything but desolate and forgotten in this place."[32] NWP leader Alice Paul was repeatedly interrogated by a prison psychiatrist, who wanted to prove that she was mentally ill rather than deeply dedicated to the cause of woman suffrage. She defied her interrogators and insisted that her opinions were political, not paranoid.

Preparedness and Patriotism

While anti-war women and militant suffragists persisted in their protests, the majority of American women threw themselves into the war effort. Wilson had described the United States' role in idealistic terms, claiming World War I as a "war for democracy" to spread American ideals throughout the world. Following his lead, the majority of Americans believed that their country was simply fighting for the ideals of peace and freedom and against barbarism. They were sure that their government's purposes were good and that stronger government meant a better civic life. They hoped that war could be the fruition of many progressive hopes, and they were eager to help to make it so. (See Visual Sources: Uncle Sam Wants You: Women and World War I Posters, pp. 454–59.)

Activist women also viewed supporting the war as an opportunity to demonstrate not merely their patriotism but their claims to full citizenship. Carrie Chapman Catt set aside her long history of peace advocacy to lead NAWSA into active support for the war. "I am a pacifist, but not for peace without honor," she wrote in April 1917. "I'd be willing, if necessary, to die for my country."[33] Initially the federal government was slow to take up women's offer of service, but Catt and others who supported the war pushed for the creation of the Women's Committee of the Council for National Defense (WCND) in 1917. Anna Howard Shaw, former NAWSA president, was made its head. Although the WCND was intended as purely advisory, the women appointed were determined to make it a channel for delivering women's energies to the war effort.

The WCND set up state and local branches of their organization, which in turn used women's organizations such as the Young Women's Christian Association, the Woman's Christian Temperance Union, and the General Federation of Women's Clubs to mobilize women's voluntary war work. The WCND even had a

◆ **Japanese Women's Auxiliary to the Los Angeles Red Cross**
During World War I women actively supported mobilization by conserving food and raising
funds for the Liberty Loan campaign, a major source of financing for the war. They also supported the American Red Cross, which not only sent nurses to the front but also provided
warm garments and medical supplies for the troops. African Americans and immigrants,
eager to express their patriotism, participated in these efforts. The women in this photograph
were members of the Japanese Women's Auxiliary to the Los Angeles Red Cross, a group that
took much pride in its work and its demonstration of loyalty to the United States. *Seaver Center for Western History Research.*

subdivision for "colored women," with African American poet Alice Dunbar-
Nelson as its field representative. Women labor activists served on another sub-
committee on Women in Industry; this was transformed after the war into the
U.S. Woman's Bureau, led by Mary Van Kleeck.

Women's pro-war activities took many forms. Following the model of suffrage
parades, they organized grand public marches to raise money for wartime "Liberty
Bonds." They drew up plans to organize America's housewives to conserve meat,
sugar, and wheat for the war effort. They raised relief funds for refugees in Europe.
Several thousand women, organized by the American Red Cross, served as nurses
and ambulance drivers on the battlefields of France.

Women were also active in what was called "Americanization" work (see
Chapter 6). These were efforts to accelerate the assimilation of immigrants into
American society, especially those, such as Germans and Italians, who were suspected of loyalty to America's opponents rather than to its allies. In the Southwest,
particular attention was focused on Mexican immigrants, who were regarded
as potentially dangerous radicals because of the 1910 revolution in Mexico.

Throughout the nation's cities, native-born women reformers taught English language, home, and health classes for immigrant women, while also instructing them in wartime food conservation measures.

But the biggest contribution that women made to the war effort was through their labor. Although the United States did not enter the war until 1917, by 1915 the economy was already beginning to speed up to provision the Allies and prepare for possible American involvement. As European immigration was slowed to a halt by the naval war in the Atlantic, the accelerating needs of the labor force were met instead by white women workers and then by black men and women. The female labor force increased to more than 10 million during the war years, and many women found new and better-paying opportunities in the railroad, steel, and other heavy industries. Harriot Stanton Blatch characterized the situation with brutal honesty: "When men go awarring, women go to work. War compels women to work. That is one of its merits."[34]

The Great Migration

World War I was an especially monumental turning point for African Americans. Many seized the opportunity provided by demand for wartime labor to flee southern segregation and exploitation and migrate north. Two to three times as many southern black people, perhaps 500,000, migrated in the decade after 1910 as in the decade before. The black population of Chicago increased 150 percent, Detroit 600 percent, New York City 66 percent. This profound shift in population between 1914 and 1920, from the South to the North and from rural to urban life, is known as the "Great Migration."

Unlike European and Asian migrations, in which men represented the vast majority of migrants, women totalled almost half the number of African American migrants. Their reasons for migrating were in part economic. Black women found it easier to move into job opportunities than black men. For the first time, African American women, who had been almost exclusively employed in domestic and agricultural labor, entered factory work, although usually in the dirtiest and most dangerous jobs and only for the brief period of wartime mobilization. "I'll never work in nobody's kitchen but my own anymore," one black woman optimistically declared.[35] Even in domestic labor, a woman could earn more in a day up North than in a week in the South. Going north also meant escaping the constant threat of sexual harassment to which they were exposed in the white homes in which they worked, and with it the lynching that loomed for any black man who tried to protect his wife or daughters. A twenty-five-year-old mother of eight asked the African American newspaper, the *Chicago Defender,* for help in migrating. "I want to get out of this dog hold," she wrote, "because I don't know what I am raising [my children] up for in this place."[36] (See Documents: African American Women and the Great Migration, pp. 466–73.)

The new migrants needed aid in finding jobs and housing and adjusting to northern urban life. The National Association of Colored Women acted quickly to lift the burden, establishing a Women Wage Earners Association to assist migrating black women workers. The YWCA also responded by increasing the funding of its Division of Colored Work, designating $200,000 for work with young women in African American communities, and tripling the number of independent black branches. In 1919, the Women's Trade Union League, which had heretofore ignored the needs of African Americans, devoted attention to black immigrants' needs by hiring Irene Goins of Chicago as a special organizer for black women workers.

For the most part, however, black migrants met hostility and segregation among whites in the North. In 1915, *Birth of a Nation,* one of the first great epics of the American film industry, presented a thoroughly racist account of American history, including a defense of lynching, to packed houses of white filmgoers throughout the North and South. During and after the war, pent-up racial antagonism exploded in a series of race riots. In 1917 Ida B. Wells-Barnett risked her life to go to East St. Louis, Illinois, to investigate the 150 black people who were, in her words, "slaughtered" in a riot there. In 1919, another deadly riot erupted in Chicago, after a white mob killed an African American child who had wandered onto a whites-only beach. But despite the violence and disappointment African Americans faced in the North, migration offered black women and their families improved economic opportunities and an escape from the dead-end life of the South.

Winning Woman Suffrage

The United States entered World War I just as momentum for woman suffrage was peaking. Militant suffragists of the NWP demonstrated daily outside the White House, while the NAWSA, under Carrie Chapman Catt's leadership, steadily lobbied Congress. The victory of woman suffrage in the second New York referendum in 1917 boosted prospects for national victory. Catt had predicted that once New York women were enfranchised, the state's congressional delegation, the largest in the country, would swing over to woman suffrage and "the backbone of the opposition will be largely bent if not broken."[37] She was right. Two months after woman suffrage won in New York, the House of Representatives passed a constitutional amendment establishing full voting rights for all American women. The NWP named it the Susan B. Anthony Amendment to signify the long battle that had to be fought to win it (see Chapter 4).

From the House, the Anthony Amendment went to the Senate, where it confronted the power and resistance of southern Democrats. With the Fourteenth and Fifteenth Amendments still a rankling sore (see Chapter 5), southern Democrats were opposed to any further federal involvement in voting rights. President Wilson, who finally yielded to pressure from suffragists, went to the Senate to appeal for passage. "We have made partners of women in this war," he pleaded. "Shall we admit them only to a partnership of suffering and sacrifice and toil and not to a partnership of privilege and right?"[38] Nonetheless, when the Senate voted in October 1918, the amendment fell two votes short of passage.

That same month, the war ended in victory for the Allies. Wilson left for Paris to negotiate the peace and fight for the establishment of a "League of Nations," a multinational organization to achieve, in his words, "mutual guarantees of political independence and territorial integrity to great and small states alike."[39] A small army of American women activists went with him in hopes of influencing the outcome of the peace conference. Many of these American women then traveled to Zurich to fulfill the promise they had made in The Hague in 1915 to reconvene the international women's peace movement after the war. When Wilson returned to the United States with the Versailles Treaty, which included establishment of the League of Nations among its provisions, he was unable to convince a skeptical Congress to ratify it, a defeat that literally destroyed him. In October 1919, he suffered a disabling stroke, and for the last year of his presidency, first lady Edith Bolling Galt Wilson took on many of the tasks of her husband's office (and was widely maligned for overstepping her bounds).

Through all this, suffragists still had to find the final votes they needed in Congress. In the November 1918 elections, they campaigned against senators who voted against them, only to lose a crucial vote when a senatorial supporter died and was replaced by an opponent. Finally, in June 1919, the necessary votes were in place. "By that time I was so accustomed to worry and hard work, I could not get used to a situation in which neither was needed," recalled Maud Wood Park, NAWSA manager of congressional lobbying. As suffragists listened from the gallery of the Senate—Carrie Chapman Catt, who had vowed never to sit through another such debate, could not bear to attend—Senator Elison Smith of South Carolina let loose with one last burst of anti-suffrage oratory. "The southern man who votes for the Susan B. Anthony amendment votes to ratify the fifteenth amendment," he declaimed. "If it was a crime to enfranchise the male of [an alien and ignorant] race, why is it not a crime to enfranchise the other half?"[40] But by now the outcome was a foregone conclusion, and the amendment passed.

Given the rightward drift of postwar politics, ratification was a long and grueling process, and NAWSA's structure of strong state divisions was crucial in winning endorsement from the necessary thirty-six states. Of these, the only Deep South states were Texas and Kentucky. (Georgia, Louisiana, Mississippi, and North Carolina did not formally ratify the woman suffrage amendment until the 1970s!) The final battle came down to Tennessee, one of the only southern states with a viable two-party system. The decisive vote came from a young Republican legislator named Harry Burn, in response to his mother's urging. "Don't forget to be a good boy," she wrote him, "and help Mrs. Catt put the 'Rat' in Ratification."[41]

On August 26, 1920, seventy-two years after the Seneca Falls convention, the Nineteenth Amendment was added to the U.S. Constitution. Patterned after the Fifteenth Amendment, it reads, "The right of citizens of the United States to vote shall not be denied or abridged . . . on account of sex" (see the Appendix, p. A-15). But all American women's struggles for political equality were not yet complete. The courts ruled that the amendment did not affect the political status of women in the American colonies of Puerto Rico and the Philippines, who had to undertake their own campaigns—eight and sixteen years respectively—for voting rights. Most African American women in the South found that when they tried to register to vote, they were stopped by the same devices used against black men. And for all American women, the battle for parity and power within the Democratic and Republican parties had just begun. It would take another seven decades for voting women to become a force to be reckoned with in American politics and for politicians to begin to recognize them as such.

CONCLUSION: New Conditions, New Challenges

The Progressive period marked the end of one era in American women's history and the beginning of another. The gradual move of American women into public life that had begun in the middle of the nineteenth century reached its apex in the first decades of the twentieth. In few other periods of American history did women achieve greater public visibility and political influence. The inclusion of women's equal political rights in the U.S. Constitution, after almost three-quarters of a century of effort, crowned a host of women's other Progressive era achievements.

By the same token, crucial changes were taking place just under the surface. Not only were the numbers of female workers continuing to rise but the place of paid labor in women's lives was shifting dramatically. Women had entered the Progressive era under the banner of motherhood; they were leaving it, unbeknownst to many of them, under the banner of worker. The sexual revolution and birth control movement of these years also signified grand changes to come in women's lives. All of these developments would play out in the next decades as women faced different sorts of challenges and began to envision new collective goals.

Parades, Picketing, and Power: Women in Public Space

ALTHOUGH AMERICAN WOMEN were never as tightly restricted to the private sphere of the home as nineteenth-century cultural prescriptions suggested, by the turn of the century, women's presence in the public arena had notably expanded. Working-class women had jobs in factories, shops, and offices and filled crowded city streets. They frequented dance halls and amusement parks. Leisure-class women shopped in department stores, attended college, and participated in reform activities. In this essay, we analyze women's increased public visibility by examining the ways in which two groups of women activists—working-class women strikers and leisure-class suffragists—took to the streets to march and picket, literally opening up new spaces for women in the society. Whether they were agitating for economic rights or for the vote, their public visibility had political and cultural significance. The bold occupation of public space was an important demonstration of women's legitimacy as political actors.

THE STRIKERS

Women laborers had participated in strikes and public demonstrations as early as the mill girls of Lowell, Massachusetts, in the 1830s (see Chapter 3). Nonetheless, when New York City women shirtwaist workers began picketing in front of their factories in 1909, many observers found their behavior shocking. These young Jewish and Italian women were not only challenging their employers but transgressing against conventional notions of appropriate feminine behavior. When the demonstrations expanded to a general strike of the entire industry and the leisure-class women of the Women's Trade Union League (WTUL) became involved, the newspaper coverage became more sympathetic. From this point on, the events of the strike were widely reported in the popular press. The women made good copy, and their leaders eagerly sought publicity for the cause.

By 1909, newspapers had the technology to illustrate their stories with photographs. Given the limitations of that technology, these pictures were usually posed and static; the dramatic moments captured on film that would become the hallmark of modern photojournalism were a thing of the future. The hybrid illustration in Figure 7.1 appeared in the *New York Evening Journal* on November 10, 1909. The photograph shows, as the newspaper caption puts it, "Girl Strikers: each of whom has been arrested five times for picketing." This somewhat formal picture

447

◆ **Figure 7.1 "Girl Strikers,"** *New York Evening Journal,* **November 10, 1909**

◆ **Figure 7.2 Members of the Rochester, New York, Branch of the Garment Workers Union, 1913**
From the Albert R. Stone Negative Collection, Rochester Museum & Science Center, Rochester, New York.

is coupled with a drawing showing the action of police arresting the resisting women.

The photograph reveals something widely commented on in the newspaper reports. The women look fashionably dressed and, in particular, sport elaborate hats. People hostile to the strikers pointed to their clothing as evidence that the women were not suffering from dire poverty. Male union leaders and WTUL officials retorted that the clothes were cheap and bought through scrimping and going without food. Clara Lemlich was the only working woman to respond in the newspapers: "We're human, all of us girls, and we're young. We like new hats as well as any other young women. Why shouldn't we?"[42] Where critics of the strikers saw women dressed above their station, behaving in unladylike ways on the public streets, the strikers saw themselves as attractive, modern young women, willing to fight for their rights and a decent standard of living, dressed in their best to reflect the seriousness of their purpose and action.[43] Compare the photograph with the drawing. What response to the strikers did the newspaper editors seek to encourage by publishing this hybrid image?

The shirtwaist strike sparked dozens of garment industry strikes in other cities. Figure 7.2 portrays members of the Rochester, New York, branch of the Garment Workers Union as they picketed in the winter of 1912 for a cut in hours (but not pay), an end to subcontracting, and the union's right to represent the workers in negotiations with their employers. After four months—and the death of one seventeen-year-old striker shot by an excited employer—the workers won all their demands except for union recognition. This image, in which the strikers are the only women in sight, suggests something of the transgressive meaning of women marching on picket lines. During the 1909 New York City shirtwaist strike, the police conducted raids on brothels in the factory neighborhoods, pushing prostitutes into the street to mingle with the picketers. This effort to call into question the sexual respectability of the union women proved a theme in many strikes. But note how the Rochester women posed themselves for this photograph. What attitude do they project about their right to take to the streets?

Women were also central to another monumental strike that took place in the textile mills of Lawrence, Massachusetts, in 1912 (see p. 414). Textile workers in that community represented as many as forty nationalities, and half of them were women and children. The strike began in January when a group of Polish women discovered that their paychecks had been cut by 32 cents. Working women figured prominently in the subsequent marches, parades, and rallies. Housewives joined them, demonstrating in public spaces customarily occupied by women, such as front stoops, church steps, and doorways, and drawing on their female networks of neighbors and kin to promote the strike. These immigrant housewives, highly sensitive to the pay cut, called the struggle the "three loaves" strike because that was the amount of bread that the lost wages would have bought. Figure 7.3 indicates the buoyancy and camaraderie of the strikers as they linked

◆ **Figure 7.3 Immigrant Housewives during the "Three Loaves" Strike, Lawrence, Massachusetts, 1912**
Collection of the Immigrant City Archives, Lawrence, MA.

arms and marched, well aware of the camera that recorded their defiance of public decorum. How does this image differ from those in Figures 7.1 and 7.2? Why do you suppose the women are dressed so differently?

THE SUFFRAGISTS

For leisure-class suffragists to move into public space with their demonstrations was also difficult but for different reasons, as they were so bound by standards of domestic propriety. The reputation for "respectability" that was key to their difference from the working class seemed endangered by such bold, forthright public activity. Precisely because public parades were such a radical move for leisure-class women, these demonstrations drew enormous crowds eager to see a mass violation of ladylike norms.

New York City, home to one of the largest and most well-funded suffrage movements, also featured the most dramatic parades. The 1910 and 1911 parades, held right after the settlement of the shirtwaist strike and the deadly Triangle Shirtwaist Company fire respectively, were inspired by the public demonstrations of working women, which leisure-class allies had supported. In the 1911 suffrage march, labor organizer Leonora O'Reilly was a featured speaker. Banners highlighted both political and economic rights, and working girls were prominent in the ranks of the paraders. Harriot Stanton Blatch, chief organizer of the marches, understood the symbolic possibilities of suffrage parades. "What could be more stirring than hundreds of women, carrying banners, marching—marching—marching! The public would be aroused, the press would spread the story far and wide, and the interest of our own workers would be fired."[44]

In 1912 and 1913, the New York City parades were many times more spectacular, no longer foregrounding working women but emphasizing instead the participation of women of all classes (though not always of all races) cooperating for the common cause of woman suffrage. Male supporters also marched. A bill authorizing a referendum to grant full voting rights to the women of New York was before the state legislature, and the parade was intended to impress voters and legislators alike with suffragists' determination and power. As Figure 7.4 indicates, the crowds watching the 1913 parade on Fifth Avenue were ten and twelve deep. What can you tell of their attitude toward the parade? How do the dress and organization of the marchers emphasize their unanimity and discipline?

Parades soon spread to other states. Figure 7.5 captures a 1914 Suffrage Day parade in Minneapolis/St. Paul, Minnesota. With two thousand marchers, the procession stretched out for over a mile. Reflecting the large immigrant population of the state, the parade included the Scandinavian contingent shown here, with women dressed in national costumes carrying the Swedish and Norwegian flags. Norway had just enfranchised women the year before, the second country in Europe to do so, following Finland's example in 1906. A Scandinavian suffrage club

◆ Figure 7.4 **Suffragists Marching down Fifth Avenue, New York City, 1913**

Milstein Division of United States History, Local History and Genealogy, The New York Public Library, Astor, Lenox, and Tilden Foundations.

◆ Figure 7.5 **Suffrage Day Parade, Minneapolis/St. Paul, Minnesota, 1914**
Minnesota Historical Society.

had been established in Minnesota in 1907; other Minnesota suffrage groups included the Women Workers' Suffrage Club, the Everywoman Suffrage Club (consisting of African American women), and a Women's Welfare League. The diversity in Minnesota's campaign reflected the widening circle of support for woman suffrage that coalesced after 1910 (see p. 427). What does the featuring of traditional ethnic costumes signify in a movement for women's political equality?

The most significant and highly publicized suffrage parade was held in Washington, D.C., in March 1913. This was not only the first suffrage parade to represent the movement on a national level but was also one of the first such demonstrations held in the nation's capital on any issue. Extremely well organized by the young Alice Paul, just beginning her career as the leader of suffragism's militant wing (see p. 429), the parade drew five thousand women from around the country. Banners identified some groups of marchers by their professions, from factory worker to lawyer. Other participants walked with women's clubs. Still others rode on floats that depicted women in roles of mother, worker, and citizen. The organizers required African American women to march at the back of the parade. The parade culminated at the steps of the U.S. Treasury building, where marchers enacted an allegorical pageant, with individual women performing the roles of America, Peace, Liberty, Hope, Justice, and Charity.[45] The *Washington Post* described the event as "Miles of Fluttering Femininity Present Entrancing Suffrage Appeal."[46] Although condescending, the newspaper's comments vindicated the

◆ **Figure 7.6 Suffrage Parade down Pennsylvania Avenue, Washington, D.C., March 1913**
Brown Brothers.

organizers' hopes that the attractiveness of the parade and its participants proved that suffrage and femininity were compatible.

The photograph in Figure 7.6 captures the start of the parade. The coordinated clothing of this group of marchers indicates the attention to matters of style. The woman to the far right is dressed in academic regalia, worn proudly by women college graduates in suffrage parades. To the left is Inez Milholland, the beautiful lawyer and suffragist, leading the parade from her white horse, as she had in New York City. The most striking aspect of the image, however, is the backdrop of the national Capitol. Although Washington, D.C., officials tried to locate the march in a less central location, Paul was adamant that it take place on Pennsylvania Avenue, in the customary place for official parades, and on the day before the presidential inauguration of Woodrow Wilson. What is the significance of the juxtaposition of the parade and the Capitol building in this image?

Ironically, the parade's greatest contribution to the suffrage cause may have been its disruption by enormous crowds of drunken men, the kind who always showed up for a presidential inauguration. The *Baltimore American* reported that the women "practically fought their way foot by foot up Pennsylvania Avenue through a surging throng."[47] Newspapers all over the country criticized not just the rowdy crowds but the police for failing to protect the marchers. The debacle led to a congressional hearing, which the suffragists skillfully exploited to generate favorable publicity for their cause. Even former NAWSA president Anna Howard Shaw, who generally disapproved of radical tactics, knew how to make the most of the episode: "Do you suppose that if we were voters the police would have allowed the hoodlums to possess the streets while we marched?"[48]

◆ Figure 7.7 **National Woman's Party Picketers at the White House, 1918**
Library of Congress, LC-USZ62-31799.

A final example in 1917 of women's claim to public space for political ends comes full circle, back to picketing. Figure 7.7 shows the suffrage militants of the National Woman's Party picketing the White House during World War 1 (see p. 440). College graduates, they identified themselves by their alma maters. Just as the working-class women illustrated in Figures 7.1 to 7.3 had hoped to attract publicity to their cause, these radical suffragists sought to embarrass President Wilson by graphically pointing out the hypocrisy of a war fought for democracy while women at home were not enfranchised. More moderate suffragists criticized the radicals' tactics, but how might images such as this one have played a role in bringing Wilson around to support of the suffrage amendment?

QUESTIONS FOR ANALYSIS

1. Compare the photographs illustrating the strikers (Figures 7.1 to 7.3) and the suffragists (Figures 7.4 to 7.7). How did both groups take to the streets, and what commonalities and differences do their uses of public space reveal?

2. A major motivation behind picketing and parading was to capture publicity. What other purposes could these activities serve? What possibilities and dangers did the courting of publicity pose for strikers? For suffragists?

3. What does the popularity among women activists of these mass demonstrations suggest about the public involvement of women in the Progressive era?

VISUAL SOURCES

Uncle Sam Wants You: Women and World War I Posters

P RIOR TO WORLD WAR I, the federal government communicated with citizens primarily through press releases printed in newspapers. In April 1917, however, President Woodrow Wilson formed the Committee on Public Information (CPI) to promote public support for the war. The CPI established a Department of Pictorial Publicity, which drew on a well-established tradition of using posters for advertising as well as on the skills of well-known magazine illustrators. The federal government used other methods to build support for war needs such as conserving food, recruiting soldiers for the military and workers for war industries, and supporting Liberty Bond and Red Cross fund drives, but the posters were the most colorful and abundant device. Over 20 million copies of 2,500 different posters were produced during the war. State governments and civic associations such as the Red Cross also created these dramatic advertisements to "sell the war."

Wartime propaganda aimed at creating a strong sense of identification with the nation and an eagerness to support the military effort. Although building the army itself required the coercion of the draft, the government turned to persuasive measures when possible in keeping with the notion that the United States was going to "war for democracy." The posters reproduced here need to be understood as part of this massive drive to imbue Americans with intense loyalty and patriotism. A strong anti-war movement in the country opposed the war, but dissent was repressed and many protestors were imprisoned and, if not citizens, deported (see p. 440).

Women's efforts were central to the nation's call for patriotism. In the midst of the final stages of their drive for citizenship, many women saw themselves, if not quite as regular soldiers, as members of a volunteer army that blanketed the nation in support of various wartime mobilization drives. These activities required exceptional administrative skills, and for some leisure-class women, this became full-time work.

Posters, of course, do not convey the complexity of these women's volunteer activity. The messages were simple. Women were urged to do their part as a demonstration of their citizenship, and their images were widely used to encourage all Americans to support the war. Given the eagerness with which women rushed into the public sphere to support the war, it is ironic that the majority of these images depicted traditional notions of womanhood.

Images of women have been used to represent the United States since the nation was founded. (See Visual Sources: Gendering Images of the Revolution, pp. 110–18.) Posters used female representations to give a feminine face to war aims. A beautiful woman flanked by the United States flag or dressed in "the stars and stripes" represented the patriotism of a nation at war. Figure 7.8 depicts a beseeching woman wearing a cap that clearly echoes the American flag. In the backdrop is a European city with its church towers in flames, a potent reminder to Americans safe at home of the devastating war across the Atlantic. The poster in Figure 7.9 features a female form to indicate that America's honor needed fighting men to protect it. What conventional ideas of femininity do these posters mobilize to bolster their messages?

Posters also traded on images of female sexuality. The saucy young woman dressed in a military uniform in Figure 7.10, an image created by well-known artist Howard Chandler Christy, provocatively exclaims, "I Wish I Were a Man." What does this image suggest about modern notions of female sexuality emerging in the prewar years? How does the cross-dressed figure communicate the proper roles of men and women in wartime?

Even when posters encouraged women to participate in war activities by buying Liberty Bonds, supporting the Red Cross, knitting socks for soldiers, or conserving food, the images rarely challenged traditional ideas of women's proper place. Figure 7.11, for example, is a recruitment poster for the Land Army, a voluntary organization formed to mobilize women as temporary farmworkers. How does it link labor on the home front to the war? How are the women agricultural laborers represented?

◆ Figure 7.8 **"Let's End It—Quick with Liberty Bonds"** *(top)*
Library of Congress, LC-USZC4-9462.

◆ Figure 7.9 **"It's Up To You. Protect the Nation's Honor. Enlist Now"** *(bottom)*
Library of Congress, LC-USZ62-87685.

◆ Figure 7.10 **"Gee!! I Wish I Were a Man.
I'd Join the Navy"**
Library of Congress, LC-USZ62-42150.

◆ Figure 7.11 **"The Woman's Land Army of
America Training School"**
Library of Congress, LC-USZ62-42546.

Food conservation was the aspect of home front war support effort most explicitly targeted at women. Future president Herbert Hoover headed up the U.S. Food Administration, and women were the rank and file of his "army." Female energy was marshalled through a variety of clubs and organizations, including local branches of the Women's Council for National Defense (see p. 441). Women volunteers all over the country went house-to-house, encouraging housewives to pledge to uphold principles of food conservation. Each household that agreed received a window card that, in the words of one food administrator, carried the message "to the passer-by that the inmates of this home were pledged to support the government, the Food Administration, the cause of Americans, and the Allies at the front."[49] Women's groups also conducted public lessons on conservation and distributed recipe books. Figure 7.12, issued by the U.S. Food Administration and designed to encourage women to substitute corn for wheat, portrays a housewife in her kitchen. How is she helping the military effort through her domestic work?

◆ Figure 7.12 "Corn—The Food of the Nation—Serve Some Way Every Meal"
© ZUMA/CORBIS.

Some posters depicted women supporting the war effort in the workforce. The government distributed one featuring a typist, now almost wholly a female occupation, with the caption, "The Kaiser is afraid of you!" On occasion, posters acknowledged women who crossed conventional gender barriers when they took jobs in war work. These images were usually issued by the Young Women's Christian Association (YWCA), which produced its own posters. During the war, the YWCA continued its prewar activism on behalf of young working women and distributed the poster depicted in Figure 7.13 as part of its fund-raising campaign. In keeping with YWCA literature that praised women factory workers' vital contribution to defense, this image emphasizes female strength and solidarity. Note too the graphic style of this image. How does it compare to government posters intended to convey more conventional ideas about women's war contribution?

World War I poster art is also revealing for what it did not picture, in particular the way in which it supported existing racial hierarchies. Government and voluntary agencies worked in black communities to encourage support for war programs. Alice Dunbar-Nelson's report on "Negro Women in War Work" (see p. 471), for example, detailed the fund-raising of the National Association of Colored Women, which raised close to $5 million in the third Liberty Loan drive. Yet despite the record of black women's participation, apparently no posters represented them or other women of color. Images of European immigrants appeared in a few World War I posters, but the diversity of American women was not reflected in this popular propaganda form.

War posters also failed to depict adequately the full range of ways in which women supported the war effort. The wartime growth in the wage labor force was rarely represented, and instead of images of women performing manual labor, most women depicted in posters were either icons for the nation or wartime vol-

◆ Figure 7.13
"For Every Fighter a Woman Worker. Y.W.C.A."
Library of Congress, LC-USZC4-1419.

unteers. But if few posters challenged traditional expectations about women's domestic roles, women themselves did take advantage of wartime opportunities. Not only did working women temporarily break into traditionally male jobs, but suffragists used women's war service as a way of dramatically demonstrating their claim for full citizenship.

QUESTIONS FOR ANALYSIS

1. Figures 7.9 and 7.10 are both enlistment posters aimed at young men. What emotional responses do the artists seek to arouse in their intended audience? How are their methods alike, and how do they differ?

2. Until recently in the United States, only men officially served in combat, and it could be argued that by virtue of asking men to risk death, wartime gave them a heightened claim on citizenship. To what extent do these posters reinforce this notion? To what extent do they challenge it?

3. The Library of Congress's online catalog of prints and photographs offers an extensive number of World War I posters. Go to <loc.gov/rr/print/catalog .htmls>, find the World War I poster collection, and search for other poster images of women. What insights does your research give you about the representation of American women in World War I?

Modernizing Womanhood

A S THE DRIVE FOR THE VOTE HEATED UP in the years before World War I, another less sharply defined movement emerged among more radical women, who called themselves feminists (see p. 433). While women like Charlotte Perkins Gilman and Crystal Eastman supported the suffrage campaign, their ideas moved beyond women's political rights to include themes of economic independence and more modern sexual relationships and marriages. Many feminists had socialist leanings and were associated with the struggles of working-class women; a few were union activists themselves. Self-consciously rebellious, they viewed themselves as breaking from the suffocating conventions of respectable female behavior, demanding instead to be recognized, in the words of Edna Kenton, as "people of flesh and blood and brain, feeling, seeing, judging and directing equally with men, all the great social forces."[50]

In 1912, twenty-five feminists in New York founded a club they called Heterodoxy because it "demanded of a member that she should not be orthodox in her opinions."[51] Over the next two decades, Heterodoxy provided a lively environment for feminists to share their ideas. It was this group, under the leadership of Marie Jenney Howe, that called the first mass meeting on feminism, held in New York City's Cooper Union Hall on February 17, 1914 (see p. 434). The range of ideas embodied in feminism, as well as the interest of many sympathetic males in the movement, is revealed in this newspaper account.

"Talk on Feminism Stirs Great Crowd," *New York Times* (1914)

What is Feminism? Twelve speakers, six men and six women, attempted to answer the question in Cooper Union last night in what was called the first feminist mass meeting ever had. The People's Institute made the arrangements for the discussion. The auditorium was filled almost to capacity, and it was remarked that there were more men than women in the audience. The applause

was frequent, and hearty. Many definitions of feminism were given, differing in details, but agreeing in the essential fact that the movement sought freedom for women.

There was Rose Young, who said that feminism to her was "some fight, some fate, and some fun," and there was Edwin Bjorkman, who said that feminism meant "that woman shall have the same right as man to be different." Henrietta Rodman said that when feminism was the vogue

Source: *New York Times*, February 18, 1914, p. 2.

women would lose such privileges as "the right to alimony and the right to be supported all of her life," and Will Irwin added that feminism would disprove "all of the bunk talked about the home and fireside."

George Middletown considered the subject of feminism from several points of view. He said in part:

"Feminism means trouble: trouble means agitation; agitation means movement; movement means life; life means adjustment and readjustment — so does feminism. Feminism is not a femaleness with fewer petticoats; it does not seek to crinoline men. It asks [for] a new fashion in the social garments of each. Feminism is a spiritual attitude. It recognizes that men and women are made of the same soul stuff. It places this above biological bosh.

"In another aspect feminism is an educational ideal. It asks that children be educated according to temperament and not according to maleness and femaleness. It asks that a girl be educated for work and not for sex. Feminism seeks to change social opinion toward the sex relation, not to advocate license, but to recognize liberty."

Rose Young, when her turn to speak came, said:

"To me feminism means that woman wants to develop her own womanhood. It means that she wants to push on to the finest, fullest, freest expression of herself. She wants to be an individual. When you mention individualism to some people they immediately see a picture of original sin, but the freeing of the individuality of woman does not mean original sin; it means the finding of her own soul.

"The first thing that we have to overcome is custom and convention, and the common attitude of mind, and then this fear of individuality will pass away. We have to compel conviction that woman is a human being."

This idea of the assertion of individuality by woman was dwelt upon by Edwin Bjorkman. He said that feminism meant that "woman should have the right to be a full-fledged personality and not merely a social unit."

"We want woman to have the same right as man to experiment with her own life," he said. . . .

"Feminism means revolution, and I am a revolutionist," said Frances Perkins.° "I believe in revolutions as a principle. It does good to everybody."

Max Eastman, as his contribution to the discussion, said:

"Feminism is the name for the newly discovered and highly surprising fact that it is just as important for a woman to be happy as a man. And one woman will be happy by going out and seeking adventures of her own and another will be happy staying at home and thinking about babies and baked beans. Both should be allowed to do what they want to do. There'll be a great deal more fun for everybody when women are universally active and free and independent."

Marie Jenney Howe, who was the Chairman of the meeting, said that feminism was "the entire woman movement," and she added that while men were held in prison by convention, custom, and tradition, "women were confined to one room in the prison and had to watch the men walk about in the corridors in comparative freedom."

"Feminism is simply part of the great world fight for freedom and justice and equality, and might better be called humanism," said George Creel.

"The basis of feminism, the basis of suffragism, the basis of all the modern movements making for progress lies in the labor movement," said Mrs. Frank Cochran, the only speaker who used her husband's name.

° At the time of the meeting a New York social reformer, Frances Perkins in 1933 became the first woman to head a federal cabinet office.

ALTHOUGH FEMINISTS most often published in radical journals, their writings also appeared in mass magazines. In 1913 *McClure's Magazine* noted that "no movement of this century is more significant or more deep-rooted than the movement to readjust the social position of women," and began a "department for women" to "represent the ideas of the more advanced thinkers of the feminist movement." High-profile suffrage activist and lawyer Inez Milholland wrote the articles. The following is an extract from her second essay.

INEZ MILHOLLAND
The Changing Home (1913)

PROPERTY RIGHTS IN WOMEN ARE DISAPPEARING

. . . The past fifty years, with their key discoveries in science, have unlocked the secrets of earth and air, have given us modern production and distribution, have brought the ends of the world together in an entirely new sort of neighborhood, with the beginnings of a new common understanding—have, in a word, expanded man's thought, feeling, and social power as the explorations of the sixteenth and seventeenth centuries expanded his geography.

These discoveries and the resultant harnessing of newly discovered natural laws, have made possible the "social surplus" of which the Socialists say so much. For the first time in human history, the race can produce enough of the necessaries of life to go round. While we have not yet arrived at such a fair distribution, the tendency of modern social and political effort is distinctly taking that direction all over the world. And, coincidentally with the struggles of workers everywhere for a share in the fruits of life under the new conditions, we see woman, with individual economic independence at last in sight, stirring and striving to free herself from property-subjection to man in industry, and in marriage itself.

THE HOME HAS BEEN REMOVED FROM THE WOMAN

It is still said, in some quarters, that "woman's place is the home"; but it is becoming increasingly difficult to understand the phrase. For the home, in the earlier sense of the term, has been pretty effectually removed from the woman. In the traditional idyllic home which apparently still exists in the fancy of many conservative thinkers (but which probably never existed as generally as these thinkers imagine), woman spun, wove, and made clothing, milked and churned, put up foods, and so on. Her duties were many, arduous, sometimes dignified and important. Her "sphere" was defined with some clearness. Within it she exercised a real authority. In addition, she bore and reared children. And she found time for all!

To-day, if woman is to "go back to the home" in the only sense that the phrase can possibly carry, she will have to follow it into the canning factory, the packing-house, the cotton and woolen mills, the clothing factory, the up-State dairy, the railroad that handles the dairy products, the candy factory, etc. As a matter of fact, she has already been forced in considerable numbers to follow these tasks into their new industrial environ-

SOURCE: "The Changing Home," *McClure's Magazine*, March 1913, 206–19.

ment. But, whereas in the home she had some authority and certain partnership rights, in industry she has no voice except as she can make herself heard through the medium of a trade union or (less directly) of the vote.

So the "home" has, in part, been removed, and the eight million women actually engaged in industry to-day indicate with some force that woman has had to go with it. To order her "back to the home" is, therefore, nonsense. It is like ordering the cab-driver, displaced by the taxicab chauffeur, back to the stage-coach to compete with the railroad. . . .

MARRIAGE BY INTIMIDATION

No one, of course,—least of all the advanced feminist thinkers,—questions the imperative beauty and value of romantic love. Indeed, the hope is that marriage, far from being undermined or destroyed, can be made real and lasting. . . . What thoughtful women are distinctly beginning to object to is the time-honored belief that it is decent for a woman to bestow her sex, legally or illegally, in exchange for a guarantee of food, shelter, and clothing.

That millions of women have had to do precisely this in the past is too commonly known to be gainsaid. They have had to do it sometimes because there was no other way in which they could live according to reasonable standards of what living is, and sometimes, often, because the prevailing masculine ideal of the ornamental comparatively useless woman has withheld from them the training and equipment that would have enabled them to cope with life as it is.

But, now that the changing economic conditions have forced woman in some degree to meet life squarely and directly, and at the same time have begun to make some sort of economic independence seem possible for almost any individual, she is making the interesting discovery that she can in some measure subsist without throwing herself, legally or illicitly, on the mercy of the individual man. Accordingly, she is pressing and striving to increase her economic opportunity, even to gain some real economic authority; and at the same time she is getting a grip on the lever of political power. . . .

THE NEW POWER OF THE WAGE-EARNING WOMAN

. . . [T]hat this new condition carries with it a new social attitude toward divorce goes without saying. The promise of the new relationship between man and woman is that the deeply rooted, perennial mating instinct may begin to work more spontaneously and finely in conditions permitting freer choice. It is beginning to be recognized that real marriage can not be brought into existence through fear of want or through other social intimidation. . . .

A mere casual survey of current books and plays makes it evident that a calm, intelligent study of these elemental facts is rapidly taking the place of our traditional attitude of outward conformity tempered by inner panic. We are beginning to perceive that we can not successfully fit all of life into a preconceived mold; that our real task is to try, soberly and patiently, to learn what this strange substance we call life really is.

T HE THEME OF SEXUAL LIBERATION, evident in Milholland's *McClure's* article, appeared repeatedly in feminist writing and was often accompanied by a call for the legalization of birth control. In this article from the radical journal *Birth Control Review*, Crystal Eastman discusses the far-reaching implications of women's control over reproduction. Eastman's concern for economic as well as sexual liberation reflects both her socialist and feminist sensibilities.

CRYSTAL EASTMAN
Birth Control in the Feminism Program (1918)

Feminism means different things to different people, I suppose. To women with a taste for politics and reform it means the right to vote and hold office. To women physically strong and adventuresome it means freedom to enter all kinds of athletic contests and games, to compete with men in aviation, to drive racing cars, . . . to enter dangerous trades, etc. To many it means social and sex freedom, doing away with exclusively feminine virtues. To most of all it means economic freedom,—not the ideal economic freedom dreamed of by revolutionary socialism, but such economic freedom as it is possible for a human being to achieve under the existing system of competitive production and distribution,—in short such freedom to choose one's way of making a living as men now enjoy, and definite economic rewards for one's work when it happens to be "home-making." This is to me the central fact of feminism. Until women learn to want economic independence, i.e., the ability to earn their own living independently of husbands, fathers, brothers or lovers,—and until they work out a way to get this independence without denying themselves the joys of love and motherhood, it seems to me feminism has no roots. Its manifestations are often delightful and stimulating but they are sporadic, they effect no lasting change in the attitude of men to women, or of women to themselves.

Whether other feminists would agree with me that the economic is the fundamental aspect of feminism, I don't know. But on this side we are surely agreed, that Birth Control is an elementary essential in all aspects of feminism. Whether we are the special followers of Alice Paul, or Ruth Law, or Ellen Key, or Olive Schreiner, we must all be followers of Margaret Sanger. Feminists are not nuns. That should be established. We want to love and to be loved, and most of us want children, one or two at least. But we want our love to be joyous and free—not clouded with ignorance and fear. And we want our children to be deliberately, eagerly called into being, when we are at our best, not crowded upon us in times of poverty and weakness. We want this precious sex knowledge not just for ourselves, the conscious feminists; we want it for all the millions of unconscious feminists that swarm the earth,—we want it for all women.

Life is a big battle for the complete feminist even when she can regulate the size of her family. Women who are creative, or who have administrative gifts, or business ability, and who are ambitious to achieve and fulfill themselves in these lines, if they also have the normal desire to be mothers, must make up their minds to be a sort of supermen, I think. They must develop greater powers of concentration, a stronger will to "keep at it," a more determined ambition than men of equal gifts, in order to make up for the time and energy and thought and devotion that child-bearing and rearing, even in the most "advanced" families, seems inexorably to demand of the mother. But if we add to this handicap complete uncertainty as to when children may come, how often they come or how many there shall be, the thing becomes impossible. I would almost say that the whole structure of the feminist's dream of society rests upon the rapid extension of scientific knowledge about birth control.

SOURCE: *Birth Control Review,* January 1918, reproduced in Blanche Wiesen Cook, ed., *Crystal Eastman on Women and Revolution* (New York: Oxford University Press, 1978), 46–49.

QUESTIONS FOR ANALYSIS

1. What role does women's economic independence play in feminist thought?
2. Why is birth control so crucial to the transformation in women's lives that feminists anticipated?
3. What changes in relationships and marriage did feminists promote?
4. Feminists were self-consciously "modern." What evidence do you see for this sensibility in these documents?

D O C U M E N T S

African American Women and the Great Migration

BETWEEN 1910 AND 1930 AFRICAN AMERICAN MEN AND WOMEN left the rural South in extraordinary numbers, some for cities in their own region but many more for urban centers in the North and Midwest. This move profoundly shaped the black experience. The number of women migrants nearly equaled that of men. For both men and women the impulse to leave stemmed from a combination of factors, with the lure of jobs in the North during the war and postwar years particularly important.

THE EXPERIENCE OF MIGRATION

POOR AFRICAN AMERICANS left behind few private papers for the historical record, so historians are fortunate to be able to turn to letters that southern migrants wrote to black newspapers like the *Chicago Defender* and the *Atlanta Journal,* as well as to letters written to potential employers and friends and family back home. The letters reproduced here were collected in 1919 and published in the *Journal of Negro History.*° Letter A, written by an Anniston, Alabama, man in 1917, makes it clear that the Great Migration was a family affair and that women expected to join men in getting paid work, a point made in many men's letters.

Women's letters reveal a variety of concerns. A wife hopes to find out about work for her family in letter B, which also suggests the desperate conditions of poor southern blacks and their fear of reprisal from southern whites for leaving. Her unwillingness to "say more" makes it frustrating for the historian. Would a franker letter refer to the sexual assault so many black women experienced? Or to her fear for the men of her family and the omnipresent threat of violence or lynching? More commonly, women who wrote concentrated on economic issues and detailed their own work experience and skills, which were usually in some form of domestic service (letter C).

Just like immigrants from overseas, many African Americans made the trek out of the South through a process of chain migration, with one member of the family going first and others following. Women were crucial to this process, as

---

°The names of the writers are not provided in these letters because the editor wished to protect their privacy and perhaps to prevent identification by whites from their hometowns.

they were often responsible for saving meager resources and taking care of things at home before the family could move north to follow a male relative. In some localities, large groups of people combined their resources in "migration clubs," to raise funds and facilitate the difficult transition to northern urban life. Letter D reveals the efforts of Louisiana women to migrate together.

Women who wrote letters seeking jobs expected to find familiar work as domestics, but as wartime labor shortages increased, factories began to hire African American women in manufacturing jobs. Letter E details work in a meat-packing house. Written by a woman who had already migrated to Chicago to a friend back home, encouraging letters like this helped fuel further migration.

A. Letter from Anniston, Alabama, April 26, 1917

Dear Sir: Seeing in the Chicago Defender that you wanted men to work and that you are not to rob them of their half loaf; interested me very much. So much that I am inquiring for a job; one for my wife, auntie and myself. My wife is a seamster, my auntie a cook I do janitor work or common labor. We all will do the work you give us. Please reply early.

B. Letter from McCoy, Louisiana, April 16, 1917

Dear Editor [of the *Chicago Defender*]: I have been takeing your wonderful paper and I have saved [each edition] from the first I have received and my heart is upset night and day. I am praying every day to see some one that I may get a pass [a free railway ticket] for me, my child and husband I have a daughter 17 who can work well and myself. please sir direct me to the place where I may be able to see the parties that I and my family whom have read the defender so much until they are anxious to come dear editor we are working people but we cant hardly live here I would say more but we are back in the jungles and we have to lie low but please sir answer and I pray you give me a homeward consolation as we haven't money enough to pay our fares.

C. Letter from Biloxi, Mississippi, April 27, 1917

Dear Sir: I would like to get in touch with you a pece of advise I am unable to under go hard work as I have a fracture ancle but in the mene time I am able to help my selft a great dele. I am a good cook and can give good recmendation can serve in small family that has light work, if I could get something in that line I could work my daughters a long with me. She is 21 years and I have a husband all so and he is a fireman and want a positions and too small boy need to be in school now if you all see where there is some open for me that I may be able too better my condission anser at once and we will com as we are in a land of starvation.

From a willen workin woman. I hope that you will healp me as I want to get out of this land

SOURCE: *Journal of Negro History,* October 1919, 329, 426, 457–58, and July 1919, 318, 333.

of surfing [suffering] I no there is som thing that I can do here there is nothing for me to do I may be able to get in some furm where I don't have to stand on my feet all day I don't know just whah but I hope the Lord will find a place now let me here from you all at once.

D. Letter from New Orleans, Louisiana, April 23, 1917

I am a reader of the Defender and I am askeso much about the great Northern drive on the 15th of May.° We want more understanding about it for there is a great many wants to get ready for that day & and the depot agent never gives us any satisfaction when we ask for they don't want us to leave here, I want to ask you to please publish in your next Saturdays paper just what the fair will be on that day so we all will know & can be ready. So many women here are wanting to go that day. They are all working women and we cant get work here so much now, the white women tell us we just want to make money to go North and we do so please kindly ans. this in your next paper.

°Unfortunately, details of this event do not appear in the historical record.

E. Letter from Chicago, Illinois [undated]

My dear Sister: I was agreeably surprised to hear from you and to hear from home. I am well and thankful to say I am doing well. The weather and everything else was a surprise to me when I came. I got here in time to attend one of the greatest revivals in the history of my life—over 500 people joined the church. We had a Holy Ghost shower. You know I like to have run wild. It was snowing some nights and if you didnt hurry you could not get standing room. Please remember me kindly to any who ask of me. The people are rushing here by the thousands and I know if you come and rent a big house you can get all the roomers you want. You write me exactly when you are coming. I am not keeping house yet I am living with my brother and his wife. My son is in California but will be home soon. He spends his winter in California. I can get a nice place for you to stop until you can look around and see what you want. I am quite busy. I work in Swifts packing Co. in the sausage department. My daughter and I work for the same company—We get $1.50 a day and we pack so many sausages we dont have much time to play but it is a matter of a dollar with me and I feel that God made the path and I am walking therein.

Tell your husband work is plentiful here and he wont have to loaf if he want to work. . . . Well goodbye from your sister in Christ.

P.S. My brother moved the week after I came. When you fully decide to come write me and let me know what day you expect to leave and over what road and if I dont meet you I will have some one ther to meet you and look after you. I will send you a paper as soon as one come along they send out extras two and three times a day.

LIFE IN THE NORTH

MIGRANT WOMEN AND MEN escaped the brutal conditions of the South, but the North was not always the promised land. The cost of living was high and decent housing largely unobtainable as African Americans were forced into over-crowded areas of substandard housing. Schools, restaurants, and other public places were not legally segregated, but blacks found hardening lines of racial separation in most northern cities.

Violence, in the form of race riots, erupted in both northern and southern cities during the war and in the immediate postwar years. The report of the Chicago Commission on Race Relations, prompted by that city's devastating 1919 riot, is a rich source documenting the lives of Chicago blacks. The interview below with a transplanted Georgia family, "Mr. and Mrs. J_____" (the commission protected the privacy of its interviewees by using initials rather than full names), offers particular insights into the wife's experiences.

CHICAGO COMMISSION ON RACE RELATIONS
Report (1922)

Motives for coming to Chicago.—Reading in the *Atlanta Journal,* a Negro newspaper, of the wonderful industrial opportunities offered Negroes; the husband came to Chicago in February, 1917. Finding conditions satisfactory, he had his wife sell the stock and household goods and join him here in April of the same year. He secured work at the Stock Yards, working eight hours at $3 a day....

The family stayed in a rooming-house on East Thirtieth Street. This place catered to such an undesirable element that the wife remained in her room with their daughter all day. She thought the city too was cold, dirty, and noisy to live in. Having nothing to do and not knowing anyone, she was so lonely that she cried daily and begged her husband to put her in three rooms of their own or go back home. Because of the high cost of living, they were compelled to wait some time before they had saved enough to begin housekeeping.

SOURCE: Chicago Commission on Race Relations, *The Negro in Chicago: A Study of Race Relations and a Race Riot* (Chicago: University of Chicago Press, 1922), 170–72.

Housing experience.—Their first home was on South Park Avenue. They bought about $500 worth of furniture, on which they are still paying. The wife then worked for a time at the Pullman Yards, cleaning cars at $1.50 a day for ten hours' work. Their house leaked and was damp and cold, so the family moved to another house.... [Their six-room apartment] is warm, but dark and poorly ventilated....

The daughter has married a man twenty-three years old, who migrated first to Pittsburgh, Pennsylvania, then to Chicago. He works at the Stock Yards. They occupy a room and use the other part of the house, paying half the rent and boarding themselves. A nephew ... also boards with Mr. and Mrs. J_____, $8.00 a week. He is now unemployed, but has been doing foundry work. Mrs. J_____ occasionally does laundry work at $4 a day.

How they live.—The cost of living includes rent $25; gas $5.40 a month; coal $18 a year; insurance $9.60 a month; clothing $500 a year; transportation $3.12 a month; church and club dues $3 a month; hairdresser $1.50 a month. Little is spent for recreation and the care of health.

Relation to the community. — The whole family belongs to the Salem Baptist Church and attends twice a week. The wife is a member of the Pastor's Aid and the Willing Workers Club, also the Elk's Lodge. The husband is a member of the Knights of Pythias.° He goes to the parks, bathing-beaches, and baseball games for amusement. The family spends much of its time in church and helped to establish the "Come and See" Baptist Mission. . . . They have gone to a show only once or twice since they came to the city. During the summer they spend Sunday afternoons at the East Twenty-ninth Street Beach.

Heavier clothes were necessary because of the change of climate, and more fresh meat is used because of the lack of garden space and the high cost of green vegetables.

The wife thinks that northern Negroes have better manners, but are not as friendly as the colored people in the South. She says people do not visit each other, and one is never invited to dine at a friend's house. She thinks they cannot afford it with food so high. She thinks people were better

° A fraternal organization that provided members with a social outlet as well as insurance against ill health and death.

in the South than they are here and says they had to be good there for they had nothing else to do but go to church.

She feels a greater freedom here because of the right to vote, the better treatment accorded by white people, the lack of "Jim Crow" laws. She likes the North because of the protection afforded by the law and the better working conditions. "You don't have an overseer always standing over you," she remarked. . . .

Economic sufficiency. — With all this, Mrs. J_____ gets more pleasure from her income because the necessities of life here were luxuries in Georgia, and though such things are dear here there is money to pay for them. Houses are more modern, but not good enough for the rent paid. They had to pay $2 more than the white family that moved out when they moved in. . . .

Sentiments on the migration. — Mrs. J_____ says "some colored people have come up here and forgotten to stay close to God," hence they have "gone to destruction." She hopes that an equal chance in industry will be given to all: that more houses will be provided for the people and rent will be charged for the worth of the house; and the cost of living generally will be reduced. She does not expect to return to Georgia and is advising friends to come to Chicago.

THE WAR YEARS opened up more work opportunities as the following essay by Alice Dunbar-Nelson, the Women's National Council of Defense field representative for black women, indicates. Primarily designed to praise the contributions of black women to the war effort, the essay mostly concerns middle-class black women volunteering in the Red Cross or Young Women's Christian Association or raising money for war bonds. In this passage, however, Dunbar-Nelson summarizes the impact of migration and war on women's job opportunities. The widow of poet Paul Dunbar, Dunbar-Nelson was already an important author when this essay was published. She went on to become one of the founding figures of the Harlem Renaissance (see Chapter 8).

ALICE DUNBAR-NELSON
Come Out of the Kitchen, Mary (1919)

For generations colored women have been working the fields of the South. They have been the domestic servants of both the South and the North, accepting the positions of personal service open to them. Hard work and unpleasant work has been their lot, but they have been almost entirely excluded from our shops and factories. Tradition and race prejudice have played the largest part in their exclusion. The tardy development of the South and the failure of the colored woman to demand industrial opportunities have added further values [factors]. Clearly, also, two hundred years of slavery and fifty years of industrial boycott in both the North and the South, following the Civil War, have done little to encourage or to develop industrial aptitudes. For these reasons, the colored women have not entered the ranks of the industrial army in the past.

But war expediency, for a time at least, partially opened the door of industry to them. . . .

"Come out of the kitchen, Mary," was the slogan of the colored woman in war time. She doffed her cap and apron and donned her overalls. Some States, such as Maryland and Florida, specialized in courses in motor mechanics and automobile driving. The munition factories took the girls in gladly. Grim statistics prove that their scale of wages were definitely lower than a man's doing the same work, and sad to say a considerable fraction below that of white girls in the same service, although Delaware reports some very high-priced, skilled ammunition testers, averaging seven to twelve dollars a day. The colored girls blossomed out as switchboard operators, stock takers, wrappers, elevator operators, subway porters, ticket choppers, track-walkers, trained signalers, yard-walkers. They went into every possible kind of factory devoted to the production of war materials, from the most dangerous posts in munition plants to the delicate sewing in aeroplane factories. Colored girls and colored women drove motor trucks, unloaded freight cars, dug ditches, handled hardware around shipways and hardware houses, packed boxes. They struggled with the discomforts of ice and fertilizing plants. They learned the delicate intricacies of all kinds of machines, and the colored woman running the elevator or speeding a railroad on its way by signals was a common sight. . . .

A strange thing about . . . [women's industrial work] was that there was no perceptible racial disintegration and the colored women bore their changed status and higher economic independence with much more equanimity than white women on a corresponding scale of living. The reason for this may perhaps be found in the fact that the colored woman had a heritage of 300 years of work back of her. Her children were used to being left to shift for themselves; her home was used to being cared for after sundown. The careful supervision of the War Work Council and the Council of Defense over the health and hours of the woman in industry averted the cataclysm of lowered vitality and eventual unfitness for maternity.

The possible economic effect of this entrance into the unknown fields of industry on the part of the colored woman will be that when pre-war conditions return and she is displaced by men and is forced to make her way back into domestic service, the latter will be placed on a strictly business basis and the vocation of housekeeping and home-making will be raised to the dignity of a profession.

SOURCE: Alice Dunbar-Nelson, "Negro Women in War Work," in *The American Negro in the World War* (1919; repr., New York: Arno Press, 1969), 394–97.

ALTHOUGH ALICE DUNBAR-NELSON SEEMED RESIGNED to black women's re-turn to domestic work after the war—if perhaps on better terms—black sociologist Forrester B. Washington was far more openly critical of this likely outcome.

FORRESTER B. WASHINGTON
The Last to Be Employed . . . the First to Be Released (1919)

Everyone is aware that almost as soon as the armistice was signed, the cancellation of war orders began, and factories engaged in production dependent upon the continuation of hostilities commenced to release their women employe[e]s. But it is not generally known that in the majority of plants in Chicago the first persons to be released were colored women. If only those were discharged who had taken soldiers' positions, it is doubtful if any serious distress would be caused the colored people; but the fact is that many colored people who had obtained their positions as a result of the labor vacuum caused by the cessation of immigration a year or two before we entered the war are now being discharged as well as those hired more recently. The history of the experiences of colored women in the present war should make fair-minded Americans blush with shame. They have been universally the last to be employed. They were the marginal workers of industry all through the war. They have been given, with few exceptions, the most undesirable and lowest paid work, and now that the war is over they are the first to be released.

It is especially significant that Chicago, which now has the third largest negro population in the country, should be the most inconsiderate in its treatment of the colored woman worker. As a matter of fact, the country as a whole has not treated the colored working woman according to the spirit of democracy. The essential difference between Chicago and elsewhere is that in the other cities the colored woman made some little progress into the skilled and so-called semi-skilled industries. In Chicago, while she did get into many occupations into which she had never gained entrance before, they were only the marginal occupations. She became the bus girl in the dairy lunches, the elevator girl, the ironer in the laundry, etc. Now she is being discharged rapidly from even these menial and low-paid positions. . . .

The American employer in his treatment of colored women wage-earners should square himself with that democratic ideal of which he made so much during the war. During those perilous times white and black women looked alike in the factory when they were striving to keep the industry of the country up to 100 per cent production, just as white and black soldiers looked alike going over the top to preserve the honor of the country. Moreover, organized labor cannot afford to sink below the high standard to which it rose during the war.

If either the American employer or the American laborer continues to deny the colored woman an opportunity to make a decent living, the Bolshevik cannot be blamed for proclaiming their affirmation of democratic principles a sham.

SOURCE: Forrester B. Washington, "Reconstruction and the Colored Woman," *Life and Labor* 9, no. 1 (Jan. 1919): 3–7, reproduced in Eric Arnesen, *Black Protest and the Great Migration: A Brief History with Documents* (Boston: Bedford, 2003).

QUESTIONS FOR ANALYSIS

1. What insights do these documents give you about African American women's motivation for migration? About their subsequent experiences in the workforce?

2. What advantages did these women find in the North? What challenges and hardships?

3. Judging from these documents, how would you characterize the impact of World War I on African American women?

4. What comparisons can you draw between women's experiences during the Great Migration and the turn-of-the-century wave of European immigration discussed in Chapter 6?

NOTES

1. Nancy S. Dye, "Introduction," in Nancy S. Dye and Noralee Frankel, eds., *Gender, Class, Race, and Reform in the Progressive Era* (Lexington: University Press of Kentucky, 1991), 1.

2. Lynn Wiener, *From Working Girl to Working Mother: The Female Labor Force in the United States, 1820–1980* (Chapel Hill: University of North Carolina Press, 1985), 4.

3. "Female/Male Income Ratio, 1890–1995," http://www.econ.utah.edu/maloney/genchrt1.gif.

4. Grace Coyle, "Women in the Clerical Occupations," *Annals of the American Academy of Political and Social Science,* May 1929, 181.

5. Nancy Cott, *The Grounding of Modern Feminism* (New Haven: Yale University Press, 1987), 350.

6. Virginia G. Drachman, " 'My "Partner" in Law and Life': Marriage in the Lives of Women Lawyers in Late Nineteenth- and Early Twentieth-Century America," *Law & Social Inquiry* 14, no. 2. (Spring 1989): 221–50.

7. Barbara Mayer Wertheim, *We Were There: The Story of Working Women in America* (New York: Pantheon, 1977), 271.

8. Quoted in Elizabeth Anne Payne, *Reform Labor and Feminism: Margaret Dreier Robins and the Women's Trade Union League* (Urbana: University of Illinois Press, 1988), 48.

9. Quoted in Meredith Tax, *The Rising of the Woman: Feminist Solidarity and Class Conflict, 1880–1917* (New York: Monthly Review Press, 1980), 222.

10. Ibid., 235.

11. Excerpted in Susan B. Anthony and Ida H. Harper, eds., *History of Woman Suffrage* (Rochester, NY: Susan B. Anthony, 1902), 4:178.

12. An early use of this term can be found in Seth Koven and Sonya Michel, eds., *Mothers of a New World: Maternalist Politics and the Origins of Welfare States* (New York: Routledge, 1993).

13. Agnes Nestor, *Woman's Labor Leader* (Rockford, IL.: Bellevue Books, 1954), 88.

14. Quoted in Alice Kessler-Harris, *Out to Work: A History of Wage-Earning Women in the United States* (New York: Oxford University Press, 1982), 198.

15. Quoted in Sherry Katz, "Socialist Women and Progressive Reform," in William Deverell and Tom Sitton, eds., *California Progressivism Revisited* (Berkeley: University of California, 1994), 125.

16. Quoted in Darlene Clark Hine and Kathleen Thompson, *A Shining Thread of Hope: The History of Black Women in America* (New York: Broadway Books, 1998), 202.

17. From May 2, 1901, letter to Carlos Montezuma; quoted in Ruth Spack, "Dis/engagement: Zitkala-Sa's Letters to Carlos Montezuma, 1901–1902," *Melus,* vol. 26 (April 2001): 173.

18. "What Will Woman Suffrage Convention Do for the Working Woman," 1908, reprinted in Dawn Keetley and John Pettegrew, eds., *Public Women, Public Words: A Documentary History of American Feminism,* vol. 2, *1900–1960* (Lanham, MD: Rowman and Littlefield, 2002), 170.

19. Quoted in Rebecca Mead, *How the Vote Was Won: Woman Suffrage in the Western United States, 1868–1914* (New York: New York University Press, 2004), 123–24.

20. Quoted in Paula Giddings, *When and Where I Enter* (New York: William Morrow, 1984), 126.

21. "The South, Suffrage, and the Educational Requirement," excerpted in Keetley and Pettegrew, *Public Women, Public Words,* 2:157.

22. Adele Hunt Logan, "Woman Suffrage," excerpted in Keetley and Pettegrew, *Public Women, Public Words,* 2:164.

23. From *Votes for Women,* October 1909, quoted in John Putnam, "A Test of Chiffon Politics: Gender Politics in Seattle, 1897–1917," *Pacific Historical Review* 69, no. 4 (November 2000): 598.

24. *Winning Equal Suffrage in California: Reports of Committees of the College Equal Suffrage League of Northern California in the Campaign of 1911* (San Francisco: National College Equal Suffrage League, 1913), 11.

25. Alice Park to editor, *Woman's Journal* 13 (October 1911), Park Collection, Huntington Library, San Marino, California.

26. Quoted in Christine Stansell, *American Moderns: Bohemian New York and the Creation of a New Century* (New York: Metropolitan Books, 2000), 228.

27. Rosalyn Fraad Baxandall, ed., *Words of Fire: The Life and Writing of Elizabeth Gurley Flynn* (New Brunswick: Rutgers University Press, 1987), 14.

28. Rheta Childe Dorr, *A Woman of Fifty* (New York: Funk and Wagnalls, 1924), 286–69.

29. Carrie Chapman Catt, *New York Times,* February 6, 1915, quoted in Harriet Human Alonso, *Peace as a Women's Issue: History of the U.S. Movement for World Peace and Women's Rights* (Syracuse: Syracuse University Press, 1993), 61.

30. Mary Heaton Vorse, *A Footnote to Folly: Reminiscences of Mary Heaton Vorse* (New York: Farrar & Rinehart, 1935), 82.

31. Alfreda M. Duster, ed., *Crusade for Justice: The Autobiography of Ida B. Wells* (Chicago: University of Chicago Press, 1970), 370.

32. Quoted in Doris Stevens, *Jailed for Freedom* (New York: Boni and Liveright, 1920), 190–91.

33. Carrie Chapman Catt, "Organized Womanhood," *Woman Voter,* April 1917, 9.

34. Harriott Stanton Blatch, *Mobilizing Woman Power* (New York: Woman's Press, 1918), 88–90.

35. Quoted in Maurine Greenwald, *Women, War, and Work: The Impact of World War I on Women Workers in the United States* (Westport, CT: Greenwood Press, 1980), 24.

36. Quote from *Chicago Defender,* Mobile, Alabama, April 25, 1917, in Susan Ware, ed., *Modern American Women: A Documentary History,* 2nd. ed. (New York: McGraw-Hill, 1997), 58.

37. Quoted in Eleanor Flexner, *Century of Struggle: The Woman's Rights Movement in the United States* (Cambridge: Belknap Press, 1959), 291.

38. Ibid., 322.

39. Woodrow Wilson, Fourteen Points speech, in Arthur S. Link et al., eds., *The Papers of Woodrow Wilson,* vol. 45 (Princeton, NJ: Princeton University Press, 1984), 536.

The text of the speech is also available online at http://usinfo.state.gov/usa/infousa/facts/democrac/51.htm.

40. Maud Wood Park, *Front Door Lobby* (Boston: Beacon Press, 1960), 259, 262.

41. Quoted in Flexner, *Century of Struggle*, 336.

42. Quoted in Susan Glenn, *Daughters of the Shtetl: Life and Labor in the Immigrant Generation* (Ithaca: Cornell University Press, 1991), 165.

43. Nan Enstad, *Ladies of Labor, Girls of Adventure: Working Women, Popular Culture, and Labor Politics at the Turn of the Twentieth Century* (New York: Columbia University Press, 1999), 84–160.

44. Harriott Stanton Blatch and Alma Lutz, *Challenging Years: The Memoirs of Harriott Stanton Blatch* (New York: G. P. Putnam's Sons, 1940), 129.

45. Sarah J. Moore, "Making a Spectacle of Suffrage: The National Woman Suffrage Pageant, 1913," *Journal of American Culture* 20 (1997): 89–103.

46. Linda J. Lumsden, "Beauty and the Beasts: Significance of Press Coverage of the 1913 National Suffrage Parade," *Journalism and Mass Culture Quarterly* 77 (2000): 595.

47. Quoted in Flexner, *Century of Struggle*, 269.

48. Quoted in Lumsden, "Beauty and the Beasts," 595, 597.

49. Ralph Merritt, Federal Food Commissioner for California, to "The Volunteer Enlistment Sergeant" [1917], Seaver Center, Natural History Museum, State Council of Defense, Women's Committee Records, Box 14.

50. Quoted in Cott, *Grounding of Modern Feminism,* 36.

51. Ibid., 38.

SUGGESTED REFERENCES

General Works   No period in U.S. women's history has generated greater and more varied scholarship than 1900–1920. For a general overview on women and Progressivism, see the collection edited by Noralee Frankel and Nancy S. Dye, *Gender, Class, Race, and Reform in the Progressive Era* (1991); and Dorothy and Carl. J. Schneider, *American Women in the Progressive Era, 1990–1920* (1993).

Women Workers   Overviews of the history of working women include Claudia Goldin, *Understanding the Gender Gap: An Economic History of American Women* (1992); Alice Kessler Harris, *Out to Work: A History of Wage-Earning Women in the United States,* 20th anniv. ed. (2003); and Leslie Woodcock Tentler, *Wage-Earning Women: Industrial Work and Family Life in the United States, 1900–1930* (1979). In *Daughters of the Shtetl: Life and Labor in the Immigrant Generation* (1991), Susan A. Glenn explores Jewish and Italian immigrant women in the garment industry and addresses the sources of their militancy. Nan Enstad brings the tools of cultural history to bear on women's labor history in *Ladies of Labor, Girls of Adventure: Working Women, Popular Culture, and Labor Politics at the Turn of the Twentieth Cen-*

tury (1999). Eileen Boris examines wage earning in domestic settings in *Home to Work: Motherhood and the Politics of Industrial Homework in the United States* (1994).

On women in the clerical field, see Sharon Harman Strom, *Beyond the Type-writer: Gender, Class, and the Origins of Modern American Office Work, 1900–1920* (1992). On women in the legal profession, see Virginia Drachman, *Sisters in Law: Women Lawyers in Modern American History* (1998). Susan M. Reverby surveys the nursing profession in *Ordered to Care: The Dilemma of American Nursing, 1850–1945* (1987). Rosalind Rosenberg looks at the first generation of professional women social scientists in *Beyond Separate Spheres: Intellectual Roots of Modern Feminism* (1982). Stephanie Shaw has written a general history of black professional women workers in the Jim Crow era in *What a Woman Ought to Be and Do* (1995). Darlene Clark Hine considers the history of black women in nursing in *Black Women in White: Racial Conflict and Cooperation in the Nursing Profession, 1890–1950* (1989).

Women's labor activism in the Progressive era is well studied. Meredith Tax's *The Rising of the Women: Feminist Solidarity and Class Conflict, 1880–1917* (2001) provided the title for a section of Chapter 7. David Von Drehle offers fresh insights into the New York City Triangle Shirtwaist Company fire in *Triangle: The Fire That Changed America* (2003). Also see Annelise Orleck, *Common Sense and a Little Fire: Women and Working-Class Politics in the United States, 1900–1965* (1995). The Women's Trade Union League is the subject of Nancy Schrom Dye's *As Equals and as Sisters: Feminism, the Labor Movement, and the Women's Trade Union League of New York* (1980).

Social Housekeeping   The term "female dominion" used for women's social re-form activism in this period comes from Robyn Muncy, *Creating a Female Dominion in American Reform, 1890–1935* (1991). On "maternalism," see the collection com-piled by Seth Koven and Sonya Michel, *Mothers of a New World: Maternalist Politics and the Origins of Welfare States* (1993). Two studies of child welfare programs in this period are Linda Gordon, *Pitied but Not Entitled: Single Mothers and the History of Welfare, 1890–1935* (1994); and Molly Ladd-Taylor, *Mother-Work: Women, Child Welfare, and the State, 1890–1930* (1994). Mothers' pensions are the subject of Joanne Goodwin's study, *Gender and the Politics of Welfare Reform: Mothers' Pensions in Chicago, 1911–1929* (1997). Protective labor legislation is one of the few aspects of U.S. women's history that has been examined in a comparative historical context; see Ulla Wikander, Alice Kessler-Harris, and Jane Lewis, eds., *Protecting Women: Labor Legislation in Europe, the United States, and Australia, 1880–1920* (1995). Vivien Hart, *Bound By Our Constitution: Women, Workers and the Minimum Wage* (1994), also uses comparative tools.

For women and political parties, Melanie Gustafson has written a comprehen-sive history of *Women and the Republican Party, 1854–1924* (2001). (There is no comparable history of women and the Democratic Party.) See Mari Jo Buhle's *Women and American Socialism, 1870–1920* (1981) for coverage of the American So-cialist Party.

On African American women in the Progressive era, see Cynthia Neverdon-Morton, *Afro-American Women of the South and the Advancement of the Race, 1895–1925* (1989); also Jacqueline Anne Rouse, *Lugenia Burns Hope: Black Southern Reformer* (1989). Much of the material on this subject is in article form. Important anthologies include Vicki Ruiz and Ellen Carol DuBois, eds., *Unequal Sisters: A Multicultural Reader in U.S. Women's History,* 3rd ed. (2000); Sharon Harley and Rosalyn Terborg Penn, eds., *The Afro-American Woman's Struggles and Images* (1978); and Darlene Clark Hine et al., *"We Specialize in the Wholly Impossible": A Reader in Black Women's History* (1995). On Native American activism during the Progressive era, see Frederick Hoxie, *Talking Back to Civilization: Indian Voices from the Progressive Era* (2001). The Society for American Indians is examined in Hazel Herzberg, *The Search for an American Indian Identity: Modern Pan-Indian Movements* (1981).

Woman Suffrage   The history of woman suffrage is another well-studied topic. For an unequaled overview of this complex subject, see Eleanor Flexner and Ellen Fitzpatrick, *Century of Struggle: The Woman's Rights Movement in the United States,* enl. ed. (1996). Additional scholarship is found in Jean Baker, ed., *Votes for Women: The Struggle for Suffrage Revisited* (2002); and Marjorie Spruill Wheeler, ed., *One Woman, One Vote: Rediscovering the Woman Suffrage Movement* (1995). Sara Hunter Graham examines the National American Woman Suffrage Association in *Woman Suffrage and the New Democracy* (1996). For the radical wing of militant suffragists, see Linda G. Ford's *Iron-Jawed Angels: The Suffrage Militancy of the National Woman's Party, 1912–1920* (1991); also Christine Lunardini, *From Equal Suffrage to Equal Rights: Alice Paul and the National Woman's Party, 1910–1928* (1986). Rosalyn Terborg-Penn considers black women's suffrage involvement in *African American Women in the Struggle for the Vote, 1850–1920* (1998). On the New York suffrage movement, see Ellen Carol DuBois, *Harriot Stanton Blatch and the Winning of Woman Suffrage* (1997). Gayle Gullett focuses on the California movement in *Becoming Citizens: The Emergence and Development of the California Women's Movement, 1880–1911* (2000). On the theatricality of the woman suffrage parades, see Susan A. Glenn, *Female Spectacle: The Theatrical Roots of Modern Feminism* (2000). The anti-suffrage movement is the subject of Susan E. Marshall, *Splintered Sisterhood: Gender and Class in the Campaign against Woman Suffrage* (1997).

The Rise of Feminism   On the feminist movement that emerged in the 1910s, the place to start is Nancy F. Cott, *The Grounding of Modern Feminism* (1987). Christine Stansell considers the Greenwich Village milieu in *American Moderns: Bohemian New York and the Creation of a New Century* (2000). Ellen Kay Trimberger examines one New York feminist marriage of the period in *Intimate Warriors: Portrait of a Modern Marriage, 1899–1944* (1991). Linda Gordon studies the birth control movement in *The Moral Property of Women: A History of Birth Control Politics in America* (2002). The most recent major biography of Margaret Sanger is Ellen Chesler's *Woman of Valor: Margaret Sanger and the Birth Control Movement in America* (1992). On Charlotte Perkins Gilman, see Ann Lane's biography, *To Herland and Beyond: The Life and Work of Charlotte Perkins Gilman* (1990).

Women and World War I   On the topic of women during World War I, see Maurine W. Greenwald, *Women, War, and Work: The Impact of World War I on Women Workers in the United States* (1980). Carrie Brown's *Rosie's Mom: Forgotten Women Workers of the First World War* (2002) includes extraordinary photographs. Kathleen Kennedy examines female dissenters in this period in *Disloyal Mothers and Scurrilous Citizens: Women and Subversion during World War I* (1999). Harriet Hyman Alonso is the major historian of the women's peace movement; see her *Peace as a Woman's Issue: A History of the U.S. Movement for World Peace and Women's Rights* (1993).

On the Great Migration of African Americans in this period, see Elizabeth Clark-Lewis, *Living In, Living Out: African American Domestics and the Great Migration* (1994); and Joe William Trotter, Jr., ed., *The Great Migration in Historical Perspective: New Dimensions of Race, Class, and Gender* (1991).

Selected Web Sites

Web resources on the Progressive era are also plentiful. The Women and Social Movements in the United States, 1600 to 2000, site, now sponsored by Alexander Street Press and available by library subscription, offers numerous rich document collections in this period: <**alexanderstreet6.com/wasm/index.html**>. On the Triangle Shirtwaist Company fire in New York City, 1909–1910, see <**ilr.cornell .edu/trianglefire**>. The Lawrence, Massachusetts, strike the next year is the subject of a section of the interesting UK-based Web site Spartacus: <**spartacus.schoolnet .co.uk/USAlawrence.htm**>. For an online exhibit on the history of American sweatshops, see <**americanhistory.si.edu/sweatshops/index.htm**>.

Online materials about the woman suffrage movement are extensive as well. The Library of Congress provides two sites: one that offers photographs and other visuals, <**memory.loc.gov/ammem/vfwhtml/vfwhome.html**>, and one that features materials from the library's extensive collection from the National American Woman Suffrage Association, <**memory.loc.gov/ammem/naw/nawshome.html**>. The Bancroft Library of the University of California, Berkeley, has put its suffragist oral histories online, including a late-life interview with Alice Paul: <**bancroft .berkeley.edu/ROHO/projects/suffragists.html**>. Political scientist Jo Freeman's personal Web site includes an interesting set of cartoons on the role of women in the 1912 presidential election: <**jofreeman.com/polhistory/1912.htm**>.

On African American history in this period, see the Library of Congress Web site on the Great Migration, <**lcweb.loc.goy/exhibits/african/afam011.html**>, as well as a special site on the fascinating black businesswoman and social activist, Madame C. J. Walker, <**madamcjwalker.com**>. The Margaret Sanger Papers project has a Web site at <**nyu.edu/projects/sanger/index.html**>. The Charlotte Perkins Gilman Society provides a site that includes guides to further online resources: <**cortland.edu/gilman/**>.

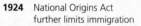

8

Change and Continuity

WOMEN IN PROSPERITY, DEPRESSION, AND WAR, 1920–1945

FROM ONE PERSPECTIVE, WOMEN'S EXPERIENCES IN the period from 1920 to 1945 seem marked more by change than continuity. Popular culture icons graphically capture the differences between the decades. The young, devil-may-care "flapper" with her short dress, rouged face, and rolled stockings symbolized the "New Woman" of the 1920s. Rebelling against the restraint of Victorian womanhood, the flapper eagerly embraced the growing consumer culture, with its emphasis on leisure and materialism, of this largely prosperous era. For the following decade, the most powerful icon is Dorothea Lange's widely reproduced photograph, "Migrant Mother," who symbolized Americans' dignified suffering as they weathered the devastating economic crisis of the 1930s. The migrant mother embodied too the popular assumption that woman's most important role during the Great Depression was an extension of her traditional responsibilities of maintaining the home and family. Images of women during World War II seemingly point in yet a third direction. "Rosie the Riveter" — the cheerful, robust woman in overalls working in the defense industry, taking on new and challenging work to serve her country in time of need— emphasized female independence and strength outside the home.

But although each decade had its distinctive qualities, overarching developments, especially in work and politics, link these seeming disparities into the larger trends in American women's history. In the immediate aftermath of the Nineteenth Amendment, women plunged into the responsibilities of active citizenship and struggled to carve out a base for political power and influence. Female participation in the paid labor market continued to grow, especially with respect to the growing numbers of working women who were also wives and mothers. Finally, cultural expectations for women shifted in two crucially related areas, consumerism and sexuality. Both of these shifts had implications for women's family lives as well. Yet despite these changes in women's lives, another theme also emerges, that of continuity with the past. Racial and ethnic prejudice continued to limit women's opportunities in the workforce and access to political influence. And for all women, traditional expectations about women's primary role in the home persisted, serving as the filter through which change would affect their lives.

PROSPERITY DECADE: THE 1920s

Looking on the surface, the 1920s appear as a decade of progress and prosperity. Industrial growth and international economic expansion created a society more affluent than ever before. An explosion of consumer goods, from mass-produced cars to gleaming bathroom fixtures and electrical kitchen appliances, helped to transform daily lives and gave women more power and pleasure as consumers. Underlying the bright prosperity of the decade, however, were darker currents. Many Americans continued to live below or near the poverty line. Farm families suffered from low prices and high indebtedness for most of the decade, and many rural women endured harsh, isolated lives. Cities provided more opportunities, but here too poor wages and living conditions, especially for Mexican Americans and African Americans, separated the haves from the have nots.

Relatively few commentators in the 1920s delved beneath the surface image of prosperity to analyze the lives of those who did not participate in the boom times. The same superficiality characterized the widely held image of the New Woman. In the popular mind, women had

1935	National Youth Administration (NYA) created
1935	National Labor Relations (Wagner) Act passed
1935	Social Security Act passed
1935	Works Progress Administration created
1935	Congress of Industrial Organizations founded
1936	*United States v. One Package of Japanese Pessaries legalizes the dissemination of contraceptive information*
1936	**Mary McLeod Bethune appointed to head Division of Negro Affairs, NYA**
1937	Japan invades China
1937	**Women create the Emergency Brigade in Flint, Michigan, strike**
1938	Fair Labor Standards Act passed
1939	World War II breaks out in Europe
1941	Fair Employment Practices Commission established
1941	United States enters World War II after Japan attacks Pearl Harbor
1942	**Women recruited into war industries**
1942	**Women's Army Corps given formal military status**
1942	Japanese immigrants and their citizen children interned
1942-1945	**Rationing increases women's domestic responsibilities**
1943	Congress extends the right of naturalization to Chinese immigrants
1945	Harry S Truman becomes president after Roosevelt's death
1945	United States drops atomic bombs on Hiroshima and Nagasaki
1945	Japan surrenders, ending World War II

481

become liberated—by the freedom of wartime, by the exercise of the vote, by participation in the workforce, and by experiments with a new sexual morality. The image was an exaggerated generalization of the experience of young, urban, prosperous white women who were glamorized in the popular media. But contemporaries were correct that most women's lives had changed significantly since the nineteenth century, even though the goals of autonomy and equality remained elusive for most of them.

The New Woman in Politics

In 1920 women political activists were poised for a great adventure. With the energy they had brought to the suffrage campaign, women from all groups were now prepared to make women's votes count. African American women focused on using the new national amendment to extend suffrage in the South and on lobbying for a federal antilynching law. White women formed the League of Women Voters (LWV) in 1920, which emphasized lobbying, voter education, and get-out-the-vote drives in the overall mission to train women to be good citizens. An astute recognition of the growing importance of national organizations' lobbying efforts in Washington, D.C., led fourteen women's organizations to form the Women's Joint Congressional Committee, with the goal of promoting legislation backed by the member organizations. On the local and state levels, women also pursued their agendas, supporting child and women's labor laws, health and safety legislation, municipal reform, and a broad extension of women's legal rights. The lobbying efforts of these women's groups underline the importance of women activists in pioneering twentieth-century interest-group politics.

In addition to working through their organizations, activist women debated among themselves as to how, and whether, they should act within the Democratic and Republican parties. The argument that women were unsullied by the corruption of political parties had been a common one in the suffrage battle, and many women had grave reservations about working within the established party system. Indeed, like its precursor, the National American Woman Suffrage Association, the LWV was established as a strictly nonpartisan group that refrained from supporting political parties or their candidates. While some former suffragists attempted to exert influence within the Republican and Democratic parties, others followed Alice Paul's lead into the National Woman's Party (NWP). Always a single-issue party, the NWP focused exclusively on passage of an Equal Rights Amendment (ERA). First introduced in Congress in 1923, the ERA stated: "Men and women shall have equal rights throughout the United States and every place subject to its jurisdiction."

At first glance, the optimism of white women activists seems justified. In 1920 both Democrats and Republicans recognized women's issues in their platforms, presumably taking women at their word that they planned to use their combined votes as a powerful political tool. And they opened up places within the organizational structure of their parties for female members, although the positions granted were rarely equal in terms of power or influence. As the *New York Times* magazine, *Current History,* summed it up, "Where there is dignity of office but little else, or where there is routine work, little glory, and low pay, men prove willing to admit women to an equal share in the spoils of office."[1] Women became officeholders as well, with a rare handful elected to Congress (seven in 1928) and more serving in the various states (an estimate in 1928 was one thousand appointed or elected), especially in positions earmarked as women's jobs, such as secretary of education and secretary of state. Women were more numerous in local government, in part because many of these positions were nonpartisan and thus seemingly more in keeping with ideas that women should operate "above politics." Despite these inroads, female officeholders generally worked within the context of prevailing assumptions that women should keep to women's issues, or "municipal housekeeping," the same assumption that limited their ability to wield much power within their political parties.

Women reformers also had mixed success in their lobbying activities. Many states passed laws urged by women activists, including those that expanded women's legal rights and those directed at social reform, such as child labor laws and wage and hour laws for women. At the federal level, the women's lobby saw an early success in the Sheppard-Towner Act of 1921, which gave matching funds for states to provide health care and other services for mothers and children. Yet by the end of the decade, progress had slowed, especially on the national level. The Child Labor Amendment—passionately advocated after the Supreme Court invalidated a second national child labor law in 1921—failed to be ratified, and most national legislation supported by women lobbyists was unsuccessful. Congress cut the Sheppard-Towner Act's appropriations and ended its once promising program in 1929. Moreover, the women's rights movement itself was in shambles, with women divided among themselves as to tactics and goals. By decade's end, many women activists were disillusioned and embittered.

Ironically, some of the problems hindering a sustained feminist movement grew out of the success of the suffrage battle. Before national suffrage was achieved, a great many women—equally excluded from this basic right of citizenship—came under the same umbrella of "votes for women." Once the Nineteenth Amendment was ratified, the lines that divided women—class, race, age, ideology—became more significant. By gaining the individual right they had so vigorously sought, they laid the groundwork for the fracturing of female communities. As one activist ruefully put it in 1923, "The American woman's movement, and her interest in great moral and social questions, is splintered into a hundred fragments under as many warring leaders."[2]

This was particularly evident in the ferocious debate over the Equal Rights Amendment (see boxes, "Arguing for the ERA" and "Arguing against the ERA"). Under the leadership of Alice Paul, the NWP focused so exclusively on the ERA as a means of achieving political and economic equality with men that it appropriated the newly coined term "feminism" to refer to its specific agenda (see Chapter 7). Women interested in broader social reform, especially the protective labor laws that they had worked so hard to achieve in the states, were alarmed at this "blanket amendment," which they feared would undermine protective laws for women. Although not unsympathetic to the plight of working-class women, ERA

ALICE PAUL
Arguing for the ERA

At the height of the Equal Rights Amendment battle, foes and supporters debated each other in print. In March 1924 the Congressional Digest *featured an exchange between Alice Paul and Mary Van Kleeck, "Is Blanket Amendment Best Method in Equal Rights Campaign?" Here, Paul (1895–1977), founder of the National Woman's Party and foremost supporter of the ERA, argues for the amendment.*

The Woman's Party is striving to remove every artificial handicap placed upon women by law and by custom. In order to remove those handicaps which the law can touch, it is endeavoring to secure the adoption of the Equal Rights Amendment to the United States Constitution.

There are a number of reasons for working for a national Equal Rights Amendment instead of endeavoring to establish Equal Rights by state action alone, as has been the course pursued during the past seventy-five years:

1. **A National Amendment Is More Inclusive Than State Legislation.**
   The amendment would at one stroke compel both federal and state governments to observe the principle of Equal Rights, for the Federal Constitution is the "supreme law of the land." The amendment would override all existing legislation which denies women Equal Rights with men and would render invalid every future attempt on the part of any legislators or administrators to interfere with these rights.

2. **A National Amendment Is More Permanent Than State Legislation.**
   The national amendment would establish the principle of Equal Rights permanently in our country, in so far as anything can be established permanently by law. Equal Rights measures passed by state legislatures, on the other hand, are subject to reversal by later legislatures.

supporters countered that such legislation treated women as invalids and could limit their economic opportunity. The controversy revealed differing attitudes about women's nature and the meaning of equality. Social reformers such as Julia Lathrop and Frances Perkins also cared about extending women's legal rights, but they nonetheless stressed the distinctiveness of their sex. They believed that biological attributes justified protective legislation. Moreover, their sense of women's moral superiority and special maternal qualities, rooted in the nineteenth-century ideology of separate spheres, shaped their commitment to social reform.

3. **The Campaign for a National Amendment Obviates the Costly and Difficult State Referendums Which Frequently Occur in Securing State Legislation.**

   Equal Rights measures passed by the legislatures must be submitted to a state referendum, when the existing discriminations are written in the state constitution and can only be removed by amending the Constitution. Furthermore, referendums are frequently forced by an initiative petition upon bills which have passed the state legislatures. No referendum is necessary, on the other hand, in the case of a national amendment. Everyone who worked in the suffrage campaign is familiar with the great cost and difficulty of state referendums and the value of a national amendment in obviating this expensive and laborious method of achieving a reform.

4. **The Campaign for a National Amendment Unites the Resources of Women, Which Are Divided in Campaigns for State Legislation.**

   In the campaign for a national amendment the strength of the Equal Rights forces is concentrated upon Congress and is therefore more effective than when divided among forty-eight state campaigns.

5. **A National Amendment Is a More Dignified Way to Establish Equal Rights Than Is State Legislation.**

   The principle of Equal Rights for men and women is so important that it should be written into the frame-work of our National Government as one of the principles upon which our government is founded. The matter is far too important to our nation's welfare and honor to leave it to the states for favorable or unfavorable action, or for complete neglect, as they see fit.

SOURCE: "Who Won the Debate over the Equal Rights Amendment in the 1920s?" Women and Social Movements in the United States, 1775–2000, Center for the Study of Women and Gender at the State University of New York at Binghamton, http://womhist.binghamton.edu/era/doc16.htm (accessed March 17, 2004).

Other factors besides differences over the ERA struggle would hamstring the development of a strong feminist movement. Young, middle-class, white women often seemed more interested in the pleasures of consumption and leisure than in the social commitment involved in pursuing women's rights and social reform. If these women felt both ERA and anti-ERA supporters were quaintly old-fashioned, black women reformers found their white counterparts largely unresponsive to their concerns. This split emerged most concretely at a 1921 NWP meeting, where sixty black women representing the National Association of Colored Women were

MARY VAN KLEECK
Arguing against the ERA

Mary Van Kleeck (1883–1972), a noted labor reformer who had served as the first head of the Women's Bureau in the Department of Labor, was the director of industrial studies at the Russell Sage Foundation. Like other activists concerned about women workers, she adamantly opposed the ERA because of its perceived threat to protective labor laws for women.

We who oppose the suggested amendment are heartily in accord with what we believe to be the purpose of its advocates, namely, to free women for largest service in the life of the nation, by sweeping away those man-made restrictions, which are based wholly on out-worn traditions and prejudiced views of the status and capacity of women. We oppose the amendment because we do not believe that it will accomplish that purpose.

We hold that many important steps toward the goal of removing all sex-prejudice are beyond the reach of law and would be unaffected by this amendment, such as the opening of colleges and universities to women; the enlargement of professional and vocational opportunities; and the abandonment of the social customs which restrict women's activities.

We believe that if this amendment were passed many separate statutes in state and in nation would be required to put its intent into effect. These statutes, we are convinced by experience, can be enacted without any constitutional amendment. A long list of those actually passed since women have had the vote has been compiled by the National League of Women Voters. The time taken to enact and ratify the amendment would only postpone the passage of these laws which we must have anyway.

A vague provision in the Constitution always necessitates interpretation by the courts. If this vague provision for equal rights for men and women were to be included in the Constitution, the time-consuming efforts of judges to define its meaning for each new statute may be expected

refused convention time to raise the subject of the failure of southern states to acknowledge the voting rights of black women. Alice Paul insisted that this was a "race issue," not a "woman's issue." The African Americans, led by Addie Hunton, field secretary for the National Association for the Advancement of Colored People (NAACP), countered by reminding the convention that "five million

to nullify for the next century the effect of present and future laws designed to open up larger opportunities to women. Some of our laws which do not apply alike to men and therefore appear to perpetuate legal discriminations against women — such as mothers' pensions and certain provisions for the support of children — do so only superficially. Actually these laws are intended to protect the home or to safeguard children. They do not contemplate an artificial segregation of women as a group apart from their social relationships. In sweeping away laws like these on the superficial ground that they perpetuate sex disabilities, we should be deliberately depriving the legislature of the power to protect children and to preserve the right of mothers to be safeguarded in the family group. The wheat and the tares are so close together in all social legislation that we would better let them grow until a skilled gardener can root out the tares one by one; otherwise we may lose our wheat.

The amendment would jeopardize laws like these for women in industry because they do not also apply to men. The proposal to include men in them will indefinitely postpone their extension[.] Yet in the opinion of women in industry these laws which insure tolerable conditions of work should come first in any genuine bill of equal rights for women. Women in industry ask for the substance of freedom. They are unwilling to trust a hoe to those who do not know the difference between wheat and tares.

We hold that the amendment is unnecessary because the right of suffrage has already given women the power to secure legislation and accomplish all that the amendment is supposed to make possible. No constitutional barrier to the enactment of these laws has been interposed, which would be removed by this amendment. We hold that besides being unnecessary it is dangerous because its vagueness jeopardizes what we have and indefinitely retards what we have still to gain.

SOURCE: "Who Won the Debate over the Equal Rights Amendment in the 1920s?" Women and Social Movements in the United States, 1775–2000, Center for the Study of Women and Gender at the State University of New York at Binghamton, http://womhist.binghamton.edu/era/doc16.htm (accessed March 17, 2004).

women in the United States cannot be denied their rights without all the women of the United States feeling the effect of that denial. No women are free until all women are free."[3] Although this and other setbacks in the effort to secure the vote in the South led African American women to deemphasize the voting issue, they persisted in their broad agenda of improving the lives of all African Americans; in particular, they continued their antilynching activities by working for federal legislation and even forging an alliance with southern white women. Though some women could come together in interracial cooperation, the limited vision of white leaders such as Paul as to what constituted "women's issues" shut off possibilities for a broader, more inclusive conception of a feminist movement.

While the difficulties women reformers faced arose in part from women's disunity, a far more serious problem was the decade's conservative political climate. Observers in the 1920s, citing declining overall voting participation during the decade (roughly half of those eligible voted), assumed that women's nonvoting accounted for the decline, arguing that women lost political clout as a result. With only sparse data of voting by sex available, many historians have echoed this assumption. More recent studies, however, maintain that women's participation in elections varied significantly by location and by election. Women in states that only recently had enfranchised them seem to have participated in fewer numbers than those living in states such as California, where women had longer experience with the electoral process. Notably, men's voting decreased in this period as well, following a long-standing trend of declining engagement in partisan politics. That both men and women were failing to vote in large numbers points to a political climate of disaffected or disinterested citizenry, and it is this broader context of American politics, not women's failures as voters, that offers the most compelling explanation for the difficulties women reformers faced.[4]

A related problem was a political climate hostile to reform that made it impossible to sustain the prewar enthusiasm for progressive measures. On the national scene, the Republicans dominated the White House and Congress, and, reflecting in part the party's ties to corporate business interests, resisted efforts to expand federal regulatory powers. Federal prohibition of alcohol, following ratification of the Eighteenth Amendment in 1919, further increased many Americans' wariness of intrusive social reforms. Prohibition met with vigorous opposition. Many Americans resented and circumvented the law, and others worried that the ineffectual effort to control alcohol consumption had fostered contempt for the legal system. That women reformers were so closely associated with the controversial amendment surely fueled hostility to the social reforms women activists promoted in the 1920s. Finally, the widening prosperity of the period may well have influenced many Americans to turn toward new consumer and leisure pleasures and away from political engagement and concern for the nation's poor.

Perhaps most damaging to reform and especially women's part in it was the "Red Scare" of 1919 to 1921. Prompted initially by the Russian Revolution of 1917 and the fear that the fledgling U.S. Communist Party was plotting a revolution to topple this nation's government, Americans succumbed to a hysteria in which wild-eyed Bolsheviks seemed to be lurking around every corner. The Red Scare led to the deportation of "suspicious" immigrants, the suppression of the labor movement, and massive violations of civil liberties. It also helped to fuel the growth of the second Ku Klux Klan, an organization opposed to immigrants, Catholics, Jews, and blacks that achieved significant popularity and influence in the early 1920s. Finally, the Red Scare contributed to the passage of restrictive immigration laws of the 1920s and became a weapon for opponents of reform legislation, who could now argue that efforts to increase government's role in regulating the economy or protecting workers and the poor would lead America down the same path as Russia.

Critics particularly focused on a number of women's groups, including those in the Women's Joint Congressional Committee and the Women's International League for Peace and Freedom, which they argued were spreading bolshevism in the United States. Jane Addams in particular came in for forceful criticism. Opponents' attempts to discredit women reformers with claims that they were Bolsheviks point to a further dilemma facing women activists. Preeminent among the opponents of reform were right-wing women's organizations. The Women Sentinels of the Republic was a small but vocal group that opposed social reform as the forerunner of bolshevism. The Daughters of the American Revolution, initially interested in women's social reform efforts, had by mid-decade also taken up the antiradical hysteria. Women in an auxiliary of the all-male Ku Klux Klan supported some reforms such as Prohibition but, like other right-wing women's groups, promoted what was called "one-hundred-percent Americanism" and were suspicious of the liberal goals of the women's lobby.

With these counterpressures, then, it is not surprising that the reform agenda of women's groups stalled at the nation's capitol, and it is impressive that women activists accomplished as much as they did on the local and state level. In the process they helped to keep the reform spirit alive, if not well, and created a crucial bridge to the social welfare reforms of the 1930s introduced by President Franklin D. Roosevelt's New Deal.

Women at Work

Although women's expanding political opportunities contributed to the sense of a New Woman in the 1920s, changes in work were equally important—and were similarly mixed in offering women genuine independence. World War I had brought short-term opportunities in a variety of jobs for women, but these opportunities were not sustained. After the war, as before, women's work was characterized by sex segregation, clustered in job categories dominated by women. In the 1920s, 86 percent of women workers concentrated into ten job classifications, jobs in which they made less money and had lower status and fewer skills than men. (See Chart 8.1 for women's occupational distribution from 1900 to 1940; for more data on women's participation in the labor force, see Tables 2–4 in the Appendix.) As one historian neatly summed it up, "Women were invited into the workforce and again invited not to expect too much of it."[5]

The growing acceptance of women in the workforce is evident in the hard statistics. Their participation in paid labor grew from 21 percent in 1900 to 25 percent in 1930. Not only did more women work, but the percentage of married women in the labor force doubled, rising from 5.6 to 11.7 percent. This increase resulted in part from compulsory education laws that kept children from taking jobs to help out the family, a factor that particularly affected immigrant wives, as

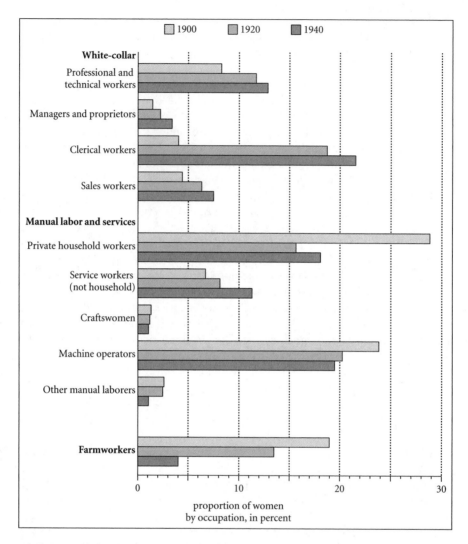

◆ Chart 8.1 **Women's Occupations, 1900–1940**
SOURCES: U.S. Bureau of the Census, Historical Statistics of the United States, *Part 1, table D 182–232;* Statistical Abstract of the United States, 1985 *(Washington, DC: GPO, 1984), table 673; 1991 (Washington, DC: GPO, 1991), table 652.*

well as from rising consumer standards, which gave families incentives for married women to work.

Despite the dramatic increase in the number of married women in the labor force, only 10 percent of all wives worked during the 1920s. Yet their presence signaled a trend that would grow steadily in the future, and in the 1920s the development was significant enough to spark heated controversies. Marriage experts such as Ernest Groves announced that "when the woman herself earns and her maintenance is not entirely at the mercy of her husband's will, diminishing masculine authority necessarily follows."[6] Even observers sympathetic to working wives tended to criticize those who pursued careers, as opposed to women who joined the workforce to help make ends meet in poorer households. Wives who did work often acknowledged hesitation and doubt, but nonetheless, as one newspaper woman put it, stuck to their work: "My reasons are simple and selfish. My monthly paycheck is a welcome addition to the family budget, and a degree of financial independence is heartwarming to one who has tried the sentimental role of partner-homemaker with its uneconomic 'allowance' dole. Housework as a life job bores me and enrages me. Writing, even such hack work as I do, lights up windows for my soul."[7]

But how many women had work that could provide such illumination? As Visual Sources: Women at Work (see pp. 534–47) reveals, even as more and more women entered the labor force, the idea of women's proper place shaped profoundly their work experiences and opportunities. Factory work continued to be a major source of employment, especially among immigrant daughters, but the most rapidly expanding field was clerical work. The emergence of the modern corporation in the late nineteenth century transformed office work and office personnel. By 1910, women already dominated stenographic and typing positions, and in the 1920s they increased their presence as clerks and bookkeepers. As clerical work became increasingly dominated by women, or "feminized," assumptions about these positions changed as well. While men might enter the lower rungs of white-collar work as the first stepping stone to climbing their way up the corporate ladder, jobs that women filled rarely had the same potential for upward mobility.

Status and salaries were low within the white-collar hierarchy, but nonetheless many women viewed these jobs as welcome opportunities and flocked to the commercial courses offered in the public high schools. European immigrant daughters, whose level of education was improving in part because of mandatory education laws, now had more options than factory work. Middle-class workers—who would have found factory work and domestic service demeaning—also staffed the modern office, and their high visibility helped to improve the respectability of women working.

Women of color, however, faced office doors that were largely closed to them. Black women found positions only in a small number of black-owned firms. Mary Helen Washington reported on her aunt's migration from Indianapolis to Cleveland in search of a good job. She was "trained as a bookkeeper and was so good at her work that her white employer at Guardian Savings of Indianapolis allowed her to work at the branch in a black area. The Cleveland Trust Company was not so liberal, however, so in Cleveland, she went to work in what is known in the black community as 'private family' [as a domestic servant]."[8] Japanese and Chinese American women also experienced discrimination in finding office work.

Similar patterns of sexual and racial discrimination appeared in the professions. The professional woman attracted much publicity in the 1920s as an exemplar of the New Woman, yet the percentage of working women in the professions was still small (see Chart 8.1). Women professionals tended to cluster in teaching, nursing, and the expanding field of social work. Even in these increasingly feminized fields, women met with discrimination. Although eight of ten teachers were women, for example, only one in sixty-three superintendents were female. For women of color, the barriers were particularly high, and they made few inroads in this period. The percentage of black women working in the professions, for example, barely rose from 2.5 percent in 1920 to 3.4 percent in 1930.

While educated women struggled to find meaningful work in the professions, the vast majority of American women worked at far less satisfying labor. Black women had been optimistic that migration to the North would provide well-paid factory work. But even in the boom time of World War I, their jobs were the least desirable ones and usually did not last after the war had ended and soldiers had returned to the workforce. In the 1920s, some black women managed to find jobs in industries such as Chicago's packing plants and slaughterhouses, where researcher Alma Herbst found them seasonally employed in the hog-killing and beef-casing department and working "under repulsive conditions."[9] In both northern and southern factories, black women were segregated from white women, who generally refused to work with African Americans. Invariably, these white women had better jobs and better pay.

After the war, most African American women worked in the fields of agricultural labor, laundry work, and domestic service. Seeking to improve control over their work lives, they increasingly refused jobs as live-in servants. The change to day work allowed these women to carve out a small degree of control over their work lives and their private time. As Mayme Gibson put it, "When I got work by the days I'd work in jobs where I'd be doing all the cleaning, my way. Nobody's be looking over your shoulder, saying what you was to do. People took daywork to finally get to work by theyself; to get away from people telling you how to do every little thing."[10] While day work offered an improvement over live-in situations, nonetheless domestic work continued to be highly exploitative, with poor wages and conditions.

Like black women, Mexican American women were heavily concentrated in domestic labor. In 1930, the first date in which census figures reported people of Mexican descent separately, 44 percent of Mexican women who worked were servants. Some urban women found semiskilled factory work. A 1928 study of Los Angeles reported "that in some cases the wife or mother sought the work; in others, the young daughters. In either case, poverty was the immediate incentive." Most worked in "packing houses and canneries of various kinds, followed by the clothing, need trades, and laundries."[11] Outside the cities, many Mexicanas and their American-born daughters worked with their families in agricultural labor. Next to black women, Japanese women were the most likely women of color to work outside the home; about 30 percent worked for wages. Most were married and, like Mexican Americans, worked either as family farm laborers or as domestic servants.

For all women of color, even the educated, the double burden of race and gender translated into few job options. In contrast, most white women, especially native-born ones who had office and professional employment, had cleaner, better paying, less demanding work. Despite these significant differences, all women faced a hierarchical labor market that devalued women's work. As Emily Blair put it at the end of the decade, summarizing her and other feminists' disappointment over women's failure to make significant economic advances in the 1920s, "The best man continued to win, and women, even the best, worked for and under him. Women were welcome to come in as workers, but not as co-makers of the world. For all their numbers they seldom rose to positions of responsibility or power."[12]

The New Woman in the Home

As significant as changes in the public realm of politics and work were for women, the most dramatic transformation in women's lives emerged in the private worlds of home, family, and personal relationships. Contemporaries in the 1920s either celebrated or condemned what was widely viewed as a female sexual revolution. At the center of the revolution was the young, emancipated flapper with her bobbed hair, skimpy clothes, and penchant for outrageous dancing and drinking. Although the image of the flapper glamorized in movies and the pages of popular novelist F. Scott Fitzgerald was exaggerated, many young women across class and racial lines eagerly adopted the flapper clothing style and danced to jazz music their elders found alarmingly erotic. Even more unnerving was their sexual activity. Rejecting the Victorian moral code, young unmarried women increasingly engaged in "petting"—a term that encompassed a wide range of sexual play short of intercourse. And the generation who came of age in the 1920s was significantly more likely than their mothers to have engaged in premarital intercourse.

But if daughters were experimenting sexually, many of their mothers, too, were carving out new roles in what historians have called the "affectionate family." Smaller families were becoming the norm for the urban middle class, but fewer children did not mean less maternal responsibility. Modern mothers, aided by a bounty of household appliances made possible by the widespread electrification of homes in this period, were expected to maintain their homes and raise their children with new efficiency and skill (see Chart 8.2). Increasingly important was their role as consumers. *Photoplay* ran an ad that summed up popular opinion of the New Woman in the home: "Home Manager—Purchasing Agent—Art Director—Wife. She is the active partner in the business of running a home. She buys most of the things which go to make home life happy, healthful, and beautiful."[13] The rosy images of advertising aside, most homemakers continued to have time-consuming responsibilities. Indeed, expectations about careful shopping, cleaner homes, and healthier children may have increased, rather than lightened, women's domestic burdens. Also in the 1920s, a new emphasis on the marriage partnership being a mutually satisfying sexual relationship emerged. A 1930 sociological study, *New Girls for Old*, encapsulated the new way of thinking: "After hundreds of years of mild complaisance to wifely duties, modern women have awakened to the

◆ Movies, Sex, and Consumerism

Movie moderns like Joan Crawford, pictured here in a scene from *Our Dancing Daughters* (1929), conveyed a sense of physical freedom, energy, and independence. They helped to promote new notions of female sexuality that were often tied to the burgeoning consumer culture. Here the screen itself simulates a department store window as Crawford's character Diana stands in front of her mother's perfume collection extravagantly displayed in a luxurious dressing room. *Courtesy of the Academy of Motion Picture Arts and Sciences.*

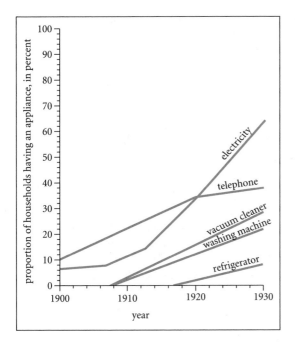

◆ Chart 8.2 **Household Appliances, 1900–1930**

knowledge that they are sexual beings. And with this new insight the sex side of marriage has assumed sudden importance."[14]

Changing ideas about female sexuality were furthered in part by the increasing availability and respectability of reliable birth control, especially the diaphragm. When reformer Margaret Sanger began her drive to legalize the dissemination of contraceptives in 1912, she initially concentrated on helping poor women to control their fertility as a means of mitigating the harshness of their lives (see Chapter 7). By the 1920s, however, discouraged by conservative opposition to her plans for birth control clinics for the poor, she began to target elite and middle-class audiences and to emphasize the erotic potential for women by separating sex from reproduction. Sanger was instrumental in liberalizing state laws to make contraceptives more available, although the requirement that a physician dispense contraceptives meant that they were more likely to be readily available to prosperous white women.

Sanger's approach to female sexuality had been deeply influenced by British psychologist Havelock Ellis, one of the most eminent among a growing circle of "sexologists." Although similar to Sigmund Freud, the founder of modern psychoanalysis, in emphasizing the erotic natures of all humans, Ellis and others, including Sanger, tended to romanticize sexuality by investing it with mystical qualities and insisting that sexual gratification was necessary for emotional health. In the prewar years, their ideas caught on among the feminists (see Chapter 7) who clustered in bohemian centers like New York's Greenwich Village. Criticizing Victorian sexual codes and bourgeois marriage itself, they insisted on women's economic and sexual freedom. By writing plays and novels reflecting these new ideas about female sexuality, these women, along with academic social scientists who were teaching the new sexual ideology in college courses, helped to redefine the ideal of womanhood.

Young working-class women were another source of challenges to Victorian notions of sexual restraint. Poorly paid yet eager to take advantage of early twentieth-century urban commercial entertainments like dance halls and amusement parks, these young women inhabited a culture that sanctioned "treating," whereby male suitors would entertain them and buy them gifts in exchange for sexual favors. The relative freedom of the urban environment and the desire for "cheap amusements" prompted women to map out a new sexual terrain.[15] (See Documents: Young Women Speak Out, pp. 519–25.)

By the 1930s, these changes evident in both working-class women and radical elites had filtered to a broad middle-class audience. Crucial to the popularization of these ideas was the rapid expansion of the mass media, especially motion pictures. Popular movies featured stars like Clara Bow who had "IT"—the catch phrase for sexual appeal—and attracted audiences with displays of female flesh and passionate love scenes. Despite heightened attention to sexuality, movies rarely condoned adultery or promiscuity, however. While the plots might titillate with the escapades of "bad" girls, these women usually paid for their sins; the heroines who resisted temptation were rewarded at the end by marriage or a renewal of their marriage commitment.

Movies thus sent an ambivalent message. On the one hand, they encouraged women to view themselves as more sexual creatures. On the other, by keeping the focus on marriage, films also reflected a desire to contain female eroticism in acceptable channels. Another way in which movies and other forms of mass media, most notably advertising, simultaneously promoted a new sexuality while limiting it was the close association drawn between sexuality and consumer goods. Although advertising featured a variety of images of women, one of the most ubiquitous was the glamorous female, made sexy by the products she purchased.

Not surprisingly, the 1920s also witnessed an explosion of beauty shops, expanding from five thousand in 1920 to forty thousand in 1930, along with a corresponding 400 percent leap in the sale of cosmetics. Thus, just as women were being encouraged to explore their sexuality, they were also being encouraged to identify it with particular standards of beauty and with the purchase of consumer goods and to see its goal as the happily adjusted marriage. In the process, the radical egalitarian potential of women's sexual liberation was muted.

There were other indications that the sexual revolution was less revolutionary than it seemed. Young women might engage in petting, for example, but prevailing norms discouraged intercourse except as a prelude to marriage between engaged couples. A double standard for men and women persisted, and women could get a reputation for being "fast," which could damage their marriage prospects. Moreover, not everyone embraced the new sexuality. Divorce case records in the 1920s reveal some wives, traditionally reared, could not comfortably accept the new sexual code, much to the dismay of their husbands, who had anticipated a highly sexualized marriage. Among Italian immigrant daughters, a very low rate of illegitimacy persisted into the 1930s, an indication that many of these young women remained outside the peer culture that sanctioned sexual activity for unmarried women.[16]

For many African American women reformers, who had labored for decades to protect black women from sexual exploitation and to counter the stereotype of black women as promiscuous, celebrating female sexuality was problematic. During the Harlem Renaissance, a major cultural movement of black authors and artists who sought to articulate a distinct black contribution to American culture, women writers such as Jessie Fauset, Nella Larsen, and Zora Neale Hurston similarly were sensitive to the portrayal of black women's sexuality. But in another major expression of black culture, female jazz and blues singers such as Bessie Smith, Ida Cox, and Ma Rainey often presented an exuberant sense of women's enjoyment of their sexuality that spoke of resistance to sexual objectification and domination by men. Some songs featured a woman demanding that her lover pay attention to her needs, such as "One Hour Mamma," in which Ida Cox reminded her partner that she wanted "a slow and easy man" who "needn't ever take the lead" and who "love me like I like to be."[17]

The sexual dimension of the New Woman, like her participation in politics and the workforce, was complex. New developments in both public and private spheres ushered in significant changes, although these were filtered through the lens of class, race, and ethnicity and were accompanied by continued emphasis on women's roles as wives and mothers. A coalescence of factors in the 1920s—an expanding role in the workplace, new political opportunities, a more sexualized marriage, and the growing importance of the consumer culture—did not give women full economic and political equality or personal autonomy, but it did give their lives a modern contour, putting in motion the trends that would characterize women's lives for the rest of the twentieth century.

DEPRESSION DECADE: THE 1930s

Although the fabled prosperity of the 1920s was never as widespread as popular memory has it, the contrast between that decade and the economic hardships faced by Americans in the 1930s is striking. In 1933 unemployment figures had reached 25 percent and the U.S. gross national product (GNP) had been cut almost in half. A stunning stock market crash in late October 1929 had helped precipitate the Great Depression, particularly by damaging the nation's banking system, but long-standing weaknesses in the economy accounted for its length and severity. A prolonged agricultural depression and a decline in certain "sick" industries such as textiles and mining were just two points of underlying vulnerability. An unequal distribution of the nation's wealth—in 1929, 40 percent of the population received only 12.5 percent of aggregate family income, while the top 5 percent of the population received 30 percent—meant that once the Depression began, the majority of people were unable to spend the amount of money that was needed to revive the economy. The Great Depression became self-perpetuating, and for ten years it left what one observer has called "an invisible scar" running through the lives of millions of Americans.

If our most familiar female icon of the 1920s is the flamboyant flapper, then the counterpart for the Depression decade of the 1930s is Dorothea Lange's haunting photograph of Florence Owens, "Migrant Mother." Owens was part of a massive exodus of farm families from the southwestern plains states, where farmers, already suffering from low crop prices in the 1920s, were devastated by a prolonged drought in the 1930s that had created the "dust bowl" and countless family tragedies. The image potently evokes the hardships embodied in the sterile statistics of the era, a period in which overall unemployment rose as high as 30 percent, banks closed by the thousands, and hundreds of thousands of Americans lost their homes and farms. Even if a woman was not part of the down and out, she could identify with the fear and uncertainty of the migrant woman. But just as the flapper only scratches the surface of the experience of women in the 1920s, so too the migrant mother was just one facet of a complex mosaic of American womanhood.

At Home in Hard Times

Even more so than in good times, class and race proved powerful determinants of women's experience in the Great Depression. While elite and middle-class families experienced downward mobility and emotional and material hardships, it was the nation's working-class and farm families who suffered most from the economic crisis. Not only did they face a greater likelihood of losing their jobs or farms, but they also had fewer resources to draw on in hard times. African Americans were among the greatest losers. They were the first fired in industrial jobs and the hardest hit among the rural southern Americans so devastated by the farm crisis. Mexican and Asian American farmers and workers in the West and Southwest also experienced high rates of unemployment and low wages. Like African Americans, they met with discrimination from city, state, and federal agencies that provided relief payments to the impoverished. Indeed, resistance to subsidizing unemployed immigrant workers led to a drive to deport Mexican immigrants, especially in Texas and California. In the 1930s, Los Angeles lost one-third of its Mexican population, many of whom were citizen children of immigrant parents. This deportation movement led to significant disruption in communities, placing heavy burdens on women and families already coping with economic dislocations.

The Depression was also a heavily gendered experience. Despite the fact that women's participation in the workforce had been steadily increasing in the early twentieth century, most observers continued to regard women's proper place as in the home and to interpret the unemployment crisis of the 1930s primarily as a male dilemma. Policy makers, sociologists, and popular writers alike emphasized "the forgotten man" and worried about the psychological impact of unemployment for American traditions of masculine individualism. Sociological studies such as *The Unemployed Man and His Family* (1940) emphasized the familial

◆ **Migrant Mother**

This evocative 1936 photograph of Florence Owens by Farm Security Administration photographer Dorothea Lange captured one of the tragic outcomes of the Great Depression: the massive migration of farm families from the drought-ravaged Great Plains. At least 350,000 victims of the dust bowl headed west in the 1930s, half of them settling in rural areas where they worked for low wages as migratory farm laborers. In 1960, Lange reminisced about the photograph: "She told me her age, that she was thirty-two. She said that they had been living on frozen vegetables [picked from] surrounding fields, and birds that the children killed. She had just sold the tires from her car to buy food. There she sat in that lean-to tent with her children huddled around her, and seemed to know that my pictures might help her, and so she helped me. There was a sort of equality about it." *Library of Congress LC-USF34-009058-C.*

499

disruption that resulted when men lost jobs and often sacrificed their dominant position in the household. Observers may have been correct that the crisis was harder on men than on women. As sociologists Helen and Robert Lynd put it in their widely read 1937 study of "Middletown" (Muncie, Indiana), "The men, cut adrift from their usual routine, lost much of their sense of time and dawdled helplessly and dully about the streets; while in the homes the women's world remained largely intact and the round of cooking, housecleaning, and mending became if anything more absorbing."[18]

These tasks became more absorbing because so many women had to juggle fewer resources and become adept at "making do." Magazines ran articles on cooking with cheaper ingredients, and ads aimed at female consumers touted money-saving products and offered advice for preparing nutritious "7 cents' breakfasts." For poor women, the burdens of homemaking were exacerbated by problems of poor sanitation and substandard housing—problems especially for minority women and poor white rural women. In many social groups, homemaking often became more complicated and stressful by the presence of extended kin, as families coped with reduced income by combining households.

Other issues shaped the households women inhabited. Unemployment for men often strained marriages, especially ones that had been patriarchal. Desertion rates rose, but rates for divorce, an expensive proposition, did not. Another measure of the Depression's impact was the decline in fertility rates, dropping, for example, from eighty-nine to seventy-six live births per thousand women of childbearing age between the years 1930 and 1933 (see Chart 1 in the Appendix). The trend toward smaller families and the use of contraception, evident among more prosperous families in the 1920s, spread to many in the working class in the 1930s, as fewer children became an economic necessity and after access to legal birth control was facilitated by a 1936 decision (*United States v. One Package of Japanese Pessaries*) invalidating federal laws that had prohibited the dissemination of contraceptive information.

Women and Work

Although contemporaries viewed women's responsibilities primarily as maintaining the home in hard times, women as workers constitute an important part of the Depression story. Hostility toward married women working intensified in the 1930s, evident in public opinion polls such as the one conducted by George Gallup in 1936, which asked if married women should work if their husbands were employed; 82 percent of the respondents said "no," although there was less opposition to wives in very low-income families who worked.[19] Legislation reflected this hostility. The 1932 National Economy Act required that when workforce reductions had to take place, the first let go should be those who already had a family member in the government's employ, which did not specifically target women but led to the firing of thousands of them. State and local governments echoed this trend, as did many private companies. Most school districts did not hire wives as teachers, and half of them fired women when they married. For those women who did work, wages contracted in the 1930s, and they continued to earn less than men, receiving in 1935, for example, 65 cents for every dollar of men's wages.[20]

Despite this discrimination, women's desire and need to work increased and their participation in the workforce grew modestly, inching up from 25 percent in 1930 to 27 percent in 1940. More striking was the increase of women workers who were married. In 1930, 12 percent of wives worked; in 1940, 17 percent.[21] While women also experienced devastating unemployment, especially in the early hard years of the Depression, white women at least found jobs far more quickly than their male counterparts. Sex segregation in the workforce ironically assisted them. Heavy industrial jobs, the domain of men (where women counted for less than 2 percent of all workers), were the most affected by the Depression, while light industry, usually associated with female operatives, recovered more quickly as the decade progressed. More significantly, opportunities in clerical work expanded in part because the federal agencies of the New Deal designed to cope with the Depression almost doubled the number of federal employees.

In contrast to white women, black women lost jobs during the 1930s. One traditional field for black women—farm labor—constricted as hundreds of thousands of sharecroppers and wage workers were thrown out of work in the South. Mechanization further eliminated farm jobs. At the same time, opportunities in the other major area of employment for black women—domestic work—shrank and competition grew. In New York City and elsewhere, "slave markets" provided a particularly potent example of the harsh conditions. Black women would stand on street corners waiting for white women to drive by and hire them for a day's heavy labor for less than $2.00. Whatever their jobs, black women were almost certain to earn less than other groups. The average wages per week of white women in Texas factories, for example, were $7.45, while Mexican women took home $5.40 and black women only $3.75.[22]

The patterns of work in the 1930s underlined the broad trends becoming clear in the previous decade. Participation of women, especially married women, in the workforce increased, but did so in sex-segregated labor markets that limited women's occupational mobility and income. Moreover, that market was further segregated by race and ethnicity, with white women dominating the rapidly expanding clerical workforce. Jobs in agriculture decreased, but they were still a significant source of work for women of color, as were domestic labor and semiskilled industrial work, especially that related to garment and food processing. The restricted nature of women's job opportunities would not be challenged—and then only temporarily—until the United States entered World War II in 1941.

Women's New Deal

As American women and men coped with hard times, they sought strong political leadership. They found it in President Franklin D. Roosevelt. In 1932, as the Depression deepened, Roosevelt defeated incumbent Republican Herbert Hoover handily and came to Washington, D.C., with a clear mandate to act forcefully to bring about recovery and relieve suffering. He brought to the presidency a

◆ **Eleanor Roosevelt and the Women's Press Corp**
Eleanor Roosevelt, seated at center, is surrounded by women reporters, who particularly appreciated the First Lady because of the access she gave them to the White House. She instituted women-only press conferences that helped them counter the prevailing sexism they
faced in their profession and allowed her to publicize her interest in New Deal programs and
social reform. As one appreciative newspaper woman characterized the respect Mrs. Roosevelt gave women reporters, "Never was there such a gift from heaven for the working press."
Stock Montage.

charisma and a willingness to experiment with programs that directly assisted the
needy. Labeling these programs a "New Deal" for Americans, Roosevelt easily
pushed an enormous amount of legislation through Congress. Roosevelt's New
Deal agencies contributed to his immense popularity, a popularity that the efforts
of his wife, Eleanor Roosevelt, enhanced. A gifted woman, with a long-standing
commitment to social reform, Eleanor called herself "the eyes and ears of the New
Deal," perhaps an implicit reference to her husband's limited physical mobility.
(He was severely crippled from polio.) She crisscrossed the nation promoting the

New Deal, pushed Roosevelt to pay more attention to the plight of African Americans, and gathered around her a group of activist women particularly concerned about the hardships women and children faced during the Depression. (See Documents: Women's Networks in the New Deal, pp. 526–33.) Despite her efforts, however, most New Deal programs slighted or discriminated against women.

The National Industrial Recovery Act (NIRA) reflected the way in which the New Deal reinforced existing assumptions about women's subordinate role in the workforce. Passed in 1933 and designed to stimulate recovery, this pivotal piece of legislation established codes that set wages, hours, and prices in the nation's major economic sectors. Jobs described as "light and repetitive" were those usually assigned to women, and 25 percent of the codes explicitly permitted differential wages between men and women, anywhere from 5 to 25 cents per hour. Clerical workers in many fields were excluded, and farm and domestic workers were not covered at all: one cook wrote to President Roosevelt "that the large and unprotected class of Domestics were not thought of. I keenly felt for my kind who [sic] you spoke of the robbery of the Bankers but never mentioned the robbery of the Housewives."[23]

Despite such shortcomings, the New Deal did help some women workers, especially in its efforts to provide protection for organized labor. The 1920s had been a low point for unions, which suffered from the postwar Red Scare and corporate antiunions drives. Union membership stood at a mere 12 percent of the workforce at the end of the decade. The NIRA, however, contained provisions that legitimized unions and helped to spark hundreds of organizing drives that tapped into the widespread discontent of workers. Women were particularly active in the International Ladies Garment Workers' Union, which conducted organizing drives in sixty cities, increasing its size by 500 percent between 1933 and 1934. When in 1935 the Supreme Court, arguing that it represented an unconstitutional delegation of power to the executive, invalidated the NIRA, the New Deal replaced its labor provisions with the National Labor Relations (Wagner) Act. This legislation again galvanized unionization campaigns and contributed to the success of a new national union federation, the Congress of Industrial Organizations (CIO), which in 1935 had broken off from the more conservative American Federation of Labor (AFL). The CIO, influenced in part by the significant presence of Communist Party members among its organizers, many of whom were women, concentrated on mass production industries. Women especially benefited from union inroads in light industries such as manufacture of tobacco and paper products. In 1924, 200,000 women belonged to a union; by 1938, the figure was 800,000, a 300 percent gain.

Women actively participated in strikes, both as workers and as wives of male strikers. In 1933, poor wages and working conditions led to a long and bitter strike by eighteen thousand cotton workers in California, most of whom were Mexicans associated with the Cannery and Agricultural Workers Industrial Union. Women participated by preparing and distributing food among the strikers, but they were also active on the picket line. They taunted strikebreakers, urging them to join the strike, yelling out in Spanish, "Come on out, quit work, we'll feed you. If you don't, we'll poison all of you." This confrontation ended in violence as many women armed themselves with knives and lead pipes.[24]

Women also played a crucial role in the 1937 Flint, Michigan, sit-down strike against General Motors. When the men sat down at their machines, their wives as well as women workers (who were not included in the occupation of the factory because of concerns about sexual propriety) organized the Women's Emergency Brigade. They fulfilled the traditional female role of providing food for the men, but then they moved beyond to stage a women's march of seven thousand and to create other diversions that allowed men to expand their sit-down strike to another GM plant. Brigade leader, autoworker, and socialist Genora Johnson Dollinger explained, "This was an independent move. It was not under the direction of the union or its administrators—I just talked it over with a few women—the active ones—and told them this is what we had to do."[25] The successful strike ended with GM's recognition of the United Auto Workers union. Perhaps predictably, the strike also ended with men assuming women would resume their customary positions in the home, saying, according to Dollinger, "Well, you women did a wonderful job, but now your duty is back there getting those kids in school, getting the wash done, and regular meals again."[26] Both as auxiliary supporters and as workers, then, women played an important role in the radicalism that so shaped the 1930s.

The federal government's new involvement in protecting working-class Americans through labor legislation was matched by its unprecedented intervention in providing relief for those made destitute by the Depression. Although most policy makers perceived of the unemployment crisis as primarily a male one, an inner circle of female New Dealers, aided by Eleanor Roosevelt, insisted that the government pay attention to the "forgotten woman." (See Documents: Women's Networks in the New Deal, pp. 526–33.) A central figure was Ellen S. Woodward, who headed the Women's and Professional Projects Division of several agencies that provided federal relief for the unemployed—the Federal Emergency Relief Administration (FERA), Civil Works Administration (CWA), and Works Projects Administration (WPA). Woodward worked hard to get women included in programs that created jobs for the unemployed. A small number of professional women, such as librarians, social workers, teachers, and nurses, were accommodated in federal projects, and some artists and writers found employment in programs such as the Federal Theater Project headed by Hallie Flanagan. But the vast majority (almost 80 percent in 1935) of women needing help were unskilled, and for them the work-relief jobs clustered in traditional women's work of sewing, canning, and domestic labor.

These work-relief programs offered invaluable assistance to poor women. Reporter Lorena Hickok, not known for her sentimentality, described their impact on women in Florida sewing rooms: "I don't think you have any idea of what they have done to women themselves. They come in sullen, dejected, half starved. Working in pleasant surroundings, having some money and food have done wonders to restore their health and morale."[27] In addition to offering individual em-

◆ **WPA Training for Household Workers**
Most telling of the ways in which New Deal programs reinforced existing stereotypes concerning minority women were the programs for domestic training. When Ellen S. Woodward set about to deal with the problem of unemployed domestics, she wanted to have a training program that would elevate these women's position and give them both dignity and skills. But by shunting minority women to these programs, the New Deal reinforced both race- and sex-segregated labor patterns. *Franklin D. Roosevelt Library.*

ployment, these programs benefited the community. Between 1933 and 1937, women made over 122 million articles that were distributed to the poor free of charge. They provided the food for highly successful free school lunch programs. Librarians created card catalogs and oversaw Braille transcription projects. Handicraft programs drew on regional variations. In Texas, women were given leather to make coats and jackets; in Arizona, Native American women fashioned copperware: in Florida, women produced hats, handbags, and rugs for the tourist industry.

Yet, despite these benefits and Woodward's promise that "women are going to get a square deal," the programs were riddled with discrimination against women. Most programs focused on male unemployment and treated women as subordinate earners who ideally should be in the home. To be eligible for work relief, they needed to prove that they were heads of family, and if a husband was physically able to work, whether he had found work or not, women were unlikely to be given federal jobs. Single women without families were also less likely to find work on federal projects. "They say they can't place me as I do not have a family. What are we single girls going to do?"[28] wrote one woman to the White House, which received four hundred letters a month from women about the problems they faced. Some young women found jobs with the National Youth Administration (NYA), but they were excluded from the Civilian Conservation Corps, which put 2.5 million young men to work conserving the nation's parks and natural resources. Only after Eleanor Roosevelt intervened were similar camps set up for women, but these accommodated only eight thousand young women.

This type of discrimination provoked protest from women's groups as well as the unemployed. One woman wrote to the Roosevelts to complain: "I should like to know why it is that men can be placed so easily and not women."[29] The answer to that question lay in part with local administrators, who often resisted finding work for women, particularly work that challenged traditional notions of women's proper domestic roles. When women found positions, the jobs invariably fell into low-paying categories. New Deal agencies, then, not only followed sex segregation policies based on traditional notions of women's proper place in the home, but they also helped to institutionalize them.

Similarly, New Deal agencies replicated the discrimination based on race and ethnicity found in the private labor market. Relief policies were designed to help the poor, and indeed, most minority groups benefited from them to some degree. But despite official guidelines that tried to limit discrimination, federal agencies rarely challenged the policies of local administrators. On many Native American reservations, officials often were indifferent to the problem of work relief for women. In the racially segregated South, local New Deal agencies resisted giving black women jobs during harvest periods when cheap farm labor was in demand. When African American women could get federal jobs, they were usually in segregated programs. When white and black women were assigned to integrated sewing rooms, black women were routinely given the more arduous and menial work. Skilled black women faced similar problems. Natalie Middletown of Cleveland received a high score on a clerical test, but she had few employment opportunities, finally receiving a job through the NYA, where she was not allowed to type or handle money but rather worked in a dusty attic sorting files, at a pay and job classification lower than white women's.[30] In San Antonio, a three-part caste system was in operation. African American women were formally segregated from projects that could employ white or Mexican women, but an informal process kept white and Mexican women from working together in sewing or canning rooms.

That the New Deal both assisted women and reinforced their inequality as wage workers was most dramatically evident in the Social Security Act of 1935.

This path-breaking legislation owed much to women reformers like Secretary of Labor Frances Perkins (see p. 526). It provided a federal pension plan and federal-state matching fund program for unemployment assistance and for aid to dependent mothers and children. Neither domestic workers nor farm workers—two major employment options for poor women—were covered by the program, however, and women who chose to work in the home as mothers and housewives were similarly excluded. A 1939 amendment to Social Security further institutionalized inequality. Married working women were taxed at the same rate as their husbands, but because there was a family limit to benefits, a wife's benefits were reduced if her wages and her husband's exceeded the family limits. In addition, widows and their children received benefits when a husband and father died, but a married woman's dependents did not. In common with other New Deal programs, then, Social Security operated under the assumption of women's subordinate place in the labor market and their primary role in the home.

Despite its mixed record in terms of racial and gender discrimination, the New Deal did assist a wide variety of Americans in coping with the devastating effects of the Great Depression. It facilitated the growth of unions, put millions of people to work, and institutionalized the modest welfare provisions of the Social Security Act. One thing it failed to accomplish was to end the Depression. The return of prosperity would not come until the advent of World War II, when the demand for war production set American factories back to work and created full employment.

WORKING FOR VICTORY: WOMEN AND WAR, 1941–1945

In the late 1930s, as the militarism of Germany, Italy, and Japan rose to a crescendo, most Americans adamantly opposed being drawn into war. Once Adolf Hitler invaded Poland in 1939, however, France and Britain, the United States' allies in World War I, declared war on the Axis powers, Germany and Italy. Despite an official neutrality mandated by Congress, the United States offered financial and other material assistance to its former allies and began its own defense buildup. Public sentiment remained high against becoming involved in the war, but December 7, 1941, shattered that resistance. When Japan, which had signed an alliance with the Axis, executed a devastating surprise air attack on the American naval base and fleet at Pearl Harbor, Hawaii, killing 2,400 Americans, Congress declared war on Japan. Within days, Germany and Italy declared war on the United States, and the United States in turn declared war on those nations. The United States entered a global conflagration being fought in Europe, Asia, and Africa that would last until victory was declared in 1945.

The global war and the massive mobilization it entailed had a tremendous impact on American women. By undercutting patterns of sex-segregated labor, perfectly symbolized by the poster image of "Rosie the Riveter," and offering women new independence and responsibilities, it produced significant changes, both in the workplace and in the domestic arena. Yet to a striking degree Americans continued to reiterate traditional notions about woman's proper sphere in the home even as they challenged these ideas in daily life. And, as was the case during the Depression, race, ethnicity, and gender discrimination continued to shape American women's experience.

Women in the Military

Despite a long tradition of exceptional American women edging their way onto the battlefield, donning the nation's uniform was a particularly male act that served to shape definitions of ideal masculinity. As the American military establishment geared up for World War II, it initially resisted incorporating women into the service. Eventually, military necessity, as well as pressure from women's groups under the leadership of Congresswoman Edith Nourse Rogers of Massachusetts, led to the acceptance of female military recruits. Thousands of men were thus made available for combat. The WACs (Women's Army Corps) attracted 140,000 recruits; 100,000 served in the navy's WAVES (Women Accepted for Volunteer Emergency Service); 23,000 were in MCWR (Marine Corps Women's Reserve); and 13,000 enlisted with SPARS (Coast Guard Women's Reserve). Another 76,000 served as army or navy nurses.

Women's jobs typically followed the conventional patterns of peacetime. While some women worked as mechanics and welders and in other skilled jobs that broke the gender barrier, most filled jobs as clerks, telephone operators, dieticians, and in other routine assignments. In defending the idea of female recruits, Army Assistant Chief John H. Hildring aptly summed up common expectations about female military service: "We have found difficulty in getting enlisted men to perform tedious duties anywhere nearly as well as women will do it."[31] A particularly vital role filled by women was nursing, often in exceptionally dangerous circumstances, just behind the front in all the major theaters of the war—North Africa, Europe, and Asia. While the military welcomed nurses, it resisted commissioning women as doctors—despite the severe shortage of physicians—until April 1943, fifteen months after America's entry into the war.

Black women experienced racial discrimination at the hands of the federal government's segregated military establishment. Because the navy prohibited African American men from serving in any but menial positions, it also refused to incorporate black women into its ranks until 1944, almost at the end of the war. Black nurses were commissioned in the army, and 10 percent of the WACs were African Americans, but they lived and worked in segregated units and had less access to training and skilled jobs than white women. Black nurses were allowed to attend only to African Americans or prisoners of war, and they were often assigned to menial, not skilled, patient services.

All women in the service encountered a public that was ambivalent about the gender challenges presented by women in uniform. Oveta Culp Hobby, a prominent Houston woman who became director of the WACs, had to counter pervasive rumors of sexual immorality and drunkenness among service women. Although some of the rumors focused on lesbianism and the "queer damozels of the Isle of

◆ Breaking Down the Sex and Color Lines: African American WAC Officers in World War II

This 1943 photograph features a group of African American nurses drilling at the first Women's Army Corps Training Center in Fort Des Moines, Iowa. Leading the group is Charity Adams, a former teacher from South Carolina who rose to the rank of major in the WACs. Her autobiography details pride in her accomplishments and the women who served with her, but also unstinting criticism of the segregation she and other black women experienced. After reporting a particularly brutal exchange with a white male colonel who criticized her severely for attending an officer's club—for, as he put it, she might be an officer, but "you are still colored and I want you to remember that"—Adams commented, "I suspect that I knew it all before, but having lived under circumstances in which I had learned how to avoid confrontation and humiliation, I had not fully recognized what obstacles we had to overcome." *National Archives NWDNS-111-SC-238651.*

Lesbos" among recruits, most critics alleged promiscuity among heterosexual women.[32] As a result, the WACs distributed publicity praising the women's high moral character, but the agency also refused to distribute contraceptives to women in the service, in contrast to the policy adopted for men that was designed to prevent the spread of venereal disease. For women and men alike, the military also adopted a harsh policy toward homosexuality, making "homosexual tendencies," as diagnosed by a psychiatrist, sufficient grounds for dismissal from the service. However, although World War II military service offered many women and men opportunities to participate in a discreet lesbian and gay subculture, relatively few service people were discharged on these grounds.

Equally as pressing as concerns about sexual immorality was the worry that these women were sacrificing their femininity by usurping men's roles. In an effort to put these fears to rest, the *New York Times* reported in 1945 that the WAC "will always be a civilian at heart." Her service "will increase her femininity," and, the *Times* predicted, "the most important post-war plans of the majority of women in the WAC include just what all women want—their own homes and families."[33] Similarly, Colonel Hobby, while insisting that women in the service be treated with respect, reiterated traditional notions of women's proper place by asserting that military women were developing "new poise and charm," and that they "were only performing the duties that women would ordinarily do in civilian life."[34]

One duty that women rarely took on in civilian life was eagerly embraced by the women pilots of WASP (Women Airforce Service Pilots). The U.S. government refused to militarize this agency, a measure of just how threatening the idea of women performing high-status "male" jobs was. Instead, these pilots were civil servants without military rank, privileges, or uniforms. Drawing on an eager applicant pool of over 25,000 women, the WASPs accepted 1,074, all of whom had pilot's licenses and experience, unlike most men accepted for training as military pilots. Of these, two were Mexican American, two Chinese American, and one Native American. The lone African American who applied was urged to withdraw her application by WASP director Jacqueline Cochran, who explained that she wanted to avoid controversy at a time when the program had not yet been officially put in place.

WASP pilots ferried and tested plans and participated in maneuvers and training. Although they did not participate in combat, thirty-eight women lost their lives on duty. The WASPs performed invaluable services, but they were disbanded in December 1944, before the end of the war, because of pressure from civilian male pilots and veteran groups, which resented potential female competition in an elite male field. WASPs were not eligible for veteran benefits until a congressional act passed in 1977 finally gave them partial recognition for what they had accomplished.

Women, War, and Work

Just as the military establishment was reluctant to incorporate women into the armed services, so too did employers not initially welcome female workers in defense industries. In a similar fashion, the federal government's War Manpower Agency largely excluded women advisors from policy-making decisions about war production. But by mid-1942, as male workers were drafted into the army, the reality of labor scarcity started to erode resistance to female war workers. Women became the objects of a massive propaganda campaign to urge them to do their bit for Uncle Sam. Writers for popular magazines such as the *Saturday Evening Post* adopted story lines and recommendations from the government's Office of War Information to reinforce the importance of women taking advantage of training programs and employment opportunities. Posters and newsreels echoed the message: "The More Women at Work the Sooner We'll Win."

Women responded eagerly to expanded job opportunities, not just in defense industries but in other sectors of the economy as well. (See Visual Sources: Women at Work, pp. 534–47.) After the hardships of the Depression, with some 3 million women unemployed as late as 1940, a burgeoning demand for labor put the unemployed to work and created jobs that provided new opportunities for women coming into the labor market for the first time. Between 1940 and 1945, almost 5 million new female workers entered the labor force, representing a 43 percent increase in women workers.[35] In 1944, an estimated 37 percent of adult women worked in the paid labor force. In a particularly important trend that foreshadowed postwar developments, older, married women provided the largest numbers of new workers, while there was little change in women between 20 and 30 years of age. Traditional jobs in light industry and clerical work expanded, and for white women, professional positions also became more readily available. As male farmers went off to war, women increased their presence in agriculture by 8 percent, as women, many of them organized in the U.S. Department of Agriculture's Women's Land Army, helped to harvest the nation's crops.

Women's participation in the defense industry was particularly significant because it broke down sex-segregated labor patterns. Women were trained in skilled jobs such as welders, riveters, and electricians. Their successes were widely touted, but publicity about these many Rosie the Riveters emphasized that women had maintained their femininity. One plant personnel manager, for example, commented that "we like the girls to be neat and trim and well put together. It helps their morale. It helps our prestige too."[36] Further, defense jobs were for the war's duration only, something women were doing allegedly for service, not for their own economic or personal goals. Thus, what could have been a dramatic development that challenged sex segregation in the labor market was robbed of its more radical potential.

Nonetheless, defense work did improve women's economic situation. The federal government's National War Labor Board (NWLB) issued General Order Number 16 (November 1942), which called for paying women wages equal to men's when they were doing comparable work. Women's groups had pressured the NWLB, but the main motivation for the order was a desire not to undercut men's wages while women were temporarily taking on male jobs. Unions adopted a similar approach. Women's participation in unions rose from 9.4 percent of union members before the war to 22 percent in 1944. Although some left-wing unions' nondiscriminatory policies stemmed from genuinely egalitarian goals, most unions supported equal pay primarily with the goal of preserving male privileges. Moreover, older patterns of male and female classifications for jobs persisted, as well as seniority-based pay scales that served to assure higher wages for men.

For African American women, war job opportunities presented a mixed lot. Defense industries resisted hiring black women until it became absolutely necessary. In Detroit's war industries in 1943, of 96,000 jobs filled by women, women of color held only 1,000.[37] Not until later that year did wartime manufacturers begin to hire black women. These possibilities for breaking into better-paying industrial work—the first since World War I—were undeniably exciting and helped to create another large migration out of the South. This time, in addition to the cities of the Midwest and North, African Americans branched out into the West, especially southern California. In this burgeoning center of defense manufacturing, as many as 12,000 African Americans arrived monthly in the peak year of 1943 (see Map 8.1).

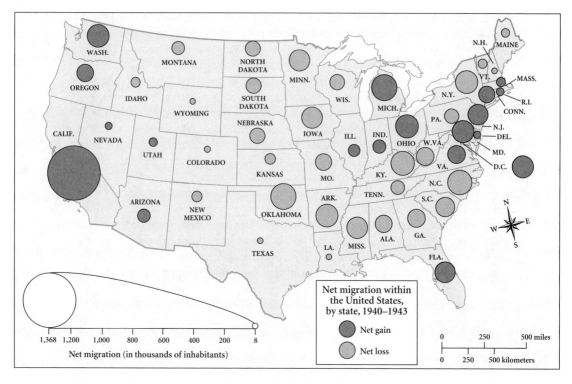

◆ **Map 8.1 A New Wave of Internal Migration, 1940–1943**
Almost 15 million people changed residence during the war years, with half of them moving to another state. While the movement of African Americans out of the rural South was the most dramatic example of this internal migration, whites, Mexican Americans, and Native Americans also headed for the nation's cities. Migrants found exciting job opportunities in defense industries, but they had to cope with the stresses of relocating and overcrowded, often inadequate housing, problems that fell especially on women's shoulders.

War jobs allowed many black women to escape the drudgery and poor wages of domestic work. However, they were often denied training and, even with training, assigned to less desirable positions, such as work in foundries and outside labor gangs. Although some of the treatment they received reflected employer racism, white women frequently resisted working with black women, in particular refusing to share toilet, shower, and meal facilities. In some cases, white women even went on strike over these issues, reflecting more a concern to maintain social distance between the races and a deep-seated belief that black women were "unclean" than fears about economic competition.[38]

Many black women protested the discrimination they encountered. Black organizations such as the NAACP fostered this new militancy, as did black newspapers. In Los Angeles, publisher Carlotta Bass used the pages of the *Eagle* to call for more jobs for African Americans. In concert with the NAACP, Bass organized a rally in July 1942 that marched on the local U.S. Employment Services office to insist that black women be given jobs in war industries, a tactic that eventually helped to integrate southern California defense plants. Black women also turned to the Fair Employment Practices Commission (FEPC), filing 25 percent of the complaints it received. This federal agency, charged with assuring that defense industries and training programs did not discriminate, had been created in 1941 in response to determined black protest and a threat to lead a march on Washington, D.C. A significant development in the history of civil rights, the FEPC nonetheless had limited success. The imperative of keeping war production up to speed meant that the FEPC had few tools for disciplining discriminating companies, and it rarely succeeded in forcing defense contractors to hire black women.

But black women nonetheless benefited significantly from war opportunities. The percentage of black women employed in domestic service decreased from 60 percent in 1940 to 45 percent in 1944, and their participation in the industrial workforce increased from 7 to 18 percent for the same period. They also obtained more white-collar work in the federal government, especially in Washington. However, black women's low seniority usually meant that as the war wound down, they were the first fired. Margaret Wright, a skilled worker for Lockheed Aircraft, a major defense contractor, was laid off at the war's end, and later she sadly recalled that "I had to fall back on the only other thing that I knew, and that was doing domestic work."[39] By 1950, some of the gains made in breaking away from domestic work had eroded: 50 percent of African American working women were still in domestic service. After the war, however, some women were able to hold on to higher paying industrial and clerical work. Even for those who were shunted back to domestic work, the migration from the impoverished rural South offered at least the hope for a better life.

Other women of color found expanded opportunities in the war years and faced less discrimination than African Americans. In the Midwest, Mexicans, who before the war had difficulty finding industrial work and were routinely asked for their citizenship papers, found that employers "stopped asking for proof of legalization because they needed all the workers they could find for the war effort."[40] Not only did these women secure jobs in defense industries, but they also found that the labor scarcity improved their circumstances in other industrial jobs. Food processing, which was traditionally characterized by low status and pay, was vital to the war effort, and the United Cannery, Agricultural, Packing, and Allied Workers of America union in California was able to use the war emergency to push usually resistant employers for pay concessions and other benefits, including in one instance a plant nursery for children of employees.

So, too, Native American women's employment expanded during the war. About one-fifth of adult women on reservations left to take jobs, and those who stayed behind increased their duties, helping to maintain farming and tribal concerns such as the timber industry. The Bureau of Indian Affairs, under John

◆ **Keeping the Home Fires Burning**
Much war-time publicity was given to women who took jobs in the defense industry or
served in the military, but another valued role for women was the faithful wife or mother
who patriotically sent off her menfolk to fight. Magazine articles offered advice on the types
of letters women should write to help maintain their fighting men's morale. Here, Rose Ong,
a San Francisco seamstress, is shown with pictures of her six sons, all of whom were in the
military. For Mrs. Ong and her family, World War II marked a watershed of new acceptance
into mainstream American life. *National Archives 208 MO-74R-19075.*

Collier, a New Dealer who had constructed a more humanitarian and liberal Native American policy that nonetheless perpetuated a patronizing attitude toward
Indians, publicized Native American contributions to the war effort, as did the
journals of the off-reservation boarding schools, which supplied most of the
young women who went into defense work.[41]

For Chinese American women, the war offered unusual opportunities. Jobs in
defense industries represented a significant economic improvement over working in family businesses or in food processing or garment industries. Unlike
many other groups of women, Chinese American defense industry workers were

young and unmarried. Before the war, these second-generation women had found most jobs outside Chinatown closed to them, despite their American education and English language proficiency. Their improved job prospects stemmed in part from the labor scarcity but also from a reduction in the racial prejudice against the Chinese now that they were U.S. allies in the war against Japan. Even on the West Coast, where Asian Americans were most densely populated and where prejudice ran extremely high, the Chinese became the "good" Asians. Symbolic of this change in attitude was the 1943 congressional decision to abolish the legal strictures prohibiting Chinese aliens from becoming naturalized citizens. For Chinese women and their families, then, World War II facilitated more integration into mainstream American society as well as improved economic opportunities.[42]

For Japanese American women, the situation in contrast was bleak. Following decades of anti-Japanese sentiment on the West Coast, the Japanese bombing of Pearl Harbor touched off a firestorm of suspicion directed at the Japanese in this country. Despite the absence of any evidence of sabotage or disloyalty, President Roosevelt, encouraged by military leaders and western politicians, issued Executive Order 9066, mandating the internment of over 110,000 people of Japanese descent, more than two-thirds of whom were native-born American citizens. In ten remote camps located in California, Arizona, Utah, Colorado, Wyoming, Idaho, and Arkansas the Nisei (the Japanese term for second-generation Japanese Americans) and their parents (the Issei) lived in stark barracks behind barbed wire. Prisoners without trial, incarcerated primarily because of race, the internees found the experience bewildering and humiliating.

Women continued as best they could with their familial duties, trying to supplement the unappetizing and inadequate food provided in the mess tent, keeping clothes clean without the benefit of running water in their barracks, and above all, struggling to keep the family unit together in the face of the disruption of relocation and camp life. Ironically, internment may have offered slight benefits to young Nisei women. They worked in the camps as clerks or teachers for the same low wages as their fathers and brothers, giving them some small taste of economic equality and independence. Within the camps, peer groups exerted strong pressure as teenaged girls tried to keep up with the latest fashions on the outside and socialized with young men. The strong patriarchal authority of the Japanese household further eroded when Nisei daughters and sons began to leave the camps in 1942 after the government determined that an individual Nisei's loyalty could be sufficiently investigated and determined. Some obtained permission to go to college in regions outside the West. An estimated 40 percent of these were women. Others secured jobs in the Midwest and on the East Coast, with the most likely type of work being domestic service, although some found employment in manufacturing. After Nisei men were urged to volunteer for military service to "prove" their loyalty, some Nisei women followed suit and became WACs or military nurses. They often left the camps with parents disapproving or ambivalent at best. One woman who planned to be a teacher noted that "Mother and Father do not want me to go out. However, I want to go so very much that sometimes I feel that I'd go even if they disowned me. What shall I do? I realize the hard living conditions outside but I think I can take it."[43]

War and Everyday Life

Far removed from the experience of Japanese internment, most American women faced very different sorts of pressures connected to everyday life on the homefront. When men went off to join the military, wives often followed them while they were in training stateside, living in makeshift accommodations and coping with a sense of impermanency and of an uncertain future.[44] Other women migrated either alone or with their families in search of better-paying jobs in cities, confronting the challenges of adjustment to new surroundings. These included scarce housing in boom areas, a particularly pressing problem for black women and Mexicans, who were also subject to housing discrimination.

But the new environment could be liberating as well, especially for single women. New jobs offered higher income and a sense of independence that undoubtedly led to more sexual experimentation. As one young war worker expressed it, "Chicago was just humming, no matter where I went. The bars were jammed, and unless you were an absolute dog you could pick up anyone you wanted to." Observers worried about this trend, pointing out that it was not prostitutes but "amateurs" who were undermining morality and spreading sexually transmitted disease.[45] Although promiscuity was probably not as great as critics feared, women did experience more personal freedom. Particularly notable were opportunities for lesbian women. Leaving provincial hometowns for large cities, they found other women who identified as lesbians. "Lisa Ben" moved from a ranch in northern California to a job in Los Angeles, ending up in a boarding house occupied by young single women and asking herself, "Gee, I wonder if these are some of the girls I would very dearly love to meet." They apparently were, and Ben stayed in Los Angeles after the war and became part of the discreet lesbian bar scene that emerged there and in other major cities during the war years.[46]

Despite the sexual experimentation, conventional expectations about marriage and family remained unaltered. The number of marriages escalated, with the Census Bureau estimating that between 1940 and 1943 a million more families were formed than would have been expected in peacetime. Fertility spiked as well, after the low levels of the Depression, with births per one thousand rising from 19.4 in 1940 to 24.5 in 1945 (see Chart 1 in the Appendix). Popular culture reiterated respect for the domestic ideal. While movie heroines were often portrayed as self-reliant and independent war workers or army nurses, the message remained that women at war were only temporarily outside their proper place of home and family.

Whether they worked or not, married women's responsibilities in the household continued. Although released from the extreme restraints of making do in the hard times of the 1930s, homemaking remained difficult. Consumer goods such as sugar, meat, and shoes were rationed, and housewives had to organize their shopping carefully. Home appliances that might have lightened their load were not being produced because factories and workers were needed for war production—though manufacturers continued their advertising campaigns to keep up consumer desire. A vacuum cleaner company promised, "A day is coming when this war will be done. And on that day, like you, Mrs. America, Eureka will put aside its uniform and return to the ways of peace . . . building household appliances."[47]

For women who worked, household burdens proved particularly difficult. Limited hours for shopping after their workday ended was one source of frustration. Nor could women expect any help from absent husbands and sons during their "second shift" at home. Child care posed another problem. Some corporations, faced with high turnover and absenteeism, offered nurseries. The federal government mounted a limited program of daycare centers, but these were underutilized, in part because women associated federal programs with New Deal assistance to the down and out and in part because of cultural resistance to the idea of strangers taking care of one's children. Most women relied on friends and family members for help with child care.

As the war drew to a close in 1945, fears over the implications of Rosie the Riveter and her colleagues for the postwar family reached a crescendo. Anthropologist Margaret Mead reported that soldiers contemplating their return to the United States worried, "Well, mostly we've been wondering whether it's true that women are smoking pipes at home."[48] Some Americans foresaw that women were in the workforce to stay, and agencies like the U.S. Department of Labor's Women's Bureau remained concerned about improving their wages and opportunities. But most opinion makers emphasized reinstating women to their rightful place, the home, so that returning GIs could anticipate full employment and a stable family life. Industrial leader Frederick Crawford pronounced that "from a humanitarian point of view, too many women should not stay in the labor force. The home is the basic American institution."[49]

Surveys of women working during the war indicated that a significant number—a Women's Bureau survey reported three of four women—had hoped to continue to work outside the home after the war.[50] But with demobilization women were laid off in large numbers. Gladys Poese Ehlmann recalled the shock of her dismissal from Emerson Electric Company in St. Louis, explaining that "the war was over on August 14 and we went in on the 15th. They lined us up and had our paychecks ready for us."[51] Accounting for 60 percent of the dismissals in heavy industry, women were fired at a rate 75 percent higher than men. But although women's participation in the workforce dropped, this decline was short-lived. Women lost better-paid positions and most of those high-status jobs that had challenged sex-segregated labor patterns. But within a few years of the armistice, 32 percent of women were back in the labor force, and more than half of them were married. The war had not eroded cultural ideas about women's primary role in the home and their secondary status as wage earners, but it had been a vehicle for sustaining and even accelerating a process of increased female participation in the work place.

CONCLUSION: The New Woman in Ideal and Reality

The images called up at the start of this chapter—of 1920s flapper, 1930s migrant mother, and 1940s Rosie the Riveter—capture the distinctive qualities of these three decades. But while the eras of prosperity, depression, and war affected women in different ways, we can still discern broad trends for the period as a whole that reveal the trajectory of twentieth-century women's lives.

Between 1920 and 1945, women worked in greater numbers, and more wives and mothers contributed to this trend, but they did so in the context of discriminatory sex-segregated labor patterns and unequal opportunities for women of color. In another aspect of public life, politics, women also witnessed important changes. Women now had the vote in all states, with the significant exception of African American women in the South, who like southern black men were largely disenfranchised. Other legal rights—property, divorce, jury service—had been expanded in most states.

Although women did not sustain the ambitious hopes that followed the successful suffrage campaign, they could claim smaller victories. Reformers in the 1920s struggled against a repressive political climate to sustain their social justice agenda and, in the Depression years, became active and valued participants in the New Deal. Not as influential in the war years, they nonetheless left a permanent mark on public policy, especially in their Women's Bureau and Social Security activities.

Patterns in the home are less clearly defined. The Depression and war had contradictory effects on marriage, divorce, and fertility rates. Trends of the 1920s toward increased emphasis on female sexuality persisted, but they did so in the context of an abiding cultural ideal that assumed that this sexuality would be confined in the context of marriage and the home.

As Americans faced the realities of a complex postwar world, these themes of women's lives at home and in the workplace and political arena would do more than continue. They would eventually erupt in dramatic challenges to prevailing notions of women's proper place.

DOCUMENTS

Young Women Speak Out

Historians have many ways of exploring the new patterns in women's lives concerning sexuality, marriage, and work in the 1920s. Magazine and newspaper articles repeatedly analyzed the "New Woman." Movies featured "dancing daughters" and working girls. Advertisements encouraged women to enjoy new freedoms and new consumer goods. Sociologists conducted surveys and studies, such as Phyllis Blanchard and Carlyn Manasses's appropriately titled *New Girls for Old* (1930), which spoke frankly about sexuality.

To hear what young women themselves had to say about the New Woman, we can turn to evidence historians rarely examine: advice columns. The first modern sustained advice column appeared in the *New York Evening Journal* in 1898, largely a sales gimmick intended to attract women readers who might purchase products on the advertising pages. Marie Manning, writing under the name of Beatrice Fairfax, became an instant success because, according to Fairfax, the column was "the only medium through which they could discuss their perplexities and get an impartial answer from an unknown and unprejudiced person."[52]

In the 1920s and 1930s, young women continued to seek such help. The themes vary in the following letters—one set from *Photoplay* and probably written by white women, and another from a San Francisco Japanese newspaper, the *New World*—but as you read the letters, consider how together they reveal the struggles women encountered as they adjusted to new social expectations and sought outside, rather than parental, assistance.

LETTERS TO CAROLYN VAN WYCK

In the 1920s, Carolyn Van Wyck's column ran in *Photoplay*, a glossy magazine that featured articles on movies and the stars' lives, advice on clothes and cosmetics, and even articles on household furnishings to help readers emulate the lives of their favorite movie personalities. Van Wyck's answers incorporated both modern and more conventional ideas about women's roles. She was sympathetic to the desire to flirt and have a good time but consistently warned young women against being "cheap." She spoke approvingly of a "wise divorce," which she described as much fairer and squarer than a "miserable marriage." Yet she generally reinforced the notion of marriage as the ultimate goal for young women, arguing in 1927 that it is the "happy ending (no matter what you young moderns say!) of the love story."

Van Wyck solicited letters on specific topics. In March 1927, the theme, as she described it, was, "Should a Wife Work? Working Girls when they get married often want to be working wives. They don't want kitchen duty and no wages but a real outside job and real wages. Then the fun begins, for many a husband objects to such arrangement. Now I'm stepping into the fray." The letter for that issue:

Dear Carolyn Van Wyck:

I'm married and just eighteen. My husband is only a boy of nineteen, so you can imagine how strange we feel, away from family and friends. He is making a small salary, and I'd like to work to help out. He says that it's because I feel I'm not getting what I want of our marriage. It isn't true. I love him more than life and I want to work to help him. He thinks I'd rather work than be with him. I would work only during his working hours. I have a chance at a job that needs only my afternoons. I worked before I was married. I honestly believe we'd be happier if we had more money. Still my husband protests. Please advise me.

M. T.

In response, Van Wyck agreed that wives should work if they wanted to, but she insisted that the woman who loves her husband "must see that their common interests always supersede her personal interest in her work."[53] Compare this young wife's predicament to the young wife in the 1925 advertisement in *Good Housekeeping* (see Figure 8.1, p. 535).

IF YOUNG MARRIED COUPLES were struggling with issues of money and relationships, so too were young single working women. One letter addressed what Van Wyck claimed was a common concern: "Whether or not to be a gold-digger!" She thought the interest was probably generated by the popular 1925 book, *Gentlemen Prefer Blondes,* with the oft-quoted line from the heroine Lorelei Lee, "a kiss on the hand is thrilling, but a diamond bracelet lasts forever."

Dear Carolyn Van Wyck:

What do you think of golddiggers? Do you think a girl should be one? I was brought up in the country and taught no nice girl would take gifts from a man, unless she was engaged to him, much less deliberately work him for presents. Now I am alone, a working girl in a large city. The girls in my office are constantly augmenting their incomes through men's pocketbooks, and getting away with it. They call me an idiot for not doing the same. What do you think?

M. A. B.

Van Wyck responded at length, criticizing the trend, and concluded, "For what does it profit a girl if she lose all the real beauty of life and win a fur coat?"

YET ANOTHER WORKING WOMAN felt her friends were too modern in paying their own way on dates.

Dear Carolyn Van Wyck:

I live in a small city and most of the girls in my crowd work. I myself am a wage earner. We are all eager to get a good time out of life, but here's the trouble. Many of my friends pay their own way when they go out with boys. The boys, you see, don't make much money. And they argue that, if the girl pays her share, they can have snappier parties. Somehow I can't seem to do that—perhaps that is why my friends have more dates than I. I'm not entirely manless, but I wonder if I'd have more fun if I were less old-fashioned on this money matter. Please tell me. Do you think a girl should pay her own way?

Myrtle

Van Wyck was sympathetic to the desire to be thoughtful of young men's pocketbooks, but she insisted in August 1927 that "men . . . like to own a sense of importance, of power. And paying the dinner check, tipping not wisely but too well, bringing an occasional nosegay of valley lilies or a box of French bon-bons, is their way of flaunting this sense. And so, Myrtle, continue to be old-fashioned!"

PERHAPS EVEN MORE PRESSING an issue than who paid for dates was women's sexual behavior, a common theme in Van Wyck's column. The following letter in March 1926 encapsulates the dilemma of the desire to explore sexuality in the context of a persistent sexual double standard.

Dear Carolyn Van Wyck:

Petting is my biggest problem. The boys all seem to do it and don't seem to come back if you don't do it also. We girls are at our wits' end to know what to do. All the boys want to pet. I've been out with nearly fifty different ones and every one does it. I thought sometimes it was my fault but when I tried hardest to keep from it they were all the worse. As yet I've never been out with anyone that got beyond my control. It may sound simple, but the minute I say that it is mean to take advantage because they are stronger they all seem to respect my wishes. I've tried getting mad; but it doesn't do any good. I don't seem to know what I want out of life. I want the thrills. I get a kick out of petting and I think all girls do no matter how much they deny it. What's to be done? The boys all like it and I can't seem to make myself dislike it and am not afraid of any of the men I know. . . . It makes me wonder how on earth you are to get a husband who respects you because you don't pet if you get turned down every time because you won't, before they have time to appreciate your sterling qualities. I'm sure that I don't want to marry anyone who is too slow to want to pet. But I want to discover what is right. Please help me.

[unsigned]

In this case, Van Wyck once again sympathized with the problem the writer faced and claimed she must make her own decision. She added, however, "It seems to me much better to be known as a flat tire and keep romance in one's mind than to be called a hot date and have fear in one's heart."

LETTERS TO DEIDRE

SOME ETHNIC NEWSPAPERS also had advice columns directed toward young people, which emphasized letters from young women. In San Francisco's *New World Sun,* Mary Oyama Mittwer was "Dear Deidre" in the 1930s, a decade later than the *Photoplay* columns reproduced on the preceding pages. Her correspondents were Nisei, young second-generation Japanese American men and women. These writers' questions repeated many of the same issues that mainstream young women raised with Carolyn Van Wyck, but they did so in the context of assimilation and intergenerational conflicts that reflected their immigrant background. Both urban and rural Nisei from numerous states wrote to "Dear Deidre," and they often offered advice of their own to fellow letter writers. Deidre was generally sympathetic to young women's desire to be up-to-date and "modern," but she consistently urged them to find a medium between Japanese and American values.[54]

Letters concerning intergenerational tensions surfaced frequently in letters to Deidre. In a 1937 column entitled "Parents Tell Nisei Too Much What to Do," a twenty-year-old college sophomore wrote:

Dear Deidre:
I feel myself quite dependent upon my parents. Therefore, my next question is: Am I dominated over by my parents? For instance, when she (my mother) tells me how I should dress, how I should make up, dress my hair, how I should or should not act in public, where I should go, what I should do, and every bit of anything that concerns me. Most of the time she is right. If ever I should oppose any of her advice, she would say that she has experienced more and that she does not want me to get into trouble.

According to Japanese teachings, children should listen to what parents say and do as they say, which is to be "Oya koh-ko." She tells me that parents teach good things most of the time and SOMETIMES they make mistakes. If you can give me answers by personal letter or through your daily column, I would be very happy and then may seek out a way to prevent my parent's domineering over me—if I can....

Yours truly,
S. N.

Deidre's response undoubtedly disappointed S. N. She noted that when children are truly adults and out on their own, parents should recognize their maturity. But Deidre did not consider a twenty-year-old college student fully adult and remarked that "as for your parents, I hardly think that they are trying to dominate or to oppress you; and no doubt your mother's advice is sound and most of what she says is right. Yes, and she is more experienced than you in the knowledge of the world (having seen more), and you are wise to be 'oya koh-ko' and to follow her counsel."

LIKE S. N'S LETTER, "An Educated Girl Faces a Problem," published in 1937, reveals distinctive issues the Nisei generation faced. The marriages of most mothers of Nisei women had been arranged ones, and few Issei (first generation) had received much education. Progressive Miss, as the writer called herself, had an invalid father and was the eldest of three sisters, and thus had a responsibility for their welfare. She cast her problem, however, in the context of a decision about whether to marry a man she was attracted to but with whom she had little in common.

Miss Deidre:

. . . Now to get back to my problem, it's this: To marry or not to marry my current love and boy friend. To go back a little to ancient history, my ex-boy friend and first love, many years back, was a brilliant and well educated man. Our friendship and love, while it lasted, was quite perfect and beautiful, but for some perverse reason on my part, we broke up.

After that, I went around with several others, but not very seriously. Most of my pals of the opposite sex were all college graduates and the above-average type of men. I respected and admired them, but did not fall in love. Finally, I met my second and current boyfriend, who is totally unlike any that I have ever known before. I like him *very much* although we have little in common. He is fond of me and perfectly devoted.

The thing that worries me is: can marriage be based upon mere liking or "love" so-called—when there is so very, very little in common?

Progressive Miss

Instead of offering advice to Progressive Miss, Deidre published two long letters from readers, one who called herself Farmer's Daughter and the other Voice of the Rockies. The first writer urged Progressive Miss to marry the man, emphasizing that he could offer her a comfortable life. And, reflecting traditional Japanese ideas about familial responsibility, she also commented that Progressive Miss's financially secure marriage could allow her to pave the way for her younger sisters' marriages. Voice of the Rockies also encouraged Progressive Miss to marry, but she emphasized instead an idealized notion of romantic love and the way in which time would allow it to blossom.

———

WHILE PROGRESSIVE MISS worried about the basis for a good marriage, Modern Miss raised questions about marriage itself. In "Defense of Nisei 'Bachelorettes,'" written in 1936, she was reacting to a column in the newspaper about Nisei "spinsters."

Dear friend Deidre:

So many of our Nisei young men are surprisingly backward in this respect and are too afraid or lack the open mind to think out such ideas for themselves without being influenced to a great extent by the old Japanese ideas. It makes me chuckle when I hear these old dodoes smugly calling themselves "Americanized" when they are anything but Americanized or modern in their thinking.

Now, to get back to the point about "bachelorettes": I have no use for any rash person, man or woman, who makes such sweeping statements as: "ALL women are born to fulfill biological duties to this world," etc. Ridiculous! Any one with common sense realizes that there are exceptions to every statement and rule. ALL women are NOT necessarily "born for marriage." Most women, yes, I grant; but NOT "all women." Are all men born to be fathers? No, well, then, for the same reason, all women are not born to be mothers. . . .

In the sensible American society of today there is no stigma attached to the unmarried women. In conservative Japanese society and in our backward Nisei society there seems to be a sort of "unwritten question mark" hovering over

the unmarried misses' heads, like a sort of an invisible halo. Why this silly fact should be, I don't know, unless it's a hangover from the unprogressive old Japanese thinking, or rather I should say the OLD Oriental mode of thinking.

What makes me laugh is that some of our elders think that all our bachelorettes are either: (a) dying to get married, (2) unhappy, restless and dissatisfied, or else (3) thinking of catching a man and getting married from the time they are born.

The fact is: (1) they are NOT dying to get married—far from it; they love their own work, are independent and don't intend to get married until they find the RIGHT man (which is more than some of our Issei women did), (2) Our bachelorettes are happy and having a good time out of life. Oftentimes, they are happier than those disillusioned, frustrated-in-life, young matrons who married too soon (or to the wrong man) because they feared public opinion and being labeled an "oldo missu," (3) ALL girls do NOT necessarily think of getting married. Although many do, still there are exceptions who have no intention whatsoever of getting married or even wanting to get married.

I know several charming, talented, gifted girls who have NO intention of marrying, because they want to devote their life to their work, and because they have not so far met a man of equal talent and ability whom they might be able to fall in love with. In other words, they won't marry until they can meet a man they can love BETTER than their careers. Don't think they lack boy-friends because they have admirers, swains and proposals galore. They turn down proposals because they are afraid that marriage will hinder their work, or that too much interest in a man will turn their mind away from their art. So much for that . . .

Modern Miss

Deidre's response was to acknowledge that there were many "charming and talented misses who had no particular desire for marriage. We have known extreme cases where one or two have looked upon matrimony, as a yoke of bondage to be avoided as long as possible! At any rate, it is our personal opinion that no one need worry about the 'old maid problem.' Sooner or later they all get married anyway. It's just a case of some girls taking a longer time to make up their minds than others. No need for busybodies on the sidelines to worry . . . yokei na osewa!"

QUESTIONS FOR ANALYSIS

1. To what extent do the letters to Carolyn Van Wyck and Deidre support the notion of a "New Woman" in the 1920s and 1930s?

2. To what extent do they contradict this notion?

3. Compare the themes emphasized in the two sets of letters. In what ways do Nisei women's concerns reflect their family's immigrant past?

4. Why might young women write to total strangers about such pressing personal questions, rather than turn to parents and friends?

DOCUMENTS

Women's Networks in the New Deal

D
URING THE PROGRESSIVE ERA of the early twentieth century, white women reformers operated within a political network of shared goals. Their common "maternalist" outlook advocated a special female interest in expanding state power in support of humanitarian reform (see Chapter 7). Through a multitude of organizations, ranging from the National Consumers League to the National Women's Trade Union League, they worked together to support the abolition of child labor, mothers' pensions, women's wage and hour laws, and the suffrage campaign. In addition to well-known activists in this "female dominion" of reform, like Jane Addams and Florence Kelley, thousands of women supported the reform agenda through local clubs and membership in the General Federation of Women's Clubs. In 1912, when the federal Children's Bureau was established, its head, Julia Lathrop, not only solicited support from other women reformers in the bureau's campaign to stop child labor, but also mobilized women's clubs throughout the country to lobby for funding and support for the bureau.

During the 1920s, when the climate for reform was less hospitable, the women's dominion nonetheless persisted, working through the Women's Joint Congressional Committee to achieve temporary successes like the Sheppard-Towner Act (see p. 483). But it was not until the election of Franklin D. Roosevelt in 1932 and his implementation of the New Deal that women activists had a significant opportunity to influence national public policy. The Roosevelt administration appointed numerous women with experience in progressive-era organizations to high federal positions, helping to create a network of almost thirty women in Washington, D.C., who collaborated on a female-focused social reform agenda. Although many of them were concerned with advancing women's rights, broad-ranging social reform, rather than feminism, was their primary agenda. As Secretary of Labor Frances Perkins explained, "I was much more deeply touched by the problems of poverty, the sorrows of the world, the neglected individuals, the neglected groups, and the people who didn't get on well in this great and good civilization."[55] Despite these women's high profile in public life, then, an organized movement for women's equal rights would not appear until well after World War II.

Former Hull House volunteer and executive secretary of the New York Consumers League, Perkins occupied the most powerful position of the group, becoming the first woman to serve in a president's cabinet. Her department was a force behind New Deal legislation that secured the rights of organized labor, and it was crucial in developing Social Security (1935) and the Fair Labor Standards Act (1938). Even more ambitious than the women-backed labor legislation of the Progressive era, which had mostly focused on the states, the Fair Labor Standards Act established federal minimum wages and maximum hours for women and men, as well as finally restricted child labor.

Another major appointment, Ellen Sullivan Woodward, headed up women's programs under various New Deal agencies (1933–1936) targeted toward the unemployed. Woodward later served as a member of the Social Security Board (1938–1946). One of Woodward's first undertakings, a White House conference in November 1933 on the Emergency Needs of Women, brought in representatives from women's organizations to discuss the problems of over 300,000 to 400,000 women in need of urgent assistance. Woodward, following ideas similar to Julia Lathrop's linkage of the Children's Bureau and women's clubs, hoped to "mobilize women's inherent capacities for community housekeeping."[56]

Women's prominent place in the New Deal in part stemmed from practical politics. Male Democrats recognized that female voters could help the party and the New Deal, as the following excerpts by Molly Dewson and Gladys Tillett indicate. Another crucial factor was the presence of Eleanor Roosevelt. Before her husband became president, Eleanor had been involved in social welfare reform in New York. Her work with the Women's Trade Union League had brought her into contact with working-class women such as Rose Schneiderman, who became a personal friend and staunch supporter of the New Deal. Eleanor Roosevelt brought unprecedented activism and ability to the role of first lady. Highly visible in public, she wrote daily news columns, contributed frequently to women's magazines, spoke often on the radio, gave weekly press conferences, and nurtured the group of women activists who supported social reform. Roosevelt was also, for her time, unusually progressive in her concern for racial justice, far more so than her husband. African American women were not part of the same network as Perkins and Woodward, but Eleanor was close to and supportive of Mary McLeod Bethune, a black educator who used her position as head of the National Youth Administration's Division of Minority Affairs to push the New Deal to pay more attention to African Americans' needs.

The documents that follow reflect a profound sense of excitement about opportunities in the New Deal for advancing the cause of social reform and optimism about women's participation in government and politics. But even before World War II directed the nation's attention away from domestic problems, by the late 1930s the New Deal began to lose momentum, and with it women's roles in Roosevelt's administration and in the Democratic party diminished.

ELEANOR ROOSEVELT

I N A 1940 *GOOD HOUSEKEEPING* ARTICLE, Eleanor Roosevelt attempted to answer the question, "What have women accomplished for human betterment with the vote?" She acknowledged that women had made only partial progress in having political influence, but consider the ways in which Roosevelt argues that women in government had helped to bring about significant change.

No revolution has come about because women have been given the vote, and it is perfectly true that many women are not thrilled by their opportunity to take part in political-party work. . . .

The women, however, are gradually increasing their activities. There are more women in civil-service positions and there are more women in rather inconspicuous but important positions in city, state, and federal governments where technical knowledge is required.

When I went to Washington, I was so much impressed by the work they were doing that I started to have parties for women executives in various departments, and I discovered an astonishing number of women doing very important work, but getting comparatively little recognition because government is still a man's world.

SOURCE: Mrs. Franklin D. Roosevelt, "Women in Politics," *Good Housekeeping,* March 1940, 45, 68.

As a result of this, however, I find the influence of women emerging into a more important sphere. There was a time when no one asked: "What will the women think about this." Now that question comes up often. . . .

Looking for concrete achievements, I feel we can really credit to the women only one over this period of years, and that is the one already mentioned — the government's attitude of concern for the welfare of human beings. On the whole, more interest is now taken in social questions. The government is concerned about housing, about the care of citizens who temporarily are unable to take care of themselves, about the care of handicapped children, whether handicapped by poor homes or by straitened circumstances. This is the general change, which I attribute to the fact that men had to appeal for the vote of the women and have therefore taken a greater interest in subjects they feel may draw women to their support.

ROSE SCHNEIDERMAN

R OSE SCHNEIDERMAN HAD WORKED her way from cap maker in a sweat shop to president of the Women's Trade Union League. But she considered her appointment in 1933 to the National Recovery Administration (NRA), the administrative board of the National Industrial Recovery Act, "the high spot in my career," in part because of the act's assistance to organized labor. In this passage from her autobiography *All for One* (1967), she describes the code-making process of the NRA. What accounts for her obvious excitement about being a New Dealer?

The object of the three advisory boards was to formulate codes for all the different industries for the President's approval. These codes would set up conditions of employment, wages and hours, and would also contain a provision known as 7-A, giving workers the right of collective bargaining by representatives of their own choosing. To do

SOURCE: Rose Schneiderman with Lucy Goldthwaite, *All for One* (New York: Paul S. Eriksson, 1967), 195–99.

this, hearings, presided over by deputy administrators, were held for every industry. A member of each of the three advisory boards was present at each hearing to safeguard the interest of his constituents. Employers and trade union leaders appeared as witnesses. I was appointed to represent the Labor Board when codes affecting working women were discussed.

Of course, I was very excited and pleased about my appointment. . . . The next two years were the most exhilarating and inspiring of my life. Working hours were of no account. Most of the time there were hearings all day long and in the evening, too. I left the office late every night, tired but happy over the job the Labor Board was doing.

Eleanor Roosevelt took part in everything that was happening. She was intensely interested in the housing situation and in the distribution of food to the needy and the work of the W.P.A. [Works Progress Administration]. But with it all, there was always time for friendship and to help those who needed her.

It was fun to be included in some of the White House parties. Shortly after F.D.R. was elected, the Gridiron Club, composed of newspapermen, gave one of its famous dinners to which no woman has ever been invited. Mrs. Roosevelt decided that she would give one for the newspaper women in Washington and for a few other friends, so while the President was the guest of honor at the men's dinner, we had a very gay evening with satirical skits on current events as amusing, I am sure, as those given by men at their dinner.

MOLLY DEWSON

MOLLY DEWSON, WHO HAD BEEN ACTIVE in the New York Consumers League, became the head of the Women's Division of the Democratic National Committee in 1932. In that duty, she played an important role in bringing out the female vote for Franklin D. Roosevelt in his first election. Her reward was patronage for women. She succeeded in getting women appointed to positions in the Democratic Party and also to government positions. Two of her most significant lobbying efforts were on behalf of Frances Perkins and Ellen S. Woodward. Another important activity was her "Reporter Plan" to maintain support for the New Deal among women. The plan called for each county to appoint women to serve as "Reporters of each Federal agency." Their role was to educate themselves about that agency's activities and to share that understanding in local communities through speeches, discussion groups, and the like. Dewson eventually accepted federal appointments herself, most notably serving on the Social Security Board from 1937 to 1938. How does this segment of her unpublished 1949 autobiography explain its title, "An Aid to the End"?

I was going to put my energies into organizing the women to learn specifically what F.D.R. was trying to accomplish and tell others about it so that he would have understanding support in the states, but until January [1933?] I would work to get worthwhile government positions for Democratic women who had demonstrated the capacity to fill them adequately. There were some sixty-five on my list of "key women" whose political work deserved recognition either by the federal or the state governments and whose assistance in future party work was essential. . . .

[Dewson provides pages of typed lists of women appointed to a wide range of government positions including Ruth Byran Owen of Florida, minister to Denmark; Judge Florence F. Allen of

SOURCE: Molly Dewson, "An Aid to an End," in Women in National Politics microfilm collection, Schlesinger Library, reel A3, vols. 39 and 40, pp. 124, 130, 135, 140–41.

Ohio, who was appointed to the U.S. Sixth Circuit Court; Antoinette Funk, New Mexico's Assistant Commissioner, General Land Office; and Edna Bushman, Deputy Collector, Internal Revenue, San Jose, Texas. Another lengthy list details women appointees to special New Deal agencies, an accomplishment she particularly valued because of her deep commitment to social reform.]

Many additional and important, although temporary, appointments were made in the New Deal agencies created to meet the national emergency, to move the country off its dead center, to end certain deplorable practices, to care for those wiped out by the Great Depression and to give people a basic modicum of security. Skilled executives, trained specialists and lawyers were necessary to develop and administer these agencies. . . .

In three years Roosevelt had set a new trend. At last women had their foot inside the door. We had the opportunity to demonstrate our ability to see what was needed and to get the job done while working harmoniously with men.

I believe the work of the women I have listed compared well with that of the best men and was much better than the average man's performance. But it is true that the number of trained and experienced women to choose from is still very much smaller than the pool of well-equipped men. Also women are bucking a deeply founded prejudice. It takes at least a generation for an idea to penetrate, yet it is fast becoming a commonplace for women to strike out in all fields whether it is an economic necessity or not.

One day in 1935 Mary Anderson [head of the Women's Bureau] and I were sitting side by side at a small luncheon in the women's University Club. I said, "This is a pleasant dining room for private parties." Mary answered nostalgically, "I have very pleasant memories of this place. The women in the top government positions used to lunch here regularly on certain days. Now there are so many of them they would need a hall, so we don't get together any more."

GLADYS AVERY TILLETT

G LADYS AVERY TILLETT FROM NORTH CAROLINA had been a suffragist before she became active in the Democratic Party in the 1920s. In this oral history interview published in 1976, she relates how Molly Dewson brought her into the National Democratic Party. Notice how Tillett also reiterates a constant theme of New Deal women: her great respect for Eleanor Roosevelt.

The thirties were a great time for women to become politically involved. It was in '34 that I met Molly Dewson—she was quite a power behind the scenes with Roosevelt—and she pulled me into the national scene. She got me to cover the state with what she called the Reporter Plan, which was a way to let people know what the New

Deal really meant. So I became state chairman of the Reporters and learned a lot from that remarkable woman—she attended our first regional conference, and often she would have us to Washington to talk about various things. It helped to see and hear women who were policymakers.

She came to speak, and Frances Perkins came. It was Molly who talked me into running the Women's Speakers Bureau in the '36 campaign. Now, Roosevelt had a lot of faith in her be-

SOURCE: Jeane Westin, *Making Do: How Women Survived the '30s* (Chicago: Follett Publishing Co., 1976), 302–3.

cause she had helped him win in '32—so when she asked me to join in the reelection effort I was really honored. . . .

One of my great pleasures was meeting Mrs. Roosevelt. She had such a genuine quality. You know, she helped women, and we thought highly of her—she just gave all our efforts a life.

She was so free of prejudice toward women, blacks or anyone—many black women adored her. And you know she always had a great deal of courage when she came to the South. She was always willing to take a stand, and there were stands to take about blacks and women.

You see, women were new in politics and had to struggle to establish themselves. It was the beginning of the women's movement because being in on the political picture helped women see what they could achieve.

MARY MCLEOD BETHUNE

AFRICAN AMERICAN WOMEN LEADERS in the 1930s continued to work for women's rights in the context of the broader struggle for justice for all members of their race. Mary McLeod Bethune was in this tradition. A prominent educator, Bethune had founded Bethune-Cookman College, served as president of the National Association of Colored Women, and established the National Council of Negro Women in 1935. Bethune began her New Deal experience as an advisor to the National Youth Administration, but soon became the director of the Division of Minority Affairs, later called the Division of Negro Affairs. Years later, Bethune recounted that in making her decision to take up that responsibility, she had "visualized dozens of Negro women coming after me, filling positions of high trust and strategic importance. God, I knew, would give me the requisite strength, wisdom and administrative ability to do the job."[57] In that role, Bethune energetically tried to expand black leadership in the NYA and to pressure the Roosevelt administration to provide equal opportunities for blacks in all New Deal programs, not just in the NYA. What does the following document indicate about Bethune's commitment to the New Deal?

Proceedings of the Second National Youth Administration Advisory Committee Meeting (1936)

I want first of all to express on the part of the Negro people, our appreciation for the vision of our illustrious President, and his committee, in extending to the nation this NYA program. In my opinion, and I think I am thinking in terms of thinking Negro people, I believe it to be one of the most stabilizing projects for the benefit of the American of tomorrow, than possibly any one thing that we have done. . . .

The Negro views with deep interest the national program for all youth and approves most highly its objectives. More particularly is the Negro interested in those phases of the program,

SOURCE: Audrey Thomas McCluskey and Elaine M. Smith, eds., *Mary McLeod Bethune: Building a Better World, Essays and Documents* (Bloomington: Indiana University Press, 1999), 216.

which for the first time in the history of the nation, affords to Negro youth through Federal benefits, larger opportunities for education, productive work and cultural and wholesome recreation.

DESPITE THE NEW DEAL'S ultimate shortcomings in addressing the inequities blacks experienced, Bethune remained a loyal supporter of both Roosevelts. In describing Eleanor Roosevelt, she claimed that she "has done more to better race relations and to give the 'human touch' to the affairs of state and the democratic struggle than any other woman I have known."[58]

The following is a formal letter to President Roosevelt. Written in 1940, as the United States began mobilizing its industrial productivity anticipating the advent of war, Bethune wrote in her position of president of the National Council of Negro Women. Although not a participant in the white women's New Deal, Bethune had a strong base of power among black women's organizations. What is she asking of Roosevelt in this letter? What claims does she make about African American women and why?

My dear Mr. President:

At a time like this, when the basic principles of democracy are being challenged at home and abroad, when racial and religious hatreds are being engendered, it is vitally important that the Negro, as a minority group in this nation, express anew his faith in your leadership and his unswerving adherence to a program of national defense adequate to insure the perpetuation of the principles of democracy. I approach you as one of a vast army of Negro women who recognize that we must face the dangers that confront us with a united patriotism.

We, as a race, have been fighting for a more equitable share of those opportunities which are fundamental to every American citizen who would enjoy the economic and family security which a true democracy guarantees. Now we come as a group of loyal, self-sacrificing women who feel they have a right and a solemn duty to serve their nation.

In the ranks of Negro womanhood in America are to be found ability and capacity for leadership, for administrative as well as routine tasks, for the types of service so necessary in a program of national defense. These are citizens whose past records at home and in war service abroad, whose unquestioned loyalty to their country and its ideals, and whose sincere and enthusiastic desire to serve you and the nation indicate how deeply they are concerned that a more realistic American democracy, as visioned by those not blinded by racial prejudices, shall be maintained and perpetuated.

I offer my own services without reservation, and urge you, in the planning and work which lies ahead, to make such use of the services of qualified Negro women as will assure the thirteen and a half million Negroes in America that they, too, have earned the right to be numbered among the active forces who are working towards the protection of our democratic stronghold.

Faithfully yours,
Mary McLeod Bethune
President

SOURCE: McCluskey, 173–74.

QUESTIONS FOR ANALYSIS

1. Frances Perkins once commented, "Those of us who worked to put together the New Deal are bound together by spiritual ties no one else can understand." What was the basis for the bond of the New Deal's women's network?

2. What distinctive contribution did Eleanor Roosevelt think women had brought to public life since getting the vote?

3. To what extent are the concerns expressed by Mary McLeod Bethune different from those of the white women associated with the Roosevelt administration?

4. Although the women's network did not forge an organized feminist movement, it did further some feminist aims. How do these documents reflect the concern to advance women's rights?

VISUAL SOURCES

Women at Work

SINCE 1830, EVERY PERIOD in American history has seen a rise in the numbers of working women, but during the years from 1920 through 1945 growth in numbers also meant fundamental changes in women's labor force participation. By 1920, 24.4 percent of women worked, and by 1947, two years after the war, when employment patterns had stabilized, that figure was 27.6 percent. For the period 1920–1945, we can see specific developments, even marks of "progress"—the expansion of the clerical field and contraction of agricultural work; the increased presence of wives and mothers in paid labor; women's growing presence in unions; and an expansion of women's opportunities in skilled factory work. Categories of class, race, and ethnicity continued to segment the female labor market, however, and popular values concerning women's work continued to view women as subordinate wage earners—an attitude that reinforced a sex-segregated labor market that devalued all working women as "temporary" and unskilled, regardless of their status. Even at the height of World War II, when demands for women's labor dramatically broke through traditional employment barriers, this static idea of women's proper place continued to shape profoundly their work experiences and opportunities.

The visual sources reproduced here feature two types of images. The first are advertisements from popular magazines; the second are documentary photographs. Comparing the two reveals the growing disparity between the reality of women's work and cultural values that continued to stress that women's proper place was in the home.

ADVERTISEMENTS

The advertising industry in the 1920s experienced an extraordinary boom, as advertising agencies adopted some of the techniques developed during World War I to promote the war effort and applied them to the business of selling to consumers the vastly expanded products that rolled off the assembly lines of American factories. Growing more sophisticated, advertisers recognized that women had become the family's purchasing agent, and so they targeted the female buyer with ads featuring women placed in general family journals such as the *Saturday Evening Post* or in women's magazines such as *Good Housekeeping*.

These advertisements depicted women almost exclusively as housewives in the context of their home and children or as purchasers of personal products and fashions. The relatively infrequent depictions or acknowledgment of women's paid

"John was worried about bills—Till I Helped Him"

Earned $600 in 4 Months

Mrs. Ray Altschuler, of New York, earned $600.00 in four months. Mrs. Alice Loomis, in far off Hawaii, virtually paid for her home —by telephone calls and pleasant chats with people interested in entertaining and inspiring reading.

Mrs. Florence M. Caffee, of Wyoming, reports that her work for us has earned her several hundred dollars.

Thousands are earning money, and exercising a cultural influence in their communities, by pleasant spare time work through telephone calls, letters and personal chats. Our instructions by mail make it easy for you. If an addition to the monthly income will be welcome, let us explain without obligation, our money-making plan.

Mail Coupon Today!

SHE was a young wife who thought her husband could miraculously stretch his income to meet all of her desires. When the sober awakening came, she learned that a wage-earner can bring in only so much. She found out too why so many women are joining hands with the men of the household to make dreams come true. Instead of frittering away her spare hours, she is now a money-earner through the IMC way.

This case is typical of hundreds of couples who have found in our plan a means to become savers instead of owers. The time seems to have passed when one person's income is sufficient for the needs of a family. Let us tell you of this plan that enables thousands of men and women, boys and girls, to turn their spare time into cash —without experience, without capital, without interfering with their regular duties.

Dept. GH-H825
International Magazine Co., Inc.
119 West 40th Street, N. Y. C.

YES, I would like to earn some extra money in my spare time. Without obligation to me, please send the details of your money-making plan.

Name...................................

Street and Number.......................

City........................State.........

◆ Figure 8.1 **A Young Wife Earns Extra Money**
Good Housekeeping, *August 1925, p. 174.*

labor fell into predictable patterns. Consider Figure 8.1, a 1925 ad encouraging women to sell magazine subscriptions. Although the text suggests that wives can contribute to the family income "in their spare time" and by "joining hands with the men of the household to make dreams come true," both the image and the text suggest women's distinctly subordinate status. In the image, the woman's body is elevated slightly above "John's," but her downcast eyes and the way in which she leans in toward her husband reinforce her subordinate "helping" role. John may be worried, but we see his face clearly and his posture still evokes strength. What do the image and the text together suggest about attitudes towards wives and husbands as "money earners"? What is the significance of the way in which the ad correlates women's paid labor to family goals?

When ads depicted women in the workplace, by far the most common image was that of the secretary, a reflection of the burgeoning ranks and high visibility of office workers in the years after World War I. In the 1870s, before the development of the modern corporation, almost all clerical workers had been men; by 1920, the vast majority were women. In Figure 8.2, Palmolive soap directed its attention to the "Business Girl." In this 1928 image, the demure and tidy appearance of the

◆ **Figure 8.2 The Business Girl and Palmolive Soap**
"The Business Girl Knows," Item #BH1018. Ad'Access. 1999. Rare Book, Manuscript, and Special Collections Library, Duke University. http://scriptorium.lib.duke.edu/adaccess/.

The Business Girl Knows

The Dollars-and-Cents Value of "That Schoolgirl Complexion"

THE universal rule for daily skin cleansing with soap and water is founded on one important factor: *A true complexion soap is meant.*

Thus millions use Palmolive, a soap made for ONE purpose ONLY; to safeguard and protect the skin. Remember this when purchasing soap for facial use.

AS beauty is rated a dollars-and-cents asset by women of the stage and screen, so too it is rated today by women in the business world. Note there the lovely complexions that you see.

The rule for *gaining* a good complexion is the same as for *keeping* one—soap and water, as advised by virtually every leading authority on skin care. This to keep the skin and pores clean and free of beauty-impairing accumulations.

The one secret is in the *kind* of soap one uses. Only a true complexion soap can be wisely employed on the skin. Other soaps may be too harsh.

The rule for "That Schoolgirl Complexion"

Thus millions use Palmolive, in this way—a soap made for ONE purpose only, to safeguard the skin. A good complexion is worth too much for experiment.

Wash your face gently with soothing Palmolive Soap, massaging the lather softly into the skin. Rinse thoroughly, first with warm water, then with cold. If your skin is inclined to be dry, apply a touch of good cold cream—that is all.

Do this regularly, and particularly in the evening. Use powder and rouge if you wish. But never leave them on over night. They clog the pores, often enlarge them. Blackheads and disfigurements often follow. They must be washed away.

Avoid this mistake

Do not use ordinary soaps in the treatment given above. Do not think any green soap, or one represented as of olive and palm oils, is the same as Palmolive.

It costs but 10c the cake! So little that millions let it do for their bodies what it does for their faces. Obtain a cake, then note the difference one week makes. The Palmolive-Peet Co., Chicago, Illinois.

Retail Price 10c   *Palmolive Soap is untouched by human hands until you break the wrapper—it is never sold unwrapped.*

Palmolive Radio Hour: Broadcast every Friday night—10 to 11 P.M., eastern time; 9 to 10 P.M. central time, over station WEAF and 28 stations associated with National Broadcasting Co.

KEEP THAT SCHOOLGIRL COMPLEXION

young woman reflected the respectability of clerical work for young, white, unmarried women and the importance of a feminine appearance. How does the text distinguish Palmolive from other soaps? What message is the advertiser trying to convey by emphasizing "dollars-and-cents value" and "that schoolgirl complexion"?

The rare ad images of professional women in the 1920s and 1930s were almost always of a nurse promoting products related to health and cleanliness. Figure 8.3, a 1937 ad for the scouring powder Bon Ami, depicts a beautiful, even glamorous, young woman in a crisp nursing uniform. Juxtaposed with her elegance is the labor she's performing— cleaning a bathtub. Why did Bon Ami choose the figure of a nurse to help sell its product? What does the image suggest about popular perceptions of the profession of nursing?

It is not surprising that professional women would be largely absent from advertising. The percentage of women who were doctors and lawyers actually declined in this period, while "feminized" professions— nurses, teachers, librarians, and social workers—expanded. Not all women benefited equally from these increased opportunities. In particular, the professions continued to discriminate against African American women, regardless of their educational achievements. Exceptions were black social workers with the Urban League and YWCA who aided the many migrants from the South. Teachers were a major foundation of the black middle class, but they found it difficult to get work in the North. Black nurses faced similar discrimination and found it difficult to get public health jobs (see Chapter 7).

Despite the importance of these black professional women to their own communities, in magazines directed at white audiences, the only images of black working women were as domestic servants. The 1935 ad shown in Figure 8.4 illustrates a short

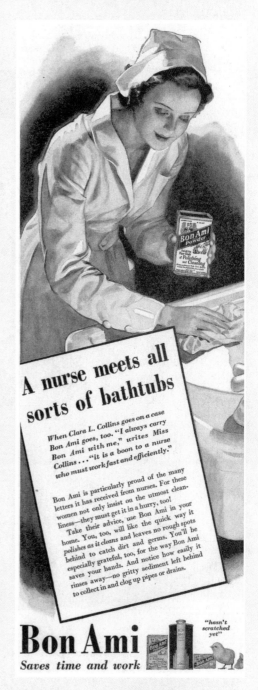

◆ **Figure 8.3 A Nurse Meets All Sorts of Bathtubs**
Saturday Evening Post, *1937.*

◆ Figure 8.4 **Ella May Learns about Red Cross Towels**

◆ Figure 8.5 **Mrs. Lansing Booth's Double Shift: Defense Worker and Mother**
Saturday Evening Post, *September 25, 1943, p. 65.*

story of a white woman, Helen, and her frustration with her black maid, Ella May, who "plumb forgot" to wash out her dish rag and towels. The problem is resolved when Helen's friend, Marian, who does her own housework and is therefore more knowledgeable about helpful products, urges Helen to give Ella May Red Cross towels for messy jobs. Note that the photographic image of Ella May at the top indicates a chastened look as she listens to her employer criticize her, while in the cartoon image below she is smiling happily. Why did the advertiser choose to introduce a black maid into the story, rather than a simpler approach of having one housewife educate another about the virtues of paper towels? What does the ad suggest about popular perceptions of black domestic workers?

If ads in the 1920s and 1930s portrayed working women in customarily subordinate and sex-segregated jobs, advertisements in the World War II era branched out significantly. White women appeared engaged in defense factory work and in a variety of jobs traditionally viewed as the preserve of men. Texts accompanying the ads often explained that women had stepped in to fill the void left by male workers who joined the military, and the women depicted were young and attractive, indicating that doing "men's work" did not endanger femininity. That married women were taking defense jobs was a common theme in wartime ads. In the 1943 ad reproduced in Figure 8.5, for example, a housewife is shown operating a drill press in a large war plant where she works six days a week. But consider the other images and the text. How do they suggest that her job is only temporary? What popular interpretation of married women's wartime work does this ad reveal?

DOCUMENTARY PHOTOGRAPHS

Documentary photographs of ordinary working women multiplied dramatically in the post–World War I years. Producing images was made easier by technological advancements such as the availability of rolls of film and faster lenses that allowed photographers to capture people and events more spontaneously. The interest of federal agencies in investigating and documenting work and social life also fostered more attention to photographing ordinary Americans. After its inception in 1920, the Women's Bureau of the U.S. Department of Labor not only conducted surveys but also commissioned photographs of a wide range of employment situations. During the Great Depression, the New Deal's Farm Security Administration (FSA) became a potent force in documenting the lives of Americans throughout the nation. Created in part to promote the New Deal itself, the FSA's photography project dramatically conveyed both the nation's pervasive poverty and the efforts of the federal government to help Americans weather the crisis. Many FSA photographers were exceptionally talented and brought artistic skill as well as compassion for their subjects to their work. Of these, a number were women. Marion Post Wolcott recorded the details of people's daily lives, particularly women's work. Dorothea Lange, who called herself a "photographer-investigator," was especially noted for her documentation of migrant workers in the West, with "Migrant Mother" perhaps the most famous photograph (see p. 499). Even after the

◆ Figure 8.6 **Ben Shahn, "Picking Cotton," 1935**
Library of Congress LC-USF-3301-006218.

Depression ended, the government stayed in the business of photographing Americans at work as part of its Office of War Information propaganda effort.

Figures 8.6 and 8.7 capture an aspect of women's work ignored in advertisements: farm labor and food processing. The numbers of Americans involved in agricultural labor declined steadily in the twentieth century, a reflection of both the mechanization of farm work and the growing importance of the industrial and commercial sectors of the economy. Whereas in 1880, the U.S. Census had listed 19 percent of adult working women as employed in agriculture, by 1920 that figure was 13 percent, and by 1940, 3 percent. However, these statistics do not take into account the many rural women who labored without pay in family-owned farms, performing both household tasks and field work.

Among hired agricultural laborers, race was a determining factor. In 1930, more than 20 percent of African American, Japanese, and Mexican working women were farm laborers, as opposed to 5 percent of working white women. Filipinas and Native American women also commonly worked in the fields. Rural

◆ Figure 8.7 **Dorothea Lange, "Women Packing Apricots," 1938**
Library of Congress LC-USF34-018316-E.

Japanese and Mexican women, who worked on their small family-held farms in the West, supplemented the family income by working for wages in local food-processing plants. In the South, black women and their families continued as sharecroppers, struggling through the crushing conditions of drought and depression to eke a living out of the land.

Both Figures 8.6 and 8.7 were produced under the auspices of the FSA. The well-known painter Ben Shahn took the haunting photograph in Figure 8.6 in 1935. While many pictures of field workers emphasized the backbreaking nature of their labor, Shahn chose to photograph a young black girl as she paused at her work as a cotton picker. What impact is Shahn striving for with this image in an Arkansas cotton field? In what ways does his photograph increase the viewer's empathy for the young woman?

Mexican immigrant women had the double burden of working while trying to maintain their families in harsh, substandard living conditions. In addition to working in the fields, they also clustered in jobs packing fruits and vegetables, as

◆ Figure 8.8 **Marion Post Wolcott, "Negro Domestic Servant," 1939**
Library of Congress LC-USF34TO1-051738-D.

Figure 8.7 indicates. This 1938 picture, taken in Brentwood, California, by Dorothea Lange, seems less obviously posed than Figure 8.6, but here too, the women are aware of the photographer. In another photograph taken at the same time, Lange captured a wider view of the packing shed that emphasized unpleasant working conditions and showed the women and a handful of men hard at work. For this photograph Lange focused on the women themselves. Why? What was Lange attempting to capture? What does the image suggest about the way in which these women created a communal spirit despite the arduous nature of fruit-packing work?

Figure 8.8, a 1939 photograph of an Atlanta, Georgia, domestic servant taken by Marion Post Wolcott, captures one of the most common yet least frequently photographed forms of paid female labor, domestic service. Although in the twentieth century, the percentage of women employed as domestics declined over-all, for the years 1920 through 1945, roughly 20 percent of all women workers still fell into this category. One of the most significant developments for this period was a shift from living-in to day work. With the spread of day work, middle- and upper-class housewives adopted a pattern of hiring part-time or daily workers, which lessened the domestic worker's reliance on employment in one household at the expense perhaps of security. This new pattern also made it possible for even lower-middle-class women to hire some household help from time to time.

The other most important development in the field of household work was its changing racial character. Excluded by racism from other opportunities, poor women of color congregated in domestic service just as clerical work opened up for white women (see p. 491). By 1920, the percentage of native-born and foreign-born white women domestics had dropped dramatically, leaving the field to be dominated by women of color. In 1920, 40 percent of black women were domestic workers, a percentage that rose to almost 60 percent in 1940. Native Americans and Mexican Americans also clustered in domestic work, although better job opportunities for these groups expanded during World War II to a greater extent than for African Americans.

This racial pattern points to the importance of hierarchical relationships in constructing a multicultural history of American women. The definition of middle-class status for white women included freedom from household drudgery, a freedom gained by the purchase of household appliances and by the employment of other women to do the domestic labor. Many middle-class and elite white women's ability to entertain, to enjoy leisure, or to take paid employment often depended on their ability to secure the cheap, easily exploitable labor of women of color. The image in Figure 8.8 hints at this dynamic, as the work of the black maid—in doing the dishes in the sink, keeping the kitchen spotless, and caring for the white infant—offers her employer freedom from household tasks. Might the photographer be calling our attention to the fact that the black woman, who was surely old enough to have her own child, was caring for a white baby instead of her own? How does this photograph's representation of a black servant contrast with the advertisement in Figure 8.4?

As in the case of domestic labor, race and sex were powerful determinants of women's employment in manufacturing jobs. Following World War I, some black women maintained a toehold in industrial employment, but most needed to revert to domestic work. Many white women remained in factory work, but sex-segregated patterns were reestablished, confining most women to jobs described as "light and repetitive" that paid less than male industrial work. In the 1920s, roughly three of ten working women were in light manufacturing, grouped together in areas such as the garment trade, textiles, and cigar making.

For most of the 1920s, an era of weak unions, few women (one in thirty-four) participated in organized labor. A new militancy emerged late in the decade, however, when textile workers in North Carolina rebelled in spontaneous strike, setting off a "Piedmont revolt" of union organizing that persisted into the 1930s and 1940s. Figure 8.9, an FSA photograph taken by Jack Delano in 1941, shows the

◆ Figure 8.9 **Jack Delano, "Striking Georgia Textile Workers," 1941**
Library of Congress LC-USF33-020936-M2.

determined stance of United Textile Workers' Union women picketing in Greensboro, Georgia, as a lone policeman or perhaps company guard looks on. Other unions, mostly notably the International Ladies Garment Workers' Union, made even more headway in the Depression, prompting organizer Anna Weinstein to say, "Now the girls have a power stronger than the bosses to back them. We are no longer robots. We are independent. We are strong. No longer can a boss cheat us out of pay. We now have the courage to tell him he is doing wrong and he must stop."[59]

Although the Greensboro women are not elegantly dressed, their clothing does not reveal that they are factory workers. What do their clothing choices suggest about their image of themselves as strikers? Compare this photograph with the depiction of striking shirtwaist workers in 1909 (see Figure 7.1, p. 448). How does the ability to capture women actively on the picket line enhance the photographer's power to depict striking women's militancy? What does the photograph reveal of Delano's own attitude toward the strikers?

While the Great Depression was hard on all industrial workers, light industries tended to recover more quickly than heavy industry jobs, which employed

◆ Figure 8.10 **Women's Bureau, "Model Sewing Factory," 1937**
National Archives 86G-2E-9.

men almost exclusively. And, even though the National Industrial Recovery Act often embodied discriminatory wage rates, they benefited many women workers by establishing federal guidelines for minimum wages and hours (see p. 503). Figure 8.10 shows a photograph of a model garment workshop taken by the Women's Bureau in 1937. By featuring an orderly and clean factory environment, what interpretation might the Women's Bureau hope to convey about the value of employer attention to working conditions?

In contrast to this model factory, the harsh times of the Depression also created more opportunities for exploitative labor. A glutted labor market and the presence of poor Mexican women in the West and Southwest led garment manufacturers to return to the late nineteenth-century practice of putting out piecework to women in their homes. Figure 8.11 shows Mexican American women in Texas working on fabric cut in New York City and sent to them in bundles. The photographer makes it clear that the three women are gathered in a home. But the positions of the women and the bundles of cloth indicate that the women are engaged in commercial sewing. The man's hat hanging on the wall suggests that there might be a male breadwinner in the family but that women's paid labor is

◆ Figure 8.11 **Mexican American Garment Workers in Texas, 1934**
National Archives 86G-6E-8.

nonetheless necessary. Compare this to a photograph with a similar theme from the turn of the century, Jacob Riis's "In the Home of an Italian Ragpicker" (see Figure 6.1, p. 387). What similarities do you find in these depictions of piecework? How have conditions changed? How does the work environment of these Texan women compare to the garment factory dating from the same era in Figure 8.10?

Women's job opportunities significantly improved during World War II. The 1945 image of two female riveters engaged in defense work in Figure 8.12 suggests the dramatic changes in women's work during the war. The imperatives of defense industry not only challenged traditional sex segregation and gave white women an opportunity to work in highly skilled industrial jobs, but they also created inroads in racial hierarchies that had limited most African American women to domestic labor. While magazine advertisements like Figure 8.5 continued to depict white women exclusively, documentary photographers, most of whom worked for the FSA, created an extensive record of white and black women's defense work during World War II. These images were usually posed and intended to highlight women's patriotic participation in the war effort.

The image in Figure 8.12 originally appeared in the black journal *Opportunity* and, like many wartime defense work photographs, was to some extent idealized. Defense firms resisted hiring any women in the first half year after Pearl Harbor, and even after a severe labor shortage forced them to turn to white women, the firms still balked at hiring black women, who were the last hired and first fired, tended to have the least skilled and least desirable industrial jobs, and encountered significant discrimination from white employees as well as employers (see p. 512). Yet none of these tensions surface in this photograph of two women riveting. In what ways does this posed image indicate a collegial working relationship between the women? Why might a black magazine choose this particular image to represent black women defense workers?

Wartime photographs of working women documented their contribution to the war effort, but neither the government nor employers expected women's expanded job opportunities to be permanent, an assumption that was also reflected in wartime advertisements (see Figure 8.5). But World War II labor shortages did result in some permanent changes. Although few women maintained the same level of skilled industrial work after the war, many were able to continue in some industrial jobs, especially in the textile and auto industries. Wartime need also helped to open up the clerical field to many women of color. African American, Chinese American, and Nisei women, for example, obtained

◆ Figure 8.12 **Rosie the Riveters, 1945**
General Research Division, Schomburg Center for Research in Black Culture, The New York Public Library, Astor, Lenox, and Tilden Foundations.

jobs working for the federal government during the war, and for black women in particular civil service was an important avenue of employment in the postwar period. These small gains, however, should not obscure the fact that sex- and race-segregated labor patterns that relegated women to lower-paid and lower-skilled jobs continued to be the norm in the post–World War II years.

QUESTIONS FOR ANALYSIS

1. What do the advertising images suggest about popular attitudes concerning women and work?

2. In what ways are the advertising images similar to those of the documentary photographs? How are they different?

3. What sorts of jobs were most likely to be considered women's work? Why is sex-segregated labor such an important concept for understanding the broader meaning of women's increased participation in the workforce in this period?

4. How did the Great Depression and World War II affect women's work lives?

5. How did the job experiences of white women and women of color vary? In what ways were they similar?

NOTES

1. Dorothy M. Brown, *Setting a Course: American Women in the 1920s* (Boston: Twayne, 1987), 69.

2. Ibid., 50.

3. Paula Giddings, *When and Where I Enter: The Impact of Black Women on Race and Sex in America* (New York: William Morrow, 1984), 169.

4. Kristi Andersen, *After Suffrage: Women in Partisan and Electoral Politics before the New Deal* (Chicago: University of Chicago Press, 1996); Nancy F. Cott, *The Grounding of Modern Feminism* (New Haven: Yale University Press, 1987), 104–8, 318–19.

5. Alice Kessler-Harris, *Out to Work: A History of Wage-Earning Women in the United States* (New York: Oxford University Press, 1982), 248.

6. Lynn Y. Weiner, *From Working Girl to Working Mother: The Female Labor Force in the United States, 1820–1980* (Chapel Hill: University of North Carolina, 1985), 104.

7. Lois Scharf, *To Work and to Wed: Female Employment, Feminism, and the Great Depression* (Westport, CT: Greenwood Press, 1980), 33.

8. Sharon Hartman Strom, *Beyond the Typewriter: Gender, Class, and the Origins of Modern American Office Work, 1900–1930* (Urbana: University of Illinois Press, 1992), 299–300.

9. Jacqueline Jones, *Labor of Love, Labor of Sorrow: Black Women, Work, and the Family, from Slavery to the Present* (New York: Basic Books, 1985), 177.

10. Elizabeth Clark-Lewis, *Living In, Living Out: African American Domestics in Washington, D.C., 1910–1940* (Washington, DC: Smithsonian Institution Press, 1994), 157.

11. Paul S. Taylor, "Mexican Women in Los Angeles Industry in 1928," *Atzlan* 11 (1980): 116 (originally written in 1929).

12. Emily Newell Blair, "Discouraged Feminists," *Outlook and Independent* 158 (July 8, 1931): 303.

13. *Photoplay* 29 (February 1926): 105.

14. Phyllis Blanchard and Carlyn Manasses, *New Girls for Old* (New York: Macaulay, 1930), 196.

15. Kathy Lee Peiss, *Cheap Amusements: Working Women and Leisure in Turn-of-the-Century New York* (Philadelphia: Temple University Press, 1986).

16. Elaine Tyler May, *Great Expectations: Marriage and Divorce in Post-Victorian America* (Chicago: University of Chicago Press, 1980); John D'Emilio and Estelle B. Freedman, *Intimate Matters: A History of Sexuality in America* (New York: Harper & Row, 1988).

17. Hazel V. Carby, " 'It Jus' Be's Dat Way Sometime': The Sexual Politics of Women's Blues," in *Radical America* 20 (1986), 9–22.

18. Robert S. and Helen Merrell Lynd, *Middletown in Transition: A Study in Cultural Conflicts* (New York: Harcourt, 1937), 178–79.

19. Kessler-Harris, *Out to Work,* 257.

20. Susan Ware, *Holding Their Own: American Women in the 1930s* (Boston: Twayne, 1982), 27.

21. Weiner, *From Working Girl to Working Mother,* 4–6.

22. Jones, *Labor of Love,* 209.

23. Scharf, *To Work and to Wed,* 114.

24. Devra Weber, *Dark Sweat, White Gold: California Farm Workers, Cotton, and the New Deal* (Berkeley: University of California Press, 1994), 95–96.

25. Ware, *Holding Their Own,* 47.

26. Ibid.

27. Martha H. Swain, *Ellen S. Woodward: New Deal Advocate for Women* (Jackson: University Press of Missouri, 1995), 53.

28. Ibid., 63.

29. Ibid., 48.

30. Kimberly L. Phillips, *Alabama North: African-American Migrants, Community, and Working-Class Activism in Cleveland, 1915–45* (Urbana: University of Illinois Press, 1999), 197.

31. Susan M. Hartmann, *The Home Front and Beyond: American Women in the 1940s* (Boston: Twayne, 1982), 35.

32. Melissa A. Herbert, "Amazons or Butterflies: The Recruitment of Women into the Military during World War II," *Minerva* 9 (1991): 50–68.

33. Ibid., 7.

34. Hartmann, *The Home Front and Beyond,* 42.

35. Kessler-Harris, *Out to Work,* 276.

36. Ibid., 288.

37. Karen Tucker Anderson, "Last Hired, First Fired: Black Women Workers during World War II," *Journal of American History* 69 (1982): 85.

38. Eileen Boris, " 'You Wouldn't Want One of 'Em Dancing with Your Wife': Racialized Bodies on the Job in World War II," *American Quarterly* 50 (1998): 77–108.

39. Paul Spickard, "Work and Hope: African American Women in Southern California during World War II," *Journal of the West* 32 (1993): 75.

40. Richard Santillán, "Rosita the Riveter: Midwest Mexican American Women during World War II, 1941–1945," *Perspectives in Mexican American Studies* 2 (1989): 132.

41. Grace Mary Gouveia, " 'We Also Serve': American Indian Women's Role in World War II," *Michigan Historical Review* 20 (1994): 153–82.

42. Xiaojian Zhao, "Chinese American Women Defense Workers in World War II," *California History* 25 (1996): 138–53.

43. Valerie Matsumoto, "Japanese American Women during World War II," in Ellen Carol DuBois and Vicki L. Ruiz, eds., *Unequal Sisters: A Multicultural Reader in U.S. Women's History* (New York: Routledge, 1990), 380.

44. Elaine Tyler May, "Rosie the Riveter Gets Married," in Lewis A. Erenberg and Susan E. Hirsch, eds., *The War in American Culture: Society and Consciousness during World War* II (Chicago: University of Chicago Press, 1996), 128.

45. D'Emilio and Freedman, *Intimate Matters,* 261.

46. Ibid., 290.

47. Hartmann, *The Home Front and Beyond,* 200.

48. Margaret Mead, "The Women in the War," in Jack Goodman, ed., *While You Were Gone: A Report on Wartime Life in the United States* (New York: Simon and Schuster, 1946), 278.

49. May, "Rosie the Riveter Gets Married," 140.

50. Julia Kirk Blackwelder, *Now Hiring: The Feminization of Work in the United States, 1900–1995* (College Station: Texas A&M University Press, 1997), 137.

51. Nancy Baker Wise and Christy Wise, *A Mouthful of Rivets: Women at Work in World War II* (San Francisco: Jossey-Bass, 1994), 182.

52. Lynne Olson, "Dear Beatrice Fairfax," *American Heritage* (May/June 1992): 93.

53. Ibid.

54. Valerie Matsumoto, "Redefining Expectations: Nisei Women in the 1930s," *California History* 73 (1974): 44–53, and "Desperately Seeking 'Deidre': Gender Roles, Multicultural Relations, and Nisei Women Writers of the 1930s," *Frontiers* 12 (1991): 19–32.

55. Susan Ware, *Beyond Suffrage: Women in the New Deal* (Cambridge: Harvard University Press, 1981), 15.

56. Swain, *Ellen S. Woodward,* 45.

57. Mary McLeod Bethune, "My Secret Talks with FDR," *Ebony* IV, April 1949, 42–51.

58. Ibid.

59. James R. Green, *The World of the Worker: Labor in Twentieth-Century America* (New York: Hill and Wang, 1980), 167.

SUGGESTED REFERENCES

General Works   A number of broad studies offer insights to women's experiences for the period 1920–1945. For politics, see Robyn Muncy, *Creating a Female Dominion in American Reform, 1890–1935* (1991); and Lois Scharf and Joan M. Jensen, eds., *Decades of Discontent: The Women's Movement, 1920–1940* (1987). On issues of sexuality and marriage, see, for example, Beth Bailey, *From Front Porch to Back Seat: Courtship in Twentieth-Century America* (1988); Ellen Chesler, *Woman of Valor: Margaret Sanger and the Birth Control Movement in America* (1992); Lillian Faderman, *Odd Girls and Twilight Lovers: A History of Lesbian Life in Twentieth-Century America* (1991); and John D'Emilio and Estelle B. Freedman, *Intimate Matters: A History of Sexuality in America,* 2nd ed. (1997). For women's work lives, see Julie Kirk Blackwelder, *Now Hiring: The Feminization of Work in the United States, 1900–1995* (1997); Miriam Cohen, *Workshop to Office: Two Generations of Italian American Women in New York City, 1900–1950* (1993); Evelyn Nakano Glenn, *Issei, Nisei, War Bride: Three Generations of Japanese American Women in Domestic Service* (1986); Barbara J. Harris, *Beyond Her Sphere: Women and the Professions in American*

History (1978); Darlene Clark Hines, *Black Women in White: Racial Conflict and Co-operation in the Nursing Profession, 1890–1950* (1989); Susan Estabrook Kennedy, *If All We Did Was to Weep at Home: A History of White Working-Class Women in America* (1979); Alice Kessler-Harris, *Out to Work: A History of Wage-Earning Women in the United States* (2003); and Phyllis Palmer, *Domesticity and Dirt: Housewives and Domestic Servants in the United States, 1920–1945* (1989). For African American women, see Paula Giddings, *When and Where I Enter: The Impact of Black Women on Race and Sex in America* (1984); Jacqueline Jones, *Labor of Love, Labor of Sorrow: Black Women, Work, and the Family, from Slavery to the Present* (1986); and Kimberley L. Phillips, *Alabama North: African-American Migrants, Community, and Working-Class Activism in Cleveland, 1915–45* (1999). Valerie J. Matsumoto, *Farming the Home Place: A Japanese American Community in California, 1919–1982* (1993); Judy Yung, *Chinese Women of America: A Pictorial History* (1986); and Judy Yung, *Unbound Feet: A Social History of Chinese Women in San Francisco* (1995) treat the experiences of Asian American women. For Mexican American women, see Vicki L. Ruiz, *From Out of the Shadows: Mexican Women in Twentieth-Century America* (1998); and George Sánchez, *Becoming Mexican American: Ethnicity, Culture, and and Identity in Chicano Los Angeles, 1900–1945* (1993).

The 1920s   For sources that specifically address the 1920s, see Dorothy M. Brown's general study, *Setting a Course: American Women in the 1920s* (1987). For postsuffrage political issues, Kristi Andersen, *After Suffrage: Women in Partisan and Electoral Politics before the New Deal* (1996); Nancy F. Cott, *The Grounding of Modern Feminism* (1987); and J. Stanley Lemons, *The Woman Citizen: Social Feminism in the 1920s* (1990) are especially valuable. Excellent insights on work are available in Susan Porter Benson, *Counter Cultures: Saleswomen, Managers, and Customers in American Department Stores, 1890–1940* (1986); Elizabeth Clark-Lewis, *Living In, Living Out: African American Domestics in Washington, D.C., 1910–1940* (1994); Margery W. Davies, *Woman's Place Is at the Typewriter: Office Work and Office Workers, 1870–1930* (1982); Lisa M. Fine, *The Souls of the Skyscraper: Female Clerical Workers in Chicago, 1870–1930* (1990); Angel Kwolek-Folland, *Engendering Business: Men and Women in the Corporate Office, 1870–1930* (1994); and Sharon Hartman Strom, *Beyond the Typewriter: Gender, Class, and the Origins of Modern American Office Work, 1900–1930* (1992). Themes of consumption and sexuality are analyzed in Hazel V. Carby, "'It Jus' Be's Dat Way Sometime': The Sexual Politics of Women's Blues," *Radical America* 20 (1986): 9–22; Kathy Peiss, *Hope in a Jar: The Making of America's Beauty Culture* (1998); and Ellen Kay Trimberger, "Feminism, Men, and Modern Love: Greenwich Village, 1900–1925," in Ann Snitown, Christine Stansell, and Sharon Tompson, eds., *Powers of Desire: The Politics of Sexuality* (1983).

The 1930s   An excellent general study of women in the Depression is Susan Ware, *Holding Their Own: American Women in the 1930s* (1982). See also Jeane Westin, *Making Do: How Women Survived the '30s* (1976). On women and work, see Lois Scharf, *To Work and to Wed: Female Employment, Feminism, and the Great Depression* (1980); and Devra Weber, *Dark Sweat, White Gold: California Farm Workers, Cotton,* *and the New Deal* (1994). Studies that explore women and the New Deal include Julie Kirk Blackwelder, *Women of the Depression: Caste and Culture in San Antonio, 1929–1939* (1984); Julie Boddy, "Photographing Women: The Farm Security Administration Work of Marion Post Wolcott," in Lois Scharf and Joan M. Jensen, eds., *Decades of Discontent: The Women's Movement, 1920–1940* (1987); Blanche Wiesen Cook, *Eleanor Roosevelt,* 2 vols. (1992, 1999); Joyce Ross, "Mary McLeod Bethune and the National Youth Administration: A Case Study of Power Relationships in the Black Cabinet of Franklin D. Roosevelt," *Journal of Negro History* 60 (1975): 1–28; Sandra Schackel, *Social Housekeepers: Women Shaping Public Policy in New Mexico, 1920–1940* (1992); Martha H. Swain, *Ellen S. Woodward: New Deal Advocate for Women* (1995); Susan Ware, *Beyond Suffrage: Women in the New Deal* (1981); and Susan Ware, *Partner and I: Molly Dewson, Feminism, and New Deal Politics* (1987). A valuable essay on the experience of Japanese American women is Valerie Matsumoto, "Redefining Expectations: Nisei Women in the 1930s," *California History* 73 (1994): 44–53.

World War II   For World War II, see the following general works: Karen Anderson, *Wartime Women: Sex Roles, Family Relations, and the Status of Women during World War II* (1981); D'Ann Campbell, *Women at War with America: Private Lives in a Patriotic Era* (1984); Susan M. Hartmann, *The Home Front and Beyond: American Women in the 1940s* (1982); and Margaret Higonnet et al., eds., *Behind the Lines: Gender and the Two World Wars* (1987). Women's military service is treated in Grace Mary Gouveia, " 'We Also Serve': American Indian Women's Role in World War II," *Michigan Historical Review* 20 (1994): 153–82; Gail M. Gutierrez, "The Sting of Discrimination: Women Airforce Service Pilots (WASP)," *Journal of the West* 35 (1996): 153–82; Melissa A. Herbert, "Amazons or Butterflies: The Recruitment of Women into the Military during World War II," *Minerva* 9 (1991): 50–68; and Martha S. Putney, *When the Nation Was in Need: Blacks in the Women's Army Corps during World War II* (1992). Valuable accounts of women in the workforce are Karen Tucker Anderson, "Last Hired, First Fired: Black Women Workers during World War II," *Journal of American History* 69 (1982): 82–97; Eileen Boris, " 'You Wouldn't Want one of 'Em Dancing with Your Wife': Racialized Bodies on the Job in World War II," *American Quarterly* 50 (1998): 77–108; Sherna Gluck, *Rosie the Riveter Revisited: Women, the War, and Social Change* (1988); Vicki L. Ruiz, *Cannery Women, Cannery Lives: Mexican Women, Unionization, and the California Food Processing Industry, 1930–1950* (1987); Richard Santillán, "Rosita the Riveter: Midwest Mexican American Women during World War II, 1941–1945," *Perspectives in Mexican American Studies* 2 (1989): 115–47; Paul Spickard, "Work and Hope: African American Women in Southern California during World War II," *Journal of the West* 28 (1993): 70–79; and Nancy Baker Wise and Christy Wise, *A Mouthful of Rivets: Women at Work in World War II* (1994). Studies dealing with minority women's experiences in wartime include Maureen Honey, ed., *Bitter Fruit: African American Women in World War II* (1999); Valerie Matsumoto, "Japanese American Women during World War II," *Frontiers* 8 (1984): 6–14; and Xiaojian Zhao, "Chinese American Women Defense Workers in World War II," *California History* 25 (1996): 138–53. On reconversion, see Elaine Tyler May, "Rosie the Riveter Gets Married," in Lewis A. Erenberg and Susan E. Hirsch, eds., *The War in American Culture: Society and Consciousness during World War II* (1996).

Selected Web Sites

The Women and Social Movements Web site was created by the Center for the Historical Study of Women and Gender at the State University of New York at Binghamton, <**womhist.binghamton.edu**>. Of the many document sets it provides, the following are particularly relevant to this chapter's themes: Equal Rights Debate in the 1920s; The Red Scare and Women's Peace Activism, 1920s; National Woman's Party and the Enfranchisement of Black Women, 1919–1924; Puerto Rican Women Garment Workers and the New Deal, 1933; Women and Civil Liberties in the San Antonio Pecan Workers Strike, 1938.

The Library of Congress's American Memory site, <**memory.loc.gov**>, offers a number of valuable collections, including photographs of the Farm Security Administration, many of which appear in this chapter. For the 1920s, see Prosperity and Thrift: The Coolidge Era and the Consumer Economy, 1921–1929, <**memory.loc.gov/ammem/coolhtml/coolhome.html**>. In this searchable database, there are several digitalized books and articles concerning women including Christine Frederick's *Selling Mrs. Consumer;* Sophonisba P. Breckinridge, *Women in the Twentieth Century: A Study of Their Political, Social, and Economic Activities;* and Pearl Idelia Ellis, "Americanization through Homemaking," a pamphlet describing Americanization efforts among Mexican women.

In addition to the American Memory collections, for the Depression era, the New Deal Network is a rich source, with a searchable database that includes numerous topics related to women, <**newdeal.feri.org/**>.

For World War II, see the *American Experience* documentary on women WASP pilots, *Fly Girls,* <**pbs.org/wgbh/amex/flygirls/index.html**>. The site provides a summary of the film, a timeline, images, and videoclips.

9

Beyond the Feminine Mystique

WOMEN'S LIVES, 1945–1965

I N DECEMBER 1955, A MIDDLE-AGED AFRICAN AMERICAN woman in Montgomery, Alabama, was arrested for refusing to give up her seat to a white passenger. Rosa Parks's protest against segregation sparked the Montgomery bus boycott, one of the pivotal events of a resurgent postwar civil rights movement. Parks's story signals the importance of women in the civil rights movement, certainly, but Parks, a department store seamstress, is also significant because she was a working woman. In the postwar era, female participation in the paid labor force expanded dramatically and became a defining characteristic of many more women's lives.

Parks's life is one indication of how the period of 1945 to 1965 was rife with tensions and contradictions. Mainstream cultural values of "the feminine mystique" emphasized women's domestic and maternal roles. Yet women worked outside the home and participated in civic activism that encompassed labor unions, politics, and civil and women's rights. Other contradictions are evident in the contrast between Americans' celebration of unprecedented prosperity and their deep anxieties about the Cold War and nuclear arms race. Cold War fears contributed to a repressive social and political climate that inhibited dissenting voices and reinforced traditional expectations about women's familial roles. Yet despite the conservative temper of this era, the civil rights movement gathered steam, and the seeds of a resurgent feminism took root.

FAMILY CULTURE AND GENDER ROLES

Two overarching themes shaped Americans' lives in the postwar era. The first, the Cold War between the Soviet Union and the United States, led to a sense of insecurity and anxiety that encouraged conformity to political and social norms. The second, the United States' extraordinary prosperity, prompted tremendous optimism about the nation's material progress. Both anxiety and affluence contributed to a popular conception of the family as a source of social stability and prosperity and reinforced traditional notions of women's place in the home.

The New Affluence and the Family

One startling measure of the nation's post–World War II prosperity was the growth in the gross domestic product (GDP), from $213 billion in 1945 to more than $500 billion in 1960. Not everyone enjoyed this new affluence. Many Americans, but especially nonwhite minorities, continued to live more economically marginalized lives than the affluent classes, and by 1959, 22 percent of all Americans still lived below the poverty line. Yet most Americans experienced a rising standard of living, with average family income almost doubling in the years between 1945 and 1960. Veterans pursued upward mobility through the Servicemen Readjustment Act of 1944, or the GI Bill, which provided federal assistance through home and student loans to returning military personnel. The GI Bill was particularly significant for assisting children of European immigrants in leaving behind the poverty of urban ethnic enclaves to become middle-class suburbanites. Although educational and economic differences still created clear class distinctions between blue-collar and white-collar workers, many of the former benefited from their unions' success in negotiating improved benefits, such as health insurance and automatic cost-of-living wage adjustments.

Affluence contributed to an emphasis on domesticity and the nuclear family. With more discretionary funds, Americans spent money on homes, raising the percentage of homeownership in the country from 43 percent in 1940 to 62 percent in 1960. Many of these homes were located in mushrooming new suburban developments that created a haven for the new domesticity—a haven restricted to white Americans, however, as much postwar housing remained racially segregated both by law and custom. To furnish their homes and garages, families bought electrical appliances, cars, and the exciting new form of at-home entertainment, televisions. New housing construction, road building, and consumer goods fueled the burgeoning postwar economy, and advertisers, manufacturers, and public policy makers all considered consumer purchasing power crucial to prosperity. They extolled the family as the bedrock of the nation's economic well-being and targeted women as its purchasing agent. *Life* magazine captured the essence of this understanding with a 1958 cover that featured thirty-six babies and the caption, "Kids—Built-in Recession Cure."

Figures on marriage and fertility for the postwar era suggest Americans' enthusiasm for family and domestic life. Temporarily reversing the long trend since early in the nineteenth century toward fewer children, family size between the war and the early 1960s went up, creating a "baby boom" (see Chart 9.1 and the Appendix, p. A-36). More Americans married and married younger, further spiking the birthrate. In the 1930s, women gave birth to 2.4 children on average; in the 1950s, that number increased to 3.2. More babies were born between 1948 and 1953 than had been born in the previous thirty years. A brief downturn in the divorce rate, unique in the twentieth century, also signaled an increased commitment to family life in this period. Pent-up desires for traditional family life denied to many in the Great Depression and war years undoubtedly played a part, while

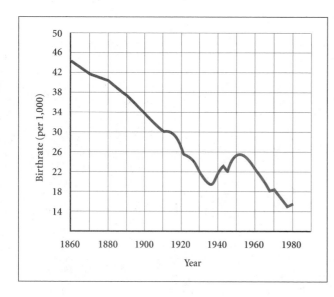

◆ Chart 9.1 **The American Birthrate, 1860–1980**

the pervasive celebration of family life in popular culture may also have shaped young couples' decisions.

The Cold War and the Family

While prosperous families lay at the heart of America's material success, a stable family order was also credited with a crucial role in giving the United States the upper hand in the Cold War. World War II had barely ended before the two former allies, the Soviet Union and the United States, began facing off for what became a global struggle lasting almost fifty years. Representing the conflicting systems of capitalism and communism, each side attempted to achieve dominance in world geopolitics. In the United States, President Harry S Truman articulated the doctrine of "containment," which called for resisting the spread of Communist governments in countries around the world. The Cold War became hot in Korea between 1950 and 1952, in the first major overseas armed conflict in American history not authorized by congressional declaration. The newly formed United Nations sent troops, primarily supplied by the United States, to defend the U.S.-backed government in the south of Korea against encroachment by the Communist regime in the north. The war ended with a cease-fire that left Korea divided by a demilitarized zone between North and South Korea that is still in existence. The Cold War also spawned an escalating nuclear arms race. The terrible power of atomic destruction unleashed when the United States dropped bombs on Hiroshima and Nagasaki, Japan, became a mushrooming threat to the peoples of the world as the U.S. and Soviet governments matched their militant rhetoric with competition to acquire nuclear weapons.

The Cold War had a chilling effect on U.S. domestic politics. In the late 1940s and early 1950s, the nation was immersed in a hunt for Communists within its borders, led by U.S. Senator Joseph McCarthy. McCarthy's search for Communists in high places was more symptom than cause of the new witch-hunts. Other politicians and leaders also called for purging American institutions of "internal subversives." The most notorious manifestations of the period's "Red Scare" were a federal loyalty program that scrutinized thousands of public employees and widely publicized congressional hearings held by the House Un-American Activities Committee (HUAC) to investigate Communist influence in American life. Women and men lost jobs and had their civil liberties violated on the basis of flimsy evidence. In 1950, U.S. Representative Helen Gahagan Douglas was "red-baited" and pushed from politics because of her support for causes such as rent control laws and federal regulation of oil drilling. Douglas lost a hotly contested U.S. Senate race in California to future president Richard M. Nixon, who hinted at what he thought were her pro-Communist sympathies by saying that "she was pink down to her underwear."[1] Unions and mainstream liberal organizations, including the American Association of University Women and the National Council of Negro Women, purged their membership of Communists and "fellow travelers," people deemed sympathetic to communism. The intensity of the Red Scare began to ebb after 1954 when Senator McCarthy, overreaching himself by investigating the U.S. army, was formally censured by the Senate for unbecoming conduct. But anxieties about subversion and dissent continued to shape the political climate for many years to come.

One key aspect of the postwar culture of conformity was an emphasis on the family as a bastion of social order, one that would help Americans resist the menace of communism and provide shelter in the midst of an uncertain world. Employers and returning soldiers had been eager to send women back to the home to restore traditional gender patterns. Meshing with anxieties flowing from the disruptions of World War II, Cold War fears about atomic annihilation and Soviet expansion reinforced what was a kind of revived cult of domesticity. And just as social stability was credited to family order, social problems were attributed to family

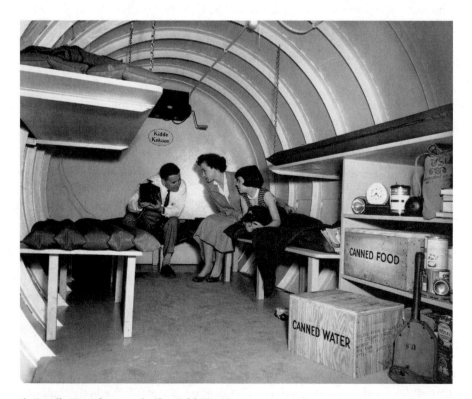

◆ **Family Togetherness in the Cold War Era**

As the Cold War spread fears of nuclear warfare, many Americans, encouraged by the federal government, built fallout shelters in their front and back yards. Magazines and newspapers frequently ran articles that featured pictures of 1950s families posed in their shelters, reflecting the strong emphasis on family culture in the era. This 1955 image depicts mother, father, and daughter in a "Kidde Kokoon," a shelter manufactured by Walter Kidde Nuclear Laboratories of Garden City, New York. The shelter cost $3,000 and was outfitted with such items as canned food and water, chemical toilet, radiation detector, and face respirator. © *CORBIS.*

dysfunction. An apparent postwar rise in crime among children, referred to as "juvenile delinquency," was blamed on working mothers and weak fathers.

A corollary of this idealization of the family was the continuation of wartime fears of sexual promiscuity among women and the heightened visibility of homosexuals. The 1953 publication of Alfred Kinsey's *Sexual Behavior in the Human Female,* the follow-up to Kinsey's *Sexual Behavior in the Human Male* (1948), shocked many Americans with its statistics: 50 percent of the women surveyed admitted to premarital intercourse, 90 percent to "petting," and 28 percent to what Kinsey termed "homosexual tendencies." Kinsey's findings—as well as other evidence, such as the growth of an urban lesbian subculture centered in working-class bars and a rise in premarital pregnancies—signaled changes in sexual behavior. Yet taboos against female sexuality outside of heterosexual marriage remained strong, as did a double standard that excused male sexual adventures before marriage while prizing premarital female virginity. In the face of challenges to these norms, leading experts championed early marriages to reduce premarital experimentation and firm gender roles in the home to ensure the heterosexuality of children.

With this concentration on the family came a strong emphasis on rigid gender roles—on men's role as breadwinners and women's as wives and mothers. Many psychologists insisted that "maturity" entailed a willing acceptance of one's biologically based social roles. Parents who turned to the best-selling childrearing book *Baby and Child Care* (1946) by Dr. Benjamin Spock learned that working mothers damaged their children: "If a mother realizes clearly how vital [a mother's] care is to a small child, it may make it easier for her to decide that the extra money she might earn, or the satisfaction she might receive from an outside job, is not so important, after all."[2] In educational films such as *A Date with Your Family,* high school students viewed a mother and daughter dutifully catering to men as they prepared and served a meal. And in movies such as *The Best of Everything* (1959), filmgoers followed a plot that not only depicted career women's sterile lives but also warned young women that "love, even when it's bad, is the best of everything." While some television shows pictured men struggling to control their scheming and adventuresome wives, in others women appeared as content wives and mothers. (See Visual Sources: Television's Prescriptions for Women, pp. 593–608.)

Rethinking the Feminine Mystique

In 1963 Betty Friedan captured the essence of this postwar ideology of female domestic containment in her best-selling book *The Feminine Mystique.* Arguing that millions of American women were suffering from "the problem that has no name," a malaise brought about by the limited aspirations to which society restricted women, Friedan indicted the "feminine mystique" of popular culture. Excoriating mass media for encouraging women to develop a sense of personal creativity through the use of cake mixes and floor waxes, she similarly lambasted psychologists for prescribing tranquilizers for "neurotic" women rather than examining the social basis of their unhappiness. She criticized popular magazines for

BETTY FRIEDAN
The Problem That Has No Name

In The Feminine Mystique *(1963), Betty Friedan (b. 1921) condemned the media, educators, professionals, and the culture as a whole for defining domesticity and motherhood as the only appropriate goals for women. These two excerpts suggest the compelling argument Friedan presented for challenging conventional expectations about women's proper roles.*

If I am right, the problem that has no name stirring in the minds of so many American women today is not a matter of loss of femininity or too much education, or the demands of domesticity. It is far more important than anyone recognizes. It is the key to these other new and old problems which have been torturing women and their husbands and children, and puzzling their doctors and educators for years. It may well be the key to our future as a nation and a culture. We can no longer ignore that voice within women that says: "I want something more than my husband and my children and my home." . . .

. . . With a vision of the happy modern housewife as she is described by the magazines and television, by the functional sociologists, the sex-directed educators, and the manipulators dancing before my eyes, I went in search of one of those mystical creatures. Like Diogenes with the lamp, I went as a reporter from suburb to suburb, searching for a woman of ability and education who was fulfilled as a housewife. . . .

In one upper-income development where I interviewed, there were twenty-eight wives. Some were college graduates in their thirties or early forties; the younger wives had usually quit college to marry. Their husbands were, to a rather high degree, engrossed in challenging professional work. Only one of these wives worked professionally; most had made a career of motherhood with a dash of community activity. Nineteen out of the twenty-eight had had natural childbirth. . . . Twenty of the twenty-

disseminating the feminine mystique at every turn, while denying that women were interested in reading about political, international, and social issues. Friedan argued that this permeation of the feminine mystique meant that most women were denied a sense of an autonomous self. The success of *The Feminine Mystique*—it sold over 3 million copies—clearly indicated that she had tapped into many women's frustrations over the domestic role they were expected to perform and the limitations imposed by their containment in the home (see box, "The Problem That Has No Name").

eight breastfed their babies. At or near forty, many of these women were pregnant. The mystique of feminine fulfillment was so literally followed in this community that if a little girl said: "When I grow up, I'm going to be a doctor," her mother would correct her: "No, dear, you're a girl. You're going to be a wife and mother, like mummy."

But what was mummy really like? Sixteen out of the twenty-eight were in analysis or analytical psychotherapy. Eighteen were taking tranquilizers; several had tried suicide; and some had been hospitalized for varying periods, for depression or vaguely diagnosed psychotic states. ("You'd be surprised at the number of these happy suburban wives who simply go berserk one night, and run shrieking through the street without any clothes on," said the local doctor, not a psychiatrist, who had been called in, in such emergencies.) Of the women who breastfed their babies, one had continued, desperately, until the child was so undernourished that her doctor intervened by force. Twelve were engaged in extramarital affairs in fact or in fantasy.

These were fine, intelligent American women, to be envied for their homes, husbands, children, and for their personal gifts of mind and spirit. Why were so many of them driven women? Later, when I saw this same pattern repeated over and over again in similar suburbs, I knew it could hardly be coincidence. These women were alike mainly in one regard: they had uncommon gifts of intelligence nourished by at least the beginnings of higher education—and the life they were leading as suburban housewives denied them the full use of their gifts.

It was in these women that I first began to notice the tell-tale signs of the problem that has no name; their voices were full and flat, or nervous and jittery; they were listless and bored, or frantically "busy" around the house or community. They talked about "fulfillment" in the wife-and-mother terms of the mystique, but they were desperately eager to talk about this other "problem" with which they seemed very familiar indeed.

SOURCE: Betty Friedan, *The Feminine Mystique* (1963; repr., New York: Dell, 1974), 27, 224–26.

Despite the powerful impact of Friedan's book, recent critics have rightly pointed out that she vastly overstated the pervasiveness and uniformity of this restrictive domestic ideal. Rarely acknowledging that the women she described were affluent and white, she glossed over the significant differences that class, race, and ethnicity produced and neglected the increasing number of women entering the paid workforce. Among black women, working wives and mothers had long been valued and understood as virtually essential for their families to achieve middle-class status. Images and articles promoting the feminine mystique were largely absent from *Ebony,* the major African American popular magazine of the period. Instead, *Ebony* featured women who fought racial discrimination and achieved success in business, politics, and the arts, although it was careful to note the importance of these women's family roles and their attention "to the needs of their husbands and children."[3]

Even among middle-class white women, Friedan overstated her case. Articles in popular magazines directed at white women often depicted successful career women, including those who combined work and marriage. Writers encouraged women to be active in community affairs and held up as models women who achieved "great pride and accomplishment and the satisfaction of 'doing a job.'"[4] Moreover, in contrast to Friedan's claim that magazines ignored women's discontent, they gave extensive attention to wives' dissatisfaction with their married lives and their housework obligations. In advice columns like "Can This Marriage Be Saved?" letter writers testified to the drudgery of household chores and the stresses entailed in unrelenting domesticity. Nevertheless, the advice dispensed uniformly encouraged women to find psychological tools to help them adjust to the gendered expectations of middle-class marriage, rather than challenge the expectations themselves.[5]

The most ironic corrective to Friedan's assessment is that the author was not the simple housewife and unwitting victim of domestic confinement that she claimed to be. Friedan had a background in radical politics, had been a journalist for the United Electrical, Radio and Machine Workers Union, and in the 1940s and 1950s had frequently written about racial and gender discrimination in the workforce. Thus she knew about women workers but chose not to discuss them in her book. She obscured her past probably because of the anti-Communist preoccupations of the era and because portraying herself as an angry casualty of the feminine mystique made for a more marketable book.

But these limitations do not decrease *The Feminine Mystique*'s value as a historical source. Not only was the book important in the revival of feminism in the 1960s, but it also captured a crucial aspect of mainstream Cold War cultural values about women. The ideology of the feminine mystique is best understood as a prescription for female behavior promulgated by those Americans most eager to reinforce traditional gender roles as a means of creating social order. This eagerness may well have stemmed from the challenges posed to conventional expectations about women's roles.

Women and Work

These challenges were most evident in women's changing employment patterns. As the baby boom suggests, women embraced motherhood in the 1950s, but they also poured into the paid labor market in what many observers at the time called a "revolutionary" development. In 1940, 25 percent of women worked; by 1960 the figure had climbed to 35 percent.

More dramatic was the growth in the percentage of married women in the labor force. In 1940, only 17 percent of wives worked; by 1960, 32 percent of wives earned wages. By 1960, married women constituted fully 61 percent of the female labor force (see the Appendix, p. A-38). While all groups of women held jobs outside the home, particularly significant was the growth in wage earning of middle-class white married women, the very group assumed to be most in the grip of the feminine mystique. White wives' participation in the workforce more than doubled between 1940 and 1960, rising from 14 to 30 percent, while for black wives, the increase was smaller but began at a higher level, going from 32 percent in 1940 to 47 percent in 1960. In a dramatic reversal of older patterns, educated women were more likely to work than those without high school and college degrees.

Mothers also increased their participation in the workforce, with one of the most significant developments a trend toward older women entering the workforce when their children reached school age. By having children at younger ages, mothers found themselves positioned to join the labor force. Because advances in health care meant Americans were living longer, women could expect to work for twenty or more years after their children began going to school.

The expanded availability of jobs, created by a burgeoning economy and fueled by the growth of the consumer culture, also affected women's work patterns. White-collar fields dominated by women for decades—clerical work, sales, nursing, social work, and teaching—grew dramatically. Service sector jobs—so-called pink-collar work, such as food service, personal care, and beauty salon work—also multiplied and became increasingly feminized. In blue-collar employment, women had lost many skilled positions in heavy manufacturing at the end of World War II, but they found other fields opening up: the lower ranks of the printing industry, positions in industrial assembly, and jobs as delivery personnel and bus and taxi drivers.

Improvements in the opportunities for women of color were particularly notable. Although the absolute numbers were small, black women in the 1950s attended college at a rate higher than either white women or black men. After decades of discrimination, they found more white-collar clerical work opening up to them, as did Latinas and Chinese and Japanese American women. Because of their high degree of education, Nisei (second-generation Japanese American) women also made strides in teaching, social work, and civil service.

For all these improvements, poor women of color still had limited options. Although the percentage of black women workers employed as domestics dropped significantly, from 60 percent in 1940 to 42 percent in 1950, a substantial minority continued to work in low-paid, devalued labor, as did many Latina and Asian women. Immigrant women, because of lack of language and other skills as well as discrimination, found few jobs available to them. In 1943 Congress repealed the Chinese Exclusion Act of 1882 (see Chapter 6), in deference to America's World War II alliance with China. Chinese women, approximately 40,000 of them between 1948 and 1965, took advantage of the repeal as well as of other legislation, such as the War Brides Act of 1945 and the 1953 Refugee Relief Act, to immigrate to the United States. Most clustered in Chinatowns in the nation's cities, especially New York and San Francisco. There they worked in family enterprises as well as the garment industry, which was a crucial source of much needed income. Puerto

◆ **Puerto Rican Garment Worker in New York City**
After World War II, Puerto Rican immigration to the United States swelled dramatically, facilitated by cheap airfares to New York City and the fact that Puerto Ricans were citizens because their nation was an American-controlled territory. Women migrated in large numbers, lured by plentiful low-skilled manufacturing and garment industry jobs. *The Records of the Offices of the Government of Puerto Rico in the U.S. Centro de Estudios Puertor-riqueños, Hunter College, CUNY. Photographer Unknown.*

Rican women, part of a vastly expanded post–World War II migration from that Caribbean island mostly to New York City, also concentrated in the garment trade, which as an industry was suffering from decline in this period, resulting in low wages, poor conditions, and erratic employment. These poorer women's restricted options underline an important characteristic of the "revolutionary" aspect of women's work after World War II. While certainly many women of color had new opportunities, the most dramatic change was the entrance into the labor market of white married women who could take advantage of new service and clerical jobs that offered "respectable" employment.

Women's increased employment also stemmed from changes in employment practices. Well aware of the expanding labor market and concerned about finding qualified workers, employers not only willingly hired women, but they also dropped the "marriage bar" that had operated in many fields. While in the past, bosses resisted hiring wives and mothers because of beliefs that they were unreliable and belonged in the home, now they hired women who wanted to work regardless of their household responsibilities. Moreover, they restructured the nature of the work market by making part-time jobs widely available for the first time to tap a rich vein of labor power.

Employers who enticed married women with more flexible schedules and other incentives had encouragement from administrators in the U.S. Department of Labor, including its Women's Bureau, and other public policy makers. Maintaining economic prosperity and keeping the upper hand over the Soviet Union in the Cold War motivated employment experts to evaluate the labor market carefully. Many insisted that "womanpower" needed to be exploited efficiently as a means of promoting U.S. productivity and competitiveness. Alice Leopold, head of the Women's Bureau in the mid-1950s, emphasized the need to compete with communism by training American women in new skills. "Women," she noted, "are becoming increasingly important in the development of our country's industry, in scientific research, in the education field, and in the social sciences."[6]

This recognition framed the work of two important agencies in the 1950s. The National Manpower Council (NMC), a private group with close ties to government agencies and corporations, used conferences and publications to draw attention to women's employment. At a 1951 conference on "Women in the Defense Decade," in the midst of the Korean War, the American Council on Education tackled the "urgent question . . . about just how and in what respects women could serve the defense of the nation,"[7] leading to the creation in 1953 of the Commission on the Education of Women (CEW).

In both groups, organizers walked a tightrope between what they viewed as national needs and the dominant ideology about women's place. Sensitive to the prevailing gender norms, they took care not to be viewed as undermining traditional roles. A 1955 CEW report explicitly stated that its recommendations concerning women "must not detract from the importance of their roles as wives and mothers."[8] Yet both groups also encouraged training and education for women and criticized discriminatory labor patterns that limited full use of the nation's womanpower.

Despite the attention both the NMC and the CEW paid to promoting women's opportunities in the workforce, changes in attitudes were slow in coming. It was not until the 1960s that public education stopped consistently tracking women into clerical and similar endeavors. And little headway occurred in breaking down discrimination in the labor field. Neither the NMC nor the CEW addressed the limited economic opportunities of women of color, focusing instead almost exclusively on white women. And for all women, sex-segregated labor patterns, and the inequality embedded in them, persisted. Indeed, one historian argues that by emphasizing part-time work, the NMC reinforced women's marginal status in the workplace.[9] These groups legitimated married women's participation in the workforce but barely scratched the surface of the discrimination women faced.

Changes in the labor market and encouragement on the part of employers and the government are crucial factors in understanding the growth in women's work outside the home, but this development was also fundamentally a question of personal choice. What led women to create this demographic shift? Scattered evidence suggests the complicated processes that undergirded these choices. Nurses, the largest category of female professional labor, described themselves as taking advantage of new work opportunities to serve their community.[10] At the same time, they emphasized that their home responsibilities came first, and it was

◆ Working Mothers

In 1953 *Life* ran an article on four working mothers that emphasized that this new trend stemmed from women's desire to "improve living conditions." Pauline Painkos (left), a working-class suburban wife employed as a machine operator at a Johnson & Johnson factory, hates "having to leave her baby," but feels her income is vital to maintaining their "unpretentious standard of living." Grace Sullivan (right), a teacher "who spends her days with other people's children," claims "I am a better mother because I work—and anyway I am gone only while they are away." The *Life* photographer detailed Sullivan's contribution to the family's income by showing her "at home, surrounded by articles bought with her own money." *TimeLife Pictures/Getty Images.*

only the flexibility of nursing that allowed them to work for wages. In contrast, many working-class women apparently felt less need to justify working, admitting they took paid labor to get out of the house, in addition to providing assistance to their families.

The degree of family need may have been the crucial factor in most married women's decision to seek employment. Poor women of color—as they had done for decades—worked to make ends meet. For others, paid labor made life easier for their families and, in particular, enabled them to participate in the burgeoning consumer economy and enter the middle class. A survey of unionized women indicated that a significant number of them took jobs to finance their children's education or to make house payments. Contemporary observers echoed these explanations. A 1957 Ford Foundation study, *Womanpower,* reported that "the desire to achieve a richer life for the family has such widespread approval that it provides a generally acceptable reason for married women whose responsibilities at home do not absorb all their time and energy to go to work."[11] Similarly, in 1956 *Look* magazine concluded: "No longer a psychological immigrant to man's world, she works rather casually as a third of the U.S. labor force, and less toward a big career than as a way of filling a hope chest or buying a new home freezer. She gracefully concedes the top job rungs to men."[12] *Look*'s assessment fittingly summed up prevailing assumptions about women's work. Acknowledging a significant shift in labor patterns, it minimized its impact on women's role in the home, a belief that sustained the persistent discrimination that the rising tide of working women encountered.

WOMEN'S ACTIVISM IN CONSERVATIVE TIMES

No matter how observers minimized the implications of women's work outside the home, it represented a potentially significant challenge to cultural norms. Still other evidence of women's engagement in the public world outside the home was the wide range of activism that flourished in the postwar era. Organized feminism remained weak, but women participated in a variety of efforts to improve their work lives and to contribute to their communities. Their activism, like women's participation in the workforce, laid the seeds for challenging the prevailing ideas of women's role in the family, the workplace, and public life.

Working-Class Women and Unions

While the increased participation of middle-class women in the labor market was one of the most striking characteristics of the postwar era, working-class women's struggle to maintain the gains they had made during World War II was an important aspect of women's activism in the period historians dub the "doldrums" of feminism. Unionized women in industry led the way in challenging layoffs, poor pay, restricted job opportunities, and other discriminatory policies. And in some industries, black and white women came together to challenge racial discrimination that African American women faced in the workplace.

Women of the United Packinghouse Workers of America (UPWA) exemplified a female activism that not only sought to improve working women's opportunities in the 1950s but also laid the groundwork for working-class women's participation in the feminist movement of the 1960s. Like many other Congress of Industrial Organization (CIO) unions, the UPWA had theoretically embraced an egalitarian stance in the 1930s and 1940s and actively recruited black men and white and black women (see Chapter 8). Women, however, did not always find their union sympathetic to their concerns. As in most industries during World War II, sex-segregated labor patterns broke down in the big meatpacking houses, with women taking on heavy work formerly reserved for men. But after the war, the companies largely reverted to prewar job classifications that limited women's opportunities and wages, and union men did not challenge employers' decisions to lay off women in large numbers, regardless of their seniority rights.

Despite the UPWA's failure to support women during postwar reconversion, the national leadership had become more sympathetic by the 1950s, in part because women made up a significant percentage (approximately 20 percent) of the union. Women drew on the union's Anti-discrimination Department—which also addressed racial discrimination—to bolster their efforts at improving their work lives. This department organized women's conferences, sponsored a woman's column in the union's newspaper, and served as a clearing house for grievances.

African American women became some of the most militant female activists in many unions. Women like UPWA member Addie Wyatt of Chicago often built upon their positions as community leaders. As Wyatt recalled, in her church, "women were always leaders. They were preachers, they were officers . . . and whatever was necessary in the church to do, women and men always did it in partnership. And I always thought that was right."[13] As Wyatt rose to prominence in the union—eventually becoming president of her local chapter—she turned her attention to the struggle for racial justice and served as a labor advisor to civil rights leader Martin Luther King Jr. Other black UPWA women were active on the local level, drawing their colleagues into drives against segregation and other discriminatory policies in their communities.

Part of the focus of Wyatt and other black women was to challenge the discrimination black women faced in the packing houses. Joined by many white women union members, they successfully protested racial discrimination in hiring as well as the packers' policy of racially segregating departments, whereby white women had cleaner, better paid positions such as bacon slicers, while black women were relegated to dirty work such as cleaning feces from sausage casings.

These women concentrated on breaking down racial barriers, but they also recognized some of their shared concerns as working women. They addressed the problems that kept women from being active in the union and made clear connections between women's domestic lives and their work lives. At a 1954 conference, UPWA leader Marian Simmons pointed out, for example, that "merely satisfying the needs of women on the job would not be enough. Just now with women working in the plants and having to go home to all the household drudgery and assuming the full responsibility of taking care of children during non-working hours and providing for their keep during working hours, it is impossible for her to exercise her full freedom and equality. We have to map out a plan by which women can be free to exercise [their] full talents and inclinations."[14]

UPWA women tackled a number of issues specifically focused on women's employment concerns. They negotiated contracts calling for equal pay for equal work—a provision that affected relatively few women, however, as it applied to men and women doing the same jobs, when most women were clustered in lower paying "women's work." The next logical step in achieving better wages for women—challenging the gendered structure of the workplace—was more problematic, in part because men resisted but also because women were divided on the issue. UPWA women had long supported the concept of protective labor legislation for women and opposed the Equal Rights Amendment, which they viewed as something for elite working women that did not speak to their concerns (see Chapter 8). Slow to challenge sex-typed work, they sought rather to improve women's wages and conditions within their separate work sphere.

Women in the electrical industry were the most militant female workers in the postwar era. During World War II, as their numbers increased in the industry to half of the workforce, women were able to pressure their CIO union, the United Electrical, Radio and Machine Workers (UE), to address wage differentials and other forms of discrimination. After the war, when employers reverted to the prewar patterns of sexsegregated labor and women suffered widespread layoffs, women persisted in pressuring the UE for fairer treatment. By 1947, they had achieved nondiscrimination clauses for sex, race, color, creed, and national origin in seven hundred local contracts.

The anti-Communist Red Scare gave an ironic boost to women electrical workers' efforts to counter discrimination. The UE, with a strong Communist presence, found itself under attack by the government, employers, and its parent union, the CIO, in the postwar years. To demonstrate its own freedom from "subversives," the CIO expelled the UE as well as other Communist-influenced unions in 1949. When the CIO set up a new union, the International Union of Electrical Workers (IUE), the UE had to compete for members. Well aware of the high numbers of women in the electrical industry, whom the IUE also actively recruited by speaking to women's concerns, the UE redoubled its efforts to address the discrimination women faced and deepened its rhetoric of social justice. Most significant was the forty-page pamphlet it issued in 1952, "UE Fights for Women Workers," a work recently discovered to have been written anonymously by Betty Friedan. (See Documents: Feminism in the UE, pp. 609–12.) The pamphlet called for ending separate men's and women's job categories, upgrading women's wages, and allowing them access to higher skilled jobs. As one historian puts it, "The program was a prescription for a gender-blind workplace."[15]

Women in the UE were ahead of their times. Most women unionists in the late 1940s and 1950s concentrated on improving their work opportunities and wages, primarily in the context of jobs carved out as women's work. They called for fair treatment as workers but rarely framed their analysis in terms of women's equality. Class more than gender was their lens for understanding their circumstances, although certainly black women had a more complicated analysis due to the racial inequality they routinely faced. But the struggles of this era and the recalcitrance of both corporate employers and male unionists would culminate in a far more activist movement for women's rights in the 1960s and beyond.

◆ Women and Union Activism
Like women in the UPWA and the UE, women in the United Auto Workers union (UAW) fought hard in the postwar era to counter discriminatory employment practices. One of the most militant groups emerged in 1947 in the Detroit area, where women created Region 1-A's Women's Committee, which spawned similar committees elsewhere. This photograph captures Region 1-A's Women's Committee conference in November 1955, a period in which tensions over the impact of automation on women was one of several issues that concerned female union leaders. Although only one African American is present in this picture, black women were active in the UAW and pursued twin goals of workers' rights for African Americans and for women. *Walter P. Reuther Library, Wayne State University.*

Middle-Class Women and Voluntary Associations

More affluent women were also activists in the postwar years. The cultural values that discouraged middle-class women from working outside the home sanctioned the long tradition of their participation in voluntary associations outside the domestic sphere. In the postwar era, middle-class women participated in a wide range of civic and political activities, sometimes in mixed-sex groups such as the American Civil Liberties Union (ACLU), the National Association for the Advancement of Colored People (NAACP), or Parent-Teacher Associations (PTAs), and sometimes in all-female groups such as the Young Women's Christian Association (YWCA) and the League of Women Voters (LWV). As was the case with working-class union leaders, middle-class women's organizations rarely tackled questions of women's rights, but their activism nonetheless belies the stereotype of the bored or self-satisfied housewife cut off from the larger world outside the home.

In the 1950s, the focus of many women's organizations shifted away from their prewar engagement with gender issues (see Chapter 8). Both the strength of the domestic ideal and Cold War anxieties about the Communist menace put pressure on organizations to moderate their interest in women's rights and social reform more generally. Changing demographics also fostered the retreat from previous agendas. Both the LWV and the American Association of University Women (AAUW) expanded dramatically in the postwar era, bringing an influx of suburban housewives who had less interest in women's issues than did older members. The LWV moved away from endorsing legislation and narrowed its focus to voter education and local civic issues, and the AAUW membership showed less interest in an action-oriented agenda to promote women's educational advancement and focused instead on local study groups.

In other organizations, interest in promoting women's rights was redirected to a growing concern with the civil rights movement. The YWCA's long-standing concern with working-class women helped prepare it to focus on racial inequality. Spurred by black women in its ranks, it eliminated its own organizational segregation and forged alliances in support of black women's civil rights efforts. In the context of the 1950s, this modern reform activity led critics to label YWCA women as "subversive." Other organizations with religious affiliations, such as the National Council of Catholic Women and the National Council of Jewish Women (NCJW), also became involved in racial justice issues. The NCJW's interest in civil rights was particularly deepened by the shock of the Holocaust. The extermination of 6 million Jews by Adolf Hitler's Nazi regime fostered a belief that racism in all its forms needed to be combated vigorously.

The National Council of Negro Women (NCNW) also witnessed significant changes in this era. Founded during the Great Depression by Mary McLeod Bethune (see Chapter 8) with the idea of creating a political pressure group that could agitate for black women's political and economic advancement, the NCNW fell on hard times in the 1950s. It had difficulty attracting young women, in part because it had gained the reputation of being interested only in black professional women. By the mid-1960s, the NCNW revived, but it did so by downplaying women's rights in favor of community service and civil rights.

While women recentered established organizations, they also found outlets for civic activism in new associations. Cold War issues brought women with very different political sensibilities into the political arena during the 1950s. Historians are just beginning to explore women's roles in right-wing political organizations, but clearly some conservative grassroots activists came from the ranks of middle-class women. They participated in groups such as the Minute Women of the USA, Pro-America, and Women for Constitutional Government, founded to tackle what they viewed as pervasive Communist subversion of American ideals. In their local communities, these women investigated politicians, teachers, and school boards and focused attention on national political issues, including U.S. participation in the United Nations, which they viewed as undermining America's sovereignty and too sympathetic to communism. They promoted their ideas within the main-stream organizations to which they belonged, such as the PTA, and they red-baited liberal groups such as the AAUW and the YWCA. Women in these small radical groups networked with more moderate right-wing organizations such as the Daughters of the American Revolution (see Chapter 8) and helped to fuel and per-petuate the Red Scare. Even after the intensity of the Red Scare abated, women continued to be active in conservative anti-Communist groups and became im-portant contributors to the growth of the right wing within the Republican Party in ensuing decades (see Chapter 10).

On the other side of the political spectrum was a new entry in the long-standing female pacifist tradition. Women Strike for Peace (WSP) burst on the scene on November 1, 1961, a day on which over fifty thousand American women in at least forty communities joined in a one-day peace demonstration protesting the nuclear arms race and the Soviet Union's and the United States' proposed re-sumption of atmospheric testing of bombs after a three-year moratorium. In the next year, the WSP sponsored peace vigils, petition drives, forums, and letter-writing campaigns. Although the media often characterized WSP members as "simple housewives and mothers," many had a long history of activism. Some had connections to the Communist Party, and many had been active in the Committee for a Sane Nuclear Policy (SANE), an organization of men and women founded to challenge the proliferation of nuclear weaponry, which had been damaged by red-baiting. Other members had abandoned the Women's International League for Peace and Freedom (see Chapter 7), which they found too hierarchical in struc-ture to achieve its aims.

Despite WSP members' concerted efforts to present themselves just as con-cerned middle-class mothers, their peace activism drew the attention of HUAC, which summoned fourteen women to a congressional hearing in December 1962. As WSP women prepared to be grilled on their political affiliations and opinions, they determined that they would not give in to any HUAC demands that they identify Communists in the organization. When the committee called its first wit-ness, Blanche Posner, a volunteer in WSP's New York office, all the WSP women stood with her as a gesture of solidarity. Much to the consternation of the inter-rogators, they applauded witnesses' comments and seemed not so much defiant as slightly mocking. The women frequently suggested to their questioners that the "male mind" simply could not understand their refusal to have a structured or-ganization with clearly defined leaders and membership lists. They repeatedly in-voked their maternal role. As Posner put it, "I don't know, sir, why I am here, but I

◆ **Women Strike for Peace**

The anti-nuclear group Women Strike for Peace (WSP) began by literally striking—walking out of their kitchens and off their jobs. As the group's numbers swelled, women engaged in lobbying, petitioning, and picketing. This 1962 photo captures WSP members' attempt to stop atmospheric testing in Nevada. *Swarthmore College Peace Collection; photo by Harvey Richards.*

do know why you are here, because you don't quite understand the nature of this movement. This movement was inspired and motivated by mothers' love for their children. . . . When they were putting their breakfast on the table, they saw not only the Wheaties and milk, but they also saw [radioactive traces of] strontium 90 and iodine 131. . . . They feared for the health and life of their children. This is the only motivation."[16]

The women's conduct made the hearings a media embarrassment for HUAC. Major newspapers featured stories with such titles as "Peace Gals Make Red Hunters Look Silly" and "It's Ladies Day at Capitol: Hoots, Howls and Charm."[17] The hearings strengthened rather than crippled the WSP, and in the following year they claimed some credit for President John F. Kennedy's decision to agree to a limited test ban treaty with the Soviet Union. The organization went on to play an important role in the early years of the anti–Vietnam War movement, but its rhetoric of maternalism gradually subsided as WSP women felt the powerful influence of the younger activists of the women's liberation movement (see Chapter 10).

That a group with such radical political ideas could make use of a rhetoric that aligned so well with the feminine mystique sheds light on the complexity and contradictions of postwar female activism. Like other working- and middle-class women activists, WSP members wielded public influence and power but did not overtly challenge the primacy of women's domestic roles. The influence of the feminine mystique, coupled with the anti-Communist climate that stifled dissent, explains why women's activism was not accompanied by feminist questioning of women's unequal position in American society.

A MASS MOVEMENT FOR CIVIL RIGHTS

Women who supported the civil rights movement through their unions or through middle-class organizations like the YWCA were responding to one of the most potent movements for social change of the twentieth century, the civil rights campaign of the postwar years. Going against the tide of the era's political conservatism, black women and men fought against the system of white supremacy in the South. Joined by white liberals sympathetic to their cause, they achieved substantial gains but met with much frustration as well. Women were major activists in the civil rights movement of this period, although for both whites and blacks, women's rights took a back seat to the issue of race. Nonetheless, the civil rights movement proved a seedbed for the resurgence of feminism in the late 1960s.

As late as a week before the most famous public moment of the civil rights movement—the August 28, 1963, March on Washington, which attracted an unprecedented 200,000 black and white demonstrators—no woman had been invited to speak from the platform. At the last minute, Rosa Parks and a few other women were added to the program, but their participation was clearly an afterthought. The charismatic Martin Luther King Jr. overshadowed all other speakers, male and female, with his "I Have a Dream" speech. Historians have only recently begun to reconstruct women's substantial contributions to the postwar civil rights movement. Some were blue-collar unionists, others college and high school students; some were well-educated professionals, others illiterate sharecroppers. In their search for racial justice, they rarely focused on specific concerns of women, but their gender shaped the nature of the activism they engaged in—both creating opportunities and imposing limits—as they helped to forge the modern civil rights movement. (See Documents: Women in the Civil Rights Movement, pp. 613–21.)

Challenging Segregation

At first the movement focused specifically on the South, where widespread racial violence and economic exploitation left millions of African Americans economically, socially, and politically deprived. Racism, moreover, was institutionalized. Since the late nineteenth century, southern states enforced Jim Crow laws disfranchising virtually all African Americans and establishing a rigid system of segregation where everything from water fountains to public schools was designated either for "whites" or "colored." This legalized apartheid system, which denied blacks virtually any protection under the law, came under relentless attack in the postwar era.

World War II helped to set the stage for radical racial change. Continuing migration out of the South, new job opportunities, and military service gave black men and women heightened expectations. By successfully lobbying the federal government to establish the Fair Employment Practices Commission in 1941, African American leaders established a beachhead, albeit one with limited impact, in the struggle to force the national government to take responsibility for enforcing the Fourteenth and Fifteenth Amendments (see Chapter 8). And as more African Americans moved outside the South to regions where they could finally vote, they expanded their political base and gained influence with national politicians in both parties. This influence helped to bring about the racial desegregation of the army during the Korean War. The Cold War, too, created a new climate of opinion. The shocking inequities faced by African Americans became a common refrain in the Soviets' argument that American democracy was a sham.

In the immediate postwar period, national organizations, especially the NAACP and the Congress of Racial Equality (CORE, founded during World War II), battled disfranchisement and segregation, joined by unions such as the UPWA that worked to counter economic discrimination against black people. The postwar movement against segregation is usually dated from the all-important 1954 Supreme Court decision in *Brown v. Board of Education of Topeka,* a case brought by the NAACP on behalf of elementary school student Linda Brown and others. The *Brown* decision effectively overturned the 1896 decision *Plessy v. Ferguson,* which had legitimized the southern pretense of a "separate but equal" system of segregation (see Chapter 7). By ruling that segregated schools were inherently unequal and thus violated the Fourteenth Amendment, the decision infused African Americans with new hope, and their efforts to organize resistance to the southern racial system multiplied (see the Appendix, pp. A-28–A-29).

Thurgood Marshall, who later became the first black Supreme Court justice, led the NAACP team that won the *Brown* case. Constance Baker Motley, the first African American woman to be appointed to the federal judiciary (1966), was the only woman on the legal team. Black women were even more at the forefront of the many local struggles to compel school boards to comply with the Court's decision. Of all these confrontations, the one that drew the most national attention took place in Little Rock, Arkansas. There, in 1957, nine black students, six of them young women, registered to attend the strictly segregated Central High School. For their determination, the young people and their families were subjected to considerable violence. One of the young women, Melba Patillo, later recalled that she was threatened with sexual assault as she walked back from school but did not dare tell her parents for fear they would withdraw her from the desegregation effort. Arkansas governor Orval Faubus sent the state national guard to block the black students' entry. It was not until President Dwight D. Eisenhower, concerned about the defiance of federal law, sent U.S. troops to provide protection for the students that they were able to enter the school. Their victory, however, was only temporary. In the following year, Faubus closed the school system rather than integrate it, a tactic that was not checked by the federal courts for several years. Although parts of the Upper South did desegregate their school systems voluntarily, by 1964 only 2 percent of southern blacks attended integrated schools, a measure of the deep resistance *Brown* evoked among many southern whites.

Throughout the Little Rock students' ordeal, one local woman organized their efforts and provided much needed support. Daisy Bates was in many ways typical of black female activists throughout the twentieth century. A successful businesswoman and civic activist—she and her husband owned the local black newspaper, the *State Press*—Bates had long been active in the NAACP, serving as president of the Arkansas branch in 1953. While federal troops remained to guard the students throughout the school year, each day Bates ushered the students to their high school and provided crucial leadership to the black community.

Efforts to integrate higher education also were hard-fought battles in which women had high visibility. In 1956, Autherine Lucy became the first black student to be admitted to the University of Alabama, only to be expelled three days later "for her own protection" against relentless white brutality and official intransigence. Seven years later Vivian Malone, along with a black male student, succeeded in integrating that university. At the University of Georgia, Charlayne Hunter, later a nationally prominent television newswoman, broke the racial barrier of that state's higher education system in 1961.

A year after the *Brown* case, the Montgomery, Alabama, bus boycott became the second great watershed in invigorating the postwar civil rights movement. African Americans stayed off the buses of Montgomery for 381 days until the U.S. Supreme Court struck down the city's system of segregated public buses. The boycott had its origins on December 1, 1955, when Rosa Parks—whose historic action was described at the start of this chapter—refused to give up her seat in the front of the bus to a white passenger, a daily humiliation required of black bus riders. Parks was not simply a tired woman whose arrest unwittingly sparked a massive protest. She had been active in the local NAACP for fifteen years, and her decision to make this stand against segregation was part of a lifelong commitment to racial justice. For some time local NAACP leaders had wanted to find a good test case to challenge Montgomery's bus segregation in the courts. An earlier incident that involved a young, unmarried pregnant woman was deemed unacceptable. Parks, a respectable, hardworking, middle-aged woman, fit the bill perfectly.

On the night of Parks's arrest, a group working independently of the NAACP sprung into action. The Women's Political Caucus (WPC), consisting primarily of black professional women, had been founded in 1946 to focus on challenging disfranchisement and segregation in Montgomery. According to one member, well before Parks's arrest, "We had all the plans and we were just waiting for the right time."[18] WPC president Jo Ann Robinson utilized the organization's extensive network to duplicate and distribute flyers announcing a boycott. At a community meeting the evening after Parks's arrest, the boycott was formally organized and endorsed. Shortly afterwards a twenty-six-year-old minister newly arrived in town, Martin Luther King Jr., was selected to head up the newly created boycott agency, the Montgomery Improvement Association (MIA).

Men, particularly ministers, who traditionally were at the center of black southern leadership, predominated in the MIA, and women largely were excluded from formal leadership positions, an exclusion they rarely questioned. But women were nonetheless pivotal to the success of the boycott. Not only did they initiate the boycott itself, but they formed its backbone. Ever since 1884 when Ida B. Wells (see Chapter 5) had challenged her ejection from a Tennessee railroad car, black women had been in the forefront of battles to desegregate public transportation. It was women, much more than men, who depended on public transportation to travel long distances to their jobs as domestic servants in white households. During the Montgomery bus boycott, some were able to take advantage of a carpool system created by women activists, but most walked. In addition to their personal sacrifices, other women helped the boycott by raising funds and providing food for mass meetings. As one WPC leader put it, the "grassroots support" was "a hundred percent among the women."[19]

Women as "Bridge Leaders"

Montgomery women demonstrated a pattern repeated in other civil rights activities. Men monopolized the formal leadership roles and mediated among the community, the media, and government officials. Women were far more likely to have unofficial positions, yet they served vital functions in organizing and inspiring their local communities. One scholar terms this pattern "bridge leadership."[20] The role of bridge leader became increasingly significant as the struggle took on a new trajectory. While not neglecting the older methods of pursuing legal battles in the courts and lobbying legislators, the movement increasingly became a *mass* movement. In boycotts, sit-ins, demonstrations, and marches, women repeatedly served as bridge leaders.

Ella Baker exemplified the bridge leader. A well-educated southerner who migrated to New York in the 1920s, Baker became active in the NAACP, eventually becoming director of the branch offices. An extraordinary woman and gifted speaker, Baker was committed to bringing about social change by mobilizing grassroots resistance. In 1957 she began to work for the Southern Christian Leadership Conference (SCLC), an organization of black ministers under the direction of Martin Luther King Jr. The SCLC reluctantly appointed Baker an "acting" executive director until a suitable male executive could be found. She accepted the position but clearly chafed at the male-dominated leadership structure and hierarchical style. As she later put it, "I had known . . . that there would never be any role for me in a leadership capacity with SCLC. Why? First, I'm a woman. Also, I'm not a minister."[21]

Perhaps Baker's most lasting contribution was her central role in the establishment of the Student Nonviolent Coordinating Committee (SNCC, pronounced "snick"). SNCC had emerged from yet another kind of mass protest, the sit-in movement that started in 1960 in Greensboro, North Carolina, when four male students took seats at the "whites only" lunch counter at the local Woolworth's store, determined to "sit in" until they were served. Their protest eventually drew in hundreds of students, women and men, blacks and whites. Their goal

ELLA BAKER
Bigger Than a Hamburger

Ella Baker (1903–1986), one of the most influential activists in the civil rights movement, served a particularly important role in advising Student Nonviolent Coordinating Committee members. In this 1960 article, she describes their goals.

The Student Leadership Conference made it crystal clear that current sit-ins and other demonstrations are concerned with something much bigger than a hamburger or even a giant-sized Coke.

Whatever may be the difference in approach to their goal, the Negro and white students, North and South, are seeking to rid America of the scourge of racial segregation and discrimination—not only at lunch counters, but in every aspect of life.

In reports, casual conversations, discussion groups, and speeches, the sense and the spirit of the following statement that appeared in the initial newsletter of the students at Barber-Scotia College, Concord, N.C., were re-echoed time and again: "We want the world to know that we no longer accept the inferior position of second-class citizenship. We are willing to go to jail, be ridiculed, spat upon and even suffer physical violence to obtain First Class Citizenship."

By and large, this feeling that they have a destined date with freedom, was not limited to a drive for personal freedom, or even freedom for the Negro in the South. Repeatedly it was emphasized that the movement

was both economic disruption and publicity for the movement. They showcased the tactics of nonviolent resistance, a doctrine popularized by King but originating with the Indian nationalist leader Mahatma Gandhi. Students stoically withstood taunts and physical abuse in a steadfast determination to overcome oppression. The successful Greensboro sit-in sparked a wave of sit-ins in fifty-four cities that helped to desegregate many public facilities in the Upper South. The Deep South, however, especially Alabama and Mississippi, remained resistant.

In her role as SCLC acting director, Baker convened a meeting of over three hundred college students to help form an organization to orchestrate their future efforts. Following Baker's precept that strong leaders were not necessary for a strong movement, SNCC emerged as a nonhierarchical organization, with rotating officers. Although women were active in all the civil rights organizations, SNCC gave women the greatest opportunity to participate and influence the civil rights movement (see box, "Bigger Than a Hamburger").

concerned with the moral implications of racial discrimination for the "whole world" and the "Human Race."

This universality of approach was linked with a perceptive recognition that "it is important to keep the movement democratic and to avoid struggles for personal leadership."

It was further evident that desire for supportive cooperation from adult leaders and the adult community was also tempered by apprehension that adults might try to "capture" the student movement. The students showed willingness to be met on the basis of equality, but were intolerant of anything that smacked of manipulation or domination.

This inclination toward group-centered leadership, rather than toward a leader-centered group pattern of organization, was refreshing indeed to those of the older group who bear the scars of the battle, the frustrations and the disillusionment that come when the prophetic leader turns out to have heavy feet of clay.

However hopeful might be the signs in the direction of group-centeredness, the fact that many schools and communities, especially in the South, have not provided adequate experience for young Negroes to assume initiative and think and act independently accentuated the need for guarding the student movement against well-meaning, but nevertheless unhealthy, over-protectiveness.

Here is an opportunity for adult and youth to work together and provide genuine leadership—the development of the individual to his highest potential for the benefit of the group. . . .

SOURCE: "Bigger Than a Hamburger," *Southern Patriot*, June 1960, p. 4.

SNCC men and women participated in the Freedom Rides of 1961, which CORE organized to challenge segregated interstate bus travel and bus terminals in the South. On May 14, 1961, a group consisting of black and white men and women boarded a bus in Washington, D.C., headed to New Orleans. In Anniston and Birmingham, Alabama, the activists encountered vicious mob violence. A pivotal bridge leader in the Freedom Rides was Diane Nash, a young black SNCC activist, who had earlier led the Nashville sit-ins. (See Documents: Women in the Civil Rights Movement, pp. 613–21.) After the violence in Birmingham, some SCLC leaders called for an end to the rides, but Nash interceded, insisting that "if they stop us with violence, the movement is dead."[22] The rides continued. The unwillingness of Alabama's officials to protect the freedom riders eventually led President John F. Kennedy to send federal marshals to Alabama to protect them. He later ordered the Interstate Commerce Commission to enforce desegregation on interstate bus routes. Even though they never made it to New Orleans, the riders had succeeded in integrating interstate bus travel.

Voter Registration and Freedom Summer

Women activists like Nash faced violence, harassment, and degrading jail conditions. By far the most challenging—and dangerous—activities were the voter organizing drives that took place deep in the rural South. In 1960 SNCC had begun a voter registration drive in Mississippi where, although African Americans represented 45 percent of the population, only 5 percent of black adults were registered to vote. In 1962, registration efforts heated up after SCLC, SNCC, NAACP, and CORE established the Council of Federated Organizations (COFO) to oversee voting registration drives in Mississippi.

As they struggled to overcome the reluctance of local blacks to risk their livelihood or personal safety to register to vote, the activists also encountered stiff resistance from local whites. Viewed as outside agitators, they experienced harassment, intimidation, and deadly violence. But they were usually able to rely on a small number of local community leaders—often women—who provided shelter, moral support, and valuable personal contacts, at great personal risk to themselves. (See Documents: Women in the Civil Rights Movement, pp. 613–21.)

The most famous of these local leaders was Fannie Lou Hamer of Sunflower County, Mississippi. Hamer worked on a large cotton plantation. There, despite only a sixth-grade education, her natural capacities as a leader eventually elevated her to a position as a kind of forewoman for her boss and an influential person in the local black community. Motivated by the desire to make blacks full citizens, Hamer joined SNCC and, after a year of effort, finally registered to vote in 1963. "We just got to stand up now as Negroes for ourselves and for our freedom," she insisted, "and if it don't do me any good, I do know the young people it will do good."[23] Despite the loss of her job and threats to her life, she became an organizer and spokeswoman for the Mississippi voter registration effort. She was renowned for her outspoken and charismatic style and for her passion and skill as a politically inspirational singer. Hamer was an exemplar of the rural black southern women who were pillars of the southern civil rights movement. But appreciation for their strength must not obscure the considerable personal sacrifices these women endured. Until she died in 1977, Hamer suffered both physically and emotionally from the ramifications of a brutal 1963 beating she received as punishment for her commitment to voting rights for blacks.

Despite such heroism, southern black voter registration was stalled by fear, violence, and the determined resistance of white political leaders. In the spring of 1964, COFO devised a plan to import one thousand volunteers from outside the South, primarily white students, to register black voters in the Deep South. Freedom Summer, as the plan was called, was meant not only to infuse new energy into the voter registration drive but to use these white students to focus media and federal attention on southern recalcitrance. Trained in nonviolent resistance and warned about the dangers involved, the first volunteers arrived in June 1964.

Violence shadowed Freedom Summer. Four volunteers were killed, eighty beaten, and more than a thousand arrested. Thirty-seven churches were bombed and burned.

The recruitment of white northern students created tension within the movement. Some of these highly educated whites tried to assume leadership positions and had to be reminded that they had come to help, not to take charge. The presence of white women raised particular issues. A handful of southern white women had been active in the civil rights movement from the very beginning, including older women like Virginia Foster Durr and Anne Braden, who had a lifelong commitment to challenging segregation, and younger activists like Joan Browning, who was a freedom rider, and Casey Hayden, who was an early member of SNCC. (See Documents: Women in the Civil Rights Movement, pp. 613–21.) During Freedom Summer, however, the number of white women, estimated at somewhere between one-third and one-half of the volunteers, increased dramatically. Any sort of closeness or intimacy between black men and white women constituted a highly charged trigger for white racists' anger. Both white women and black men had their own reasons for engaging in these flirtations and sexual liaisons, but black women deeply resented them, and they contributed to racial divisions in the early years of the women's liberation movement (see Chapter 10).

The climax of southern voter registration efforts and Freedom Summer was a bold challenge to the lily-white Mississippi Democratic Party. Encouraged by, among others, Ella Baker, Mississippi black voters organized a delegation of the Mississippi Freedom Democratic Party to attend the Democratic National Convention in Atlantic City in August 1964. They demanded that they replace the all-white regular state group as the Mississippi delegation. Hamer testified about the violence and beatings she suffered in order to register to vote. Despite the extraordinary power of her story, the party leadership, including President Lyndon Johnson and Vice President Hubert Humphrey, with the tacit approval of more moderate black leaders, chose to seat the all-white delegation and to offer the civil rights alternative a mere two "at-large" seats (seats that did not represent a specific district). The Mississippi Freedom Party rejected this proposal as a compromise that did not address the illegality of Mississippi's systematic denial of blacks' access to the political process. Hamer, deeply disillusioned, returned to Mississippi, where she nonetheless continued her activism on behalf of southern black economic and political empowerment. But the civil rights movement as a whole never recovered its optimism after the disappointment in Atlantic City.

Sexism in the Movement

When Hamer returned home in the fall of 1964, SNCC was faltering, beset by a wide range of tensions, including the influx of new white members who had stayed on after Freedom Summer and questions about the viability of nonviolent resistance in the face of relentless persecution. A discussion paper written by Casey Hayden and Mary King, two longtime, highly respected white members of SNCC, drew parallels between the subordination of blacks and the subordination of

◆ **Fannie Lou Hamer**

Fannie Lou Hamer, one of the most charismatic civil rights figures, was active in SNCC in Mississippi and came to national attention as a delegate of the Mississippi Freedom Democratic Party to the 1964 Democratic National Convention in Atlantic City. Under pressure from President Johnson, the networks cut off live coverage of Hamer's passionate speech, in which she asked "Is this America?," but it later made network news. *Matt Herron.*

women in society. Hayden and King criticized SNCC for not "recognizing that women are the crucial factor that keeps the movement running on a day-to-day basis [or giving women] equal say-so when it comes to day-to-day decision making."[24] The paper received virtually no attention at the time, but historians now regard it as an important document linking women's participation in the civil rights movement to the women's liberation movement of the late 1960s (see box, "Women in the Movement").

Was SNCC sexist? Were women relegated to minor positions and not taken seriously by male leaders? Many black women had established themselves as a powerful presence in SNCC, but white women, especially the new student volunteers, were viewed, and usually viewed themselves, as playing supportive roles. In retrospect it seems that males monopolized formal leadership positions, but few women now claim that they experienced any resentment at the time. For black women, race was of utmost importance, and few acted in the context of bettering the position of black women specifically. Even those white women who criticized male domination of the movement remember above all that participating in the civil rights movement proved personally and politically liberating. As Harriet Tanzman, a University of Wisconsin student who first went south during Freedom Summer, explained, "I was able to do things I never knew I could do. I mean it took the best of us, the movement, whether we were eighteen or twenty-five. It empowered our lives."[25]

In numerous ways, the civil rights movement was fundamental in helping to revive the feminist movement. It gave middle-class white women exposure to role models of female public activism and leadership, like Ella Baker and Fannie Lou Hamer, and opportunities to envision themselves operating outside the rigid gender norms of middle-class culture. What might be called implicit feminist impulses underlay their willingness to undertake the risks of civil rights activism. Rita Schwerner Bender (the wife of Mickey Schwerner, one of four activists killed during Freedom Summer) was a member of CORE in Brooklyn before heading to Mississippi in 1964. In 1994, she recalled her decision to join the movement. "I did not see myself as saving anyone, but I did have a view of saving myself from a split-level house."[26] The empowerment that Tanzman and other women described later led many to challenge the patriarchal nature of their society.

Tensions within SNCC exacerbated by Freedom Summer and its aftermath were part of a larger change in the direction of the civil rights movement. The Atlantic City disappointment exposed the degree to which the Kennedy administration temporized about protecting African Americans' constitutional rights. Repeatedly, as activists faced violence and intimidation, the Justice Department intervened only when forced by massive media exposure of violence against peaceful demonstrators. Despite years of agitation, Congress resisted passing a Civil Rights Act until 1964, when President Lyndon Johnson pushed it through as a homage to the assassinated John F. Kennedy. Brutality to demonstrators in Selma, Alabama, was followed by congressional passage of the Voting Rights Act of 1965, which threw out the literacy tests used to keep blacks out of southern Democratic parties and authorized the U.S. Attorney General to intervene in counties where less than 50 percent of the black voting-age population was registered. But for many young blacks, this was too little too late. Breaking from more moderate leaders like Martin Luther King Jr., in the late 1960s militant blacks turned from the goal of integration to "black power," an explicitly male-dominated phase of the civil rights movement. Rejecting the "beloved community" of black/white unity in the first, heady days of civil rights radicalism, SNCC demanded that whites leave the organization to be run entirely by blacks for goals of their own choosing (see Chapter 10).

A Widening Circle of Civil Rights Activists

As African Americans mounted their civil rights struggle, another minority group, Mexican Americans, intensified its drive to fight prejudice and attain legitimacy in American society. Here, too, women made significant contributions that have been obscured by the attention given to male leaders.

After World War II, Mexican Americans in Texas, California, and some states in the Midwest sought to improve their communities, increase their political influ-

CASEY HAYDEN AND MARY KING
Women in the Movement

Casey Hayden (b. 1939) and Mary King (b. 1940) anonymously distributed this "Position Paper: Nov. 1964" during a SNCC retreat in Waveland, Mississippi. Their list of concerns symbolizes the close connection between young white women's civil rights activism and the emergence of the women's liberation movement later in the decade.

Staff was involved in crucial [SNCC] constitutional revisions at the Atlanta staff meeting in October. A large committee was appointed to present revisions to the staff. The committee was all men.

Two organizers were working together to form a farmers league. Without asking any questions, the male organizer immediately assigned the clerical work to the female organizer although both had had equal experience in organizing campaigns.

Although there are some women in Mississippi projects who have been working as long as some of the men, the leadership group in COFO is all men.

A woman in a field office wondered why she was held responsible for day-to-day decisions, only to find out later that she had been appointed project director but not told.

A fall 1964 personnel and resources report on Mississippi projects lists the number of people on each project. The section on Laurel, however, lists not the number of persons, but "three girls."

One of SNCC's main administrative officers apologizes for appointment of a woman as interim project director in a key Mississippi project area. . . .

Any woman in SNCC, no matter what her position or experience, has been asked to take minutes in a meeting when she and other women are outnumbered by men.

The names of several new attorneys entering a state project this past summer were posted in a central movement office. The first initial and last name of each lawyer was listed. Next to one name was written: (girl)

ence, and challenge de facto segregation and economic and educational discrimination. One of the most dynamic organizations of the period was the Community Service Organization (CSO), which was founded in 1947 and based primarily in California. The CSO had wide-ranging goals of fostering civil rights, improving health care and living conditions, and developing leadership skills in urban Mexican communities. Historians estimate that close to half of its membership was fe-

Capable, responsible, and experienced women who are in leadership positions can expect to have to defer to a man on their project for final decision-making.

A session at the recent October staff meeting in Atlanta was the first large meeting in the past couple of years where a woman was asked to chair.

Undoubtedly this list will seem strange to some, petty to others, laughable to most. The list could continue as far as there are women in the movement. Except that most women don't talk about these kinds of incidents, because the whole subject is [not] discussible—strange to some, petty to others, laughable to most. The average white person finds it difficult to understand why the Negro resents being called "boy," or being thought of as "musical" and "athletic," because the average white person doesn't realize that *he assumes he is superior*. And naturally he doesn't understand the problem of paternalism. So too the average SNCC worker finds it difficult to discuss the woman problem because of the assumptions of male superiority. Assumptions of male superiority are as widespread and deep rooted and every much as crippling to the woman as the assumptions of white supremacy are to the Negro. Consider why it is in SNCC that women who are competent, qualified, and experienced, are automatically assigned to the "female" kinds of jobs such as typing, desk work, telephone work, filing, library work, cooking, and the assistant kind of administrative work but rarely the "executive" kind. . . .

This paper is presented anyway because it needs to be made know[n] that many women in the movement are not "happy and contented" with their status. . . . What can be done? Probably nothing right away. . . . [But] maybe sometime in the future the whole of the women in this movement will become so alert as to force the rest of the movement to stop the discrimination and start the slow process of changing values and ideas so that all of us gradually come to understand that this is no more a man's world than it is a white world.

November, 1964

SOURCE: Alexander Bloom and Wini Breines, eds., *"Takin' It to the Streets": A Sixties Reader* (New York: Oxford University Press, 1995), 45–47.

male, most of whom participated with their husbands. Men dominated the formal leadership positions, while women played subordinate but nonetheless vital roles, including most of the clerical work. Helen Chávez, wife of César Chávez, who became the most significant Chicano activist of his time, recalled that daily she recorded in longhand her husband's dictated reports and that for meetings, "I would address all the envelopes and address the postcards."[27] Women also turned their energies to citizenship education programs, voter registration drives, and fund-raising. In the latter, their efforts reflected the gendered nature of their activism. They often raised money through sales of items such as Mexican *tamales* or *pan dulce* (sweet rolls). The CSO *Reporter* described another quintessential 1950s social gathering that these Mexican American women adapted to their cause: "A series of Tupper Ware parties with a percentage of sales given to CSO are being conducted under the able leadership of Ursula Gutierrez."[28]

Some Mexican women worked outside these patterns of gendered activism. Dolores Huerta began her career doing volunteer work for the Mexican American community, but later served as a paid lobbyist for CSO and, in 1962, cofounded the United Farm Workers with César Chávez. Another prominent woman, Hope Mendoza, had been active in the International Ladies' Garment Workers Union and, like women in the UE and UPWA, was militant in her defense of women workers. Chairing CSO's labor relations committee, she brought her labor expertise and extensive contacts to the CSO's efforts to support Mexican American workers. Among other things, she educated workers to the value of unions, raised funds, and interviewed politicians seeking the CSO's endorsement. Mendoza's high-profile activities were exceptional, but many other women in the CSO shared her union experience. Although most women in the organization stayed within traditional female boundaries, many more women followed the more assertive paths of Huerta and Mendoza in the late 1960s and 1970s as the Chicano movement for Mexican American empowerment gathered force.

◆ **Dolores Huerta**

Dolores Huerta is most famous for her role as cofounder with César Chávez of the United Farm Workers in 1962. Huerta played a leading role in organizing workers and negotiating contracts. In the late 1960s, she spearheaded a national boycott of grapes that forced growers to sign a contract with the union. Here she is shown in 1970 speaking to farm workers in Salinas, California. *Walter P. Reuther Library, Wayne State University.*

WOMEN AND PUBLIC POLICY

While the civil rights movement forged ahead, encouraging many young women to begin to question the cultural assumptions that reinforced women's subordination, other women focused on public policy issues, especially discrimination in the workforce. The creation of the President's Commission on the Status of Women in 1961 proved a turning point. It not only focused renewed attention on the problems working women faced, but it also helped to create a network of women activists who eventually helped form the National Organization for Women, a linchpin for what came to be called "second wave" feminism.°

The Continuing Battle over the ERA

The community of women interested in promoting women's legal rights and economic opportunities faced many obstacles in the years following World War II. With the feminine mystique holding sway over much of American culture and the Red Scare promoting conformity, the social and political climate hampered serious questioning of women's roles. Nonetheless, professional lobbyists for organizations like the YWCA, the AAUW, and the National Federation of Business and Professional Women (BPW) formed a female network attentive to policy developments in Washington that kept alive concerns over women's rights. Throughout the late 1940s and 1950s, however, these women were divided by the long-standing debate over the Equal Rights Amendment (ERA). Their division on this issue discouraged fresh approaches to questions concerning women's growing, yet fundamentally unequal, participation in the workforce.

The battle lines were similar to those of the 1920s, when the ERA was first introduced (see Chapter 8). The National Woman's Party, with strong support from career women in the BPW, argued for the amendment as a device that would strike down all manner of laws and policies that fettered women's rights as free and equal individuals. Opposing the ERA were most of the staff of the federal Women's Bureau and the women's organizations traditionally allied with it, such as the League of Women Voters and the YWCA. Women labor union leaders formed a particularly adamant group in opposition to the ERA.

All of these opponents believed that the ERA endangered protective labor legislation, which ever since its inception in the Progressive era had emphasized women's distinctiveness, especially in their maternal function (see Chapter 7). By the 1950s, Women's Bureau leaders had retreated somewhat from their emphasis on promoting more protective legislation in the various states and had moved toward fostering equal pay laws and challenging some discriminatory policies. They no longer had to defend special minimum wage and maximum hour laws for women since the Fair Labor Standards Act of 1938 had extended these protections

---

° "Second wave" to distinguish this era of women's rights activism from the "first wave," beginning in 1848 with the Seneca Falls Declaration of Sentiments and ending in 1920 with ratification of the Nineteenth Amendment.

to men. Under the Republican administration of Dwight D. Eisenhower, Republican politicians joined with anti-union conservative business interests to support the ERA because they viewed protective labor legislation as an intrusion of the government into the labor market. Alice Leopold, appointed by Eisenhower as the new head of the Women's Bureau, was a supporter of the amendment. Nonetheless, Women's Bureau staffers and their traditional allies continued to condemn the ERA, their commitment heightened by the anti-union climate of the 1950s and by the affiliation of some with the Democratic Party, which remained resolutely anti-ERA.

A Turning Point: The President's Commission on the Status of Women

It was in part to deflect attention away from the ERA that Esther Peterson, who became head of the Women's Bureau in 1961, proposed a commission on the status of women. Appointed by liberal Democrat John F. Kennedy, Peterson had strong union ties and enthusiastically supported the new president's program for revived activism on the part of the federal government, especially on behalf of disadvantaged Americans. Kennedy pledged to get the "country moving again" with a "New Frontier" to continue the liberal reforms started by Franklin Roosevelt's Depression-era New Deal. Peterson prevailed on Kennedy to establish the President's Commission on the Status of Women (PCSW) in late 1961, with the hope that it would particularly advance the cause of working women.

Eleven men and fifteen women drawn from leaders in women's organizations, unions, business, education, and politics comprised the PCSW, which was chaired by former first lady Eleanor Roosevelt. Supplementing the commission were dozens of subcommittees that brought many women activists into the process of research and deliberation on issues ranging from inequities in wage rates and limited job opportunities to the particular problems of poor black women and of working mothers. As activists like Peterson pushed an agenda to assist working women, many members of the commission worried lest their efforts be interpreted as undermining women's maternal roles by encouraging them to work. Indeed, the executive order creating the commission revealed the contradictions implicit in its task. The commission was responsible for "developing recommendations for overcoming discriminations in government and private employment on the basis of sex and for developing recommendations for services which will enable women to continue their roles as wives and mothers while making a maximum contribution to the world around them."[29]

Not surprisingly, the PCSW's final report, published in 1963, outlined moderate proposals for the most part. It recommended child care tax benefits for lower income working mothers and improved maternity benefits. It called for state and federal governments to promote women's education and job training and endorsed equal pay for equal work. The PCSW recommended an executive order to require private employers to give women "equal opportunities," a strikingly vague mandate already established for federal employment. It proposed expanding provisions of existing legislation to improve women's social security benefits and bring more women under the coverage of the Fair Labor Standards Act of 1938, a change that would particularly benefit poor black and Chicana women. In keeping with the Women's Bureau's long-standing commitment to protective legislation, it endorsed a limit of a forty-hour work week for women, with overtime pay beyond forty hours. The PCSW also addressed the need for states to repeal outdated laws that limited the rights of women to serve on juries or control their own property.

The commission did not endorse the ERA but offered as an alternative a recommendation that the Fourteenth Amendment (see the Appendix, p. A-14) be understood as protecting women's equal rights. Pauli Murray, an African American civil rights attorney who served on the Subcommittee on Political and Civil Rights and had long been active in promoting black and women's rights, formulated this argument for the PCSW, explicitly drawing a connection between the discrimination women faced and the civil rights movement, claiming that "arbitrary discrimination against women violated the Fourteenth Amendment in the same way racial bias did."[30] Despite Murray's insightful analysis, the commission omitted any discussion of a race-gender analogy—presumably because it was too controversial—and simply urged the Supreme Court to legitimate the Fourteenth Amendment's applicability to women, which it did within the decade (see Chapter 10).

One legacy of the PCSW was passage of federal "equal work for equal pay" legislation. The Women's Bureau had supported such legislation for over a decade but had met with opposition both from the National Woman's Party because of its single-minded focus on the ERA and from business interests worried about labor costs. But in the context of the Kennedy administration's sympathy to organized labor and a strong endorsement by the PCSW report, Congress passed the Equal Pay Act in 1963. The act offered significantly less than the Women's Bureau or its female union supporters had hoped for. It rejected the concept of equal pay for comparable work, substituting instead the proviso that women working in identical jobs with men—a relatively small class of workers—must be paid equally. The act also limited its applicability to those occupations already covered by the 1938 Fair Labor Standards Act, a measure that failed to include women's jobs in the agricultural and domestic service sectors. Despite its limits, the Equal Pay Act resulted in concrete gains for some women and at least theoretically committed the federal government to the recognition that women's labor had equal value to men's.

Still, few concrete results followed the commission's recommendations. Its importance was in the way in which it focused attention, however ambivalently, on the varied discriminations that women faced. It was instrumental in encouraging many activists to retreat from an interpretation that emphasized sexual difference and the need for laws to protect women toward an approach that favored equal rights and promoted the government's role in challenging discrimination against women. Equally significant was that not only did the PCSW's deliberations encourage a network of women activists interested in promoting women's rights, but it also spawned dozens of state commissions on the status of women, which in turn created a community of women throughout the country addressing similar concerns. As Pauli Murray explained, "Like-minded women found one another,

◆ **Pauli Murray and Esther Peterson, November 1963**
Both Pauli Murray (left) and Esther Peterson (right) were pivotal figures for the 1961 PCSW. Peterson, as head of the Women's Bureau, convinced President Kennedy to convene the commission and helped to shape its deliberations. Murray served on the Subcommittee on Political and Civil Rights and constructed an innovative argument for using the Fourteenth Amendment to guarantee women's equal rights. Providence Journal *photograph.*

bonds developed through working together, and an informal feminist network emerged to act as leaven in the broader movement that followed."[31]

Toward a Feminist Revival

That "feminist network" was encouraged by a dramatic legislative milestone: the passage of the Civil Rights Act of 1964. Pressure from the civil rights movement had led to a call for an omnibus federal act forbidding discrimination on the grounds of race. While Congress was debating the legislation, members of the National Woman's Party encouraged U.S. Representative from Virginia Howard Smith, a supporter of the ERA, to propose an amendment to the bill that would extend federal civil rights protection to women. Smith did so, in large measure because as a white southerner he opposed the Civil Rights Act and thought the inclusion of sex would undermine support for the legislation. Once the bill was introduced in the House, however, the few women congressional representatives, notably Martha Griffiths of Michigan, backed it, with support from many women activists such as Pauli Murray, who saw the amendment as a way of fighting both "Jim Crow" and "Jane Crow."

The Women's Bureau staff initially withheld support for the amendment because they feared that if the act applied to women it would undermine state protective legislation, but also because they worried it would damage the African American cause, which they viewed as the more serious form of discrimination. Once the measure went to the Senate, however, President Johnson backed the amendment to assure the entire bill's swift passage, and Peterson and Women's Bureau allies came on board. Title VII of the Civil Rights Act of 1964, which prohibits employment discrimination based on race, sex, national origin, or religion, became law.

The Equal Employment Opportunity Commission (EEOC), the agency established to implement Title VII, estimated that in the first year of its operation, grievances about sex discrimination constituted 37 percent of its complaints. Women, many of them rank-and-file union members, complained about unequal benefits and pay, discrimination in hiring and firing, restrictive state protective legislation, and separate union seniority lists. The commission, however, concentrated on racial discrimination and gave little priority to women's complaints, making the EEOC an ineffective tool to counter sexual discrimination in the workplace.

Discontent with the failures of the EEOC erupted in the 1966 Third Annual Conference on the Status of Women. By then, a groundswell of women, forged by the PCSW and the state commissions, had emerged who were insisting on women's equal rights. Their consciousness had also been raised by the 1963 publication of Betty Friedan's *The Feminine Mystique.* Their frustrations were compounded because the sponsor of the conference, the Women's Bureau, continued its traditional support for protective legislation, measures that were increasingly disadvantageous or irrelevant to women's work lives. The bureau blocked efforts to use the conference as a forum to mount an attack on the EEOC. As a result, a group of sixteen women had an impromptu meeting to create an outside pressure group, which they modeled on the NAACP, and the National Organization for Women (NOW) was founded. At the time, they could hardly have predicted that their actions would help create the "second wave" of American feminism (see Chapter 10).

The original sixteen, as well as the larger group that formed the first board of NOW, represented a fairly diverse set of people. One man, former EEOC commissioner Richard Graham, participated; the rest were women. Some, like Pauli Murray, had been active in the civil rights movement. Others, like Caroline Davis and Dorothy Haener, were union leaders. Aileen Hernandez, a black woman and former EEOC member, had also come from the ranks of labor. Catherine East was on the Women's Bureau staff, and Martha Griffiths was a congresswoman. Friedan, who became the first president of NOW, had been invited to the conference by women she called "Washington's Feminist Underground."

The women who organized NOW built on the foundations established by the women activists who during the doldrums of feminism had participated in unions, government agencies, and civic associations. NOW soon took women in new directions by demanding "action to bring American women into full participation in the mainstream of American society now."[32] But, as Chapter 10 reveals, even as NOW was being formed, changes in the political, social, and cultural environment would give new meaning to those words and lead the organization—and feminism—in directions that even its founders had not been able to imagine.

CONCLUSION: The Limits of the Feminine Mystique

American women in the postwar era lived in conservative times. Cold War fears stifled dissent, labeled labor unions and civil rights activity "subversive," and contained women and men in rigid gender roles to maintain family and social order. Certainly many women's lives were limited by this dominant ideology, yet women's lives were more diverse and complex than mainstream cultural prescriptions indicate. Women's place might have been in the home, but it was also in the workforce, as both public officials and employers eagerly sought to fuel American productivity and achieve the upper hand in the Cold War. Women may have been shunted into sex-segregated jobs, but participation in the workforce and the discrimination experienced there would have long-term implications for their consciousness.

Other signs that women's roles were not as constrained as popular images of the era suggest are evident in women's central role as bridge leaders in the burgeoning civil rights movement, as well as the persistent efforts of working-class union women to fight for fair treatment on the job. Middle-class women, too, in a wide range of voluntary associations and political activity represented women's desire to engage as citizens in the world outside their homes. These different forms of activism, combined with initiatives from the federal government's Women's Bureau, especially the President's Commission on the Status of Women, helped lay the groundwork for the resurgence of feminism in the late 1960s that would have a powerful impact on many women's domestic and public lives.

Television's Prescriptions for Women

Thanks to cable networks like Nickelodeon and TV Land, viewers today have access to some well-known 1950s television programs and commercials. Some critics explain the popularity of these shows and advertisements by suggesting that they are camp entertainment for some present-day viewers, amusing in their outdated, unintended humor, but that for others they evoke a nostalgic sense of simpler, more innocent times. Historians who study 1950s television delve more deeply into the medium and its message and, as with any other historical source, examine both the televised images and the assumptions of the people who created programming and advertising. This essay explores women and television in the 1950s by looking first at the way in which television programming and advertising targeted and understood the female viewer and second at the images of women conveyed in the decade's situation comedies. While advertising tended to reinforce key aspects of the feminine mystique, especially a relentless depiction of white middle-class women's role in the home, situation comedies of the 1950s displayed a more diverse and complex rendering of women and their families.

Television was a novelty until after World War II. Some national programming began to appear in 1947, and then during the years 1948–1950, the new medium took off: by 1951 there were 107 stations in 52 cities. Rising prosperity and a burgeoning consumer culture facilitated Americans' eager embrace of TV. By 1955, 65 percent of the nation's households had televisions, and by 1960 that figure had grown to 90 percent. National networks dominated television from the medium's inception, and network executives, along with their programs' sponsors, viewed television's purpose as the selling of products. This commercial motivation encouraged the networks to promote television as family entertainment and in the process to reinforce conventional notions of women's roles as housewives and mothers.

Many observers in the postwar years argued that television viewing would bring families together, thus stabilizing the home. Women's magazines ran articles discussing how women might integrate the "box" into their homes. While some authors addressed decorating problems that arose in making room for a large appliance, others explored the placement of the television in the context of family leisure-time patterns. They noted that the TV set was quickly displacing the piano as a source of family entertainment and that it was usurping the role of the fireplace as the focal point for social interaction. The TV had become, many argued, an electric hearth, the heart of family "togetherness."

ADVERTISEMENTS

This sense of the television appeared in many advertisements for television sets. Figure 9.1 depicts a comfortable middle-class home with an elegant TV as part of its attractive furniture. The family clusters around the Motorola TV in a semicircle, watching a program designed for family viewing, the variety show starring singer

◆ **Figure 9.1**
Advertisement for Motorola Television, 1951
Gaslight Advertising Archives, Inc.

What **Motorola TV** means to *your* family!

to Mom
it means beauty for her home with Fashion Award cabinet designs . . . and entertainment all day long!

to Dad
it means relaxation after work . . . his favorite sports, the news, variety shows . . . low cost fun at home.

to the Kids
it means a new world of magic and fun-filled education . . . with 2 simple controls they can operate themselves.

to the Older Folks
it means hours of happiness . . . without leaving home . . . in big, clear, easy-to-see pictures.

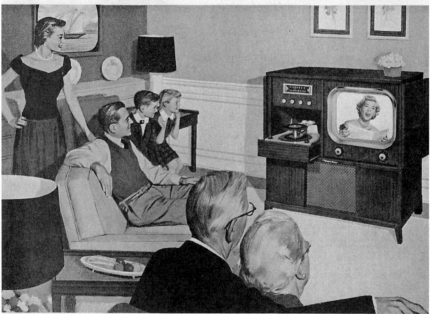

MODEL 20F2 COMBINATION IN MAHOGANY 20 INCH SCREEN

ONLY MOTOROLA GIVES YOU THESE EXCLUSIVE FEATURES . . . IN FASHION AWARD CABINETS!

GLARE GUARD
THE CURVED ANTI-REFLECTION SCREEN

NEWEST TV IMPROVEMENT. The *curved* surface of the Motorola Glare-Guard screen directs reflections *down*—out of the viewer's eyes . . . cuts annoying room-light reflection glare for new tele-viewing enjoyment.

TWO SIMPLE CONTROLS. Sharp, steady pictures with just two simple controls. Turn it on . . . select your station . . . that's all! Built-in-Antenna. Rectangular black picture tubes.

THREE-SPEED RECORD CHANGER. Automatically plays all size 78, 45 and 33⅓ rpm speed records without complicated adjustments. Single, feather-light tone arm, permanent needle.

"GOLDEN VOICE" AM AND FM RADIO. New "Music Lover" sound system faithfully brings you true pitch and tone in both musical and voice reproduction, from lowest bass to highest treble.

LONG LIFE "DEPENDA-BILT" CHASSIS. Factory tested . . . we play it before we ship it . . . to make sure that it brings you long, reliable TV reception. It's built to perform better . . . longer!

SEE YOUR CLASSIFIED DIRECTORY FOR THE NAME OF YOUR NEAREST MOTOROLA DEALER • *Specifications subject to change without notice.*

Dinah Shore (who was the television spokeswoman for Chevrolet cars), suggesting another element of the flourishing consumer market of the period. That the mother alone is standing is typical of many depictions of television viewers. Why do you think advertisers chose to show the mother standing? What does the posture and position of the woman in Figure 9.1 suggest about her role in the family? How does the text above the image reinforce the television's familial function?

Although the television industry generally assumed that its family audience was white and largely middle class, manufacturers did aggressively market television sets to African Americans and routinely ran ads in *Ebony*, a popular black magazine founded in 1942. Blacks were negatively stereotyped in television programming (as shown in Figures 9.7 and 9.8), but they were interested in buying sets, perhaps because they could enjoy entertainment in their homes rather than suffer the indignity of segregation in public venues. Some ads were identical to those that appeared in white mainstream periodicals, such as a May 1953 advertisement in *Ebony* that featured glamorous white brides framed by an Admiral TV set, with text noting that a television made a "memorable wedding gift."

Other advertisers attempted to adapt to their black audience. Figure 9.2 is an example of one of a number of 1953 RCA Victor advertisements that featured African Americans watching television. Another ad in this series depicts, yet again, the Dinah Shore television show, but this one displays black singer Eartha Kitt, a frequent performer on network variety shows. Notice that the woman is once again standing, this time in the effort to help her husband select a station, now

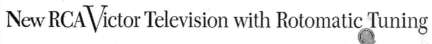

New RCA Victor Television with Rotomatic Tuning

brings you more to see — less to do

More detail—a stronger, sharper picture wherever you live. ROTOMATIC *gets* it, MAGIC MONITOR *holds* it!

More stations—with TV's big new expansion.

Less "dialing"—every station already *tuned on target*, all ROTOMATIC on one knob!

Less "adjusting"—MAGIC MONITOR *automatically* ties in finest "Golden Throat" sound, screens out static and interference, controls power level.

Lowest prices ever!
17-inch TV as low as **$179**95   21-inch TV as low as **$229**95

Above, the new 17-inch CRAIG, ebony finish, $179.95. 178349. Built-in UHF tuning, optional at extra cost.

...and you set the style!

◆ Figure 9.2 **Advertisement for RCA Victor Television, 1953**

made easier by an automatic dial. Compare Figures 9.1 and 9.2. How do these advertisements for televisions reinforce conventional roles for male and female viewers?

Televisions were often depicted as bringing families together, but some critics worried that the new medium would create new sources of familial conflict, as parents and children and husbands and wives collided over control of the set. Television advertisers themselves often tackled this theme. Their solution, as Figure 9.3

◆ **Figure 9.3**
Advertisement for General Electric Television, 1955
Gaslight Advertising Archives, Inc.

indicates, was multiple television sets! Consider the two-part construction of this 1955 General Electric ad. Why would the advertiser choose a cartoon to portray family conflict? How does the photograph depict stereotypical gender roles?

Women's primary roles as housewives became a predominant theme for network executives and sponsors in the early years of television. They were eager to attract women viewers because of their responsibilities as family purchasing agents. As one executive noted, "We're after a specific audience, the young housewife—one cut above the teenager—with two to four kids, who has to buy the clothing, the food, the soaps, the home remedies."[33] As the television industry saw it, the dilemma was whether daytime programming geared to this specific audience would be compatible with women's patterns of household labor. Unlike radio, they feared, television needed to be watched with some degree of concentration. These hesitations were finally overcome by 1952, when the networks began to offer a full range of daytime programs that included soap operas, quiz shows, and magazine-style variety shows. As the 1955 *Ladies' Home Journal* ad in Figure 9.4 indicates, they explicitly marketed their daytime lineup to women by emphasizing that the programs did not interfere with their household duties. Read the descriptions of the seven shows watched by the young housewife in a single morning. How do they attempt to persuade women that television watching hastens rather than hinders their household work? What assumptions does this advertisement make about women's domestic labor?

Although soap operas were a direct carryover from radio, the magazine-style variety show was a new format for daytime programming. NBC's *Today* program, which debuted in 1952, aired between 7 and 9 A.M. and offered short segments of news and entertainment designed for the whole family, plus features on fashion and homemaking directed toward women. *Today* and copycat shows proved immensely successful in attracting a female audience. As *Variety* explained it, "The housewife with her multiple chores, it would seem, wants her TV distractions on a 'catch as catch can' basis.... [And the new shows] are all geared to the 'take it awhile leave it awhile' school of entertainment projection and practically all are reaping a bonanza for the networks."[34] Inspired by the success of their morning program, in 1954 NBC introduced *Home*, a magazine-style show expressly for women. Figure 9.5 is a 1955 advertisement in *Ladies' Home Journal* that asks, "What better way to keep house than with the *Home* program?"

As the ad's text suggests, *Home* was geared towards what the networks assumed women wanted—information that would assist them in their household responsibilities—and the program was explicitly modeled after women's magazines. Announcer Hugh Downs introduced the first show by saying, "You're looking at NBC's newest television studio in New York: a studio especially designed for *Home*. And from this television laboratory—which is what it really is—each weekday at this hour, 11:00 A.M., a staff of electronic editors is going to bring you news and information that applies to your home and your family."[35] *Home* featured an innovative revolving circular set outfitted with a workshop area, garden, and kitchen. Actress Arlene Francis was "editor-in-chief" of the show, and she served as emcee, or femcee, as women hosts were often dubbed in this period.

WHERE
DID THE
MORNING GO?

Time for lunch already?
Where did the morning go?
The chores are done, the
house is tidy . . . but it hasn't
seemed like a terribly
tiring morning.

First there was breakfast, and that was pleasant. We all got the news from "TODAY," and Dave Garroway had some fascinating guests. The children were still laughing about J. Fred Muggs when they left for school.

Then I sat Kathy down in front of "DING DONG SCHOOL" and I didn't have to worry about her while I tidied up. Miss Frances got her interested in finger-painting, and after the program Kathy just went on playing quietly.

"WAY OF THE WORLD" had the second installment of the new story, and I couldn't miss that. It's like a magazine serial — you keep looking forward to the next episode. And beautifully acted, with new stars for every new story.

I think I started the ironing while I watched "THE SHEILAH GRAHAM SHOW". First she discussed the latest Hollywood news and gossip. Then she interviewed William Holden, and showed parts of his exciting new movie.

And I finished the ironing while I watched "HOME". I couldn't *count* the good ideas I've had from Arlene Francis and her expert assistants on health, home decorating, gardening and food. I added a few things to my shopping list.

Any morning of any day, "THE TENNESSEE ERNIE FORD SHOW" can brighten things up for me. Tennessee Ernie and his talented friends joke, sing and share the fun with everyone . . . at the studio and at home.

And then "FEATHER YOUR NEST", where that lovely couple won a living room suite, and Bud Collyer and Janis Carter were so nice to them. And I think that it's a wonderful idea that viewers at home can win prizes, too.

The morning was a pleasure instead of drudgery. And yet I have everything done . . . I haven't really wasted a second. It's the way I like to have the morning go.

EXCITING THINGS ARE HAPPENING ON

NBC
TELEVISION
a service of (RCA)

◆ **Figure 9.4**
Ladies' Home
Journal
Advertisement
for NBC, 1955
Gaslight Advertising
Archives, Inc.

According to *Newsweek,* which reported on the show's debut, Francis's staff included a gardening expert, a child psychologist, a food editor, an advisor on fashion and beauty, and an interior design specialist. *Newsweek* also noted that NBC's president, Sylvester Laflin (Pat) Weaver, sought to tap the advertising market that women's magazines enjoyed. "It is inconceivable to me," Weaver noted, "that all that advertising money spent on women's products . . . has been allowed

◆ Figure 9.5 **Ladies' Home Journal Advertisement for NBC's Home Program, 1955**
From Daniel Delis Hill, Advertising to the American Woman, 1900–1999 *(Columbus: Ohio State University Press, 2002).*

Arlene Francis invites you to keep house with **H⌂ME**

HOME, with lovely Arlene Francis as hostess, is the NBC television program which concerns itself with everything that matters most to you: your home, your family, your world, yourself.

- • Food
- • Health
- • Beauty
- • Child Care
- • Diets

- • Fashion
- • Decorating
- • Gardening
- • Vacations
- • Sewing

HOME comes to you from a special circular stage which contains everything from a kitchen sink to a real garden. From this stage, Arlene Francis, assisted by Hugh Downes and a staff of expert editors, brings you a full hour daily of entertaining and informative services:

The good, the new, the useful . . . pass in review before your eyes, every weekday on HOME. What more enjoyable way to see and hear the things that interest you most, than on television? What better way to keep house than with the HOME program, over the NBC Television network?

see your newspaper for local time and channel

to escape [from television]."³⁶ In keeping with that idea, *Home* segments were generally tied to specific sponsors and commercials, and indeed NBC described the program's set as "a machine for selling."³⁷ Despite the emphasis on home and family, the show also provided coverage of current events and some controversial topics of the day, such as "crisis in the schools" and the "menace of tranquilizers," themes that were believed to particularly interest women. What does the list of "entertaining and informative services" provided in the ad indicate about NBC's assumptions concerning women's interests?

♦ Figure 9.6 **Advertisement for Betty Crocker, 1952**
Courtesy of General Mills Archives.

The line between programming and commercials was often blurred in shows geared to "Mrs. Consumer." This was evident in programs featuring Betty Crocker, General Mills' mythical spokeswoman, who was portrayed by a series of actresses on both radio and television. Figure 9.6 features actress Adelaide Hawley, who appeared in the 1952 ABC daytime programs *Bride and Groom* and *Betty Crocker Star Matinee*. In the former, a couple was married on-screen and Betty gave tips to brides on fixing their grooms' favorite foods, foods that featured General Mills products. Her television appearances featured this verse:

American homemakers
Keepers of the hearth
Whose hands and hearts are filled
With the day-to-day cares and joys
That, taken with one another
Make homemaking a woman's
Most rewarding life.[38]

How does Figure 9.6 illustrate this verse? What does it suggest about the relationship between popular media and the "feminine mystique"?

SITUATION COMEDIES

Advertisements for television and television programs offer one avenue for exploring assumptions about women's roles in the 1950s. The content of popular shows is another. This section examines the depiction of women in situation comedies, or "sitcoms," which, in contrast to the genres discussed above, were shown in the evening and geared to the whole family. The images reproduced here, of course, do not adequately convey the dynamic medium of TV. They do not capture motion, dialogue, or laugh tracks. Missing, too, is the importance of audience familiarity with the shows' characters, another crucial aspect shaping how Americans experienced sitcoms. These photographs, mostly publicity stills, nonetheless stand as emblems of popular sitcoms' depiction of women and the family in this era. With a very few exceptions, such as *Our Miss Brooks*, a comedy starring Eve Arden as a schoolteacher, adult white women characters in sitcoms did not work outside the home and were portrayed as house-wives, despite the number of married women entering the paid workforce. Beyond this common thread, these programs offered strikingly diverse images of the American family.

The networks adopted many situation comedies from successful radio programs. Two of these starred African Americans. *Beulah* aired on ABC from 1950 to 1953 and portrayed a maid and the white family she worked for, the Hendersons. Over the life of the series on radio and television, three well-known black actresses played Beulah: Louise Beavers, Hattie McDaniel, and Ethel Waters. Figure 9.7 shows Louise Beavers as Beulah. Two other black characters appeared regularly in the series: Beulah's boyfriend, Bill, an oafish man who ran a fix-it shop but seemed to spend most of his time in his girlfriend's kitchen, and Oriole, her scatterbrained friend who worked for the white family next door. Although some of the comedy derived from Beulah's persistent, yet fruitless, efforts

◆ **Figure 9.7 Scene from *Beulah***
Photofest.

to convince Bill to marry her, the major focus of the series was Beulah's nurturing her white family and solving their small dilemmas. A classic "mammy" figure, her catch phrase was "Somebody bawl fo' Beulah?" In one episode her southern cuisine (she was described as the "queen of the kitchen") helped Mr. Henderson impress a business client. In another, she taught Donnie, the family's son, to jive dance.

Although some African Americans took pleasure in seeing an African American star on television, other individuals and groups, including the NAACP, criticized the series for perpetuating degrading stereotypes. Does Beulah appear to be part of the family? In what ways does Figure 9.7 reinforce racial hierarchies of the day? Contrast this image with the slave nurse in Figure 3.12 (p. 195).

A more famous sitcom with black cast members was *Amos 'n' Andy* (1949–1953), which starred men but featured a number of women. On the original radio show, two white men who had created the series played the title characters, but on television the cast was all African American. Even before the show aired, the NAACP launched a protest over bringing the radio program, which many blacks found degrading because of its racist stereotypes, to television. In response to this pressure, CBS modified Amos, one of the title characters, by making him and his wife, Ruby, models of middle-class propriety. To fill the comedic void,

◆ **Figure 9.8 Scene from *Amos 'n' Andy***
Everett Collection.

however, the series gave enhanced attention to George ("The Kingfish") Stephens, with his fractured English and his scams to avoid work and get rich quick. The unambitious and none-too-smart Andy served as the victim of many of his schemes.

The major female character was the Kingfish's wife, Sapphire, played by Emestine Wade, who had also performed the role in radio. For the most part Sapphire was a shrew, a caricature of the domineering wife who routinely threw her husband out of the house. In Figure 9.8, she is shown waiting to pounce on the Kingfish as he attempts to sneak into their home. An even more negative portrayal of black women emerged with Sapphire's large and loud-mouthed mother, "Mama." As the Kingfish described her, "Andy, you take de venom of a cobra, de disposition of a alligator and de nastiness of a rhinoceros." . . . "Put 'em all together dey spell Mother!" [39] Partially as a result of NAACP pressure and partly because of declining ratings, CBS canceled the show in 1953. Compare Sapphire and her husband to the loving black couple shown in Figure 9.2. What might account for the striking differences in these two popular culture depictions? After at first perpetuating negative stereotypes of black women as either mammies or shrews, sitcoms subsequently treated them as invisible. African Americans would not reappear in sitcoms for another decade, and it was not until 1968, when Diahann Carroll appeared as a nurse in *Julia,* that a black woman starred in a series.

A number of early sitcoms featured white immigrant families, most notably *The Goldbergs* (1949–1954). CBS adopted the show from the popular radio program of the same name, which starred Gertrude Berg as Molly Goldberg. Berg also wrote the scripts for the program, which she said was modeled after the experiences of her mother and grandmother. The show explored the domestic crises of a Jewish family living in the Bronx and their circle of neighbors. Molly dominated the show, and part of the humor was her accented English and eccentric phrasing. "Enter, whoever. If it's nobody, I'll call back." [40]

A stereotypical Jewish mother, Molly eagerly turned her nurturing skills to solve friends' and family members' problems. Each show began with Molly leaning out her apartment window to shout across the airshaft, "Yoo-hoo, Mrs. Bloom." Inside the family circle, a key theme was the aspiration for assimilation and the American middle-class dream. Significantly, assimilation was often cast in terms of consumption. In one show Molly disapproves of her daughter-in-law's plan to buy a washing machine on the installment plan. "I know Papa and me never bought anything unless we had the money to pay for it." Her son convinces her she is wrong, and by the end she is suggesting that the family buy two cars in order to "live above our means—the American way."[41]

Figure 9.9 shows Molly in her dining room, where she is serving the guest of honor, well-known television personality Arthur Godfrey. Molly is depicted as nurturing and the family as close-knit. The room's decor is old-fashioned, as is Molly for the most part. At a time when many upwardly mobile Jews were leaving the crowded cities and the ethnic neighborhoods their parents and grandparents had created, the cozy world of the Goldbergs was increasingly anachronistic. Why might this disparity contribute to the appeal of the program?

A less sentimental rendering of the urban family was *The Honeymooners* (1955–1956), in which Jackie Gleason played bus driver Ralph Kramden, a

◆ Figure 9.9 **Scene from *The Goldbergs***
Photofest.

◆ Figure 9.10 **Scene from *The Honeymooners***
Photofest.

dreamer who always missed realizing his hopes for a more comfortable life. Audrey Meadows played Alice, his long-suffering and practical wife. Marital bickering between the two was a constant in the series. The stance of Alice in Figure 9.10 as she looks disapprovingly at Ralph, with their friends Norton and his wife Trixie in the background, conveys some of this tension. One of Ralph's catch phrases, "One of these days, Alice, one of these days, pow! Right in the kisser!," suggests even more. Plots frequently involved Alice's disappointment over their limited income and the drabness of the apartment, completely devoid of the consumer goods that most Americans were eagerly acquiring in this period. The show generally closed with a harmonious resolution, but the overarching tone was nonetheless one of male-female conflict, with Alice fighting back.

Marital disputes also served as the focal point for the humor in one of the most beloved sitcoms of early television, *I Love Lucy* (1951–1961). Lucille Ball's character Lucy is married to Ricky Ricardo, played by Ball's real-life husband, Cuban bandleader Desi Arnaz. In the process of the show, they have a baby, Little Ricky, whose TV birth coincided with the birth of the couple's real son. Lucy seemingly represents a stereotypical dizzy female. Childish and impractical, she is juxtaposed to Ricky's usually mature demeanor. She constantly is forced to defer to his decisions as head of the family and resorts to wheedling, deception, and "feminine wiles" to get her way. But like the Kramdens, the Ricardos' marital disagreements prove fodder for most plots. She eternally desires a job in show business and constantly hankers for consumer items, from kitchen appliances to Parisian frocks. Ricky proves the obstacle on both counts.

Many plots focus on Lucy's schemes to get a job, yet repeatedly she humiliates herself as she fails in each attempt. A particularly revealing episode for its comments on male-female roles is the show in which Lucy and her best friend, Ethel, wager with Ricky and Ethel's husband, Fred, that men's work is easier than women's labor in the home. They trade places, and while Ricky and Fred make a mess of homemaking (Figure 9.11, top), Lucy and Ethel look for work. In the middle image of Figure 9.11, a clerk in an employment agency reads a list of jobs, and the women realize they have no training for any of them except perhaps candy-making. They get jobs making chocolates, but their incompetence leads to their demotion to packing on an assembly line. At first, they do well, but as the conveyer belt speeds up, they fall behind and start eating the chocolate instead of packing it to try to keep up (Figure 9.11, bottom). At the end of the episode, both men and women agree to call the bet off and to return to their accustomed roles.

Some critics argue that, far from reinforcing the feminine mystique, with its emphasis on women's roles as housewives and mothers, *Lucy* subverts it. For if Lucy is a housewife, she is not a contented one, as her quest for employment suggests. Conversely, others maintain that despite her aspirations, she fails at her forays into the workplace, and the storylines generally end with her return to her housewifery role and her acceptance of Ricky's authority. Do you think the images shown in Figure 9.11 suggest subversion or reinforcement of the feminine mystique? How do you suppose contemporary audiences interpreted the squabbles between Lucy and Ricky?

Sitcoms that featured working-class or minority families had almost disappeared by the mid-1950s. And, with the exception of *I Love Lucy,* so too had programs that traded on marital bickering and themes concerning domestic power. As more and more real American women went into the workforce, the networks offered up sitcoms that idealized the family and reinforced women's prescribed role in the home. Unlike Lucy, the mothers in *The Adventures of Ozzie and Harriet, The Donna Reed Show, Leave It to Beaver,* and *Father Knows Best* led contented lives with serene marriages. Their husbands were successful breadwinners and their homes spacious and well furnished. They were rarely depicted as performing arduous household labor, but their immaculate houses were a reflection of their womanly skills.

Although ostensibly comedies, the humor in these sitcoms was sometimes barely discernible. Plots usually revolved around the dilemmas of childrearing as parents strove to teach children social and moral lessons. *Father Knows Best* (1954–1963), the first of this genre, led the way among sitcoms that promoted

◆ Figure 9.11 **Scenes from *I Love Lucy***
Photofest.

family values. Figure 9.12 shows the mother, Margaret Anderson (played by Jane Wyatt), joining in a prayer around the family dinner table. In what ways are the Andersons similar to and different from the families shown in the other sitcoms?

Father Knows Best was aptly named. In the episode titled "Kathy Becomes a Girl," the youngest daughter Kathy learns that boys do not like tomboys. As her father explains, "Being dependent—a little helpless now and then" was a sure ploy designed to win men.[42] An even more telling statement about the ideal female role came in a show that uncharacteristically featured Margaret expressing a degree of dissatisfaction with her lot. As her children and her husband are winning trophies for various activities, Margaret is forced to acknowledge that she has never received a medal for anything. To compensate, she takes up fishing and plans to compete in a tournament. Her chances are good, her coach tells her, because so few women compete. Ready for the competition, she falls, injures herself, and misses the contest. Her children seek to cheer her up with a series of tributes to her motherly skills and homemade awards, such as a frying pan emblazoned with the title "Most Valuable Mother." The episode received a 1958–1959 directing Emmy.

◆ **Figure 9.12 Scene from *Father Knows Best***
Everett Collection.

Neither advertising nor sitcom images should be taken as an accurate reflection of American women. What they offer are insights into how television portrayed women. The inherently commercial nature of television facilitated advertising and programming that featured women's role as housewives and the purchasers of consumer goods for her family. Sitcoms, too, had close commercial links. When Molly Goldberg left her window at the start of the show, she returned to her kitchen and launched into a commercial for Sanka coffee, the program's sponsor. Although early sitcoms acknowledged some diversity among Americans, with a few exceptions most women were portrayed in their domestic roles. As the example of *Lucy* indicates, tensions over these roles often served as the comedic plot. But despite the reality of women's increased participation in the workforce, by the second half of the decade TV sitcoms idealized the middle-class family and the stay-at-home mother, and thus served as a powerful reinforcement of the cultural prescriptions of the feminine mystique.

QUESTIONS FOR ANALYSIS

1. What messages do the spatial arrangements, figure positions, and clothing styles in the advertisements (Figures 9.1–9.6) suggest about popular perceptions of the middle-class family and women's role in it?

2. Why did advertisers think these ads would sell consumer goods and network programming?

3. To what extent do the images from the sitcoms (Figures 9.7–9.12) reflect American diversity in terms of ethnicity, race, or class?

4. In what ways have television messages about gender roles changed since the 1950s?

D O C U M E N T S

Feminism in the UE

A<small>T A TIME WHEN COLD WAR FEARS</small> stifled dissent and reinforced traditional gender roles, women in a handful of industrial unions stood out for their efforts to achieve fair play for working women. Not surprisingly, unions such as the United Packinghouse Workers of America (UPWA), the United Auto Workers (UAW), and the United Electrical, Radio and Machine Workers (UE), which represented workers in industries with a high percentage of women, were among the most vociferous supporters of women's right to fair wages and opportunities. Women leaders in all three unions fought to prevent postwar layoffs that targeted women first, to negotiate for improved wages, and to demand that their unions take women's concerns seriously. UE women, however, were unusual in their early criticism of sexsegregated labor patterns that designated most industrial labor as either "men's" or "women's" work, as can be seen in the following extract from a 1952 UE publication.

While this pamphlet is striking for its forward-looking demands for women's work rights and its recognition of the double burden of African American women, it is also significant because its anonymous author was Betty Friedan, who eleven years later published the path-breaking *The Feminine Mystique*. In that book Friedan presented herself as a suburban housewife, similar to the women she was describing, who were trapped by the "problem that has no name." She indicated that an alumnae survey of her Smith College classmates she conducted sparked her work, and ten years after *The Feminine Mystique* appeared she explicitly stated that she "wasn't even conscious of the woman problem" until she started writing the book.[43] Historian Daniel Horowitz's research into Friedan's formative influences, however, reveals that Friedan's college course work and employment as a journalist for the nation's most radical union, among other experiences, gave her ample exposure to serious questioning about women's work and family roles.

Friedan not only obscured her radical past when she wrote *The Feminine Mystique,* but she neglected her earlier subjects. Zeroing in on affluent women trapped by domesticity, Friedan ignored working women and women of color in her 1963 blockbuster. New insights into Friedan's past raise many questions, but perhaps the most significant implication is that we see more clearly the connection between working-class unionized women's activism in the 1940s and 1950s and the roots of the feminist movement of the 1960s.

BETTY FRIEDAN
UE Fights for Women Workers (1952)

HOW INDUSTRY EXPLOITS WORKERS

In advertisements across the land, industry glorifies the American woman—in her gleaming GE kitchen, at her Westinghouse Laundromat, before her Sylvania television set. Nothing is too good for her—unless she works for GE, or Westinghouse, or Sylvania or thousands of other corporations throughout the U.S.A.

As an employee, regardless of her skill she is rated lower than common labor (male). She is assigned to jobs which, according to government studies, involve greater physical strain and skill than many jobs done by men—but she is paid less than the underpaid sweeper, the least skilled men in the plant. She is speeded up until she may faint at her machine, to barely earn her daily bread.

Wage discrimination against women workers exists in every industry where women are employed. It exists because it pays off in billions of dollars in extra profits for the companies. According to the 1950 census, the average wage of women in factories was $1,285 a year less than men. Multiply this by the 4,171,000 women in factories and you get the staggering total of 5.4 billion dollars. In just one year, U.S. corporations made five billion four hundred million dollars in extra profits from their exploitation of women.

Here are just a few examples of the double standard on wages in the electrical manufacturing industry:

At a large GE plant, women who make up one-fourth of the workers are hired in at $1.22 an hour, while men are hired in at $1.47, except for common labor, which is $1.43. Most of the women work on production jobs whose highest rate is $1.34—nine cents less than the rate of an untrained sweeper. Women doing the same work as men on punch press, motor winding, stator bar insulating, wiring, electronic-tube assembly, are getting from 20 to 30 cents an hour less. GE pockets the difference—a profit on sex.

At a large Westinghouse plant, the minimum hiring-in rate for women is $1.33 [an hour]. The hiring-in rate for men starts at $1.51. The highest rated job held by a woman pays $1.54, only $3\frac{1}{2}$ cents more than the male sweeper. Only a few women are in labor grades 5 and 6, equal to or slightly higher than the bottom sweeper's rate on the male key sheet. Most of the women are in Grades 1 to 4, below the starting point of the male key sheet. . . .

In the lamp industry, all production work is done by women, who make up three-fourths of the total working force. These women production workers are hired in at from five to twenty cents less than men, and the highest rate they can make is several cents less than the male common labor rate. As a result, the companies make $2,619 per year on every employee in the lamp industry, compared to $1,540 per employee in motor and generator plants where only one-quarter of the workers are women. An extra profit, on sex! . . .

Today, the UE is engaged in an intensified campaign to end the rate discrimination against women. For these rates below common labor threaten every rate in the plant. The companies, as part of their general rate-cutting offensive, are putting in new machines and processes to be run by women at rates below common labor, replacing higher-paid men. And because the women's base rate is so low, they are at the mercy of the company's speed-up drive—the women are being used as a wedge to speed up and cut rates of all workers.

That's why in collective bargaining today, a major UE demand is to abolish all rates below common labor and end the rate discrimination

SOURCE: United Electrical, Radio and Machine Workers of America, *UE Fights for Women Workers*, UE Publication No. 232, June 1952.

against women. The full weight of the union is being thrown behind this battle. . . .

SPECIAL SITUATION OF NEGRO WOMEN

The situation of Negro women workers today is even more shocking. For the discrimination that keeps Negro men at the bottom of the pay scale forces their wives to work to supplement the pitifully inadequate income of the family.

But Negro women are barred from almost all jobs except low-paying domestic service in private homes, or menial outside jobs as janitresses and scrubwomen. In the basic sections of the electrical, radio and machine industry, as in industry generally, Negro women are not employed. In map plants and others where Negro women have been hired as a source of cheap labor, they suffer the exploitation of all women working under discriminatory rates of pay because of their sex.

Census figures show the special economic problems of Negro women: 41.4% of Negro married women continue to work compared to 25.3 percent of white married women.

As of March, 1950, 20.7 percent of Negro women with children under six had to work as compared with 11.2 percent of white women.

Altogether in 1950, 46 out of every hundred Negro women were in the labor force as compared to 32 out of every hundred white women.

Out of 451 job classifications, 3/4 of all women workers were concentrated in the 23 lowest paid job categories. But almost 4/5 of Negro women workers were employed in 5 of the lowest paid of the 451 job classifications.

In 1950, the average earnings of Negro women were $474 a year, compared to $1,062 for white women, $1,471 for Negro men, and $2,709 for white men. The compounding of the two kinds of discrimination against Negro workers who are women is shown by the fact that the average earnings of Negro women are barely 1/6 the average earnings of white men.

UE's fair practices committees in many local unions have been fighting the discrimination against hiring Negro women in the electrical and machine industry, and the discriminatory practices that restrict Negro women to the most menial, lowest-paid jobs. But electrical apparatus plants and other basic sections of the industry still discriminate on a large scale against Negro women, and for the most part today Negro women are not employed in the industry. Negro women workers have a real stake in the UE's fight to end rate exploitation of women in the industry, but their problems also require a special fight to lift the double bars against hiring of Negro women. . . .

THE WHOLE UNION'S FIGHT

One third of the UE membership are women. If all the women who work in UE plants belonged to the union, the percentage would be even higher. This single fact shows how important for the strength of the union is the fight to end discrimination against women in our plants.

The companies want to keep the women segregated, on separate lower paying jobs with separate seniority, so that they may use them as part of their plan to drive down wages and destroy union gains under their war program. In the layoffs that are resulting from the war economy and the big business runaway shop drive, they want to pit women against men, married women against single workers, older women against younger. Segregation of women is the handle of a dangerous union-smashing weapon in the hands of the company. The only way to fight it is to end the segregation, integrate the women's jobs in their proper place in the rate structure, make it possible for women to be upgraded to any job in the plant, and establish identical seniority rights based on length of service without regard to age, sex, marital status, race or color.

Women in UE are determined to win the rates and job rights to which they are entitled. They have been meeting in conferences all over the country to discuss urgent problems of meeting the high cost of living on paychecks even lower than other workers . . . of physical suffering caused by growing speedup in the plant, coupled with care of home and children after the full workday. They resolved to fight to end the double wage standard that enables the companies to make an extra profit on their sex while they have such a hard time getting along. And these UE women have real fighting power, as they have demonstrated on many a picket-line across the country.

But fighting the exploitation of women is men's business too, as more and more men workers faced with rate cuts and speedup in GE, Westinghouse and other plants now realize. In every local and shop, and in the national chains, the whole weight of the unions is being thrown into the fight to end the double wage standard against women. . . .

UE'S PROGRAM FOR WOMEN

Reslot all jobs done by women up from common labor rates, under a single rate structure, to eliminate discrimination as compared to jobs done by men.

Post all job opportunities for upgrading according to seniority, regardless of race or sex, providing adequate training for women to qualify for new job openings.

Make the company provide adequate health and safety safeguards for all workers.

Eliminate double seniority lists for men and women wherever they exist.

Give special attention to problems of married women growing out of family responsibility, such as shifts and absenteeism.

Eliminate discriminatory hiring practices against married women, Negro women, etc., where they exist.

Campaign for government-financed child care centers for working mothers as were provided in World War II.

Press fight against speedup which is causing accidents and ill health among women workers.

Guarantee the life and militancy of the union by developing, training and electing women to all levels of leadership.

See that Fair Practices Committees are functioning in every shop.

QUESTIONS FOR ANALYSIS

1. What sorts of discrimination against women does this UE pamphlet outline, and what solutions does it offer?
2. Why does it include a special discussion on black women?
3. What arguments does it offer to convince men to support women's work rights?
4. What indications does it give that the UE was a radical union that challenged the power of industrial capitalism?
5. One historian remarks that this pamphlet is "a remarkable manual for fighting wage discrimination that is, ironically, as relevant today as it was in 1952."[44] Do you agree?

DOCUMENTS

Women in the Civil Rights Movement

As historians examine the lives of American women of the last half of the twentieth century, they are able to draw on a wider variety and number of sources than historians researching earlier periods. The documents presented in this essay are either autobiographical accounts or oral histories. Both types offer us the woman's own words and understanding of her participation in the civil rights movement. But, as with all types of historical sources, the reader needs to evaluate the document's strengths and shortcomings. How does the narrator's commitment shape her recollection? Does she have an ax to grind? Is she anxious to justify or exaggerate her actions? Need we be concerned that her memory is accurate? And in the case of oral histories, has the interviewer unduly influenced the narrative?

AUTOBIOGRAPHICAL ACCOUNTS

Septima Clark (1898–1987), a Charleston, South Carolina, schoolteacher, had been active in the civil rights movement before she went to the Highlander Folk School in 1954 in Tennessee, a left-wing, biracial institution interested in labor and community organizing. She became Highlander's director of education and established, with Esau Jenkins and Miles Horton, an innovative Citizenship School for prospective voters. Like Ella Baker (see pp. 577–79), Clark emphasized grassroots mobilization and the importance of listening to the needs and interests of the people the civil rights movement was trying to engage. Clark's program, which was later transferred to the Southern Christian Leadership Council (SCLC), trained hundreds of local activists—more than half of them women—who in turn ran their own workshops.

The key to the program was teaching blacks how to read and write so they could attempt the difficult process of registering to vote. The southern states used a poll tax system to keep both poor blacks and whites from registering to vote, but the most widespread technique was a literacy test that included trick questions and such devices as asking the prospective voter to interpret a selected passage from the state constitutions.

In the following passage from her second autobiography, *Ready from Within*, originally published in 1986, Clark describes a school set up in the early 1960s at the Dorchester Cooperative Community Center in McIntosh, Georgia, where recruits from all over the South were brought for workshops. What were the most serious problems Clark and her group encountered?

SEPTIMA CLARK

Once a month, for five days, we'd work with the people we had recruited, some of whom were just off the farms. . . . We went into various communities and found people who could read well aloud and write legibly. They didn't have to have a certificate of any kind. I sat down and wrote out a flyer saying that the teachers we need in a Citizenship School should be people who are respected by the members of the community, who can read well aloud, and who can write their names in cursive writing. These are the ones that we looked for.

We brought those people to the [Dorchester Cooperative Community] center in Liberty County, Georgia. While they were there, we gave them the plan for teaching in a citizenship school. We had a day-by-day plan, which started the first night with them talking, telling us what they would like to learn. The next morning we started off with asking them: "Do you have an employment office in your town? Where is it located? What hours is it open? Have you been there to get work?"

The answers to those things we wrote down on dry cleaner's bags, so they could read them. We didn't have any blackboards. That afternoon we would ask them about the government in their home town. They knew very little about it. They didn't know anything about the policemen or the mayor or anything like that. We had to give them a plan of how these people were elected, of how people who had registered to vote could put these people in office, and of how they were the ones who were over you.

We were trying to make teachers out of these people who could barely read and write. But they could teach. If they could read at all, we could teach them that c-o-n-s-t-i-t-u-t-i-o-n spells constitution. We'd have a long discussion all morning about what the constitution was. We were never telling anybody. We used a very non-directive approach.

The people who left Dorchester went home to teach and to work in voter registration drives. They went home, and they didn't take it anymore. They started their own citizenship classes, discussing the problems in their own towns. "How come the pavement stops where the black section begins?" Asking questions like that, and then knowing who to go to talk to about that, or where to protest it.

The first night at the Liberty County Center we would always ask people to tell the needs of the people in their community. The first night they gave us their input, and the next morning we started teaching from what they wanted to do.

But what they wanted varied. We had to change. Down in the southern part of Georgia some women wanted to know how to make out bank checks. One woman told the workshop that somebody had been able to withdraw a lot of money from her account because she did not know how to make out her own check and check up on her own account. . . .

So we started teaching banking. We brought in a banker, and he put the whole form up on the board and showed them how to put in the date and how to write it out. He told them, "Don't leave a space at the end of the check. Somebody else could write another number in there. When you finish putting down the amount, take a line and carry it all the way to the dollar mark."

[Clark summed up the impact of the voter registration drive and the 1965 Voting Rights Act, which had eliminated the literacy test.]

After that, people in Alabama did not have to answer twenty-four questions. They could register to vote if they could sign their name in cursive. It didn't take us but twenty minutes in Selma, Alabama, to teach a woman to write her

SOURCE: Cynthia Stokes Brown, ed., *Ready from Within: Septima Clark and the Civil Rights Movement* (1986; repr., Trenton, NJ: Africa World Press, Inc., 1990), 63–70, 77–79.

name. The white students took her to the court-house. She wrote her name in cursive writing and came back with a number that meant she could register to vote. This is the way we did it.

We had 150 of those schools in Selma, paying those teachers $1.25 an hour, two hours, each morning, five days a week. The Marshall Field Foundation furnished the money for that, and we did it for three solid months. At the end of three months, we had 7002 persons with a number that gave them the right to vote when the federal man came down in August. We worked from May 18 to August 15. That was in 1965, because in 1966 we went to the vote. . . .

In Selma, anybody who came to our meeting lost their job. Fifty or more did. Some of them got their jobs back later, but some never did. . . . But even with that kind of harassment, the Citizenship Schools really got into full force. There were 897 going from 1957 to 1970. In 1964 there were 195 going at one time. They were in people's kitchens, in beauty parlors, and under trees in the summer-time. I went all over the South, sometimes visiting three Citizenship Schools in one day, checking to be sure they weren't using textbooks, but were teaching people to read those election laws and to write their names in cursive writing.

One time I heard Andy Young say that the Citizenship Schools were the base on which the whole civil rights movement was built. And that's probably true. . . .

[Clark, like Ella Baker, later expressed frustration over the male domination of the civil rights movement.]

I was on the Executive Staff of SCLC, but the men on it didn't listen to me too well. They liked to send me into many places, because I could always make a path in to get people to listen to what I have to say. But those men didn't have any faith in women, none whatsoever. They just thought that women were sex symbols and had no contributions to make. That's why Rev. Abernathy would say continuously, "Why is Mrs. Clark on this staff?"

Dr. King would say, "Well, she has expanded our program. She has taken it into eleven deep south states." Rev. Abernathy'd come right back the next time and ask again. I had a great feeling that Dr. King didn't think much of women either. . . .

But in those days I didn't criticize Dr. King, other than asking him not to lead all the marches [so other leaders could be developed]. I adored him. I supported him in every way I could because I greatly respected his courage, his service to others, and his non-violence. The way I think about him now comes from my experience in the women's movement. But in those days, of course, in the black church men were always in charge. It was just the way things were. . . .

I see this as one of the weaknesses of the civil rights movement, the way the men looked at the women. . . .

Out of these experiences I felt I wanted to be active in the women's liberation movement.

[At the encouragement of a white civil rights activist, Virginia Durr, Clark went on to participate in the National Organization for Women.]

Although the vast majority of civil rights activists were black, whites, many of them women, also participated. Sandra (Casey) Hayden (b. 1939) came from a small town in Texas where she lived with her divorced mother and grandmother, both strong women and highly influential in her life. Her activism began at the University of Texas through the Young Women's Christian Association (YWCA), an organization that fostered social activism on many college campuses in the 1950s and that Hayden described as a place where she was "grounded in a democratic manner of work, exposed to and educated about race." She was an early and valued member of the Student Nonviolent Coordinating Committee (SNCC). In this passage from an autobiographical essay, "Fields of Blue" (2000), she discusses some of her activities in Atlanta as the organization's northern coordinator during 1963. What is the significance of her emphasis on the ideal of community?

CASEY HAYDEN

I threw myself into my work, developing Friends of SNCC groups on campuses and in cities. Initially, SNCC was kept alive largely through spontaneous donations. Now we were looking for sustaining support. This position was a good fit for me. I was trained to organize and administer programs, had been on a northern campus and knew what was needed to sustain support there, and had an enormous number of contacts by now through the Y, the NSA [National Student Association], SDS [Students for a Democratic Society, discussed in Chapter 10], the Northern Student Movement, and all the traveling I'd done. I sent out field reports and instructions on how to organize, created mailing lists and key supporter lists, answered piles of correspondence and endless phone calls, responded to emergencies in the field, and laid the groundwork for Dinkly Romilly and Betty Garman, white women I knew from other organizations, who followed me in this position. . . . I did all my own work in SNCC. At this point, bringing into being a program and a network, I did the head work and the hands-on work. I thought we turned hierarchy upside down by throwing out that division of labor. This was true for me throughout my years with the organization. I was never a secretary in SNCC and never had one. I worked long hours with no days off, feeling responsible for the staff in the field whose lives were daily at risk. I visited the field, including

Greenwood, where I attended the First Greenwood Mississippi Freedom Folk Festival. Traveling in an integrated car, we took turns hiding under blankets on the floor in the back. Once there, we sat with local people on planks in an open field to listen to local talent, and Pete Seeger and Bob Dylan. Whites in pick-ups circled the field, rifles on display in racks on the rear windows. . . .

In meetings and out, I saw our first task as creating relationships among ourselves, holding our community together. A style, an ethic, was implied. I stuck around endlessly, we all did, until some level of understanding was reached, at which point we could act. This was called coming to consensus. Once this broad consensus was reached, I didn't argue with people about what they should do. There was more than enough to do, and plenty of room for experimentation. If folks were willing to risk their lives, that was enough. They should be able to choose how they would die. I did try to do what I said I'd do. That was accountability, synonymous with self-discipline. To my recollection everyone operated like this, for some time.

Integration worked both ways. I was breaking the barrier between people with my own body, integrating the black community. I thought I was getting the better side of the deal. . . . Our struggle was to break down the system, the walls, of segregation. This implied no barriers in our relations with each other. Once we broke down the barriers between ourselves, we were in a new space together, in community. This was our radi-

SOURCE: Constance Curry et al., *Deep in Our Hearts: Nine White Women in the Freedom Movement* (Athens: University of Georgia Press, 2000), 349–50, 365–66.

cal truth. Our radical truth was an experience, not an idea. That was SNCC's great genius.

[Hayden comments on the SNCC position paper she coauthored in 1964 with another white woman, Mary King (see box, pp. 584–85).]

The paper aimed to bring forward the fact that sexism was comparable to racism, a novel idea at the time—so novel, in fact, that the word sexism didn't exist in our lexicon. . . . [A]s the paper has entered the literature of feminism over the years, some historians have wondered if it exposed a struggle for power or leadership. Nonsense. We [the authors] were all white. None of us were after leadership. That was for blacks. I believe we were speaking not for our private self-interest, but for all women, to share what we saw: that gender is a social construct, as is race. There was no written feminist critique on the left in our generation. We were the first. It is a good critique, in many ways, and brave, a fine example of how the tools developed in analyzing racism were translated, inside SNCC itself, into an analysis of gender. We had pierced the racist bubble and were seeing clearly. All things were open to question. As Bernice Reagon has said, "SNCC was where it could happen."

ORAL HISTORIES

ALTHOUGH WE HAVE ONLY a handful of memoirs written by women civil rights activists, a growing collection of oral histories has expanded historians' access to a wide range of women who participated in the movement. Oral accounts, like memoirs, if recorded long after the events described, are sometimes marred by faulty memories or influenced by the person conducting the interview. Nonetheless, they give invaluable insights into the experiences and feelings of historical actors whose voices are often unheard in more traditional documentary sources.

This first selection is drawn from an interview conducted by historian and filmmaker Henry Hampton with Diane Nash (Bevel), one of the best known of the women SNCC activists. Nash (b. 1938), an African American who left Chicago to attend Fisk University in Nashville, describes her early involvement in the movement, at the Nashville sit-ins in 1960. Why is this account so powerful?

DIANE NASH

The sit-ins were really highly charged, emotionally. In our non-violent workshops, we had decided to be respectful of the opposition, and try to keep issues geared toward desegregation, not get sidetracked. The first sit-in we had was really funny, because the waitresses were nervous. They must have dropped two thousand dollars' worth of dishes that day. It was almost a cartoon. One in particular, she was so nervous, she picked up dishes and she dropped one, and she'd pick up another one, and she'd drop it. It was really funny, and we were sitting there trying not to laugh, because we thought that laughing would be insulting and we didn't want to create that kind of atmosphere. At the same time we were scared to death. . . .

SOURCE: Henry Hampton and Steve Fayer, comps., *Voices of Freedom: An Oral History of the Civil Rights Movement from the 1950s through the 1980s* (New York: Bantam, 1990), 57–59, 82–83.

After we had started sitting in, we were surprised and delighted to hear reports of other cities joining in the sit-ins. And I think we started feeling that power of the idea whose time had come. Before we did the things that we did, we had no inkling that the movement would become as widespread as it did. I can remember being in the dorm any number of times and hearing the newscast, that Orangeburg had demonstrations, or Knoxville, or other towns. And we were really excited. We'd applaud, and say yea. When you are that age, you don't feel powerful. I remember realizing that with what we were doing, trying to abolish segregation, we were coming up against governors, judges, politicians, businessmen, and I remember thinking, "I'm only twenty-two years old, what do I know, what am I doing?" And I felt very vulnerable. So when we heard these newscasts, that other cities had demonstrations, it really helped. Because there were more of us. And it was very important.

The movement had a way of reaching inside you and bringing out things that even you didn't know were there. Such as courage. When it was time to go to jail, I was much too busy to be afraid.

[As a SNCC activist, in 1961 Nash became involved in the Freedom Rides. Here, she describes her leadership role when violence threatened to stop the rides and Nash insisted that they go forward (see p. 579).]

A contingent of students left Nashville to pick up the Freedom Ride where it had been stopped. Some of the students gave me sealed letters to be mailed in case they were killed. That's how prepared they were for death.

The students who were going to pick up the Freedom Ride elected me coordinator. As coordinator, part of my responsibility was to stay in touch with the Justice Department. Our whole way of operating was that we took ultimate responsibility for what we were going to do. But it was felt that they should be advised, in Washington, of what our plans were. Some people hoped for protection from the federal government. I think Jim Lawson cautioned against relying on federal protection.

I was also to keep the press informed, and communities that were participating, such as Birmingham, Montgomery, Jackson, and Nashville. And I coordinated the training and recruitment of more people to take up the Freedom Ride.

[Nash later became a rider herself and was jailed in Jackson, Mississippi, in 1961.]

O RAL HISTORIES ARE PARTICULARLY VALUABLE for capturing the stories of older rural women who offered indispensable aid to the activists who came to their communities. In this selection, published in 1983, Mary Dora Jones reminisces about taking in Freedom Summer workers in Marks, Mississippi. The interviewer is the Pulitzer Prize–winning journalist Howell Raines who later became executive editor of the *New York Times*. What does Jones's account convey about disagreements within the African American community and the dangers facing those African Americans who supported the civil rights activists?

MARY DORA JONES

MARY DORA JONES: I had about several blacks and four whites in my house, wouldn't nobody else take 'em.

RAINES: In Marks?

JONES: Right . . . they really move. They comes in, they mean business. They didn't mind dyin', and as I see they really mean business, I just love that for 'em, because they was there to help us. And since they was there to help us, I was there to help them. . . .

RAINES: Did that cause you any problems in the community. . . . opening your home up?

JONES: Oh, really, because they talkin' about burnin' my house down. . . . Some of the black folks got the news that they were gonna burn it down. . . . My neighbors was afraid of gettin' killed. People standin' behind buildin's, peepin' out behind the buildin's, to see what's goin' on. So I just told 'em. "Dyin' is all right. Ain't but one thing 'bout dyin'. That's make sho' you right, 'cause you gon' die anyway." . . . If they had burnt it down, it was just a house burned down.

RAINES: That's the attitude that changed the South.

JONES: So that's the way I thought about it. So those kids, some of 'em from California, some of 'em from Iowa, some of 'em from Cincinnati, they worked, and they sho' had them white people up there shook up.

RAINES: . . . youngsters that came in, particularly the white ones from outside the South, did they have a hard time adjusting . . . ?

JONES: They had a hard time adjustin' because most all of the blacks up there didn't want to see 'em comin' . . . said they ain't lettin' no damn civil rights come. "If they come up here to my house, I'm gon' shoot 'em."

See this is what the black folks were sayin', and those kids had went to the preachers' houses,

they had done went to the deacons' houses, they had done went to the teachers' houses, all tryin' to get in. Some of 'em come in around five o'clock that evenin', landed in my house. I give 'em my house, "My house is yo' house." I was workin' for a man, he was workin' at the Post Office, and he and his wife was beggin' me everyday, "Don't fool with them Communists."

RAINES: The white people?

JONES: That's what they was tellin' me, those kids was Communists. I said, "Well, I tell you what. I don't think they no more Communist than right here where I am, because if they Communists, then you Communists. They cain't hurt me no mo' than I already been hurt." Anything that helped the peoples, then I'm right there. So I didn't stop, although I got him scared to fire me. He would have fired me, but I got him scared to fire me. . . .

RAINES: This was your white boss?

JONES: This was my white boss I was working for. His wife was sick, and every day the wife would talk to me about those people, askin' me where they lived. I said, "Well, they ain't livin' at yo' house. Why you want to know where they live?" So she said, "They ain't livin' with you?" And I said, "Well, I'm payin' the last note on the house," just like that. And I never did tell her.

Finally one day she brought me home, and it was a car sittin' there in my driveway, and two white men was in there, and there were some sittin' on the porch. She put me out and she went on back. When I went to work the next morning, she say, "Mary, was them, ah, civil rights people at yo' house?" I said, "Now when you turned around and stopped and they were sittin' there, you oughta been askin' 'em what they was. They'da told you."

And I never did tell 'em anything. So it went on some, she said, "Ain't but one thing I hate about it, this intermarriage." And I said, "Well, ain't no need in worryin' about that, because if you wanna worry about that, you oughta been talkin' to your granddaddy. . . ."

SOURCE: Howell Raines, *My Soul Is Rested: Movement Days in the Deep South* (New York: Putnam, 1977), 279–81.

EARLINE BOYD of Hattiesburg, Mississippi, had been involved in the NAACP in her community even before civil rights activists came to her town for the voter registration drive. In this interview, conducted in 1991 by Dr. Charles Bolton of the University of Southern Mississippi's Civil Rights in Mississippi Oral History Project, she describes some of the harassment African Americans active in civil rights faced. What insights does she offer about women's participation in the movement?

EARLINE BOYD

EARLINE BOYD: There was the pressure on people about jobs or they would try and intimidate them in different ways.

I remember one man lost his job. He had been working for one of the white funeral homes here and his wife was very active in it. When they found out that she was marching that day going to the courthouse—that's where we were marching to that particular day—when he went back to work the people—I don't remember exactly what they said to him, but I do know that she his wife told him just to give that job up and not to go back anymore. So evidently they had said things to him, had made him know that they did not want him. He didn't go; it was his wife who was doing the marching and was active in the movement.

So it was hard on people and a lot of people was afraid, you know, to take a step towards trying to work with the movement. I don't remem-

ber where I was working then, but it didn't have any effect on me, on my job at the time. And I would just go whenever they had it and it was kind of hard. Now some people probably, well, the ones that was working for people who didn't want them to go, I'm sure they gave them a lot of hard times. So that was my way of getting started in the movement.

DR. CHARLES BOLTON: Were a lot of women involved? It sounds like the women maybe were more involved than the men.

BOYD: There were more women involved than men in the movement.

BOLTON: Why do you think that is?

BOYD: Well, I guess the man was the person who was really head of the household and needed a job. Women worked but I guess they felt like it would be easier for them to go and not lose their job than for men. Even so, like I said about this man who lost his job when the person that he was working for found out that his wife was going, then he started talking to him. And of course, his wife was working for herself and had her own day care center. So it wouldn't bother her. And he stopped working there, and I don't know where he went to work after that. But later on I do remember that he started working for himself too.

SOURCE: "Civil Rights in Mississippi Digital Archive," Mississippi Oral History Program of The University of Southern Mississippi, interview conducted August 29, 1991, http://anna.lib.usm.edu/%7Espcol/crda/oh/ohboydrp.html (accessed January 29, 2003).

QUESTIONS FOR ANALYSIS

1. What insights do these accounts offer about the distinct experiences of women in the civil rights movement?

2. What kinds of leadership skills did these movement women display?

3. Can you find specific examples in these documents that suggest any of the pitfalls historians face in drawing upon remembrances as sources?

4. To what extent do these documents reveal the obstacles facing civil rights activists?

5. What clues do these documents provide as to the relationship between the civil rights movement and the emergence of the feminist movement in the late 1960s?

NOTES

1. James T. Patterson, *Grand Expectations: The United States, 1945–1974* (New York: Oxford University Press, 1996), 223.

2. Jessica Weiss, *To Have and to Hold: Marriage, the Baby Boom, and Social Change* (Chicago: University of Chicago Press, 2000), 57.

3. "Wright Girls Combine Careers and Marriage," *Ebony,* January 1951, 74.

4. Joanne Meyerowitz, "Beyond the Feminine Mystique: A Reassessment of Postwar Mass Culture, 1946–1958," in Joanne Meyerowitz, ed., *Not June Cleaver: Women and Gender in Postwar America, 1945–1960* (Philadelphia: Temple University Press, 1994), 240.

5. Eva Moskowitz, "'It's Good to Blow Your Top': Women's Magazines and a Discourse of Discontent, 1945–1960," *Journal of Women's History* 8 (Fall 1996): 66–98.

6. Alice Kessler-Harris, *Out to Work: A History of Wage-Earning Women* (New York: Oxford University Press, 1982), 304.

7. Susan M. Hartmann, "Women's Employment and the Domestic Ideal in the Early Cold War Years," in Meyerowitz, *Not June Cleaver,* 88.

8. Ibid., 90.

9. Julia Kirk Blackwelder, *Now Hiring: The Feminization of Work in the United States, 1900–1995* (College Station: Texas A&M University Press, 1997), 162–63.

10. Susan Rimby Leighow, "An 'Obligation to Participate': Married Nurses Labor Force Participation in the 1950s," in Meyerowitz, *Not June Cleaver,* 37–56.

11. Weiss, *To Have and to Hold,* 55.

12. Sara M. Evans, *Born for Liberty: A History of Women in America* (New York: Free Press, 1989), 254.

13. Bruce Fehn, "African-American Women and the Struggle for Equality in the Meatpacking Industry, 1940–1960," *Journal of Women's History* 10 (Spring 1998): 50.

14. Ibid., 58–59.

15. Lisa Kannenberg, "The Impact of the Cold War on Women's Trade Union Activism: The UE Experience," *Labor History* 34 (Winter 1993): 318.

16. Amy Swerdlow, *Women Strike for Peace: Traditional Motherhood and Radical Politics in the 1960s* (Chicago: University of Chicago Press, 1993), 110.

17. Ibid., 117.

18. Belinda Robnett, *How Long? How Long? African-American Women in the Struggle for Civil Rights* (New York: Oxford University Press, 1997), 59.

19. Ibid., 67.

20. Ibid., 17–32.

21. Ibid., 94.

22. Ibid., 104.

23. Clayborne Carson, *In Struggle: SNCC and the Black Awakening of the 1960s* (Cambridge: Harvard University Press, 1995), 74.

24. Sara Evans, *Personal Politics: The Roots of Women's Liberation in the Civil Rights Movement and the New Left* (New York: Knopf, 1979), 86–87.

25. Debra L. Schultz, *Going South: Jewish Women in the Civil Rights Movement* (New York: New York University Press, 2001), 83.

26. Ibid., 9.

27. Margaret Rose, "Gender and Civic Activism in Mexican American Barrios in California: The Community Service Organization, 1947–1962," in Meyerowitz, *Not June Cleaver,* 181.

28. Ibid., 190.

29. Patricia G. Zelman, *Women, Work, and National Policy: The Kennedy-Johnson Years* (Ann Arbor: UMI Research Press, 1982), 28.

30. Linda Kerber, *No Constitutional Right to Be Ladies* (New York: Hill and Wong, 1998), 192.

31. Alice Kessler-Harris, *In Pursuit of Equity: Women, Men, and the Quest for Economic Citizenship in Twentieth-Century America* (New York: Oxford University Press, 2001), 234.

32. Ruth Rosen, *The World Split Open: How the Modern Women's Movement Changed America* (New York: Viking, 2000), 75.

33. William Boddy, *Fifties Television: The Industry and Its Critics* (Urbana: University of Illinois Press, 1990), 20.

34. Lynn Spigel, *Make Room for TV: Television and the Family Ideal in Postwar America* (Chicago: University of Chicago Press, 1992), 80.

35. Bernard M. Timberg, "Why NBC Killed Arlene Francis's *Home* Show," *Television Quarterly* 30 (Winter 2000): 80.

36. *Newsweek,* March 15, 1954, 93.

37. Spigel, *Make Room for TV,* 83.

38. Jim Hall, *Mighty Minutes: An Illustrated History of Television's Best Commercials* (New York: Harmony, 1984), 47.

39. Melvin Patrick Ely, *The Adventures of Amos 'n' Andy* (New York: Free Press, 1991), 211.

40. Robin P. Means Coleman, *African American Viewers and the Black Situation Comedy: Situating Racial Humor* (New York: Garland, 2000), 61.

41. Rick Mitz, *The Great TV Sitcom Book* (New York: Richard Marek, Publishers, 1992), 14.

42. Susan J. Douglas, *Where the Girls Are: Growing Up Female with the Mass Media* (New York: Times Books, 1994), 36.

43. Betty Friedan, *The Feminine Mystique,* 20th ann. ed. (New York: Norton, 1983), 5.

44. Kannenberg, "The Impact of the Cold War," 318.

SUGGESTED REFERENCES

General Works Two books offer overviews of women's history for this era: Rochelle Gatlin, *American Women Since 1945* (1987), and Eugenia Kaledin, *American*

Women in the 1950s (1984). A lively oral history is Brett Harvey, *The Fifties: A Women's Oral History* (1993). Joanne Meyerowitz, ed., *Not June Cleaver: Women and Gender in Postwar America, 1945–1960* (1994), offers a valuable anthology of recent historical essays that challenge the primacy of the feminine mystique for understanding the period.

Marriage, Family, and Cold War Culture   A starting point for understanding the impact of the Cold War on American families is Elaine Tyler May, *Homeward Bound: American Families in the Cold War Era* (1988). Other insights on marriage, sexuality, and the family may be found in Wini Breines, *Young, White, and Miserable: Growing Up Female in the Fifties* (1992); Stephanie Coontz, *The Way We Never Were: American Families and the Nostalgia Trap* (1992); Lillian Faderman, *Odd Girls and Twilight Lovers: A History of Lesbian Life in Twentieth-Century America* (1991); Steven Mintz and Susan Kellogg, *Domestic Revolutions: A Social History of American Family Life* (1988); Eva Moskowitz, "'It's Good to Blow Your Top': Women's Magazines and a Discourse of Discontent, 1945–1960," *Journal of Women's History* 8 (1996): 66–98; and Jessica Weiss, *To Have and To Hold: Marriage, the Baby Boom, and Social Change* (2000). For a valuable primary source on working-class women, see sociologist Mirra Komarovsky's *Blue-Collar Marriage* (1967).

Popular culture is engagingly discussed by Susan J. Douglas in *Where the Girls Are: Growing Up Female with the Mass Media* (1994). See also William Boddy, *Fifties Television: The Industry and Its Critics* (1990); Robin P. Means Coleman, *African American Viewers and the Black Situation Comedy: Situating Racial Humor* (2000); Gerald Jones, *"Honey, I'm Home!" Sitcoms: Selling the American Dream* (1992); George Lipsitz, "The Meaning of Memory: Family, Class, and Ethnicity in Early Network Television Programs," in Lynn Spigel and Denise Mann, eds., *Private Screenings: Television and the Female Consumer* (1992); and Lynn Spigel, *Make Room for TV: Television and the Family Ideal in Postwar America* (1992).

For the feminine mystique, begin with Betty Friedan, *The Feminine Mystique* 20th ann. ed. (1983), followed by Daniel Horowitz's insightful assessment, *Betty Friedan and the Making of* The Feminine Mystique (1998); Susan M. Hartmann, "Women's Employment and the Domestic Ideal in the Early Cold War Years," in Meyerowitz, *Not June Cleaver*, 84–102; and Joanne Meyerowitz, "Beyond the Feminine Mystique: A Reassessment of Postwar Mass Culture, 1946–1958," in Meyerowitz, *Not June Cleaver*, 229–62.

Women and Work   Three important overviews of women and work that include valuable material on the postwar era are Julia Kirk Blackwelder, *Now Hiring: The Feminization of Work in the United States, 1900–1995* (1997); Alice Kessler-Harris, *Out to Work: A History of Wage-Earning Women* (1982); Lynn Y. Weiner, *From Working Girl to Working Mother: The Female Labor Force in the United* States (1985). A number of books analyze women's participation in the labor movement: see Dorothy Sue Cobble's *Dishing It Out: Waitresses and Their Unions in the Twentieth Century* (1991) and *The Other Women's Movement: Workplace Justice and Social Rights in Modern America* (2004); Dennis A. Deslippe, *"Rights, Not Roses": Unions* *and the Rise of Working-Class Feminism, 1945–1980* (2000); and Nancy F. Gabin, *Feminism in the Labor Movement: Women and the United Auto Workers, 1935–1975* (1990). Specialized articles on the topic include Bruce Fehn, " 'Chickens Come Home to Roost': Industrial Reorganization, Seniority, and Gender Conflict in the United Packinghouse Workers of America, 1956–1966," *Labor History* 34 (1993): 324–41; Lisa Kannenberg, "The Impact of the Cold War on Women's Trade Union Activism: The EU Experience," *Labor History* 34 (1993): 309–23; and Leah F. Vosko and David Witwer, " 'Not a Man's Union': Women Teamsters in the United States during the 1940s and 1950s," *Journal of Women's History* 13 (2001): 169–92. On African American women and work, see Bruce Fehn, "African-American Women and the Struggle for Equality in the Meatpacking Industry, 1940–1960," *Journal of Women's History* 10 (1998): 45–69; Paula Giddings, *When and Where I Enter: The Impact of Black Women on Race and Sex in America* (1984); and Jacqueline Jones, *Labor of Love, Labor of Sorrow: Black Women, Work, and the Family, from Slavery to the Present* (1985).

Middle-Class Women's Activism   For an overview of this subject, consult Leila J. Rupp and Verta Taylor, *Survival in the Doldrums: The American Women's Rights Movement, 1945 to the 1960s* (1987). Specialized studies include Susan Levine, *Degrees of Equality: The American Association of University Women and the Challenge of Twentieth-Century Feminism* (1995); Faith Rogow, *Gone to Another Meeting: The National Council of Jewish Women, 1893–1993* (1993); Susan Lynn, *Progressive Women in the Conservative Times: Racial Justice, Peace, and Feminism, 1945 to the 1960s* (1992); Amy Swerdlow, *Women Strike for Peace: Traditional Motherhood and Radical Politics in the 1960s* (1993); Susan Ware, "American Women in the 1950s: Nonpartisan Politics and Women's Politicization," in Louise A. Tilly and Patricia Gurin, eds., *Women, Politics, and Change* (1990), 281–99; and Deborah Gray White, *Too Heavy a Load: Black Women in Defense of Themselves, 1894–1994* (1999). For the importance of women to conservative politics, see Lisa McGirr, *Suburban Warriors: The Origins of the New American Right* (2001), and a conference paper by Laura Pierce, " 'Civic Watchdogs in High Heels': Women's Patriotic Organizations and Anti-Communism in the United States, 1945–1965" (paper presented at meeting of the Organization of American Historians, Memphis, 2003).

Women and Civil Rights   After being largely invisible in the history of the civil rights movement, women activists are the subject of a growing literature. A number of general works offer insights about women's experiences. See especially Charles M. Payne, *I've Got the Light of Freedom: The Organizing Tradition and the Mississippi Freedom Struggle* (1995), and the oral history collections of Henry Hampton and Steve Fayer, comps., *Voices of Freedom: An Oral History of the Civil Rights Movement from the 1950s through the 1980s* (1990), and Howell Raines, *My Soul Is Rested: Movement Days in the Deep South Remembered* (1983). For the concept of bridge leaders, see Belinda Robnett, *How Long? How Long? African-American Women in the Struggle for Civil Rights* (1997). A useful anthology of articles is Vicki L. Crawford, Jacqueline Anne Rouse, and Barbara Woods, eds., *Women in the Civil Rights*

Movement: Trailblazers and Torchbearers, 1941–1964 (1990), but see also articles such as Bernice McNair Barnett, "Invisible Southern Black Women Leaders in the Civil Rights Movement: The Triple Constraints of Gender, Race, and Class," *Gender and Society* 7 (1993): 162–82; Carolyn Calloway-Thomas and Thurmon Garner, "Daisy Bates and the Little Rock School Crisis: Forging the Way," *Journal of Black History* 26 (1996): 616–28; Aprele Elliott, "Ella Baker: Free Agent in the Civil Rights Movement," *Journal of Black Studies* 26 (1996): 593–603; and Cynthia Griggs Fleming, "Black Women Activists and the Student Nonviolent Coordinating Committee: The Case of Ruby Doris Smith Robinson," *Journal of Women's History* 4 (1993): 64–82. Biographies of major leaders include Douglas Brinkley, *Rosa Parks* (2000); Chan Kai Lee, *For Freedom's Sake: The Life of Fannie Lou Hamer* (2000); and Barbara Ransby, *Ella Baker and the Black Freedom Movement: A Radical Democratic Vision* (1993). Valuable autobiographies are Cynthia Stokes Brown, ed., *Ready from Within: Septima Clark and the Civil Rights Movement* (1990), and Jo Ann Robinson, *The Montgomery Bus Boycott and the Women Who Started It: The Memoir of Jo Ann Gibson Robinson* (1987). For white women in the movement, see Joan C. Browning, "Trends in Feminism and Historiography: Invisible Revolutionaries: White Women in Civil Rights Historiography," *Journal of Women's History* 8 (1996): 186–204; Constance Curry et al., *Deep in Our Hearts: Nine White Women in the Freedom Movement* (2000); Virginia Foster Durr, *"Outside the Magic Circle": The Autobiography of Virginia Foster Durr* (1985); Catherine Fosl, *Subversive Southerner: Anne Braden and the Struggle for Racial Justice in the Cold War South* (2002); and Debra L. Schultz, *Going South: Jewish Women in the Civil Rights Movement* (2001). For a crucial assessment of the relationship between the civil rights movement and second wave feminism, see Sara Evans, *Personal Politics: The Roots of Women's Liberation in the Civil Rights Movement and the New Left* (1979).

Scholarship on Mexican American women for this period is still sparse, but see Vicki Ruiz, *From Out of the Shadows: Mexican Women in Twentieth-Century America* (1999); Margaret Rose, "Women in the United Farm Workers: A Study of Chicana and Mexicana Participation in a Labor Union, 1950–1990," PhD dissertation UCLA, 1988; Margaret Rose, "Gender and Civic Activism in Mexican American Barrios in California: The Community Service Organization, 1947–1962," in Meyerowitz, *Not June Cleaver,* 177–200; and Richard Santillán, "Midwestern Mexican American Women and the Struggle for Gender Equality: A Historical Overview, 1920s–1960s," *Perspectives in Mexican American Studies* 5 (1995): 79–119.

Women and Public Policy   A number of books address the issues that framed the President's Commission on the Status of Women. See Cynthia Harrison, *On Account of Sex: The Politics of Women's Issues, 1945–1968* (1988); Linda Kerber, *No Constitutional Right to Be Ladies* (1998); Alice Kessler-Harris, *In Pursuit of Equity: Women, Men, and the Quest for Economic Citizenship in Twentieth-Century America* (2001); Kathleen A. Laughlin, *Women's Work and Public Policy: A History of the Women's Bureau, U.S. Department of Labor, 1945–1970* (2000); Judith Sealander, *As Minority Becomes Majority: Federal Reaction to the Phenomenon of Women in the Work Force, 1920–1963* (1983); and Patricia G. Zelman, *Women, Work, and National Policy: The*

Kennedy-Johnson Years (1982). The history of NOW is yet to be written, but see Ruth Rosen, *The World Split Open: How the Modern Women's Movement Changed America* (2000), and Friedan's own account in *It Changed My Life: Writings on the Women's Movement* (1976).

Selected Web Sites

For classic educational short films of the 1950s, such as *A Date with Your Family,* and advertising features, see the Prelinger Archive, which offers hundreds of download-able films: <**archive.org/movies/prelinger.php**>. Of the many Web sites for the civil rights movement, a particularly rich one is the Mississippi Oral History Project, cre-ated by the Center for Oral History and Cultural Heritage at The University of Southern Mississippi: <**usm.edu/msoralhistory/**>. For Web pages on the history of feminism, see Toni Carabillo's Feminist Chronicles, 1953–1993, sponsored by the Feminist Majority, at <**feminist.org/research/chronicles/chronicl/.html**>. This searchable database has hundreds of documents and is particularly rich on the his-tory of NOW.

10

Modern Feminism and American Society

1965 TO THE PRESENT

L IKE 1848, 1968 WAS A YEAR OF CASCADING DEVELOPments in American history, which inaugurated a new epoch in the history of American women. In January, South Vietnamese Communist forces unleashed a surprise military offensive against U.S. troops who were there to shore up an unpopular, undemocratic government. In April, Martin Luther King Jr. was assassinated in Memphis, Tennessee, and with him died the nonviolent phase of the modern civil rights movement. In June, Robert Kennedy, whose campaign for the Democratic presidential nomination championed the African American and Chicano civil rights movements, was also shot and killed. In August, protest moved decisively from the electoral arena to the streets as thousands of young people demanded that the Democratic National Convention in Chicago repudiate military involvement in Vietnam. Political upheaval was worldwide as students and young workers demonstrated in the capital cities of France, Czechoslovakia, and Mexico, demanding greater democracy and more openness from their own governments.

And what of American women? They campaigned for Kennedy, the brother of the late president John F. Kennedy, and mourned his and King's deaths. Some served in Vietnam, nursing wounded and dying American men. In the many giant demonstrations against the war, women were fully half of the rank and file. What marks this year as a watershed in U.S. women's history, however, was that women were not only politically active alongside men but they struck out in new directions in pursuit of their own demands for freedom. Exhilarated to be part of the ambitious activism of the period but frustrated by their exclusion from its leadership, women began to insist that equality and liberation should characterize the relations between the sexes, as well as among races and nations. As African American writer and activist Toni Cade (later Bambara) put it, "mutinous cadres of women" in all sorts of protest organizations "[were] getting salty about having to . . . fix the coffee while the men wrote the position papers and decided on policy."[1]

Out of this combination of excitement and frustration came "women's liberation," a new kind of feminism rooted in 1960s experiences and perspectives. Initially concentrated on gaining equality for women within the protest movements of black power, Chicanismo, and the New Left, women's liberation soon challenged the condition of women in the larger society. In conjunction with the National Organization for Women (NOW), women's liberation made feminism into a mass movement. Sometimes called "the second wave," this modern feminism outlived its 1960s origins to become one of the most important social and political forces of the late twentieth century. An ironic measure of its radicalism and historical impact was the anti-feminist movement that emerged in the late 1970s in reaction, advocating the defense and reinstitution of traditional womanhood. Ultimately unable to reverse the changes in women's lives that feminism championed, anti-feminism nonetheless had a tremendous impact on mainstream American political life, all the way up to and including the presidency.

Feminism provides an essential framework for understanding the recent history of American women, indeed of American politics and culture, but it was not the only engine of change. The modern feminist movement was as much a response to as a cause of deep social changes affecting women, especially the maturation of the female labor force and corresponding shifts in American family life. Developments in the market that had transformed women's lives within the United States a century before reverberated globally by the end of the millennium.

1974	Watergate scandal forces Nixon's resignation
1975	**United Nations sponsors first International Women's Conference in Mexico City**
1977	**National Women's Conference held in Houston**
1978	Supreme Court sustains affirmative action in *University of California Regents v. Bakke*
1980	Ronald Reagan elected president
1981	**Sandra Day O'Connor becomes first woman appointed to Supreme Court**
1982	**ERA fails ratification**
1990s	**"Third wave" feminism flourishes**
1991	**Clarence Thomas–Anita Hill hearings held**
1992	**Bill Clinton elected president along with record number of women to Congress**
1995	**United Nations International Women's Conference held in Beijing**
1996	**Personal Responsibility and Work Opportunities Act passed**
1998-1999	Clinton impeached and acquitted
2000	Highly contested presidential election resolved by Supreme Court in favor of George W. Bush
2001	Terrorists destroy New York's World Trade Center and attack Pentagon
2003	United States and allies invade Iraq
2004	**March for Women's Lives draws 1 million pro-choice activists to Washington, D.C.**
2004	**Gay marriages begin in California and Massachusetts**
2004	George W. Bush reelected president

Renewed immigration and increased globalization made the dramatic changes in and shifting expectations about American women's lives into a phenomenon of worldwide significance.

THE ERA OF WOMEN'S LIBERATION

In 1960, "feminism" was a term of derision or contempt, if it was used at all. By decade's end, Americans were hearing a great deal about this new phenomenon. Rooted in the social upheavals surrounding the civil rights movement, the Vietnam War, and the counterculture, the reemergence of feminism in the second half of the 1960s signaled the beginning of a new era in women's history.

The creation of NOW in 1966 (see Chapter 9) put women's civil rights on the political map. Self-consciously modeling their organization after the National Association for the Advancement of Colored People, NOW founders expected to act primarily as a lobbying and litigating group. Historians often describe NOW as representing "liberal" feminism because it focused on bringing about women's equality through legal and political means, a process that paralleled other twentieth-century liberal reform movements. By contrast, the feminism known as "women's liberation" considered itself revolutionary, seeking changes that went beyond civil rights to cultural transformation.

Sexual Revolution, Black Power, and the War in Vietnam

All of the upheavals collectively known as "the sixties" played a role in the emergence of women's liberation. The introduction in 1960 of the birth control pill, along with the confidence that modern medicine had conquered all sexually transmitted diseases (proven tragically wrong by the AIDS epidemic two decades later), forged a conviction that sexual relations no longer had unwanted consequences and could be indulged in casually and freely. The sixties atmosphere of sexual liberation pushed women past the limits of their mother's generation, especially beyond marriage as their goal and their fate. But the ethic of sexual liberation set different sorts of restraints on women. What sexual liberation meant before women's liberation is captured in images of women in miniskirts and go-go boots, with exaggerated eye makeup and long straight hair, signaling their availability to men. Women were not supposed to be sexual adventurers themselves so much as be rewards for the men who crashed through the barricades of respectability.

By the late 1960s, sexual liberation had been expanded by young people into a broader challenge to the very foundations of their parents' way of life. The "counterculture," as this diffuse phenomenon was known, went beyond the "hippie" lifestyle of sex, drugs, and rock 'n' roll to experiment with new forms of living. Instead of following in the path of the hard-working, male-headed, nuclear family of the 1950s, the counterculture encouraged the creation of "communes," groups determined to find different forms of intimacy and interdependence. These deliberately created communities (latter-day versions of the utopian communities of the

1830s and 1840s—see Chapter 4) retained more of the gender divisions of the larger society than they cared to admit. Nonetheless, the countercultural ambition to replace the traditional middle-class family structure set the stage for an explicitly feminist revolt against norms of domesticity and motherhood.

Changes in the civil rights movement also had an impact on the emergence of women's liberation. Deeply frustrated by the slow federal response to their demands, dispirited by a wave of black ghetto riots in the summer of 1965, and traumatized by the King and Kennedy assassinations in 1968, African American activists turned away from the goal of racial integration and concentrated instead on cultivating black leadership, sensibility, and mass empowerment. Their spirit of militant, collective anti-racism spread to other communities of color. Young Mexican American civil rights advocates created the era of Chicano nationalism. Native Americans formed the All-Indian Nation, and Asian Americans established a Pan Asian movement. Coming together under the term "third world" (borrowed from the term for developing countries outside the Cold War era orbits of the Western, or first world, and Soviet, or second world), these activists saw themselves as part of a larger uprising against America's traditions of white supremacy.

Of all these forms of militant anti-racism, the most influential was black power. In contrast to earlier, southern-based civil rights activism, the black power movement thrived in the urban ghettoes of the North. Black power advocates adopted a black nationalist philosophy, which although it did not call for an independent state, did seek to consolidate a sense of peoplehood among African Americans. A major inspiration for black power was the philosophy of Malcolm X, a renegade leader of the Nation of Islam (commonly known as the Black Muslims) who challenged the goal of integration and the message of black inferiority it subtly conveyed. He was assassinated in 1965. In 1966 the Student Non-Violent Coordinating Committee became a black power organization, voting to expel its white members and embracing the goal of black self-determination. That same year, the Black Panther Party was formed in Oakland, California, and quickly became notorious for insisting on the right to community self-defense, with weapons if necessary, against police abuse. Under the banner of black power, writers and young black militants wore African-inspired clothes and "natural" hairstyles, and dropped their European, or "slave," names. In 1971, New Jersey–born Paulette Williams renamed herself Ntozake Shange, then went on to write the prize-winning play "for colored girls who have considered suicide when the rainbow is enuf."

The impact of the black power movement on the emergence of women's liberation was complex. On the one hand, black power had a decidedly masculine caste, in contrast to the earlier phases of civil rights activism, in which African American women had been prominent as local leaders (see Chapter 9). Black nationalism tended to cast women as mothers of a new peoplehood rather than as political actors themselves. Black men were to lead and defend their people; black women were to give birth to and nurture them. Nonetheless, there were significant female figures in the black power era, notably Angela Davis, a philosophy professor who went underground for a year to escape FBI charges that she had aided a black prisoner revolt in Marin County, California.

◆ Angela Davis and Black Power

The face of Angela Davis, framed by the halo of her natural Afro hairstyle, is one of the signature female images of the era. Sought by the FBI for her alleged role in a 1970 revolt of black militant prisoners in Marin County, California, she gave herself up after a few months in hiding and spent over a year in federal prison. There, using only the resources available, she wrote one of the earliest historical analyses of the position of women within slavery. In 1972 she was acquitted of all charges. © *Bettmann/ CORBIS.*

Yet, the black power emphasis on self-determination rather than integration, on the group rather than the individual, provided the model for the emerging women's liberation movement. Black power ideas inspired women's liberation by insisting that only when the oppressed and the activist were one and the same, when subordinate people sought to liberate themselves rather than look to powerful saviors, could true freedom be won.

Even more than sexual liberation and black power, however, the U.S. war in Vietnam, the nation's longest armed conflict, provided the immediate context for the appearance of the women's liberation movement. U.S. armed forces began to trickle into Vietnam in 1961, as part of President Kennedy's decision to intervene in the Cold War era civil war there between a Communist government in the north and an anti-Communist regime in the south. In 1965, President Lyndon B. Johnson began sending large numbers of combat troops and bombing Hanoi, the capital of North Vietnam. By the time that U.S. forces withdrew in 1973, approximately 2.8 million Americans had served in Vietnam. Of these, an estimated seven thousand were women. Among the approximately sixty thousand Americans who died in Vietnam were eight military nurses and fifty-six women working with organizations ranging from the Red Cross to the CIA.

In general, however, the war in Vietnam—fighting in it or fighting against it—was an intensely male experience. Combat forces were not only all male but built around life-and-death male comradeship. Military training denigrated weakness or fear as feminine. For many U.S. soldiers in Vietnam, the only nonenemy Vietnamese and the only women they encountered came from the large prostitute population that grew up around U.S. army facilities. By the mid-1960s, the possibility of being called up through the draft hung like a cloud over the lives of nearly all young men in the United States. As opposition against the war grew, men could pursue alternative forms of heroism: by refusing to be drafted, by publicly burning their draft cards, or by leaving the United States. Women who opposed the war were their supporters. "Hell no. We won't go," was the slogan of men in the draft resistance movement. "Girls say yes to guys who say no" was the female equivalent.

The major organization behind anti-war protests was Students for a Democratic Society (SDS). Formed in 1962 by forty college students meeting at Port Huron, Michigan, SDS protested against America's hypocritical claim to be the bastion of democracy. Impatient with what they regarded as the outdated, class-based politics of the previous generation of left-wing activists (the "Old Left"), SDS activists declared themselves the "New Left." After white students left SNCC, many joined SDS.

Even more than SNCC, SDS tended strongly to reserve leadership roles for men. By 1967, white SDS women began to meet separately from men, following the model of the black power movement. "Women must not make the same mistake that blacks did at first of allowing others . . . to define our issues, methods and goals," an anonymous group of women SDSers announced. (New Leftists often did not sign their manifestos; personal claims to authorship were considered insufficiently collective.) "The time has come for us to take the initiative in organizing ourselves for our own liberation."[2]

By 1969, an estimated 2 million Americans, women and men both, had taken to the streets in cities all over the country to protest the war. The spring of 1970, when anti-war demonstrations closed down most college campuses, culminated in the killing by national guard troops of four students at Kent State University in Ohio, among them two women, and two young men at Jackson State University in Mississippi. Rebellion at home combined with mounting American casualties in Vietnam to increase the pressure on President Richard Nixon to find some way out of what now appeared to be an unwinnable war.

Significantly, the first national political event at which the women's liberation movement made its appearance was a women's anti-war demonstration, organized in January 1968 by Women Strike for Peace (WSP) (see Chapter 9). Named the "Jeanette Rankin Brigade" in honor of the first woman elected to the U.S. Congress, who had cast her vote against both world wars (see Chapter 7), the Washington, D.C., demonstration drew five thousand women, including eighty-seven-year-old Rankin. A group of younger women, determined to leave behind older traditions of female activism, organized a protest within a protest. They criticized the WSP for the link between pacifism and motherhood on which it had relied throughout the 1950s. "You have resisted our roles of supportive girlfriends and tearful widows," reads the leaflet they distributed. "Now you must resist

◆ Women against War

Although the most common images of anti-war protesters in the Vietnam era focus on college students, Americans of all sorts protested the war in Indochina. Among the first were members of Women Strike for Peace, a group that had taken up the anti-nuclear cause in the 1950s (see Chapter 9). This photograph of an April 1972 "die in" in New York City captures the dramatic techniques prevalent in anti-war demonstrations of the 1960s and 1970s. Here, WSP women are protesting President Nixon's bombing of Cambodia while specifically targeting ITT (International Telephone & Telegraph) because of its defense contracts with the military. *Swarthmore Peace Collection; photo by Dorothy Marder.*

approaching Congress playing these same roles that are synonymous with power-lessness."[3]

What Was Women's Liberation?

Women's liberationists approached the challenge of greater freedom for women in a manner radically different from that which NOW had laid out two years before. Well educated, confident of an affluent future, politically alienated, and disdainful of sexual restraints, young people of the 1960s had no faith in the older generation's ability to create a better world. "We want something more, much more, than the same gray, meaningless, alienating jobs that men are forced to sacrifice their lives to," wrote Robin Morgan in criticism of NOW's goal of integrating women into the American mainstream.[4] The young women who had come through the movements of the sixties envisioned a different kind of emancipatory politics for their sex. Their goal—and in many ways their achievement—was to revolutionize consciousness and culture, not to reform law and public policy. They did not form a single overarching organization but rather declared themselves a "movement," determined to bring about a dramatic shift in the fabric of history.

Even the label "feminism" seemed too old-fashioned and circumscribed to describe their movement, so they adopted a term of their own making. "Women's liberation" pointed to freedom for women without limits and without pragmatic considerations of what was politically feasible. Small women's liberation groups surfaced in 1968 and 1969 in many places throughout the country. Much has been written about New York City, but early and influential groups emerged as well in smaller (often college) towns such as Chapel Hill in North Carolina, Iowa City, and Gainesville, Florida. Women's liberation periodicals published in Seattle and Baltimore were read in Los Angeles and Boston. The spontaneity of this development and the lack of centralized direction or national organization were hallmarks of women's liberation.

Women's liberation can be clustered into three components: consciousness-raising, theory making, and social action. Consciousness-raising consisted of small groups of women—perhaps a dozen women meeting weekly—sharing personal and private aspects of their lives in order to understand female subordination. Accumulating their personal experiences into collective truths could free women from the belief that their lives were abnormal or that they were to blame personally for their alienation from norms of femininity. Topics ranged widely: What do you feel about menstruation? How do men see you? Were you a "nice girl"? Did you ever want to be a boy? What did you want to do with your life when you were little? Groups worked hard to create space for all women to speak and to avoid any sense that there was a "right" or "wrong" experience. Ultimately, consciousness-raising rested on the conviction that "the personal is political," that the massive power inequities that women still suffered could be found in the tiniest details of daily existence. No longer was it trivial that husbands refused to change the baby's diapers, that construction workers harassed women on the street, or that women felt inhibited from telling their boyfriends what they wanted sexually.

Groups of women's liberationists also worked to raise consciousness among a larger female public through dramatic public actions. They picketed and sat in at magazines from *Playboy* to *Ladies' Home Journal* in protest of their perpetuation of degrading stereotypes of women. The most famous such protest took place in Atlantic City, New Jersey, at the 1968 Miss America pageant, the site of a notorious "bra-burning" episode that has come down through history as a symbol for women's liberation. In reality, bras were not burnt at the demonstration but were dramatically thrown into a "freedom trash can," along with other "articles of torture." The women's liberationists did their best to make it clear that the Miss America pageant advertised not only a sexually objective and degrading notion of womanhood but also racism (no black woman had ever been chosen for the pageant) and militarism (see box, "No More Miss America!").

No More Miss America!

In 1968 a group of feminists staged a protest against the Miss America pageant in Atlantic City, New Jersey. They issued a statement, "No More Miss America!," in which they set out their plans for the demonstration, which included "Picket Lines; Guerrilla Theater; Leafleting; Lobbying Visits to the contestants urging our sisters to reject the Pageant Farce and join us; a huge Freedom Trash Can (into which we will throw bras, girdles, curlers, false eyelashes, wigs, and representative issues of Cosmopolitan, Ladies' Home Journal, Family Circle*)," and formulated a ten-point list of demands.*

The Degrading Mindless-Boob-Girlie Symbol. The Pageant contestants epitomize the roles we are all forced to play as women. The parade down the runway blares the metaphor of the 4-H Club county fair, where the nervous animals are judged for teeth, fleece, etc., and where the best "Specimen" gets the blue ribbon. So are women in our society forced daily to compete for male approval, enslaved by ludicrous "beauty" standards we ourselves are conditioned to take seriously.

Racism with Roses. Since its inception in 1921, the Pageant has not had one Black finalist, and this has not been for a lack of test-case contestants. There has never been a Puerto Rican, Alaskan, Hawaiian, or Mexican-American winner. Nor has there ever been a *true* Miss America—an American Indian.

Miss America as Military Death Mascot. The highlight of her reign each year is a cheerleader-tour of American troops abroad—last year she went to Vietnam to pep-talk our husbands, fathers, sons and boyfriends into dying and killing with a better spirit. She personifies the "unstained patriotic American womanhood our boys are fighting for." The Living Bra and the Dead Soldier. We refuse to be used as Mascots for Murder.

The Consumer Con-Game. Miss America is a walking commercial for the Pageant's sponsors. Wind her up and she plugs your product on promotion tours and TV—all in an "honest, objective" endorsement. What a shill.

Competition Rigged and Unrigged. We deplore the encouragement of an American myth that oppresses men as well as women: the win-or-you're-worthless competitive disease. The "beauty contest" creates only one winner to be "used" and forty-nine losers who are "useless."

The Woman as Pop Culture Obsolescent Theme. Spindle, mutilate, and then discard tomorrow. What is so ignored as last year's Miss America? This only reflects the gospel of our Society, according to Saint Male: women must be young, juicy, malleable—hence age discrimination and the cult of youth. And we women are brainwashed into believing this ourselves!

The Unbeatable Madonna-Whore Combination. Miss America and Playboy's centerfold are sisters over the skin. To win approval, we must be both sexy and wholesome, delicate but able to cope, demure yet titillatingly bitchy. Deviation of any sort brings, we are told, disaster: "You won't get a man!!"

The Irrelevant Crown on the Throne of Mediocrity. Miss America represents what women are supposed to be: inoffensive, bland, apolitical. If you are tall, short, over or under what weight The Man prescribes you should be, forget it. Personality, articulateness, intelligence, and commitment—unwise. Conformity is the key to the crown—and, by extension, to success in our Society.

Miss America as Dream Equivalent To—? In this reputedly democratic society, where every little boy supposedly can grow up to be President, what can every little girl hope to grow to be? Miss America. That's where it's at. Real power to control our own lives is restricted to men, while women get patronizing pseudo-power, an ermine cloak and a bunch of flowers; men are judged by their actions, women by appearance.

Miss America as Big Sister Watching You. The pageant exercises Thought Control, attempts to sear the Image onto our minds, to further make women oppressed and men oppressors; to enslave us all the more in high-heeled, low-status roles; to inculcate false values in young girls; women as beasts of buying; to seduce us to our selves before our own oppression.

SOURCE: Alexander Bloom and Wini Breines, eds., *Takin' It to the Streets: A Sixties Reader*, 2nd ed. (New York: Oxford University Press, 2002), 405–6.

Of all the changes in women's lives that came out of these consciousness-raising efforts, perhaps the most pervasive was the revisioning of sexuality from a thoroughly female point of view. No longer were women willing to regard their own sexuality solely in terms of how sexy they appeared to men. Instead women concentrated on exploring their own desires. They suggested that intercourse might not be as good a way for women to experience sexual pleasure as for men. Rejecting widespread diagnoses of female frigidity, women's liberation celebrated the possibilities of the clitoris. "What we must do is redefine our sexuality," wrote Anne Koedt in her widely read article, "The Myth of the Vaginal Orgasm." "We must discard the 'normal' concepts of sex and create new guidelines which take into account mutual enjoyment."[5] Masturbation, long a favorite topic among young men, now became a subject of experimentation and discussion among women.

The most radical change in sexual thinking and behavior had to do with lesbianism. (See Visual Sources: Lesbians in Postwar America, pp. 677–84.) The powerful new assertion of women's sexual desires, coupled with the exploration of the richness of women's relationships, encouraged many in women's liberation to pursue sexual relations with each other. "We were putting our energy into each other and slowly falling in love with each other," explains Marilyn Webb of Washington, D.C.[6] At the 1970 Congress to Unite Women in New York City, a group of lesbians took over the meeting, proudly declaring themselves the "Lavender Menace" and challenging the women in the audience to acknowledge, accept, and even explore same-sex love. The legitimation of lesbianism within women's liberation was facilitated by the argument that loving woman was as much a political identity as a sexual one. "Feminism is the theory, lesbianism is the practice," declared New Yorker Ti-Grace Atkinson.[7]

In popular memory, the link between women's liberation and lesbianism is very strong, but most women liberationists remained heterosexual. Indeed, women's liberation encouraged utopian ambitions for revolutionizing the intimate relations between men and women so that they could be genuine and full partners, and women need no longer choose between their own needs and ambitions and their love of men. Some marriages were shattered by the rise of women's liberation, but others were initiated or remade on an explicit basis of equality and mutuality. The women's liberation practice was for women not to take their husband's names upon marriage.

Women's liberation theory grew from consciousness-raising. The central project was to understand the structures of universal male dominance. "Our society, like all other historical civilizations, is a patriarchy," declared feminist writer Kate Millett in *Sexual Politics* (1970).[8] One of the boldest statements came from Shulamith Firestone, a twenty-four-year-old whose book *The Dialectic of Sex: The Case for Feminist Revolution* (1970) became an international best-seller. Like many radical feminists, Firestone worked from a left-wing framework garnered from her background as a student radical. Marxist theorists spoke of the dialectic, or contradiction, of class; Firestone wrote of the "dialectic of sex." The most basic human conflict was not economic but sexual, she contended, and its roots were nothing less than the biological distinction between the sexes. Firestone envisioned a future of mechanical wombs that would free women from the biological prison of their maternal role. In subsequent decades, as reproductive medicine made extraordinary breakthroughs, aspects of Firestone's predictions, which at the time seemed the stuff of science fiction, actually came into being.

Other theorists took the opposite tack, challenging the idea that differences between men and women were rooted in nature and thus fundamentally unchangeable. They documented the different ways that various societies formulated this distinction and how vigorously our own society worked to teach young children to be appropriately masculine or feminine. Part of the problem, they observed, lay with the word "sex" itself. Because it referred both to the biological capacity for human reproduction and the behavioral and psychological differences of men and women, it confused what was anatomical and what was social. To distinguish the two, women's liberation writers revived the obscure grammatical term "gender" to describe what anthropologist Gayle Rubin described in 1975 as "a set of arrangements by which the biological raw material of human sex and procreation is shaped by human, social intervention."[9]

The Agenda of Women's Liberation

The third component of women's liberation was social action. Determined to implement fundamental changes in gender relations, women's liberation groups sought to address the long-standing but unacknowledged oppression of women. Rape and other sorts of violence against women were brought dramatically into public light. Before women's liberation, rape victims were often suspected of dressing or behaving in provocative ways, and their testimony was distrusted by police and courts. Husbands were legally sheltered from rape prosecution on the grounds that sexual service was a wife's conjugal obligation. As women broke the silence around rape, it soon became clear how many sexual assaults went unreported. Women's liberationists held "speak-outs" to go public with their own experience as rape victims and established crisis centers to help other women find support. They undertook state-by-state campaigns to make sexual assault within marriage a crime. They established shelters for wives who were battered and exposed the common police practice of keeping the lid on domestic violence.

Another indication of women's determination to uproot patriarchy emerged in their protest against the medical system's treatment of women. The authority of physicians, roughly 90 percent of whom were then male, routinely went unchallenged, and women's complaints were often treated as psychological rather than physical symptoms. Focusing less on women becoming doctors and more on wresting the control of women's health from the hands of professionals altogether, women's liberationists learned the skills of midwifery and encouraged women to give birth at home, not in obstetrical wards. Carol Downer of Los Angeles specialized in teaching women how to do safe self-abortions at early stages of pregnancy. The Boston Women's Health Collective, none of whose members were doctors, became expert on the topics of women's bodies and needs and produced a short book, *Women and Their Bodies* (1970), which eventually became *Our Bodies,*

Ourselves. Its approach to women's health proved so empowering that it outgrew the resources of the original collective and was turned over to a commercial publisher for broader distribution.

Women's liberation affected some of its most dramatic changes in the area of higher education. Charging that the standard college curriculum ignored women's presence, many doctoral theses were begun in the early 1970s on the history of women, comparative anthropology of sex roles, and forgotten women writers and artists. Time-honored generalizations were reexamined for their applicability to women. "Did women have a Renaissance?," asked historian Joan Kelley Gadol. (The answer was no.) Entire disciplines were examined for hidden assumptions about the gendered nature of reason and intellectual authority. The natural and physical sciences were found to be particularly unfriendly to women. Simultaneously, Title IX of the federal Education Amendments Act of 1972 increased pressure on university administrations to hire women to remedy the colossal gender inequity in faculty staffing. Women's studies programs were established, initially on the very margins of legitimate academic study. The first such programs were founded in 1969 at Cornell University and San Diego State University. By 1973, there were over eighty programs and one thousand courses around the country.

Women's liberation was also concerned with women's experiences as wage earners, joining with NOW to put equality in the work world on the political agenda. The growing number of working mothers led to the demand for greater resources for day care, ranging from small-scale cooperatives to employer- and federally funded programs. Women's liberationists drew attention to the centrality of office and service work both to women's lives and to the American economy. The movement criticized the treatment of secretaries as "office wives" rather than as workers and challenged the long-standing disinterest of the American labor movement in organizing women's white- and pink-collar labor, as opposed to men's blue-collar jobs. The Chicago Women's Liberation Union was particularly active in these areas, sponsoring both the Action Committee for Day Care to promote public support for child care and Women Employed to help clerical workers organize for better pay, wider job opportunities, and general respect as workers.

Diversity and Race

The range of social action projects pursued by women's liberation suggests the diversity of women's experiences, needs, and demands. Concerns with racial and ethnic diversity also reflected the influence of the civil rights movement on the first generation of women's liberation activists. Early anthologies such as *Sisterhood Is Powerful* (1970) included selections from African American, Latina/Chicana, Asian American, and Native American women to substantiate the claim that sisterhood was all-inclusive. Nonetheless, there was little transracial organizing within women's liberation. While white women followed a gender separatist model and withdrew from New Left groups to form their own all-female collectives, women of color tended to remain within mixed-sex (but racially separatist) organizations.

For African American women, the concentration on male-female unity was especially strong in response to the 1965 publication of a federal report, "The Negro Family: A Case for National Action," authored by Daniel Patrick Moynihan, then assistant secretary in the U.S. Department of Labor. The Moynihan Report characterized the competence and power of African American women, in their families and in their communities, as "pathological," one of the factors holding back black Americans. The report was intended to aid in the advancement of African Americans, but written as it was before the emergence of women's liberation, it did so by blaming black women for single-parent households and rising male unemployment. Here was a federally authorized report calling for greater male dominance in the black community as a way to bring it into line with the larger society.

But the Moynihan Report alone would not have had such a powerful impact if it had not been for long-standing strains of racial antagonism within the history of American feminism, reaching back through the white-dominated women's movement of the early twentieth century to the Reconstruction era split over black suffrage (see Chapters 5 and 7). White women's liberationists did not think of themselves as bound by this history, but black women were well aware of it. Further exacerbating relations with white women was black women's resentment at sexual relations between black men and white women in the civil rights movement. Put simply, African American women did not trust white advocates of women's liberation to be truly inclusive in their struggle for freedom for women. One of the major challenges confronting the revived feminist movement was to face this history, overcome this distrust, and create a more inclusive, diverse women's freedom movement.

Despite their mistrust of white women's liberationists, women of color shared an interest in many feminist issues. Within the women's caucuses that they formed in their mixed-sex groups, they discussed and wrote about male chauvinism, reproductive freedom, and sexual exploitation. Simmering resentments about the treatment of women within SNCC led to the formation of a Black Women's Liberation Committee in 1968. "We can't talk about freedom and liberation," explained one of its founders, Frances Beal, "and talk about putting women down."[10] The group later expanded to include Puerto Rican and Asian American women and renamed itself the Third World Women's Alliance. A group of black women also organized in Mount Vernon, New York, to challenge black male nationalists' hostility to contraception and to defend their own right to reproductive self-determination. The first anthology of African American feminist writings, *The Black Woman,* was published in 1970.

Chicanas also began to explore feminist ideas at this time. They felt unwelcome in white-dominated women's groups but were charged by male comrades with being *vendidas* (traitorous sellouts) for allegedly following Anglo ideas. Chicanas particularly resented the argument that the truly authentic and politically devoted Mexican American woman was one who remained focused on her family. Undaunted, Anna NietoGomez and other Chicanas at California State University at Long Beach founded the *Hijas [Daughters] de Cuauhtemoc* in 1971, named after a 1911 Mexican women's rights group that the Cal State students rediscovered. The new *Hijas* organized for greater access to birth control within Mexican American communities and against the abuses of the social welfare system. In 1971, the *Hijas* and six hundred other Chicanas from all over the country gathered in Houston for the First National Chicana Conference, crowding into workshops on "Sex and the Chicana" and "Marriage Chicana Style."

Walking a careful line between embracing and challenging the premises of women's liberation, between promoting and criticizing their own communities and cultures, these women of color raised fundamental issues. They asked in what way white women wanted to be equal, and to whom. "Equal to white men in their power and ability to oppress Third World people?" is the way that the Third World Women's Alliance posed the question.[11] While women's liberation theory emphasized the overwhelming role of patriarchal power in the subordination of women, women of color insisted that the reality of inequality was more complex and that their lives were shaped by the intersections of race, class, and sex. In her important 1969 analysis, "Double Jeopardy: To Be Black and Female," Frances Beal concentrated on the role of American capitalism, which placed black women at the bottom of the economic ladder, below both black men and white women.

The feminism of women of color took a major step forward with the publication in 1977 of "A Black Feminist Statement," authored by the Combahee River Collective. The Collective, an outgrowth of the mid-1970s National Black Feminist Organization, was a Boston group of African Americans, many of them lesbians, who selected a name commemorating the Civil War leadership of Harriet Tubman (see Chapter 4). They insisted that their "sexual identity combined with their racial identity to make their whole life situation and the focus of their political struggles unique."[12] They named their approach, which focused on their own oppression rather than the suffering of others, as "identity politics." Their formulation encouraged a multiplicity of feminist voices, reflecting a diversity of women's experiences, rather than the unitary statement of a single, common "women's oppression" that had characterized the early white-dominated women's liberation years.

Following this identity politics approach to women's oppression, the 1981 anthology *This Bridge Called My Back: Writings by Radical Women of Color* brought together the unabashedly feminist writings of Chicanas and African Americans with Native American and Asian American women. "What began as a reaction to the racism of white feminists soon became a positive affirmation of the commitment of women of color to our *own* feminism," according to editors Cherríe Moraga and Gloria Anzaldúa.[13] The anthology's contributors, many of them lesbians, were not intimidated by the disapproval of male comrades, dedicating themselves to the strengthening of bonds between women. While they criticized white feminists for treating them as token symbols of women's universal victimization and for failing to recognize the power and resources that their home cultures provided them, they challenged the sexism and homophobia of their fathers, brothers, husbands, and political comrades. The challenge, according to Japanese American writer Mitsuye Yamada, is to "affirm our own culture while working within it to change it."[14]

◆ **Gloria Anzaldúa**

Poet, writer, and cultural theorist Gloria Anzaldúa was one of the first openly lesbian Chicana writers. Coeditor with Cherríe Moraga of the now-classic multicultural anthology *This Bridge Called My Back,* and author of the path-breaking *Borderlands/La Frontera: The New Mestiza* (see Documents: Feminist Revival in the 1990s, pp. 665–69), she was instrumental in revisioning feminism to embrace the concerns of lesbians and women of color. She died in 2004. *Photo copyright © by Annie Valva.*

Over time, these new, diverse approaches to women's lives and demands helped to shift the center of feminist energy and authority away from the white middle-class women with whom it had begun. One measure of the importance of the feminism of women of color is the tremendous efflorescence in their fiction. The writings of Toni Morrison, Sandra Cisneros, Amy Tan, and Louise Erdrich, among others, played a major role in bringing the feminist message and perspective to the masses of American women.

Feminism in the Seventies

As the various strands of women's liberation flourished, NOW continued its work on women's economic and political equality. One of its most visible early achievements was to force local newspapers to end their practice of sex-segregated help-wanted advertisements. To commemorate the fiftieth anniversary of the Nineteenth Amendment granting woman suffrage, on August 26, 1970, NOW organized a national "Women's Strike for Equality" day, focused on abortion rights, child care, and equal educational and economic opportunity. Especially outside of large cities and college towns, women inspired by the high media visibility of women's liberation turned to the only organization they could find, NOW, in the process changing it from a lobbying group to a mass membership organization. Like women's liberation, NOW was pressed to represent American women in all their diversity, especially in a series of confrontations about the prominence of lesbians in the organization. By 1974, NOW boasted seven hundred chapters, forty thousand members, and an annual budget of $300,000.

Thus women's liberation and NOW moved closer to form a common feminist movement, with the former contributing the issues and the militant stance and the latter the organizational structure and focus on institutional and legislative change. By 1970, 40 percent of American women were willing to say to pollsters that they favored "efforts to change and strengthen women's status in society."[15] Working women particularly favored changes, and African American women were twice as likely as white women to be supportive. *Ms.,*° a mainstream national feminist magazine, began publication in 1972. Under the editorship of journalist Gloria Steinem, the magazine featured high production values and commercial advertisements carefully chosen for their nonexploitative portrayal of women. Feminist bookstores, record companies, and publishing houses, restaurants and theater groups, battered women's shelters and child care centers were set up. Other feminist programs found a place in established institutions: birthing centers in hospitals, women's caucuses in political parties and trade unions, child care programs in corporations, rape task forces in police departments, women's studies programs in universities.

In the early 1970s, a raft of important federal legislation was passed on women's rights issues, including legislation clarifying the inclusion of women in the 1963 Equal Pay Act and the obligation of the Equal Employment Opportunity Commission, created in 1964, to deal with sex discrimination. Feminists succeeded in introducing Title IX of the Education Amendments Act of 1972, which prohibits sex discrimination in federally funded educational programs. Title IX passed with very little fanfare but eventually created a revolution in high school and college athletics by requiring that women's sports be funded at equivalent levels to men's sports.

As these legislative gains indicated, the established political system was being transformed by energies from the protest movements of the 1960s, including feminism. The 1972 Democratic National Convention had three times as many women delegates as in 1968. New Yorker Shirley Chisholm, who in 1968 had been the first African American woman elected to the U.S. Congress, four years later mounted a serious campaign for the Democratic nomination for president, the first woman and the first African American to do so.

The Democrats' eventual nominee in 1972 was George McGovern, the Senate's most outspoken opponent of the Vietnam War. President Richard M. Nixon

°The term "Ms." was revived by feminists in the 1970s so that women would no longer need to advertise their marital status by having to choose between the appellations "Miss" and "Mrs."

◆ **College Women Athletes Go the Distance**
In this photograph from the 2000 NCAA (National Collegiate Athletic Association) Outdoor Track and Field Championships in Durham, North Carolina, college women athletes are shown running the women's 5,000-meter race. Kara Wheeler (number 515) of the University of Colorado won the event. In the center is Amy Yoder of the University of Arkansas and on the right Marty Hernandez of Brigham Young University. The passage in 1972 of Title IX, which prohibits sex discrimination in federally funded programs, transformed the world of female athletics. Since 1972, women's participation in college sports has increased by 400 percent and in high school sports by 800 percent. Despite these developments, women's programs still lag behind men's: currently male athletic programs at NCAA institutions receive 36 percent more funding than women's. *AP/Photo/Erik Perel.*

ran a relentlessly negative campaign for reelection against him. Not content with aboveboard politics, the Committee to Reelect the President (known by the acronym CREEP) arranged for a covert break-in of the Democratic National Committee's headquarters at the Watergate apartment complex in Washington, D.C., to find documents to use against McGovern, but the burglars were caught by police. The positions that McGovern took were too liberal for the majority of Americans. Nixon won reelection in a landslide, but the repercussions of the Watergate episode were slowly unraveling his presidency.

Recognizing that the nation was profoundly war weary, the president became determined to find a way to end the war without losing it. In search of "peace with honor," Nixon simultaneously negotiated with and bombed the North Vietnamese, but his actions only deepened protests at home. Exactly one week after his second inauguration, Nixon announced a cease-fire with the North Vietnamese and began to withdraw American troops. Meanwhile, the Watergate burglars went on trial and evidence of high-level involvement in the episode began to accumulate.

Despite the administration's increasingly frantic cover-up efforts, public outrage grew at what increasingly came to be seen as the illegal use of presidential power. In the summer of 1974, Congress began to draw up articles of impeachment; to avoid this fate, Richard Nixon became the only American president to resign during his term in office. The lasting legacies of the Watergate scandal were profound, including both widespread public distrust of government and recognition of the political power wielded by the news media.

The Equal Rights Amendment and Reproductive Rights

The two issues that carried the impact of feminism into the very center of national politics from the 1970s on were the Equal Rights Amendment (ERA) and reproductive rights. The ERA, which amended the Constitution to prohibit the denial of legal equality on the basis of gender discrimination, had first been proposed in 1923 (see Chapter 8). Organized labor had long opposed the ERA for endangering protective labor legislation, but in the wake of the feminist upheaval of the sixties, the composition of the forces for and against the ERA changed dramatically. In 1973, urged on by female labor activists, the American Federation of Labor–Congress of Industrial Organizations (AFL-CIO) formally switched its position. Working women became a mainstay of the pro-ERA movement.

This switch in labor's attitude toward the ERA flowed directly from profound changes in the place and prospects of women in the labor force. Equal access to all occupations and equal pay for equal work were the most widely supported elements of the feminist agenda, and the ERA appeared to be just the tool to ensure economic justice for women. In 1972, the ERA easily passed both houses of Congress, and within a year thirty of the necessary thirty-six states had ratified the amendment. Victory seemed imminent. Few could foresee the long and protracted battle over the ERA and how it would lead to the emergence of an anti-feminist movement.

As the ERA appeared to be nearing ratification, legal equality was making gains in the courts. A group of feminist lawyers, led by future Supreme Court Justice Ruth Bader Ginsburg, revived the century-old New Departure argument (see Chapter 5) that the Equal Protection Clause of the Fourteenth Amendment could be used to protect women from discrimination. The Supreme Court began to rule that legal discrimination by gender was unconstitutional, including in cases where the law favored women over men. The first of these cases, *Reed v. Reed* (1971), involved an Idaho state law that gave fathers preference over mothers in control over the estate of a deceased child. The Court found this discrimination by gender irrelevant to the purposes of the law and ruled it unconstitutional. (See the Appendix, p. A-31.)

While the ERA effort pursued the long-standing feminist goal of legal equality, the campaign to decriminalize abortion highlighted the newest dimension of modern feminism, women's quest for sexual self-determination. Since no form of contraception was 100 percent reliable (except the birth control pill, the side effects of which posed complications), legal and safe access to abortion was important to heterosexually active women who wanted to have full control over whether, when, and how often they became pregnant. By 1970, when it was estimated that 1 million American women a year had illegal abortions, an abortion reform movement surfaced that sought to widen the legal loophole that allowed doctors to perform medically necessary abortions.[16] The feminist movement aimed to go further, insisting that abortion was not a matter of medical practice or criminal law but a highly personal decision that belonged only to the woman who was pregnant. The movement to reform abortion laws was thus transformed by the rising tide of feminism into the movement to repeal them.

Starting in 1967 in Colorado, some states began to liberalize their abortion laws, and in 1971, New York State completely decriminalized abortion in the first six months of pregnancy. But as the majority of state legislatures resisted these changes, abortion activists turned to the courts to challenge abortion laws. Norma McCorvey, a young single pregnant mother, was willing to be the plaintiff in such a case, even though it meant she would have to carry her pregnancy to term. Under the pseudonym "Jane Roe," she and her lawyers challenged the highly restrictive abortion laws of Texas. They won at the lower level, but the state of Texas appealed the decision to the U.S. Supreme Court.

On January 22, 1973, the Supreme Court ruled seven to two in favor of Jane Roe (see the Appendix, pp. A-31–A-32). *Roe v. Wade* was the most important Supreme Court case concerning women's rights since *Minor v. Happersett,* a century before (see the Appendix, p. A-25). The decision effectively threw out as unconstitutional all state laws making abortion a crime. But the decision was not without its troubling aspects and effectively invited the states to rewrite their laws to restrict abortion more narrowly, after the first trimester of pregnancy. With this inviting loophole, the battle for abortion rights began in earnest.

Meanwhile, women of color were beginning to draw attention to another aspect of the problem of reproductive freedom. Throughout the 1960s, many poor women, especially those dependent on government aid, were subject to tremendous pressure from physicians and social workers to allow themselves to be sterilized by tubal ligation, often while lying on the delivery table in the midst of labor. Among women on welfare, on Native American reservations, and in the U.S colony of Puerto Rico, sterilization statistics reached as high as one-third of women of childbearing age, a figure that activists equated to racial genocide. In 1974, the Department of Health, Education and Welfare issued guidelines requiring a three-day waiting period between granting consent and getting the operation. Even so, a great deal of patient advocacy at the local level was necessary to ensure that women understood the situation and had granted truly informed consent. This fight against "sterilization abuse" was important in clarifying that women must be able to make their own choices about their reproductive lives rather than have decisions forced on them by public regulations, institutional policy, or economic exigency. The campaign against sterilization abuse enlarged the abortion repeal movement into something larger and more basic, a movement for comprehensive reproductive rights for all women.

◆ Fighting for Reproductive Rights

By the mid-1970s, feminists' understanding of reproductive rights had moved beyond access to contraception and abortion to encompass the campaign against coercive sterilization, an abuse with its origins in public health officials' desire to control the childbearing of women in the welfare system. As this poster suggests, unwanted sterilization especially affected women of color: Native Americans, blacks, Puerto Ricans, and Chicanas. Because of the efforts of groups like CARASA (Committee for Abortion Rights and Against Sterilization), the U.S. Department of Health, Education and Welfare created guidelines that eventually halted these practices.

IN DEFENSE OF TRADITIONAL WOMANHOOD

As of 1968, the obstacles faced by insurgent feminism stemmed mostly from traditional beliefs and long-established sexism. Within a decade, however, a much more determined and organized resistance began to surface, concentrated especially on stopping ratification of the ERA and reversing the Supreme Court decision in *Roe v. Wade*. The political gains of anti-feminism were reinforced by a cultural and media blacklash, which called into question the desirability of feminist life choices.

The rank and file of the anti-feminist movement were women. Mostly white, devoutly Christian, married and with children, they rose in defense of traditional gender relations and what came to be called "family values." Ironically, the anti-feminist movement, like the feminist movement against which it was arrayed, pushed concerns about women's social role and status to the forefront of American political life. Indeed, the prominence of women in the anti-feminist and larger conservative movements is one of the most striking measures of the changing place of women in American life in the late twentieth century.

STOP-ERA and the New Right

Unlike the labor-based criticisms of the ERA of the past, opposition to the ERA in the 1970s came from the far right of the Republican Party. Throughout the 1950s and 1960s, right-wing leaders had dedicated themselves to halting the spread of communism. Starting in the early 1970s, however, a self-proclaimed "New Right " (a kind of mirror image of the New Left of the 1960s) switched to domestic issues and contested the recent and dramatic gains of the civil rights and feminist movements (and later the gay rights movement). The Republican Party, eager to break out of its image as the party of the rich, found this focus on these social issues extremely useful in attracting new adherents. Anti-feminism was a crucial factor in the conservative offensive that marked American political life in the late twentieth century.

Activist Phyllis Schlafly almost single-handedly put New Right anti-feminism on the political map. One of the most important female conservative leaders in U.S. history, Schlafly had been unable as a woman to make her mark on right-wing politics until she discovered the ERA issue in 1972. She formed a new organization, STOP (Stop Taking Our Privileges)-ERA, into which she recruited women who felt marginalized by the feminist upsurge. A lawyer and author as well as mother of six, her highly public career contradicted her message, which was that American society was best served and women were happiest when they remained full-time housewives and mothers (see box, "What's Wrong with 'Equal Rights' for Women").

Schlafly maintained that ratification of the ERA would wreak social chaos by eroding fundamental gender distinctions. Her charge that the ERA would forbid separate men's and women's public toilets got much attention, but her claim that

PHYLLIS SCHLAFLY
What's Wrong with "Equal Rights" for Women

Phyllis Schlafly (b. 1924) began her conservative activism in the 1950s when she fervently embraced the anti-Communist campaign. In the 1970s, she took up the cause of anti-feminism and founded the organization STOP-ERA. In this 1972 article published in her own newsletter, The Phyllis Schlafly Report, *Schlafly details her objections to the Equal Rights Amendment and feminism.*

THE FRAUD OF THE EQUAL RIGHTS AMENDMENT

In the last couple of years, a noisy movement has sprung up agitating for "women's rights." Suddenly, everywhere we are afflicted with aggressive females on television talk shows yapping about how mistreated American women are, suggesting that marriage has put us in some kind of "slavery," that housework is menial and degrading, and—perish the thought— that women are discriminated against. New "women's liberation" organizations are popping up, agitating and demonstrating, serving demands on public officials, getting wide press coverage always, and purporting to speak for some 100,000,000 American women.

It's time to set the record straight. The claim that American women are downtrodden and unfairly treated is the fraud of the century. The truth is that American women never had it so good. Why should we lower ourselves to "equal rights" when we already have the status of special privilege?

The proposed Equal Rights Amendment states: "Equality of rights under the law shall not be denied or abridged by the United States or by any state on account of sex." So what's wrong with that? Well, here are a few examples of what's wrong with it.

This Amendment will absolutely and positively make women subject to the draft. Why any woman would support such a ridiculous and un-American proposal as this is beyond comprehension. Why any Congressman who had any regard for his wife, sister, or daughter would support such a proposition is just as hard to understand. Foxholes are bad enough for men, but they certainly are *not* the place for women—and we should reject any proposal which would put them there in the name of "equal rights." . . .

Another bad effect of the Equal Rights Amendment is that it will abolish a woman's right to child support and alimony, and substitute what the women's libbers think is a more "equal" policy, that "such decisions should be within the discretion of the Court and should be made on the economic situation and need of the parties in the case."

Under present American laws, the man is *always* required to support his wife and each child he caused to be brought into the world. Why should women abandon these good laws—by trading them for something so nebulous and uncertain as the "discretion of the Court"?

The law now requires a husband to support his wife as best as his financial situation permits, but a wife is not required to support her husband (unless he is about to become a public charge). A husband cannot demand that his wife go to work to help pay for family expenses. He has the duty of financial support under our laws and customs. Why should we abandon these mandatory wife-support and child-support laws so that a wife would have an "equal" obligation to take a job?

By law and custom in America, in case of divorce, the mother always is given custody of her children unless there is overwhelming evidence of mistreatment, neglect or bad character. This is our special privilege because of the high rank that is placed on motherhood in our society. Do women really want to give up this special privilege and lower themselves to "equal rights," so that the mother gets one child and the father gets the other? I think not. . . .

What "Women's Lib" Really Means

Many women are under the mistaken impression that "women's lib" means more job employment opportunities for women, equal pay for equal work, appointments of women to high positions, admitting more women to medical schools, and other desirable objectives which all women favor. We all support these purposes, as well as any necessary legislation which would bring them about.

But all this is only a sweet syrup which covers the deadly poison masquerading as "women's lib." The women's libbers are radicals who are waging a total assault on the family, on marriage, and on children.

Source: William H. Chafe et al., *A History of Our Time: Readings on Postwar America*, 6th ed. (New York: Oxford University Press, 2003), 211–13. (Original source: *The Phyllis Schlafly Report* 5, no. 7 (February 1972), noted as reprinted with permission of the author.)

◆ Map 10.1 **The Battle over the ERA**

The ERA quickly won support in 1972 and 1973 but then stalled. ERAmerica, a coalition of women's groups formed in 1976, lobbied extensively, especially in North Carolina, Florida, and Illinois, but failed to sway the conservative legislatures in those states. After Indiana ratified in 1977, the amendment still lacked three states' votes toward the three-fourths majority required for a constitutional amendment. Subsequent efforts to revive the ERA were unsuccessful.

the ERA would extend the draft to women proved more troubling. She also insisted that instead of ending sex discrimination, the ERA would deprive women of crucial privileges such as the expectation of economic support from their husbands. Schlafly's claims put the pro-ERA forces on the defensive. Ironically, many of her concerns, such as women going into the armed services, came to pass despite the defeat of the ERA. The erosion in the position and status of the housewife was the consequence not of a change in the Constitution but of underlying economic and social developments.

By lobbying forcefully in crucial state legislatures, STOP-ERA slowed the pace of ratification to a crawl. NOW fought back by urging feminists to refuse to travel to or do business in states that refused to ratify the ERA, but to no avail. In 1977, Indiana was the last state to ratify. Congress extended the period for ratification by four years, but it made no difference. In 1982, the ERA went down to defeat, three states short of ratification, with both pro- and anti-forces exhausted but also battle-strengthened (see Map 10.1).

From Anti-Abortion to Pro-Life

The campaign to undo *Roe v. Wade* was not as successful as STOP-ERA and failed to recriminalize abortion, but its impact on the larger political environment was, if anything, greater. To the anti-abortion movement, legalized abortion represented the triumph of untrammeled individualism over women's sacred vocation of motherhood. Opponents staked their ground on the rights of the fetus, framing the women who sought abortions either as murderously selfish or victimized by abortion advocates. To indicate the larger issues at stake, the anti-abortion movement renamed itself "pro-life"—prompting the pro-abortion forces to christen themselves, in equally expansive language, "pro-choice."

The anti-abortion movement has consistently been based in religious sentiment. It got its start in 1971 when the Catholic Church sponsored the formation of the National Right to Life Committee. A sophisticated media campaign, including films of late-term fetuses *in utero* and photographs of tiny fetal hands, built popular support. (Pro-choicers retaliated with the image of a wire hanger, to symbolize deaths from illegal abortions.) Starting in the late 1970s, leadership of the anti-abortion movement shifted to fundamentalist Protestants. Activists marched in front of abortion clinics that had sprung up since *Roe v. Wade.* They intimidated so many physicians from providing abortions that women in 80 percent of the nation's counties lost access to abortion.[17] In 1995, the movement secured a tremendous public relations victory when Norma McCorvey, the Roe of *Roe v. Wade,* renounced her support for abortion. In cities across the country, pro-choicers and pro-lifers engaged in angry face-to-face encounters. Eventually, the heightened rhetoric of the pro-lifers, which characterized legalized abortion as a "holocaust" of unborn babies, spilled into physical violence, as clinics were bombed and abortion providers were murdered from Boston to California.

In the 1980s, Congress and state legislatures started to pass new legal limitations on who could get abortions, when, and under what conditions. These laws required underage girls to obtain parental permission for an abortion, denied public funds for abortion, and mandated waiting periods and elaborate counseling. As cases challenging these laws made their way through the court system, the fate of abortion rights seemed increasingly precarious. In the 1989 *Webster v. Reproductive Health Services* and the 1992 *Planned Parenthood v. Casey* cases, the Supreme Court ruled that many of these restrictions were constitutional, stopping just short of overturning *Roe v. Wade* altogether (see the Appendix, p. A-34). More recent cases have focused on local ordinances forbidding aggressive pro-life picketing at clinics and a Nebraska law prohibiting late-term ("partial-birth") abortions, which a five-to-four Court majority struck down in 2000 as unconstitutionally vague. In 2003, President George W. Bush signed a federal law banning late-term abortions that President Bill Clinton had previously vetoed. (In the fall of 2004, several federal judges ruled the law unconstitutional.)

Simultaneous with the gains that conservatives were making against the ERA and abortion rights, a more diffuse anti-feminism began to surface. In her best-selling book, *Backlash: The Undeclared War on American Women* (1991), Susan

Faludi explored claims that circulated widely in the 1980s about the unhappiness and disappointment that women who had chosen feminist lifestyles were allegedly suffering. One particularly inflammatory sociological study, reported on by *Newsweek* in 1986, stated that if a woman was over forty and single, her chances for marriage were less than her chances of being killed by a terrorist.[18] Frightening if exaggerated statistics and news stories also appeared about an infertility "epidemic" among women who delayed childbearing, the economic costs to women of the rising divorce rate, and widespread psychological depression among unmarried career women. Not only was there no remaining task for feminism, according to the backlash mentality, but the movement's achievements had cost women dearly.

As feminism fell back into disfavor, young women in the 1990s took up the challenge of developing what is sometimes called the "third wave." (See Documents: Feminist Revival in the 1990s, pp. 665–76.) They had learned from the conflicts of the seventies to create much more racially diverse politics. They built on the previous generation's success at combating sexual violence and defending women's right to greater sexual pleasure, and they advanced a more consistently positive approach to female sexuality. All this was important as the controversies over the character and direction of modern women's lives were becoming central to national politics.

Women's Issues and Presidential Politics

The cultural backlash against feminism coincided with profound political changes. Ronald Reagan, whose 1980 election reflected the rising fortunes of the New Right, was America's first anti-abortion president. Among his many friendly gestures to the pro-life movement was the 1988 announcement of an Emancipation Proclamation for Unborn Children. But the "Reagan Revolution" could not reverse feminist gains. As America's first divorced president, he may have even benefited from them. It fell to Reagan in 1981 to appoint the first woman justice to the Supreme Court, Sandra Day O'Connor. To the consternation of many opponents of abortion, O'Connor often cast the swing vote in abortion cases, usually willing to uphold the constitutionality of numerous restrictions but not to vote against the essential holding in *Roe v. Wade,* that women's constitutionally protected right to privacy included the right to choose an abortion.

From this point on, every major presidential candidate had to take a position on abortion, with Republicans favoring the pro-life side and Democrats the pro-choice. Supreme Court nominations became key in the battle over abortion. One of the most dramatic fights took place in 1991, when President George H. W. Bush nominated Clarence Thomas to fill the seat vacated by the great civil rights leader, Thurgood Marshall. During the nomination process, Anita Hill—like Thomas, an African American lawyer—charged that Thomas had sexually harassed her when they worked together at the Equal Employment Opportunity Commission. Television audiences sat riveted while Hill told intimate and embarrassing details of Thomas's unwanted sexual advances before the entirely male Senate Judiciary Committee. Thomas angrily denied the charges and claimed that he was being

◆ Congresswomen on the March

The October 1991 Senate hearings to confirm Clarence Thomas to the Supreme Court highlighted not only the issue of sexual harassment but the persistent underrepresentation of women in Congress. The Senate had only two women members, and the committee that heard Hill's testimony was entirely male. On October 9, seven female members of the House of Representatives, enraged by the treatment that Hill was receiving in the "men's club" atmosphere of the hearings, marched up the Capitol steps to demand that the Senate delay the hearings and investigate Hill's charges. The delegation was led by Barbara Boxer of California, who a year later became a U.S. senator. *Paul Hosefros/NYT Pictures.*

subjected to a "high-tech lynching for uppity blacks." The senators, unwilling to appreciate the gravity of Hill's charges, voted in favor of Thomas, who went on to become one of the court's most consistently conservative and anti-abortion justices. The Thomas-Hill incident catapulted the issue of sexual harassment into public consciousness. In the wake of the hearings, national polls confirmed the widespread experience of sexual harassment on the job, with four of ten women saying that they had faced unwanted sexual advances from men at work.

The Thomas-Hill incident also contributed to the growing power and assertiveness of women in electoral politics. In the 1992 elections, the number of women elected to the Senate increased from three to seven and in the House from thirty to forty-eight; the figures have been steadily rising ever since. Carol Moseley Braun, an Illinois state legislator, became the first African American female senator. More than a half century after women had won the right to vote, a female voting bloc had finally emerged, with women more likely to vote Democratic and men Republican.[19] "The gravitation of men and women to different political camps appears to be the outstanding demographic development in American politics over the past twenty years," claimed the *Atlantic Monthly* in 1996.[20] Men and women evidenced basic differences not only over clearly feminist issues but over the general role of government, especially with respect to social services, with women favoring more and men favoring less.

In the 1992 election, women supported Democrat Bill Clinton over President George H. W. Bush, but only by a few percentage points. During his first administration, Clinton's strength among women voters grew. Betty Ford and Rosalynn

Carter had supported the ERA when they were first ladies, but Hillary Rodham Clinton was America's first First Lady to have worked full-time for a living. To supporters, but even more to opponents, the Clintons as individuals and as a couple embodied the massive changes that had taken place in America's gender and marital practices over the last quarter century. President Clinton appointed women to prominent federal offices, from Janet Reno as attorney general to Madeleine Albright as secretary of state, making her the first woman to be ranked so high in the presidential order of succession. For the Supreme Court's second female member, he chose Ruth Bader Ginsburg. By the time of the 1996 presidential election, the female vote for a second Clinton administration was eleven points higher than the male vote.

Then, in 1998, President Clinton became embroiled in a scandal over a sexual affair with a twenty-one-year-old White House intern named Monica Lewinsky. On the grounds that he had publicly lied about the relationship, he became the second president in American history (after Andrew Johnson in 1868) to be tried on articles of impeachment. Feminism played a complicated, even ironic role in this episode. Although many previous presidents had been notorious adulterers, thirty years of feminism had called into question the long-standing assumption that men in power could engage in extramarital sex with impunity, and the proponents of impeachment made ample use of this new revulsion at the double standard. Nonetheless, in striking contrast to the position most feminist groups had taken on the Thomas-Hill affair, they stood by Clinton, probably because of his consistent defense of abortion rights.

The first president of the twenty-first century, George W. Bush, has pursued a mixed path with respect to women in politics. In small and large ways, he has continued to wear away at abortion rights, including the withdrawal of $34 million in congressionally authorized funds from United Nations family planning programs, claiming that these moneys would facilitate the availability of abortions to women around the world. His opposition to stem cell research derived from fetal tissue, a position strongly held by the pro-life movement, has proved particularly controversial for interfering with scientific breakthroughs in the treatment of diabetes, Alzheimer's, and other diseases. His nominees for judicial appointments to the federal bench have been overwhelmingly pro-life advocates. Yet, he nominated a significant number of women to important government positions, including on the courts. One of his closest aides was Condoleezza Rice, a black woman who held the highly nontraditional role of national security advisor.

National security issues moved center stage as a result of the September 11, 2001, terrorist attacks on the United States in which Al Qaeda extremists hijacked four commercial airliners. Two destroyed the World Trade Center in New York City, another seriously damaged the Pentagon, and a fourth crashed in a Pennsylvania field. Among the more than three thousand people who died were women such as CeeCee Lyles and Debby Welse, flight attendants who joined passengers in preparing to bring down the fourth plane before it could be flown into the White House, its likely target. The U.S. decision to go to war against the Afghan Taliban regime for harboring Al Qaeda was justified in part by the Taliban's barbaric treat-

◆ March for Women's Lives

On April 25, 2004, numerous feminist groups staged one of the largest demonstrations ever to take place in Washington, D.C. Estimates of attendance at the "March for Women's Lives" ranged from 500,000 to over a million. Sparked by President George W. Bush's anti-abortion policies, pro-choice demonstrators called for equal access to reproductive services, noting that restrictions particularly hurt poor women. They also demanded a restoration of federal funds pledged through the United Nations to birth control programs around the world. As was the case with the 1913 woman suffrage march in Washington, D.C. (see Figure 7.6, p. 452), demonstrators chose the nation's capitol as a highly symbolic place to make their political demands. © *ZUMA/CORBIS.*

ment of Afghan women, to which women's groups in the United States had been trying to draw attention for some time. In the presidential election of 2004, Democratic Party candidate John Kerry largely agreed with President Bush on the need to protect the nation from terrorism and to win the war in Iraq, but he argued for a more multilateral approach. The shadow of the sixties loomed over the election, owing to Kerry's history as a leader of the anti–Vietnam War movement. An inflammatory new issue, the legalization of gay marriage, was also crucial (see Figure 10.6, p. 684). Referenda banning the practice passed in eleven states, including Ohio, where the president won the electoral college votes that gave him the election. Women voted more for Kerry than did men, but the gender gap was not as large as it had been in previous elections.

WOMEN, WORK, AND FAMILY

This intense political conflict over women's roles, family life, and sexual mores was a measure of how deeply women's place in American society and the U.S. economy had changed. By the start of the twenty-first century, the majority of women worked most of their adult lives outside the home, a development of enormous consequence for American family life. Women at the high and low ends of the economic ladder dealt with these conflicts very differently. The dramatic upswing in immigration after 1965, one of several ways in which globalization increasingly shaped the lives of American women, further complicated the portrait of women's work and family lives at millennium's end.

Women in the Labor Force

For almost two centuries, the numbers and percentages of women in the labor force has been rising steadily, but in the last third of the twentieth century, this steady quantitative change became a dramatic qualitative change. This development took place in the context of broad economic transformations, beginning with the move abroad of much of America's manufacturing sector to be replaced by a labor force of service workers and a rapidly growing high-tech sector. Between 1970 and 2000, employment rates, stock market averages, and average incomes went up and down, but what remained steady was increasing inequality in wealth. By 1996, the United States was the most economically stratified industrial nation in the world. Meanwhile, standards of consumption were going up — the majority of American households now had VCRs and computers. It was in this context that the place of work in women's lives was undergoing major alterations. By 1990, women constituted almost half of paid labor, drawn into the workforce by economic pressures as well as by shifting attitudes and practices. The working mother was now the norm (see the Appendix, p. A-38).

From one perspective, women workers were moving in the direction of equality with men. The median wage for full-time women workers increased from 59 percent of men's average earnings in 1970 to 77 percent in 2002. The wage gap between white and black women also narrowed, although the combined impact of race and gender discrimination left black women earning 64 percent and Hispanic women 52 percent of the average earnings of white men. In the professions, the infusion of women was stunning. The percentage of medical degrees awarded to women jumped from 10 percent in 1977 to 41 percent in 1997, and of law degrees from 22 percent to 44 percent in that same period. By century's end, women were the majority of graduates in veterinary medicine and pharmacy programs. Even in the corporate world, the substantial barrier against women in high positions, called the "glass ceiling" because it was invisible until hit, began to give way. The percentage of major corporations with female executives quintupled from 5 percent in 1970 to 25 percent in 2002. The narrowing of the gender gap in wages reflected not only women's gains but men's losses as the number of high-paying jobs in the skilled manufacturing sector, in which men predominated, declined significantly.

Looked at more closely, however, the experience of working women was decidedly more mixed. While barriers were falling in male-dominated occupations and professions, close to 75 percent of women continued to work in female-dominated jobs. These sectors of the labor force were generally less well paid and constituted the major downward drag on women's aggregate earning figures. Eighty percent of clerical and administrative support jobs, 90 percent of private household labor, and almost 70 percent of institutional service work continued to be performed by women. As one observer writes, "for women and men to be equally represented throughout all occupations in the economy today, 53 out of every 100 workers would have to change jobs."[21]

For women seeking to break into male-dominated jobs, affirmative action programs were a major resource. In 1971, the Republican administration of President Nixon issued guidelines for federally contracted employment that went beyond banning discrimination by race and gender to authorize "affirmative action" in hiring. State and local governments and private corporations followed suit, and universities instituted affirmative action admission plans to qualify more women and minorities for professional employment. Affirmative action campaigns also opened up jobs in steel factories, construction trades, and police and fire departments. A measure of the impact of these programs was the political and legal reaction against them. In 1978, the Supreme Court ruled in *University of California Regents v. Bakke* that race—and by implication gender—could be used as one of many criteria for admission to the University of California, but that an affirmative action "quota" was unconstitutional (see the Appendix, p. A-33). Dismantling affirmative action programs, which were recast as "reverse discrimination," became a major plank of the conservative Republican platform. In 2003, the Supreme Court continued to walk a narrow line, ruling that the University of Michigan Law School could consider race among other factors in admissions, but that the undergraduate admission ranking, which awarded points to underrepresented racial groups, was unconstitutional.

Other approaches were necessary to improve the wages for women in female-dominated occupations. As late as the 1980s, jobs predominantly held by women were paid close to 30 percent less than those in which men were the majority. The "comparable worth" approach proposed to rectify this inequity by systematically upgrading the pay rates of female-dominated job classifications. State and city governments instituted pay equity programs throughout the 1980s. Labor unions, especially those in the clerical and service sectors, also became resources for women in female-dominated industries. While union membership in general declined sharply, in part because of hostile Republican administrations, women's proportion of the membership rose from 19 percent in 1962 to 42 percent in 2002. Groups of female workers that were never before considered candidates for unionization formed militant labor organizations that took male labor leaders by surprise. For instance, the Association of Flight Attendants, formed in 1973 and accepted into the AFL-CIO in 1984, successfully fought demeaning aspects of this occupation such as age and weight requirements and the job title of "airline hostess." Unions in service jobs and public employment especially benefited by the growth in female unionization.

Changes in Family and Personal Life

The tremendous growth in women's labor force participation led to profound changes in women's family and personal lives. Lifelong marriage became far less common as a goal and as an experience in the last third of the twentieth century. One historian refers to this as the "disestablishment" of the institution of marriage in favor of the "pluralization" of sexual and familial arrangements.[22] With women's increasing capacity for self-support and the widespread acceptability of cohabitation among unmarried couples, the rates of marriage declined. The divorce rate rose so steeply that one out of every two marriages ended in divorce (although most divorced people remarried). By the late 1990s, only one out of four households included a married couple. The steepest rise was among those who had never married, the percentage of which in 1998 was three times that of 1970.° The numbers of African American women who never married was fifteen to twenty percentage points higher than in the general population.

The increasing acceptability of lesbianism was an important element in the growing numbers of unmarried women. Formal statistics on numbers of lesbians are almost impossible to come by, but the 2000 census included approximately 5.5 million same-sex couples. There was also considerable change among heterosexual married couples, largely as a result of women's growing labor force participation. As young women concentrated on jobs and careers, the average age at which they married rose to 25.1 in 2002, the highest in American history. By the late 1990s, the majority of married couples included two wage earners, the wife as well as the husband. Increasingly the dual-income marriage was replacing the male-breadwinner structure as the most reliable way for a family to improve its standard of living.

The decline in marriage as a way of life pointed in two quite different directions for women, depending on economic status. At the upper end of the income ladder, women were able to support themselves, engage in sexual relationships, become homeowners, and have children without marriage. As early feminist calls for publicly funded child care went unheeded, women in professional, corporate, and managerial jobs turned to low-wage women to care for their children, clean their homes, and tend to their aging parents. A century-long decline in the private domestic sector was dramatically reversed.

At the lower end, women supporting themselves and their children on a single female income found themselves much poorer. Female-headed families were six times as likely to be living below the poverty level as two-parent families. Observers disagreed on how to deal with this development, which sociologists labeled

---

° The actual percentage varies depending on the age cohort. Thus, for women 30–34, 21.6 percent are never married, while from 35–40, the percentage goes down to 14.3 percent.

"the feminization of poverty." Conservatives mounted a national campaign to revive marriage and bring men's wages back into women's lives, while liberals called for higher wages for women and better access to social services.

Childbearing and childrearing also underwent significant change. Women had fewer children, had them later, had more of them outside of marriage, and were more likely never to have them at all. In 1998, one out of five women in their mid-forties was childless, twice the rate of two decades earlier. Increasingly, the functions of childbearing and childrearing were being separated off from marriage, so that neither was the prerequisite for the other. Women were more likely to marry without having children and more likely to have children without marrying. In 2002 one out of three children was born to an unmarried mother. Although much attention was paid to unmarried teenage pregnancies, in fact their numbers were declining while the numbers of adult women who were having children outside of marriage were rising. Unmarried motherhood was still much more common among African American women, but the rate among white women was gaining.

The growth in single motherhood and female-headed households took place as funds for social services, on which the poorest of these women relied, were being reduced. The welfare rights movement of the late 1960s had encouraged poor women to regard federal welfare programs, especially Aid to Families with Dependent Children (AFDC), as entitlements. By the mid-1970s, 3.6 million families, or more than 5 percent of the American population, relied on AFDC. This program had been designed in the 1930s when stay-at-home motherhood was the standard, but American attitudes had changed dramatically, no longer assuming that mothers had to be kept at home with their children (see Chapter 8). As working mothers became the norm, AFDC became problematic, and poor single mothers on welfare became political targets.

The attack on AFDC, begun in the Reagan years, culminated in 1996 when President Clinton signed the Personal Responsibility and Work Opportunities Act, claiming to "end welfare as we know it." The law limited poor women and children to receive federal welfare assistance for no more than five years. By 2000, the welfare rolls had been cut in half. Poor single mothers were now required to take any job available to them, no matter how low the pay; most of these jobs lacked any health benefits to replace the federal programs from which these families had been removed. Overall, more women were in the labor force but were not out of poverty. In 2003, census bureau data indicated that one-fifth of all homes headed by working single mothers were below the poverty line of approximately $18,000 in annual income.

Poor women faced special challenges, but modern mothering was difficult for working women at all economic levels. The problem of balancing home and work life became the most persistent and difficult personal dilemma for many American women. As one historian writes, "Women remain caught between a world of work, which assumes that there is someone behind every worker who is available to take care of family needs, and the tenacious presumption that women have primary responsibility for children and household."[23] Only at the higher end of the economic

◆ **Sally Forth, a Working Mother**

In 1953, when *Life* magazine ran the photographs on page 566, working mothers were still considered a novelty in popular culture. By the 1980s, they had become a staple in television, movies, advertisements, and even comics. The comic strip *Sally Forth* details the work and family life of a professional woman, who has a supportive husband, Ted, and a precocious ten-year-old daughter, Hillary. Created by Greg Howard, *Sally Forth* began syndication in 1982 and continues to be highly popular, appearing in over seven hundred newspapers. *Reprinted with special permission of King Features Syndicate.*

scale did working mothers turn to paid nannies to care for their children in their own homes. The children of most working mothers were cared for by the children's fathers, their grandparents, other people caring for children out of their own homes, or at daycare centers. In contrast to the mothers of the 1950s, who were discontent because they spent too much time at home raising children, late twentieth-century mothers worried about their divided lives, about not having enough time with their children, and about falling behind at the workplace.

Women and the New Immigration

The last third of the twentieth century saw important changes in the racial and ethnic composition of American womanhood. In 1965 Congress passed the Immigration and Nationality Act. This law opened up the gates of immigration closed since 1924; it also shifted from quotas based on countries of origin to categories based on occupational skills, family ties, and political refugee status. For the first time in over forty years, large numbers of immigrants began to flow into the United States (see the Appendix, p. A-40). Many new immigrants lacked formal immigration papers, either because they overstayed temporary visas or because they crossed into the country without papers in the first place. One estimate is that in 1988 there were 2 million so-called undocumented immigrants in the United States.[24]

In terms of gender, post-1965 immigration differed dramatically from the 1880–1920 wave (see Chapter 6). By 1995, women were the majority of legal immigrants, drawn to the United States as immigrants have always been by the hope of greater individual opportunity but now within an international labor market of low-waged women. (See Visual Sources: American Women in the World, pp. 685–92.) Unlike earlier generations, immigrant women were more likely than native-born women to work outside the home for wages. The new immigrants also differed dramatically in their lands of origin. Instead of eastern and southern Europe, half of the new immigrants came from Mexico and Central and Latin America, and a quarter from Asia.

The boom in immigration led to the revival of anti-immigrant sentiment, much of it focused on immigrants' reliance on publicly funded social services. Women and children were the special targets of these attacks because they made much greater use of educational, health, and welfare services than did men. In 1994, a voter initiative barring immigrants and their children from public schools and hospitals was passed in California but thrown out by the courts as unconstitutional. Two years later, the carefully titled federal Illegal Immigration Reform and Immigrant Responsibility Act barred immigrants, even those with legal status, from federal welfare programs for five years after their arrival. Such legislation did not reduce poor immigrants' dependence on public services so much as shift it to other programs. Thus, immigrant women who were denied prenatal care turned to emergency rooms to have their babies and required costly neonatal intervention when their American-born (hence citizen) children were sickly or underweight.

Despite the growing political hostility that they faced, immigrant women made important and varied contributions to American society. At one end of the occupational ladder, immigrant women brought with them professional skills. Filipinas and Korean women became a major presence in the nursing profession. Chinese and Indian female immigrants also went into professional occupations. At the other end, immigrant women flowed into the lowest rungs of the female labor force ladder, where their low-paid labor made services and manufactured goods affordable for middle-class Americans. In the garment industry, the majority of workers were Latino and Asian women. Low pay, long hours, and dangerous working conditions recalled the immigrant sweatshops of a century before (see Chapter 7). Immigrant women also poured into the booming service sector. In institutional service work such as cooking and cleaning in hospitals and hotels, they usually did the dirtiest work and had the least desirable working shifts. Starting with the 1990 "Justice for Janitors" campaign in Los Angeles, immigrant women workers helped to spark a union revival in the service industry. Blanca Gallegos, spokeswoman for the Hotel and Restaurant Employees Union, explained, "If you're working hard, you shouldn't be living in poverty. . . . It presents a lot of difficulties for women, especially for single mothers."[25]

Immigrant women also were the overwhelming number of private domestic workers. The cheapness of the labor of immigrant women was a crucial factor in the ability of middle-class women to take jobs outside the household. One of the many ironies of the predominance of immigrant women in private domestic labor, especially the thriving nanny sector of the field, was that market forces drove native-born women to entrust the raising of their children to immigrant women unfamiliar with American culture who were not primarily English speakers. Thus the relationship between worker and employer was skewed toward cultural conflict and misunderstanding. The hidden economy of immigrant domestic workers became a political issue in 1993 when President Clinton's 1993 nomination of Zoe Baird for U.S. Attorney General floundered on the discovery that she had employed two immigrant maids without legal status and had not paid social security taxes on their wages.

The immigrant women drawn to the United States were part of the larger phenomenon of globalization. This term refers to the process by which corporations have grown so large and powerful that they increasingly dominate separate national economies, exacerbating inequalities and eroding cultural differences among the peoples of the world. The collapse of the Soviet Union in 1989 left international capitalism an unchallenged system, thus accelerating globalization. American corporations set up factories abroad, where U.S. government regulations and trade unions could be evaded and labor costs were much lower. In this way, the foreign women who work for American corporations — across the Mexican border making clothing, in China making children's toys, and in Vietnam making athletic shoes — can be considered part of the history of the United States through women's eyes.

Another side to globalization has encouraged American women to collaborate with women activists in the Middle East, Asia, and Africa to advance the legal, economic, and reproductive rights of women the world over. The agenda and reach of feminism has thus been broadened far beyond what the founders of NOW or women's liberation could have imagined, giving greater reality to their initial vision of universal sisterhood.

CONCLUSION: Women Face a New Century

At the very core of the dramatic changes in women's lives and expectations since 1968 were women's accelerating participation in the paid labor force and the subsequent erosion of traditional family patterns. Politically and culturally, the radical movements of the sixties and early seventies — from black power, the counterculture, and the anti-war movement to Chicano, Native American, and Asian American nationalism — also were fundamental to women's history, reigniting a long-dormant feminist tradition and encouraging a new generation to rethink the meaning of freedom for women. And not only feminism but also the anti-feminist movement have had a powerful impact on women's lives and American history, making debates about sex, gender, and family increasingly central to national politics.

It might seem that feminism caused the deep economic and social changes in American women's lives, but it is more accurate to say that it resulted from them. Feminism gave millions of women a framework for interpreting their lives and served as a catalyst for mobilizing women for social and political change. Above all, from the special perspective of this book — revisioning American history through women's eyes — the modern feminist revival marked a tremendous increase in women's determination to take an active, conscious role in the shaping of American society.

DOCUMENTS

Feminist Revival in the 1990s

T HE DEFEAT OF THE ERA in 1982 seems symbolic of the way in which the feminist movement itself stalled in the early 1980s. The anti-feminism that Susan Faludi detailed in her 1991 bestseller *Backlash* (see p. 653) undermined a strong movement on behalf of women, but there were also problems within feminism. Membership in NOW dropped off, *Ms.* magazine struggled to stay afloat, and younger women seemed increasingly indifferent. But in the early years of the 1990s, a disparate group of young women started calling attention to a resurgent feminism. Many of these women adopted the description "third wave" feminism, drawing on the terms often used to describe nineteenth-century feminism (the first wave) and the movement of the 1960s and 1970s (the second wave). Others rejected the term, noting that it implied a sharp and misleading generational boundary and that it linked historical feminism too tightly to specific movements associated primarily with white women. While the term "third wave" may be problematic, feminism was definitely resurgent in the 1990s.

As older organizations like NOW began to see membership rise again, new organizations sprang into action, including the Third Wave Foundation, founded in 1992, whose Web page proclaims, "By empowering young women, Third Wave is building a lasting foundation for social activism around the country."[26] Anthologies of writings, most of them personal accounts that hark back in genre to the consciousness-raising essays of the 1970s, flourished. Women also pursued feminist agendas in popular culture, especially in the world of punk and hip-hop music. Unafraid to be outrageous, new feminist magazines like *Bitch* and *Bust* appeared, supplemented by inexpensively reproduced, small-run magazines ("zines") and Web pages self-published by young women and devoted to women's issues, reflecting how important Internet technologies have been to a renewed feminist movement.

Why and how did feminism renew itself? In part, the conservative political climate associated with the New Right startled many young women out of their complacent belief that the barriers to women's rights had been torn down. The Thomas-Hill hearings (see p. 654) and the *Webster* decision (see p. 653) proved especially important in reviving feminism by highlighting sexual harassment on the job and new challenges to reproductive freedom. Third-wave feminism also grew out of critiques of the second wave. A major theme was that the movement's focus had been too narrowly constrained by the white women who dominated it and that it had a limited ability to speak to the concerns of women of color. These young women were also motivated to respond to what the popular press criticized as the feminist cult of victimhood, especially in the arena of sexuality, which undercut the goal of women's empowerment. Many commentators—especially those from an older feminist generation—note that the third-wave feminists often have a simplistic sense of the complex contours of the second wave. But although their history may be flawed at times, the new feminists are redefining feminism in ways that make it more relevant to modern young women.

A central characteristic of this redefinition is the insistence that feminism acknowledge the multiple identities of women. To focus exclusively on the analytic category of gender without also paying attention to such factors as race, ethnicity, age, class, and sexual orientation limits feminism's usefulness in interpreting women's lives or in becoming an agent for social change. The writings of U.S. women of color have been central to this reformulation of feminist ideology. Particularly important has been Gloria Anzaldúa, a prize-winning poet and writer who was coeditor of the path-breaking 1981 collection *This Bridge Called My Back* (see p. 642). In this passage from her book *Borderlands/La Frontera: The New Mestiza* (1987), Anzaldúa artfully integrates Spanish phrases to draw the reader into the experience of "the borderland" of her location as a Chicana. The title of this passage translates as "Toward a New Consciousness." What multiple identities does Anzaldúa identify, and how are these crucial to the shaping of a new consciousness?

Gloria Anzaldúa
La Conciencia de la Mestiza (1987)

Por la mujer de mi raza
Hablará el espi'ritu.°

Jose Vasconcelos, Mexican philosopher, envisaged *una raza mestiza, una mezcla de razas afines, una raza de color—la primera raza síntesis del globo.* He called it a cosmic race, *la raza cósmica,* a fifth race embracing the four major races of the world. Opposite to the theory of the pure Ayran, and to the policy of racial purity that white America practices, his theory is one of inclusivity. At the confluence of two or more genetic streams, with chromosomes constantly "crossing over," this mixture of races, rather than resulting in an infe-

rior being, provides hybrid progeny, a mutable, more malleable species with a rich gene pool. From this racial, ideological, cultural and biological cross-pollination, an "alien" consciousness is presently in the making—a new *mestiza* consciousness, *una conciencia de mujer.* It is a consciousness of the Borderlands.

"Una Lucha de Fronteras" ("A Struggle of Borders")

Because I, a *mestiza,*
Continually walk out of one culture
and into another,
because I am in all cultures at the same time,
alma entre dos mundos, tres, cuatro,
me zumba la cabeza con lo contradictorio.
Estoy norteada por todas las voces que me
        Haban
simultáneamente.

The ambivalence from the clash of voices results in mental and emotional states of perplexity.

°Anzaldúa did not offer English translations for her Spanish phrases and sentences. We follow the same practice so as to preserve her intentions of intermixing American and Mexican cultures.

SOURCE: Dawn Keetley and John Pettegrew, eds., *Public Women, Public Words: A Documentary History of American Feminism, 1960 to the Present* (Madison, WI: Madison House, 2002), 3: 347–49.

Internal strife results in insecurity and indecisiveness. The mestiza's dual or multiple personality is plagued by psychic restlessness.

In a constant state of mental nepantilism, an Aztec word meaning torn between ways, *la mestiza* is a product of the transfer of the cultural and spiritual values of one group to another. Being tricultural, monolingual, bilingual, or multilingual, speaking a patois, and in a state of perpetual transition the *mestiza* faces the dilemma of the mixed breed: which collectivity does the daughter of a darkskinned mother listen to? . . .

The new *mestiza* copes by developing a tolerance for contradictions, a tolerance for ambiguity. She learns to be an Indian in Mexican culture, to be Mexican from an Anglo point of view. She learns to juggle cultures. She has a plural personality, she operates in a pluralistic mode—nothing is thrust out, the good the bad and the ugly, nothing rejected, nothing abandoned. Not only does she sustain contradictions, she turns the ambivalence into something else.

She can be jarred out of ambivalence by an intense, and often painful, emotional event which inverts or resolves the ambivalence. I'm not sure exactly how. The work takes place underground—subconsciously. It is work that the soul performs. . . .

En unas pocas centurias, the future will belong to the mestiza. Because the future depends on the breaking down of paradigms, it depends on the straddling of two or more cultures. By creating a new mythos—that is, a change in the way we perceive reality, the way we see ourselves, and the ways we behave—*la mestiza* creates a new consciousness.

The work of *mestiza* consciousness is to break down the subject-object duality that keeps her a prisoner and to show in the flesh and through the images in her work how duality is transcended. The answer to the problem between the white race and the colored, between male and females, lies in healing the split that originates in the very foundation of our lives, our culture, our languages, our thoughts. A massive uprooting of dualistic thinking in the individual and collective consciousness is the beginning of a long struggle, but one that could, in our best hopes, bring us to the end of rape, of violence, of war.

I DEAS SIMILAR TO ANZALDÚA'S NOTIONS of the fluidity of identity appear repeatedly in the anthologies of self-described third-wave feminists. In this contribution to the anthology *Listen Up: Voices from the Next Feminist Generation,* first published in 1995, Korean American writer JeeYeun Lee discusses the necessity and difficulties of creating a truly inclusive feminist movement. Why does Lee conclude that "no simplistic identity politics is ever possible"?

JeeYeun Lee
Beyond Bean Counting (1995)

I came out as a woman, an Asian American and a bisexual within a relatively short span of time,

SOURCE: Barbara Findlen, ed., *Listen Up: Voices from the Next Feminist Generation* (Seattle: Seal Press, 2001), 67–73.

and ever since then I have been guilty of the crime of bean counting, as Bill Clinton oh-so-eloquently phrased it. Every time I am in a room of people gathered for any reason, I automatically count those whom I can identify as women, men, people of color, Asian Americans, mixed-race people, whites, gays, lesbians, bisexuals, heterosexuals, people with disabilities. . . .

Such is the nature of feminism today: an uneasy balancing act between the imperatives of outreach and inclusion on one hand, and the risk of tokenism and further marginalization on the other. This dynamic has indelibly shaped my personal experiences with feminism, starting from my very first encounter with organized feminism. This encounter happened to be, literally, Feminist Studies 101 at the university I attended. . . .

[Lee found the course "exhilarating" and "exciting" but also an "intensely uncomfortable experience." She was frustrated by the complete absence of material on Asian American women, "nothing anywhere." While grateful for the empowering insights the class gave her about feminism, she felt that she would have "been turned off from feminism altogether had it not been for later classes that dealt specifically with women of color."]

I want to emphasize that the feminism that I and other young women come to today is one that is at least sensitive to issues of exclusion. If perhaps twenty years ago charges of racism, classism and homophobia were not taken seriously, today they are the cause of extreme anguish and soul-searching. I am profoundly grateful to older feminists of color and their white allies who struggled to bring U.S. feminist movements to this point. At the same time, I think that this current sensitivity often breeds tokenism, guilt, suspicion and self-righteousness that have very material repercussions on women's groups. . . .

In this age when "political correctness" has been appropriated by conservative forces as a derogatory term, it is extremely difficult to honestly discuss and confront any ideas and practices that perpetuate dominant norms—and none of us is innocent of such collusion. . . .

Issues of exclusion are not the sole province of white feminists. I learned this very vividly at a 1993 retreat organized by the Asian Pacifica Lesbian Network. It has become somewhat common

lately to speak of "Asian and Pacific Islanders" or "Asian/Pacific Americans" or, as in this case, "Asian Pacifica." This is meant to be inclusive, to recognize some issues held in common by people from Asia and people from the Pacific Islands. Two women of Native Hawaiian descent and some Asian American allies confronted the group at this retreat to ask for more than lip service in the organization's name: If the group was seriously committed to being an inclusive coalition, we needed to educate ourselves about and actively advocate Pacific Islander issues. And because I don't want to relegate them to a footnote, I will mention here a few of these issues: the demand for sovereignty for Native Hawaiians, whose government was illegally overthrown by the U.S. in 1893; fighting stereotypes of women and men that are different from those of Asian people; decrying U.S. imperialist possession and occupation of the islands of Guam, the Virgin Islands, American Samoa, the Marshall Islands, Micronesia, the Northern Mariana Islands and several others.

This was a retreat where one would suppose everyone had so much in common—after all, we were all queer API women, right? Any such myth was effectively destroyed by the realities of our experiences and issues: We were women of different ethnic backgrounds, with very different issues among East Asians, South Asians, Southeast Asians and Pacific Islanders; women of mixed race and heritage; women who identified as lesbians and those who identified as bisexuals: women who were immigrants, refugees, illegal aliens or second generation or more; older women, physically challenged women, women adopted by white families, women from the Midwest. Such tangible differences brought home the fact that no simplistic identity politics is ever possible, that we had to conceive of ourselves as a coalition first and foremost: as one woman on a panel said, our identity as queer API women must be a *coalitional* identity. Initially, I thought that I had finally found a home where I could relax and let down my guard. This was true to a certain degree, but I discovered that this was the home where I would have to work the hardest because I cared the most. I would have to be committed to push myself and push others to deal with all of our differences, so that we could be safe for each other. . . .

All this is to say that I and other young women have found most feminist movements today to be at this point, where there is at least a stated emphasis on inclusion and outreach with the accompanying risk of tokenism. I firmly believe that it is always the margins that push us further in our politics. Women of color do not struggle in feminist movements simply to add cultural diversity, to add the viewpoints of different kinds of women. Women of color feminist theories challenge the fundamental premises of feminism, such as the very definition of "women," and call for recognition of the constructed racial nature of all experiences of gender. . . .

These days, whenever someone says the word "women" to me, my mind goes blank. What "women"? What is this "women" thing you're talking about? Does that mean me? Does that mean my mother, my roommates, the white woman next door, the checkout clerk at the supermarket, my aunts in Korea, half of the world's population? I ask people to specify and specify, until I can figure out exactly what they're talking about, and I try to remember to apply the same standards to myself, to deny myself the slightest possibility of romanticization. Sisterhood may be global, but who is in that sisterhood? None of us can afford to assume anything about anybody else. This thing called "feminism" takes a great deal of hard work, and I think this is one of the primary hallmarks of young feminists' activism today: We realize that coming together and working together are by no means natural or easy.

MULTIPLE IDENTITIES mean multiple concerns. The following selection is drawn from *Manifesta: Young Women, Feminism, and the Future* (2000), coedited by Jennifer Baumgardner and Amy Richards, two prominent white activists who founded the Third Wave Foundation. It celebrates the wide-ranging issues feminists embraced in the 1990s. What is the significance of their comments concerning the phrase, "I'm not a feminist, but . . ."?

JENNIFER BAUMGARDNER AND AMY RICHARDS
The Feminist Diaspora (1999)

Relationships, marriage, bisexuality, STDs, abortion, and having children were the topics our friends were thinking about on the night of our dinner party. Among the subjects with which our dinner companions have also grappled were

immigration problems, access to education, racism as manifest by white women befriending black women to get over their white guilt, taking care of an aging relative, credit-card debt, depression, and body image. Every woman's life touches many issues, some of which demand urgent attention at different times.

On every Third Wave Foundation membership card, for example, there is a place that asks,

SOURCE: Jennifer Baumgardner and Amy Richards, eds. *Manifesta: Young Women, Feminism, and the Future* (New York: Farrar, Strauss and Giroux, 2000), 47–48.

"My issues are ?," and no two cards have ever listed the same answer. Among the responses provided, members list "Jewish progressive life," "war crimes," "student financial aid," "interracial dating," "issues of the South Asian Diaspora," "universal health care," "mothering as a teenager," "condom distribution," "chauvinistic fathers," "fat oppression," and "white and male supremacy." Those are just the tip of the iceberg of what young women are thinking about. And, when you scratch the surface of why someone cares about a certain issue, it's almost always because such issues have affected that person or someone he or she cares about. Whether it's a glance at the Third Wave Foundation's membership cards or at a plenary session of the Fourth World Conference on Women in Beijing, at an Honor the Earth board meeting or our dinner party, there is never one feminist issue that dwarfs all others. There will never be one platform for action that all women agree on. But that doesn't mean feminism is confused. What it does mean is that feminism is as various as the women it represents. What weaves a feminist movement together is consciousness of inequities and a commitment to changing them.

As two young women who believe in the importance of a political vision and have faith in our peers, we want to begin to articulate why a generation leading revolutionary lives is best known for saying, "I'm not a feminist, but . . ." Third Wave women have been seen as nonfeminist when they are actually living feminist lives. Some of this confusion is due to the fact that most young women don't get together to talk about "Feminism" with a capital F. We don't use terms like "the politics of housework" or "the gender gap" as much as we simply describe our lives and our expectations. To a degree, the lack of a Third Wave feminist terminology keeps us from building a potent movement, which is why we need to connect our pro-woman ethics to a political vision. And yet, even without the rip-roaring political culture that characterized the sixties and the seventies, Third Wave women are laying the groundwork for a movement of our own.

A QUITE DIFFERENT VERSION of feminism emerged in popular music. When Madonna first burst on the scene in the mid-1980s, many labeled her as a new feminist icon. Her outrageous, sexual style seemed to convey her control of her own sexuality rather than present her as a sex object. Other powerful female performers also convey what might be called feminist sensibilities. Many black female rap performers, including Queen Latifah, reject the term "feminist" but nonetheless appeal to young women because of their critique of racism and sexism. Queen Latifah's music video "Ladies First" (1989) includes historical references to African American women such as Sojourner Truth and Angela Davis. As Queen Latifah puts it, "I wanted to show the strength of black women in history—strong black women. Those were good examples. I wanted to show what we've done. We've done a lot, it's just that people don't know it. Sisters have been in the midst of these things for a long time, but we just don't get to see it that much."[27]

The most overtly feminist young women in music are the Riot Grrrls, a phenomenon that emerged in Washington, D.C., and Olympia, Washington, in 1991. There, young white women began to challenge the male domination of the punk rock scene with all-female bands such as Bikini Kill and Heavens to Betsy. Their lyrics often focus on themes of sexual abuse, an oppressive beauty culture, and patriarchal oppression. Enthusiasm for Grrrl power spread, leading to zines, Internet sites, and even a national convention in Washington, D.C. As important as the music was to empowering the female artists, zines and other forms of interaction spread the enthusiasm well beyond the musicians themselves. As one young woman explains, "Zines are so important because so many girls feel isolated and don't have other girls to support them in their beliefs. Zines connect them to other girls who will listen and believe and care if they say they've been raped or molested and harassed. Zines provide an outlet for girls to get their feelings and lives out there and share them with others."[28]

Women associated with the Riot Grrrls reveal something of the complexity of third-wave feminism. They are not afraid of the concept of "girlishness" — both in their name and their penchant for little girl clothing and images — but they reject the notions of powerlessness that mainstream culture associates with "girls." Older feminists had railed against the term "girl" to describe an adult female because it infantilized women; Riot Grrrls transformed the term. As one young woman puts it, " 'Grrrl' puts the growl back in our pussycat throats."[29]

The following declaration of Riot Grrrls' philosophy appeared originally in a *Bikini Kill* zine in 1991. How would you characterize their philosophy?

KATHLEEN HANNA
Riot Grrrl Manifesto (1991)

BECAUSE us girls crave records and books and fanzines that speak to US that WE feel included in and can understand in our own ways.

BECAUSE we wanna make it easier for girls to see/hear each other's work so that we can share strategies and criticize-applaud each other.

BECAUSE we must take over the means of production in order to create our own moanings.

BECAUSE viewing our work as being connected to our girlfriends-politics-real lives is essential if we are gonna figure out how [what] we are doing impacts, reflects, perpetuates, or DISRUPTS the status quo.

BECAUSE we recognize fantasies of Instant Macho Gun Revolution as impractical lies meant to keep us simply dreaming instead of becoming our dreams AND THUS seek to create revolution in our own lives every single day by envisioning

and creating alternatives to the bullshit christian capitalist way of doing things.

BECAUSE we want and need to encourage and be encouraged in the face of all our own insecurities, in the face of beergutboyrock that tells us we can't play our instruments, in the face of "authorities" who say our bands/zines/etc. are the worst in the U.S. and BECAUSE we don't wanna assimilate to someone else's (boy) standards of what is or isn't.

BECAUSE we are unwilling to falter under claims that we are reactionary "reverse sexists" AND NOT THE TRUEPUNKROCKSOUL CRUSADERS THAT WE KNOW we really are.

BECAUSE we know that life is much more than physical survival and are patently aware that the punk rock "you can do anything" idea is crucial to the coming angry grrrl rock revolution that seeks to save the psychic and cultural lives of girls and women everywhere, according to their own terms, not ours.

SOURCE: Jessica Rosenberg and Gitana Garofalo, "Riot Grrrl: Revolutions from Within," *Signs* 23 (January 1998): 812–13.

BECAUSE we are interested in creating non-hierarchical ways of being AND making music, friends, and scenes based on communication + understanding, instead of competition + good/bad categorizations.

BECAUSE doing/reading/seeing/hearing cool things that validate and challenge us can help us gain the strength and sense of community that we need in order to figure out how bullshit like racism, able-bodyism, ageism, speciesism, classism, thinism, sexism, antisemitism and heterosexism figures in our own lives.

BECAUSE we see fostering and supporting girl scenes and girl artists of all kinds as integral to this process.

BECAUSE we hate capitalism in all its forms and see our main goal as sharing information and staying alive, instead of making profits or being cool according to traditional standards.

BECAUSE we are angry at a society that tells us Girl = Dumb, Girl = Bad, Girl = Weak.

BECAUSE we are unwilling to let our real and valid anger be diffused and/or turned against us via the internalization of sexism as witnessed in girl/girl jealousism and self-defeating girltype behaviors.

BECAUSE I believe with my wholeheartmindbody that girls constitute a revolutionary soul force that can, and will, change the world for real.

OTHER YOUNG FEMINISTS challenged the way in which the media and male-dominated culture had sexually objectified women and undermined their ability to embrace eroticism. They criticized their feminist foremothers, who, they argued, emphasized freeing women from their sexual oppression and their victimization by men and Madison Avenue to the exclusion of the joys and power of female sexuality. This critique was often based on a misleading stereotype of 1970s feminists that emphasized unshaven legs, Birkenstock sandals, and rigid rules for appropriate feminist behavior. Prominent black writer and activist Rebecca Walker, the daughter of well-known novelist Alice Walker, is one of the women most responsible for popularizing the term "third wave." She offers a far more sophisticated manifesto for reclaiming female sexuality in an essay published in the anthology *Listen Up* (1995). As she details her own sexual coming of age, she asks, "What do young women need to make sex a dynamic, affirming, safe and pleasurable part of our lives?" What answers does she suggest?

REBECCA WALKER
Lusting for Freedom (1995)

When I think back, it is that impulse I am most proud of. The impulse that told me that I deserve to live free of shame, that my body is not my

SOURCE: Findlen, *Listen Up*, 19–24.

enemy and that pleasure is my friend and my right. Without this core, not even fully jelled in my teenage mind but powerful nonetheless, how else would I have learned to follow and cultivate my own desire? How else would I have learned to listen to and develop the language of my own body? How else would I have learned to initiate, sustain and develop healthy intimacy, that most valuable of human essences? I am proud that I did not stay in relationships when I couldn't grow. I moved on when the rest of me would emerge physically or intellectually and say, Enough! There isn't enough room in this outfit for all of us. . . .

It is obvious that the suppression of sexual agency and exploration, from within or from without, is often used as a method of social control and domination. Witness widespread genital mutilation and the homophobia that dictatorially mandates heterosexuality; imagine the stolen power of the millions affected by just these two global murderers of self-authorization and determination. Without being able to respond to and honor the desires of our bodies and our selves, we become cut off from our instincts for pleasure, dissatisfied living under rules and thoughts that are not our own. When we deny ourselves safe and shameless exploration and access to reliable information, we damage our ability to even know what sexual pleasure feels or looks like.

Sex in silence and filled with shame is sex where our agency is denied. This is sex where we, young women, are powerless and at the mercy of our own desires. For giving our bodies what they want and crave, for exploring ourselves and others, we are punished like Eve reaching for more knowledge. We are called sluts and whores. We are considered impure or psychotic. Information about birth control is kept from us. Laws denying our right to control our bodies are enacted. We learn much of what we know from television, which debases sex and humiliates women.

We must decide that this is no longer acceptable, for sex is one of the places where we do our learning solo. Pried away from our parents and other authority figures, we look for answers about ourselves and how the world relates to us. We search for proper boundaries and create our very own slippery moral codes. We can begin to take control of this process and show responsibility only if we are encouraged to own our right to have a safe and self-created sexuality. The question is not whether young women are going to have sex, for this is far beyond any parental or societal control. The question is rather, what do young women need to make sex a dynamic, affirming, safe and pleasurable part of our lives? How do we build the bridge between sex and sexuality, between the isolated act and the powerful element that, when honed, can be an important tool for self-actualization?

Fortunately, there is no magic recipe for a healthy sexuality; each person comes into her or his own sexual power through a different route and at her or his own pace. There are, however, some basic requirements for sexual awareness and safe sexual practice. To begin with, young women need a safe space in which to explore our own bodies. A woman needs to be able to feel the soft smoothness of her belly, the exquisite softness of her inner thigh, the full roundness of her breasts. We need to learn that bodily pleasure belongs to us; it is our birthright.

Sex could also stand to be liberated from pussy and dick and fucking, as well as from marriage and procreation. It can be more: more sensual, more spiritual, more about communication and healing. Women and men both must learn to explore sexuality by making love in ways that are different from what we see on television and in the movies. If sex is about communicating, let us think about what we want to say and how will we say it. We need more words, images, ideas.

Finally, young women are more than inexperienced minors, more than property of the state or of legal guardians. We are growing, thinking, inquisitive, self-possessed beings who need information about sex and access to birth control and abortion. We deserve to have our self-esteem nurtured and our personal agency encouraged. We need "protection" only from poverty and violence.

And even beyond all of the many things that will have to change in the outside world to help people in general and young women in particular grow more in touch with their sexual power, we also need to have the courage to look closely and lovingly at our sexual history and practice. Where is the meaning? What dynamics have we created or participated in? Why did we do that? How did we feel? How much of the way we think about ourselves is based in someone else's perception or label of our sexual experiences?

It has meant a lot to me to affirm and acknowledge my experiences and to integrate them into an empowering understanding of where I have been and where I am going. Hiding in shame or running fast to keep from looking is a waste of what is most precious about life: its infinite ability to expand and give us more knowledge, more insight and more complexity.

THIRD-WAVE FEMINIST PERSPECTIVES have made their way into mainstream popular culture. The HBO series *Sex and the City,* set in New York and based on the newspaper columns of Candace Bushnell, has often been cited as an exemplar of modern feminist consciousness. The four main characters are independent young women with successful careers, who have achieved their success without sacrificing femininity or denying themselves sexual joy and empowerment. In the following *New York Times* op-ed column, journalist Catherine Orenstein critiques the television series. How does her perspective embody both her own generation's feminism and that of the feminists of the 1960s and 1970s?

CATHERINE ORENSTEIN
What Carrie Could Learn from Mary (2003)

Thanks to HBO's *Sex and the City,* now wrapping up its sixth and final season, female sensibility has a new face. Four faces, to be precise: prim Charlotte, no-nonsense Miranda, slutty Samantha, and every-girl Carrie, the sex columnist played by Sarah Jessica Parker who is the show's thematic center. Perched on Jimmy Choos and wrapped in Gucci, sipping pink cosmopolitans with an assortment of handsome suitors, the women are witty, glamorous, independent and sexually liberated — in short, who wouldn't want to be them?

Me, for one. The show may deserve a nod for spotlighting women's conversation, for treating sexuality frankly, and for rendering the traditionally stigmatized state of being a single woman more acceptable — indeed, chic. But under the guise of being salaciously liberating and radically feminist, the vision of modern femininity in *Sex and the City* is in fact surprisingly retrograde. The heroines spend most of their time on shopping, cocktails, and one-night stands. Charlotte dreams of bridesmaids' dresses. Miranda frigidly "dates" her TiVo, while nymphomaniac Samantha—a blond bimbo who combines old-fashioned objectification with postmodern "do me" feminism—plows through the Kama Sutra. And in one episode Carrie discovers that she has only $957 in savings—but $40,000 in designer shoes in her closet.

More dated still, especially for a show that supposedly celebrates the joys of single life and female friendship, is its preoccupation with snag-

SOURCE: *New York Times,* September 5, 2003, p. A19.

ging a man. The characters are a walking compendium of modern female angst—the quest for a relationship, the ticking of the biological clock, the fear of aging out of the marriage market. Not that these aren't sometimes true and even potentially funny themes of single life. But when did haute couture fashion and prêt-à-porter [ready-to-wear] men come to eclipse all the other elements of independent womanhood?

As a single writer living in New York City, I can't help but compare *Sex and the City* to yesteryear's *Mary Tyler Moore Show*, whose heroine—like Carrie, a 30-something single journalist—had cool clothes and plenty of suitors, but also story deadlines, a grouchy boss, and male friends (not just "gay boyfriends" as on *Sex*). The show, which had its debut in 1970, was infused with the optimism and vigor of second-wave feminism. It opened with Mary leaving a boyfriend for the big city—Minneapolis—and landing a job as a television producer. She tackled substantial issues like freedom of the press and sexism in the workplace. Sure, there were also jokes about her single status. And she and sidekick Rhoda were once so desperate for dates that they joined a club for divorcées even though neither of them had ever been married. But the jokes came with a light-hearted confidence in Mary's future. Whether or not she married, her theme song promised, she would "make it after all."

Other single heroines of the past seem comparatively forward thinking today as well, including Murphy Brown, the reporter and single mom played by Candace Bergen, and even Helen Gurley Brown, whose 1962 best seller *Sex and the Single Girl* was the titular and thematic foremother to *Sex and the City*. While Ms. Gurley Brown's flirt-to-get-what-you-want brand of feminism seems quaint today, she never confused her means with her ends. She didn't sit around sipping cosmopolitans, she became editor in chief of *Cosmopolitan* Magazine.

It's no coincidence that these icons of single femininity are all journalists. In the early 20th century, journalism was one of the few careers open to women, and the expanding ranks of "girl reporters" inspired stereotype-defying single heroines: Rosalind Russell as an ace reporter in 1940's *His Girl Friday,* Katharine Hepburn as a foreign correspondent in 1942's *Woman of the Year,* not to mention that famed comic-strip journalist Brenda Starr.

By contrast, the heroines of *Sex and the City* are vapid, materialistic, and hysterical. The show makes short shrift of their intellect, they have no causes, no families—with the exception of Miranda, who has a son—and their jobs (what little we see of them) seem to exist to enable office trysts. Like Candace Bushnell's columns in the *New York Observer* upon which the show was based, their lives are flattened backdrops for their dates, and their dates, like their shoes, are accessories—nice looking, often uncomfortable, and seasonal.

In part this is what makes them popular. They're a caricature of a complicated generation of women—myself included—now coming into our 30's: the daughters of women's lib. Born in the years that the Ivy Leagues went co-ed and abortion became legal, we've been raised on promises of equality, we've been blessed with opportunities, and we've delayed marriage and motherhood longer than any other generation. We have the luxury, or so we may think, of taking feminism's gains for granted.

Sex and the City glamorizes this condition—but to what end? Lacking substance and dimension, defined by sex appeal and revolving around men, Carrie and her friends are stuck in a surprisingly old-fashioned, Jane Austenian trap: having failed to leverage youth and beauty into something more substantial, they are now in danger of becoming spinsters. Indeed, they are already there, according to a recent *New York Times* article that compared them to the sexagenarians of *The Golden Girls*.

Before the series comes to an end, it would be gratifying to see Carrie and her friends grow up into something more than restless partyers, man-hunters and shoe-shoppers, and find something more enduring to glamorize: a cause, a family, a career that is more than a backdrop for sex, or even just a story worthy of the girl reporter's legacy. Something that broadens our idea of what makes a woman sexy. Something worthy of the feminism our mothers bequeathed us.

QUESTIONS FOR ANALYSIS

1. What do the documents suggest are the most important characteristics of the feminist revival of the 1990s? How is it different from the movement of the 1960s and 1970s?

2. Baumgardner and Richards claim that, despite the many faces of contemporary feminism, the movement is "not confused." Do you agree?

3. Do you agree with the idea that pop star Madonna is a feminist icon? What about the women of *Sex and the City*? What other figures in popular culture might be included in an assessment of women and feminism?

4. Do the documents offer compelling reasons for young women to identify with the term "feminism"?

Lesbians in Postwar America

WORLD WAR II PROVED A TURNING POINT in the creation of urban lesbian communities, as Chapter 8 suggests. In the years immediately after the war, however, the emphasis on conformity and rigid gender roles put significant pressure on all homosexuals to keep their sexual lives private, to stay closeted. At a time when the ideas of the Feminine Mystique held sway in mainstream culture, women who refused the role of wife and mother were considered pathological and subversive. Homosexuals who congregated at bars or other public places were subject to police harassment and arrest. The military aggressively sought to identify and discharge gay men and women, driving homosexuals to exercise extreme care to avoid exposure. In civilian work as well, gay men and women faced discrimination. Despite these pressures, lesbians continued to develop distinct underground subcultures that by the 1970s emerged as open, public communities.

White lesbians—the group we know the most about—must be differentiated by class. During and after World War II, young urban working-class women eager to connect with other lesbians met in bars in out-of-the-way locales, usually in poor neighborhoods. There they created a subculture based on distinct roles of "butch" and "femme," the former dressing like men and adopting a masculine, tough style and the latter looking and acting highly feminized. While these personae superficially mirrored heterosexual gender expectations, scholars point out that lesbian sexual behavior emphasizes the woman's pleasure, not the man's; hence the butch-femme roles inverted the cultural assumptions that shaped heterosexual sex of the era. As the more openly lesbian of the two roles, the butch was especially important in helping to define a lesbian identity, at the same time that butch women were the targets of rampant homophobia and outright violence.

In contrast to working-class women, middle-class lesbians had family and financial resources that allowed them to hide their sexual lives and choices from public view, thus appearing to conform to dominant social norms. They tended to avoid the bar scene, in part because of the danger of arrest and exposure but also because some found the butch-femme phenomenon distasteful and the apparent mimicking of heterosexual roles insulting. They also worried that the exaggerated styles of butch and femme would draw only unwelcome attention to lesbians and foster homophobia. Propriety was as important to their subculture as the butch-femme norm was to working-class women, so their preference was for private parties and for dress styles that did not draw attention. The Daughters of Bilitis,° the

° The society's name derived from a late nineteenth-century French work, *Songs of Bilitis*, by Pierre Louys, which contained poems about love between women.

first national lesbian rights society, was founded in 1955 by eight women in San Francisco; the group's magazine, the *Ladder,* urged lesbians to adopt "a mode of behavior and dress acceptable to society."[30] The group, whose stated goal was "to fight for understanding of the homophile minority," spread from San Francisco to a handful of other major cities, but it remained a small organization with a discreet public profile.

Anxiety about respectability among middle-class women was driven to some extent by economic concerns. Without the financial support of husbands, lesbians had to be self-supporting, and to remain professionally employed, they needed (with rare exceptions) to stay in the closet. Their anxiety also had a political dimension. The hysterical hunt for Communists in the late 1940s and 1950s (see Chapter 9) was accompanied by an attack on lesbians and gay men as security risks and subversive presences in government employment. In 1953 the federal government amended its loyalty program to include "sexual perversion" as grounds for dismissal from government jobs. Federal applicants for jobs were asked, "Have you ever had, or have you now, homosexual tendencies?," and the *Federal Personnel Manual* insisted that "persons about whom there is evidence that they have engaged in or solicited others to engage in homosexual or sexually perverted acts with them, without evidence of rehabilitation . . . are not suitable for Federal employment."[31] While the majority of people affected were men, women too felt the pervasive risk of exposure. Many middle-class lesbians had government jobs as teachers, librarians, or social workers, so holding on to their jobs meant keeping their sexual identities private. Private employers also were reluctant to hire or retain homosexuals.

Resentment of economic discrimination led to the first public protests mounted by gays and lesbians in the 1950s. The Mattachine Society,° founded in 1951 in Los Angeles, was dominated by men, although as it spread to other cities more lesbians entered its ranks. In the early 1960s, Washington, D.C.'s Mattachine Society, clearly influenced by the African American civil rights movement, became especially vocal in its criticism of discrimination. It attempted to recruit African Americans, although the membership remained overwhelmingly white. Figure 10.1 is a photograph of a 1965 Mattachine Society picket line in front of the White House, one of a series of demonstrations focused on government employment discrimination against homosexuals. The photograph was taken by Kay Tobin Lahusen, and the woman in front in the picture is Barbara Gittings. Both are long-time gay rights activists. What do the clothing and the demeanor of the women picketers suggest about lesbians who worked for the government? The date of this demonstration was the year following the Civil Rights Act of 1964, which prohibited employment discrimination on the basis of race, religion, national origin, or gender (see Chapter 9). To what extent does the image suggest a connection between this protest and the civil rights movement?

° The group's name came from *mattacino,* an Italian term for a court jester who was willing to tell the king the truth.

While a path-breaking step towards legal and social equality, these pickets represented a very small number of middle-class gays and lesbians willing to take their cause to the public. In the late 1960s, with the so-called Stonewall riot, a more broad-based gay movement emerged. The impetus was a police raid on a New York City working-class gay bar, the Stonewall, on June 27, 1969. Instead of the customary acquiescence, men, and a small number of women, fought back with beer cans and bottles. During the subsequent two-day riot, the protesters chanted "gay power," a slogan modeled after "black power." The results were electrifying. The gay liberation movement spread quickly throughout the nation's cities; public demonstrations often were held in conjunction with protests against the Vietnam War.

Figure 10.2, a 1970 poster for the Gay Liberation Front (GLF), captures the spirit of the new movement that attracted young lesbians and gay men. What message do you think the GLF hoped to convey with the poster? How does this image contrast with Figure 10.1? What does it suggest about the changing nature of gay protest?

◆ Figure 10.1 **Mattachine Society Picket Line in Front of the White House, 1965**
Photo by Kay Tobin Lahusen.

The lesbian community was transformed not only by gay power but by the simultaneous movements for women's liberation and black power. In the early 1970s, many young lesbians worked from within the feminist movement, arguing that the root of discrimination against lesbians could be found in the oppression of women, and that an ideological commitment to women loving women was the only way to quash patriarchal power and achieve female liberation (see p. 638). Novelist Rita Mae Brown expressed this view powerfully, writing that "I became a lesbian because the culture that I live in is violently anti-woman. How could I, a woman, participate in a culture that denies my humanity? . . . To give a man support and love before giving it to a sister is to support that culture, that power system."[32] With their passionate commitment to creating a "lesbian nation," these radicals advocated lesbianism based on political ideology. This ideology, which reflected the growth of a style of politics based on group identity, sometimes led to

◆ Figure 10.2
**Gay Liberation
Front Poster, 1970**
*Courtesy of the June L.
Mazer Lesbian Archives.*

conflict between gay men and women and also between heterosexual and lesbian feminists, even as it strengthened lesbian communities.

Another area of tension concerned women of color. Although white lesbians made claims for a common lesbian identity, few lesbians of color joined white women's organizations, preferring to separate into their own groups, which spoke to their concerns not only with homophobia and sexism but with racism as well. The Combahee River Collective was perhaps the most well-known (see p. 642), but other groups proliferated in urban areas throughout the United States. In 1978, women in Los Angeles founded Lesbians of Color at the first convention of the National Lesbian Feminist Organization. They described their goals as follows: "We come together to fight our oppression as women of color and as lesbians. We come together to validate and support one another's personal/political struggles and growth."[33]

Figure 10.3, probably dating from 1982, is a flyer publicizing the group's annual dance. The flyer is an excellent example of what historians call "ephemera," from "ephemeral," or fleeting. It was not intended as a permanent document, but librarians and other specialists working in archives who have long recognized the historical value of ephemera have collected such material from a wide range of social action groups, thus giving us a better record of how groups publicized their efforts at community building and social change. Why do you suppose Los Angeles Lesbians of Color chose to emphasize "international working women's day"? What other clues to the organization does the flyer convey?

Unlike other radical movements with postwar roots, lesbian and gay activism continued to grow through the 1970s, and it could claim considerable progress both in spearheading legal protections against discrimination and in creating environments in which homosexuals could express their sexual identity openly. In the 1980s, a time of renewed conservatism, gay men and lesbians became particular targets for the conservative reaction against the "rights revolution" of the preceding decade. In the name of family values, fundamentalist religious groups mounted organized campaigns against the legal protections and public visibility won by gays and lesbians.

Despite this backlash, lesbian communities and their struggle for equal rights and social visibility persisted, and limited acceptance began to grow in mainstream America. A major factor was the AIDS epidemic, which began to spread through the U.S. gay male population in the early 1980s and increased public awareness of the numbers and diversity of the homosexual population and of its heroic response to the toll the disease was taking. Although few lesbians contracted AIDS, they were affected as the popular image of homosexuality became associated less with reckless pleasure seeking and more with communities of caring and loss. Lesbians were involved in the creation of institutions to serve the gay community and efforts to force the public health system to respond to the AIDS crisis.

Both cause and reflection of this shifting environment was the growth of gay families, a development that particularly affected lesbians beginning in the 1980s. Lesbians were mothers to children born during prior

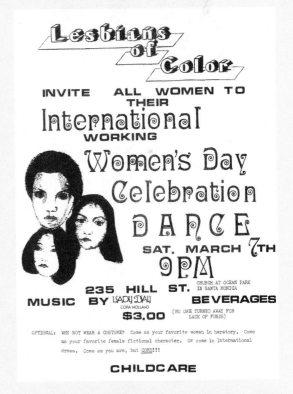

◆ Figure 10.3 **Lesbians of Color Dance Flyer, 1982**
Courtesy of Lesbian Legacy Collection of the ONE Archives, Los Angeles. Artist unknown.

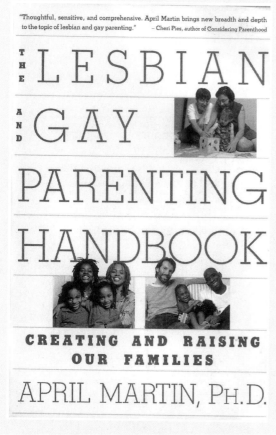

◆ Figure 10.4 **Cover of April Martin, *The Lesbian and Gay Parenting Handbook: Creating and Raising Our Families*, 1993**
Courtesy of HarperCollins.

heterosexual marriages, to adopted children, to children fathered by male (often gay) friends, and to children conceived through artificial insemination.° As early as 1993, gay families were numerous enough that Harper-Collins, a mainstream publisher, issued *The Lesbian and Gay Parenting Handbook: Creating and Raising Our Families* by April Martin. What does the cover of this book, shown in Figure 10.4, convey about lesbian families in the 1990s? What special issues might lesbian parents face that are different from those of heterosexual families?

For lesbians, one of the most stunning examples of changing cultural norms took place in 1997 when popular comedian Ellen DeGeneres not only announced publicly that she was a lesbian but had her character in the TV situation comedy *Ellen* come out as well. The coming-out episode reached the third largest audience in television history. But it also generated controversy from both directions. Conservative religious organizations took out a large advertisement in the entertainment industry's publication *Variety,* denouncing the program "as a slap in the face to American families."[34] Meanwhile, some pro-gay critics faulted DeGeneres for not going far enough. They criticized her for saying that she did not like the term "lesbian" and pointed out that the episode's humor was largely based on her awkward adjustment to the surprising realization of her sexual orientation. The show was primarily a media event, but it was a historically important one.

Figure 10.5 reproduces the April 14, 1997, cover of the popular weekly magazine, *Time.* Why might *Time* have decided to feature DeGeneres on its cover? In

---

° Statistics about lesbian parenting are very limited at present, but the U.S. census estimated in 2000 that one-third of gay and lesbian couples were raising children.

the accompanying article, DeGeneres claimed that "I never wanted to be the lesbian actress. I never wanted to be the spokesperson for the gay community. Ever. I did it for my own truth."[35] To what extent does media attention such as this cover suggest that Ellen's coming out nonetheless represented a political act?

For lesbian activists at the start of the twenty-first century, their civil rights remain a pressing issue. They share with gay men a concern about employment and health care. They particularly struggle over family issues— the rights to keep custody of and to adopt children, to gain employment benefits for their partners routinely offered to married heterosexuals, and increasingly the full rights of marriage for their own committed relationships. Many larger employers began to offer partner benefits, such as health insurance. Over two hundred cities have enacted ordinances that prohibit discrimination based on sexual preference in employment and housing.

◆ Figure 10.5 **Ellen DeGeneres, Cover of *Time*, April 14, 1997**
Time Life Pictures/Getty Images.

The most dramatic development for gay and lesbian rights came in 2003 when the Massachusetts Supreme Court held that same-sex couples were entitled to the "protections, benefits, and obligations of civil marriage." Then, in early 2004, officials in a number of states, including New York, California, and Oregon, began performing highly publicized gay marriages. Pending court challenges, the San Francisco marriage applications noted, "Marriage of lesbian and gay couples may not be recognized as valid by any jurisdiction other than San Francisco, and may not be recognized as valid by any employer," and that "if you are a same-gender couple, you are encouraged to seek legal advice regarding the effect of entering into marriage."[36] In August 2004, the California Supreme Court voided the nearly four thousand marriages performed in San Francisco as counter to state law that restricts marriage to opposite-sex partnerships. The court did not rule on the constitutionality of the law, however. Figure 10.6 depicts the ceremony performed on February 12, 2004, at San Francisco City Hall in which Del Martin, eighty-three, and Phyllis Lyon, seventy-nine, were pronounced "spouses for life." Martin and Lyon, two of the founders of the Daughters of Bilitis, had been a couple for

◆ **Figure 10.6 Marriage Ceremony of Del Martin (right) and Phyllis Lyon (left) at San Francisco City Hall, February 12, 2004**
Courtesy of the San Francisco Chronicle.

fifty-one years. The photograph appeared the following day on the front page of the *Los Angeles Times*. Theirs was the first wedding to be performed in San Francisco, but are there other reasons that the *Los Angeles Times* may have featured this particular couple and this specific image?

QUESTIONS FOR ANALYSIS

1. Compare the images of lesbian protests in Figures 10.1 and 10.2 with the earlier protests involving women shown in "Visual Sources: Parades, Picketing, and Power: Women in Public Space," pages 447–53. In what ways does women's use of public space for protesting seem to have changed? How has it remained the same?

2. What do these images suggest about the changes in lesbian experience over the past fifty years?

3. To what extent do they suggest the degree of diversity among American lesbians?

American Women in the World

LIKE MUCH WRITTEN HISTORY, *Through Women's Eyes* has taken as its framework a single nation, the United States and its colonial antecedents. But the presence and importance of the surrounding world has been implicit throughout this national saga, beginning in the seventeenth century with the interactions among indigenous peoples, European traders and settlers, and African slaves. Waves of immigration, international commerce in raw materials and finished goods, political and intellectual influences from abroad, and wars of defense, expansion, and international conflict have all been regular features of American history as reflected in the experience and actions of women. For any period, it is possible—and useful—to revision American history so that this international context emerges from the background into the spotlight. The visual images in this final source essay are an exercise in just this change of focus.

While American history has always existed in international context, that context became more obvious and important in the last decades of the twentieth century through the process known as globalization. The collapse of the Soviet Union and the consequent end of the Cold War in 1989 left the United States the world's only superpower and the free market system unchallenged by socialism. The result has been an internationally integrated capitalist system in which financial investment, consumer goods, and workers all move from nation to nation with increasing fluidity. At the end of the nineteenth century, capitalist competition within the United States began to give way to corporate centralization. At the start of the twenty-first century, that process has reached beyond national boundaries, so that giant corporations are now termed "multinationals," with economic structures exceeding the capacity of any single nation, even the United States, to regulate or restrain. The benefits and costs of these exchanges are distributed very unevenly, both among nations and within them. From the viewpoint of the American economy, globalization has brought both greater wealth and more inequality: a flood of cheap consumer goods, the export of many manufacturing jobs to Asia and Latin America, and a burgeoning immigrant working class doing the most menial jobs.

Economic globalization has profoundly affected women both inside and outside America's borders. American manufacturing jobs, once highly unionized and (in the garment industry) filled by women workers, have been exported abroad, particularly in the wake of free trade policies such as the North American Free Trade Agreement (NAFTA), signed in 1994 by Canada, Mexico, and the United States. In foreign factories run by or subcontracted to companies with familiar brand names like Nike and Gap, garments are produced at a fraction of the wages

◆ Figure 10.7 **Anti-sweatshop Campaign Poster, 1996**

Marilyn Anderson.

paid to American workers and then shipped to the United States for sale. In Central America these factories, which can also be found all over Asia, are known as *maquilas;* in Mexico, as *maquiladoras.* Their workers are preponderantly female, many of them mothers whose earnings are crucial to their families' well-being.

Given the multinational character of the companies involved, unions and other activist groups in the United States have joined together with foreign workers to mount campaigns for the improvement of wages and conditions of work. In the tradition of the National Consumer Union of the Progressive era (see Chapter 7), groups like the United Students Against Sweatshops have organized buyers' boycotts of goods (such as clothing with official college logos) made abroad under exploitative conditions. A network of American women's anti-sweatshop activists, entitled STITCH: Organizers for Labor Justice, was formed in 1994.[37]

One such U.S.-based consumer campaign was organized in 1996 against the Phillips-Van Heusen Corporation. The company initially agreed to the unionization of six hundred workers in one of its Guatemalan plants, 80 percent of whom were women. But a year later, it closed the plant and, following the pattern of the early twentieth-century American garment industry, subcontracted out production to middlemen, who paid workers even lower wages to labor in sweatshop conditions. Figure 10.7 is a poster to organize American support for the union campaign. In what ways is the poster designed to appeal to the American consumer, and how effective is it?

The passage of NAFTA and the consequent loss of American manufacturing jobs were expected to have the effect of discouraging immigration into the United States, especially illegal immigration from Latin America. However, this does not seem to have happened. To cope with the post-NAFTA economic upheaval, many Mexicans and Central Americans have taken to sending family members to earn U.S. wages to send back home. Some U.S. manufacturers, searching to lower their labor costs to compete with *maquilas* and satisfy consumer demand for lower prices, have turned to low-waged immigrant labor, especially to undocumented (illegal) immigrants who cannot use the courts or public agencies for protection against their extreme exploitation. In stark contrast to the waves of immigration in the late nineteenth century, now the majority of these and other international newcomers to the United States are women.

Responses to this situation have been contradictory. From 1989 to 1994, the federal government granted legal amnesty to 2 million undocumented Mexican workers. At the same time, anti-immigrant sentiment has flourished, especially among the working-class Americans who have suffered the most from the loss of U.S. manufacturing jobs. The 1996 federal law that denied public health and educational resources to immigrants, legal

◆ Figure 10.8 **Mexican Woman Captured while Crossing the California Border, 1988**
Photo © Ken Light.

as well as illegal (see p. 663), mandated the addition of new federal officers to patrol the borders, most of them posted in the Southwest. In Figure 10.8, one of these agents is taking a mug shot of an unnamed woman who was captured crossing into California. How does the photograph put a human face on these transnational border confrontations? What comparisons do you draw between this picture and the photographs taken by Jacob Riis of women immigrants a century before? (See Visual Sources: Jacob Riis's Photographs of Immigrant Girls and Women, pp. 386–92.)

Globalization has cultural and intellectual as well as economic dimensions for women. Not only goods and labor but also information and images are transmitted around the globe. American movies, television, and popular music reach an international audience, but influence goes the other way too, facilitated by technology and corporate power. While some observers criticize the homogenization of diverse local cultures, others celebrate the ability of people from distant parts of the globe to share common understandings and a unifying culture.

The cultural impact of globalization has encouraged the internationalization of modern standards for gender equality and female independence. The American women's rights movement has been influenced by international forces since its very beginning. The activists of the 1850s corresponded with women of similar sentiments in France and England, and immigrants from Germany and Poland joined in the movement. Many Progressive era women such as Jane Addams and Carrie Chapman Catt participated in international women's networks and drew inspiration from reform efforts initiated abroad. Nothing captures the historic links between American and international feminism better than the story of International Women's Day, which was first celebrated in 1908 by American Socialist women. The celebration was carried through the international Socialist and Communist movements until American women's liberationists rediscovered it when they visited Cuba and Vietnam in the 1960s. In 1981, the U.S. Congress declared Women's History Week (later Women's History Month) as an official federal event. International Women's Day is still celebrated around the world and connects far-flung women's movements to one another.

In the late twentieth-century world, the United Nations became a major resource for the internationalization of feminism. When the UN was formed in 1946 in the immediate aftermath of World War II, it established a Commission on the Status of Women (UN-CSW). The twenty-fifth anniversary of UN-CSW coincided with the upsurge in second-wave feminist energies in the United States and Europe, and in 1975 the United Nations sponsored its first International Women's Conference in Mexico City. Fifteen hundred delegates from 133 participating countries attended; for the first time in the history of UN conferences, the majority of official participants were women. The conference helped to advance what four years later became the UN's most comprehensive document on women's rights, the Convention° on the Elimination of All Forms of Discrimination Against Women (CEDAW), which the United States has refused to sign.

The Mexico City conference inaugurated the UN Decade of Women. To begin U.S. participation, the federal government authorized funds for a national conference, which took place in Houston in 1977. An important event in the development of American feminism, the conference brought together a diverse range of attendees. One-third were women of color. Conservative women from states that had not ratified the ERA secured about 20 percent of the delegates, but despite their presence, the conference passed a comprehensive National Women's Agenda that called for action against domestic violence and rape, ratification of the ERA, reproductive freedom and lesbian rights, and a unified statement of the importance of rights for women of color.

Figure 10.9 pictures the opening event at the 1977 Houston conference, which was the last leg of a fifty-one-day torch relay that began in Seneca Falls, New York, linking the meeting to the century-and-a-half-long American women's rights tradition (see Chapter 4). Second from the left in the photo is Billie Jean King, a champion tennis player and popular advocate for feminism. Next to her is the grandniece and namesake of Susan B. Anthony. In the center is New York congresswoman Bella Abzug, crowned by one of the big, bold hats for which she was famous; Abzug was not only a leading congressional advocate of women's rights but an outspoken opponent of the war in Vietnam. The next three women—Sylvia Ortiz, Peggy Kokernot, and Michelle Cearcy—were young Houston-area athletes. At far right in the photo is Betty Friedan. How does the picture capture

---

° A United Nations convention is a kind of international treaty, which obligates signatory countries to certain actions, in this case regular reports on the status of women.

◆ Figure 10.9 **National Women's Conference in Houston, 1977**
Copyright © 1978 Diana Mara Henry.

the enthusiasm for universal sisterhood that was so strong in the first decade of the feminist revival? What do you make of the sea of American flags at a meeting connected to a UN-sponsored conference of women from around the globe?

The Mexico City conference was followed by UN-sponsored international women's conferences in Copenhagen (1980) and Nairobi (1985). In 1995, the UN sponsored the Fourth International Women's Conference in Beijing to survey the gains of the international feminist movement over the previous two decades. While feminism had faded somewhat in the United States, it was flourishing in Asia, Africa, and parts of the Middle East. The growth in scope and self-confidence of global feminism could be measured in the size and enthusiasm of the official meeting, attended by fifteen thousand participants. As in Mexico City, the UN hosted a simultaneous conference of nongovernmental organizations, entitled "Looking at the World Through Women's Eyes," which was twice as large as the meeting of official delegates. Jo Freeman, a feminist activist and political scientist, was among the hundreds of American women who attended this extraordinary event. "In every country, even the smallest or least developed, there is a greater awareness of women, women's problems and women's importance than ever before," she wrote afterwards. "In all but the most conservative of countries, the feminist message that women are people, not just wives and mothers, is taken seriously."°

Hillary Rodham Clinton also attended. Here, as at other times during her husband's presidency, she self-consciously modeled herself after Eleanor Roosevelt, who transformed the role of First Lady into a position of considerable political influence (see Chapter 8). Clinton made a major public speech at the UN conference. "By gathering in Beijing, we are focusing world attention on issues that matter most in the lives of women and their families," she declared, "access to education, health care, jobs and credit, the chance to enjoy basic legal and human rights and participate fully in the political life of their countries." "As an American," she added, "I want to speak up for women in my own country—women who are raising children on the minimum wage, women who can't afford health care or child care, women whose lives are threatened by violence, including violence in their own homes." The next year, Clinton published *It Takes a Village* (1996). Using her title to invoke traditional African childrearing structures, Clinton argued for greater collective involvement and public support for childrearing. Figure 10.10 pictures Clinton at a session at the Beijing conference to discuss greater economic support for the world's women. What does this image, as well as Clinton's words, suggest about the position of the United States toward and in the burgeoning global feminist movement?

The Beijing conference hammered out an extensive international Platform for Action that addressed diverse subjects, including poverty among the world's women; persistent educational, political, economic, and health inequality; the violation of the rights of girl children; media stereotyping; and gender inequality in environmental safeguards. The impact of armed conflict on women and the international scope of violence against women were particular areas of concern. At the 1993 World's Conference on Human Rights in Vienna, Austria, feminist activists had successfully lobbied the UN and the international community to recognize the necessity of formally designating acts of violence against women, whether hidden in the family or condoned by governments, as full-fledged human rights abuses. The 1995 Beijing conference adopted the phrase that gained currency in Vienna, "Women's rights are human rights," and has since become the identifying slogan of the international feminist movement.

This brings us to the subject of war and American women in the age of globalization. Overseas wars have traditionally exposed American men to foreign influences, but now this is also the case for American women. Women now enroll in the military for the same reasons as men—employment opportunities, education, and adventure. Furthermore, the national military draft, which never included women, has been replaced with reliance on reserve military forces, in which women form a substantial part. Thus, when America's armed service capacity is

° Freeman's report can be found at <**jofreeman.com/womenyear/beijingreport.htm**>.

United Nations Development Fund for Women
Fonds de Développement des Nations Unies pour la Femme
Fondo de Desarrollo de las Naciones Unidas para la Mujer

◆ Figure 10.10 **Fourth International Women's Conference in Beijing, 1995**
© *CORBIS.*

mobilized, as it is with increasing frequency, the face of the American military that the country and the world see is often that of a woman deployed in difficult, dangerous, and controversial overseas campaigns.

By enlarging the available pool of labor and talent, women have strengthened and modernized the American military. But the presence of women in military uniforms performing military service has also led to complications, especially in the recent series of Middle Eastern wars. In the first Gulf War against Iraq in 1991, the United States was allied with Saudi Arabia and Kuwait, two of only five countries left in the world to deny voting rights to women. In deference to their orthodox Islamic practices, the U.S. military placed limits on its own female forces, for instance, forbidding them to drive vehicles in violation of local custom. Ten years later, when the United States went to war against the Taliban regime of Afghanistan in retaliation for its harboring of the terrorist forces responsible for the September 11, 2001, attack on the United States, the stark contrast between modern American women and the drastic domestic confinement and abuse of Afghan women made the liberation of Afghan women one of the rationales for the U.S. decision to go to war (see p. 656).

Figure 10.11 is a photograph that illustrates some of these complexities in the context of the third of these conflicts, the U.S. war against Saddam Hussein's regime in Iraq, begun in March 20, 2002, and, at the time of publication of this book, still ongoing. Iraq is a more modernized and secular country than

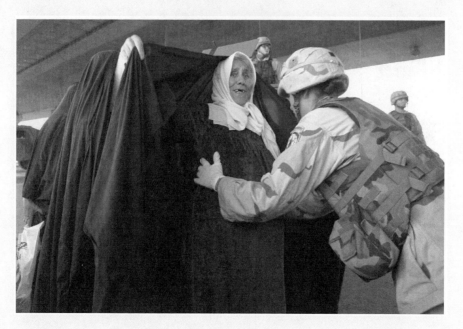

◆ Figure 10.11 **Two Women: An American Soldier and an Iraqi Civilian, 2002**
© *CORBIS.*

Afghanistan, but American television and newspapers show few images of urban
Iraqi working women or female Iraqi soldiers fighting for or against the regime of
Saddam Hussein. This photograph was one of many shot during the war by Zohra
Bensemra, an Algerian woman photographer. Although the American soldier's position and uniform make it difficult to see, the soldier, like the Iraqi she is frisking,
is a woman. Think about how the photograph emphasizes the contrast between
the Iraqi civilian and American soldier while playing on the fact that they are both
women. What does the photograph reveal about the relationships that globalization establishes among women?

QUESTIONS FOR ANALYSIS

1. In what ways does increasing global integration bring American women
   closer to women around the world?

2. In what ways does it increase the distance and inequality between them?

3. How do you think these two processes balance out?

4. How can you revision American women's history in other periods in an international context?

NOTES

1. Toni Cade, ed., *The Black Woman: An Anthology* (New York: New American Library, 1970), 107.

2. "To the Women of the Left," reprinted in Rosalyn Baxandall and Linda Gordon, eds., *Dear Sisters: Dispatches from the Women's Liberation Movement* (New York: Basic Books, 2000), 29.

3. "Burial of Weeping Womanhood," reprinted in Baxandall and Gordon, *Dear Sisters,* 25.

4. Robin Morgan, comp., *Sisterhood Is Powerful: An Anthology of Readings from the Women's Liberation Movement* (New York: Random House, 1970), xxxv.

5. Baxandall and Gordon, *Dear Sisters,* 158.

6. Quoted in Alice Echols, *Daring to Be Bad: Radical Feminism in America, 1967–1975* (Minneapolis: University of Minnesota Press, 1989), 212.

7. Ibid., 238.

8. Kate Millett, *Sexual Politics* (New York: Avon, 1970), 25.

9. Gayle Rubin, "The Traffic in Women: Notes on the 'Political Economy' of Sex," reprinted in Joan W. Scott, ed., *Feminism and Theory* (New York: Oxford University Press, 1996), 111.

10. Quoted in Benita Roth, *Separate Roads to Feminism: Black, Chicana, and White Feminist Movements in America's Second Wave* (New York: Cambridge University Press, 2004), 90.

11. Statement, Third World Women's Alliance, 1968, reprinted in Baxandall and Gordon, *Dear Sisters,* 65–66.

12. "A Black Feminist Statement," reprinted in Dawn Keetley and John Pettegrew, eds., *Public Women, Public Words: A Documentary History of American Feminism* (Madison, WI: Madison House, 2002), 3:77.

13. Cherríe Moraga and Gloria Anzaldúa, eds., *This Bridge Called My Back: Writings by Radical Women of Color* (Watertown, MA: Persephone Press, 1981), xxiii.

14. Ibid., 73.

15. Cited in Myra Marx Ferree and Beth B. Hess, *Controversy and Coalition: The New Feminist Movement across Three Decades of Change,* 3rd ed. (New York: Routledge, 2000), 8.

16. Flora Davis, *Moving the Mountain: The Women's Movement in America since 1960* (Urbana: University of Illinois Press, 1999), 158.

17. Ibid., 163.

18. Eloise Salholz, "The Marriage Crunch," *Newsweek,* June 2, 1986, 55.

19. Anna Greenberg, "Deconstructing the Gender Gap," http://www.ksg.harvard .edu/prg/greenb/gengap.htm (accessed August 30, 2004).

20. Steven Stark, "Gap Politics," *Atlantic Magazine,* July 1996, 71–80.

21. Nancy MacLean, "The Hidden History of Affirmative Action: Working Women's Struggles in the 1970s and the Gender of Class," *Feminist Studies* (Spring 1999): 50.

22. Nancy Cott, *Public Vows: A History of Marriage and the Nation* (Cambridge: Harvard University Press, 2000), 212.

23. Sarah M. Evans, *Tidal Wave: How Women Changed America at Century's End* (New York: Free Press, 2003), 234.

24. Doreen Mattingly, " 'Working Men' and 'Dependent Wives': Gender, 'Race,' and the Regulation of Migration from Mexico," in Cathy J. Cohen et al., eds., *Women Transforming Politics: An Alternative Reader* (New York: New York University Press, 1997), 51.

25. Quoted in *The Daily Bruin,* March 9, 2000, http://www.dailybruin.ucla.edu/db/issues/00/03.09/news.janitors.html (accessed August 30, 2004).

26. Third Wave Foundation, http://www.thirdwavefoundation.org (accessed September 1, 2004).

27. Robin Roberts, " 'Ladies First': Queen Latifah's Afrocentric Feminist Music Video," *African American Review* 28 (1994): 245–58.

28. Jessica Rosenberg and Gitana Garofalo, "Riot Grrrl: Revolutions from Within," *Signs* 23 (1998): 810.

29. Laurel Gilbert and Crystal Kile, *Surfergrrrls: Look Ethel! An Internet Guide for Us* (1996), quoted in Ednie Kaeh Garrison, "U.S. Feminism-Grrrl Style! Youth (Sub)Cultures and the Technologics of the Third Wave," *Feminist Studies* 26 (Spring 2000): 141.

30. Lillian Faderman, *Odd Girls and Twilight Lovers: A History of Lesbian Life in Twentieth-Century America* (New York: Columbia University Press, 1991), 180.

31. David K. Johnson, *The Lavender Scare: The Cold War Persecution of Gays and Lesbians in the Federal Government* (Chicago: University of Chicago Press, 2004), 196.

32. Quoted in Faderman, *Odd Girls and Twilight Lovers,* 207.

33. Lesbians of Color Network, undated leaflet, from ONE Archives, Lesbian of Color Folder.

34. Susan J. Hubert, "What's Wrong with This Picture? The Politics of Ellen's Coming Out Party," *Journal of Popular Culture* 33 (1999): 31.

35. Bruce Handy, "He Called Me Ellen Degenerate?," *Time,* April 17, 1994, 82.

36. *Los Angeles Times,* February 13, 2004, pp. A1, A28.

37. The STITCH Web site is found at http://www.stitchonline.org.

SUGGESTED REFERENCES

General Works   Three scholars of U.S. women's history have recently published studies of women's history in the last third of the twentieth century that emphasize the powerful influence of the feminist revival: Sara M. Evans, *Tidal Wave: How Women Changed America at Century's End* (2003); Estelle B. Freedman, *No Turning*

Back: The History of Feminism and the Future of Women (2002), which situates U.S. women's history in a global context; and Ruth Rosen, *The World Split Open: How the Modern Women's Movement Changed America* (2000).

Feminist Movements   One of the earliest studies of women's liberation, published while the movement was still thriving, is *The Politics of Women's Liberation* (1975) by feminist activist and political scientist Jo Freeman. Sarah Evans's influential *Personal Politics: The Roots of Women's Liberation in the Civil Rights Movement and the New Left* (1979) examines the influence of the civil rights and New Left movements on the rediscovery of feminism in the late 1960s. Alice Echols's collection of essays, *Shaky Ground: The Sixties and Its Aftershocks* (2002), considers relations of gender and race within the counterculture. Echols has also written a critical historical analysis of the tensions between different early women's liberation approaches in *Daring to Be Bad: Radical Feminism in America, 1967–1975* (1989). Flora Davis's *Moving the Mountain: The Women's Movement in America since 1960* (1999) is a more narrative history that interweaves the history of women's liberation with that of the National Organization for Women. In *Controversy and Coalition: The New Feminist Movement across Three Decades of Change,* 3rd ed. (2000), Myra Marx Ferree and Beth B. Hess go beyond the emergence of women's liberation to trace the development and influence of contemporary feminism through the rest of the century. Judith Ezekiel's *Feminism in the Heartland* (2002) examines women's liberation in Dayton, Ohio. Amy Erdman Farrell provides a history of *Ms.* magazine in *Yours in Sisterhood: Ms. Magazine and the Promise of Popular Feminism* (1998).

Two newer collections of historical documents from the women's liberation movement are Dawn Keetley and John Pettegrew, eds., *Public Women, Public Words: A Documentary History of American Feminism,* vol. 3, *1960 to the Present* (2002), and Rosalyn Baxandall and Linda Gordon, eds., *Dear Sisters: Dispatches from the Women's Liberation Movement* (2000). Individual memoirs have begun to appear, for instance, Susan Brownmiller, *In Our Time: A Memoir of Revolution* (1999), and Karla Jay, *Tales of the Lavender Menace: A Memoir of Liberation* (1999). Rachel Blau DuPlessis and Ann Snitow, eds., *The Feminist Memoir Project: Voices from Women's Liberation* (1998), offers a collection of briefer reminiscences. Florence Howe, ed., *The Politics of Women's Studies: Testimony from Thirty Founding Mothers* (2000), focuses on one of the more lasting aspects of the second wave.

The starting point for a history of lesbians is Lillian Faderman, *Odd Girls and Twilight Lovers: A History of Lesbian Life in Twentieth-Century America* (1991). For a path-breaking study of a working-class lesbian community, see Elizabeth Lapovsky Kennedy and Madeline D. Davis, *Boots of Leather, Slippers of Gold: The History of a Lesbian Community* (1993). John D'Emilio, *Sexual Politics, Sexual Communities: The Making of a Homosexual Minority in the United States, 1940–1970,* 2nd ed. (1998), and David K. Johnson, *The Lavender Scare: The Cold War Persecution of Gays and Lesbians in the Federal Government* (2004), offer insights on early gay efforts to counter discrimination, and Martin Duberman explores the origins of the gay liberation movement in *Stonewall* (1993).

The first source for the role of women of color and their response to the rise of women's liberation is Toni Cade's collection, *The Black Woman: An Anthology* (1970). Michele Wallace's *Black Macho and the Myth of the Superwoman* (1990) is a new edition of a controversial 1979 critique of sexism in the black liberation movement. Gloria T. Hull et al., *All the Women Are White, All the Blacks Are Men, but Some of Us Are Brave* (1982), offers excerpts from many pioneering black feminist writings, and Patricia Hill Collins's *Black Feminist Thought: Knowledge, Consciousness, and the Politics of Empowerment* (2000) analyzes this literature. *Ain't I a Woman: Black Women and Feminism* by bell hooks (1981) is one of the earliest modern African American feminist analyses. A very interesting dialogue between black and white feminists is found in Gloria I. Joseph and Jill Lewis, *Common Differences: Conflicts in Black and White Feminist Perspectives* (1981).

Alma García, ed., *Chicana Feminist Thought: The Basic Historical Writings* (1997), is the best primary source for feminism within the Chicano/Chicana movement. For a range of writings from all groups of women of color, see Cherríe Moraga and Gloria Anzaldúa, eds., *This Bridge Called My Back: Writings by Radical Women of Color* (1979), and the subsequent volume, edited by Anzaldúa and AnaLouise Keating, *This Bridge We Call Home: Radical Visions for Transformation* (2002). In *Separate Roads to Feminism: Black, Chicana, and White Feminist Movements in America's Second Wave* (2004), Benita Roth offers a very useful comparative analysis of the three movements.

Third-wave feminism is well covered in Jennifer Baumgardner and Amy Richards, eds., *Manifesta: Young Women, Feminism, and the Future* (2000); Barbara Findlen, ed., *Listen Up: Voices from the Next Feminist Generation,* 2nd ed. (2001); and Daisy Hernández and Bushra Rehman, eds., *Colonize This! Young Women of Color on Today's Feminism* (2002). Two articles on the subject are Kimberly Springer, "Third Wave Black Feminism?" *Signs* 27 (2002): 1059–82, and Gayle Wald, "Just a Girl? Rock Music, Feminism, and the Cultural Construction of Female Youth," *Signs* 23 (1998): 585–610.

In Defense of Traditional Womanhood   On the general cultural atmosphere of the anti-feminist reaction to women's liberation, see Susan Faludi's influential *Backlash: The Undeclared War against American Women* (1991). In *Women of the New Right* (1987), Rebecca E. Klatch looks at the larger history of women in the conservative movement. Carol Felsenthal offers a biography of the movement's major figure in *The Sweetheart of the Silent Majority: The Biography of Phyllis Schlafly* (1981). On the battle over the ERA, see Mary Frances Berry, *Why ERA Failed: Politics, Women's Rights, and the Amending Process of the Constitution* (1986), and Jane J. Mansbridge, *Why We Lost the ERA* (1986). On the anti-abortion movement, see Dallas A. Blanchard, *The Anti-Abortion Movement and the Rise of the Religious Right: From Polite to Fiery Protest* (1994); Kristin Luker, *Abortion and the Politics of Motherhood* (1984); and Rickie Solinger, ed., *Abortion Wars: A Half Century of Struggle, 1950–2000* (1998). In *Contested Lives: The Abortion Debate in an American Community* (1998), Faye D. Ginsburg provides a fascinating study of women in both the pro-choice and anti-abortion movements in a single midwestern community.

On the Thomas-Hill hearings, see *Race-ing Justice, En-gendering Power: Essays on Anita Hill, Clarence Thomas, and the Construction of Social Reality*, edited by Toni Morrison (1992). On the sex and gender dimensions of the impeachment of President Clinton, see Lauren Berlant and Lisa Duggan, eds., *Our Monica, Ourselves: The Clinton Affair and the National Interest* (2001).

Women, Work, and Family   On women in the labor force, an excellent overview that extends to the late twentieth century is Julia Kirk Blackwelder, *Now Hiring: The Feminization of Work in the United States, 1900–1995* (1997). Arlie Russell Hochschild, *Second Shift: Working Parents and the Revolution at Home* (2003), examines the double responsibilities of working mothers. Barbara Ehrenreich, *Nickel and Dimed: On (Not) Getting By in America* (2001), offers a compelling portrait of women in low-wage jobs.

On changes in family and personal life, see Stephanie Coontz, *The Way We Really Are: Coming to Terms with America's Changing Families* (1997). Sociologist Judith Stacey has written two books on this subject: *Brave New Families: Stories of Domestic Upheaval in Late Twentieth-Century America* (1998) and *In the Name of the Family: Rethinking Family Values in the Postmodern Age* (1996).

On women and the new immigration, see Barbara Ehrenreich and Arlie Russell Hochschild, eds., *Global Woman: Nannies, Maids, and Sex Workers in the New Economy* (2003). On globalization, see Miriam Ching Yoon Louie, *Sweatshop Warriors: Immigrant Women Workers Take on the Global Factory* (2001).

Selected Web Sites

Veterans of the Chicago Women's Liberation Union (1969–1977) have put together an excellent Web site that includes written and photographic reminiscences of activists, documentation of the organization's varied projects, and classic writings of the women's liberation period: <**cwluherstory.com/**>. Duke University also has an extensive set of digitized documents from the women's liberation period at <**scriptorium.lib.duke.edu/wlm/**>. For historical and contemporary materials about Chicana feminism, see <**chicanas.com/**>. At the University of California, Santa Barbara, Sherri Barnes has assembled a Web site on black feminism: <**library.ucsb.edu/subjects/blackfeminism/introduction.html**>. The Third Wave Foundation provides resources for younger feminists at <**thirdwave foundation.org/**>.

There are enormous amounts of material on the Web about the abortion controversy. A gateway to sites representing the pro-life movement is <**members .tripod.com/~jproj/linklife.html**>. The National Organization for Women has a pro-choice page at <**now.org/issues/abortion/**> and a page on the ERA at <**now .org/issues/economic/cea/history.html**>.

The U.S. Department of Labor has made it easy to access resources on women workers: <**dol.gov/dol/audience/aud-women.htm**>. Estelle Freedman has assembled a Web site to accompany her book *No Turning Back* (2002), which situates the past and present issues facing U.S. women in an international environment: <**noturningback.stanford.edu/resources.html**>. The United Nations Division of Women is a fine place to start to learn about the global growth in the feminist movement: <**un.org/womenwatch/daw/**>.

The Declaration of Independence

IN CONGRESS, JULY 4, 1776,
THE UNANIMOUS DECLARATION OF THE
THIRTEEN UNITED STATES OF AMERICA

When in the Course of human events, it becomes necessary for one people to dissolve the political bands which have connected them with another, and to assume among the Powers of the earth, the separate and equal station to which the Laws of Nature and of Nature's God entitle them, a decent respect to the opinions of mankind requires that they should declare the causes which impel them to the separation.

We hold these truths to be self-evident, that all men are created equal, that they are endowed by their Creator with certain unalienable rights, that among these are Life, Liberty, and the pursuit of Happiness. That to secure these rights, Governments are instituted among Men, deriving their just powers from the consent of the governed. That whenever any Form of Government becomes destructive of these ends, it is the Right of the People to alter or to abolish it, and to institute new Government, laying its foundation on such principles and organizing its powers in such form, as to them shall seem most likely to effect their Safety and Happiness. Prudence, indeed, will dictate that Governments long established should not be changed for light and transient causes; and accordingly all experience hath shown, that mankind are more disposed to suffer, while evils are sufferable, than to right themselves by abolishing the forms to which they are accustomed. But when a long train of abuses and usurpations, pursuing invariably the same Object evinces a de-

sign to reduce them under absolute Despotism, it is their right, it is their duty, to throw off such Government, and to provide new Guards for their future security. — Such has been the patient sufferance of these Colonies; and such is now the necessity which constrains them to alter their former Systems of Government. The history of the present King of Great Britain is a history of repeated injuries and usurpations, all having in direct object the establishment of an absolute Tyranny over these States. To prove this, let Facts be submitted to a candid world.

He has refused his Assent to Laws, the most wholesome and necessary for the public good.

He has forbidden his Governors to pass Laws of immediate and pressing importance, unless suspended in their operation till his Assent should be obtained; and, when so suspended, he has utterly neglected to attend to them.

He has refused to pass other Laws for the accommodation of large districts of people, unless those people would relinquish the right of Representation in the Legislature, a right inestimable to them and formidable to tyrants only.

He has called together legislative bodies at places unusual, uncomfortable, and distant from the depository of their public Records, for the sole purpose of fatiguing them into compliance with his measures.

He has dissolved Representative Houses repeatedly, for opposing with manly firmness his invasions on the rights of the people.

He has refused for a long time, after such dissolutions, to cause others to be elected; whereby the Legislative powers, incapable of Annihilation, have returned to the People at large for their exercise; the State remaining in the mean time exposed to all the dangers of invasion from without and convulsions within.

He has endeavoured to prevent the population of these States; for that purpose obstructing the Laws of Naturalization of Foreigners; refusing to pass others to encourage their migrations hither, and raising the conditions of new Appropriations of Lands.

He has obstructed the Administration of Justice, by refusing his Assent to Laws for establishing Judiciary powers.

He has made Judges dependent on his Will alone, for the tenure of their offices, and the amount and payment of their salaries.

He has erected a multitude of New Offices, and sent hither swarms of Officers to harass our People, and eat out their substance.

He has kept among us, in times of peace, Standing Armies without the Consent of our legislature.

He has combined with others to subject us to a jurisdiction foreign to our constitution, and unacknowledged by our laws; giving his Assent to their Acts of pretended Legislation:

For quartering large bodies of armed troops among us:

For protecting them, by a mock Trial, from Punishment for any Murders which they should commit on the Inhabitants of these States:

For cutting off our Trade with all parts of the world:

For imposing taxes on us without our Consent:

For depriving us, in many cases, of the benefits of Trial by jury:

For transporting us beyond Seas to be tried for pretended offences:

For abolishing the free System of English Laws in a neighbouring Province, establishing therein an Arbitrary government, and enlarging its Boundaries so as to render it at once an example and fit instrument for introducing the same absolute rule into these Colonies:

For taking away our Charters, abolishing our most valuable Laws, and altering fundamentally the Forms of our Governments:

For suspending our own Legislatures, and declaring themselves invested with Power to legislate for us in all cases whatsoever.

He has abdicated Government here, by declaring us out of his Protection and waging War against us.

He has plundered our seas, ravaged our Coasts, burnt our towns, and destroyed the lives of our people.

He is at this time transporting large armies of foreign mercenaries to compleat the works of death, desolation, and tyranny, already begun with circumstances of Cruelty & perfidy scarcely paralleled in the most barbarous ages, and totally unworthy the Head of a civilized nation.

He has constrained our fellow Citizens taken Captive on the high Seas to bear Arms against their Country, to become the executioners of their friends and Brethren, or to fall themselves by their Hands.

He has excited domestic insurrections amongst us, and has endeavoured to bring on the inhabitants of our frontiers, the merciless Indian Savages, whose known rule of warfare, is an undistinguished destruction of all ages, sexes, and conditions.

In every stage of these Oppressions We have Petitioned for Redress in the most humble terms: Our repeated Petitions have been answered only by repeated injury. A Prince, whose character is thus marked by every act which may define a Tyrant, is unfit to be the ruler of a free people.

Nor have We been wanting in attention to our British brethren. We have warned them from time to time of attempts by their legislature to extend an unwarrantable jurisdiction over us. We have reminded them of the circumstances of our emigration and settlement here. We have appealed to their native justice and magnanimity, and we have conjured them by the ties of our common kindred to disavow these usurpations, which, would inevitably interrupt our connections and correspondence. They too have been deaf to the voice of justice and of consanguinity. We must, therefore, acquiesce in the necessity, which denounces our Separation, and hold them, as we hold the rest of mankind, Enemies in War, in Peace Friends.

We, therefore, the Representatives of the United States of America, in General Congress, Assembled, appealing to the Supreme Judge of the world for the rectitude of our intentions, do, in the Name, and by Authority of the good People of these Colonies, solemnly publish and declare, That these United Colonies are, and of Right ought to be FREE AND INDEPENDENT STATES; that they are Absolved from all Allegiance to the British Crown, and that all political connection between them and the State of Great Britain, is and ought to be totally dissolved; and that as Free and Independent States, they have full Power to levy War, conclude Peace, contract Alliances, establish Commerce, and to do all other Acts and Things which Independent States may of right do. And for the support of this Declaration, with a firm reliance on the Protection of Divine Providence, we mutually pledge to each other our Lives, our Fortunes, and our sacred Honor.

John Hancock

Button Gwinnett	George Wythe	James Wilson	Josiah Bartlett
Lyman Hall	Richard Henry Lee	Geo. Ross	Wm. Whipple
Geo. Walton	Th. Jefferson	Caesar Rodney	Matthew Thornton
Wm. Hooper	Benja. Harrison	Geo. Read	Saml. Adams
Joseph Hewes	Thos. Nelson, Jr.	Thos. M'Kean	John Adams
John Penn	Francis Lightfoot Lee	Wm. Floyd	Robt. Treat Paine
Edward Rutledge	Carter Braxton	Phil. Livingston	Elbridge Gerry
Thos. Heyward, Junr.	Robt. Morris	Frans. Lewis	Step. Hopkins
Thomas Lynch, Junr.	Benjamin Rush	Lewis Morris	William Ellery
Arthur Middleton	Benja. Franklin	Richd. Stockton	Roger Sherman
Samuel Chase	John Morton	John Witherspoon	Sam'el Huntington
Wm. Paca	Geo. Clymer	Fras. Hopkinson	Wm. Williams
Thos. Stone	Jas. Smith	John Hart	Oliver Wolcott
Charles Carroll	Geo. Taylor	Abra. Clark	
of Carrollton			

The Constitution of the United States of America

AGREED TO BY PHILADELPHIA
CONVENTION, SEPTEMBER 17, 1787
IMPLEMENTED MARCH 4, 1789

We the People of the United States, in Order to form a more perfect Union, establish Justice, insure domestic Tranquility, provide for the common defence, promote the general Welfare, and secure the Blessings of Liberty to ourselves and our Posterity, do ordain and establish this Constitution for the United States of America.

ARTICLE I

Section 1. All legislative Powers herein granted shall be vested in a Congress of the United States, which shall consist of a Senate and a House of Representatives.

Section 2. The House of Representatives shall be composed of Members chosen every second Year by the People of the several States, and the Electors in each State shall have the Qualifications requisite for Electors of the most numerous Branch of the State Legislature.

No Person shall be a Representative who shall not have attained to the Age of twenty-five Years, and been seven Years a Citizen of the United States, and who shall not, when elected, be an Inhabitant of that State in which he shall be chosen.

Representatives and direct Taxes shall be apportioned among the several States which may be included within this Union, according to their respective Numbers, *which shall be determined by adding to the whole Number of free Persons, including those bound to Service for a Term of Years, and excluding Indians not taxed, three fifths of all other Persons.*[1] The actual Enumeration shall be made within three Years after the first Meeting of the Congress of the United States, and within every subsequent Term of ten Years, in such Manner as they shall by Law direct. The Number of Representatives shall not exceed one for every thirty Thousand, but each State shall have at Least one Representative; and *until such enumeration shall be made, the State of New Hampshire shall be entitled to chuse three, Massachusetts eight, Rhode Island and Providence Plantations one, Connecticut five, New-York six, New Jersey four, Pennsylvania eight, Delaware one, Maryland six, Virginia ten, North Carolina five, South Carolina five, and Georgia three.*

When vacancies happen in the Representation from any State, the Executive Authority thereof shall issue Writs of Election to fill such Vacancies.

The House of Representatives shall chuse their Speaker and other Officers; and shall have the sole Power of Impeachment.

Section 3. The Senate of the United States shall be composed of two Senators from each State, *chosen by the Legislature thereof,*[2] for six Years; and each Senator shall have one Vote.

Note: The Constitution became effective March 4, 1789. Provisions in italics are no longer relevant or have been changed by constitutional amendment.

[1]Changed by Section 2 of the Fourteenth Amendment.
[2]Changed by Section 1 of the Seventeenth Amendment.

Immediately after they shall be assembled in Consequence of the first Election, they shall be divided as equally as may be into three Classes. The Seats of the Senators of the first Class shall be vacated at the Expiration of the second Year, of the second Class at the Expiration of the fourth Year, and of the third Class at the Expiration of the sixth Year, so that one-third may be chosen every second Year; and if Vacancies happen by Resignation, or otherwise, during the Recess of the Legislature of any State, the Executive thereof may make temporary Appointments until the next Meeting of the Legislature, which shall then fill such Vacancies.[3]

No person shall be a Senator who shall not have attained to the Age of thirty Years, and been nine Years a Citizen of the United States, and who shall not, when elected, be an Inhabitant of that State for which he shall be chosen.

The Vice President of the United States shall be President of the Senate, but shall have no Vote, unless they be equally divided.

The Senate shall chuse their other Officers, and also a President pro tempore, in the absence of the Vice President, or when he shall exercise the Office of President of the United States.

The Senate shall have the sole Power to try all Impeachments. When sitting for that Purpose, they shall be on Oath or Affirmation. When the President of the United States is tried, the Chief Justice shall preside: And no Person shall be convicted without the Concurrence of two thirds of the Members present.

Judgment in Cases of Impeachment shall not extend further than to removal from Office, and disqualification to hold and enjoy any Office of honor, Trust or Profit under the United States: but the Party convicted shall nevertheless be liable and subject to Indictment, Trial, Judgment and Punishment, according to Law.

Section 4. The Times, Places and Manner of holding Elections for Senators and Representatives, shall be prescribed in each State by the Legislature thereof; but the Congress may at any time by Law make or alter such Regulations, except as to the Places of Chusing Senators.

The Congress shall assemble at least once in every Year, and such Meeting *shall be on the first Monday in December, unless they shall by Law appoint a different Day.*[4]

Section 5. Each House shall be the Judge of the Elections, Returns and Qualifications of its own Members, and a Majority of each shall constitute a Quorum to do Business; but a smaller number may adjourn from day to day, and may be authorized to compel the Attendance of absent Members, in such Manner, and under such Penalties, as each House may provide.

Each House may determine the Rules of its Proceedings, punish its Members for disorderly Behavior, and, with the Concurrence of two thirds, expel a Member.

Each House shall keep a Journal of its Proceedings, and from time to time publish the same, excepting such Parts as may in their Judgment require Secrecy; and the Yeas and Nays of the Members of either House on any question shall, at the Desire of one-fifth of those Present, be entered on the Journal.

Neither House, during the Session of Congress, shall, without the Consent of the other, adjourn for more than three days, nor to any other Place than that in which the two Houses shall be sitting.

Section 6. The Senators and Representatives shall receive a Compensation for their Services, to be ascertained by Law, and paid out of the Treasury of the United States. They shall in all Cases, except Treason, Felony and Breach of the Peace, be privileged from Arrest during their Attendance at the Session of their respective Houses, and in going to and returning from the same; and for

---

[3]Changed by Clause 2 of the Seventeenth Amendment.

[4]Changed by Section 2 of the Twentieth Amendment.

any Speech or Debate in either House, they shall not be questioned in any other Place.

No Senator or Representative shall, during the Time for which he was elected, be appointed to any civil Office under the Authority of the United States, which shall have been created, or the Emoluments whereof shall have been increased, during such time; and no Person holding any Office under the United States, shall be a Member of either House during his Continuance in Office.

Section 7.   All Bills for raising Revenue shall originate in the House of Representatives; but the Senate may propose or concur with Amendments as on other Bills.

Every Bill which shall have passed the House of Representatives and the Senate, shall, before it becomes a Law, be presented to the President of the United States; If he approve he shall sign it, but if not he shall return it, with his Objections to that House in which it shall have originated, who shall enter the Objections at large on their Journal, and proceed to reconsider it. If after such Reconsideration two thirds of that House shall agree to pass the Bill, it shall be sent, together with the Objections, to the other House, by which it shall likewise be reconsidered, and if approved by two thirds of that House, it shall become a Law. But in all such Cases the Votes of both Houses shall be determined by Yeas and Nays, and the Names of the Persons voting for and against the Bill shall be entered on the Journal of each House respectively. If any Bill shall not be returned by the President within ten Days (Sundays excepted) after it shall have been presented to him, the Same shall be a Law, in like Manner as if he had signed it, unless the Congress by their Adjournment prevent its Return, in which Case it shall not be a Law.

Every Order, Resolution, or Vote to which the Concurrence of the Senate and the House of Representatives may be necessary (except on a question of Adjournment) shall be presented to the President of the United States; and before the Same shall take Effect, shall be approved by him, or being disapproved by him, shall be repassed by two thirds of the Senate and House of Representatives, according to the Rules and Limitations prescribed in the Case of a Bill.

Section 8.   The Congress shall have Power to lay and collect Taxes, Duties, Imposts and Excises, to pay the Debts and provide for the common Defence and general Welfare of the United States; but all Duties, Imposts and Excises shall be uniform throughout the United States;

To borrow money on the credit of the United States;

To regulate Commerce with foreign Nations, and among the several States, and with the Indian Tribes;

To establish an uniform Rule of Naturalization, and uniform Laws on the subject of Bankruptcies throughout the United States;

To coin Money, regulate the Value thereof, and of foreign Coin, and fix the Standard of Weights and Measures;

To provide for the Punishment of counterfeiting the Securities and current Coin of the United States;

To establish Post Offices and post Roads;

To promote the Progress of Science and useful Arts, by securing for limited Times to Authors and Inventors the exclusive Right to their respective Writings and Discoveries;

To constitute Tribunals inferior to the supreme Court;

To define and punish Piracies and Felonies committed on the high Seas, and Offenses against the Law of Nations;

To declare War, grant Letters of Marque and Reprisal, and make Rules concerning Captures on Land and Water;

To raise and support Armies, but no Appropriation of Money to that Use shall be for a longer Term than two Years;

To provide and maintain a Navy;

To make Rules for the Government and Regulation of the land and naval Forces;

To provide for calling forth the Militia to execute the Laws of the Union, suppress Insurrections and repel Invasions;

To provide for organizing, arming, and disciplining the Militia, and for governing such Part of them as may be employed in the Service of the United States, reserving to the States respectively, the Appointment of the Officers, and the Authority of training the Militia according to the discipline prescribed by Congress;

To exercise exclusive Legislation in all Cases whatsoever, over such District (not exceeding ten Miles square) as may, by Cession of particular States, and the acceptance of Congress, become the Seat of Government of the United States, and to exercise like Authority over all Places purchased by the Consent of the Legislature of the State in which the Same shall be, for the Erection of Forts, Magazines, Arsenals, dock-Yards, and other needful Buildings;—And

To make all Laws which shall be necessary and proper for carrying into Execution the foregoing Powers, and all other Powers vested by this Constitution in the Government of the United States, or in any Department or Officer thereof.

Section 9. The Migration or Importation of such Persons as any of the States now existing shall think proper to admit, shall not be prohibited by the Congress prior to the Year one thousand eight hundred and eight but a tax or duty may be imposed on such Importation, not exceeding ten dollars for each Person.

The privilege of the Writ of Habeas Corpus shall not be suspended, unless when in Cases of Rebellion or Invasion the public Safety may require it.

No Bill of Attainder or ex post facto Law shall be passed.

No capitation, or other direct, Tax shall be laid, unless in Proportion to the Census or Enumeration herein before directed to be taken.[5]

No Tax or Duty shall be laid on Articles exported from any State.

No Preference shall be given by any Regulation of Commerce or Revenue to the Ports of one State over those of another: nor shall Vessels bound to, or from, one State, be obliged to enter, clear, or pay Duties in another.

No Money shall be drawn from the Treasury, but in Consequence of Appropriations made by law; and a regular Statement and Account of the Receipts and Expenditures of all public Money shall be published from time to time.

No Title of Nobility shall be granted by the United States: And no Person holding any Office of Profit or Trust under them, shall, without the Consent of the Congress, accept of any present, Emolument, Office, or Title, of any kind whatever, from any King, Prince, or foreign State.

Section 10. No State shall enter into any Treaty, Alliance, or Confederation; grant Letters of Marque and Reprisal; coin Money; emit Bills of Credit; make any Thing but gold and silver Coin a Tender in Payment of Debts; pass any Bill of Attainder, ex post facto Law, or Law impairing the Obligation of Contracts, or grant any Title of Nobility.

No State shall, without the Consent of the Congress, lay any Imposts or Duties on Imports or Exports, except what may be absolutely necessary for executing its inspection Laws: and the net Produce of all Duties and Imposts, laid by any State on Imports or Exports, shall be for the Use of the Treasury of the United States; and all such Laws shall be subject to the Revision and Control of the Congress.

No State shall, without the Consent of the Congress, lay any duty of Tonnage, keep Troops, or Ships of War in time of Peace, enter into any Agreement or Compact with another State, or with a foreign Power, or engage in War, unless actually invaded, or in such imminent Danger as will not admit of delay.

ARTICLE II

Section 1. The executive Power shall be vested in a President of the United States of America. He

---

[5]Changed by the Sixteenth Amendment.

shall hold his Office during the Term of four Years, and, together with the Vice President, chosen for the same Term, be elected, as follows:

Each State shall appoint, in such Manner as the Legislature thereof may direct, a Number of Electors, equal to the whole Number of Senators and Representatives to which the State may be entitled in the Congress; but no Senator or Representative, or Person holding an Office of Trust or Profit under the United States, shall be appointed an Elector.

The Electors shall meet in their respective States, and vote by Ballot for two Persons, of whom one at least shall not be an Inhabitant of the same State with themselves. And they shall make a List of all the Persons voted for, and of the Number of Votes for each; which List they shall sign and certify, and transmit sealed to the Seat of the Government of the United States, directed to the President of the Senate. The President of the Senate shall, in the Presence of the Senate and House of Representatives, open all the Certificates, and the Votes shall then be counted. The Person having the greatest Number of Votes shall be the President, if such Number be a Majority of the whole Number of Electors appointed; and if there be more than one who have such Majority, and have an equal Number of Votes, then the House of Representatives shall immediately chuse by Ballot one of them for President; and if no Person have a Majority, then from the five highest on the List the said House shall in like Manner chuse the President. But in chusing the President, the Votes shall be taken by States, the Representation from each State having one Vote; a quorum for this Purpose shall consist of a Member or Members from two thirds of the States, and a Majority of all the States shall be necessary to a Choice. In every Case, after the Choice of the President, the Person having the greatest Number of Votes of the Electors shall be the Vice President. But if there should remain two or more who have equal Votes, the Senate shall chuse from them by Ballot the Vice President.[6]

The Congress may determine the Time of chusing the Electors, and the Day on which they shall give their Votes; which Day shall be the same throughout the United States.

No Person except a natural born Citizen, or a Citizen of the United States, at the time of the Adoption of this Constitution, shall be eligible to the Office of President; neither shall any Person be eligible to that Office who shall not have attained to the Age of thirty five Years, and been fourteen Years a Resident within the United States.

In Case of the Removal of the President from Office, or of his Death, Resignation, or Inability to discharge the Powers and Duties of the said Office, the same shall devolve on the Vice President, *and the Congress may by Law provide for the Case of Removal, Death, Resignation, or Inability, both of the President and Vice President, declaring what Officer shall then act as President, and such Officer shall act accordingly, until the Disability be removed, or a President shall be elected.*[7]

The President shall, at stated Times, receive for his Services a Compensation, which shall neither be increased nor diminished during the Period for which he shall have been elected, and he shall not receive within that Period any other Emolument from the United States, or any of them.

Before he enter on the Execution of his Office, he shall take the following Oath or Affirmation:—"I do solemnly swear (or affirm) that I will faithfully execute the Office of President of the United States, and will to the best of my Ability, preserve, protect and defend the Constitution of the United States."

Section 2.   The President shall be Commander in Chief of the Army and Navy of the United States, and of the Militia of the several States, when called into the actual Service of the United States; he may require the Opinion, in writing, of the principal Officer in each of the executive Departments, upon any Subject relating to the Duties of their respective Offices, and he shall have

---

[6]Superseded by the Twelfth Amendment.

[7]Modified by the Twenty-fifth Amendment.

Power to Grant Reprieves and Pardons for Offences against the United States, except in Cases of Impeachment.

He shall have Power, by and with the Advice and Consent of the Senate, to make Treaties, provided two thirds of the Senators present concur; and he shall nominate, and by and with the Advice and Consent of the Senate, shall appoint Ambassadors, other public Ministers and Consuls, Judges of the supreme Court, and all other Officers of the United States, whose Appointments are not herein otherwise provided for, and which shall be established by Law: but the Congress may by Law vest the Appointment of such inferior Officers, as they think proper, in the President alone, in the Courts of Law, or in the Heads of Departments.

The President shall have Power to fill up all Vacancies that may happen during the Recess of the Senate, by granting Commissions which shall expire at the End of their next Session.

Section 3.   He shall from time to time give to the Congress Information of the State of the Union, and recommend to their Consideration such Measures as he shall judge necessary and expedient; he may, on extraordinary Occasions, convene both Houses, or either of them, and in Case of Disagreement between them, with Respect to the Time of Adjournment, he may adjourn them to such Time as he shall think proper; he shall receive Ambassadors and other public Ministers; he shall take Care that the Laws be faithfully executed, and shall Commission all the Officers of the United States.

Section 4.   The President, Vice President and all civil Officers of the United States, shall be removed from Office on Impeachment for, and Conviction of, Treason, Bribery, or other high Crimes and Misdemeanors.

Article III

Section 1.   The judicial Power of the United States, shall be vested in one supreme Court, and in such inferior Courts as the Congress may from time to time ordain and establish. The Judges, both of the supreme and inferior Courts, shall hold their Offices during good Behaviour, and shall, at stated Times, receive for their Services a Compensation, which shall not be diminished during their Continuance in Office.

Section 2.   The judicial Power shall extend to all Cases, in Law and Equity, arising under this Constitution, the Laws of the United States, and Treaties made, or which shall be made, under their Authority;—to all Cases affecting Ambassadors, other public Ministers and Consuls;—to all Cases of admiralty and maritime Jurisdiction;—to Controversies to which the United States shall be a Party;—to Controversies between two or more States;—*between a State and Citizens of another State;*[8]—between Citizens of different States;—between Citizens of the same State claiming Lands under Grants of different States, and between a State, or the Citizens thereof, and foreign States, Citizens or Subjects.

In all Cases affecting Ambassadors, other public Ministers and Consuls, and those in which a State shall be Party, the supreme Court shall have original Jurisdiction. In all the other Cases before mentioned, the supreme Court shall have appellate Jurisdiction, both as to Law and Fact, with such Exceptions, and under such Regulations as the Congress shall make.

The trial of all Crimes, except in Cases of Impeachment, shall be by Jury; and such Trial shall be held in the State where said Crimes shall have been committed; but when not committed within any State, the Trial shall be at such Place or Places as the Congress may by Law have directed.

Section 3.   Treason against the United States, shall consist only in levying War against them, or in adhering to their Enemies, giving them Aid and Comfort. No Person shall be convicted of Treason unless on the Testimony of two Witnesses to the same overt Act, or on Confession in open Court.

---

[8]Restricted by the Eleventh Amendment.

The Congress shall have Power to declare the Punishment of Treason, but no Attainder of Treason shall work Corruption of Blood, or Forfeiture except during the Life of the Person attainted.

ARTICLE IV

Section 1.   Full Faith and Credit shall be given in each State to the public Acts, Records, and judicial Proceedings of every other State. And the Congress may by general Laws prescribe the Manner in which such Acts, Records, and Proceedings shall be proved, and the Effect thereof.

Section 2.   The Citizens of each State shall be entitled to all Privileges and Immunities of Citizens in the several States.

A Person charged in any State with Treason, Felony, or other Crime, who shall flee from Justice, and be found in another State, shall on demand of the executive Authority of the State from which he fled, be delivered up, to be removed to the State having Jurisdiction of the Crime.

No Person held to Service or Labour in one State, under the Laws thereof, escaping into another, shall, in Consequence of any Law or Regulation therein, be discharged from such Service or Labour, but shall be delivered up on Claim of the Party to whom such Service or Labour may be due.[9]

Section 3.   New States may be admitted by the Congress into this Union; but no new State shall be formed or erected within the Jurisdiction of any other State; nor any State be formed by the Junction of two or more States, or parts of States, without the Consent of the Legislatures of the States concerned as well as of the Congress.

The Congress shall have Power to dispose of and make all needful Rules and Regulations respecting the Territory or other Property belonging to the United States; and nothing in this Constitution shall be so construed as to Prejudice any Claims of the United States, or of any particular State.

[9]Superseded by the Thirteenth Amendment.

Section 4.   The United States shall guarantee to every State in this Union a Republican Form of Government, and shall protect each of them against Invasion; and on Application of the Legislature, or of the Executive (when the Legislature cannot be convened) against domestic Violence.

ARTICLE V

The Congress, whenever two thirds of both Houses shall deem it necessary, shall propose Amendments to this Constitution, or, on the Application of the Legislatures of two thirds of the several States, shall call a Convention for proposing Amendments, which, in either Case, shall be valid to all Intents and Purposes, as Part of this Constitution, when ratified by the Legislatures of three fourths of the several States, or by Conventions in three fourths thereof, as the one or the other Mode of Ratification may be proposed by the Congress; Provided that no Amendment which may be made prior to the Year One thousand eight hundred and eight shall in any Manner affect the first and fourth Clauses in the Ninth Section of the first Article; and that no State, without its Consent, shall be deprived of its equal Suffrage in the Senate.

ARTICLE VI

All Debts contracted and Engagements entered into, before the Adoption of this Constitution, shall be as valid against the United States under this Constitution, as under the Confederation.

This Constitution, and the Laws of the United States which shall be made in Pursuance thereof; and all Treaties made, or which shall be made, under the Authority of the United States, shall be the supreme Law of the Land; and the Judges in every State shall be bound thereby, any Thing in the Constitution or Laws of any State to the Contrary notwithstanding.

The Senators and Representatives before mentioned, and the Members of the several State Legislatures, and all executive and judicial Officers, both of the United States and of the several

States, shall be bound by Oath or Affirmation, to support this Constitution; but no religious Test shall ever be required as a Qualification to any Office or public Trust under the United States.

Article VII

The Ratification of the Conventions of nine States shall be sufficient for the Establishment of this Constitution between the States so ratifying the Same.

Done in Convention by the Unanimous Consent of the States present the Seventeenth Day of September in the Year of our Lord one thousand seven hundred and Eighty seven and of the Independence of the United States of America the Twelfth. In Witness whereof We have hereunto subscribed our Names.

Go. Washington
President and deputy from Virginia

New Hampshire
John Langdon
Nicholas Gilman

Massachusetts
Nathaniel Gorham
Rufus King

Connecticut
Wm. Saml. Johnson
Roger Sherman

New York
Alexander Hamilton

New Jersey
Wil. Livingston
David Brearley
Wm. Paterson
Jona. Dayton

Pennsylvania
B. Franklin
Thomas Mifflin
Robt. Morris
Geo. Clymer
Thos. FitzSimons
Jared Ingersoll
James Wilson
Gouv. Morris

Delaware
Geo. Read
Gunning Bedford jun
John Dickinson
Richard Bassett
Jaco. Broom

Maryland
James McHenry
Dan. of St. Thos. Jenifer
Danl. Carroll

Virginia
John Blair
James Madison, Jr.

North Carolina
Wm. Blount
Richd. Dobbs Spaight
Hu Williamson

South Carolina
J. Rutledge
Charles Cotesworth Pinckney
Pierce Butler

Georgia
William Few
Abr. Baldwin

Amendments to the Constitution

AMENDMENT I [1791][1]

Congress shall make no law respecting an establishment of religion, or prohibiting the free exercise thereof; or abridging the freedom of speech, or of the press; or the right of the people peaceably to assemble, and to petition the government for a redress of grievances.

AMENDMENT II [1791]

A well-regulated militia being necessary to the security of a free State, the right of the people to keep and bear arms shall not be infringed.

AMENDMENT III [1791]

No soldier shall, in time of peace, be quartered in any house without the consent of the owner, nor in time of war, but in a manner to be prescribed by law.

AMENDMENT IV [1791]

The right of the people to be secure in their persons, houses, papers, and effects, against unreasonable searches and seizures, shall not be violated, and no warrants shall issue but upon probable cause, supported by oath or affirmation, and particularly describing the place to be searched, and the persons or things to be seized.

AMENDMENT V [1791]

No person shall be held to answer for a capital, or otherwise infamous crime, unless on a presentment or indictment of a grand jury, except in cases arising in the land or naval forces, or in the militia, when in actual service in time of war or public danger; nor shall any person be subject for the same offence to be twice put in jeopardy of life or limb; nor shall be compelled in any criminal case to be a witness against himself, nor be deprived of life, liberty, or property, without due process of law; nor shall private property be taken for public use without just compensation.

AMENDMENT VI [1791]

In all criminal prosecutions, the accused shall enjoy the right to a speedy and public trial, by an impartial jury of the State and district wherein the crime shall have been committed, which district shall have been previously ascertained by law, and to be informed of the nature and cause of the accusation; to be confronted with the witnesses against him; to have compulsory process for obtaining witnesses in his favor, and to have the assistance of counsel for his defence.

AMENDMENT VII [1791]

In suits at common law, where the value in controversy shall exceed twenty dollars, the right of trial by jury shall be preserved, and no fact tried by a jury shall be otherwise reexamined in any court of the United States, than according to the rules of the common law.

---

[1]The dates in brackets indicate when the amendment was ratified.

AMENDMENT VIII [1791]

Excessive bail shall not be required, nor excessive fines imposed, nor cruel and unusual punishments inflicted.

AMENDMENT IX [1791]

The enumeration in the Constitution, of certain rights, shall not be construed to deny or disparage others retained by the people.

AMENDMENT X [1791]

The powers not delegated to the United States by the Constitution, nor prohibited by it to the States, are reserved to the States respectively, or to the people.

AMENDMENT XI [1798]

The judicial power of the United States shall not be construed to extend to any suit in law or equity, commenced or prosecuted against one of the United States by citizens of another State, or by citizens or subjects of any foreign state.

AMENDMENT XII [1804]

The electors shall meet in their respective States, and vote by ballot for President and Vice-President, one of whom, at least, shall not be an inhabitant of the same State with themselves; they shall name in their ballots the person voted for as President, and in distinct ballots the person voted for as Vice-President, and they shall make distinct lists of all persons voted for as President, and of all persons voted for as Vice-President, and of the number of votes for each, which lists they shall sign and certify, and transmit sealed to the seat of government of the United States, directed to the President of the Senate;—the President of the Senate shall, in the presence of the Senate and House of Representatives, open all the certificates and the votes shall then be counted;—the person having the greatest number of votes for President shall be the President, if such number be a majority of the whole number of electors appointed; and if no person have such majority, then from the persons having the highest numbers not exceeding three on the list of those voted for as President, the House of Representatives shall choose immediately, by ballot, the President. But in choosing the President, the votes shall be taken by States, the representation from each State having one vote; a quorum for this purpose shall consist of a member or members from two-thirds of the States, and a majority of all the States shall be necessary to a choice. And if the House of Representatives shall not choose a President whenever the right of choice shall devolve upon them, before *the fourth day of March* next following, then the Vice-President shall act as President, as in the case of the death or other constitutional disability of the President.[2]

The person having the greatest number of votes as Vice-President shall be the Vice-President, if such number be a majority of the whole number of electors appointed; and if no person have a majority, then from the two highest numbers on the list the Senate shall choose the Vice-President; a quorum for the purpose shall consist of two-thirds of the whole number of Senators, and a majority of the whole number shall be necessary to a choice. But no person constitutionally ineligible to the office of President shall be eligible to that of Vice-President of the United States.

AMENDMENT XIII [1865]

Section 1. Neither slavery nor involuntary servitude, except as a punishment for crime whereof the party shall have been duly convicted, shall exist within the United States, or any place subject to their jurisdiction.

---

[2]Superseded by Section 3 of the Twentieth Amendment.

Section 2.   Congress shall have power to enforce this article by appropriate legislation.

AMENDMENT XIV [1868]

Section 1.   All persons born or naturalized in the United States, and subject to the jurisdiction thereof, are citizens of the United States and of the State wherein they reside. No State shall make or enforce any law which shall abridge the privileges or immunities of citizens of the United States; nor shall any State deprive any person of life, liberty, or property, without due process of law; nor deny to any person within its jurisdiction the equal protection of the laws.

Section 2.   Representatives shall be appointed among the several States according to their respective numbers, counting the whole number of persons in each State, excluding Indians not taxed. But when the right to vote at any election for the choice of electors for President and Vice-President of the United States, Representatives in Congress, the executive and judicial officers of a State, or the members of the legislature thereof, is denied to any of the male inhabitants of such State, being twenty-one years of age and citizens of the United States, or in any way abridged, except for participation in rebellion, or other crime, the basis of representation therein shall be reduced in the proportion which the number of such male citizens shall bear to the whole number of male citizens twenty-one years of age in such State.

Section 3.   No person shall be a Senator or Representative in Congress, or Elector of President and Vice-President, or hold any office, civil or military, under the United States, or under any State, who, having previously taken an oath, as a member of Congress, or as an officer of the United States, or as a member of any State legislature, or as an executive or judicial officer of any State, to support the Constitution of the United States, shall have engaged in insurrection or rebellion against the same, or given aid or comfort to the enemies thereof. Congress may, by a vote of two-thirds of each house, remove such disability.

Section 4.   The validity of the public debt of the United States, authorized by law, including debts incurred for payment of pensions and bounties for services in suppressing insurrection or rebellion, shall not be questioned. But neither the United States nor any State shall assume or pay any debt or obligation incurred in aid of insurrection or rebellion against the United States, or any claim for the loss or emancipation of any slave; but all such debts, obligations, and claims shall be held illegal and void.

Section 5.   The Congress shall have power to enforce, by appropriate legislation, the provisions of this article.

AMENDMENT XV [1870]

Section 1.   The right of citizens of the United States to vote shall not be denied or abridged by the United States or by any State on account of race, color, or previous condition of servitude.

Section 2.   The Congress shall have power to enforce this article by appropriate legislation.

AMENDMENT XVI [1913]

The Congress shall have power to lay and collect taxes on incomes, from whatever source derived, without apportionment among the several States, and without regard to any census or enumeration.

AMENDMENT XVII [1913]

Section 1.   The Senate of the United States shall be composed of two Senators from each State, elected by the people thereof, for six years; and each Senator shall have one vote. The electors in each State shall have the qualifications requisite for electors of [voters for] the most numerous branch of the State legislatures.

Section 2. When vacancies happen in the representation of any State in the Senate, the executive authority of such State shall issue writs of election to fill such vacancies: Provided, that the Legislature of any State may empower the executive thereof to make temporary appointments until the people fill the vacancies by election as the Legislature may direct.

Section 3. This amendment shall not be so construed as to affect the election or term of any Senator chosen before it becomes valid as part of the Constitution.

Amendment XVIII
[1919; repealed 1933 by Amendment XXI]

Section 1. After one year from the ratification of this article the manufacture, sale, or transportation of intoxicating liquors within, the importation thereof into, or the exportation thereof from the United States and all territory subject to the jurisdiction thereof, for beverage purposes, is hereby prohibited.

Section 2. The Congress and the several States shall have concurrent power to enforce this article by appropriate legislation.

Section 3. This article shall be inoperative unless it shall have been ratified as an amendment to the Constitution by the legislatures of the several States, as provided by the Constitution, within seven years from the date of the submission thereof to the States by the Congress.

Amendment XIX [1920]

Section 1. The right of citizens of the United States to vote shall not be denied or abridged by the United States or by any State on account of sex.

Section 2. Congress shall have the power to enforce this article by appropriate legislation.

Amendment XX [1933]

Section 1. The terms of the President and Vice-President shall end at noon on the twentieth day of January, and the terms of Senators and Representatives at noon on the third day of January, of the years in which such terms would have ended if this article had not been ratified; and the terms of their successors shall then began.

Section 2. The Congress shall assemble at least once in every year, and such meeting shall begin at noon on the third day of January, unless they shall by law appoint a different day.

Section 3. If, at the time fixed for the beginning of the term of the President, the President-elect shall have died, the Vice-President-elect shall become President. If a President shall not have been chosen before the time fixed for the beginning of his term, or if the President-elect shall have failed to qualify, then the Vice-President-elect shall act as President until a President shall have qualified; and the Congress may by law provide for the case wherein neither a President-elect nor a Vice-President-elect shall have qualified, declaring who shall then act as President, or the manner in which one who is to act shall be selected, and such person shall act accordingly until a President or Vice-President shall have qualified.

Section 4. The Congress may by law provide for the case of the death of any of the persons from whom the House of Representatives may choose a President whenever the right of choice shall have devolved upon them, and for the case of the death of any of the persons from whom the Senate may choose a Vice-President whenever the right of choice shall have devolved upon them.

Section 5. Sections 1 and 2 shall take effect on the 15th day of October following the ratification of this article.

Section 6. This article shall be inoperative unless it shall have been ratified as an amendment to the Constitution by the Legislatures of three-fourths of the several States within seven years from the date of its submission.

AMENDMENT XXI [1933]

Section 1.   The eighteenth article of amendment to the Constitution of the United States is hereby repealed.

Section 2.   The transportation or importation into any State, Territory, or Possession of the United States for delivery or use therein of intoxicating liquors, in violation of the laws thereof, is hereby prohibited.

Section 3.   This article shall be inoperative unless it shall have been ratified as an amendment to the Constitution by conventions in the several States, as provided in the Constitution, within seven years from the date of the submission thereof to the States by the Congress.

AMENDMENT XXII [1951]

Section 1.   No person shall be elected to the office of the President more than twice, and no person who has held the office of President, or acted as President, for more than two years of a term to which some other person was elected President shall be elected to the office of President more than once. But this article shall not apply to any person holding the office of President when this Article was proposed by the Congress, and shall not prevent any person who may be holding the office of President, or acting as President, during the term within which this Article becomes operative from holding the office of President or acting as President during the remainder of such term.

Section 2.   This article shall be inoperative unless it shall have been ratified as an amendment to the Constitution by the legislatures of three-fourths of the several States within seven years

from the date of its submission to the States by the Congress.

AMENDMENT XXIII [1961]

Section 1.   The District constituting the seat of Government of the United States shall appoint in such manner as the Congress may direct: A number of electors of President and Vice-President equal to the whole number of Senators and Representatives in Congress to which the District would be entitled if it were a State, but in no event more than the least populous State; they shall be in addition to those appointed by the States, but they shall be considered for the purposes of the election of President and Vice-President, to be electors appointed by a State; and they shall meet in the District and perform such duties as provided by the twelfth article of amendment.

Section 2.   The Congress shall have the power to enforce this article by appropriate legislation.

AMENDMENT XXIV [1964]

Section 1.   The right of citizens of the United States to vote in any primary or other election for President or Vice-President, for electors for President or Vice-President, or for Senator or Representative in Congress, shall not be denied or abridged by the United States or any State by reason of failure to pay any poll tax or other tax.

Section 2.   The Congress shall have the power to enforce this article by appropriate legislation.

AMENDMENT XXV [1967]

Section 1.   In case of the removal of the President from office or of his death or resignation, the Vice-President shall become President.

Section 2.   Whenever there is a vacancy in the office of the Vice-President, the President shall nominate a Vice-President who shall take office upon confirmation by a majority vote of both Houses of Congress.

Section 3.   Whenever the President transmits to the President pro tempore of the Senate and the Speaker of the House of Representatives his written declaration that he is unable to discharge the powers and duties of his office, and until he transmits to them a written declaration to the contrary, such powers and duties shall be discharged by the Vice-President as Acting President.

Section 4.   Whenever the Vice-President and a majority of either the principal officers of the executive departments or of such other body as Congress may by law provide, transmit to the President pro tempore of the Senate and the Speaker of the House of Representatives their written declaration that the President is unable to discharge the powers and duties of his office, the Vice-President shall immediately assume the powers and duties of the office as Acting President.

Thereafter, when the President transmits to the President pro tempore of the Senate and the Speaker of the House of Representatives his written declaration that no inability exists, he shall resume the powers and duties of his office unless the Vice-President and a majority of either the principal officers of the executive department[s] or of such other body as Congress may by law provide, transmit within four days to the President pro tempore of the Senate and the Speaker

of the House of Representatives their written declaration that the President is unable to discharge the powers and duties of his office. Thereupon Congress shall decide the issue, assembling within forty-eight hours for that purpose if not in session. If the Congress, within twenty-one days after receipt of the latter written declaration, or, if Congress is not in session, within twenty-one days after Congress is required to assemble, determines by two-thirds vote of both Houses that the President is unable to discharge the powers and duties of his office, the Vice-President shall continue to discharge the same as Acting President; otherwise, the President shall resume the powers and duties of his office.

AMENDMENT **XXVI** [1971]

Section 1.   The right of citizens of the United States, who are eighteen years of age or older, to vote shall not be denied or abridged by the United States or by any State on account of age.

Section 2.   The Congress shall have power to enforce this article by appropriate legislation.

AMENDMENT **XXVII** [1992]

No law, varying the compensation for the services of the Senators and Representatives, shall take effect, until an election of Representatives shall have intervened.

Seneca Falls Declaration of Sentiments and Resolutions

IN 1848, ELIZABETH CADY STANTON, Lucretia Mott, and Martha Coffin Wright, among others, called a meeting in Stanton's hometown of Seneca Falls, New York, to discuss "the social, civil and religious condition of Woman." Over three hundred men and women attended, and one hundred signed a comprehensive document that detailed the discriminations women endured and demanded women's rights, most controversially the vote. "The Declaration of Sentiments" was forthrightly modeled on the Declaration of Independence (see p. A-1), which is telling evidence of the Seneca Falls signers' understanding that the liberties and rights promised by the American Revolution had not been extended to the female half of the population.

DECLARATION OF SENTIMENTS

When, in the course of human events, it becomes necessary for one portion of the family of man to assume among the people of the earth a position different from that which they have hitherto occupied, but one to which the laws of nature and of nature's God entitle them, a decent respect to the opinions of mankind requires that they should declare the causes that impel them to such a course.

We hold these truths to be self-evident: that all men and women are created equal; that they are endowed by their Creator with certain inalienable rights; that among these are life, liberty, and the pursuit of happiness; that to secure these rights governments are instituted, deriving their just powers from the consent of the governed.

Whenever any form of government becomes destructive of these ends, it is the right of those who suffer from it to refuse allegiance to it, and to insist upon the institution of a new government, laying its foundations on such principles, and organizing its powers in such form, as to them shall seem most likely to effect their safety and happiness. Prudence, indeed, will dictate that governments long established should not be changed for light and transient causes; and accordingly all experience hath shown that mankind are more disposed to suffer, while evils are sufferable, than to right themselves by abolishing the forms to which they were accustomed. But when a long train of abuses and usurpations, pursuing invariably the same object evinces a design to reduce them under absolute despotism, it is their duty to throw off such government, and to provide new guards for their future security. Such has been the patient sufferance of the women under this government, and such is now the necessity which constrains them to demand the equal station to which they are entitled.

SOURCE: Susan B. Anthony, Elizabeth Cady Stanton, and Matilda Joslyn Gage, eds., *History of Woman Suffrage* (Rochester, NY: S. B. Anthony, 1889).

The history of mankind is a history of repeated injuries and usurpations on the part of man toward woman, having in direct object the establishment of an absolute tyranny over her. To prove this, let facts be submitted to a candid world.

He has never permitted her to exercise her inalienable right to the elective franchise. He has compelled her to submit to laws, in the formation of which she had no voice. He has withheld from her rights which are given to the most ignorant and degraded men—both natives and foreigners.

Having deprived her of this first right of a citizen, the elective franchise, thereby leaving her without representation in the halls of legislation, he has opposed her on all sides.

He has made her, if married, in the eye of the law, civilly dead.

He has taken from her all right in property, even to the wages she earns.

He has made her, morally, an irresponsible being, as she can commit many crimes with impunity, provided they be done in the presence of her husband. In the covenant of marriage, she is compelled to promise obedience to her husband, he becoming, to all intents and purposes, her master—the law giving him power to deprive her of her liberty, and to administer chastisement.

He has so framed the laws of divorce, as to what shall be the proper causes, and in case of separation, to whom the guardianship of the children shall be given, as to be wholly regardless of the happiness of women—the law, in all cases, going upon a false supposition of the supremacy of man, and giving all power into his hands.

After depriving her of all rights as a married woman, if single, and the owner of property, he has taxed her to support a government which recognizes her only when her property can be made profitable to it.

He has monopolized nearly all the profitable employments, and from those she is permitted to follow, she receives but a scanty remuneration. He closes against her all the avenues to wealth and distinction which he considers most honorable to himself. As a teacher of theology, medicine, or law, she is not known.

He has denied her the facilities for obtaining a thorough education, all colleges being closed against her.

He allows her in Church, as well as State, but in a subordinate position, claiming Apostolic authority for her exclusion from the ministry, and, with some exceptions, from any public participation in the affairs of the Church.

He has created a false public sentiment by giving to the world a different code of morals for men and women, by which moral delinquencies which exclude women from society, are not only tolerated, but deemed of little account in man.

He has usurped the prerogative of Jehovah himself, claiming it as his right to assign for her a sphere of action, when that belongs to her conscience and to her God.

He has endeavored, in every way that he could, to destroy her confidence in her own powers, to lessen her self-respect, and to make her willing to lead a dependent and abject life.

Now, in view of this entire disfranchisement of one-half the people of this country, their social and religious degradation—in view of the unjust laws above mentioned, and because women do feel themselves aggrieved, oppressed, and fraudulently deprived of their most sacred rights, we insist that they have immediate admission to all the rights and privileges which belong to them as citizens of the United States.

In entering upon the great work before us, we anticipate no small amount of misconception, misrepresentation, and ridicule; but we shall use every instrumentality within our power to effect our object. We shall employ agents, circulate tracts, petition the State and National legislatures, and endeavor to enlist the pulpit and the press in our behalf. We hope this Convention will be followed by a series of Conventions embracing every part of the country.

RESOLUTIONS

WHEREAS, The great precept of nature is conceded to be, that "man shall pursue his own true and substantial happiness." [William] Blackstone in his *Commentaries* remarks, that this law of Nature being coequal with mankind, and dictated by God himself, is of course superior in obligation to any other. It is binding over all the globe, in all countries and at all times; no human laws are of any validity if contrary to this, and such of them as are valid, derive all their force, and all their validity, and all their authority, mediately and immediately, from this original; therefore,

Resolved, That such laws as conflict, in any way, with the true and substantial happiness of woman, are contrary to the great precept of nature and of no validity, for this is "superior in obligation to any other."

Resolved, That all laws which prevent woman from occupying such a station in society as her conscience shall dictate, or which place her in a position inferior to that of man, are contrary to the great precept of nature, and therefore of no force or authority.

Resolved, That woman is man's equal—was intended to be so by the Creator, and the highest good of the race demands that she should be recognized as such.

Resolved, That the women of this country ought to be enlightened in regard to the laws under which they live, that they may no longer publish their degradation by declaring themselves satisfied with their present position, nor their ignorance, by asserting that they have all the rights they want.

Resolved, That inasmuch as man, while claiming for himself intellectual superiority, does accord to woman moral superiority, it is pre-eminently his duty to encourage her to speak and teach, as she has an opportunity, in all religious assemblies.

Resolved, That the same amount of virtue, delicacy, and refinement of behavior that is required of woman in the social state, should also be required of man, and the same transgressions should be visited with equal severity on both man and woman.

Resolved, That the objection of indelicacy and impropriety, which is so often brought against woman when she addresses a public audience, comes with a very ill-grace from those who encourage, by their attendance, her appearance on the stage, in the concert, or in feats of the circus.

Resolved, That woman has too long rested satisfied in the circumscribed limits which corrupt customs and a perverted application of the Scriptures have marked out for her, and that it is time she should move in the enlarged sphere which her great Creator has assigned her.

Resolved, That it is the duty of the women of this country to secure to themselves their sacred right to the elective franchise.

Resolved, That the equality of human rights results necessarily from the fact of the identity of the race in capabilities and responsibilities.

Resolved, therefore, That, being invested by the Creator with the same capabilities, and the same consciousness of responsibility for their exercise, it is demonstrably the right and duty of woman, equally with man, to promote every righteous cause by every righteous means; and especially in regard to the great subjects of morals and religion, it is self-evidently her right to participate with her brother in teaching them, both in private and in public, by writing and by speaking, by any instrumentalities proper to be used, and in any assemblies proper to be held; and this being a self-evident truth growing out of the divinely implanted principles of human nature, any custom or authority adverse to it, whether modern or wearing the hoary sanction of antiquity, is to be regarded as a self-evident falsehood, and at war with mankind.

[Signers, in alphabetical order]

Caroline Barker
Eunice Barker
William G. Barker
Rachel D. Bonnel
 (Mitchell)
Joel D. Bunker
William Burroughs
E. W. Capron
Jacob P. Chamberlain
Elizabeth Conklin
Mary Conklin
P. A. Culvert
Cynthia Davis
Thomas Dell
William S. Dell
Elias J. Doty
Susan R. Doty
Frederick Douglass
Julia Ann Drake
Harriet Cady Eaton
Elisha Foote
Eunice Newton Foote
Mary Ann Frink
Cynthia Fuller
Experience Gibbs
Mary Gilbert

Lydia Gild
Sarah Hallowell
Mary H. Hallowell
Henry Hatley
Sarah Hoffman
Charles L. Hoskins
Jane C. Hunt
Richard P. Hunt
Margaret Jenkins
John Jones
Lucy Jones
Phebe King
Hannah J. Latham
Lovina Latham
Elizabeth Leslie
Eliza Martin
Mary Martin
Delia Mathews
Dorothy Mathews
Jacob Mathews
Elizabeth W. M'Clintock
Mary M'Clintock
Mary Ann M'Clintock
Thomas M'Clintock
Jonathan Metcalf
Nathan J. Milliken

Mary S. Mirror
Pheobe Mosher
Sarah A. Mosher
James Mott
Lucretia Mott
Lydia Mount
Catharine C. Paine
Rhoda Palmer
Saron Phillips
Sally Pitcher
Hannah Plant
Ann Porter
Amy Post
George W. Pryor
Margaret Pryor
Susan Quinn
Rebecca Race
Martha Ridley
Azaliah Schooley
Margaret Schooley
Deborah Scott
Antoinette E. Segur
Henry Seymour
Henry W. Seymour
Malvina Seymour
Catharine Shaw

Stephen Shear
Sarah Sisson
Robert Smallbridge
Elizabeth D. Smith
Sarah Smith
David Spalding
Lucy Spalding
Elizabeth Cady Stanton
Catharine F. Stebbins
Sophronia Taylor
Betsey Tewksbury
Samuel D. Tillman
Edward F. Underhill
Martha Underhill
Mary E. Vail
Isaac Van Tassel
Sarah Whitney
Maria E. Wilbur
Justin Williams
Sarah R. Woods
Charlotte Woodward
S. E. Woodworth
Martha C. Wright

Presidents of the United States

Years in Office	President	Party
1789–1797	George Washington	No party designation
1797–1801	John Adams	Federalist
1801–1809	Thomas Jefferson	Democratic-Republican
1809–1817	James Madison	Democratic-Republican
1817–1825	James Monroe	Democratic-Republican
1825–1829	John Quincy Adams	Democratic-Republican
1829–1837	Andrew Jackson	Democratic
1837–1841	Martin Van Buren	Democratic
1841	William H. Harrison	Whig
1841–1845	John Tyler	Whig
1845–1849	James K. Polk	Democratic
1849–1850	Zachary Taylor	Whig
1850–1853	Millard Fillmore	Whig
1853–1857	Franklin Pierce	Democratic
1857–1861	James Buchanan	Democratic
1861–1865	Abraham Lincoln	Republican
1865–1869	Andrew Johnson	Republican
1869–1877	Ulysses S. Grant	Republican
1877–1881	Rutherford B. Hayes	Republican
1881	James A. Garfield	Republican
1881–1885	Chester A. Arthur	Republican
1885–1889	Grover Cleveland	Democratic
1889–1893	Benjamin Harrison	Republican
1893–1897	Grover Cleveland	Democratic
1897–1901	William McKinley	Republican
1901–1909	Theodore Roosevelt	Republican
1909–1913	William H. Taft	Republican

1913–1921	Woodrow Wilson	Democratic
1921–1923	Warren G. Harding	Republican
1923–1929	Calvin Coolidge	Republican
1929–1933	Herbert C. Hoover	Republican
1933–1945	Franklin D. Roosevelt	Democratic
1945–1953	Harry S Truman	Democratic
1953–1961	Dwight D. Eisenhower	Republican
1961–1963	John F. Kennedy	Democratic
1963–1969	Lyndon B. Johnson	Democratic
1969–1974	Richard M. Nixon	Republican
1974–1977	Gerald R. Ford	Republican
1977–1981	Jimmy Carter	Democratic
1981–1989	Ronald W. Reagan	Republican
1989–1993	George H. W. Bush	Republican
1993–2001	William Jefferson Clinton	Democratic
2001–present	George W. Bush	Republican

Major U.S. Supreme Court Decisions
Through Women's Eyes

THE FOLLOWING BRIEF EXCERPTS of Supreme Court decisions, carefully abridged from the full opinions delivered by the Court, have been selected for their particular importance to the history of women in the United States. Not all of them deal solely or primarily with gender discrimination. Those decisions concerning racism and the legacy of slavery, beginning with the 1856 *Dred Scott* case, have profound implications for women. Read one after another, these decisions give evidence of both the continuity of judicial reasoning and the dramatic shifts in judicial conclusions that have characterized the nation's highest court.

Dred Scott v. Sandford involved a slave couple who claimed they had gained freedom by virtue of residence for many years on free soil. The case took almost ten years to arrive before the Court, where a seven-to-two majority ruled that the Scotts remained slaves. In his last major opinion, Chief Justice Roger Taney not only dismissed the Scotts' claims, but he sought to intervene in the raging national political debate over slavery by declaring that any federal intervention in slavery, including the 1820 Missouri Compromise (which had banned slavery from the territories in which the Scotts had lived), was unconstitutional.

Dred Scott v. Sandford (1856)

It is difficult at this day to realize the state of public opinion in relation to that unfortunate race, which prevailed in the civilized and enlightened portions of the world at the time of the Declaration of Independence, and when the Constitution of the United States was framed and adopted. . . .

They had for more than a century before been regarded as beings of an inferior order, and altogether unfit to associate with the white race, either in social or political relations; and so far inferior, that they had no rights which the white man was bound to respect; and that the negro might justly and lawfully be reduced to slavery for his benefit. . . . We refer to these historical facts for the purpose of showing the fixed opinions concerning that race, upon which the statesmen of that day spoke

and acted. It is necessary to do this, in order to determine whether the general terms used in the Constitution of the United States, as to the rights of man and the rights of the people, was intended to include them, or to give to them or their posterity the benefit of any of its provisions.

[T]he right of property in a slave is distinctly and expressly affirmed in the Constitution. . . . This is done in plain words—too plain to be misunderstood. And no word can be found in the Constitution which gives Congress a greater power over slave property, or which entitles property of that kind to less protection than property of any other description. . . .

Upon these considerations, it is the opinion of the court that the act of Congress which prohibited a citizen from holding and owning property of this kind in the territory of the United States north of the line therein mentioned, is not warranted by the Constitution, and is therefore void; and that neither Dred Scott himself, nor any of his family, were made free by being carried into this territory. . . .

THE FOURTEENTH AMENDMENT, which was designed to overturn the *Dred Scott* decision by defining national citizenship broadly enough to include the ex-slaves, became the constitutional basis for challenging both race and gender discrimination. Soon after its ratification in 1868, woman suffragists saw the amendment as a potential resource. The National Woman Suffrage Association contended that inasmuch as women were citizens, their rights as voters were automatically secured. Accordingly, Virginia Minor tried to vote in her hometown of St. Louis, Missouri, and then sued the local election official who refused her ballot. Chief Justice Morrison Waite delivered the Court's unanimous opinion that although the Fourteenth Amendment did indeed grant women equal citizenship with men, it did not make them voters. His contention, that suffrage was not a civil right but a political privilege outside the amendment's intended scope, was underscored by the passage of the Fifteenth Amendment in 1870, which was addressed explicitly to voting. Waite's reasoning applied to all citizens, not just women. After the *Minor* decision, suffragists realized they needed a separate constitutional amendment to secure women's political rights.

Minor v. Happersett (1874)

The argument is, that as a woman, born or naturalized in the United States and subject to the jurisdiction thereof, is a citizen of the United States and of the State in which she resides, she has the right of suffrage as one of the privileges and immunities of her citizenship, which the State cannot by its laws or constitution abridge.

There is no doubt that women may be citizens. They are persons, and by the fourteenth amendment "all persons born or naturalized in the United States and subject to the jurisdiction thereof" are expressly declared to be "citizens of the United States and of the State wherein they reside." . . .

If the right of suffrage is one of the necessary privileges of a citizen of the United States, then the constitution and laws of Missouri confining it to men are in violation of the Constitution of the United States, as amended, and consequently void. . . . It is clear, . . . we think, that the Constitution has not added the right of suffrage to the privileges and immunities of citizenship as they existed at the time it was adopted.

It is true that the United States guarantees to every State a republican form of government. . . . No particular government is designated as republican, neither is the exact form to be guaranteed, in any manner especially designated. . . .

[I]t is certainly now too late to contend that a government is not republican, within the meaning of this guaranty in the Constitution, because women are not made voters.

INVOKING THE FOURTEENTH AMENDMENT three decades later, Homer Plessy argued that he had been denied equal protection of the law when a Louisiana statute forced him to travel in a separate all-black railroad car. By a vote of eight to one, the Court ruled against his claims and found the emerging system of state-sponsored racial segregation that was settling on the post-slave South to be fully constitutional. Writing for the majority, Justice Henry Brown argued that because a system of segregation affected both black and white, it was not discriminatory. The famous phrase by which this argument has come to be known — "separate but equal" — appears in the brave, dissenting opinion of Justice John Harlan. Note how the Court's ruling treats racial distinction and black inferiority as facts of nature that any legal decision must recognize.

Plessy v. Ferguson (1896)

A statute which implies merely a legal distinction between the white and colored races — a distinction which is founded in the color of the two races, and which must always exist so long as white men are distinguished from the other race by color — has no tendency to destroy the legal equality of the two races. . . .

The object of the [fourteenth] amendment was undoubtedly to enforce the absolute equality of the two races before the law, but, in the nature of things, it could not have been intended to abolish distinctions based upon color, or to enforce social, as distinguished from political, equality, or a commingling of the two races upon terms unsatisfactory to either. Laws permitting, and even requiring, their separation, in places where they are liable to be brought into contact, do not necessarily imply the inferiority of either race to the other. . . .

We consider the underlying fallacy of the plaintiff's argument to consist in the assumption that the enforced separation of the two races stamps the colored race with a badge of inferiority. If this be so, it is not by reason of anything found in the act, but solely because the colored race chooses to put that construction upon it. The argument necessarily assumes that if, as has been more than once the case, and is not unlikely to be so again, the colored race should become the dominant power in the state legislature, and should enact a law in precisely similar terms, it would thereby relegate the white race to an inferior position. We imagine that the white race, at least, would not acquiesce in this assumption. The argument also assumes that social prejudices may be overcome by legislation, and that equal rights cannot be secured to the negro except by an enforced commingling of the two races. We cannot accept this proposition. . . . Legislation is powerless to eradicate racial instincts, or to abolish distinctions based upon physical differences, and the attempt to do so can only result in accentuating the difficulties of the present situation. . . .

IN MULLER V. OREGON, Curt Muller challenged the constitutionality of an Oregon law setting a maximum ten-hour working day for women employees. Starting in the 1880s, the Court had turned away from the Fourteenth Amendment's original purposes to emphasize its guarantee of the individual's right of contract in the workplace, free from state regulation. This reading made most laws setting limits on the working day unconstitutional. Arguing on behalf of Oregon, Louis Brandeis, lead counsel for the National Consumers' League, successfully pressed an argument for the law's constitutionality on the ground that it was directed only at women. Brandeis's argument circumvented the Fourteenth Amendment by contending that the federal government's constitutionally authorized police power, which permitted special regulations for the national good, allowed legislation to protect motherhood and through it "the [human] race." The Court ruled unanimously to uphold the Oregon law, with Justice David Brewer delivering the opinion. As in the *Plessy* decision, the Court held that physical difference and even inferiority are facts of nature that the law may accommodate and that are compatible with formal legal equality. Yet the decision here was hailed by many women reformers as a great victory. Brandeis was appointed to the Supreme Court in 1916, the first Jewish member of the Court.

Muller v. Oregon (1908)

We held in *Lochner v. New York* [1903] that a law providing that no laborer shall be required or permitted to work in bakeries more than sixty hours in a week or ten hours in a day was not as to men a legitimate exercise of the police power of the state, but an unreasonable, unnecessary, and arbitrary interference with the right and liberty of the individual to contract in relation to his labor, and as such was in conflict with, and void under, the Federal Constitution. That decision is invoked by plaintiff in error as decisive of the question before us. But this assumes that the difference between the sexes does not justify a different rule respecting a restriction of the hours of labor. . . .

That woman's physical structure and the performance of maternal functions place her at a disadvantage in the struggle for subsistence is obvious. This is especially true when the burdens of motherhood are upon her. Even when they are not, . . . continuance for a long time on her feet at work, repeating this from day to day, tends to injurious effects upon the body, and, as healthy mothers are essential to vigorous offspring, the physical well-being of woman becomes an object of public interest and care in order to preserve the strength and vigor of the race. . . .

Even though all restrictions on political, personal, and contractual rights were taken away, and [woman] stood, so far as statutes are concerned, upon an absolutely equal plane with [man], it would still be true that she is so constituted that she will rest upon and look to him for protection; that her physical structure and a proper discharge of her maternal functions—having in view not merely her own health, but the well-being of the race—justify legislation to protect her from the greed as well as the passion of man. The limitations which this statute places upon her contractual powers, upon her right to agree with her employer as to the time she shall labor, are not imposed solely for her benefit, but also largely for the benefit of all.

T HE IRONY OF THE *MULLER* DECISION in favor of maximum hours laws to benefit women workers on the basis of their maternal dependency is underlined by the *Adkins* case, decided fifteen years later. *Adkins v. Children's Hospital* involved a congressionally authorized procedure for setting minimum wages for women workers in the District of Columbia. Writing for a five-to-three majority (Justice Brandeis had recused himself from the case), Justice George Sutherland found the maximum hours law unconstitutional on two major grounds. First, while minimum hours laws were constitutionally sanctioned public health measures, maximum wage laws were unacceptable restraints on free trade. Second, the ratification of the Nineteenth Amendment granting woman suffrage in the years since the *Muller* decision made protections of women on the basis of their need to be sheltered by men outdated. Thus, whereas in the earlier case the Court used an appeal to nature to sustain special labor laws that benefited women, in *Adkins,* the Court relied on an evolutionary approach to overturn such regulations.

Adkins v. Children's Hospital (1923)

In the *Muller* case, the validity of an Oregon statute, forbidding the employment of any female in certain industries more than ten hours during anyone day was upheld. . . . But the ancient inequality of the sexes, otherwise than physical, as suggested in the *Muller* case has continued "with diminishing intensity." In view of the great—not to say revolutionary—changes which have taken place since that utterance, in the contractual, political and civil status of women, culminating in the Nineteenth Amendment, it is not unreasonable to say that these differences have now come almost, if not quite, to the vanishing point. . . .

[W]e cannot accept the doctrine that women of mature age, *sui juris* [able to act on their own behalf legally], require or may be subjected to restrictions upon their liberty of contract which could not lawfully be imposed in the case of men under similar circumstances. To do so would be to ignore all the implications to be drawn from the present day trend of legislation, as well as that of common thought and usage, by which woman is accorded emancipation from the old doctrine that she must be given special protection or be subjected to special restraint in her contractual and civil relationships. . . .

I N THE WATERSHED CASE of *Brown v. Board of Education of Topeka,* the Supreme Court reversed its 1896 *Plessy v. Ferguson* decision to find state-sponsored racial segregation a violation of the Fourteenth Amendment guarantee of equal protection of the laws. The unanimous ruling was written by Earl Warren, newly appointed chief justice. Linda Brown was the plaintiff in one of several cases that the court consolidated, all of which challenged the constitutionality of racially segregated public schools. The case bears certain similarities to *Muller v. Oregon.* Both made use of sociological evidence, with *Brown* relying on research into the negative impact of segregation on young black children. Also as in *Muller,* the successful lead counsel in the *Brown* decision, NAACP lawyer Thurgood Marshall, ultimately was appointed to the Supreme Court, where he became the first African American justice.

Brown v. Board of Education of Topeka (1954)

The plaintiffs contend that segregated public schools are not "equal" and cannot be made "equal," and that hence they are deprived of the equal protection of the laws....

Does segregation of children in public schools solely on the basis of race, even though the physical facilities and other "tangible" factors may be equal, deprive the children of the minority group of equal educational opportunities? We believe that it does....

To separate them from others of similar age and qualifications solely because of their race generates a feeling of inferiority as to their status in the community that may affect their hearts and minds in a way unlikely ever to be undone....

We conclude that, in the field of public education, the doctrine of "separate but equal" has no place. Separate educational facilities are inherently unequal....

Because these are class actions, because of the wide applicability of this decision, and because of the great variety of local conditions, the formulation of decrees in these cases presents problems of considerable complexity.

ESTELLE GRISWOLD, executive director of the Planned Parenthood Federation of Connecticut, was arrested for providing a married couple with birth control instruction in violation of an 1879 state law forbidding any aid given "for the purpose of preventing conception." Writing for a seven-to-two majority, Justice William O. Douglas held the law unconstitutional, developing an innovative argument for the existence of a "zone of privacy" not specifically enumerated in the Constitution but found in the surrounding "penumbra" of specified rights. Note Douglas's lofty language about the nature of marriage.

Griswold v. Connecticut (1965)

This law ... operates directly on an intimate relation of husband and wife and their physician's role in one aspect of that relation....

[S]pecific guarantees in the Bill of Rights have penumbras, formed by emanations from those guarantees that help give them life and substance.... Various guarantees create zones of privacy. The right of association contained in the penumbra of the First Amendment is one, as we have seen. ... The Ninth Amendment provides: "The enumeration in the Constitution, of certain rights, shall not be construed to deny or disparage others retained by the people." ...

The present case, then, concerns a relationship lying within the zone of privacy created by several fundamental constitutional guarantees. And it concerns a law which, in forbidding the use of contraceptives rather than regulating their manufacture or sale, seeks to achieve its goals by means having a maximum destructive impact upon that relationship. Such a law cannot stand in light of the familiar principle, so often applied by this Court, that a "governmental purpose to control or prevent activities constitutionally subject to state regulation may not be achieved by means which sweep unnecessarily broadly and thereby invade the area of protected freedoms." . . .

We deal with a right of privacy older than the Bill of Rights—older than our political parties, older than our school system. Marriage is a coming together for better or for worse, hopefully enduring, and intimate to the degree of being sacred. It is an association that promotes a way of life, not causes; a harmony in living, not political faiths; a bilateral loyalty, not commercial or social projects. . . .

L IKE THE *GRISWOLD* CASE two years earlier, *Loving v. Virginia* concerns the marriage relationship and government intrusion into it. Richard Loving was a white man who married Mildred Jeter, a black woman, in 1958 in Washington, D.C. When they moved to Virginia a year later, they were found guilty in state court of violating a 1924 Virginia law forbidding white people from marrying outside of their race, a crime known as "miscegenation." They appealed their conviction to the U.S. Supreme Court. Speaking for a unanimous Court, Chief Justice Earl Warren found this and similar laws in fifteen other states unconstitutional under the Fourteenth Amendment. The court's rejection of the argument that anti-miscegenation laws were constitutionally acceptable because they rested equally on all races echoes the logic of its ruling in *Brown v. Board of Education,* in which intent to discriminate is crucial despite the superficially neutral language of the law.

Loving v. Virginia (1967)

This case presents a constitutional question never addressed by this Court: whether a statutory scheme adopted by the State of Virginia to prevent marriages between persons solely on the basis of racial classifications violates the Equal Protection and Due Process Clauses of the Fourteenth Amendment. . . .

In upholding the constitutionality of these provisions, . . . the state court concluded that the State's legitimate purposes were "to preserve the racial integrity of its citizens," and to prevent "the corruption of blood," "a mongrel breed of citizens," and "the obliteration of racial pride," obviously an endorsement of the doctrine of White Supremacy . . . . [T]he fact of equal application does not immunize the statute from the very heavy burden of justification which the Fourteenth Amendment has traditionally required of state statutes drawn according to race. . . .

Over the years, this Court has consistently repudiated "distinctions between citizens solely because of their ancestry" as being "odious to a free people whose institutions are founded upon the doctrine of equality." At the very least, the Equal Protection Clause demands that racial classifications, especially suspect in criminal statutes, be subjected to the "most rigid scrutiny." . . .

Marriage is one of the "basic civil rights of man," fundamental to our very existence and survival. . . . Under our Constitution, the freedom to marry, or not marry, a person of another race resides with the individual and cannot be infringed by the State.

T HE *REED V. REED* CASE involved the mother of a deceased child contesting an Idaho law mandating that preference be given to the father in designating an executor for a dead child's estate. Sally Reed's case was argued by then American Civil Liberties Union lawyer Ruth Bader Ginsburg. Ginsburg revived elements of the argument made in the 1874 *Minor* case, that the Fourteenth Amendment's guarantees of equal protection before the law applied in cases of discrimination against women. This time the Court accepted the argument. The unanimous opinion was written by Chief Justice Warren Burger. Like Brandeis and Marshall, Ginsburg was later a path-breaking appointee to the Supreme Court, the second woman (after Sandra Day O'Connor) to serve.

Reed v. Reed (1971)

[W]e have concluded that the arbitrary preference established in favor of males by . . . the Idaho Code cannot stand in the face of the Fourteenth Amendment's command that no State deny the equal protection of the laws to any person within its jurisdiction.

In applying that clause, this Court has consistently recognized that the Fourteenth Amendment does not deny to States the power to treat different classes of persons in different ways. . . . The Equal Protection Clause of that amendment does, however, deny to States the power to legislate that different treatment be accorded to persons placed by a statute into different classes on the basis of criteria wholly unrelated to the objective of that statute. A classification must be reasonable, not arbitrary, and must rest upon some ground of difference having a fair and substantial relation to the object of the legislation, so that all persons similarly circumstanced shall be treated alike.

J ANE ROE WAS THE PSEUDONYM of Norma McCorvey, an unmarried pregnant mother whose name headed up a class action suit challenging an 1879 Texas law criminalizing abortion. In *Roe v. Wade,* the Court ruled seven to two in Roe's favor. Justice Harry Blackmun wrote the lead opinion, relying on the concept of privacy developed in the *Griswold* case. His opinion included a detailed history of laws prohibiting abortion to show that these were of relatively recent vintage, an approach that contrasted with the anti-historical arguments of nineteenth-century cases such as *Dred Scott* and *Minor v. Happersett.* The *Roe* decision very carefully avoids declaring that a woman's right to abortion is absolute. The limits placed on women's choice—consultation with a physician, government interest in fetal life in the third trimester—opened the way for attempts to reinstitute limits on abortion.

Roe v. Wade (1973)

We forthwith acknowledge our awareness of the sensitive and emotional nature of the abortion controversy. . . . One's philosophy, one's experiences, one's exposure to the raw edges of human existence, one's religious training, one's attitudes toward life and family and their values, and the moral standards one establishes and seeks to observe, are all likely to influence and to color one's thinking and conclusions about abortion.

In addition, population growth, pollution, poverty, and racial overtones tend to complicate and not to simplify the problem. . . .

The Constitution does not explicitly mention any right of privacy. In a line of decisions, however, . . . the Court has recognized that a right of personal privacy, or a guarantee of certain areas or zones of privacy, does exist under the Constitution. . . .

This right of privacy . . . is broad enough to encompass a woman's decision whether or not to terminate her pregnancy. The detriment that the State would impose upon the pregnant woman by denying this choice altogether is apparent. Specific and direct harm medically diagnosable even in early pregnancy may be involved. Maternity, or additional offspring, may force upon the woman a distressful life and future.

Psychological harm may be imminent. Mental and physical health may be taxed by child care. There is also the distress, for all concerned, associated with the unwanted child, and there is the problem of bringing a child into a family already unable, psychologically and otherwise, to care for it. In other cases, as in this one, the additional difficulties and continuing stigma of unwed motherhood may be involved.

[A]ppellant [in this case Jane Roe] . . . [argues] that the woman's right is absolute and that she is entitled to terminate her pregnancy at whatever time, in whatever way, and for whatever reason she alone chooses. With this we do not agree. . . . [A] State may properly assert important interests in safeguarding health, in maintaining medical standards, and in protecting potential life. At some point in pregnancy, these respective interests become sufficiently compelling to sustain regulation of the factors that govern the abortion decision. The privacy right involved, therefore, cannot be said to be absolute. . . .

The appellee . . . argue[s] that the fetus is a "person" within the language and meaning of the Fourteenth Amendment. . . . If this suggestion of personhood is established, the appellant's case, of course, collapses, for the fetus' right to life would then be guaranteed specifically by the Amendment. . . .

The Constitution does not define "person" in so many words. . . . [T]he word "person," as used in the Fourteenth Amendment, does not include the unborn.

In view of all this, we do not agree that, by adopting one theory of life, Texas may override the rights of the pregnant woman that are at stake. We repeat, however, that the State does have an important and legitimate interest in preserving and protecting the health of the pregnant woman, . . . and that it has still *another* important and legitimate interest in protecting the potentiality of human life. . . .

With respect to the State's important and legitimate interest in the health of the mother, the "compelling" point, in the light of present medical knowledge, is at . . . the end of the first trimester. . . . [F]rom and after this point, a State may regulate the abortion procedure to the extent that the regulation reasonably relates to the preservation and protection of maternal health. Examples of permissible state regulation in this area are requirements as to the qualifications of the person who is to perform the abortion; as to the licensure of that person; as to the facility in which the procedure is to be performed. . . .

[T]he attending physician, in consultation with his patient, is free to determine, without regulation by the State, that, in his medical judgment, the patient's pregnancy should be terminated. If that decision is reached, the judgment may be effectuated by an abortion free of interference by the State.

With respect to the State's important and legitimate interest in potential life, the "compelling" point is at viability. This is so because the fetus then presumably has the capability of meaningful life outside the mother's womb. State regulation protective of fetal life after viability thus has both logical and biological justifications. . . .

AFFIRMATIVE ACTION PROGRAMS were initially developed in the 1960s to aid African Americans to achieve greater educational and economic opportunity. President Richard Nixon urged them as a moderate response to the demands of militant civil rights activists. Nonetheless, these programs came under fire. In 1976, Allan Bakke, a white man, filed suit when his application for admission was rejected by the University of California at Davis Medical School on affirmative action grounds. His claim, based on the Fourteenth Amendment, became known as the "reverse discrimination" argument. The Court was sharply divided, four justices believing that Bakke was the victim of reverse discrimination, four justices believing that the Davis Medical School's affirmative action policy offered a reasonable approach to eradicating the effects of a long history of racial injustice. Justice Lewis Powell forged a five-to-four majority by writing an opinion that took both positions into account. An educational affirmative action plan premised on the goal of racial diversity could be constitutional if the system used was less rigid, less "quota"-like, than that of the Davis Medical School. The Court ordered Bakke admitted to the university's medical school.

University of California Regents v. Bakke (1978)

The Medical School of the University of California at Davis (hereinafter Davis) had two admissions programs for the entering class of 100 students— the regular admissions program and the special admissions program. . . . A separate committee, a majority of whom were members of minority groups, operated the special admissions program. The 1973 and 1974 application forms, respectively, asked candidates whether they wished to be considered as "economically and/or educationally disadvantaged" applicants and members of a "minority group" (blacks, Chicanos, Asians, American Indians). . . . Special candidates, however, did not have to meet the 2.5 grade point cutoff and were not ranked against candidates in the general admissions process. . . . Without passing on the state constitutional or federal statutory grounds the [lower] court held that petitioner's special admissions program violated the [Fourteenth Amendment] Equal Protection Clause. . . . Racial and ethnic classifications of any sort are inherently suspect and call for the most exacting judicial scrutiny. While the goal of achieving a diverse student body is sufficiently compelling to justify consideration of race in admissions decisions under some circumstances, petitioner's special admissions program, which forecloses consideration to persons like respondent, is unnecessary to the achievement of this compelling goal and therefore invalid under the Equal Protection Clause.

Aseries of cases followed *Roe v. Wade* that both upheld and limited a woman's right to seek an abortion. The plaintiff in *Webster v. Reproductive Health Services* was attorney general for the state of Missouri, appealing a lower court ruling that found restrictions on a woman's right to abortion unconstitutional, including the requirement that a woman seeking a second or third trimester abortion must have a test to make sure that the fetus was not viable (could not live outside the womb). The lower court ruled that the law violated the Supreme Court's *Roe v. Wade* decision. The Supreme Court overturned this ruling. Chief Justice William Rehnquist wrote for the five-to-three majority that while the *Roe* decision had recognized the state's obligation to protect potential life, it had been too rigid in establishing the point at which this became paramount. From Rehnquist's perspective, it was permissible for the state to act to favor childbirth even while preserving the woman's formal right to abortion.

Webster v. Reproductive Health Services (1989)

In *Roe v. Wade,* the Court recognized that the State has "important and legitimate" interests in protecting maternal health and in the potentiality of human life. During the second trimester, the State "may, if it chooses, regulate the abortion procedure in ways that are reasonably related to maternal health." . . .

[But] the rigid trimester analysis of the course of a pregnancy enunciated in *Roe* has resulted in . . . making constitutional law in this area a virtual Procrustean bed. . . . [T]he rigid *Roe* framework is hardly consistent with the notion of a Constitution cast in general terms, as ours is, and usually speaking in general principles, as ours does. . . .

[W]e do not see why the State's interest in protecting potential human life should come into existence only at the point of viability, and that there should therefore be a rigid line allowing state regulation after viability but prohibiting it before viability. . . . we are satisfied that the requirement of these tests permissibly furthers the State's interest in protecting potential human life, and we therefore believe [the article] to be constitutional.

Both appellants and the United States as *amicus curiae* [filing a brief sympathetic to the parties that appealed the decision] have urged that we overrule our decision in *Roe v. Wade.* The facts of the present case, however, differ from those at issue in *Roe.* Here, Missouri has determined that viability is the point at which its interest in potential human life must be safeguarded. . . . This case therefore affords us no occasion to revisit the holding of *Roe.* . . .

APPENDIX:
TABLES AND CHARTS

Table 1
Female Population of the United States by Race, 1790–2000

	Number of Women				Percent Distribution		
Year	Total	White	Black	Other Races	White	Black	Other Races
1790	n/a	1,556,572	n/a	n/a	n/a	n/a	n/a
1800	–	2,111,141	–	–	–	–	–
1810	–	2,873,943	–	–	–	–	–
1820	4,741,848	3,870,988	870,860	–	81.6	18.4	–
1830	6,333,531	5,171,165	1,162,366	–	81.6	18.4	–
1840	8,380,921	6,940,261	1,440,660	–	82.8	17.2	–
1850	11,354,216	9,526,666	1,827,550	–	83.9	16.1	–
1860	15,358,117	13,111,150	2,225,086	21,881	85.4	14.5	0.1
1870	19,064,806	16,560,289	2,486,746	17,771	86.9	13.0	0.1
1880	24,636,963	21,272,070	3,327,678	37,215	86.3	13.5	0.2
1890	30,710,613	26,830,879	3,753,073	126,661	87.4	12.2	0.4
1900	37,243,479	32,622,949	4,447,539	172,991	87.6	11.9	0.5
1910	44,727,298	39,579,044	4,942,228	206,026	88.5	11.0	0.5
1920	51,935,452	46,421,794	5,253,890	259,768	89.4	10.1	0.5
1930	60,807,176	54,404,615	6,035,789	366,772	89.5	9.9	0.6
1940	65,815,399	58,819,215	6,596,652	399,532	89.4	10.0	0.6
1950	76,139,192	67,894,638	7,744,182	500,372	89.2	10.2	0.7
1960	90,991,681	80,464,583	9,758,423	768,675	88.4	10.7	0.8
1970	104,299,734	91,027,988	11.831,973	1,439,773	87.3	11.3	1.4
1980	116,492,644	96,686,289	13,975,836	5,830,519	83.0	12.0	5.0
1990	127,470,455	102,210,190	15,815,909	9,444,356	80.2	12.4	7.4
2000	143,368,343	107,676,508	18,077,075	17,614,460	75.1	12.6	12.3

Source: Sandra Opdycke, *The Routledge Historical Atlas of Women in America* (New York: Routledge, 2000), p. 130; U. S. Census Bureau, *Statistical Abstract of the United States, 2001* (Washington: GPO, 2001).

Chart 1
U.S. Birthrate, 1820–2000

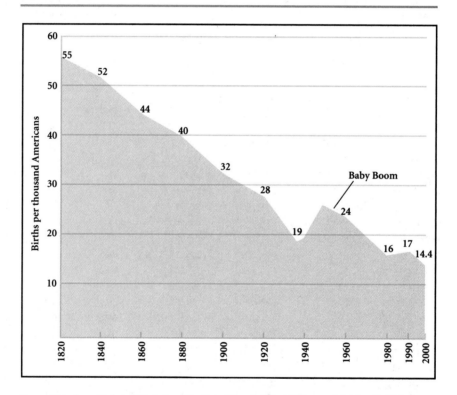

Source: Data from *Historical Statistics of the United States, Colonial Times to 1970* (1975); U.S. Census Bureau, *Statistical Abstract of the United States, 2001* (Washington: GPO, 2001).

Table 2
U.S. Women and Work, 1820–2000

Year	Percentage of Women in Paid Employment	Percentage of Paid Workers Who Are Women
1820	6.2	7.3
1830	6.4	7.4
1840	8.4	9.6
1850	10.1	10.8
1860	9.7	10.2
1870	13.7	14.8
1880	14.7	15.2
1890	18.2	17.0
1900	21.2	18.1
1910	24.8	20.0
1920	23.9	20.4
1930	24.4	21.9
1940	25.4	24.6
1950	29.1	27.8
1960	34.8	32.3
1970	43.3	38.0
1980	51.5	42.6
1990	57.4	45.2
2000	60.2	46.5

Source: U.S. Census Bureau, *Historical Statistics of the United States, Colonial Times to 1970* (Washington: GPO, 1975); *Statistical Abstract of the United States, 2002* (Washington: GPO, 2002).

Table 3
Percentage of Women in the U.S. Labor Force, by Family Status, 1890–2000

	Total Female Labor Force				Participation Rate in the Female Labor Force			
Year	Single	Widowed/ Divorced	Married	Mothers*	Single	Widowed/ Divorced	Married	Mothers*
1890	68	18	14	–	41	30	5	–
1900	67	18	15	–	41	33	6	–
1910	61	15	24	–	48	35	11	–
1920	77[†]	–[†]	23	–	44[†]	–[†]	9	–
1930	54	17	29	–	46	34	12	–
1940	49	15	36	11	48	32	17	28
1950	32	16	52	26	51	36	25	33
1960	23	6	61	27	44	13	32	37
1970	22	14	63	38	53	46	41	43
1980	26	19	55	40	64	44	50	56
1990	26	20	54	39	67	47	58	67
2000	27	20	53	39	69	61	49	73

*Mothers of children under age eighteen.

†Single women counted with widows and divorced women.

Sources: Lynn Weiner, *From Working Girl to Working Mother: The Female Labor Force in the United States, 1820–1980* (Chapel Hill: University of North Carolina, 1985), 6; Bureau of Labor Statistics, "Labor Force Participation Rates of Women by Presence and Age of Children, March 1980–2000," http://www.bls.gov/opub/rtaw/pdf/table06.pdf (accessed August 13, 2004).

Table 4
Occupational Distribution (in Percentages) of Working Women Ages Fourteen Years and Older, 1900–2000

	1900	1910	1920	1930	1940	1950	1960	1970	1980	1990	2000
Professional, Technical, and Kindred Workers	8.2	9.6	11.7	13.8	12.8	12.2	12.5	15.2	13.6	18.5	21.8
Managers, Officials, and Proprietors	1.4	2.0	2.2	0.7	3.3	4.3	0.6	3.5	7.2	11.1	14.3
Clerical and Kindred Workers	4.0	9.2	18.7	20.9	21.5	27.4	29.1	34.2	33.6	27.8	23.5
Sales Workers	4.3	5.1	6.3	6.8	7.4	8.6	7.8	7.3	11.3	13.1	13.0
Craftsmen, Foremen, and Kindred Workers	1.4	1.4	1.2	1.0	1.1	0.5	1.2	1.8	2.4	2.2	2.2
Operatives and Kindred Workers	23.8	22.9	20.2	17.4	19.5	20.0	16.2	14.9	10.1	8.0	6.4
Laborers	2.6	1.4	2.3	1.5	1.1	0.9	0.6	1.0	2.0	0.5	0.4
Private Household Workers	28.7	24.0	15.7	17.8	18.1	8.9	7.9	3.8	1.3	1.0	1.3
Service Workers (Not Household)	6.7	8.4	8.1	9.7	11.3	12.6	13.5	16.5	17.8	16.8	16.4
Farmers and Farm Managers	5.8	3.7	3.2	0.4	1.2	0.7	0.5	0.2	0.3	0.3	0.3
Farm Laborers	13.1	12.0	10.3	6.0	2.8	2.9	1.2	0.6	0.6	0.7	0.4

Source: U.S. Census Bureau, *Historical Statistics of the United States,* Part 1, table D, 182–232; *Statistical Abstract of the United States, 1985* (Washington, D.C.: GPO, 1984), table 673; 1991 (Washington, D.C.: GPO, 1991), table 652; 2000 (Washington, D.C.: GPO, 2001), table 593; "Employed Persons by Major Occupation, Sex, Race, and Hispanic Origin, Annual Averages, 1983–2002," Current Population Survey, Bureau of Labor Statistics.
Note: Data beginning in 1990 are not directly comparable with data for earlier years because of the introduction of a new occupational classification system.

Table 5
Immigration to the United States, 1900–2002

Years	Female Immigrants to the United States	Total Immigrants to the United States
1900–1909	2,492,336	8,202,388
1910–1919	2,215,582	6,347,156
1920–1929	1,881,923	4,295,510
1930–1939	386,659	699,375
1940–1949	454,291	856,608
1950–1959	1,341,404	2,499,286
1960–1969	1,786,441	3,213,749
1970–1979	2,299,713	4,366,001
1980–1989	3,224,661	6,332,218
1990–2002	6,376,805	12,759,950

Source: U.S. Census Bureau, *Historical Statistics of the United States, Colonial Times to 1970* (Washington: GPO, 1975), Series C 102–114; U.S. Department of Justice, *1978 Statistical Yearbook of the Immigration and Naturalization Service* (Washington: GPO, 1978), table 10; *1984 Statistical Yearbook of the Immigration and Naturalization Service* (Washington: GPO, 1987), table I M M 4.1; *1988 Statistical Yearbook of the Immigration and Naturalization Service* (Washington: GPO, 1989), table 11; *1994 Statistical Yearbook of the Immigration and Naturalization Service* (Washington: GPO, 2002), table 1.

Table 6
Women in the U.S. Congress, 1918–2002

Year	Number of Women			Percentage of Full Membership
	Senate	House	Total	
1918	0	1	1	0.2
1922	1	3	4	0.8
1926	0	3	3	0.6
1930	0	9	9	1.7
1934	1	7	8	1.5
1938	2	6	8	1.5
1942	1	9	10	1.9
1946	0	11	11	2.1
1950	1	9	10	1.9
1954	2	11	13	2.4
1958	1	15	16	3.0
1962	2	18	20	3.8
1966	2	11	13	2.4
1970	1	10	11	2.1
1974	0	16	16	3.0
1978	2	18	20	3.7
1982	2	21	23	4.3
1986	2	23	25	4.7
1990	2	29	31	5.8
1994	7	47	54	10.1
1998	9	54	63	11.8
2000	9	57	66	13.0
2002	14	62	76	14.2

Source: Sandra Opdycke, *The Routledge Historical Atlas of Women in America* (New York: Routledge, 2000), 133; Center for American Women and Politics, Rutgers University, http://www.rci.rutgers.edu/~cawp/Facts2.html (accessed on August 13, 2004).

Acknowledgments

Chapter 1

Excerpt from pp. 34–35 in *The Letterbook of Eliza Lucas*, edited by Elise Pinckney. Copyright © 1997 Elise Pinckney. From the Collections of the South Carolina Historical Society. Reprinted with permission.

Excerpt from pp. 433–34 in *County Court Records of Accomack-Northampton, Virginia* by Susue M. Ames (Charlottesville: University of Virginia Press, 1973). Reprinted with the permission of the University of Virginia Press.

Chapter 2

Excerpt from pp. 27–28 in *Essays on Education in the Early Republic*, edited by Frederick Rudolph. Copyright © 1965 by the President and Fellows of Harvard College. Reprinted by permission of the publishers.

Excerpts from *The Poems of Phillis Wheatley*, edited and with an introduction by Julian D. Mason Jr. Copyright © 1966 by the University of North Carolina Press. Renewed 1989. Used by permission of the publisher.

Chapter 3

B. E. Davis, "Narrative of Polly Shine," from *The American Slave: A Composite Autobiography* by George P. Rawick, supplement, Series 2, volume 9 (Texas Narratives Part 8). Copyright © 1977 by George P. Rawick. Reproduced with permission of Greenwood Publishing Group, Inc., Westport, Connecticut.

Chapter 4

Excerpts from *Occurrences in Hispanic California*, translated by Francis Price and William Ellison. © 1956 Academy of American Franciscan History. Published courtesy of the Academy of American Franciscan History.

Chapter 8

Excerpt from pp. 195–99 in *All for One* by Rose Schneiderman, with Lucy Goldthwaite. Copyright © Paul S. Eriksson. Reprinted by permission.

Excerpt from pp. 173–74 and 216 in *Mary McLeod Bethune: Building a Better World, Essays and Documents*, edited by Audrey Thomas McCluskey and Elaine M. Smith. Reprinted with permission.

Chapter 9

"Civil Rights in Mississippi Digital Archive," excerpted from Mississippi Oral History Program conducted August 29, 1991. Reprinted with permission from the Center for Oral History and Cultural Heritage, University of Southern Mississippi.

"The Problem That Has No Name," excerpted from *The Feminine Mystique* by Betty Friedan. Copyright © 1983, 1974, 1973, 1963 Betty Friedan. Used by permission of W. W. Norton & Company, Inc.

Casey Hayden and Mary King, "Position Paper: November 1964," originally published in *Takin' It to the Streets: A Sixties Reader* by Alexander Bloom and Wini Breines. Reprinted by permission.

Septima Clark excerpt from *Ready from Within: Septima Clark and the Civil Rights Movement*, edited by Cynthia Stokes Brown. Copyright © Africa World Press, Inc. Reprinted by permission.

"Northern Coordinator" excerpted from *Deep in Our Hearts: Nine White Women in the Freedom Movement* by Constance Curry et al. Copyright 2000 by Constance Curry. Reprinted by permission of the University of Georgia Press.

Diane Nash Bevel excerpt from *Voices of Freedom* by Henry Hampton. Copyright © 1995 by Henry Hampton. Used by permission of Vintage, a division of Random House, Inc.

"Mary Dora Jones" excerpted from *My Soul Is Rested* by Howard Raines. Copyright © 1977 by Howard Raines. Reprinted by permission of Penguin Group (USA) Inc.

Chapter 10

Phyllis Schlafly, "What's Wrong with 'Equal Rights' for Women." Published in *The Phyllis Schlafly Report* 5, no. 7 (February 1972). Reprinted with permission of the author.

INDEX

A note about the index:
  Letters in parentheses following pages
  refer to:
      (b) for boxed excerpts
      (d) for documents
      (i) for text illustrations
      (v) for visual sources
      (m) for maps
      (c) for charts and graphs

Abigail Adams, 104*(v)*
Abolitionism, 217–22, 223*(m)*
    beginnings of, after American Revolu-
        tion, 89–90
    legislative petitions and, 222, 223,
        223*(m)*
    party politics and, 203
Abortion, 646–48, 653–54, 656, A-31,
    A-34
    Roe v. Wade, 647, 653, 654,
        A-32–A-33*(d)*, A-34
    *Webster v. Reproductive Health Ser-
        vices*, 647, A-34*(d)*
Abzug, Bella, 688, 689*(i)*
Acoma Pueblo Indians, 2
Activism. *See* Reform movements
Adams, Abigail, 94, 95–96, 104*(v)*,
    104–5
Adams, Charity, 509*(i)*
Adams, John, 94
Adams, John Quincy, 222
Addams, Jane, 367*(i)*, 687
    antiwar movement and, 370, 440*(i)*
    bolshevism and, 489
    on immigrant women, 360
    settlement house movement and, 366,
        379–81

Subtle Problems of Charity, The,
    381–85*(d)*
Adkins v. Children's Hospital, 419,
    A-28*(d)*
Advertising, 429–30, 430*(i)*, 517,
    534–39*(v)*
    promotion of sexuality by, 493,
        494*(i)*, 496, 497
    television, 594–600*(v)*
Advice columns, 519–25*(d)*
Affirmative action, 659. See also *Univer-
    sity of California Regents v. Bakke*
AFL. *See* American Federation of Labor
African American men
    allegations of sexual crimes by,
        281–82
    disenfranchisement of, 422
African Americans. *See also* African
    American men; African American
    women; Free blacks; Racial dis-
    crimination; Slavery; Slave
    women
    abolitionist movement and, 218–19
    affirmative action and, 659
    antebellum free blacks, 157
    conditions for, in postrevolutionary
        era, 90–91
    contributions of, during Civil War,
        234, 256–58
    declining birthrate of, 295
    exclusion of, from trade unions,
        412
    during Great Depression, 498
    higher education of, 321
    historiography, xxvii–xxviii
    marriages of, 162–63, 176–79*(d)*,
        278*(i)*
    middle-class, 157, 214, 280, 423

Area ceded by
the United States
to Great Britain,
1818

Area ceded by
Great Britain,
1818

WASHINGTON

★ Olympia

Columbia R.

★ Salem

OREGON COUNTRY

OREGON

★ Boise

Snake R.

Missouri R.

★ Helena   MONTANA

NORTH DAKOTA

Bismarck ★

SOUTH DAKOTA

Pierre ★

*Agreement with Britain,
1846*

IDAHO

WYOMING

*L O U I S I A N A
P U R C H A S E
From France, 1803*

N. Platte R.

NEBRASKA

Sacramento R.

★ Carson City

★ Sacramento

San Joaquin R.

NEVADA

★ Salt Lake
City

UTAH

Cheyenne ★

★ Denver

COLORADO

S. Platte R.

Platte R.

KANSAS

*MEXICAN CESSION
1848*

CALIFORNIA

Colorado R.

PACIFIC
OCEAN

ARIZONA

★ Phoenix

★ Santa Fe

NEW
MEXICO

*TEXAS
Annexed, 1845*

Red R.

TEXAS

Rio Grande

ARCTIC OCEAN

RUSSIA

ALASKA
**Purchased from
Russia, 1867**

CANADA

Yukon R.

GADSDEN PURCHASE
from Mexico, 1853

HAWAII
*Annexed,
1898*

★ Honolulu

PACIFIC
OCEAN

Bering
Sea

Gulf of
Alaska

★ Juneau

0   250   500 miles

0   250   500 kilometers

0   50   100 miles

0   50   100 kilometers

M E X I C O

Areas ceded by Britain, 1842
(Webster-Ashburton Treaty)

CANADA

Lake Superior

Lake Huron

Lake Michigan

Lake Ontario

Lake Erie

MAINE

★ Augusta

VERMONT

Montpelier ★

Concord ★ N.H.

Connecticut R.

Boston ★

NEW YORK

MASS.

Albany ★

Hudson R.

Providence ★

Hartford ★

RHODE ISLAND

CONNECTICUT

PENN.

Delaware R.

Trenton ★ ← NEW JERSEY

Harrisburg ★

Dover ★ → DELAWARE

Susquehanna R.

Annapolis ★ → MARYLAND

WASHINGTON, D.C.

Chesapeake Bay

MINNESOTA

St. Paul ★

WISCONSIN

MICHIGAN

Lansing ★

Madison ★

IOWA

Des Moines ★

ILLINOIS

INDIANA

OHIO

Columbus ★

Indianapolis ★

WEST VIRGINIA

Charleston ★

Potomac R.

James R.

Richmond ★

VIRGINIA

Lincoln

Springfield ★

Ohio R.

Frankfort ★

KENTUCKY

Proclamation Line of 1763

THE ORIGINAL THIRTEEN COLONIES

opeka

Jefferson City ★

MISSOURI

Gained by treaty
with Britain, 1783

Cumberland R.

Nashville ★

TENNESSEE

Tennessee R.

NORTH CAROLINA

Raleigh ★

Cape Fear R.

ATLANTIC OCEAN

Missouri R.

Arkansas R.

ARKANSAS

Little Rock ★

ahoma y

OKLAHOMA

Columbia ★

SOUTH CAROLINA

Atlanta ★

Savannah R.

Mississippi R.

MISSISSIPPI

Jackson ★

ALABAMA

Montgomery ★

GEORGIA

| 0 | | 150 | | 300 miles |
| 0 | 150 | | 300 kilometers | |

LOUISIANA

Baton Rouge ★

Tallahassee ★

FLORIDA

FLORIDA
Treaty with Spain,
1819

Areas taken
from Spain
in 1810, 1813

stin

U.S. Territories

ATLANTIC OCEAN

San Juan ★

VIRGIN ISLANDS
*Acquired from
Denmark,
1916–1917*

Gulf of Mexico

PUERTO RICO
*Acquired from
Spain, 1898*

Caribbean Sea

| 0 | 50 | 100 miles |
| 0 | 50 | 100 kilometers |

BAHAMAS

CUBA

Bedford Series in History and Culture, Lynn Hunt, *University of California, Los Angeles*; David W. Blight, *Yale University*; Natalie Zemon Davis, *Princeton University*; and Ernest R. May, *Harvard University,* Advisory Editors.

Volumes in this highly praised series, including a number focused on women's history, combine first-rate scholarship, historical narrative, and important primary documents for undergraduate courses. Each book is brief, inexpensive, and focused on a specific topic or period. Package discounts are available.

Selected titles

THE SOVEREIGNTY AND GOODNESS OF GOD *by Mary Rowlandson with Related Documents*, edited with an introduction by Neal Salisbury, *Smith College*

Judith Sargent Murray: A Brief Biography with Documents, Sheila L. Skemp, *University of Mississippi*

Margaret Fuller: A Brief Biography with Documents, Eve Kornfeld, *San Diego State University*

Welfare Reform in the Early Republic: A Brief History with Documents, Seth Rockman, *Occidental College*

Women's Rights Emerges within the Antislavery Movement, 1830–1870: A Brief History with Documents, Kathryn Kish Sklar, *State University of New York, Binghamton*

HOSPITAL SKETCHES *by Louisa May Alcott*, edited with an introduction by Alice Fahs, *University of California, Irvine*

SOUTHERN HORRORS *and Other Writings: The Anti-Lynching Campaign of Ida B. Wells, 1892–1900*, edited with an introduction by Jacqueline Jones Royster, *Ohio State University*

Muller v. Oregon: A Brief History with Documents, Nancy Woloch, *Barnard College*

TWENTY YEARS AT HULL-HOUSE *by Jane Addams*, edited with an introduction by Victoria Bissell Brown, *Grinnell College*

Women's Magazines, 1940–1960: Gender Roles and the Popular Press, edited with an introduction by Nancy A. Walker, *Vanderbilt University*

The Movements of the New Left, 1950–1975: A Brief History with Documents, Van Gosse, *Franklin and Marshall College*

Historians at Work Series, Edward Countryman, *Southern Methodist University*, Advisory Editor.

Each volume in this series examines a single historical question by combining unabridged selections by distinguished historians, each with a differing perspective on the issue, with helpful learning aids. Package discounts are available.

Selected titles

Who Were the Progressives?, readings selected and introduced by Glenda Elizabeth Gilmore, *Yale University*

What Did the Internment of Japanese Americans Mean?, readings selected and introduced by Alice Yang Murray, *University of California, Santa Cruz*

"For students, teachers, and scholars, this book is at once path-breaking and accessible. It boldly and imaginatively recasts the history of women in the United States by compellingly integrating a full range of experience, approaches, and materials. Teachers will find this book ideal for their courses because students will learn from it in fresh and exciting ways."

—Daniel Horowitz, *Smith College*

"An excellent, up-to-date, and readable survey of U.S. women's history, well designed for classroom use. The abundant documentary material is keyed directly to the text and comes with smart questions, and the pictorial essays show students how to 'read' visual evidence."

—Patricia Cline Cohen, *University of California, Santa Barbara*

"I want students to understand visual and written materials as equally valid sources and learn to look at them together. . . . I eagerly await publication of this text!"

—Colette Hyman, *Winona State University*

"This book is a treasure: a wealth of historical research, wonderfully organized and lucidly written, that tells beautifully the story of what it has meant to be a woman in America from Puritan times to the present."

—Vivian Gornick

"I have been waiting for a truly satisfying overview to use in U.S. women's history courses, and I'm delighted to find one. I look forward to the opportunities for creative teaching this volume will provide."

—JACQUELYN DOWD HALL, *University of North Carolina, Chapel Hill*

"*Through Women's Eyes* will be a welcome addition to a market where nothing like it exists."

—ROBERT J. DINKIN, *California State University, Fresno*

"The topics emphasized reflect the most important research and debates among historians, in prose that is appropriate for an undergraduate audience. The balanced coverage of different groups of women is particularly well done."

—JACQUELINE K. DIRKS, *Reed College*

"This text is a wonderfully readable blend of the narrative of women's and U.S. history. I admire the way that the authors manage to organize their account around traditional themes of American history while formulating their material to answer the kinds of questions that students of women's history often pose. This effort to convey American history through women's eyes rather than to reperiodize American history to accommodate the experience of women works beautifully."

—ALICE KESSLER-HARRIS, *Columbia University*

"This effort to integrate women into the more traditional narrative is something I have tried to do for a long time, and I greatly appreciate a textbook that does the same."

—MARGUERITE RENNER, *Glendale Community College*

"*Through Women's Eyes* combines an up-to-date, inclusive account of American women's history, carefully chosen primary sources, and informative illustrations, maps, and graphs. The narrative offers students an engaging historical framework, and the collection of primary sources invites them to undertake their own critical analyses of the past. Highly recommended."

—JOANNE MEYEROWITZ, *Yale University*

"True to trends in recent scholarship, this text moves U.S. women's history beyond separate spheres onto a bustling national stage where gender is always accented by wealth and work, politics and faith, sex and health, race and ethnicity, place and time."

—VICTORIA BISSELL BROWN, *Grinnell College*

"This book fills its spectacular promise. Finally, here is a U.S. history textbook that embodies one of the foundational promises of feminist history—American history through the eyes of the majority, the women. The authors have also presented U.S. history through the eyes of diverse women, bridging at long last the agendas of both feminist historians and scholars of women of color."

—BRENDA STEVENSON, *University of California, Los Angeles*

Praise for

THROUGH WOMEN'S EYES

"This text has it all—a lively, coherently organized narrative; coverage of key developments in both national and women's history; a stunning array of primary sources; and a remarkable collection of visual images. Students will be captivated by its engaging style, user-friendly organization, and riveting images, while teachers will find it extremely effective in presenting information and encouraging students to think critically."

—SUSAN HARTMANN, *The Ohio State University*

"Integrating western, southern, and northern developments into a national narrative that includes African American, Yankee, Native American, and Mexican women, and working- and middle-class women, across the political spectrum is an incredible feat. This book will instantly become *the text* for American women's history courses across the country."

—NANCY HEWITT, *Rutgers University*

"With compelling visual sources and imaginatively selected primary documents, Ellen DuBois and Lynn Dumenil draw the reader into the historical moment. On every page, history is tangible, engaging, and real. Beautifully written and cogently argued, *Through Women's Eyes* will stand as the defining text in U.S. women's history for years to come."

—VICKI RUIZ, *University of California, Irvine*